THE COLLECTED WORKS OF

KEN WILBER

The Collected Works of Ken Wilber

THE COLLECTED WORKS OF

KEN WILBER

VOLUME EIGHT

THE MARRIAGE OF
SENSE AND SOUL

ONE TASTE

SHAMBHALA
Boston
2000

Shambhala Publications, Inc.
Horticultural Hall
300 Massachusetts Avenue
Boston, Massachusetts 02115
www.shambhala.com

9   8   7   6   5   4   3   2   1

First Edition
Printed in the United States of America
♾ This edition is printed on acid-free paper that meets the
American National Standards Institute z39.48 Standard.
Distributed in the United States by Random House, Inc.,
and in Canada by Random House of Canada Ltd

Library of Congress Cataloging-in-Publication Data
Wilber, Ken.
[Works. 1998]
The collected works of Ken Wilber.—1st ed.
p.   cm.
Includes bibliographical references and indexes.
Contents: v. 1. The spectrum of consciousness; No boundary—v. 2. The
Atman project; Up from Eden—v. 3. A sociable god; Eye to eye.
ISBN 1-57062-501-8 (v. 1: cloth: alk. paper).—
ISBN 1-57062-502-6 (v. 2.: cloth: alk. paper).—
ISBN 1-57062-503-4 (v. 3: cloth: alk. paper)
1. Consciousness.   2. Subconsciousness.   3. Self-perception.
4. Psychology—Philosophy.   5. East and West. I. Title.
BF311.W576   1999   97-45928
191—DC21   CIP
ISBN 1-57062-504-2 (v. 4: cloth: alk. paper)
ISBN 1-57062-505-0 (v. 5: cloth: alk. paper)
ISBN 1-57062-506-9 (v. 6: cloth: alk. paper)
ISBN 1-57062-507-7 (v. 7: cloth: alk. paper)
ISBN 1-57062-508-5 (v. 8: cloth: alk. paper)

CONTENTS

INTRODUCTION
TO VOLUME EIGHT

S CIENCE AND RELIGION, science and religion, science and religion. Their relationship really will drive humanity insane, if only humanity were sensitive enough. As it is, their relationship is merely fated to be one of those damnable dyads—like mind and body, consciousness and matter, facts and values—that remain annoying thorns in philosophers' sides. Ordinary men and women, on the other hand, have always drawn freely on both science (or some sort of technical-empirical knowledge) and religion (or some sort of meaning, value, transcendental purpose, or immanent presence). Still, how to fit them together: Ah, and there's the rub, as Shakespeare would say.

This volume of the *Collected Works* contains two books, *The Marriage of Sense and Soul: Integrating Science and Religion* and *One Taste* (the journals I kept while writing and publishing *Sense and Soul*). Both are devoted, in their own ways, to the relationship of science and spirituality; the former, in a scholarly fashion, the latter, according to my own personal experiences. I believe both books are advancing points that are not getting a hearing in the typical debates on these issues. I also suspect that these points will, for the most part, continue to be neglected, because they champion a direct experience of Spirit, and not simply ideas about Spirit. In other words, I am attempting to include direct contemplative and meditative spirituality in this debate, whereas most writers on the topic simply want to discuss the philosophical or scientific ideas involved: not direct experience but abstractions. It is as if a group of scholars were discussing the beaches of Hawaii, and instead of going to

Hawaii and looking for themselves, they simply pulled out a bunch of geography books and studied them. They study the maps, not the territory itself, which always seemed rather odd to me.

Surely there is room for both—direct spiritual experience, and more accurate maps and models of those experiences. The books in this volume are dedicated to both.

THE RELATION OF SCIENCE AND RELIGION

Numerous theorists have classified the typical stances that have been taken toward the relation of science and religion. All of these schemes are basically quite similar, moving from warfare, to peaceful coexistence, to mutual influence and exchange, to attempted integration.

Ian Barbour, for example, gives: (1) Conflict: science and religion are at war with each other; one is right and the other wrong, and that is that. (2) Independence: both can be "true," but their truths refer to basically separate realms, between which there is little contact. (3) Dialogue: science and religion can both benefit from a mutual dialogue, where the separate truths of each can mutually enrich the other. (4) Integration: science and religion are both part of a "big picture" that fully integrates their respective contributions.[1]

Eugenie Scott gives: (1) Warfare: science trumps religion, or religion trumps science; death to the loser. (2) Separate realms: science deals with natural facts, religion deals with spiritual issues; they neither conflict nor accord. (3) Accommodation: religion accommodates to the facts of science, using science to reinterpret, but not abandon, its core theological beliefs; a one-way street. (4) Engagement: both science and religion accommodate to each other, interacting as equal partners; a two-way street.[2]

In *Sense and Soul*, I give my own classification of the most common stances; here is a brief summary:

1. *Science denies religion.* This is still one of the most common stances among today's scientists, aggressively represented by such thinkers as Richard Dawkins, Francis Crick, and Steven Pinker. Religion is, pure and simple, either a superstitious relic from the past or, at best, a survival gimmick that nature uses to reproduce the species.

2. *Religion denies science.* The typical fundamentalist retort is that science is part of the fallen world and thus has no access to real truth.

God created the world—and the entire fossil record—in six days, and that is that. The Bible is the literal truth, and so much the worse for science if it disagrees.

3. *Science and religion deal with different realms of being and thus can peacefully coexist.* This is one of the most sophisticated stances, and it has two versions, strong and weak:

Strong version: *epistemological pluralism*—which maintains that reality consists of various dimensions or realms (such as matter, body, mind, soul, and spirit), and that science is dealing mostly with the lower realms of matter and body, and religion is dealing mostly with the higher realms of soul and spirit. In any event, both science and religion are equally part of a "big picture" that makes ample room for both, and their respective contributions can be integrated into this big picture. The traditional Great Chain of Being falls into this category (see fig. 1, p. 9). Representatives of something like this general view include Plotinus, Kant, Schelling, Coomaraswamy, Whitehead, Frithjof Schuon, Huston Smith, and Ian Barbour.

Weak version: *NOMA* ("nonoverlapping magisteria")—Stephen Jay Gould's term for the idea that science and religion are dealing with different realms, but these realms cannot be integrated into any sort of big picture since they are fundamentally incommensurate. They are both to be fully honored, but they cannot be fully integrated. By default, this is a very common stance among many scientists, who profess belief in some sort of Spirit but cannot imagine how that would actually fit with science, so they render unto Caesar what is Caesar's, and render unto God what is left over.

4. *Science itself offers arguments for Spirit's existence.* This stance claims that many scientific facts and discoveries point directly to spiritual realities, and thus science can help us directly reveal God/dess. For example, the Big Bang seems to require some sort of Creator principle; evolution appears to be following an intelligent design; the anthropic principle implies that some sort of creative intelligence is behind cosmic evolution, and so on. This is similar to Scott's one-way-street accommodation, where science is used to enrich religion, but usually not vice versa. It is also similar to what Barbour calls "natural theology" as opposed to "a theology of nature" (in the former, Spirit is found directly from a reading of nature, as with many ecophilosophers; in the latter, a revealed Spirit is used to interpret nature in spiritual terms. Barbour favors the latter, which is part of category 3). This is a very

common approach to this topic, and probably *the* most common among popular writers on the "new scientific paradigm which proves or supports mysticism."

5. *Science itself is not knowledge of the world but merely one interpretation of the world, and thus it has the same validity—no more, no less—as art and poetry.* This is, of course, the typical "postmodern" stance. Whereas the previous approach is the most common among popular writers on the topic of science-and-religion, this approach is the most common among the academic and cultural elite, who are dedicated not to constructing any sort of integration, but to deconstructing anything of worth that anybody else has to say on the issue. There are some truly important issues raised by postmodernists, and I have attempted to strongly include those points in a more integral view (see *The Marriage of Sense and Soul*, chap. 9). But left to its own devices, postmodernism is something of a dead end (see *One Taste*, Nov. 23 entry).

Now most theorists offer those kinds of classifications happy that they cover all the bases, a summary of all of that is available. I offer that classification as a summary of everything that has not worked. All of those lists—from Barbour's to mine—are lists of failures, not successes. More accurately, some of those approaches (especially 3, 4, and 5) have provided key ingredients for what might yet be a truly integrated view, but none of them have sufficiently included the core of religion that I feel must be fully brought to the integrative table, namely: direct spiritual experience. And where some theorists do at least acknowledge spiritual experience (such as Barbour),[3] they are silent as to the revolutions in cognitive science, brain science, and contemplative phenomenology, which taken together point to a much more spectacular integration of science and religion than has heretofore been suggested.

I have summarized this more integral view as "all-level, all-quadrant," and I will now briefly outline its major points.

NONOVERLAPPING MAGISTERIA?

Let us start with Stephen Jay Gould's approach—religion and science are both important but belong to different and nonoverlapping realms—which is a view that a great number of both scientists and religionists maintain. Gould states, "The *lack of conflict* between science and religion [Gould is maintaining stance 3, weak version] arises from a *lack of overlap* between their respective domains of expertise—science in the empirical constitution of the universe, and religion in the search for proper ethical values and the spiritual meaning of our lives."[4] Gould acknowledges that, of course, science and religion "bump up against each other" all the time, and that friction provides much interesting light, and often unpleasant heat. But ultimately there is neither conflict nor accord between them, because they are apples and oranges.

In order to maintain this view, Gould has to create a rather rigid dualism between nature and human: "nature" will be the realm of facts (disclosed by science), and "human" will be the realm of values and meaning (disclosed by religion). "Nature can be truly 'cruel' and 'indifferent' in the utterly inappropriate terms of our ethical discourse—because nature does not exist for us, didn't know we were coming, and doesn't give a damn about us (speaking metaphorically)." Apparently, for Gould, humans are not fully part of nature; if we were, then human would simply be something that nature is doing. But nature doesn't give a damn about us, because "us" (or the part of us that engages in religion/ethics) and "nature" (of brute fact and no values) are two *nonoverlapping* realms. "I regard such a position as liberating, not depressing, because we then gain the capacity to conduct moral discourse—and nothing could be more important—in *our own terms*, free from . . . nature's factuality."[5]

It is this awkward dualism in any of its many forms—facts and values, nature and human, science and religion, empirical and spiritual, exterior and interior, objective and subjective—that has driven the attempts to find some sort of bigger picture that seamlessly weaves together these two realms, and does not simply proclaim them to be forever fated to work different sides of the street.

It is an intensely difficult and intricate problem. The standard theological response to the dualism "empirical versus spiritual" is to claim that Spirit created the empirical world, and thus they are related in that sense. If we can accord with God (and avoid evil), then we will be saved; if we deviate from God (and commit evil), we will be damned. But then the equally standard problem: if God created the world, and the world contains evil, then didn't God create evil? If so, then isn't God responsible for evil? So why blame me? If the product is broken, the fault lies with the manufacturer. (It appears that the relation of empirical and spiritual is not so easy to solve, after all.)

The eco-spirituality theorists fare no better. Instead of a transcendent, otherworldly God who creates nature, they postulate a purely immanent, this-worldly God/dess, namely, nature and nature's evolutionary unfolding. If we can accord with nature, we will be saved; if we deviate from nature, we will be doomed. But then the same problem: If nature (via evolution) produced humans, and humans produced the ozone hole, then didn't nature produce the ozone hole? If not, then there is some part of human that is *not* part of nature, and therefore nature cannot be the ultimate ground of existence. Nature cannot be a genuine God or Goddess or Spirit—because nature is clearly *not* all-inclusive and thus must simply be a smaller slice of a much bigger pie. If so, what exactly is that Big Pie? And how, once again, do we actually heal this dualism between nature and human?

Many traditional theorists—from Plotinus to Huston Smith to Seyyed Nasr—attempt to handle these difficulties by resorting to the Great Chain of Being (a stance that is category 3, strong version). The idea is that there really aren't just two rigidly separate realms (such as matter and spirit), but at least four or five realms, infinitely shading into each other (such as matter, body, mind, soul, and spirit). The uppermost realm is the nondual ground of all the other realms, so that ultimate spirit suffers no final dualisms. However, as spirit steps down into creation, it gives rise to various dualisms that, although unavoidable in the manifest realm, can be healed and wholed in the ultimate or nondual realization of spirit itself.

Of all of the typical stances on the relation of science and religion, I have the most sympathy with that one (epistemological pluralism and the nested holarchy of truths), as I make clear in *Sense and Soul*. However, as I also point out in that book, the traditional presentation of the Great Chain suffers a series of grave limitations, many of which are no different from those faced by the simpler dualistic models, such as Gould's. For the traditionalists in effect postulate *four or five* nonoverlapping magisteria instead of just *two*, and even though those multiple magisteria (the many levels in the Great Chain) are often viewed as enveloping nests, the question still remains: What exactly is the relation of the higher realms, such as the spiritual, with the lower, such as the material?—and specifically in this sense: Is science really confined exclusively to the lower realms (matter and body), and does it, thus, have little or nothing to tell us about the higher realms themselves (soul and spirit)? Is the relation between science and religion really that of a five-floor building, where science tells us all about the lower two floors, and religion tells us all about the higher two floors? The most respected responses in this debate—from Huston Smith to Ian Barbour to Stephen

Jay Gould—are all variations on that theme (category 3, strong or weak).

But what if, instead of science telling us about one floor and religion about another, they both told us something different about each and every floor? What if science and religion were related, not as floors in a building, but as equal columns in a mansion? Not one on top of the other, but each alongside the other, all the way up and down? What then?

One thing is certain: this is an approach that has not yet been tried. Since the others have been found wanting, this might be worth investigating.

THE BRAIN OF A MYSTIC

Start with a simple example. A meditator is hooked to an EEG machine. As the meditator enters a deep contemplative state, the EEG machine shows an unmistakably novel series of brainwave patterns (such as the production of high-amplitude delta waves, which usually occur only in deep, dreamless sleep). Moreover, the meditator claims that, in her direct experience of this delta state, she is having experiences for which the word "spiritual" seems most fitting: she is experiencing a sense of expanded consciousness, an increase in love and compassion, a feeling of encountering the sacred and numinous in both herself and the world at large. Other accomplished meditators who enter this state show the same objective set of brainwave patterns and report similar subjective states of spiritual experiences. What are we to make of this?

There is already a substantial body of research indicating that something like the above scenario happens quite often.[6] Let us simply assume, for the sake of argument, that the scenario is generally true. First of all, this shows immediately that the realms of science and religion, often thought to be "nonoverlapping magisteria," are in fact overlapping like crazy.

What the standard NOMA argument (category 3, in both its strong and weak forms) tends to completely overlook is that, even if values and facts are in some sense separate realms, when a person experiences subjective values, those values have objective factual correlates in the brain itself. This is absolutely not to say that values can be reduced to brain states, or that spiritual experiences can be reduced to natural occasions. It is to say that spiritual realities (the magisteria of religion) and empirical realities (the magisteria of science) are not as compart-mentalized as the typical solutions to this debate imagine.

The integral model that I am proposing—namely, "all-level, all-quad-rant"—attempts to provide a framework in which all of those "facts," if you will, can be accommodated. The facts, that is, of both interior realities and exterior realities, "spiritual" experiences and "scientific" experiences, subjective realities and objective realities. It finds ample room for the traditional Great Chain of Being and Knowing—from mat-ter to body to mind to soul to spirit—but it plugs those realities into empirical facts in a definite and specifiable fashion, as you will see in the books in this volume.

ALL-LEVEL, ALL-QUADRANT

As a preview, let's use a few simple diagrams to outline this integral approach.

Figure 1 is the traditional Great Chain of Being. Because each senior level transcends but includes its juniors, this is actually the Great Nest of Being, as the figure shows. Notice that science (e.g., physics, biology, psychology) is indeed on the lower floors, and religion (theology, mysti-cism) is on the top floors. (This is the basis for category three, which, as we saw, is probably the most influential stance among those sympathetic with spirituality.) But this also gave the traditional Great Chain its "oth-erworldly" ontology; much of the upper floors were literally "out of this world" and had few if any points of contact with the material realm. (More specifically, the class of events marked D and E had virtually no direct correlations with A and B; hence, "otherworldly.")

The rise of modern science issued several lethal blows to that tradi-tional conception. For example, modern research clearly demonstrated that consciousness (e.g., mind), far from being merely transcendental noumenon, was in fact anchored in many ways in the organic, material brain—so much so that many modern scientists simply reduce con-sciousness to nothing but a play of neuronal systems. But we needn't follow scientific materialism to realize that consciousness is far from the disembodied essence imagined by most religious traditions. At the very least consciousness is intimately correlated with the biomaterial brain and the empirical organism, so that, whatever else their relation, science and religion are not simply "nonoverlapping magisteria."

The rise of modern science (particularly in the eighteenth century)

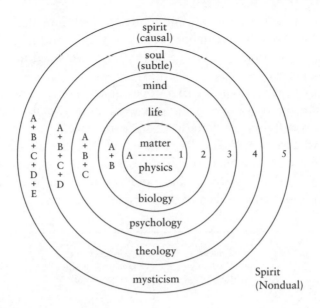

FIGURE 1. *The Great Nest of Being. Spirit is both the highest*
level (causal) and the nondual Ground of all levels.

was actually part of a whole series of events that have been described as
"modernity" (many of which I discuss in *The Marriage of Sense and*
Soul). But they can all be summarized using Max Weber's idea of the
"differentiation of the cultural value spheres" (the "values spheres" refer
essentially to art, morals, and science). Where most premodern cultures
failed to differentiate these spheres very clearly, modernity differentiated
art, morals, and science and let each pursue its own truths, in its own
way, free from intrusion or violation from the others. This resulted in
the spectacular growth of scientific knowledge, a flurry of new approaches to art, and a sustained look at morals conceived in a more
naturalistic light—resulted, that is, in many of the things that we now
call "modern."

As I try to show in the following books, these "Big Three" spheres
(art, morals, and science) basically refer to the realms of I, we, and it. Art
refers to the aesthetic/expressive realm, the subjective realm described in
first-person or "I" language. Morals refers to the ethical/normative
realm, the intersubjective realm described in second-person or "we" language. And science refers to the exterior/empirical realm, the objective
realm described in third-person or "it" language (which can actually be

divided into two realms—the individual or "it" and the collective or "its"). This gives us four major realms: I, we, it, and its. Examples of each are given in figure 2 (all of this will be explained in detail in the following pages).

In figure 2, notice that the two upper quadrants are singular or individual, and the two lower quadrants are plural or collective. The two left-hand quadrants are "interior" or "subjective," and the two right-hand quadrants are "exterior" or "objective." Notice also that all of the entities in each of the quadrants have *correlates* in the others (e.g., emotions go with limbic systems), but none of them can be *reduced* to the others without being robbed of their essential features.

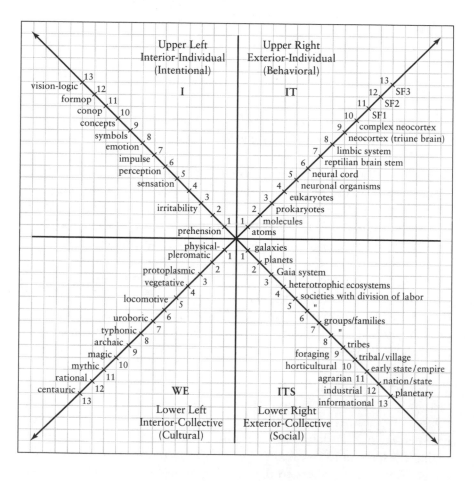

FIGURE 2. *The Four Quadrants*

Figure 1, then, is a summary of the traditional, premodern, or "religious" worldview, and figure 2 is a summary of the modern or "scientific" worldview. For the moment, let's "integrate" them by simply superimposing one on the other. Of course, it is nowhere near that simple, and I have given extensive explanations of what this integration actually involves in books such as *Sex, Ecology, Spirituality* (SES) and *Integral Psychology*. But since this is a short introductory overview, let's just superimpose the modern conception on the premodern, as shown in figure 3. Also look at figure 4, which is figure 3 labeled to show the relation of the interior states (of bodily feeling, mental ideas, and spiritual experiences) with the exterior, material realms (investigated by objective science).

If the conception shown in figures 3 and 4 is actually valid, then we will have gone a long way toward integrating a premodern religious view with a modern scientific view. We would have integrated the Great Nest of Being with the differentiations of modernity, one of the immediate gains of which would be a rather seamless integration of the religious and scientific realms and worldviews, in a way that would not violate the canons of either (or so I try to show in the following pages).

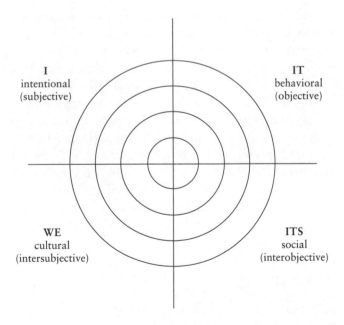

FIGURE 3. *The Great Nest with the Four Quadrants*

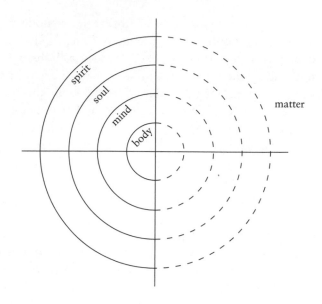

FIGURE 4. *Correlations of Interior (Consciousness) States with Exterior (Material) States*

This integral approach would also satisfy the one criterion that we earlier said had not yet been tried, namely, that science (or exterior realities) and religion (or interior realities) would develop, not with one on top of the other (as in fig. 1), but with both *alongside* each other (as the Left- and Right-Hand aspects of an "all-level, all-quadrant" approach, as shown in fig. 4). Figure 4 can therefore easily explain the tricky scenario of the meditator hooked to the EEG machine. She is experiencing very real interior, subjective, spiritual realities (Upper-Left quadrant), but these also have very real exterior, objective, empirical correlates (Upper-Right quadrant), which the EEG machine dutifully registers. Science and religion are thus giving us some of the correlative facets— interior and exterior—of spiritual realities, and that is a key ingredient of their integration in a larger and more encompassing view.

GOOD SCIENCE

Wait just a minute, says the empirical scientist. I can follow the argument right up to the point that you give actual reality to the spiritual realms. Granted meditators are experiencing *something*, but it might be nothing more than a subjective emotional state. Who says it involves *actual realities*, in the same way that science deals with realities?

Here is where *Sense and Soul* takes a few more novel turns. To begin with, up to this point I have left "science" and "religion" (or "spirituality") undefined.[7] I have simply used those terms in the general way that most people use them. But in several books (such as *A Sociable God, Eye to Eye*, and *Sense and Soul*), I carefully outline the many different meanings that have been given to "science" and "religion." (*A Sociable God*, for example, outlines nine common but dramatically different meanings of "religion.") And much of this "science and religion" debate is a garbled mess because dozens of different definitions are being used without being identified.

In the area of spirituality, for instance, we need at the very least to distinguish between horizontal or *translative* spirituality (which seeks to give meaning and solace to the separate self and thus fortify the ego) and vertical or *transformative* spirituality (which seeks to transcend the separate self in a state of nondual unity consciousness that is beyond the ego). Let us simply call those "narrow religion" and "broad religion" (or shallow and deep, depending on your preferred metaphor).

Likewise, with science, we need to distinguish between a narrow and a broad conception. Narrow science is based mostly on the exterior, physical, sensorimotor world. It is what we usually think of as the "hard sciences," such as physics, chemistry, and biology. But does this mean that science can tell us nothing about the interior domains at all? Surely there is a broader science that attempts to understand not just rocks and weasels but humans and minds? Well, in fact, we do acknowledge these types of broader sciences, sciences that are not rooted merely in the exterior, physical, sensorimotor world, but have something to do with interior states and qualitative research methodologies. We call these broader sciences the "human sciences" (the Germans call them the "geist" sciences, "geist" meaning mind or spirit). Psychology, sociology, anthropology, linguistics, semiotics, the cognitive sciences—all of these "broad sciences" attempt to use a generally "scientific" approach to the study of human consciousness. We have to be very, very careful that these approaches do not fall into merely aping the positivistic simplicity of the narrow sciences. But my point is that the difference between narrow science and broad science is already widely acknowledged. (We will return to this in a moment, but if you look at fig. 4, narrow sciences are those that study the Right-Hand or material quadrants, and broad sciences are those that attempt to study at least some aspects of the Left-Hand quadrants.)

The Marriage of Sense and Soul then proceeds to discuss just what it is that specifically defines broad religion and broad science. Start with the latter.

As we have already seen, we cannot define science—narrow or broad—by saying that it bases *all* of its knowledge on the sensorimotor world, because even narrow science (e.g., physics) uses a massive number of tools that are not empirical or sensorimotor, such as mathematics and logic. Mathematics and logic are *interior* realities (nobody has even seen the square root of negative one running around out there in the empirical world).

No, "science" is more a certain attitude of experimentation, honesty, and collaborative inquiry, and it grounds its knowledge, wherever it can, in *evidence* (whether that evidence is exterior, as in the narrow sciences, or interior, as in the broad sciences). The following three factors, I suggest, tend to define scientific inquiry in general, whether narrow or broad:

1. *A practical injunction or exemplar.* If you want to know whether it is raining or not, you must go to the window and look. The point is that "facts" are not lying around waiting for all and sundry to see. If you want to *know* this, you must *do* this—an experiment, an injunction, a pragmatic series of engagements, a social practice: these lie behind most forms of good science. This is actually the meaning of Kuhn's notion of "paradigm," which does not mean a supertheory but an exemplar or actual *practice.*

2. *An apprehension, illumination, or experience.* Once you perform the experiment or follow the injunction—once you pragmatically engage the world—then you will be introduced to a series of experiences or apprehensions that are *brought forth* by the injunction. These experiences are technically known as *data.* As William James pointed out, the real meaning of "datum" is *immediate experience.*[8] Thus, you can have physical experiences (or physical data), mental experiences (or mental data), and spiritual experiences (or spiritual data). All good science—whether narrow or broad—is anchored to some degree in data, or experiential evidence.

3. *Communal checking (either rejection or confirmation).* Once we engage the paradigm (or social practice) and bring forth a series of experiences and evidence (or data), it helps if we can check these experiences

with others who have also completed the injunction and seen the evidence. A community of peers—or those who have adequately completed the first two strands (injunction and data)—is perhaps the best check possible, and all good science tends to turn to a community of the adequate for confirmation or rejection. This is where the principle of falsifiability is very useful. Although the fallibility criterion cannot stand on its own, as Sir Karl Popper believed, it is often an important ingredient in good science. The idea is simply that bad data can be rejected by a community of the adequate. If there is no way that your belief system can be *challenged,* then there is no way to dislodge it at all, even if it is patently incorrect—and therefore whatever else you have, your beliefs are not very scientific (they are instead what is called "dogma," or a truth-claim backed only by authoritative fiat). Of course, there are many realities that are *not* open to the fallibility test—for example, you cannot reject, or even doubt, your own consciousness, as Descartes knew. But this third criterion simply says that good science constantly attempts to confirm (or reject) its knowledge claims, and the fallibility criterion is often used as one part of this third strand of good science.

DEEP RELIGION

Those three criteria are general characteristics of good science, whether narrow or broad. More specifically, they are characteristics of the way that good science, in any domain (physical, mental, spiritual), attempts to gather data and check its validity. Most forms of science also advance hypotheses to account for the data, and these hypotheses are then checked by a further application of the three strands of good science (further experiments, more data, see if they confirm or reject the hypothesis). In short, narrow science (whose data come mostly from the exterior realms or Right-Hand quadrants) and broad science (whose data come mostly from the interior realms or Left-Hand quadrants) *both attempt to be good science* (or science that follows the three strands of evidence accumulation and verification).

Let us then look briefly at religion. We have already seen that, as with science, there is a narrow religion (which seeks to fortify the separate self) and a broad or deep religion (which seeks to transcend the self). But what exactly is deep religion or *deep spirituality*, and how can it be *verified*? The claim, after all, is that in some sense deep spirituality is disclosing TRUTHS about the Kosmos, and is not merely a series of subjective emotional states. And here *The Marriage of Sense and Soul* makes its most novel and radical claim: deep spirituality is the broad science of the higher levels of human development.

THE INTEGRAL REVELATION

That is not the whole story of deep spirituality, but it is a crucial part of the story, a part that has not yet received sufficient attention. If you look at figure 1, which is the traditional Great Chain of Being, you will notice that there is a general unfolding from matter to body to mind to soul to spirit. These were traditionally (in Plotinus, for example) held to be both ontological levels of being and chronological levels of individual development (again, not in a rigid linear fashion, but in fluid and flowing waves). If you look at figure 2, you will see that the individual levels of development stop at vision-logic and the centaur. The reason figure 2 does not contain the higher, transpersonal, supramental waves of consciousness (such as soul and spirit) is that this figure simply represents average evolution up to the present, and thus it does not show the higher waves of superconscious unfolding (although individuals can develop into these higher waves in their own cases). But the claim of the great wisdom traditions is that there are indeed higher stages or waves of consciousness development, so that we have available to us not just matter and body and mind, but also soul and spirit. I have indicated these higher waves in both figures 3 and 4.

The thesis developed in a series of books (including *Eye to Eye; Sex, Ecology, Spirituality; The Eye of Spirit;* and *The Marriage of Sense and Soul*) is that deep spirituality involves the *direct investigation of the experiential evidence disclosed in the higher stages of consciousness evolution* (stages I have called psychic, subtle, causal, and nondual—which are simply summarized as "soul" and "spirit" in the figures). These deep-spiritual investigations, as I suggested in those books, follow the three strands of all good science (not narrow science, good science). They rely on specific social *practices* or injunctions (such as meditation); they rest their claims on data and *experiential* evidence; and they constantly refine and *check* these data in a community of the adequate—which is why they are correctly referred to as *contemplative sciences* (which is certainly how they understand themselves).

Thus, with reference to figure 1, deep spirituality is the broad science of those phenomena, data, and experiences labeled D and E. (In fig. 4,

D is labeled "soul" and E is labeled "spirit.") But notice—and here is part of the novel claim of this approach—the interior data and experiences of soul and spirit (in the Upper-Left quadrant) *have correlates in the sensorimotor evidence in the Upper-Right quadrant* (see fig. 4). In other words, the deep spirituality of the Upper Left, which is investigated by broad science, has correlates in the Upper Right, which is investigated by narrow science. The contemplative and phenomenological sciences (the broad sciences of the interiors) can thus join hands with *good science* for direct experiential data in the Upper Left and with *narrow science* for correlative data in the Upper Right. (I repeat, the scientific aspects—both broad and narrow—of the higher realms are *not* the whole story, but they are a crucial part of the story that has constantly been overlooked; and they are certainly an important ingredient of any truly integral approach to this topic.)[9]

Thus, an "all-level, all-quadrant" approach intimately integrates science and religion across many different fronts. It integrates deep religion with broad science by showing that deep spirituality is a broad science of the farther reaches of human potential. It also integrates deep religion with narrow science, because even deep-spiritual data and experiences— which must be understood in their own terms, and not reduced to any other level or quadrant—nonetheless have real correlates in the material brain, which can be decisively investigated with narrow science (as in the case of our meditator hooked to an EEG). It even makes room for narrow religion, as we will see in a moment. In all of these cases, an "all-level, all-quadrant" approach offers at least the possibility of a seamless intermeshing of what were previously thought to be "nonoverlapping magisteria."

VIVA LA DIFFÉRENCE!

This integral approach also respects the *vital differences* between the various types of science and religion. To say that an inquiry is following the disposition of good science is not to say what the content or actual methodology of that inquiry will be. It only says that this inquiry engages the world (injunction), which brings forth experiences of the world (data), which are then checked as carefully as possible (confirmation). But the actual form of the inquiry—its methods and its content— will vary dramatically from level to level and from quadrant to quadrant. Unlike positivism, which allowed only one method (empirical) in only one realm (sensorimotor), this approach allows as many methods and inquiries as there are levels and quadrants. In figure 4, for example, narrow science (empiric-analytic) investigates the Right-Hand quadrants; but in the interior quadrants, there are four levels in both individual and collective, giving us at least eight different methodology/ contents.

Thus, to give a very simple version, the phenomena labeled A, B, C, D, and E are all quite different entities, and methodologies have developed that deal with each of them in their own terms. In *Eye to Eye* I gave exhaustive reasons why none of these types of inquiries could be reduced to the others (I distinguished between sensorimotor experience, empiric-analytic, hermeneutic/phenomenological, mandalic, and gnostic). To the extent that all of those inquiries attempt to use injunctions (or pragmatic engagements), rest their claims in experiential evidence, and try to verify their claims as carefully as possible, they can be called "good science." But beyond that, they differ dramatically, and those differences are fully honored—and even championed—in this integral approach.

Put it yet another way: With reference to figures 3 and 4, each level (body, mind, soul, and spirit) has its own art, morals, and narrow science—its own "I" realm (UL), its own "we" realm (LL), and its own "it" realms (UR and LR). Not only does each quadrant have its own methodology; oftentimes each level within each quadrant has its own special approaches. In *The Marriage of Sense and Soul* (as well as *Eye to Eye*, SES, *Quantum Questions*, *The Eye of Spirit*, and *Integral Psychology*) there are countless examples of these different quadrant-levels and the ways in which their own uniqueness should be honored.

NARROW RELIGION

The critical response to *Sense and Soul* was enthusiastically positive, with one major exception. By far the most common criticism (and almost the only criticism) was that by downplaying and often ignoring narrow religion, I was asking altogether too much from the religious side of the marriage. The average believer, the critics said, would never give up the myths and stories that constitute perhaps 95 percent of most forms of spirituality. Not only did the professional critics hammer this point, so did most of my friends who tried giving the book to, say, their parents, only to have their parents shake their heads: "What, no resurrection of Jesus? No Moses and the covenant? No facing Mecca each day in prayer? This isn't my religion." And so on.

Well, guilty. There is no doubt that I focused almost entirely on direct spiritual experiences (of the psychic, subtle, causal, and nondual realms) and ignored the much more common religious dimension of translative spirituality. In all fairness, I did *not* deny that dimension or even suggest that it should be rejected. From *Sense and Soul*: "At the same time, this does not mean that we will lose all religious differences and local color, and fall into a uniform mush of homogenized . . . spirituality. The Great Chain is simply the skeleton of any individual's approach to the Divine, and on that skeleton each individual, and each religion, will bring appropriate flesh and bones and guts and glory. Most religions will continue to offer sacraments, solace, and myths (and other translative or horizontal consolations), in addition to the genuinely transformative practices of vertical contemplation. None of that necessarily needs to change dramatically for any religion. . . ."[10]

I did make two charges, however, which I still believe are true. One, if narrow religion makes *empirical* claims (i.e., claims about entities in the Right-Hand quadrants), then those claims must be put to the test of empirical (narrow) science. If religion claims that the earth was created in six days, let us test that empirical claim with empirical science. Most of those types of religious claims have spectacularly failed the test; you are free to believe them, but they cannot claim the sanction of either good science or deep spirituality. Two, the real core of religion is deep religion or deep spirituality, which tends to relax and lessen narrow-religion zeal, and thus, to the extent you are alive to your own higher potentials, you will find narrow religion less and less appealing.

Of course, the critics are right that most people embrace a translative or narrow religion—whether belief in the Bible, or belief in Gaia, or belief in holistic systems theory—and do not wish to radically transform the *subject* of those beliefs. In my model, those types of mental beliefs refer to the magic, mythic, rational, or vision-logic levels of development. But I also wanted to address the higher or transpersonal realms beyond those mere beliefs—the superconscious and supramental realms that constitute the core of deep spirituality and the contemplative sciences. An "all-level, all-quadrant" model makes room for all of those occasions, from premental to mental to supramental.

APPLICATIONS OF THE INTEGRAL MODEL

The October 14 entry in *One Taste* gives a short list of some of the applications that other researchers have made of this "all-level, all-quadrant" model in various fields. (Of course, the phrase "all-level, all-quadrant" is just a simple summary of the holonic approach, which actually includes quadrants, levels, lines, states, types, and realms, as will become more apparent throughout this Introduction. But it is useful to simplify all of that as "all-level, all-quadrant.")

By the time that *One Taste* was published (in early 1999), the interest in this type of integral approach had grown considerably. Part of it started when Bill Clinton read *The Marriage of Sense and Soul* and wrote a handwritten letter about it. He gave the book and letter to Al Gore, who, in a long piece in *The New Yorker* magazine, called it "one of my favorite new books."[11] The fact that the liberal *New Yorker* summarized the contents of *Sense and Soul*—without smirking—seemed to make these ideas somehow kosher to the intelligentsia. Whatever the various reasons, applications of a more integral vision have blossomed in business, education, health care, even prison reform.

I mention all this because I am asked about this issue more than any other—asked, that is, about the various types of applications of the holonic or integral model in the "real world." Here is brief sampling of what is going on.

Politics. I have been working with Drexel Sprecher, Lawrence Chickering, Don Beck, Jim Garrison, Jack Crittenden, and several others toward an all-level, all-quadrant political theory (in addition to working with the writings of political theorists too numerous to list). We have been involved with advisors to Bill Clinton, Al Gore, Tony Blair, and George W. Bush, among others. There is a surprisingly strong desire, around the world, to find a "Third Way" that unites the best of liberal and conservative—President Clinton's *Vital Center*, George W. Bush's *Compassionate Conservatism*, Germany's *Neue Mitte*, Tony Blair's *Third Way*, and Thabo Mbeki's *African Renaissance*, to name a few—and many theorists are finding an all-level, all-quadrant framework to be the sturdiest foundation for such.

Here is what I consider to be my own particular theoretical orientation, developed largely on my own, which has then become a framework for discussions with these other theorists, who bring their own original ideas for a cross-fertilization. I will first indicate my own thoughts, and then the areas where these other theorists have helped me enormously.

In the last chapter of *Up from Eden* ("Republicans, Democrats, and Mystics"), I made the observation that, when it comes to the cause of human suffering, liberals tend to believe in objective causation, whereas conservatives tend to believe in subjective causation. That is, if an individual is suffering, the typical liberal tends to blame objective social institutions (if you are poor it is because you are oppressed by society), whereas the typical conservative tends to blame subjective factors (if you are poor it is because you are lazy). Thus, the liberal recommends objective social interventions: redistribute the wealth, change social institutions so that they produce fairer outcomes, evenly slice the economic pie, aim for equality among all. The typical conservative recommends that we instill family values, demand that individuals assume more responsibility for themselves, tighten up slack moral standards (often by embracing traditional religious values), encourage a work ethic, reward achievement, and so on.

In other words, the typical liberal believes mostly in Right-Hand causation, the typical conservative believes mostly in Left-Hand causation. (Don't let the terminology of the quadrants confuse you—the political Left believes in Right-Hand causation, the political Right believes in Left-Hand causation; had I been thinking of political theory when I arbitrarily arranged the quadrants, I would probably have aligned them to match).

The important point is that the first step toward a Third Way that integrates the best of liberal and conservative is to recognize that *both* the interior quadrants and the exterior quadrants are equally real and equally important. We consequently must address both interior factors (values, meaning, morals, the development of consciousness) and exterior factors (economic conditions, material well-being, technological advance, social safety net, environment)—in short, a true Third Way would emphasize both interior development and exterior development.

Let us therefore focus for a moment on the area of consciousness development. This is, after all, the hardest part for liberals to swallow, because the discussion of "stages" or "levels" of anything (including consciousness) is deeply antagonistic to most liberals, who believe that all such "judgments" are racist, sexist, marginalizing, and so on. The typical liberal, recall, does not believe in interior causation, or even in interiors, for that matter. The typical liberal epistemology (e.g., John Locke) imagines that the mind is a *tabula rasa*, a blank slate, that is filled with pictures of the external world. If something is wrong with the interior (if you are suffering), it is because something is first wrong with the exterior (the social institutions)—because your interior comes from the exterior.

But what if the interior has its own stages of growth and development, and is not simply piped in from the external world? If a true Third Way depends upon including both interior development and exterior development, then it would behoove us to look carefully at these interior stages of consciousness unfolding. And here some surprises await the typical liberal.

This is where my work has been helpful to political theorists who are working on a Third Way (in both its liberal and conservative versions). In books such as *Integral Psychology*, I have correlated over one hundred developmental models of consciousness, East and West, ancient and modern, which helps to give us a very solid picture of the stages of development of the subjective realm—not as a rigid series of unalterable levels but as general guide to the possible waves of consciousness unfolding.

If the first step toward a truly integrated Third Way is to combine the interior and the exterior (the Left-Hand and the Right-Hand, the subjective and objective), the second step is to understand that there are *stages of the subjective*—stages, that is, of consciousness evolution. To help elucidate these stages, we can use any of the more reputable maps of interior development, such as those of Jane Loevinger, Robert Kegan, Clare Graves, William Torbert, Susanne Cook-Greuter, or Beck and Cowan's Spiral Dynamics. For this simplified overview, I will use just three broad stages: preconventional (or egocentric), conventional (or sociocentric), and postconventional (or worldcentric).

The traditional conservative ideology is rooted in a conventional, mythic-membership, sociocentric wave of development. Its values tend to be grounded in a mythic religious orientation (such as the Bible); it usually emphasizes family values and patriotism; it is strongly sociocentric (and therefore often ethnocentric); with roots as well in aristocratic and hierarchical social values and a tendency toward patriarchy and militarism. This type of mythic membership and civic virtue dominated cultural consciousness from approximately 1000 BCE to the Enlightenment in the West, whereupon a fundamentally new average mode of consciousness—the rational-egoic—emerged on an influential scale, bringing with it a new mode of political ideology, namely, liberalism.

The liberal Enlightenment understood itself to be in large measure a reaction against the mythic-membership structure and its fundamentalism, in two aspects especially: the socially oppressive power of myths with their ethnocentric prejudices (e.g., all Christians are saved, all heathens go to hell), and the nonscientific nature of the knowledge claimed by myths (e.g., the universe was created in six days). Both the active oppression instituted by mythic/ethnocentric religion and its nonscientific character were responsible for untold suffering, and the Enlightenment had as one of its goals the alleviation of this suffering. Voltaire's battle cry—which set the tone of the Enlightenment—was "Remember the cruelties!"—the suffering inflicted by the Church on millions of people in the name of a mythic God.

In place of an ethnocentric mythic-membership, based on a role identity in a hierarchy of other role identities, the Enlightenment sought an ego identity free from ethnocentric bias (the universal rights of man) and based on rational and scientific inquiry. Universal rights would fight slavery, democracy would fight monarchy, the autonomous ego would fight the herd mentality, and science would fight myth: this is how the Enlightenment understood itself (and in many cases, rightly so). In other words, *at its best* the liberal Enlightenment represented—and was a product of—the evolution of consciousness from conventional/sociocentric to postconventional/worldcentric.

Now had liberalism been just that—the product of an evolutionary advance from ethnocentric to worldcentric—it would have won the day, pure and simple. But, in fact, liberalism arose in a climate that I have called *flatland*. Flatland—or scientific materialism—is the belief that only matter (or matter/energy) is real, and that only *narrow science* has any claim to truth.[12] (Narrow science, recall, is the science of any Right-Hand domain, whether that be atomistic science of the Upper Right, or systems science of the Lower Right.) Flatland, in other words, is the belief that only the Right-Hand quadrants are real.

And liberalism, arising directly in the midst of this scientific materialism, swallowed its ideology hook, line, and sinker. In other words, *liberalism became the political champion of flatland.* The only thing that is ultimately real is the Right-Hand, material, sensorimotor world; the mind itself is just a *tabula rasa*, a blank slate that is filled with representations of the Right-Hand world; if the subjective realm is ill, it is because objective social institutions are ill; the best way to free men and women is therefore to offer them material-economic freedom; thus scientific materialism and economic equality are the major routes of ending human suffering. *The interior realms*—the entire Left-Hand domains—are simply ignored or even denied. All interiors are equal, and that ends that discussion.[13] But this desire to alleviate human suffering is applied *universally*—all people are to be treated fairly, regardless of race, color, sex, or creed (the move from ethnocentric to worldcentric). Thus, liberal political theory was coming from a higher level of development, but a development that was caught in pathological flatland. Put bluntly, liberalism was a sick version of a higher level.

That is the great irony of liberalism. Theorists have long agreed that traditional liberalism is inherently self-contradictory, because it champions equality and freedom, and you can have one or the other of those, not both. I would put this contradiction as follows: Liberalism is itself the product of a whole series of interior stages of consciousness development—from egocentric to ethnocentric to worldcentric—whereupon it turned around and denied the importance or even the existence of those interior levels of development! Liberalism, in championing only objective causation (i.e., flatland), *denied* the interior path that produced liberalism.[14] *The liberal stance itself is the product of stages that it then denies*—and there is the inherent contradiction of liberalism.

Liberalism thus refused to make any "judgments" about the interiors of individuals—no stance is better than another!—and instead focused merely on finding ways to fix the exterior, economic, social institutions, and thus it completely abandoned the interiors (values, meanings, interior development) to the conservatives. The conservatives, on the other hand, fully embraced interior development—but *only* up to the mythic-membership stage, which is nonetheless healthy as far as it goes: a healthy version of a lower level. (Mythic-membership, civic virtue, the blue meme, the conventional/conformist stage of development—these are all normal, healthy, natural, *necessary* stages of human development, and this sturdy social structure is still the main base of traditional conservative politics.)[15]

So here is the truly odd political choice that we are given today: a sick version of a higher level versus a healthy version of a lower level—liberalism versus conservatism.[16]

The point is that a truly integrated Third Way would embrace a *healthy* version of the *higher* level—namely, rooted in the postconventional/worldcentric waves of development, it would equally encourage *both* interior development and exterior development—the growth and development of consciousness and subjective well-being, *as well as* the growth and development of economic and material well-being. It would be, in other words, "all-level, all-quadrant."

Moreover, from this spacious vantage point, the *prime directive* of a genuine Third Way would be, *not* to try to get everybody to a particular level of consciousness (integral, pluralistic, liberal, or whatever), but to *ensure the health of the entire spiral of development* at all of its levels and waves. (The nature and importance of the prime directive is explored in the Introduction to Volume Seven of the *Collected Works*.) Thus the two steps toward a truly integral Third Way are: (1) uniting subjective and objective, and (2) seeing stages of the subjective and thus arriving at the prime directive.[17]

That is the general orientation that I have brought into the political discussions with the aforementioned theorists. From Chickering (*Beyond Left and Right*) and Sprecher I have adopted the important distinction between "order" and "free" wings within both conservatism and liberalism, referring to whether emphasis is placed on collective or individual ends. They also define Left as believing in objective causation and Right as believing in subjective causation.[18] This results in the widely used Chickering/Sprecher quadrants of order Right, free Right, order Left, free Left.[19] The order wings of both Left and Right wish to impose their beliefs on all, usually via government, whereas the free wings of both ideologies place the rights of individuals first. For example, those who wish the state to use its authority to reinforce conventional roles and values are order Right, while the politically correct movement and feminists who wish to use the state to enforce their version of equality are order Left. Free-market economic libertarians are generally free Right, civil libertarians are generally free Left.

Those political quadrants happen to align, in significant ways, with my four quadrants, because the upper quadrants are individual or "free," and the lower quadrants are collective or "order"; the interior quadrants are right/conservative, and the exterior quadrants are left/liberal.[20] This shows us which quadrant a particular theorist thinks is the most important (and therefore should be manipulated or addressed in attempting to achieve policy outcomes). The idea, of course, is that all four quadrants are unavoidably important in reality. Thus, an "all-level, all-quadrant" approach once again can serve as a theoretical basis for a truly integrated political orientation.

Jack Crittenden (*Beyond Individualism*) has been applying the notion of compound individuality developed in *Up from Eden* to political and educational theory, and has constantly added to my own understanding of these ideas. Don Beck's Spiral Dynamics (developed with Christopher Cowan) is a wonderful elucidation of Clare Graves's pioneering work, and has had numerous applications in the "real world," from politics to education to business, and I have benefited greatly from those many discussions as well. Beck probably has as good an understanding of the prime directive as anybody, and my own formulations have been enriched by his and Cowan's work. Michael Lerner's "Politics of Meaning," though often committed to order Left, is a powerful attempt to get liberals to look at the interior quadrants (meaning, value, spirituality), which they have classically avoided like the plague, an avoidance that has had dire consequences (e.g., the interiors have been left to the conservatives and their often reactionary, mythic-membership values, which are fine as a partial foundation of society, disastrous when left exclusively to their own devices). Jim Garrison, as president of the State of the World Forum, has had invaluable experience with how an integral vision will—and often will not—play out on the world stage. In all of this, we are looking for hints as to what a second-tier or *integral Constitution* might look like.[21]

This is a small sampling of some the political implications and applications of an "all-level, all-quadrant" approach, not merely as I have developed it, but as numerous theorists have done so, with their own original and highly significant ideas, which are now increasingly finding a mutual support.

Medicine. Nowhere are the four quadrants more immediately applicable than in medicine, and the model is being increasingly adopted by health care facilities around the world. A quick trip through the quadrants will show why an integral model can be helpful. (In this example we are talking about physical illnesses—a broken bone, cancer, heart disease, etc.—and how best to treat them, since that is the focus of most orthodox medicine.)

Orthodox or conventional medicine is a classic Upper-Right quadrant approach. It deals almost entirely with the physical organism using physical interventions: physical surgery, drugs, medication, and behavioral modification. Orthodox medicine believes essentially in the physical causes of physical illness, and therefore prescribes only physical interventions. But the holonic model claims that every physical event (UR) has at least four dimensions (the quadrants), and thus even physical illness must be looked at from all four quadrants (not to mention levels, which we will address later). The integral model does not claim that the Upper-Right quadrant is not important, only that it is, as it were, only one-fourth of the story.

The recent explosion of interest in alternative care—not to mention such disciplines as psychoneuroimmunology—has made it quite clear that the person's *interior states* (his or her emotions, psychological attitude, imagery, and intentions) play a crucial role in both the *cause* and the *cure* of even physical illness. In other words, the Upper-Left quadrant is a key ingredient in any comprehensive medical care.

But individual consciousness does not exist in a vacuum; it exists inextricably embedded in shared cultural values, beliefs, and worldviews. How a culture (LL) views a particular illness—with care and compassion or derision and scorn—can have a profound impact on how an individual copes with that illness (UL), which can directly affect the course of the physical illness itself (UR). In fact, many illnesses cannot even be *defined* without reference to a shared cultural background (just as what you consider to be a "weed" often depends on what you are trying to grow in the first place). The Lower-Left quadrant includes all of the enormous number of *intersubjective* factors that are crucial in any human interaction—it includes the shared communication between doctor and patient; the attitudes of family and friends and how they are conveyed to the patient; the cultural acceptance (or derogation) of the particular illness (e.g., AIDS); the very values of the culture that the illness itself threatens. All of those factors are to some degree causative in any physical illness and cure (simply because *every* holon has four quadrants). Of course, in practice, this quadrant needs to be limited to those factors that can be effectively engaged—perhaps doctor and patient communication skills, family and friends support groups, and a general understanding of cultural judgments and their effects on illness. Studies consistently show, for example, that cancer patients in support groups live longer than those without similar cultural support. Some of the more relevant factors from the Lower-Left quadrant are thus absolutely crucial in any comprehensive medical care.

The Lower-Right quadrant concerns all those material, economic, and social factors that are almost never counted as part of the disease entity, but in fact—like every other quadrant—are *causative* in both disease and cure. A social system that cannot deliver food will kill you (as famine-racked countries demonstrate daily, alas). But even in developed countries: If you have a lethal but treatable disease, and your insurance plan is the only source of funding you have, and your plan does not cover your disease, then you will die. The cause of your death: poverty. We usually don't think like this, because we say, "The virus killed him." The virus is part of the cause; the other three quadrants are just as much a cause. When the FDA was holding up drugs that might help AIDS, a gentleman with the disease stood before Congress and said, "Don't let my epitaph read, 'He died of red tape.' " But that is exactly right. In the real world, where every entity has all four quadrants, a virus in the UR quadrant might be the focal issue, but without a social system (LR) that can deliver treatment, you will die. That is not a separate issue; it is central to the issue, because all holons have four quadrants. The Lower-Right quadrant includes factors such as economics, insurance, social delivery systems, and even things as simple as how a hospital room is physically laid out (does it allow ease of movement, access to visitors, etc.)—not to mention items like environmental toxins.

In short, a truly effective and comprehensive medical plan would be all-quadrant, not to mention all-level (the idea is simply that each quadrant or dimension—I, we, and it—has physical, emotional, mental, and spiritual levels or waves—see figure 4—and a truly integral treatment would take all of these realities into account). Not only is this type of integral treatment more *effective*, it is for that reason more *cost-efficient*—which is why even organizational medicine is looking at it more closely. Of the hundreds of theorists doing wonderful work in this regard, I might mention John Astin, who has written perceptively on the application of holonic theory to complementary and alternative medicine;[22] Pat Odgen and Kekuni Minton;[23] Gary Schwartz and Linda Russek;[24] and Barbara Dossey and Larry Dossey, who have used holonic theory to supplement their own extensive and original work in "the great chain of healing."[25]

Business. Applications of the holonic model have recently exploded in business, perhaps, again, because the applications are so immediate and obvious. The quadrants give the four "environments" or dimensions in which a product must survive, and the levels give the types of values that will be both producing and buying the product. Research into the values hierarchy—such as Maslow's and Graves's (e.g., Spiral Dynamics), which has already had an enormous influence on business and "VALS"—can be combined with the quadrants (which show how these levels of values appear in the four different environments)—to give a truly comprehensive map of the marketplace (which covers both traditional markets and cybermarkets). Of course, this can be used in a cynical and manipulative way—business, after all, is business—but it can also be used in an enlightened and efficient fashion to more fruitfully match human beings with needed products and services (thus promoting the health of the overall spiral).

Moreover, *management training* programs based on an integral model have also begun to flourish. Daryl Paulson, in "Management: A Multidimensional/Multilevel Perspective," shows that there are four major theories of business management (Theory X, which stresses individual behavior; Theory Y, which focuses on psychological understanding; cultural management, which stresses organizational culture; and systems management, which emphasizes the social system and its governance). Paulson then shows that these four management theories are in fact the four quadrants, and that an integral model would necessarily include all four approaches. He then moves to the "all-level" part, and suggests a simplified but very useful four stages that the quadrants go through, with specific suggestions for implementing a more "all-level, all-quadrant" management.[26]

Other pioneers in this area include Geoffrey Gioja and JMJ Associates, whose Integral Leadership seminars (three general levels in the four quadrants) have been presented to dozens of Fortune 500 companies ("We believe that until recently, the transformational approach of organizational change has been the unmatched champion for producing breakthroughs, both subjective and objective. We now assert that the transformational approach has been eclipsed by the integral approach"); John Forman of R. W. Beck Associates, who uses an "all-level, all-quadrant" approach to correct the flatland distortions of systems theory; On Purpose Associates (John Cleveland, Joann Neuroth, Pete Plastrik, Deb Plastrik); Bob Anderson, Jim Stuart, and Eric Klein (co-author of *Awakening Corporate Soul*), whose Leadership Circle brings an "all-level, all-quadrant" approach to "Integral Transformation and Leadership" ("The main point is that the evolution of all of these streams of development in all of the quadrants are intimately bound up with each other. Spiritual intelligence is literacy in the practice of transformation. Spiritual intelligence is fast becoming a leadership imperative"); Leo Burke, Director and Dean of Motorola's University College of Leadership and Transcultural Studies, who oversees the training of some twenty thousand managers around the world; Ian Mitroff (*A Spiritual Audit of Corporate America*); Ron Cacioppe and Simon Albrecht ("Developing Leadership and Management Skills Using the Holonic Model and 360 Degree Feedback Process"); Don Beck of Spiral Dynamics, which has been used in situations totaling literally hundreds of thousands of people; and Jim Loehr and Tony Schwartz, who are working with an all-level, all-quadrant approach coupled with very specific change technologies built around the optimal management of energy—physical, emotional, and mental. Tony now writes the monthly Life/Work column for *Fast Company*, and can be contacted there.[27]

Education. Because I am an "integral" or "holistic" thinker, people often imagine that I support what are generally called "holistic" educational approaches, whether conventional or alternative. Alas, such is not generally the case. Many "holistic" approaches are, in my opinion, either sadly flatland (based on conventional systems theory, or merely the Lower-Right quadrant), or they stem from a philosophy that Spiral Dynamics calls "the green meme," which means a type of pluralistic approach that nobly attempts not to marginalize other approaches, but in fact marginalizes hierarchical development, and thus often ends up sabotaging actual growth and evolution. In any event, all of these typical "holistic" approaches overlook the prime directive, which is that it is the health of the overall spiral, and not any one level, that is the central ethical imperative. A truly integral education does not simply impose the green meme on everybody from day one, but rather understands that development unfolds in phase-specific waves of increasing inclusiveness. To use Gebser's version, consciousness fluidly flows from archaic to magic to mythic to rational to integral waves, and a truly integral education would emphasize, *not* just the last wave, but *all* of them as they appropriately unfold.

There are a large number of truly integral theorists working with these ideas and the applications of an all-level, all-quadrant education. In many instances, both the organizational structure of the schools (administration and faculty) and the core curriculum offered to students have been organized around an all-level, all-quadrant format. This has occurred both in conventional schools and in schools for the developmentally challenged. I hope increasingly to address this important issue in future writing.

Integral Transformative Practice. Closely related to integral education is "integral transformative practice" (ITP), which is, in a sense, integral education that includes the higher or transpersonal waves of development. Mike Murphy and George Leonard pioneered the first practical ITP in their book *The Life We Are Given*. I have continued to work closely with Mike in elucidating the theoretical underpinnings of such a practice. There are now approximately forty ITP groups around the country (if you are interested in starting or joining such, you can contact Murphy and Leonard via their publishers, Putnam). The Stanford Center for Research in Disease Prevention (of the Stanford University Medical School) is monitoring this practice, which has already had some rather extraordinary effects—testament to what an integral transformative practice can facilitate. There are many other, similar types of all-level, all-quadrant approaches being developed around the country, and I expect to see an explosion of interest in these types of more comprehensive programs, simply because they are more effective in initiating transformation.

Consciousness Studies. The dominant approach to consciousness studies in this country is still that of narrow science (i.e., a cognitive science based exclusively on the Upper-Right quadrant). As I suggest in *Integral Psychology*, a more comprehensive approach to consciousness studies would involve all four quadrants, or simply the Big Three of I, we, and it (first-person phenomenal accounts of consciousness; second-person intersubjective structures; and third-person scientific mechanisms and systems). This type of "1–2-3" of consciousness studies has already begun, as evidenced in such books as *The View from Within*, edited by Francisco Varela and Jonathan Shear, and by many articles carried regularly in the *Journal of Consciousness Studies*. The next stage of a more comprehensive approach will include not just "all-quadrant" but "all-level," and *Integral Psychology* outlines ways in which that important next step might be implemented.

Relational and Socially Engaged Spirituality. The major implication of an all-level, all-quadrant approach to spirituality is that physical, emotional, mental, and spiritual waves of being should be simultaneously exercised in self, culture, and nature—in the I, we, and it domains. There are many variations on this theme, ranging from integral transformative practice to socially engaged spirituality to relationships as spiritual path. The number of truly impressive groups and organizations pioneering these types of approaches is too large to list. But perhaps mention could be made of the work of Thich Nhat Hanh, Diana Winston, Donald Rothberg, *Tikkun*, and Robert Forman and the Forge Institute (of which I am a member), who are attempting to bring some fresh perspectives to this noble endeavor.

Integral Ecology. The approach to ecology set forth in *Sex, Ecology, Spirituality* is, critics agreed, a unique approach. Whether the critics liked the book or not, they agreed it was unique because it managed to combine ecological unity, systems theory, and nondual mystical consciousness, but without privileging the biosphere and without using the Web-of-Life notion, which I maintain is a reductionistic, flatland conception. Rather, an "all-level, all-quadrant" approach to ecology allows us to situate the biosphere, the noosphere, and the theosphere in their appropriate relationships in the Kosmos at large, and thus we can emphasize the crucial importance of the biosphere without having to *reduce* everything to the biosphere.

The key to these relationships—and the reason why they have so often been confused—can be seen in figure 4. Notice that the body (biosphere), mind (noosphere), and soul/spirit (theosphere) are all indicated on the figure. Each senior wave transcends and includes its junior, as shown by the enveloping nests. *In that sense,* it is quite correct to say that the mind transcends and includes the body, or that the noosphere transcends and includes the biosphere, or that history transcends and includes nature. The biosphere is a crucial component of the noosphere, but not vice versa (as most ecologists incorrectly suppose). That is, you can destroy the noosphere—or human minds—and the biosphere will still survive quite handsomely; but if you destroy the biosphere, all human minds are also destroyed. The reason is that the biosphere is a foundation and part of the noosphere, and *not vice versa.* By analogy, an atom is part of a molecule; if you destroy the molecule, the atom can still exist, but if you destroy the atom, the molecule is also destroyed. Same for biosphere and noosphere: on the interior realms, the biosphere is a part of the noosphere, and not the other way around (as can be clearly seen in fig. 4 and also in fig. 1). So it is *not* true that human minds (the noosphere) are part of nature (or the biosphere), but rather the reverse.

But notice, every interior event has a correlate in the exterior, sensory world—the world we often call "nature." Thus, most eco-theorists look at the external, empirical, sensory world, and they conclude that "*Everything* is a part of nature," because everything does indeed have a correlate in the Right-Hand world. So they conclude that "nature" (or the "biosphere") is the ultimate reality, and they ask that we act in accord with "nature," and thus they reduce everything to some version of ecology or the biosphere or the great Web of Life. But that is only *half* the story, the Right-Hand half. On the *interior* or Left-Hand dimensions, we see that nature—or the sensory, felt, empirical dimensions—are only a small part of the bigger story, a small slice of the Bigger Pie, a Pie that includes biosphere, noosphere, and theosphere. And although all of those interior waves have exterior correlates in the world of nature, they cannot be reduced to those exteriors, *they cannot be reduced to nature.* To do so is simply to embrace yet another version of materialism, body-ism, and one-dimensional flatland: the monochrome world of Right-Hand reality, the empirical-sensory Web of Life. That is ecological reductionism at its worst, a reductionism at the heart of many eco-philosophies.

On the other hand, an "all-level, all-quadrant" approach to ecology—as summarized in figure 4—allows us to honor the physiosphere, the biosphere, the noosphere, and theosphere, not by trying to reduce one to the others, but by acknowledging and respecting the vitally crucial role they all play in this extraordinary Kosmos.[28]

Worldviews. Because the holonic model originally arose as an attempt to coherently account for waves, streams, states, realms, and quadrants, one of its claims is to be genuinely holistic. A by-product of this attempted inclusiveness is a system that is very useful in indexing the various worldviews, philosophies, religions, and sciences that have been offered over the years. The idea, again, is not that any one of these various worldviews has the whole picture (including mine), but that the more of these worldviews can be seamlessly included in a larger vision, the more accurate the view of the Kosmos that emerges. This more encompassing view then acts as an indexing system for the various worldviews, showing their relation to each other and the irreplaceable importance of each.

There have been countless attempts, over the years, to categorize the various worldviews that are available to men and women. Plato offered brilliant accounts of the alternative philosophies present in ancient Greece. Fa-hsiang categorized the religious systems existing in T'ang China. St. Thomas Aquinas gave exhaustive representations of the most influential of the existing philosophies—to name just a few.

With the modern era, and the understanding of evolution, many theorists began to give classifications of various worldviews in terms of their *development.* One of the first, and still most influential, was that of Auguste Comte, founder of positivism, whose famous "Law of Three" stated that humanity's knowledge quest has gone through three major stages: religion, metaphysics, and science, with each stage being less primitive and more accurate (resulting, by happy chance, in the stage occupied by Comte. The constant downside of developmental theories is that the highest stage is usually, by strange coincidence, evidenced by the proponent of the theory. I hasten to point out that I have never made such claim myself, though I am often accused of it). By far the most sophisticated of these developmental classifications of knowledge was that of Georg Hegel, whose undeniably brilliant systematic philosophy found room, he believed, for every major worldview in history, East and West. (Unfortunately, as Bertrand Russell pointed out, all that Hegel actually knew about China was that it existed. This, and subtler problems with the Hegelian system, brought it tumbling down; but we can nonetheless admire Idealism for the brilliance of what it did manage to accomplish).[29] Other well-known developmental-historical models (which may involve both growth and decay) include those of Adam Smith, Karl Marx, Herbert Spencer, Oswald Spengler, Arnold Toynbee, Pitirim Sorokin, Antonio Gramsci, Teilhard de Chardin, Carroll Quigley, Jurgen Habermas, Gerhard Lenski, Jean Gebser, and Sri Aurobindo.

More recently, certain philosophers have attempted "overview" models that suggest the types of worldviews that people *can* form. One of the first was Stephen C. Pepper's *World Hypotheses* (1942), which claimed there are four of them: formistic (the world exists as categories), mechanistic (the world is cause-effect), contextual (the world is relational), and organismic (the world is interactive and relational). Schwartz and Russek (see the section "Medicine"), building on Pepper, added four more: implicit process (the world has subtler energies and consciousness), circular causality (cybernetic), creative unfolding (emergent adaptation), and integrative diversity (which attempts to integrate them all).

Another influential classification of worldviews according to available types was that of social systems theorist Talcott Parsons, who laid out worldviews along a (political) continuum of five major positions: Right Systemist, Right Marginalist, Middle Marginalist, Left Marginalist, Left Systemist. While this has some advantages, it actually covers a very narrow, middle-level range of possible worldviews, as we will see. Robert Bellah has cut his analysis at another angle, finding four major worldviews in America: republican, biblical, utilitarian, and romantic. Mark Gerzon finds six: religious, capitalist, disaffected, media, new age, and political. Samuel Huntington sees the world dominated by a clash of eight or nine major cultural worldviews (or civilizations): Western, Latin American, African, Islamic, Sinic, Hindu, Orthodox, Buddhist, and Japanese. But those are good examples of the "meta-analysis" of *types* of worldviews that many modern scholars have found useful—and they *are* useful, provided we can find a more encompassing context from which all can be accorded some sort of respect. (Ah, and there's the rub.)

The notion of levels or dimensions of reality brings yet another type of indexing system. The chakras, for example, represent the various levels of being and knowing available to humans as actual *structures* in the bodymind. (The chakra system is one of the most prominent and widespread versions of the Great Chain of Being, variations of which are found in virtually all of the world's major wisdom traditions, East and West. The chakras themselves are said to be subtle energy centers in the human body that support correlative types of knowing and being. They are generally given as seven in number, located at: the base of the body; the genital region; the abdomen; the heart region; the throat; the forehead; the crown. There are also said to be numerous auxiliary chakras above and below those. The acupuncture meridians are variations on these subtle energy currents.)

It is generally agreed that the seven chakras are simply a slightly more sophisticated version of matter (1), body (2), mind (3–4), soul (5–6), and spirit (7). But beyond that it gets a little more complicated. Accounts of the specific nature and function of each chakra vary, often considerably, because most of the main chakras perform different functions depending on whether they are "open" or "closed." The forehead chakra, for example, functions as the seat of logical rationality when closed (or operating in its outward, exoteric form), and yet, when opened (or realizing its highest function), it is the doorway to transcendental insight, mystical visions, and gnosis. For this reason, it is common to reserve the higher chakras (particularly 5, 6, and 7) for their spiritual, transcendental functions, and assign their closed functions to lower chakras (such as 3 and 4). In this example, I will therefore assign reason to the higher-mind (chakra 4), and not to its esoteric capacities (or the root of higher transcendental intelligence, chakra 6). If you have your own favorite version of the chakras, you are welcome to use that, since this example depends only on the notion of seven structural modes of consciousness, and you can fill in the details however you like.

With those qualifications in mind, I will simply define the chakras as: (1) matter; (2) biological life force, prana, emotional-sexual energy, libido, elan vital; (3) lower-mind, including power and intentionality; (4) higher-mind, including reason, and higher emotions, including love; (5) psychic opening, creative vision, nature mysticism, early stages of spiritual and transcendental consciousness; (6) subtle consciousness, gnosis, genuine archetypes, deity mysticism; (7) radiant spirit, both manifest and unmanifest, the Abyss, the empty Ground, formless mysticism.[30]

The point is that we can rather easily classify types of worldviews according to the chakra or the level of the worldview itself, and numerous theorists have done exactly that. To give a few examples that the various theorists have suggested, we have: materialistic worldviews, such as Hobbes and Marx (chakra 1): vital and pranic worldviews, such as Freud and Bergson (chakra 2); power worldviews, such as Nietzsche (chakra 3); rational worldviews, such as Descartes (chakra 4); nature mysticism, such as Thoreau (chakra 5); deity mysticism, such as St. Teresa of Ávila (chakra 6); and formless mysticism, such as Meister Eckhart (chakra 7).

As useful as those classifications are, there are certain problems that immediately stand out, and the only way to handle these difficulties is to introduce what might be called a *cross-level* analysis. We need to distinguish the level *from which* a worldview originates, and the level *to which* it is aimed. For example, Marx is often taken to be an exemplar of a type of materialism (chakra 1), but Marx himself is not coming from chakra 1 or existing at chakra 1. The only thing at chakra 1 is rocks, dirt, inert matter, and the physical dimension itself. Marx is a very rational thinker; he is coming from, or he is functioning at, chakra 4. But Marx, following Feuerbach, believed that the fundamental realities of the world are essentially material: so he is coming *from* chakra 4, but confining his attention *to* chakra 1. Similarly Freud: his early libido psychology is coming from chakra 4, but is aimed at chakra 2 (pansexualism). At the other end, so to speak: the Deists were coming from chakra 4 but aimed at chakra 6, and so on.

In other words, this allows us to trace both the level that the *subject* is coming from, and the level of reality (or *objects*) that the subject believes to be most real. This immediately enriches our capacity to classify worldviews. Moreover, it allows us to do a "double-tracking"—the level of the subject, and the levels of reality the subject acknowledges. This is sometimes referred to as the "levels of selfhood" and the "levels of reality"—or simply the level of the subject and the level of the object.[31] (This "cross-level" and "double-tracking" was introduced in *A Sociable God* and *Eye to Eye*, and refined in *Integral Psychology*.)

To use my own version of the levels of the subject (or the levels of consciousness), we have (to give an abbreviated account): sensorimotor and archaic (chakra 1); typhonic and magical (chakra 2); mythic and early mental (chakra 3); rational-egoic, centauric, and vision-logic (chakra 4); psychic (chakra 5); subtle (chakra 6); and causal (chakra 7).[32] The point is that, especially in the middle range (chakras 3, 4, and 5), the subject or self at those chakras can take as an object *any of the other chakras* (any of the other levels of reality)—can think about them, form theories about them, create artworks of them. Of course, when a lower chakra tries to grasp a higher chakra, without actually transforming to that chakra, certain inadequacies and limitations haunt the formulations, but that has never prevented people from doing so anyway, and we need to take those into account.

All of a sudden, the simple seven-level scheme is not so simple. Even if we say that only the middle chakras engage in cross-level work (the lower chakras, such as rocks, do not do so; and the higher chakras tend to be transmental, although they can certainly form mental theories— but we will leave them out for simplicity's sake), that means that chakras 3, 4, and 5 can give their attention to each of the seven chakras, forming a different worldview in each case—which gives us *twenty-five major worldviews* available from the seven structural levels of consciousness in the human bodymind.[33]

And, of course, that is just the start. If the holonic conception is "all quadrants, levels, lines, types, states, and realms," those twenty-five worldviews cover *levels* of self (or subject) and levels or *realms* of reality (or objects). We still need to include the *quadrants* in each of those levels/realms; the different *lines* or streams that move through those levels/realms; the various *types* of orientations available at each; and the many altered *states* that temporarily tap into different realms. Moreover, individuals, groups, organizations, nations, civilizations all undergo various kinds of *development* through each of those variables. All of the above factors contribute to different types of worldviews, and all of them need to be taken into account in order to offer a truly integral overview of available worldviews.

There is one final requirement. The integral vision, to be truly integral, must find a way that *all* of the major worldviews are basically *true* (even though partial). It is not that the higher levels are giving more accurate views, and the lower levels are giving falsity, superstition, or primitive nonsense. There must be a sense in which even "childish" magic and Santa-Claus myths are true. For those worldviews are simply the way *the world looks at that level*, or from that chakra, and all of the chakras are crucial ingredients of the Kosmos. At the mythic level, Santa Claus (or Zeus or Apollo or astrology) is a phenomenological reality. It will do no good to say, "Well, we have evolved beyond that stage, and so now we know that Santa Claus is not real," because if that is true—and all stages are shown to be primitive and false in light of further evolution—then we will have to admit that our own views, *right now*, are also false (because future evolution will move beyond them). But it is *not* that there is *one* level of reality (e.g., mine), and those other views are all primitive and *incorrect* versions of my one level. Each of those views is a *correct* view of a lower yet fundamentally important level of reality, not an *incorrect* view of the one real level. The notion of *development* allows us to recognize nested truths, not primitive superstitions.[34]

I am often asked, why even attempt an integration of the various worldviews? Isn't it enough to simply celebrate the rich diversity of various views, and not try to integrate them? Well, recognizing diversity is certainly a noble endeavor, and I heartily support that pluralism. But if we remain merely at the stage of celebrating diversity, we ultimately are promoting fragmentation, alienation, separation. You go your way, I go my way, we both fly apart—which is often what has happened under the reign of the pluralistic relativists, who have left us a postmodern Tower of Babel on too many fronts. It is not enough to recognize the many ways in which we are all different; we need to go further and start recognizing the many ways that we are also similar. Otherwise we simply contribute to heapism, not wholism. Building on the rich diversity offered by pluralistic relativism, we need to take the next step and weave those many strands into a beautiful web of unifying connections, an interwoven tapestry of mutual intermeshing. We need, in short, to move from pluralistic relativism to universal integralism—we need to keep trying to find the One-in-the-Many that is the form of the Kosmos itself.

That, I believe, is why we should attempt these types of integrative visions. Will we ever completely succeed? No. Should we keep trying? Always. Why? Because an *intention* to find the One-in-the-Many aligns our hearts and heads with the One-in-the-Many that is Spirit itself as it shines in the world, radiantly.

I believe that an integral approach (including quadrants, levels, lines, types, states, and realms, coupled with development) is now one of the most viable attempts to represent the One-in-the-Many, because it explicitly embraces and honors all of the worldview conceptions mentioned in this section (I will give numerous examples in a long endnote, including political analyses of Huntington, Fukuyama, Bellah, and Friedman; and spiritual worldviews as summarized by Evelyn Underhill).[35] This integral overview further acts as an *indexing system* for all these worldviews, and allows us to appreciate the special and profound contribution that each makes. And, it goes without saying, my own version of this integral vision, even if it were completely true, is destined to pass into yet further, better visions.

This integral indexing system is already being used in several applications, from "transformational websites" to "world libraries." The World Economic Forum recently invited several panels on an "all-level, all-quadrant" approach, which is perhaps an indication of its pragmatic usefulness.

Minorities Outreach. Since a truly integral model does not try to take one level or dimension of development (such as pluralistic, transpersonal, or even integral) and try to force it on everybody, but instead follows the prime directive of working for the health of the overall spiral of development, its approach to minorities is considerably different from typical liberal, conservative, or countercultural/holistic approaches. What is required is *not* to force liberal pluralism, conservative values, or holistic ideas on anybody, but to foster the conditions—both interior and exterior—that will allow individuals and cultures to develop through the spiral at their own rate, in their own way. The same is true for a more integral approach to developing countries.[36] A specific example from UNICEF is worth examining.

ALL-QUADRANTS, ALL-LEVELS, ALL-LINES: AN OVERVIEW OF UNICEF

"The Process of Integral Development" and "The Integrative Approach: All-Quadrants, All-Levels, All-Lines" are two in a series of presentations by iSchaik Development Associates, consultants for UNICEF. They outline the four quadrants, with examples from each; they summarize the major levels or waves in each quadrant; and they signal the importance of the numerous developmental lines or streams progressing in a relatively independent manner through the various waves. (See fig. 5, which was prepared by iSchaik Development Associates.) They state that "This is the bigger picture within which all the ideas and developments with which UNICEF is involved must be seen."

They then move to specifics: "In order to deepen our understanding of the complex and interrelated nature of our world, a mapping of consciousness development in social and cultural evolution is crucial. This must also have an integral approach to ensure that evolution, and thus

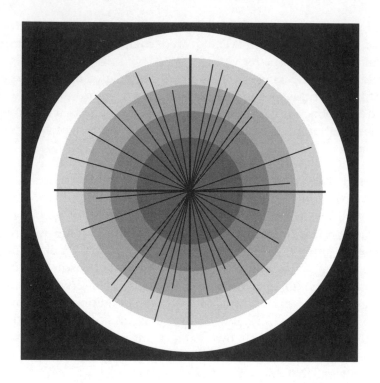

FIGURE 5. *UNICEF (iSchaik Development Associates)*

the state of children, humanity, culture and society, returns to a state of sustainable process." They point out that "this requires a framework that allows us to go deeper than the understanding of the mere objective/ surface system or web, and wider than a cultural understanding of diversity." In other words, we must go beyond standard systems analysis (which covers only the LR quadrant), and beyond a mere embrace of pluralism and diversity (which are confined to the green meme). What is required, they maintain, is an "all-quadrants, all-levels, all-lines" approach. With that, they begin a critique of the past performance of UNICEF and the UN.

"Clearly the process of development must address all four of these quadrants in an integrative fashion if it is to maintain a sustainable direction. But it is equally clear when we look at the evolution of UNICEF's involvement in this process, together with the broader process of human development and how they affect each other, that progress made so far has largely not produced sustainable change. Attempts to understand the process of change, transformation, or development without an understanding of the nature of the evolution or unfolding of (human) consciousness have little prospect for success."[37]

They then pinpoint a major reason for some of the past failures of UNICEF and the UN. "UNICEF's activities have largely operated in the Upper and Lower Right-Hand quadrants, that is, the quadrants that are objective and exterior (individual and social), and have to a large extent ignored the interior and cultural quadrants." That type of merely Right-Hand approach I have also called "monological" (another word for flatland), and so the analysis proceeds: "Possibly because of an overly monological vision of human development, UNICEF and the UN system have not been successful, or have simply not tried, at any stage, to map the larger picture in which they were involved. This monological vision may well have been necessary in the short term as human consciousness moved through, and is still moving through, the cultural stages of archaic, magic, and mythic, to the rational (and haltingly now to vision-logic or network-logic). But it is now imperative that these organizations adopt a more post or transrational approach, one that incorporates positive ideas from the rational level [and, I would add, positive contributions from *all* previous waves] but one that also transcends these to a higher or deeper post-rational level of consciousness, in all of the quadrants."

They then outline the history of UNICEF's various programs, pointing out that, as important as they were, they all focused mostly on Right-Hand initiatives.

- The 1950s were the *Era of Disease Campaigns*: "firmly in the Upper-Right quadrant, that is measurable, observable and objective."
- The 1960s were the *Decade of Development*: "emphasis now on the Lower-Right quadrant, that is 'functional fit.' "
- The 1970s were the *Era of Alternatives*: "but only alternatives that were mostly Right-Hand quadrants."
- The 1980s were the *Era of Child Survival*: but no mention of interiors or interior development.
- The 1990s were the *Decade of Children's Rights* (all seen in behavioristic terms), which quickly gave way to the *Era of Donor Fatigue*: "Donors and Governments returned to ['regressed' to] a preglobal state of nationalism stemming from problems at home and a lack of comprehension brought about from the misguided notion of all perspectives being equal ['aperspectival madness' of

pluralistic relativism]." I have often argued that each holon, in order to survive, needs a balance of justice and rights (agency) with care and responsibilities (communion), and this they echo by saying that the previous efforts of UNICEF and the UN had "no clear juxtaposition of 'rights' (justice) to jurisprudence (care and responsibility) at the global level."

Taking all of the above factors into account they conclude that:

- The 2000s are the *Era of the Integral Approach*: "This is where the sustainable process of change is seen from an integrative point of view, which explores more deeply the two Left-Hand quadrants of intention and culture. And of course for UNICEF this will have a major emphasis on children, youths, and women." The problem up to this point is that "all ideas during these five decades were monological to a degree that excluded an understanding of the needs for interior/subjective development in individuals and societies in order to make the process of change and especially transformation sustainable."

They conclude that an "all-quadrants, all-levels, all-lines" approach needs to be taken—carefully and uniquely tailored to each specific situation—in order "to ensure that actions we attempt or programs/ideas/metaphors we propose have any chance of being part of a sustainable, directional, transformative change process."

Let me point out (as do iSchaik Associates) that any such integral approach needs to be implemented with the utmost care, concern, and compassion. None of the levels or lines or quadrants are meant in any sort of rigid, predetermined, judgmental fashion. The point of developmental research is not to pigeonhole people, or judge them inferior or superior, but to act as guidelines for *possible potentials that are not being utilized.* The prime directive asks us to honor and appreciate the necessary, vital, and unique contribution provided by each and every wave of consciousness unfolding, and thus act so as to *protect and promote the health of the entire spiral,* and not any one privileged domain. At the same time, it invites us to offer, as a gentle suggestion, a conception of a more complete spectrum of consciousness, a full spiral of development, so that individuals or cultures (including ours) that are not aware of some of the deeper or higher dimensions of human possibilities may choose to act on those extraordinary resources, which in turn might help to defuse some of the recalcitrant problems that have not yielded to less integral approaches.

Those are just a few of the areas in which interest in a more integral or "all-level, all-quadrant" approach is having some immediate applications. There are others I have not mentioned: integral feminism, integral law, integral art and literary theory, even integral prison reform. Some of these approaches have been highlighted in a forthcoming book from Shambhala, assembled by a team of editors headed by Jack Crittenden, and tentatively entitled *Kindred Visions—Ken Wilber and Other Leading Integral Thinkers*, with contributions by Alex Grey, Stan Grof, Jim Garrison, Joyce Nielsen, Ed Kowalczyk, T George Harris, Marilyn Schlitz, Georg Feuerstein, Larry Dossey, Jenny Wade, Juan Pascual-Leone, Michael Lerner, James Fadiman, Roger Walsh, Leland van den Daele, Francisco Varela and Robert Shear, George Leonard, Michael Zimmerman, Father Thomas Keating, Ervin Laszlo, Thomas McCarthy for Jürgen Habermas, Eduardo Mendieta for Karl-Otto Apel, Hameed Ali, Robert Frager, Drexel Sprecher, Lawrence Chickering, Gus diZegera, Elizabeth Debold, Lama Surya Das, Rabbi Zalman Schachter-Shalomi, Mitchell Kapor, Michael Washburn, Don Beck, Frances Vaughan, Robert Forman, Mike Murphy, Max Velmans, Tony Schwartz, David Chalmers, Susanne Cook-Greuter, Howard Gardner, Robert Kegan, John Searle, and Charles Taylor, among many others. All of these men and women have contributed, in their own significant ways, to a more integral and gracious view of the Kosmos.

INTEGRAL INSTITUTE

Many of the theorists contributing to *Kindred Visions* and many of those presented in the Applications section have joined me and Paul Gerstenberger in starting the Integral Institute. We eventually plan on having branches of integral medicine, integral politics, integral spirituality, integral business, integral ecology, integral education, and so forth. The Integral Institute hopes to be a major umbrella organization for genuinely integral studies, as well as a conduit for funding for integral projects. We intend to open an Integral Center as headquarters for the Institute (in New York and/or San Francisco), and we have already started IntegralMedia with Shambhala Publications. If you are interested in joining the Institute, funding it, or applying for grants, please stay tuned to the shambhala.com website for further announcements.

ONE TASTE

To switch from the theoretical to the personal. Right after I finished writing *The Marriage of Sense and Soul*, I decided to keep a personal journal for one year. The primary reason for doing so is that most academic writing avoids any sort of personal disclosure or subjective statements, which are taken to be evidence of "biases" or "nonobjective reporting." There is some merit to that requirement, but not always, especially if the area under investigation is the subjective domain anyway. So I decided, for one year, to keep a journal that chronicled my day-to-day activities, including spiritual practice. This would allow people to judge for themselves the nature and depth—or lack thereof—of my understanding of issues about which I have written.

The journal turned out to be much more difficult and complicated than I thought. To begin with, the fact that I intended to publish it made it almost impossible to write unguardedly—and I don't mean about negative things, but about positive things. Every time something particularly good would happen to me—a nice review of a book, for example—I, as most people would, briefly noted it in the journal. But when readers saw that entry, they would immediately say, "What an egocentric person." What I failed to realize was that, because I planned on publishing the journal, every entry had an implicit frame around it that said, "I want you to know this." Thus, if I recorded *anything* that was positive about myself or my work, it gave the impression, "Here is a narcissistic creep."

When I finally realized this, it really jammed the process. If I were to make note of these positive developments in a "real" journal—i.e., that would not be published until after I died—it would be the most normal thing in the world. But to do so and then intentionally publish it while alive, well, that just doesn't work. I left a few of these positive entries in—enough to get people to yell "egocentric"—but on balance, almost all of them were left out.

The same applied to any critical comments about others that I might have. I found that these, too, didn't quite work. I left a few of them in; but on balance, I came to understand the two rules of a journal published while alive: say nothing positive about yourself and nothing negative about others.

Well, that narrows the scope, eh? What that did leave—and what I wanted to focus on anyway—was a detailed journal of my own meditative and spiritual practices; and a type of philosophical journal, or a chronicle of some of the ideas that I felt were most important as they unfolded in my own case. In that regard, I believe *One Taste* succeeds. Next to *Grace and Grit* and SES, I have received more warm and enthusiastic mail from readers of *One Taste* than from any other of my works.

What I most wanted to convey in *One Taste* was some notion of an integral life, a life that finds room for body, mind, soul, and spirit as they all unfold in self, culture, and nature. Not that I have achieved an integral life—I have never claimed that—but simply that it is an ideal worthy of aspiration. In fact, the entire message of *One Taste* is contained in the November 17 entry.

Most of our spirituality books are treatises on the spiritual life divorced from real life. When we read a book called "How to Know God" or "Finding Your Sacred Self," we do not expect to see chapters on making money, having sex, drinking wine, and vacationing in Hawaii. It is therefore profoundly jarring to see genuinely spiritual accounts right in the middle of a trip to South Beach—which is exactly why I did it. Again, not that I have mastered this integral endeavor, but simply that I wanted a journal that did not compartmentalize—that did not set spirituality against life, but instead set spirituality in the very midst of daily work, play, parties, illness, vacations, sex, money, and family—and that invited readers to be more friendly toward an integral approach in their own lives.

Of course, there are times when it is perfectly appropriate to temporarily compartmentalize in order to focus on a specific type of development—whether that be learning to cook, taking up a contemplative practice at a meditation retreat, or going on a nature hike. For spiritual development, I have always been a strong advocate of meditation, in any of its numerous forms. Thus, the second major point I wanted to get across in *One Taste* is the importance of meditation as part of an integral practice.

This is particularly crucial for strengthening consciousness and thus allowing it to remain stable as one passes from waking to dreaming to deep sleep. The more we can access this "constant consciousness" or "basic wakefulness" (which is present in all states, waking, dreaming, and sleeping), the more we become alive to Spirit's ever-present Presence. Many people reading *One Taste* reported that this was the strongest intuition or awakening that they received from the book. They had previously imagined that spirituality involved changing the *objects* of their awareness—thinking holistically instead of analytically, or trying to feel compassion instead of hatred. But they realized that true spirituality involves inquiring into the *subject* of awareness, and not simply rearranging the objects of awareness. By resting in the pure subject of consciousness, even as different states come and go, you are increasingly brought face to face with radiant Spirit itself, which is your own ultimate Subject or Self, and the Self of the Kosmos at large (at which point both subject and object embrace in One Taste).

Thus, by far the most common feedback I received from *One Taste* was "I started to meditate," or "After reading the book I went on an intensive meditation retreat," or "I vowed to strengthen my meditation practice." That is the single effect I hoped the book would have. Truly, adopting a new holistic philosophy, or thinking in integral terms, or believing in Gaia—however important those might be, are the least important when it comes to spiritual transformation. Finding out *who* believes in all those things: there is the doorway to God.

Criticism and My Response

After the applications of my work, the second most-often-asked question is, How do you handle having your work misrepresented? And my response is, not very well, I'm afraid, and I could use any pointers you might have. Since this is such a common question, I suppose I might say a few words about it.

One critic wrote, "Wilber has become one of the most influential theorists in the world today. Ironically, he is also one of the most misunderstood. One wonders whether he is famous for what he said, or what he didn't." This critic then gave a long list of beliefs that have been ascribed to me, beliefs that either I have never held, or ones that I held many years ago and have long since abandoned.

This is obviously not to say that there are no trenchant criticisms of my material; only that truly informed criticism is rare, and thus most of the time I am reduced to pleading, "That is not what I said." You don't ask that critics agree with you, only that they first report accurately the view they then attack. Quick example: this year, Stanley Krippner and Allan Combs published a piece quite critical of my work, and they proposed a model that they felt overcame its limitations. The problem is, the model they attacked was the wilber-2 model (a linear ladder model), which I have not held since 1981; and the model they proposed was essentially similar to the wilber-3 model (of structures, states, and realms), which is the model I have presented for the last fifteen years. I wrote a rebuttal, pointing out that I was misrepresented, and Combs responded with an aggressive counterattack, which ended with "Ken, we *do* understand your model. We just disagree." Yet his counterattack still gave as my model the fifteen-year-old wilber-2 model, and did not once mention wilber-3 (even though that was the model very similar to the one Combs himself was strongly defending). The claim that "We do understand your model" was thus sadly untrue.

I hesitate to use that example, because Allan Combs is a very thoughtful and sensitive scholar, and when this misrepresentation was pointed out to him, he immediately and generously took many steps to correct it. Moreover, I am a fan of Allan's work and wish him the very best. My point is simply that, if scholars as gifted as Krippner and Combs can so poorly represent my work, you can imagine how it fares in less sensitive hands. (The editors preparing the criticism section in *Kindred Visions* report that over 85 percent of the published criticisms of my work are either incorrect or misleading, which is rather startling.)

I truly understand the difficulties involved here. Often a critic will read one or two books, get excited about some of the ideas and annoyed with others, and then write a critique meant to straighten me out, often unaware that I have addressed the objections in other publications. In order to really understand my "system," a person needs to go through six or seven books, at least, and I completely understand why most people just don't want to do that. I have, over the years, tried to learn to be more gracious in my reactions to this. I can't claim complete success, but I am definitely trying.

TRUE BUT PARTIAL

One of the unforeseen effects of outlining a more integral spiritual practice is that many people were made to feel, by comparison, that they were *failing* in their own practice. This was certainly not my intent, and I regret any insensitivities involved here, so allow me to redress this situation.

Several entries in *One Taste*—June 18, for example—suggest one type of integral transformative practice that is "all-level, all-quadrant." The idea is simple enough, as I suggested earlier (namely, exercise physical, emotional, mental, and spiritual levels in self, culture, and nature). I gave numerous examples of specific exercises from each quadrant-level, and suggested that people concurrently practice as many of them as possible, thus synergistically increasing the effectiveness of each. Well, that is a fine idea, and definitely worth pursuing, but on the face of it, it also looks something like a fascist boot camp. "We *will* grow and develop! March, march, march!!!!" As Mike Murphy and I often joke, we're going to end up giving people metaphysical hernias.

My intent, rather, was simply to suggest that individuals might like to supplement their present practice with a few others from areas they were perhaps neglecting—to complement, not condemn, their present practices. For example, if you are doing psychotherapy, you might want to supplement it with meditation (or vice versa). If you are doing practices that particularly focus on self, you might want to supplement them with ones that focus on culture (relationships, group therapy, community service) or nature (outward bound, neopagan rituals, nature hikes), and so on. My intent was to *invite* people to expand their options, and *not* to condemn any practices that they were already doing.

As I have continued, in several books, to elucidate suggestions for a more integral approach to various fields, I have gotten two major reactions to this work. The first, and fortunately largest, has been enthusiastic. The second has been negative and often angry. This anger is in part a reaction to my three "angry books" (see the Introductions to Volumes Six and Seven of the *Collected Works*). But a large part of this anger is simply that some people resent a more integral approach; they feel that I am trying to force these ideas on them, that the holistic overview I have suggested somehow robs them of their freedom, that these ideas are a conceptual straightjacket against which they must fight.

In today's climate of postmodern pluralism, since there is no such thing as *objective* truth, then arguments are conducted almost entirely by attacking the *subject* who holds the beliefs. The accepted form of today's argument is thus deeply *ad hominem*: Einstein is a rotten person, therefore E does not equal mc^2. Likewise, the easiest way to fight this integral view is not to engage the ideas and evidence head on, but simply to try to discredit me as a person (the two most commons forms: I don't fit their version of spiritual, and I am apparently slightly more authoritarian than Mussolini). Those charges are made exclusively by people who have never met me, which I think speaks volumes. But I also believe that I understand this complaint, and frankly, in many ways I sympathize with it—these ideas can certainly land with an authoritarian thud.

My work is an obnoxiously imposing edifice; there is simply a hell of a lot of the damn stuff; as I mentioned above, you can't really begin to get this "system" without reading several fairly difficult books; and my occasional head-banging style doesn't help people feel at home in this wilderness. Moreover, my work is such an imposing structure, many theorists feel that in order to make their own contributions, they have to differentiate themselves from me by attacking me—the only way they can make a name for themselves is by tearing me down. All of this truly worries me, and I am constantly attempting, and often failing, to find more felicitous and economical ways to present an integral view of the Kosmos.

For the real intent of my writing is not to say, You must think in this way. The real intent is: here are some of the many important facets of this extraordinary Kosmos; have you thought about including them in your own worldview? My work is an attempt to make room in the Kosmos for all of the dimensions, levels, domains, waves, memes, modes, individuals, cultures, and so on ad infinitum. I have one major rule: *everybody* is right. More specifically, everybody—including me—has some important pieces of truth, and all of those pieces need to be honored, cherished, and included in a more gracious, spacious, and compassionate embrace. To Freudians I say, Have you looked at Buddhism? To Buddhists I say, Have you studied Freud? To liberals I say, Have you thought about how important some conservative ideas are? To conservatives I say, Can you perhaps include a more liberal perspective? And so on, and so on, and so on. . . . At no point have I ever said: Freud is wrong, Buddha is wrong, liberals are wrong, conservatives are wrong. I have only suggested that they are true but partial. My critical writings have never attacked the central beliefs of any discipline, only the claims that the particular discipline has the only truth—and on those grounds I have often been harsh. But every approach, I honestly believe, is essentially true but partial, true but partial, true but partial.

And on my own tombstone, I dearly hope that someday they will write: He was true but partial. . . .

AND IT IS ALL UNDONE

When all is said and done, and argument and theory come to rest, and the separate self lays its weary head on the pillow of its own discontent, what then? When I relax into I-I, and the infinite spaciousness of primordial purity drenches me in Being; when I relax into I-I, and the eternal Emptiness of ever-present awareness saturates the self, fills it with a Fullness that cannot even be contained; then all the agitated anxieties of life return to their source in God and Goddess, and I-I alone shine in the world that I-I alone created. Where is suffering then?, and how do you even pronounce misery? There in the Heart, where the mathematics of torture and the physics of pain can find no purchase or way to disturb, then all things bright and beautiful come out to dance in the day's glorious sun, long forgotten by the contracting ways of the loveless and forlorn self, god of its own perception, engineer of its own agony.

It is, truly, a game; what dream walkers we all are! Nothing ever really happens here, nothing moves in time or space, it is all so painfully obvious that I advert my eyes from the blinding truth. But here we are, You and I, and it is You-and-I that is the form of Spirit in this and all the worlds. For in the entire Kosmos, there is only One Self; in the entire Kosmos, there is only One Spirit—and thus the Self that is reading this page is the exactly the Self that wrote it.

Let us, then, You-and-I, recognize together who and what we are. And I will be with you until the ends of the world, and you will be with me, for there is only One Self, which is the miracle of Spirit. This is why we will be together forever, You-and-I, in the world of the Many-That-Are-One, and why we have never been separated. Just as Consciousness is singular, and the Self is One, and the Self neither comes nor goes, so You-and-I are that Self, forever and forever and endlessly forever.

Thank you deeply for coming on this journey with me, and guiding me at every point, and enlightening me through and through, and forgiving me all along, and being You-and-I.

NOTES

1. Ian G. Barbour, *Religion and Science: Historical and Contemporary Issues* (New York: HaperCollins, 1997).
2. Eugenie Scott, "The 'Science and Religion Movement,'" *Skeptical Inquirer*, July/August 1999.
3. In Barbour's central text on this topic, *Religion and Science: Historical and Contemporary Issues,* he points out that the data of religion involve spiritual experiences. "The data for a religious community consist of the distinctive experiences of individuals and the stories and rituals of a religious tradition." Unlike certain ill-informed critics who imagine that recourse to the word "data" implies some sort of positivism, Barbour realizes that "data" means any raw mate-

rial from any realm. But Barbour then devotes fewer than two pages (out of an almost four-hundred-page book) to actually discussing this data—what it is, how it is gotten, how it is verified or rejected, and so on. This large vacuum is typical of all of the approaches that I outlined in the main narrative, a vacuum that *The Marriage of Sense and Soul* attempts to fill. I will later outline why and how data fit into good science (including the parts of spiritual experience that are open to investigation by good science).

I find much of what Barbour does say to be insightful and useful, and I am in agreement with a good deal of it as far as it goes; but in slighting the actual nature of the data of religion, he falls short of the heart of the matter, in my opinion.

Barbour ends up defending a type of Whiteheadian process theology. I have elsewhere (*The Eye of Spirit*, note 11 for chap. 10; and especially *Integral Psychology*, note 15 for chap. 14) given both a modified endorsement of process philosophy and a sharp criticism of what I claim is its essentially monological nature. David Ray Griffin and I exchanged a series of e-mails on this issue, excerpts of which are published here with David's permission.

DG: "My only real problem with your discussion of Whiteheadian process thought is your criticism of it as monological. . . . Each occasion is internally influenced by EVERY prior occasion and exerts influence on EVERY future occasion. . . . How much more relational could an ontology be? Indeed, some members of the camp refer to this as 'process-relational' thought. And some of us refer to this as an 'ecological' view of the self. . . ."

KW: "You can be ecological and relational and still be monological. Traditional systems theory, for example, is a relational and ecological model, but it is entirely in third-person it-language (monological). Most ecological sciences are monological. Almost all Gaia theories are monological. And to the extent that some Whiteheadians talk about I-it prehensifications—even in relational and ecological terms—they are often stuck in monological modes."

DG: "Regarding monological: it is true that a Whiteheadian subject prehends only 'objects.' But this is by definition: whatever is prehended by a subject is by definition an object for that subject. It does not imply 'objectivity' in the (dualist) ontological sense. . . . The objects of the elementary prehensions . . . are 'objects-that-had-been-subjects,' so that the prehension (or feeling) of them is a 'feeling of feelings.' So it seems very misleading to use the term monological. . . ."

KW: "Well, it's tricky. For me, the intersubjective space is the background out of which the subject arises and in which the subject prehends objects, and that background permeates the subject (even if it entered as object), and then *henceforth*, as the new subject creatively emerges, it emerges in part from this intersubjectivity, and thus intersubjectivity at that point first enters the subject as part of the subject, not as an object-that-was-once-subject. This intersubjectivity is thus truly dialogical, not monological. Analogous to, e.g., somebody at moral stage 5 will have his thoughts all arise within that space, but that structure was *never* an object, but rather forms part of the structure in which the new subject arises moment to moment, and thus enters the subject as prehending subject, not as prehended object that was once subject."

DG: "I think I see your point—that what you call real dialogue involves a more [holonic] view of the self. But given the subtlety of the distinction between this and Whitehead's view, it seems misleading to characterize it as 'monological.' Why not distinguish between two kinds of dialogical positions—call yours 'complete' and call Whitehead's 'partial.' "

This does not mean that David agrees with my view, only that from my point of view I could distinguish these two types of dialogical process approaches— what I might call "holonic" or "quadratic" versus Whitehead's more limited view of dialogical. David does not think that Whitehead's view is partial or limited, only that from my perspective it could be characterized that way. And from my perspective, I find Whitehead's view is profound but partial, for reasons further explored in *Integral Psychology*, note 15 for chap. 14.

4. Stephen Jay Gould, "Non-Overlapping Magisteria," *Skeptical Inquirer*, July/ August 1999. His italics.

5. Ibid.; My italics.

6. See Wilber, *The Eye of Spirit*, and Charles Alexander and Ellen Langer, *Higher Stages of Human Development* (New York: Oxford University Press, 1990).

7. It is common to distinguish between "religion" (authoritarian and institutional forms) and "spirituality" (personal beliefs and experiences). In some ways that is a useful distinction, but in many ways it obscures. There are very profound personal/mystical branches of most forms of institutional religions; in fact, in many ways religion is just institutionalized spirituality (e.g., if New Age spirituality became influential and established, it would eventually be a religion). I prefer to speak instead of narrow and broad conceptions of religion/spirituality (or shallow and deep, depending on the metaphor). This is explained further in the text. My argument applies to both of them.

8. See *Eye to Eye*, chap. 2. Whenever I outline these three factors, I always emphasize that the paradigm or injunction *brings forth* data, it does not merely or solely *disclose* data. This in keeping with various post-Kantian and postmodern positions that deny the "myth of the given." It is also in line with Varela's enactive paradigm. At the same time, as discussed in *Sense and Soul*, denying the myth of the given, in any domain, is not to deny certain objectively real or intrinsic features of domains (such as their Right-Hand features). The idea that there are pure objects unaffected by perception and the idea that all realities are socially constructed are both lopsided, unsatisfactory notions. A four-quadrant epistemology steers between mere objectivism and mere subjectivism by finding room for an inherent balance of those partial truths. At the same time, due to the prevalence of extreme constructivist epistemologies, I often emphasize the objectively real components of many forms of knowing, since that is the partial but important truth that is most often being aggressively denied. See John Searle, *The Construction of Social Reality* (i.e., as opposed to the social construction of reality).

9. Even if experiences—sensory, mental, or spiritual—are mediated by cultural fac-

tors (and they are, given that all holons have four quadrants), nonetheless at the time of the apprehension, the experience is immediate. That is what I mean by immediate experience or data. The broad science of the interior domains only gives us the immediate data or immediate experiences of those interior domains. Those experiences are the ingredients for further elaboration in aesthetic/expressive and ethical/normative judgments. Thus, even with broad science, we are not reducing the interiors to merely science (broad or narrow). Science, in both its broad and narrow forms, is always merely one of the Big Three, and simply helps us investigate the immediate data or experiences that are the raw material of aesthetic and normative experiences. Charges that my approach is positivistic missed this central point (see note 10).

In the text I am focusing on just an individual—the Upper Left and Upper Right. Broad science is also part of the investigation of the Lower-Left quadrant and its realities (whereas the narrow science of the Lower Right is traditional systems theory). In all of the interior domains, broad science is *dialogical* (and *translogical*), not merely monological: here we are in the presence of phenomenology, hermeneutics, qualitative research methodology, interpretive sciences, and so on. See *Eye to Eye*, chaps. 1 and 2.

10. P. 204. One critic accused *Sense and Soul* of positivism. By failing to grasp the actual way in which my work as a whole uses the words "data," "empiricism," and "science," this critic charged that I was reducing all knowledge to positivism, a spectacularly wrongheaded criticism that students of my work immediately jumped all over (see also note 9). Another critic claimed that I misunderstood recent scientific developments because I was too heavily influenced by postmodern theories that maintain the contextuality of all knowledge, whereas empirical science was in fact connecting with real objective domains. This critic apparently failed to notice the existence of the Right-Hand quadrants, which I define in objective terms with intrinsic features. I have found that many critics have a hard time with the notion that all four quadrants can be simultaneously true (e.g., although objective facts are always set in cultural contexts, this does not deny objective facts, but simply situates them).

A few critics attacked *Sense and Soul* because they identified it with the "perennial philosophy," the idea of which they rather loathe. In fact, the pluralistic relativists, and the spiritual approaches based heavily on the green meme (see the Introduction to Volume Seven of the *Collected Works*), have for the past three decades aggressively attacked the very notion of a perennial philosophy. They tend to claim that there are no universal truths (except their own pluralistic ideas, which are universally true for all cultures), and they claim that the perennial philosophy, even if it does exist, is rigid and authoritarian (whereupon they often replace it with their own authoritarian, politically correct ideology). Nonetheless, I sympathize with some of the criticisms of the perennial philosophy. My extensive criticisms of the perennial philosophy can be found in *The Eye of Spirit*, *The Marriage of Sense and Soul*, *Integral Psychology*, *One Taste*, SES, and the Introductions to Volumes Three and Four of the *Collected Works*.

When critics identify me with the perennial philosophy, they fail to notice that the only item of the perennial philosophy that I have actually *defended* is the notion of dimensions of being and knowing, and then I only staunchly defend three of them: matter, mind, and spirit (or gross, subtle, and causal). I sometimes expand those dimensions to five (matter, body, mind, soul, and spirit), but I am willing to strongly defend only the former. That is, I claim that every major human culture, at least by the time of *Homo sapiens*, recognized these three main dimensions or realms of existence (as evidenced also in waking, dreaming, and sleeping). That is almost the *only* item of the "perennial philosophy" that I have defended. Most of the other aspects of the traditional version of the perennial philosophy (as maintained by, e.g., Frithjof Schuon, Ananda Coomaraswamy, Henry Corbin, Seyyed Nasr, Huston Smith, Marco Pallis, René Guénon, etc.)—aspects such as unchanging archetypes, involution and evolution as fixed and predetermined, the strictly hierarchical (as opposed to holonic/quadratic) nature of reality, etc.—I do not believe are either universal or true. One of the easiest ways for a green-meme critic to attack my work is to identify me with those theorists, and then attack the obviously incorrect nature of many of their ideas (ignoring the many places I have also criticized those traditionalist notions).

Although I have been a harsh critic of the perennial philosophy, I still believe that, especially in its most sophisticated forms, it is a fountain of unsurpassed wisdom, even if we have to dust it off a bit. I consider it the sheerest arrogance to merely attack this fund of wisdom (especially in light of what is usually proposed to take its place), and I also find these attacks to be one of the most vulgar forms of boomeritis: we finally have the morally superior approach, everybody before us got it wrong, and so we will simply deconstruct and trash everything not of our own wonderful making: boomeritis at its saddest (see the Introduction to Volume Seven of the *Collected Works*).

I find these types of attacks increasing in frequency and severity; probably for this reason: the green meme, which has dominated cultural studies for the last three decades, has finally begun to run out of steam, riddled with its own performative contradictions and the weariness that comes from deconstructing everything. As with every major meme or worldview, when the edifice is seriously threatened by its successor, out come the Inquisitors. The blue meme had its Spanish Inquisition, the orange meme has its Skeptical Inquisitors, and the green meme has its Politically Correct Thought Police. As the green meme begins to crumble, the green Inquisitors become particularly harsh and aggressive, which is exactly what has happened in last half decade or so (especially in universities and super-especially in alternative institutions. See, for example, the chilling book *The Shadow University: The Betrayal of Liberty on America's Campuses*, by Alan Kors and Harvey Silverglate [New York: Free Press, 1998]).

All of this is a type of good-news, bad-news joke. The good news is that none of this would be happening if the green meme weren't on its way out (as an exclusive and domineering structure of consciousness for the cultural elite). The bad news is, until that happens on a large scale (which, frankly, might not be until this generation dies), then the green Inquisitors are going to become increasingly unpleasant. But second-tier constructions are everywhere making impressive gains—in more integral views and more holistic perspectives—and thus I am cautiously optimistic that postgreen constructions will continue to blossom.

11. "The Political Scene," *The New Yorker*, Oct. 26 and Nov. 2, 1998. The book was given to Clinton by Drexel Sprecher, and the handwritten letter was to Sprecher thanking him and discussing the ideas, with a list of action items.

12. Flatland is explained in *The Marriage of Sense and Soul*, and in more detail in SES and BH. I use the term in two senses: (1) Technically, it is the belief that only Right-Hand realities are irreducibly real; the reduction of all Left-Hand events to their Right-Hand correlates. (2) I also use the word "flatland" to mean any Left-Hand belief that either comes from, or believes only in, one particular level of consciousness. Thus, behaviorists are flatland in the first sense (they believe only in objectively observable behavior), and pluralistic relativists are flatland in the second (they acknowledge only the values of the green meme).

Within flatland reductionism (in the first sense), there are two degrees: subtle reductionism, which reduces everything to the Lower-Right quadrant (dynamical process systems, chaos and complexity theories, traditional systems theory, social autopoiesis, the Web of Life, etc.), and gross reductionism, which goes even further and reduces those systems to atoms (reduces all phenomena to atomistic units in the Upper Right). Subtle reductionism is also known as exterior holism or flatland holism (in contrast to integral holism, which unites both interior holism and exterior holism). Both gross and subtle reductionism believe the entire world can be accounted for in third-person it-language (i.e., they are both monological, not dialogical or translogical). The "crime of the Enlightenment," incidentally, was subtle reductionism, not gross reductionism. The Enlightenment philosophes were the first great proponents of the *System de la Nature* and the "great interlocking order" (Charles Taylor, *Sources of the Self*; see also SES, chaps. 12 and 13).

13. This "blank slate" view of the human mind—with its correlates in a psychology of behaviorism and associationism, and an epistemology of empiricism—was adopted by liberalism for many reasons, not least of which that promised the "unlimited perfectibility" of human beings through various types of objective social engineering. All innate differences, capacities, and structures were summarily rejected, and human beings, born in a state rather akin to a blob of Silly Putty, could thus be molded by exterior institutions and forces (behaviorism, associationism) into any desired state.

David Hartley, in his *Observations on Man* (1749), had worked out a psychological theory (associationism) that viewed the mind as an assembly of sensations; this fit well the empirical theories of epistemology (Locke, Berkeley, Hume); and the entire general package was made to order for the rising political theories of liberalism. James Mill and his son John Stuart Mill embraced these ideas for a simple reason: "In psychology," John wrote of his father, "his fundamental doctrine was the formation of all human character by circumstances [objective causation], through the universal principle of association, and the consequent unlimited possibility of improving the moral and intellectual condition of mankind. . . ." This improvement could occur by behavioristic education, where the proper exteriors are imprinted on the interiors; or, especially in later versions, by more aggressive social engineering (which is why behaviorism—no matter how crude and incorrect in most respects—remained the state psychology of the Soviet Union, and it remains the implicit psychology of many forms of traditional liberalism).

As John Passmore (*A Hundred Years of Philosophy*) points out: "In one of his earliest speeches, [John Stuart] Mill announced that he shared his father's belief in perfectibility; that same faith is no less strongly expressed in the last of Mill's writings. Innate differences he always rejected out of hand, never more passionately than in his *The Subjection of Women* (1869), in which he argued that even 'the least contestable differences' between the sexes are such that they may 'very well have been produced by circumstances [objective causation] without any differences of natural capacity [subjective causation].'" Always there is the blank slate, into which a more perfect world will be poured from the outside, with no thought that there might be realities on the interior that need to be addressed as well. The "blank slate" meant radical social policy. "Associationism, in Mill's eyes, is not merely a psychological hypothesis, to be candidly examined as such: it is the essential presumption of a radical social policy."

The same was true for empiricism: not just an epistemology, but a blueprint for social action, based almost entirely on objective causation (and an implicit denial of subjective causation), which was one of the main motives for adopting it. "Empiricism, similarly, is more than an epistemological analysis; to not be an empiricist is to adhere to 'the Establishment'—to be committed to the 'sacred' doctrines and institutions." To believe in anything other than empiricism is, says Mill, "the great intellectual support of false doctrines and bad institutions." Empiricism is thus the doorway to molding human beings in an unlimited fashion (hence "perfectibility" as a social engineering agenda).

On the one hand, as we will see, this was a noble effort to move from ethnocentric notions of innate but often discriminatory "differences" (e.g., heathens are born without a soul) to a worldcentric, postconventional morality free of prejudice and bias (this is a motive I share). The fact is, much of the "Establishment"—which in Mill's time meant the mythic-membership, ethnocentric doctrines of the Church—are in fact need of trimming, and empiricism can most definitely assist us in doing so (it challenges the empirical claims of narrow religion). On the other hand, however, by denying that the interiors themselves have realities, realms, stages, and states of their own—and by, in fact, *reducing* them to imprints of the sensorimotor world—liberal philosophy and psychology would deeply sabotage their own goals. They would, with their allegiance to merely sensory empiricism and the blank slate, be prime contributors to the worldview of scientific materialism, a flatland view of the universe that in fact acts to undermine and sometimes grossly derail genuine growth and development of the interior domains. If there is an "unlimited perfectibility" of human beings, it lies, not just in shuffling exteriors, but in understanding the spiral of interior development. As we will see throughout this section, the liberal "blank slate" nobly aimed for worldcentric moral consciousness—and then crippled the path to it.

14. This is why the more "liberal" or "permissive" a society becomes, the less liberalism can flourish. When all stances are taken to be equal, and "no judgments" are made toward various stances—none are to be "marginalized"—then egocentric and ethnocentric are allowed to flourish, at which point the very existence of worldcentric liberalism becomes deeply threatened. Traditional liberalism works to undermine the foundations of traditional liberalism. See *One Taste*, Oct. 3 and 15, Dec. 10.

15. Because the mythic-membership wave (the blue meme) is a normal and necessary wave of human development, a true Third Way, based on the prime directive, would realize the absolutely necessary (if limited) role of the blue meme in any society, and not simply try to dissolve it, which the liberal green meme does every single chance it gets. Green dissolves blue, which is one of the true political nightmares in this country and abroad. See notes 35 and 36.

16. That idea is explained in several entries in *One Taste* (Oct. 3 and 15, Dec. 10).

17. The prime directive also decisively sides with a growth-to-goodness model, not a recaptured-goodness model (See *One Taste*, Dec. 10 entry). The traditional liberal believes in a state of "original goodness," which corrupt social institutions repress and oppress. While there is some truth to that notion (as explained in the *One Taste* entry), psychological research has decisively sided with the growth-to-goodness model, which points out that development generally unfolds from preconventional to conventional to postconventional. Along with "blank slate" humans, mere empiricist epistemology, and behavioristic psychology, the liberal version of "original goodness" has not found support in extensive research, leaving traditional liberalism without a believable philosophy, psychology, or ethics. An "all-level, all-quadrant" approach attempts to ground the noble aims of liberalism in a sturdier foundation, combined with the best of the conservative tradition.

As for "stages of the subjective," this actually means stages in all of the quadrants—subjective (intentional), objective (behavioral), intersubjective (cultural), and interobjective (social). The waves of development unfold in all four quadrants, and all four of those dimensions need to be taken into account. Moreover, there can be uneven development between the quadrants—highly developed technology (its) can be given to poorly developed, ethnocentric cultures (we), with nightmarish results (e.g., Kosovo)—and so on.

Thus, I technically give the two steps toward a Third Way as: (I) uniting subjective and objective; (II) seeing stages of both and thus arriving at the prime directive.

These two steps, in practice, have slightly different manifestations for liberals and conservatives, since each of those political philosophies needs to follow the two steps by supplementing their agenda with that which they presently lack. *For most conservatives* (who believe in subjective causation and in stages of the subjective, but only up to mythic-membership), stage I means being more willing to recognize the partial but genuine importance of objective causation in many circumstances and thus to act "more compassionately" toward the disadvantaged (hence, "compassionate conservatism"). Stage II—which has not yet been taken—involves moving from mythic-membership values to worldcentric values, not by abandoning the former but by enriching them (by supplements from the higher, post-orange stages). *For most liberals* (who believe in objective causation and in no stages of the interior), stage I means acknowledging subjective causation in the first place. Bill Clinton's synthesis of "opportunity and responsibility" (as applied to welfare reform and other issues) did just that; this was a fairly radical notion for a liberal, because the "responsibility" part acknowledged subjective causation (people, not institutions, are partly responsible for their own disadvantage). The joining of "responsibility" (provided by the person) and "opportunity" (provided by the government) was thus an attempt to unite subjective and objective, and this is Clinton's version of stage I (as pointed out to me by Drexel Sprecher). Stage II—which has not yet been taken—involves recognizing not just the subjective, but *stages* of the subjective (the irony, again, is that the traditional liberal stance itself *already* comes from the worldcentric stage, so this is not as daunting a challenge as it might seem; all that is required, in this case, is that liberals acknowledge *a more accurate self-conception of their own stance* and the developmental stages that produced it).

At this moment in 1999, both parties have attempted some form of stage I of the Third Way; neither party has attempted (or yet conceived) stage II, although both are struggling toward it. Right now it is a horse race to see whether liberalism or conservatism can more readily recognize and address their traditional deficiencies and thus arrive at the fully formed Third Way. Will it be harder for traditional conservatives to move from mythic-membership to worldcentric, or harder for liberals to acknowledge stages of the subjective? The party that can better address its deficiencies will arrive at a political conception of the second stage of the Third Way, will therefore fully understand and implement the prime directive—which embraces the greatest depth for the greatest span—and will thus have the inside track in the political arena for the foreseeable future.

The prime directive—namely, that the health of the entire spiral of development is the chief ethical imperative—can be derived directly from the Basic Moral Intuition, which is "preserve and promote the greatest depth for the greatest span" (see SES, index entries, Basic Moral Intuition). The prime directive does exactly that (see the Introduction to Volume Seven of the *Collected Works*).

Within this prime directive, one of the most important endeavors is to help each level, meme, or wave exist in its *healthy*, not pathological, version. Our job is not to force the blue/conservative meme to become green/liberal, but to allow blue to be as healthy *as it can be* within its own limits and domain. Don Beck, using Spiral Dynamics, and fully cognizant of the prime directive, has now found that the most reliable way to define "health" at every level or meme is: a meme is healthy if it balances, as best it can, the realities in all four quadrants (cf. the section "Medicine," later in the text). A pathology in any of the quadrants (I, we, or it) will reverberate throughout all, crippling each. The prime directive, rooted in the Basic Moral Intuition, attempts to let each meme live its own life to its own full potential (curtailed only when its agenda threatens others).

At the same time, governance implies, at some point, leadership, not followership, and true leadership is based, in part, on calling a people (and a nation and a world) to be the greatest that it can be—to develop, that is, to a greater depth or height or expansion of possibilities. And that means that leadership involves a call and an encouragement to all people not just to engage in exterior, economic, and technological development, but also to develop the interior domains to their highest potential—an encouragement to reach into the upper waves of interior development.

("The greatest depth for the greatest span" is facilitated to precisely the degree that *greater depth* is gently encouraged, or at least allowed, for all. The greater the depth or height—I often use those terms synonymously—then the greater the consciousness that can be shared and the richer the governance that can lead. A great leader is one who governs from those higher reaches, simply because the prime directive and all its implications can be better seen from that higher and wider perspective. Great leadership is thus also a call and an encouragement for all peoples, not only to be healthy at their present level, but to reach for a greater tomorrow—not just in exterior economic terms, but in interior development of freedom and moral and spiritual depth.)

The Constitution of the United States is a moral-stage 5 document. At the time it was written, perhaps ten percent of the U.S. population was actually at moral stage 5. The brilliance of this document is that it found a way to institutionalize the worldcentric, postconventional stance (moral stage 5) and let it act as a governance system for people who were not, for the most part, at that higher level. The Constitution itself thus became a *pacer of transformation*, gently encouraging every activity within its reach to stand within a worldcentric, postconventional, non-ethnocentric moral atmosphere. The brilliance of this document and its framers is hard to overstate.

The U.S. Constitution was the culmination of first-tier governance philosophy (see the Introduction to Volume Seven of the *Collected Works* for a discussion of first-tier and second-tier awareness). Even though its framers were often using second-tier thinking, the realities that they were addressing were still almost entirely first-tier, particularly the formation and relation of the *corporate states* that evolved out of *feudal empires*.

But now *global systems* and *integral meshworks* are evolving out of corporate states and value communities (to slightly modify Beck and Cowan's felicitous phrasing). What the world thus now awaits is the first genuinely second-tier form of governance and political philosophy—*a truly second-tier Constitution*. No doubt it will be "all-level, all-quadrant," or deeply integral in its structures and patterns. A genuine Third Way, in fact, is the clearing ground and one of the foundations for this integral Constitution. The question remains: Exactly how will this be conceived, understood, and embraced? What precise details, what actual specifics, where and how and when? This is the great and exhilarating call of global politics at the millenium. We are awaiting the new founding Fathers and Mothers who will call us to our more encompassing future, an integral Constitution that will act as a gentle pacer of transformation for the entire spiral of human development, honoring each and every wave as it unfolds, yet kindly inviting each and all to even greater depth. (See note 35).

18. Chickering and Sprecher assert that the influence of these (often unconscious) beliefs about subjective and objective causation is so strong that both political parties are organized around shared beliefs rather than around shared ends. Thus, both parties have order and free wings, from which arise characteristic internal tensions, in addition to the familiar conflicts between parties.

19. Drexel Sprecher is the originator of two specialized integral disciplines: generative leadership (emphasizing subjective development) and decentralized and integrated governance (emphasizing objective development). He has also designed an influential approach to political leadership training that includes exercises with injunctions, experiences, and verification to teach integral distinctions. Although the two steps toward the Third Way, as they are stated in note 17, are my own ("uniting subjective and objective; seeing stages of both and thus arriving at the prime directive"), Drexel has independently arrived at an essentially similar conception (and considerably spurred my own articulation). Sprecher sees the "two steps" toward the Third Way as being primarily economic and horizontal, then cultural and vertical. The first is the horizontal integration of the Left and Right axis of the Chickering/Sprecher matrix, the second the vertical integration of its order and freedom axis. That is one of many useful ways to conceive the two requisite steps to a Third Way; which actual details end up being the most important remains to be seen, as this dialogue among many mutually concerned parties continues to unfold.

20. Thus, if an individual is order Left, e.g., socialist (order means lower or collective quadrants, and Left means a belief in objective causation or Right-Hand quadrants), then they put most of their emphasis on factors in the Lower Right (the objective social system), and they wish governance to operate mostly by intervening in that quadrant (e.g., welfare statism). If a person is order Right, e.g., fundamentalist (order = lower or collective, and Right = a belief in subjective causation or Left-Hand quadrants), then they put most of their emphasis on the Lower Left (cultural beliefs and worldviews), and insist that everybody should share their beliefs and values, by government intervention if possible (e.g., school prayer). If a person is free Right, e.g., economic libertarian (free = upper or individual, and Right = a belief in subjective causation or Left-Hand realities), they put most of their emphasis on the Upper-Left quadrant: individuals must assume responsibility for their own success, and government should stay out of interfering with the Right-Hand (e.g., economic) quadrants altogether (except to protect those rights and freedoms). If a person is free Left, e.g., civil libertarian, they put most of their emphasis on the freedom of individual

behavior (Upper Right), and government should intervene only to protect those freedoms. There are many variations on those themes, and we must also take the levels themselves into account, but those are some simple examples.

21. An integral or "second-tier" Constitution is a governing philosophy stemming from what Clare Graves called the second tier of psychological development. (Many different theorists speak of several tiers—first, second, third, fourth, and so on. The simple Gravesian two-tier conception works just fine for the point I am making.) Using the terms of Spiral Dynamics, the United States constitution was the culmination and brilliant high point of first-tier governance (stemming from orange-to-green principles), and it established the governance systems for corporate states (and to some degree value communities). Now, in the postnational and postgreen world, we await the governance system that will allow second-tier global and holistic meshworks to flourish. We await the founding Fathers and Mothers of a second-tier or integral Constitution. See note 17.

22. John Astin, "The Integral Philosophy of Ken Wilber: Contributions to the Study of CAM [Complementary and Alternative Medicine] and Conventional Medicine." In preparation.

23. "Sensorimotor Sequencing," presented at the Psychological Trauma conference, sponsored by Boston University School of Medicine and Harvard Medical School.

24. Gary Schwartz and Linda Russek, "The Challenge of One Medicine: Theories of Health and Eight World Hypotheses," *Advances: The Journal of Mind-Body Health*.

25. See Larry Dossey, "The Great Chain of Healing: Toward an Integral Vision of Medicine (With a Bow to Ken Wilber)," in Crittenden et al. (eds.), *Kindred Visions*, forthcoming from Shambhala Publications.

26. D. Paulson, "Management: A Multidimensional/Multilevel Perspective," in Crittenden et al. (eds.), *Kindred Visions*, forthcoming from Shambhala Publications. See also D. Paulson, *Topical Antimicrobial Testing and Evaluation*, Marcel Dekker, 1999; "Successfully Marketing Skin Moisturizing Products," *Soap/Cosmetics/Chemical Specialties*, August 1999; "Developing Effective Topical Antimicrobials," *Soap/Cosmetics/Chemical Specialties*, December 1997. Daryl has published extensively on "all-level, all-quadrant" applications in various fields, including a widely appreciated elucidation of near-death experiences ("The Near-Death Experience: An Integration of Cultural, Spiritual, and Physical Perspectives," *Journal of Near Death Studies*, 18 (1) Fall 99). Daryl is also on the FDA's panel of experts on Food Safety. "We use the quadrant model to reduce infections such as *Escherichia coli* outbreaks of strain 0157-H7."

When it comes to the "all-level" part in human beings, you can use any of the reputable developmental models, from Maslow to Graves to Loevinger. Spiral Dynamics has had a great deal of success in this regard, and it now uses an "all-level, all-quadrant" refinement of its own system.

27. G. Gioja, "Creating Leaders (Beyond Transformation: An Integral Manifesto)"; On Purpose Associates (Cleveland et al.), "The Practical Philosopher: How Ken Wilber Changed Our Practice"; and L. Burke, "Not Just Money, Meaning," are

all in Crittenden et al. (eds.), *Kindred Visions*, forthcoming from Shambhala. The quote from the Leadership Circle (Bob Anderson, Jim Stuart, and Eric Klein) is taken from "The Leadership Circle: Bringing Spiritual Intelligence to the Work"; they can be contacted through Klein's publisher (*Awakening Corporate Soul*).

28. Of the many ecotheorists who have begun using a more integral approach, special mention might be made of the work of Matthew Kalman, Michael Zimmerman (*Radical Ecology*), and Gus diZerega. DiZerega and I have had our theoretical differences, but I believe we now see eye to eye on many ecological issues, and in fact we have planned some joint publications. The core of Gus's previous complaint about my work was that, because I suggested that many individuals involved in nature mysticism are often involved in prerational and even regressive occasions, I was saying that *all* nature mysticism is such, which is definitely not my opinion, as Gus now acknowledges. I do not mean to imply that Gus would agree with all my points, but I believe it is safe to say that he is comfortable with an all-level, all-quadrant approach that includes nature mysticism, deity mysticism, formless mysticism, and nondual mysticism. We also both share an appreciation of some of the many positive gains of modernity and the Enlightenment, in addition to understanding their downsides, on which most ecotheories unfairly focus.

29. See SES, BH, and MSS for an account of the strengths and weaknesses of Idealism.

30. Although I am in general agreement with much of chakra psychology, I also differ substantially on several crucial issues. The perennial philosophy (of which the chakra system is an archetypal example) tends to view these levels or planes of reality as being ontologically real and pregiven objects, independent of the subject of perception, whereas I have taken a more critical, less metaphysical, approach, incorporating some of the important insights of post-Kantian and postmodern thought (*metaphysics* essentially believes in independent object realms; *critical* thought places an emphasis on the subject that is doing the perceiving, pointing out that the structures of the subject are often crucial in the structures of the objects perceived). In my view, although features of the various realms of reality are independent of any particular observer, and are thus "objective realities" in a very real sense, they cannot be separated from the interaction that perceiving subjects bring to their disclosure. That is a technical way of saying that all existence is a four-quadrant affair, with intentional-behavioral-cultural-and-social factors inescapably built into every perception. The ontological levels of reality are not other to the levels of consciousness perceiving them. In other words, "levels of consciousness" and "levels of reality" are actually "levels of consciousness-reality" (which is why I often refer to them *both* as basic levels, basic structures, or basic waves). At the same time, we need to preserve "levels of selfhood" and "levels (or realms) of reality" as two separate variables, because a given level of self can experience a different level of reality. But that ultimately means only that one level of consciousness-reality can experience a different level of consciousness-reality. Nonetheless, because of the in-

tricacies of that critical argument, when it is important to refer to their "separate-variable" status, I often just use the simpler "levels of consciousness," on the one hand, and "levels (or realms) of reality," on the other (with the implicit assumption that I am taking a critical, not metaphysical, stance). This topic is discussed at length in a series of long endnotes in *Integral Psychology*, starting with note 3 for chapter 1. See also notes 31, 37.

31. For "levels of reality" (or "planes of reality") I also use "realms of reality" (e.g., gross realm, subtle realm, causal realm, etc.) or "spheres of reality" (e.g., biosphere, noosphere, theosphere, etc.). For "levels of selfhood" I often use "levels of consciousness" or "levels of subjectivity." But I usually refer to them *both* as basic levels, basic structures, or basic waves, since they are correlative (i.e., there are as many levels of selfhood as there are levels of reality). See notes 30, 37.

32. In classifying worldviews, I believe that we must at a minimum use quadrants, levels, lines, states, types, and realms (all six of those variables are discussed at some point in this Introduction). In my particular version of the levels or waves of consciousness (or the levels of selfhood), there are sixteen major basic waves, many of which have two or three substages. In classifying worldviews, most of those basic waves can be condensed into around nine or ten of the most important. In many cases, the substages can be ignored; however, in a few cases, the substages turn out to be crucial (e.g., the difference between early vision-logic and middle/late vision-logic is the difference between first- and second-tier thinking, the difference between pluralistic relativism and universal integralism).

There are many very useful models of the various waves and streams of "bio-psycho-socio-spiritual" development. Some of my favorites (many of which have withstood research in first-, second-, and third-world countries) include: Jane Loevinger (stages of ego development), John Broughton (genetic metaphysics), Robert Kegan (the evolving self), Howard Gardner (multiple streams), Jean Piaget (genetic epistemology), Lawrence Kohlberg (moral development), Carol Gilligan (female moral development and its four hierarchical stages), Clare Graves (value systems; Graves's work has been wonderfully extended by Beck and Cowan's Spiral Dynamics), William Perry (self/other perspectives), Robert Selman (interpersonal development), James Fowler (stages of faith), Evelyn Underhill (stages of mysticism), and Daniel P. Brown (cross-cultural stages of contemplative development). Superb approaches also include those of Michael Basseches, Juan Pascual-Leone, Commons and Richards, Kurt Fischer, Patricia Arlin, Gisela Labouvie-Vief, Jan Sinnott, Jenny Wade, Susanne Cook-Greuter, William Torbert, Deirdre Kramer, Cheryl Armon, Duane Elgin, Joel Funk, and Melvin Miller.

Of the world's contemplative traditions, all have offered overviews of the spiritual path. Some of the most sophisticated include Mahamudra Buddhism (six general stages of meditative awareness), Highest Tantra Yoga (seven phenomenological stages of unfolding enlightenment), Christian mystics such as St. Teresa of Avila (seven stages of interior development), exquisite analysis from

Kabbalah, Sufism, Neoplatonism, Kashmir Shaivism, Patanjali's *Yogasutras*, additions from neopagan and shamanic sources, among many, many others. The "stages" of spiritual development do not refer to rigid linear stages, but fluid and flowing waves of consciousness unfolding, through subtler and subtler dimensions, to the Source and Ground itself.

In *Integral Psychology* I have attempted to correlate, in a very general fashion, over one hundred of these theorists, both conventional (e.g., Loevinger, Graves) and contemplative (e.g., Plotinus, Shankara), including all of the above-mentioned theorists and researchers. Obviously these correlations can only proceed at the most generalized level, which is no excuse to avoid doing so.

The point is that all of these various conceptions immensely enrich our understanding, not only of the types of worldviews available to men and women, but the ways in which these worldviews themselves unfold, evolve, and develop. If we wish to include quadrants, waves, streams, states, types, and realms, these researchers have added enormously to our understanding of the Kosmos and the many ways that it is self-aware. (See also notes 35, 37.)

33. Seven each from those three, and one each from the other four. I am here allowing that chakra 1 is the general sensorimotor realm, which has its own archaic worldview; and that each of the higher chakras (6 and 7) have a direct, supramental, superconscious worldview. But this is just a simple example of the fact that the seven chakras actually support dozens of different worldviews, not just seven.

34. See *One Taste*, October 3 and 15 entries, for a further discussion of this theme. Of course, if junior-dimension worldviews make claims about senior dimensions, they have to be tested using the criteria of the senior dimensions. For example, if astrology makes rational-empirical claims (that is, if chakra 3 makes chakra-4 claims), then those claims need to be tested by rational-empirical means, whereupon they usually fail dramatically (astrology, for example, has consistently failed empirical tests devised by astrologers themselves; see *One Taste*, July 29 and Dec. 21 entries). But astrology is one of the numerous valid worldviews available at the mythic realm of consciousness, and it accomplishes what it is supposed to accomplish at that level—provide meaning, a sense of connection to the cosmos, and a role for the self in the vastness of the universe. It is not, however, a rational chakra-4 science with predictive power. For exactly the same reason, we needn't give much credence to what rational science has to say about chakras 5, 6, or 7.

When I claim that "all views are correct," I mean it in the general sense of every level having its own important truths that not only disclose that level, but also act as important and necessary ingredients of the higher levels (when differentiated-and-integrated, or transcended-and-included). But within any level of reality, there are more valid and less valid views, as determined *by the criteria of that level*. For example, there are good and bad astrologers. Although none of them have thus far successfully passed any rational-empirical tests, that is not the actual criteria of the mythic level. The mythic level, like all levels, attempts to provide coherence, meaning, connection to the cosmos, care of others, and pragmatic guidelines. The mythological version of this (of which astrology is a subset) is an interpretive scheme that provides meaning, ethos, mythos, and sanction for the separate self at that level. Mythology and astrology speak deeply to this level in all of us, and, when in touch with that level, provide a wonderful connection to our vital roots. Good astrologers do this in valid and worthy ways, bad astrologers do not (judged within that level). Of course, it is one thing to tap into that level, quite another to remain there. And those making higher claims for astrology, when they cannot be substantiated, are suspect in any case.

On the other hand, a rational scientist who despises every variety of mythology because it is a lower level (and cannot pass rational-empirical tests) is simply someone out of touch with his or her roots. Integrated individuals are comfortable with all of the levels of reality as manifested in and through them, and can speak the languages of all of the chakras as various situations warrant. As always, it is only the exclusive attachment to any one chakra that causes most of the problems.

3 5. If we use nine or ten major *levels*, a dozen or so major *lines*, the four *quadrants*, different *types*, various *states*, and the notion of *cross-level* phenomena, there is ample room for the major valid features of each of the worldview conceptions mentioned in this Introduction (see also note 32). For the *levels* part of the analysis, in addition to my own terms I will sometimes use the color-levels of Spiral Dynamics, which cover the levels up to centauric (*archaic*: beige; *magic*: purple; *mythic*: red/blue; *rational*: orange; early, middle, and late *centauric*: green, yellow, turquoise), and my own terms for the higher waves (*psychic*, *subtle*, *causal*, *nondual*). Spiral Dynamics is only one of many important models that can be used in such analyses, but it is based on solid research and has much to recommend it. (See the Introduction to Volume Seven of the *Collected Works* for an overview of Spiral Dynamics, along with my modest criticisms and caveats.) Here are a few examples:

Robert Bellah, Mark Gerzon, Paul Ray

Many of the various worldview theorists focus on one quadrant and outline its major stages and/or types. Robert Bellah, for example, focuses on the Lower-Left quadrant and two of its major levels: the mythic-membership (blue), with two of its principal types (republican and biblical), and the egoic-rational (orange), with two of its principal types (utilitarian and therapeutic; a subset of therapeutic is green). His analysis, I believe, is a fine sociological description of these four level-types in the LL, although his prescriptions are perhaps too heavily weighted toward blue. (See *Sex, Ecology, Spirituality* [CW6] and *Sociocultural Evolution* [CW4] for an extensive discussion of Bellah's important work.)

Gerzon's analysis finds six major "cultural states" or "belief systems" existing in America today: Patria, or the religious state (grounded in mythic-membership, blue; often Order Right); Corporatia, or the capitalist state (grounded in egoic-instrumental rationality, orange, often economic libertarians and Free Right); Disia, or the disaffected (which are generally of either preconventional or postconventional waves—purple or green—fighting the conventional blue and orange; often Order Left); Media, or the informational state (generally orange and Free Left); Gaia, or the New Age (a combination of pre- and postconventional; heavily green, often Order Left, combined with purple and red, often with regressive effect); and Officia, or the political class (which cuts across levels, but is mostly blue, orange, and green, reflecting the populations they serve). Gerzon's analysis, conducted largely through the green meme (pluralistic sensitivity), is another useful descriptive phenomenology of some of the major worldviews present in America. Notice that all of those "states" are first tier; there are no second-tier states or major centers of population around which second-tier organizations might fruitfully emerge (the Gaia or "transformation" state is heavily green/purple/red, with an extremely small minority—less than 2 percent—actively engaged in second-tier and higher concerns). Yet without a second-tier operating base, the "new patriotism" that Gerzon wisely recommends will probably remain sporadic at best.

The green meme—which constitutes approximately 20 percent of American population, and is the core of Paul Ray's misnamed "integral culture"—has a chance to move into second-tier and genuinely integral constructions (as outlined in the Introduction to Volume Seven of the *Collected Works*), but it will take an integral vision that can initially speak in green's language in order to act as catalytic converter for the transformation. It remains to be seen if this is even possible at this time. The green meme has been in charge of academia, the cultural elite, and much liberal politics for the past three decades, but it is now being challenged on all sides (its internal self-contradictions, its failed political agenda, the harsh intolerance of the politically correct thought police, its claim to be superior in a world where nothing is supposed to be superior, the nihilism and narcissism of extreme postmodernism, an aggressive marginalization of holarchies and thus its lack of an integral vision). As happens when any meme begins to lose its hegemony, its Inquisitors begin an often belligerent and reactionary defense—what might be called in this case "the mean green meme." And it is the MGM that is now one of the primary roadblocks to a truly integral, more inclusive approach. Whether the hegemony of the MGM crumbles within the next decade or two—leaving behind the many positive, important, necessary functions of the healthy green meme—or whether it holds on bitterly until the death of its adherents (the expected course if history is any judge) remains to be seen. (See the Introduction to Volume Seven of the *Collected Works* for an extensive discussion of this topic.)

Talcott Parsons

The classification scheme of Talcott Parsons (which has been fleshed out by Ralph Potter of Harvard), useful as it is, is also an example of the limitations that result when cross-level phenomena are not taken into account. Parsons's continuum (Right Systemist, Right Marginalist, Middle Marginalist, Left Marginalist, Left Systemist) is an example of a few of the types of worldviews that can be seen *from* chakra 4—they are all rational worldviews. That spectrum of views (which can also be applied to political orientation specifically) is not a *vertical* scale reaching above or below chakra 4 but a *horizontal* scale within chakra 4, stretching from systemic belief in subjective causation (Right Systemist) to systemic belief in objective causation (Left Systemist). Each level of consciousness (or chakra) has various horizontal *types* available to it (see *Integral Psychology* and the Introduction to Volume Seven of the *Collected Works* for a discussion of types). *Political orientation* (from Left to Middle to Right, defined by belief in the location of social causation, objective to mixed to subjective) is a *type* that is available at several *levels* (you can be Left or Right red, Left or Right blue, Left or Right orange, and so on—although traditionally Left and Right have often drawn larger audiences from particular levels, with Left attracting, e.g., purple and green, and Right attracting blue; the point is that, nonetheless, these are independent scales: horizontal levels versus the various typologies available within various levels. This is also why the attempt to arrange political orientation on a vertical scale corresponding with the chakras—ranging from Right Systemist at chakra 1 to Left Systemist at chakra 7—is unworkable; that scheme confuses levels and types, ignores cross-level phenomena, and thus misses the actual nature of both prerational and transrational worldviews [see below]).

Parsons's scheme is predominately a horizontal typology from within chakra 4 (i.e., some of the types of worldviews seen *from* the fourth chakra). This is why his scheme does not cover (or even recognize) the extremely important worldviews that are seen *from* chakra 1 (archaic, beige), chakra 2 (magical, purple), chakra 3 (mythic, red/blue), chakra 5 (psychic, nature mysticism), chakra 6 (deity mysticism), and chakra 7 (formless mysticism).

What is lacking in Parsons scheme is, of course, *the vertical dimension of depth* that we will see is generally missing in all of the conventional theorists discussed in this endnote (with the exception of Underhill for spiritual levels). Nonetheless, each of the schemes outlined here has an important place in an "all-level, all-quadrant" index, and each of their valid points offers irreplaceably useful perspectives.

Vertical Depth

In the main text we saw that there are a few schemes that do attempt to introduce vertical depth by using something like the chakra system itself—e.g., Marx is said to be materialism (chakra 1), Freud is pansexualism (chakra 2), Adler is a type of power psychology (chakra 3), Carl Rogers embraces humanistic psychology (chakra 4), and so on. But most of those schemes, we also saw, fail to take into account cross-level phenomena, and thus the "depth" they offer is badly skewed. Marx, Freud, and Adler are all rational thinkers; they are coming *from* chakra 4 but putting major emphasis *on* the lower chakras. But the lower chakras *themselves* have worldviews that move from *archaic* (beige, chakra 1) to *magic* (purple, chakra 2) to *mythic* (red/blue, chakra 3). At that point, the *egoic-rational* worldviews emerge (orange/green, chakra 4), and they can take as their *object* any of the other chakras. When chakra 4 believes only chakra 1 is real, we get the rational philosophy of materialism—we get a Hobbes or a Marx. When chakra 4 believes the emotional-sexual dimension is most crucial, we get a Freud. When it puts great emphasis on chakra 3, we get an Adler, and so on.

When chakra 4 looks *above* its own station and *thinks* about higher and transrational domains—*but without actually transforming to those higher domains*—then we get various *mental* philosophies *about* spirituality: we get rational Deism (4 aimed at 6), or holistic systems theory taking Gaia as Spirit (4 aimed at 5), or a philosophical concept of the Abyss or Ground of Being (4 aimed at 7), and so on. Those are all still coming from chakra 4, because the subject itself is still at chakra 4 while it thinks about the higher chakras. If the subject (or the level of selfhood) actually transforms to those higher levels of reality, then we have the worldviews *from* those higher chakras. At chakra 5, you do not think about the web of life, you have a direct experience of cosmic consciousness, where you concretely experience being one with the entire gross realm of nature. At chakra 6, you do not think about Platonic archetypes, or merely pray to Deity form, you are rather directly immersed in a living union with Divine Presence: you directly see and feel luminous-blisslove in an overpowering fashion. At chakra 7, you are plunged into the formless unmanifest, the Abyss, Emptiness, Urgrund, Ayn, nirvikalpa samadhi, and so on. The worldviews *from* those higher levels can only be seen *from* those higher levels. So we make a sharp distinction between being at, say, chakra 4 and thinking about higher chakras, and directly being at those higher chakras: the actual worldviews are dramatically different in each case.

All of the theorists in this endnote (except Underhill) are coming mostly *from* the rational level(s), and they give us a series of extremely useful worldviews *from* that perspective. But, as we will continue to see, we need to supplement their important but limited perspectives with a more "all-level, all-quadrant" view, *especially* when it comes to the *early stages* of development (purple, red, and blue) that so dominate the world's population.

Francis Fukuyama: The End of History and the Last Man

Three of the most influential analysts of world affairs today are Francis Fukuyama, Samuel Huntington, and, on a popular level, Thomas Friedman. The differences between them are illustrative of the different emphases they give to the various quadrants, levels, and lines. Fukuyama (*The End of History and the Last Man*) stresses the egoic-rational level (orange) and its *need for self-recognition* (in Maslow's needs holarchy, the self-esteem needs); he notes that the liberal-economic state has managed to deliver this mutual recognition more effectively than any other system in history; he thus believes that no further major historical changes can or will occur in that regard; so that the liberal West, in a sense, has won history, thus "ending" it.

There are many important truths in what Fukuyama says. The problem is that his analysis holds only for the egoic-rational, postconventional, worldcentric levels (orange and green), which constitute at most 30 percent of the world's population. Moreover, *every* person around the world—even those born into an egoic-rational, liberal, postconventional state—starts existence at stage 1 (the archaic, beige), and must develop through the spiral of development, a development which, five or six major stages later, will eventuate in a postconventional (orange) consciousness. *But less than a third of the world's population does so*—due to factors in all four quadrants—and thus the rest of the world (or some 70 percent of its population) does not share Mr. Fukuyama's love of, or even recognition of, the egoic-rational wave (orange meme), but prefers variations on archaic, magic, and mythic (purple, red, and blue). Thus, Fukuyama anchors his analysis in the orange meme of the Left-Hand quadrant and in the liberal-capitalistic economic factors in the Lower-Right quadrant, but that leaves out the pre-orange stages of development that hold the majority of the world's population.

Samuel P. Huntington: The Clash of Civilizations

This is where Samuel Huntington's analysis is useful. For "underneath" the world-centric, postconventional, orange and green memes, there lie the roots and foundations of the various ethnocentric civilizations. Although many of these ethnocentric civilizations contain worldcentric ideals, nonetheless the masses of people in each civilization remain heavily in purple, red, blue (and more rarely, orange) waves of consciousness unfolding. These huge civilization blocks (Huntington gives nine altogether: Western, Latin American, African, Islamic, Sinic, Hindu, Orthodox, Buddhist, and Japanese) are *anchored*, in part, in the underlying tectonic cultural plates of the Lower Left (mostly purple, red, blue, orange), which not only represent the general levels or waves through which individuals and cultures develop, but remain as unbelievably powerful archeological strata through which all developmental lines pass. Taking these major civilizations (and, I add, their underlying cultural waves and archeological strata) into account is thus a crucial part of a more integral world politics.

Huntington gives several definitions of a civilization. At one point he belittles the German distinction between civilization and culture. "German thinkers drew a sharp distinction between civilization, which involved mechanics, technology, and material factors, and culture, which involved values, ideals, and the higher intellectual, artistic, moral qualities of a society." But that is a very real distinction—it is, in fact, the Lower-Left (cultural) and Lower-Right (social) quadrants—and Huntington himself uses *both* of those (it usually doesn't pay to disagree with Germans when it comes to thinking). Huntington is objecting to the "sharp" separation of cultural and social, which I agree is a mistake; the quadrants are distinguishable but not separable, and both need to be included.

Civilizations, as Huntington defines them, are broad cultural patterns (and by "cultural" he means "sociocultural"); they are "comprehensive" ("that is, none of their constituent units can be fully understood without reference to the encompassing civilization"); they show development or evolution ("they are dynamic, they evolve, they adapt"—which can also include decay and death, and usually does); they are not political, but deeper than that ("a civilization may contain one or many political units"). I believe all of those are essentially correct, but I might be a bit more precise. In my view civilizations are amalgams of various lines or streams (such as values, cognitive styles, language, morals, ethics, customs, and traditions) as they move through various levels or waves (e.g., purple, red, blue, orange, green) as manifested in each of the quadrants (individual, behavioral, cultural, and social).

Huntington raises the issue of the evolutionary versus circular models of history. In my opinion, both are views are correct. There are evolutionary *waves* of development, within which there are *cycles*, *seasons*, or *phases* of development. The former refers to transformational development, the latter to translational development. In many (but not all) cases, the completion of a cycle opens a system (individual or collective) to a transformation (which may be either transcendental and progressive or disintegrative and regressive). (See *Integral Psychology* for a discussion of this theme.)

As we will see, although Huntington gives a fairly broad definition of civilizations, he is especially focusing on the Lower-Left quadrant, or culture in the specific sense; and his recommendations are heavily weighted to the blue meme (which is not necessarily as bad as many liberals would have us believe: remember, 70 percent of the world's population is blue or lower, and thus, when in Rome . . . Moreover, as we saw, conservatives—precisely because they recognize subjective causation and stages of the subjective up to blue—are often much more reliable and realistic judges of those realms than are liberals, who usually don't see them at all and thus are literally flying blind through the interior territories while demanding exterior changes.)

For most of humanity's history, the Left- and Right-Hand quadrants developed lockstep with each other. In the Lower Left, the evolution from archaic (beige) to magic (purple) to mythic (red/blue) to rational (orange) was accompanied, in the Lower Right, by technological development that moved, respectively, from foraging to horticultural to agrarian to industrial. Archaic worldviews went with a foraging base, late mythic worldviews went with an agrarian base, rational worldviews went with an industrial base, and so on.

But with the rise of modernity (rational-industrial), the increasing globalization of cultural evolution made a very intense type of *cross-level* phenomenon possible: for example, tribal cultures could gain access to rational-industrial technology, often with horrifying results. Moreover, the same type of cross-level access could occur *within* a given culture: Auschwitz was the product of rational-technological capacity (orange) pressed into the hands of intensely prerational (red/blue) ethnocentric aggression. Today, almost any ethnic tribe or feudal order can gain access to biological and chemical weapons that historically they would never have been able to produce themselves, and the results are literally explosive. Precisely because the Right-Hand quadrants are all *material*, these material artifacts (modes of technology to nuclear weapons) can be obtained by individuals at almost *any* level of interior, Left-Hand development, even if they themselves could never produce them. These types of phenomena make cross-level analysis of quadrants, levels, and lines absolutely mandatory in today's world politics, and it dooms analyses that do less than that.

The essential point, as I see it, is that civilizations evidence, in part, the pyramid of development, where the higher the level of development, the fewer individuals at it. This means that the bulk of the world's population, as we were saying, is at the early or foundational stages—primarily purple, red, and blue (and more rarely, orange). That is not a moral judgement; not only do all of those stages perform crucial functions in every culture, they are the necessary foundation stones for higher development. As we said, every person, in every culture, no matter how "high" or "advanced," is born at square 1, and begins the great unfolding from there. The prime directive is thus to act so as to protect and promote the health of the entire spiral of development, and not to privilege a favorite wave.

But this does mean that a new "realpolitik" will take into account the entire spiral, while realizing that the bulk of the population will remain at purple/red (preconventional) and blue (conventional)—and thus the bulk of the world's population is egocentric-to-ethnocentric, and these ethnocentric blocks will have an enormous hand in shaping world currents. Not the only hand, as we will see, but a very important one. Beck and Cowan estimate that 10 percent of the world's population is purple, 20 percent red, and 40 percent blue—thus around 70 percent of the world's population has a center of gravity at ethnocentric or lower: an extraordinary mass.

That also means that around 70 percent of the world's population falls short of the level at which Fukuyama's analysis would kick in. (When 100 percent of the world's population can be expected to reach orange in their lifetimes, that would be a type of "end of history"—but that is a century or two away, if then. Besides, there is then green, then yellow, then turquoise, then coral/psychic. . . . It appears, alas, that history might never end. . . .)

The Downside of the Green Meme

Unfortunately Huntington's analysis, brilliant and useful up to a point, is largely conducted on a flat playing field. He recognizes the existence and profound importance of these large civilization blocks, but he does not seem to acknowledge the archeological layers of development (e.g., purple, red, blue, orange, green) that are some of the crucial *strata* of these blocks. He is giving us a surface reading of the very real territories that are today present; but he is not giving us the archeological, paleontological, developmental, memetic analysis of the infrastructures of those blocks. Adding this vertical dimension to his horizontal analysis will give us a much more integral vision from which to make sounder political judgments, I believe.

Huntington then moves to his policy recommendations, and there is no question about it: they are heavily blue meme. This has often infuriated liberals (especially the MGM), because it violates their stated aims of diversity, multiculturalism, and sensitivity. But once again, as with Fukuyama's analysis, the liberal-green analysis only applies to a very small percentage of the world's population. In fact, Beck and Cowan have found that less than 10 percent of the world's population is at green (and almost *all* of that is in the Western civilization block, which is a massive embarrassment for the green multiculturalists, who champion everything *but* Western civilization).

Moreover, in order for the rest of the world to get to green, individuals have to develop from purple to red to blue to orange to green. As Beck and Cowan (and virtually all developmental researchers) constantly stress, the blue meme (by whatever name) is an absolutely crucial, unavoidable, necessary building block of higher stages (including green), and yet green does absolutely everything in its power to destroy blue wherever it finds it. As Spiral Dynamics puts it, "Green dissolves blue"—and in so doing, as Beck himself says, "Green has introduced more harm in the last thirty years than any other meme."

It is not that what green is saying is wrong; it is simply a case of very bad timing. The world at large—and much of America as well—is simply not ready for green pluralism. More than that, as Huntington quite correctly points out, no civilization in history has survived with a pluralistic agenda—but not because, as Huntington believes, that no civilization can so survive, but simply because, until more than 10 percent of the population is actually at the green wave, the cultural center of gravity will be heavily pre-green, and thus a culture that tries to ram pluralism and multiculturalism down everybody's throat is definitely going to come apart at the seams faster than you can say "deconstruction." That is what Beck means by saying that the harm green has done often outweighed the good—and that is what Huntington is also sharply criticizing.

The difference, however—and this is a big however—is that Beck is giving a post-green analysis, based on the prime directive: namely, when green dissolves blue, it cripples the spiral of development; it makes it absolutely impossible for purple and red to develop further, because there is no blue base to accept the development. Green is thus horribly damaging the overall spiral of human unfolding, here and abroad, and thus erasing much of the undeniable good that green can, and has, done on its own. The call is for all of the memes, including blue and green, to be seen as necessary parts of the overall spiral, and thus each be allowed to make its own crucial contribution to the comprehensive health of the spiral.

Huntington, on the other hand, is giving a pre-green attack on green. He is championing blue because he deeply does not like green. (He is not attacking the notion of what might be called "international pluralism," which recognizes the importance and legitimacy of the major civilization blocks—in fact, Huntington is a strong advocate of international pluralism. He is attacking multiculturalism in America, which he feels is dissolving certain necessary foundations.) This has made many liberals completely ignore the important points of Huntington's argument. For, even if Huntington's recommendations are heavily blue, that is often where we need to *begin* in many instances. Green has, inadvertently or not, damaged blue infrastructures both here and abroad, and a structural refurbishing is wisely in order (reversing, for example, what George W. Bush has called "the soft bigotry of lowered expectations").

On a sturdy blue and then orange foundation, green ideals can be built. No blue and orange, no green. Thus green's attack on blue and orange is profoundly suicidal. Not only that, but when the highly developed, postformal green wave champions any and every "multicultural" movement, it acts to *encourage* other memes *not* to grow into green. Thus, the more green succeeds, the more it destroys itself. (See the Introduction to Volume Seven of the *Collected Works*.)

Thus, it is to green's great advantage to adopt the prime directive and work for ways to facilitate the entire spiral of development, and not adopt Order-Left imperatives commanding everybody to be sensitive. And, after all, the more people at the green wave, the more people are ready to make the leap into the hyperspace of second-tier consciousness, where truly integral approaches to the world's problems can be conceived and implemented.

World Civilization

Huntington ends his blue recommendations with a dawning realization of postconventional, worldcentric, World Civilization, which not only partakes of orange/green, but begins to intuit the integral, second-tier waves. His recommendations do not stem from that level, but they do point to it.

Huntington notes that what is often called "universalism" is really just imperialism—that is, one civilization (such as the Western) tries to impose its values on all the others. That is a universalism that Huntington and I both categorically reject. But Huntington moves toward a universalism of "commonalities," which means that, in addition to recognizing and honoring the many important differences between cultures, we also attempt to cherish those things that we have in common as human beings living on a very small planet, a universalism I strongly share (what I also call unity-in-diversity, universal pluralism, unitas multiplex, universal integralism, etc.). "In a multicivilizational world, the constructive course is to renounce universalism [imperialism], accept diversity [international pluralism], and seek commonalities." I quite agree, as far as that goes.

As for a benign universalism (unitas multiplex), Huntington concludes, correctly I believe, that "if human beings are ever to develop a universal civilization, it will emerge gradually through the exploration and expansion of these commonalities. Thus . . . peoples in all civilizations should search for and attempt to expand the values, institutions, and practices they have in common with peoples of other civilizations."

He then moves toward the heart of the matter, the transformation from ethnocentric (blue) to worldcentric (even second-tier): "This effort would contribute not only to limiting the clash of civilizations but also to strengthening Civilization in the singular [*not* imperialism, but unity-in-diversity]. The singular Civilization presumably refers to a complex mix of *higher levels* of morality, religion, learning, art, philosophy, technology, material well-being, and probably other things" (my italics). In other words, as I would put it, the various developmental lines or streams ("morality, religion, learning, art," etc.) move through the developmental levels or waves (purple, red, blue, orange, green, etc.—or, in short, egocentric to ethnocentric to worldcentric), and the higher the level of development in the various lines, the greater the chance for the emergence of a world Civilization—precisely because the tectonic plates do in fact move from egocentric to ethnocentric to worldcentric (to pneumocentric). Huntington's analysis reminds us that the vast bulk of the world's population is still ethnocentric, and a realpolitik had better take that into account, if it wants to actually reach a worldcentric anything.

So Huntington then raises the crucial question to which his entire book has pointed: "How can one chart the ups and downs of humanity's development of Civilization?" He asks the question, and then the book ends.

My own suggestion, of course, is that an "all-quadrant, all-level, all-lines" approach is one of the best methods available for charting exactly that unfolding, in all its perilous ups and downs. Huntington's analysis is generally fine up to blue; but it needs to be supplemented with an analysis that leads us through orange and green and into second tier (integral vision-logic); and it needs to be itself conducted *from* the prime directive of second-tier consciousness, or so I believe, thus making more friendly the waters leading to the promised land of worldcentric Civilization and unitas multiplex.

Thomas L. Friedman: The Lexus and the Olive Tree

Thomas Friedman, though considered by some to be a mere popularizer, manages to put his finger on several items that the other analysts either miss or fail to emphasize. Friedman gives a masterly overview of why a more integral approach is necessary. Unfortunately, in my opinion, his overview is also a strictly surface analysis, consisting of six major domains or streams, but bereft of any levels or waves. (This is not peculiar to Friedman but is the standard approach in most sociocultural analysis—Huntington, Brzezinski, Paul Kennedy, Gerzon, Robert Kaplan, etc., much as their work is otherwise truly admirable).

Friedman's six streams or domains are: politics, culture, national security, finance, technology, and environment, and he maintains that in order to understand one of them, you have to try to understand all of them. He then congratulates Paul Kennedy and John Lewis Gaddis for attempting also to be more "integral" and "global," and as much as I half-applaud that move, the "global" they recommend is global flatland, the flatland web of life, which is interconnected on one level, but lacks pluridimensional depth (the standard subtle reductionism). "In an essay they jointly authored," says Friedman, "Gaddis and Kennedy bemoaned the fact that particularists are too often, in too many countries, the ones still making and analyzing foreign policy. 'These people,' the two Yale historians wrote, 'are perfectly competent at taking in parts of the picture, but they have difficulty seeing the entire thing. They pigeonhole priorities, pursuing them separately and simultaneously, with little thought to how each might undercut the other. They proceed confidently enough from tree to tree, but seem astonished to find themselves lost in the forest. The great strategists of the past kept forests as well as the trees in view. They were generalists, and they operated from an ecological perspective. They understood that the world is a web, in which adjustments made here are bound to have effects over there—that everything is interconnected. Where, though, might one find generalists today? . . . The dominant trend within universities and the think tanks is toward ever-narrower specialization: a higher premium is placed on functioning deeply within a single field than broadly across several. And yet without some awareness of the whole . . . there can be no strategy. And without strategy, there is only drift."

And without depth, there is only more drift. What needs to be added to flatland holism and the ecological web of life is the vertical dimension and the pyramid of life: *both* dimensions are crucially important. But an analysis that is bereft of the vertical dimension of the waves of consciousness unfolding is playing flatland chess, not three-dimensional chess (which happens to be the game the real world is playing), and thus the crucial height and depth dimensions slip through the analysis, so that the analysis, *by default*, proceeds from the level of subjective development of the analyst. This usually means the blue, orange, or green meme tries to understand the entire spiral of development through the lens of its own wave of perception, with less than satisfactory results.

So while I half-applaud the "web of life" interconnections ("all-quadrants, no levels") that these analysts are bringing to the picture, I suggest that a more adequate conception ("all-quadrants, all-levels") would serve strategy with even less drift.

To return to Friedman. The title of his recent book, *The Lexus and the Olive Tree*, is meant to indicate what he sees as one of the fundamental conflicts in today's world: the tension between specific cultures (similar to Huntington's "civilizations"), which are local, and increasing globalization, which is not. Techno-economic globalization (represented by the Lexus) tends to disrupt, even destroy, local traditions and cultures (represented by the olive tree), and that clash is a central factor in today's world. Friedman gives an overview of the six domains and how they play out in this central conflict, but the star of his narrative, and what he believes is a major driving force, is that of global technology, from the Lexus to cyberspace, for it is proceeding with what appears to be its own relentless logic: homogenize the world. But, like it or not, globalization is here to stay: "I believe that if you want to understand the post–Cold War world you have to start by understanding that a new international system has succeeded it—globalization. That is 'The One Big Thing' people should focus on. Globalization is not the only thing influencing events in the world today, but to the extent that there is North Star and a worldwide shaping force, it is this system. What is new is the system; what is old is power politics, chaos, clashing civilizations, and liberalism. And what is the drama of the post–Cold War world is the interaction between this new system and these old passions."

Friedman's analysis of globalization, while recognizing many streams, concentrates almost entirely on those in the Lower-Right quadrant: the social system of techno-economic globalization that is pulling the rest of train. As far as his LR-quadrant analysis goes, I believe he is generally correct (but, as we will see, the lack of vertical depth perception in the interior quadrants hobbles the analysis). His conclusions (at least in the LR) are also in line with the analysis, controversial at the time but now more accepted, of Peter Schwartz and Peter Leyden ("The Long Boom," *Wired*, July 1997), where they point out that five streams of technology, now already in motion (personal computers, telecommunications, biotechnology, nanotechnology, and alternative energy), constitute a powerful, perhaps unavoidable, drive toward global integration. Again, although I agree with that analysis as far as it goes, when it is seen within an "all-level, all-quadrant" perspective, its harsh realities are softened by the equally compelling forces in the other quadrants—not to mention refocused by an understanding of the archeological layers and tectonic plates of consciousness that will *in any event* still inhabit the global techno-net (because *everybody* is born at square 1 and will continue to move through those strata, with billions of people stretching across all of the colors of the entire spectrum of consciousness).

Friedman's (and Schwartz and Leyden's) Lower-Right quadrant focus nonetheless helps to balance the equally lopsided picture given by analysts such as Kaplan and Huntington, who almost certainly underestimate the power of the Lower-Right quadrant (especially the emergence of system networks, the impact of cyberspace, the power of global markets, the diffusion of technology—in financial, environmental, and commercial domains). There is an Eros to the Kosmos: there is a subtle, slow, relentless evolutionary drift, a migratory current to unfolding events, that, in the very long run, unfolds higher and deeper connections—egocentric to ethnocentric to worldcentric. Worldcentric, globalizing technology has Eros on its side; but that does not mean that such globalization should or will carry the Western surface values with it. Nor does it mean that a worldcentric technology will simply impose a worldcentric culture on everybody, because, once again, *everybody* is born at square 1 (archaic, beige, egocentric) and has to begin the great spiral of development from there, so that ethnocentric pockets of culture will be a part of human civilization *indefinitely* (just as, within any civilization—Western, say—there are purple street gangs, red athletic tribes, blue feudal orders, green communes—and always will be, as long as human beings are born at square 1). All of that is completely missed in these Lower-Right quadrant analyses that can only see surface techno-globalization. On the other hand, an "all-quadrant, all-levels, all-lines" perspective allows us to take the best of each analysis and set them all in a larger vision where their own important contributions (and limitations) can be better appreciated.

Evelyn Underhill: The Waves of Spiritual Experience

Let me round out this overview—which is about integrating available worldviews—with one example from the upper reaches of consciousness development and spiritual experiences. Since I have written extensively on this, I will be brief. In various publications (AP, UE, EE, TC, SES, ES, IP) I have presented considerable evidence that there are at least four different types of spiritual experiences—nature mysticism (psychic), deity mysticism (subtle), formless mysticism (causal), and nondual mysticism (nondual); and further, these evidence waves of increasing depth. I have often been accused of deriving this schema exclusively from Eastern sources, thus marginalizing (oh dear) Western traditions. This is untrue. For example, Evelyn Underhill, whose *Mysticism* is justly regarded as a classic overview of Western mystical traditions, concludes that spiritual experiences (as evidenced in the overall Western tradition) exist along a *developmental continuum* from "nature mysticism" (union with the web of life) to "metaphysical mysticism" (from archetypal illumination to formless absorption) to "divine mysticism" (states of nondual union)—in other words, virtually identical to my scheme.

But I have added what I believe is an important *cross-level* analysis (and we can see again the importance of distinguishing levels of selfhood and levels of reality), namely: a person at almost any stage of typical development (e.g., purple, red, blue, orange, green, yellow) can have an altered state of consciousness or a *peak experience* of any of the higher realms (psychic, subtle, causal, nondual). The person then *interprets* these higher experiences in the terms of the level at which the person presently resides. This inescapably calls for one of those cross-level combinatorial analyses: e.g., a person at blue can peak experience psychic, subtle, causal, nondual; so can orange, green, etc. This gives us a grid of over two-dozen very real—and very different—types of spiritual experiences. (Of course, in order for these temporary states to become enduring patterns in awareness, the person will have to grow and develop through the spiral and into these higher realms as a *permanent* realization, and not merely as a temporary or nonordinary state: passing *states* must become permanent *traits*. See *Integral Psychology* for an extensive discussion of these topics; see also note 37.)

These spiritual experiences might sound almost entirely removed from the more conventional analyses of Fukuyama, Friedman, Huntington, Kaplan, Kennedy, and crew. In fact, although often marginal, they are sometimes decisive. More than one world leader, in the course of the formative events in his or her life, has had a powerful peak experience or altered state, often religious in nature, that profoundly molded their subsequent worldviews and agendas, and not necessarily for the better (Hitler was a mystic of sorts, as was Rasputin). In some cases we deeply admire the results of this religious infusion (say, Joan of Arc or Martin Luther King, Jr.). In other cases we are repelled (Himmler, Charles Manson). This is where a cross-level analysis becomes crucial: what level is the spiritual experience coming from, and what level is doing the interpreting?

When egocentric levels receive a jolting infusion from the transpersonal realms, the result is usually a more empowered egocentric, often psychotic. When ethnocentric levels are hit with a transpersonal jolt, reborn furies result. When worldcentric levels are transfused, an Abraham Lincoln or a Ralph Waldo Emerson shines forth. An integral approach would make these factors an important part of an "all-level, all-quadrant" analysis. (And not just in world leaders. Data is impossibly unreliable here, but at the very least a majority of individuals report having had at least one major peak/spiritual experience. These events are some of the most powerful motivating forces in human psychology, whether they light the face of a Mother Teresa or drive the intense fanaticism of a jihad, and no analysis of world events that ignores them can hope to succeed.)

An Integral Constitution

All quadrants, levels, lines, states, types, and realms: the time is ripe to move world political analysis to an integral wave.

And we still stand in need of an integral Constitution of world Civilization. I believe, of course, that it will be an "all-level, all-quadrant" approach, grounded in part from what we will have learned from an articulated stage II Third Way. Beyond that, in my estimation, it would be guided by the *Basic Moral Intuition* (protect and promote the greatest depth for the greatest span), which itself embodies both the *prime directive* (facilitate the health of the entire spiral of development without privileging any particular wave) and a gentle *pacer of transformation* for the full spectrum of human resources (inviting people to grow and develop their full potentials—interior and exterior—to the best of their abilities). Those items—the integral approach, the BMI, the prime directive, and a pacer of transformation—are key ingredients, I believe, in any second-tier or integral Constitution. (See note 17.)

The translation of these ideas into a World Facilitation Federation, grounded in an integral Constitution, remains the great challenge of millennial politics.

36. This sounds a little bit like liberal inclusiveness, except that the traditional liberal, who ignores or denies stages of interior development, cannot abide many of the natural and necessary stages of interior development (particularly the conformist, law-and-order, fundamentalist stage) through which all normal human beings progress, and thus liberals act to dissolve these crucially important structures wherever they find them, which has a profoundly disruptive and regressive effect. As Spiral Dynamics puts it, green dissolves blue, and thus green often has an incredibly harmful effect on the prime directive, not only at home but in foreign policy (e.g., trying to push "human rights"—green—on countries that are at blue is, at best, a waste of time; and, at paradoxical worst, a reactionary endeavor. You handle blue rigidity not with green sensitivity but with, e.g., orange technology). See notes 15, 17, and 35.

Theorists sympathetic to a more integral orientation toward minorities (and developing countries) include Beck and Cowan, Connie Hilliard, and Maureen Silos. Contributions by all of them can be found in Crittenden et al. (eds.), *Kindred Visions*, forthcoming from Shambhala Publications.

37. Note the emphasis on the two stages of a genuine Third Way: acknowledging the subjective, then acknowledging waves of the subjective.

States and Structures

Ever since *A Sociable God*, I have emphasized the difference between *states of consciousness* and *structures of consciousness*, and I again stress this difference in *Integral Psychology*. States—including normal or natural states (e.g., waking, dreaming, sleeping) and nonnormal, nonordinary, or altered states (e.g., meditation, peak experiences, religious experiences)—are all temporary, passing phenomena: they come, stay a bit, and go, even if in cycles. Structures, on the other hand, are more enduring; they are fairly permanent patterns of consciousness and behavior. Both developmental levels and developmental lines (waves and streams) are largely composed of structures of consciousness, or holistic, self-organizing patterns with a recognizable code, regime, or agency. (This is not to be confused with the school of structuralism, with which I have, at best, tangential relations. See the Introduction to Volume Two of the *Collected Works*.)

Structures, in other words, are quite similar to enduring holons; and these basic structures or basic levels are essentially the basic levels in the Great Nest of Being. When these levels refer to the subject, we speak of levels of consciousness, levels of selfhood, or levels of subjectivity; when these levels refer to objects, we speak of levels of reality, realms of reality, or spheres of reality (see notes 30, 31).

States of consciousness, although they have structural features, tend to be more temporary and fluid. However, it is important to recognize two general categories of states, which might be called "broad" and "narrow" (not to be confused with normal and nonnormal). Allan Combs calls these *states of consciousness* and *states of mind*, the former referring to broad patterns (such as sleeping and waking) and the latter referring to moment-to-moment "small" states (such as joy, doubt, determination, etc.). Allan believes that these are related in a multi-leveled fashion, with structures of consciousness forming the broad base, within which various states of consciousness occur, and within those, various states of mind. While that is one possible scheme, I believe Allan has the relationship between states of consciousness and structures of consciousness reversed. A broad state of consciousness, such as waking, has numerous different structures of consciousness within it (e.g., the waking state includes mythic, rational, centauric, etc.), but not vice versa (e.g., you cannot be in the rational structure and then be in several different states, such as drunken or sleeping). Thus, within the broad *states* of consciousness, there exist various *structures* of consciousness.

But within those structures of consciousness, there exist various states of mind. Those structures do indeed constrain and implicitly mold all of the states of mind that occur within them (e.g., a person at concrete operational thinking will have most of his or her thoughts—and states of mind—arise *within* that structure). Thus, the overall relation of these three items, in my opinion, is: broad states of consciousness, within which there exist various structures of consciousness, within which there exist various states of mind.

At the same time, the relationships among these various states and structures is definitely holonic and intermeshing. They are not simply plunked down on top of each other like so many bricks, but are interwoven in mutually influential ways. See *Integral Psychology* for a further discussion of states and structures. See also notes 30, 31.

THE MARRIAGE OF
SENSE AND SOUL

Integrating Science and Religion

A Note to the Reader

There is nothing that will cure the senses but the soul, and nothing that will cure the soul but the senses.

—OSCAR WILDE

I T IS HARD TO SAY exactly when modern science began. Many scholars would date it at roughly 1600, when both Kepler and Galileo started using precision measurement to map the universe. But one thing is certain: starting from whatever date we choose, modern science was, in many important ways and right from the start, deeply antagonistic to established religion.

Most of the early scientists, of course, remained true believers, genuinely embracing the God of the Church; many of them sincerely believed that they were simply discovering God's archetypal laws as revealed in the book of nature. And yet, with the introduction of the scientific method, a universal acid was released that would slowly, inevitably, painfully eat into and corrode the centuries-old steel of religion, dissolving, often beyond recognition, virtually all of its central tenets and dogmas. Within the span of a mere few centuries, intelligent men and women in all walks of life could deeply and profoundly do something that would have utterly astonished previous epochs: deny the very existence of Spirit.

Despite the entreaties of the tenderhearted in both camps, the relation of science and religion in the modern world—that is, in the last three or four centuries—has changed very little since their introduction to each other in the trial of Galileo, where the scientist agreed to shut his mouth and the Church agreed not to burn him. Many wonderful exceptions aside, the plain historical fact has been that orthodox science and orthodox religion deeply distrust, and often despise, each other.

It has been a tense confrontation, a philosophical cold war of global reach. On the one hand, modern empirical science has made stunning and colossal discoveries: the cure of diseases such as typhoid, smallpox, and malaria, which racked the ancient world with untold anguish; the engineering of marvels from the airplane to the Eiffel Tower to the space shuttle; discoveries in the biological sciences that verge on the secrets of life itself; advances in computer sciences that are literally revolutionizing human existence; not to mention plopping a person on the moon. Science can accomplish such feats, its proponents maintain, because it utilizes a solid method for discovering *truth*, a method that is empirical and experimental and based on evidence, not one that relies on myths and dogmas and unverifiable proclamations. Thus science, its proponents believe, has made discoveries that have relieved more pain, saved more lives, and advanced knowledge incomparably more than any religion and its pie-in-the-sky God. Humanity's only real salvation is a reliance on scientific truth and its advance, not a projection of human potentials onto an illusory Great Other before whom we grovel and beg in the most childish and undignified of fashions.

There is a strange and curious thing about scientific truth. As its own proponents constantly explain, science is basically value-free. It tells us what *is*, not what *should be* or *ought to be*. An electron isn't good or bad, it just is; the cell's nucleus is not good or bad, it just is; a solar system isn't good or bad, it just is. Consequently science, in elucidating or describing these basic facts about the universe, has virtually nothing to tell us about good and bad, wise and unwise, desirable and undesirable. Science might offer us truth, but how to use that truth wisely: on this science is, and always has been, utterly silent. And rightly so; that is not its job, that is not what it was designed to do, and we certainly should not blame science for this silence. Truth, not wisdom or value or worth, is the province of science.

In the midst of this silence, religion speaks. Humans seem condemned to meaning, condemned to find value, depth, care, concern, worth, significance to their everyday existence. If science will not (and cannot) provide it, most men and women will look elsewhere. For literally billions of people around the world, religion provides the basic meaning of their lives, the glue of their existence, and offers them a set of guidelines about what is good (e.g., love, care, compassion) and what is not (e.g., lying, cheating, stealing, killing). On the deepest level, religion has even claimed to offer a means of contacting or communing with an ultimate Ground of Being. But by any other name, religion offers what it believes is a genuine *wisdom*.

Fact and meaning, truth and wisdom, science and religion. It is a strange and grotesque coexistence, with value-free science and value-laden religion, deeply distrustful of each other, aggressively attempting to colonize the same small planet. It is a clash of Titans, to be sure, yet neither seems strong enough to prevail decisively nor graceful enough to bow out altogether. The trial of Galileo is repeated countless times, moment to moment, around the world, and it is tearing humanity, more or less, in half.

Fools rush in where angels fear to tread; therefore, the integration of science and religion is the theme of this book. If you are an orthodox religious believer, I would ask only that you relax into the argument and see where it takes you; I do not think you will be dismayed. My primary prerequisite in this discussion is that *both* science and religion must find the argument acceptable in their own terms. For this marriage to be genuine, it must have the free consent of both spouses.

If you are an orthodox scientist, I would only suggest that, as you have a thousand times in the past when you were working on a problem, let curiosity and wonder bubble up, but in this case don't focus it on a specific solution. Simply let wonder fill your being until it takes you out of yourself and into the staggering mystery that is the existence of the world, a mystery that facts alone can never begin to fill. If Spirit does exist, it will lie in that direction, the direction of wonder, a direction that intersects the very heart of science itself. And you will find, in this adventure, that the scientific method will never be left behind in the search for an ultimate ground.

And we all know how to wonder, don't we? From the depths of a Kosmos too miraculous to believe, from the heights of a universe too wondrous to worship, from the insides of an astonishment that has no boundaries, an answer begins to suggest itself, and whispers to us lightly. If we listen very carefully, from within this infinite wonder, perhaps we can hear the gentle promise that, in the very heart of the Kosmos itself, both science and religion will be there together to welcome us home.

K.W.
Boulder, Colorado
Summer 1997

PART ONE

THE PROBLEM

1

The Challenge of Our Times

INTEGRATING SCIENCE AND RELIGION

THERE IS ARGUABLY no more important and pressing topic than the relation of science and religion in the modern world. Science is clearly one of the most profound methods that humans have yet devised for discovering *truth,* while religion remains the single greatest force for generating *meaning.* Truth and meaning, science and religion; but we still cannot figure out how to get the two of them together in a fashion that *both* find acceptable.

The reconciliation of science and religion is not merely a passing academic curiosity. These two enormous forces—truth and meaning—are at war in today's world. Modern science and premodern religion* aggressively inhabit the same globe, each vying, in its own way, for world domination. And something, sooner or later, has to give.

Science and technology have created a global and transnational framework of industrial, economic, medical, scientific, and informational systems. Yet however beneficial those systems may be, they are all, in themselves, devoid of meaning and value. As its own proponents constantly point out, science tells us what is, not what should be. Science tells us about electrons, atoms, molecules, galaxies, digital data bits, network systems: it tells us what a thing is, not whether it is good or bad, or what it should be or could be or ought to be. Thus this enormous

---

*"Premodern" is not meant in a pejorative way, only in the sense that the roots of most religions lie in the premodern world.

global scientific infrastructure is, in itself, a valueless skeleton, however functionally efficient it might be.

Into this colossal value vacuum, religion has happily rushed. Science has created this extraordinary worldwide and global framework—itself utterly devoid of meaning—but within that ubiquitous framework, sub-global pockets of premodern religions have created value and meaning for billions of people in every part of the world. And these same premodern religions often deny validity to the scientific framework within which they live, a framework that provides most of their medicine, economics, banking, information networks, transportation, and communications. Within the scientific skeleton of truth, religious meaning attempts to flourish, often by denying the scientific framework itself—rather like sawing off the branch on which you cheerily perch.

The disgust is mutual, because modern science gleefully denies virtually all of the basic tenets of religion in general. According to the typical view of modern science, religion is not much more than a holdover from the childhood of humanity, with about as much reality as, say, Santa Claus. Whether the religious claims are more literal (Moses parted the Red Sea) or more mystical (religion involves direct spiritual experience), modern science denies them all, simply because there is no credible empirical evidence for any of them.

So here is the utterly bizarre structure of today's world: a scientific framework that is global in its reach and omnipresent in its information and communication networks, forms a meaningless skeleton within which hundreds of subglobal, premodern religions create value and meaning for billions; and they each—science and religion each—tend to deny significance, even reality, to the other. This is a massive and violent schism and rupture in the internal organs of today's global culture, and this is exactly why many social analysts believe that if some sort of reconciliation between science and religion is not forthcoming, the future of humanity is, at best, precarious.

WHAT DO WE MEAN BY "RELIGION"?

The aim of this book is to suggest how we might begin to think about both science and religion in ways that allow their reconciliation and eventual integration, *on terms acceptable to both parties.*

Of course, this reconciliation of science and religion depends, in part, on exactly what we mean by "science" and "religion." We will actually devote several chapters to just this topic (Chapters 11, 12, and 13). In the meantime, a few crucial points should be noted.

Defining "religion" is itself an almost impossible task, largely because there are so many different forms of the beast that it becomes hard to spot what, if anything, they have in common. But one thing is immediately obvious: many of the specific and central claims of the world's great religions *contradict each other, but if we cannot find a common core of the world's great religions, then we will never find an integration of science and religion.*

Indeed, if we cannot find a common core that is generally acceptable to most religions, we would be forced to choose one religion and deny importance to the others; or we would have to "pick and choose" tenets from among various religions, thus alienating the great religious traditions themselves. We would never arrive at an integration of science and religion that both parties would find acceptable, because most religions would reject what was done to their beliefs in order to force this "reconciliation."

It will do no good, for example, to claim, as many Christian creationists have, that the Big Bang suggests that the world is the product of a personal creator God, when one of the most profound and influential religions in the world, Buddhism, does not believe in a personal God to begin with. Thus, we cannot use the Big Bang in order to "integrate" science and religion unless we can first find a way to reconcile Christianity and Buddhism (and the world's wisdom traditions in general). Otherwise, we are not integrating science and religion; we are simply "integrating" one narrow version of Christianity with one version of science. This is not worthy of the term "integration," and it is certainly not an integration that other religions would find acceptable.

Thus, those who wish to advocate one particular form of religion—whether it be a patriarchal God the Father, a matriarchal Great Goddess, a fundamentalist Christianity, a mythological Shintoism, a Gaia ecoreligion, a fundamentalist Islam—have often taken various modern developments in science and attempted to show that these developments just happen to fit with a very generous interpretation of their particular religion. This will not be our approach. Because the fact is, unless science can be shown to be compatible with certain deep features common to *all* of the world's major wisdom traditions, the long-sought reconciliation will remain as elusive as ever.

So before we can even attempt to integrate science and religion, we need to see if we can find a common core of the world's great wisdom traditions. This common core would have to be a general frame that, shorn of specific details and concrete contents, would nonetheless be acceptable to most religious traditions, at least in the abstract. Is there such a common core?

The answer, it appears, is yes.

THE GREAT NEST OF BEING

Huston Smith—whom many consider the world's leading authority on comparative religion—has pointed out, in his wonderful book *Forgotten Truth*, that virtually all of the world's great wisdom traditions subscribe to a belief in the Great Chain of Being. Smith is not alone in this conclusion. From Ananda Coomaraswamy to René Guénon, from Frithjof Schuon to Nicholas Berdyaev, from Michael Murphy to Roger Walsh, from Seyyed Nasr to Lex Hixon, the conclusion is consistent: the core of the premodern religious worldview is the Great Chain of Being.

According to this nearly universal view, reality is a rich tapestry of interwoven levels, *reaching from matter to body to mind to soul to spirit.* Each senior level "envelops" or "enfolds" its junior dimensions—a series of nests within nests within nests of Being—so that every thing and event in the world is interwoven with every other, and all are ultimately enveloped and enfolded by Spirit, by God, by Goddess, by Tao, by Brahman, by the Absolute itself.

As Arthur Lovejoy abundantly demonstrated in his classic treatise on the Great Chain, this view of reality has in fact "been the dominant official philosophy of the larger part of civilized humankind through most of its history." The Great Chain of Being is the worldview that "the greater number of the subtler speculative minds and of the great religious teachers [both East and West] have, in their various fashions, been engaged in." This stunning unanimity of deep religious belief led Alan Watts to state flatly that "We are hardly aware of the extreme peculiarity of our own position, and find it difficult to realize the plain fact that there has otherwise been a single philosophical consensus of universal extent. It has been held by [men and women] who report the same insights and teach the same essential doctrine whether living today or six thousand years ago, whether from New Mexico in the Far West or from Japan in the Far East."

The Great Chain of Being—that is perhaps a bit of a misnomer, because, as I said, the actual view is more like the Great Nest of Being, with each senior dimension enveloping or enfolding its junior dimension(s)—a situation often described as "transcend and include." Spirit transcends but includes soul, which transcends but includes mind, which transcends but includes the vital body, which transcends but includes matter. This is why the Great Nest is most accurately portrayed as a series of concentric spheres or circles, as I have indicated in Figure 1-1.

This is not to say that every single religious tradition from time immemorial has possessed exactly this particular scheme of matter, body, mind, soul, and spirit; there has been considerable variation within it. Some traditions have only three basic levels in the Great Nest—usually body, mind, and spirit. As Chögyam Trungpa, Rinpoche, pointed out in *Shambhala: The Sacred Path of the Warrior,* this simple hierarchy of body, mind, and spirit was nonetheless the backbone of even the earliest shamanic traditions, showing up as the hierarchy of earth, human, and heaven. This three-level scheme reappears in the Hindu and Buddhist notion of the three great states of being: *gross* (matter and body), *subtle* (mind and soul), and *causal* (spirit). Many of these traditions, on the other hand, also have extensive subdivisions of the Great Nest, sometimes breaking it down into five, seven, twelve, or even more levels and sublevels.

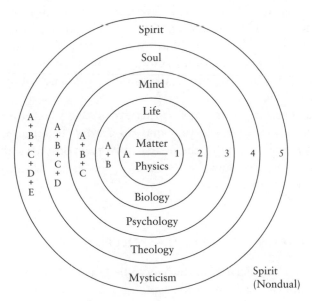

FIGURE 1-1. *The Great Nest of Being*

But the basic point has remained essentially identical: Reality is a series of nests within nests within nests, reaching from matter to mind to Spirit, with the result that all beings and all levels were ultimately enfolded in the all-pervasive and loving embrace of an ever-present Spirit.

Each senior level in the Great Nest, although it includes its juniors, nonetheless possesses emergent qualities not found on the junior level. Thus, the vital animal body *includes* matter in its makeup, but it also *adds* sensations, feelings, and emotions, which are not found in rocks. While the human mind *includes* bodily emotions in its makeup, it also *adds* higher cognitive faculties, such as reason and logic, which are not found in plants or other animals. And while the soul *includes* the mind in its makeup, it also *adds* even higher cognitions and affects, such as archetypal illumination and vision, not found in the rational mind. And so on.

In short, each higher level possesses the essential features of its lower level(s), but then adds elements not found on those levels. Each higher level, that is, *transcends* but *includes* its juniors. And this means that each level of reality has a different architecture, so to speak.

For just that reason, each level of reality, according to the great traditions, has a specific branch of knowledge associated with it (which I have also indicated in Figure 1-1): Physics studies matter. Biology studies vital bodies. Psychology and philosophy address the mind. Theology studies the soul and its relation to God. And mysticism studies the formless Godhead or pure Emptiness, the radical experience of Spirit beyond even God and the soul.

Such has been the dominant worldview, in one variation or another, for most of humankind's history and prehistory. It is the backbone of the "perennial philosophy," the nearly universal consensus about reality held by humanity for most of its time on this earth. Until, that is, the rise of modernity in the West.

THE MODERN DENIAL OF SPIRITUALITY

With the rise of modernity in the West, the Great Chain of Being almost entirely disappeared. As we will see, the modern West, after the Enlightenment, became the first major civilization in the history of humanity to deny almost entirely the existence of the Great Nest of Being.

In its place was a "flatland" conception of the universe as composed basically of matter (or matter/energy), and this material universe, including material bodies and material brains, could best be studied by science, and science alone. Thus, in the place of the Great Chain reaching from matter to God, there was now matter, period. And so it came to pass that the worldview known as *scientific materialism* became, in whole or part, the dominant official philosophy of the modern West.

Many religiously minded scholars have noted this modern "collapse" of the Great Nest of Spirit, and lamented it loudly. They have blamed this collapse on everything from the Newtonian-Cartesian paradigm to patriarchal domination, from capitalistic commodification of life's values to anti-Goddess male aggression, from hatred of the holistic web of life to a devaluation of nature in favor of analytic abstractions, from material lust and greed to obsession with monetary gain. The list of malevolent causes is indeed virtually endless.

True as those explanations might be, none of them addresses the core issues, in my opinion. As we will see, there is good reason that the Great Chain in its traditional form collapsed. The Great Nest of Spirit simply could not stand up to certain undeniable truths ushered in by modernity, and if we are to integrate both premodern religion and modern science, the truths of both parties must be brought to the union. Modernity possessed a tremendous share of new truths and new discoveries—it was far from being the Great Satan.

At the same time, the rise of modernity was beset with its own grave problems, not the least of which was the massive cultural earthquake brought about by the shuddering collapse of the Great Nest of Spirit. No longer were men and women enfolded in Spirit, they were simply awash in matter: hardly a comforting universe.

So we reach a crucial point. Our aim is to integrate premodern religion with modern science. We have already seen that the core of premodern religion is the Great Nest of Being. But what exactly is the core of modernity? *If we are to integrate premodern and modern, and if premodern is the Great Chain, then what exactly is "modern"?* The key to the long-sought integration might very well lie in this neglected direction.

What Is "Modernity"?

What specifically did modernity bring into the world that the premodern cultures by and large lacked? What made modernity so substantially *different* from the cultures and epochs that preceded it? Whatever it was, it will have to be an essential feature of the sought-for integration.

Many answers have been offered to the question "What is modernity?" Most of them are decidedly negative. Modernity, it is said, marked the death of God, the death of the Goddess, the commodification of life, the leveling of qualitative distinctions, the brutalities of capitalism, the replacement of quality by quantity, the loss of value and meaning, the fragmentation of the lifeworld, existential dread, a rampant and vulgar materialism—all of which have often been summarized in the phrase made famous by Max Weber: "the disenchantment of the world."

No doubt there is some truth to all those claims, and we will give them abundant consideration. But clearly modernity has some immensely positive aspects as well, for it also gave us the liberal democracies; the ideals of equality, freedom, and justice, regardless of race, class, creed, or gender; modern medicine, physics, biology, and chemistry; the end of slavery; the rise of feminism; and the universal rights of humankind. Those, surely, are a little more noble than the mere "disenchantment of the world."

No, we need a specific definition or description of modernity that allows for all those factors, both good (such as liberal democracies) and bad (such as the widespread loss of meaning). Various scholars, from Max Weber to Jürgen Habermas, have suggested that what specifically defines modernity is something called "the differentiation of the cultural value spheres," which especially means the differentiation of art, morals, and science. Where previously these spheres tended to be fused, modernity differentiated them and let each proceed at its own pace, with its own dignity, using its own tools, following its own discoveries, unencumbered by intrusions from the other spheres.

This differentiation allowed each sphere to make profound discoveries that, if used wisely, could lead to such "good" results as democracy, the end of slavery, the rise of feminism, and rapid advances in medical science; but discoveries that, if used unwisely, could just as easily be perverted into the "downsides" of modernity, such as scientific imperialism, the disenchantment of the world, and totalizing schemes of world domination.

The brilliance of this definition of modernity—namely, that it differentiated the value spheres of art, morals, and science—is that it allows us to see the underpinnings of *both* the good news and the bad news of modernity. In ways that will become more obvious in the following chapters, this definition allows us to understand both the *dignity* and the *disaster* of modernity, and we will explore each of them very carefully.

Premodern cultures certainly possessed art, morals, and science. The point, rather, is that these spheres tended to be relatively "undifferentiated." To give only one example now, in the Middle Ages, Galileo could not freely look through his telescope and report the results because art and morals and science were all fused under the Church, and thus the morals of the Church defined what science could—or could not—do. The Bible said (or implied) that the sun went around the earth, and that was the end of the discussion.

But with the differentiation of the value spheres, a Galileo could look through his telescope without fear of being charged with heresy and treason. Science was free to pursue its own truths unencumbered by brutal domination by the other spheres. Likewise with art and morals: Artists could, without fear of punishment, paint nonreligious themes, or even sacrilegious themes, if they wished. And moral theory was free to pursue an inquiry into the good life, whether it agreed with the Bible or not.

For all those reasons and more, these *differentiations of modernity* have also been referred to as the *dignity* of modernity, for these differentiations were in part responsible for the rise of liberal democracy, the end of slavery, the growth of feminism, and the staggering advances in the medical sciences, to name but a few of these many dignities.

As we will see, the "bad news" of modernity was that these value spheres did not just peacefully separate, they often flew apart completely. The wonderful *differentiations* of modernity went too far into actual *dissociation,* fragmentation, alienation. Dignity became disaster. The growth became a cancer. As the value spheres began to dissociate, this allowed a powerful and aggressive science to begin to invade and dominate the other spheres, crowding art and morals out of any serious consideration in approaching "reality." Science became *scientism*—scientific materialism and scientific imperialism—which soon became the dominant "official" worldview of modernity.

It was this scientific materialism that very soon pronounced the other value spheres to be worthless, "not scientific," illusory, or worse. And for precisely that reason, it was scientific materialism that *pronounced the Great Chain of Being to be nonexistent.*

According to scientific materialism, the Great Nest of matter, body, mind, soul, and spirit could be thoroughly and rudely reduced to systems of matter alone; and matter—whether in the material brain or material process systems—would account for all of reality, without remainder. Gone was mind and gone was soul and gone was Spirit—gone, in fact, was the entire Great Chain, except for its pitiful bottom rung—and in its place, as Whitehead famously lamented, there was reality as "a dull affair, soundless, scentless, colorless; merely the hurrying of material, endlessly, meaninglessly."

And so it came about that the modern West was the first major civilization in the history of the human race to deny substantial reality to the Great Nest of Being. It is into this massive and universal denial that we wish to attempt to reintroduce the spiritual dimension, but on terms acceptable to science as well.

CONCLUSION

To integrate religion and science is to integrate a premodern worldview with a modern worldview. But we saw that the essence of premodernity is the Great Chain of Being, and the essence of modernity is the differentiation of the value spheres of art, morals, and science. Thus, in order to integrate religion and science, we need to *integrate the Great Chain with the differentiations of modernity.* As we will start to see in the next chapter, this means that each of the levels in the traditional Great Chain needs to be carefully differentiated in the light of modernity. If we can do that, we will have satisfied *both* the core claim of spirituality—namely, the Great Chain—and the core claim of modernity—namely, the differentiation of the value spheres.

If this integration can be done without "cheating"—that is, without stretching and deforming either religion or science to a point where they do not recognize themselves—then this will be an integration that both parties can genuinely embrace. Such a synthesis would unite the best of premodern wisdom with the brightest of modern knowledge, bringing together truth and meaning in a way that has thus far eluded the modern mind.

2

A Deadly Dance

THE RELATION OF SCIENCE AND
RELIGION IN TODAY'S WORLD

WITH THE RISE OF MODERNITY—and the collapse of the Great Nest of Being—science and religion began an antagonistic dance. Perhaps it would be more accurate to say that science and religion entered into a fierce and complex war, a war between epochs, a war between worlds, a war between a premodern and mythological orientation to the universe and a thoroughly tough-minded and modern gaze, rational in its aspirations.

In the wake of modernity—in the wake, that is, of the multifarious events generally associated with the eighteenth-century Enlightenment and often continuing to today (events we will examine in chapter 4)— there arose four or five major stances toward the relation of science and religion. These stances are still with us, and they still dominate the discussion about science and spirituality. Yet all of them have substantial, even severe, limitations. Nonetheless, we can learn much from both their strengths and their weaknesses, their contributions and their flaws. In particular, understanding why these attempts have largely failed, and continue to fail, will help us zero in on the precise requirements of this difficult marriage.

1. Science denies any validity to religion.
   This is the standard empirical and positivist approach, which became, in numerous guises, the dominant official mood of modernity. Classic

variations on this theme have been given by Auguste Comte, Sigmund Freud, Karl Marx, and Bertrand Russell, but they all boil down to: religion is a hangover from the childhood of humanity, on exactly the same footing as the tooth fairy. It's cute for kids but deadly for adults, and its persistence into maturity—the persistence of deeply held religious beliefs into adulthood—is a sign of pathology, lack of logical clarity, or existential inauthenticity. There are no exceptions, because there is no God. And there is no God because science registers that which is real, and no microscope and no telescope have yet spotted any "God."

2. *Religion denies any validity to science.*

This is a typically fundamentalist retort to modernity, and is itself a by-product of modernity. By and large, classical religions *never* denied science—first, because science was not a threat (only with modernity does science become powerful enough to kill God); and second, because science was always held to be one of several valid modes of knowing, subservient to spiritual modes but valid nonetheless, and hence there was no reason to deny its importance.

At the same time, it should be noted that the sciences of antiquity were not nearly as impressive as what a Newton, a Galileo, or a Kepler would deliver, and thus few were the temptations to make science itself into a new religion of positivism (which is exactly what Auguste Comte would propose, with Comte himself volunteering to be, literally, the Pope of Positivism).

In any event, science in the premodern world had little inclination to deny religion and thus a drastic counterforce was uncalled for. But with the rise of modernity and its inherent claim that all religions are childish productions, many fundamentalist religions (especially Christianity and Islam) began to deny even the basic facts of science itself: evolution does not exist, the Earth was literally created in six days, radiocarbon dating is a fraud, and so on. It has been pointed out, for example, that the extremism of Islamic fundamentalists is not so much an inherent aspect of Islam (which has produced some truly glorious civilizations) as it is a product of a wild counterreaction to modernity's attempt to terrorize and kill spirituality in general. In wild panic, the fundamentalists have become counterterrorists.

This does not in any way excuse terrorism; I believe that many (but by no means all) of the religious sentiments of humankind are indeed a childish hangover and eventually need to be surrendered. Most fundamentalists, in this sense, are indeed refusing to grow up cognitively. But it does point out the intense emotions involved in this battle of modernity, this battle to find a place for both science and religion, truth and meaning, logic and God, facts and Spirit, evidence and the eternal.

3. *Science is but one of several valid modes of knowing, and thus can peacefully coexist with spiritual modes.*

This was the standard position of most classical religions and the religions of antiquity. In fact, this is just another way of describing the Great Chain of Being, and, as you can see in Figure 1–1, science and theology and mysticism all had an important and rightful place in the Great Nest of Being.

Although this view—which is now generally called *epistemological pluralism*—was the backbone of the great wisdom traditions, it collapsed with the Great Chain, upon which it depended. *When modernity rejected the Great Chain, it simultaneously rejected epistemological pluralism.* And modernity continues to reject epistemological pluralism in any of its forms because modernity most definitely continues to reject the Great Chain.

Nonetheless, for those scholars, theorists, and intelligent laypeople attempting to make sense of the universe in some sort of holistic or encompassing fashion, epistemological pluralism has remained one of the more appealing and sophisticated attempts to unite science and religion. Modernity itself aggressively discarded this view; but what we might call "countermodernity" or the "counterculture"—never much more than a small percentage of the total population, but one desperately looking for a way to heal modernity's fragmentations—would nevertheless continue to look to epistemological pluralism as one of the most refined and compelling ways to proceed.

The traditional view of epistemological pluralism was given perhaps its clearest statement by such Christian mystics as St. Bonaventure and Hugh of St. Victor: every human being has the eye of flesh, the eye of mind, and the eye of contemplation. Each of these modes of knowing discloses its own corresponding dimension of being (gross, subtle, and causal), and thus each is valid and important when addressing its own realm. This gives us a balance of empirical knowledge (science), rational knowledge (logic and mathematics), and spiritual knowledge (gnosis).

The three eyes of knowing are, of course, just a simplified version of the universal Great Chain of Being. If we picture the Great Chain as having five levels (matter, body, mind, soul, and spirit), men and women have five eyes available to them (material prehension, bodily emotion, mental ideas, the soul's archetypal cognition, and spiritual gnosis). Likewise, if the Great Chain is divided into twelve levels, we have twelve eyes, or twelve levels of awareness and knowing.

Indeed, Plotinus—arguably the greatest philosopher-mystic the world has ever known—usually gave the Great Chain twelve levels: matter, life, sensation, perception, impulse, images, concepts, logical faculty, creative reason, world soul, nous, and the One. Table 2-1 shows the typical Great Nest as presented by Plotinus and Sri Aurobindo, two of its greatest representatives (the match between them is quite striking and fairly typical).

The point is that, any way we slice the great pie—three levels, five levels, twelve levels or more—men and women have available to them *at least* the three basic eyes of knowing: the eye of flesh (empiricism), the eye of mind (rationalism), and the eye of contemplation (mysticism), each of which is important and quite valid when dealing with its own level, but gravely confused if it attempts to see into other domains. This is the very heart of epistemological pluralism, and, as far as it goes, it is indeed quite valid.

Now, if the existence of all three eyes of knowing were a commonly accepted fact in modernity, the relation of science and religion—and their peaceful coexistence—would be no problem whatsoever. Empirical science would pronounce on the facts delivered by the eye of flesh, and religion would pronounce on the facts delivered by the eye of spirit (or the eye of contemplation). But mainstream modernity has soundly and

Table 2-1.The Great Nest According to Plotinus and Aurobindo

Plotinus	Aurobindo
Absolute One (Godhead)	Satchitananda/Supermind (Godhead)
nous (intuitive mind) (subtle)	Intuitive mind/Overmind
Soul/World Soul (psychic)	Illumined World mind
Creative Reason (vision-logic)	Higher mind/Network mind
Logical faculty (formop)	Logical mind
Concepts and opinions	Concrete mind (conop)
Images	Lower mind (preop)
Pleasure/pain (emotions)	Vital-emotional; impulse
Perception	Perception
Sensation	Sensation
Vegetative life function	Vegetative
Matter	Matter (physical)

thoroughly denied reality to the eye of spirit. Modernity recognizes only the eye of reason yoked to the eye of flesh—in Whitehead's phrase, the dominant worldview of modernity is *scientific materialism,* and whether that science be the holistic science of systems theory or the subatomic physics of quantum events, science is the eye of reason linked to evidence offered by the empirical senses. *In no case is the eye of contemplation or the eye of Spirit required . . .* or even allowed.

The real difficulty, then, is not showing how empiricism, rationalism, and mysticism can all fit together in the Great Chain of Being; it is not showing how they can all be harmoniously integrated in a great spectrum of consciousness; it is not demonstrating that such a synthesis is coherent and complete. For *that,* in a sense, is the easy part. All of those statements, I believe, are true. The hard part is that modernity *does not accept the higher levels themselves* (the transmental, transrational, transpersonal, and contemplative modes), and thus it sees *no need* whatsoever for the integration. Why try to integrate science and Santa Claus?

Thus, arguing for epistemological pluralism and the different eyes of knowing (or modes of inquiry) is at best a first step. The real problem is that modernity does not accept the terms to be integrated in the first place. We will therefore have to find another path into the heart of modernity if an integration of science and religion is ever to take root in the West.

4. *Science can offer "plausibility arguments" for the existence of Spirit.*
This is a variation on epistemological pluralism, but because it has recently generated much interest—among professionals and laypeople alike—I will discuss it separately. The idea is that, as empirical science pushes into the deepest secrets of the physical world, it discovers facts and data that seem to demand some sort of Intelligence beyond the material domain.

The standard example is the Big Bang: Where did *that* come from? Since the very earliest material plasma seems to have been obeying mathematical laws that themselves did not come into being with the Big Bang, must not those laws exist "in the mind of some eternal Spirit," as Sir James Jeans, echoing Berkeley, suggested? These laws, all agree, existed prior to space and time. Thus, to the question "What existed before the Big Bang?," the answer very well might be *a nonmaterial Logos governing the patterns of creation*—what many would simply call God. And, this argument continues, since science discovered the Big Bang, science itself is pointing to God.

There are numerous variations on this argument, most of which are twists on the traditional *argument from design,* namely, that incredibly intelligent natural designs demand an incredibly intelligent Something-or-Other behind them. This is a very old argument, stretching back at least to early Greece, that has been aggressively attached to recent advances in the sciences—particularly quantum, relativistic, systems and complexity theories.

This approach is perhaps the simplest and most popular of the ways in which an alienated countermodernity has attempted to integrate science and religion. We see it in everything from *The Tao of Physics* (which maintains that modern physics discloses a worldview similar to that of Eastern mysticism) to the thoughtful writings of Paul Davies (e.g., *The Mind of God,* which maintains that "By the means of science we can truly see into the mind of God") to the Anthropic Principle (which maintains that the evolution of human beings is so improbable that the universe must have known what it was doing from the very start) to the "new holistic paradigm" approaches (which maintain that systems theory is demonstrating the same great web of life that the holistic spiritual traditions embraced).

I have a great deal of sympathy for many of those plausibility arguments. They are suggestive. They are indicative. They are certainly entertaining. But, alas, none of them can stand up to the critical philosophy of, say, Immanuel Kant or the Buddhist genius Nagarjuna, both of whom strongly demonstrated the limits of rationality in the face of the Divine. If deeply spiritual Nagarjuna is unswayed by these plausibility arguments, how must they go over with nonspiritual types? This is why the vast majority of scientists—and modernity itself—tend to take these "arguments" with mild interest at best, wild amusement at worst.

The real problem with these rational, mental, or linguistic plausibility arguments is that they are *attempting to use the eye of mind to see that which can be seen only with the eye of contemplation.* This confusion of levels (which is called a "category error") is particularly fatal when it comes to "arguments" for the existence of Spirit. It was precisely these inadequate and altogether unconvincing mental attempts to storm the spiritual palace that made modernity look with suspicion on any and all claims to be able to prove the existence of God. These arguments and "proofs" are simply not compelling to the modern mind, and to the spiritual mind they are inherently inadequate anyway. In no case, then, do these arguments deliver what they aspire to deliver, namely, any sort of actual spiritual knowledge.

Martin Gardner's response to these arguments is quite typical. Referring to the Anthropic Principle, Gardner points out that, according to its adherents, it comes in four successive forms, each stronger in its claims: the Weak Anthropic Principle, or WAP (the universe allows us to exist); the Strong Anthropic Principle, or SAP (the existence of life explains the laws of the universe); the Participatory Anthropic Principle, or PAP (conscious observers are necessary to bring the universe into existence); and the Final Anthropic Principle, or FAP (if life or consciousness ends, the universe will evaporate).

To this list Gardner, speaking for modernity, adds the Completely Ridiculous Anthropic Principle, or CRAP: any who buy the first four.

5. *Science itself is not knowledge of the world but merely an interpretation of the world, and therefore it has the same validity—no more, no less—as poetry and the arts.*

Because science refused to gracefully take its place as one among many other valid modes of knowing, this approach attempted to cripple science in its very foundations, pulling it down against its will. It tried to level the playing field by shooting science in the head and proclaiming, "There! Now we're equal."

This approach is, of course, the essence of postmodernism. It says, in effect, that the world is not *perceived,* it is only *interpreted.* Different interpretations are equally valid ways of making sense of the world, and thus no interpretation is intrinsically better than another. Science is not a privileged conception of the world but merely one among many equivalent interpretations; science does not offer "truth" but simply its own favorite prejudice; science is not a set of universal facts but merely an arbitrary imposition of its own power drives. And in all cases, science is no more grounded in reality than is any other interpretation, so that, epistemologically speaking, there is little difference between science and poetry, logic and literature, history and mythology, fact and fiction.

Thus, this postmodern view continues, science is not governed by *facts,* it is governed by *paradigms,* and paradigms are not much more than ad hoc constructions or free-floating interpretations. As we will see in the next chapter, the notion that science is governed by paradigms was made popular by Thomas Kuhn in his now-famous *The Structure of Scientific Revolutions,* which the postmodernists seized with a fury. Yet this is not at all the way Kuhn defined or described paradigms, and he strenuously denounced this abuse of his work—to no avail. But, according to this mis-Kuhnian notion of "paradigm," science is not conforming itself to actual facts, it is simply imposing its paradigms on the world at large. Since independent facts do not exist (only interpretations do), it follows, according to this account, that science is always driven by some sort of power or ideology: science itself is sexist, racist, ethnocentric, imperialistic, brutally imposing its analytic and divisive interpretations on an unwilling and innocent world. And it has no more warrant, no more final validity, than any other poetic interpretation.

Science reduced to poetry: *this is now the dominant route taken by the countercultural world in an attempt to reduce the monster of science to manageable proportions.* The postmodern attack on science, which attempts to shatter its epistemological foundations, is the reigning model of how to "counter" science in the postmodern world.

It is crucial to understand this postmodern attempt to level science and thus make room for "other paradigms," whether poetry, religion, mysticism, astrology, holism, poststructuralism, neopaganism, or whatnot. Aside from its important moments of truth (which I will highlight and incorporate), this entire postmodern attempt is nonetheless profoundly misguided and deeply confused. In attempting to shoot science in the head, it simply kills that which it should be integrating. It denies that which should be embraced. It sabotages the desired wedding by murdering one of the spouses.

Yet this postmodern attempt—to see science as paradigm-bound, and thus rush in to offer a "new paradigm"—is at the core of virtually every alternative, countercultural, and "new-paradigm" approach to science and religion. The idea is that science is undergoing a paradigm shift of momentous proportions, and this new paradigm is in fact commensurate with spiritual realities. The "new paradigm," it is claimed, will therefore unite science and religion for the first time in history, thus heralding the beginning of a world transformation, global in its sweep, that will usher in the beginning of a holistic, unified, web-of-life world.

And almost all of that, we will see, is based on a complete misreading of Thomas Kuhn.

A POSSIBLE SOLUTION

In the following chapters, I will argue that all five of those stances toward science and religion—and their possible integration—are inadequate. The first two stances—science denies religion, religion denies science—are obviously not going to be integrative. But the other three (epistemological pluralism, plausibility arguments, and postmodern/paradigm) have not proven powerful enough to integrate science and religion in a fashion that *both* parties find acceptable.

We have seen that the only way we can possibly integrate science and religion is by integrating the Great Chain with the major differentiations of modernity. *This specific integration is where all of these stances tend to fail,* yet it is this approach that very likely contains the central solution.

Let us use, as a brief example, epistemological pluralism—which, as we saw, is by far the most sophisticated of the alternatives. In the traditional view of epistemological pluralism, science is placed *on the bottom rung* of the great hierarchy. In this view, recall, science gives us the facts of the sensory level (the eye of flesh). Above that are the art, morals, and introspection of the mental realms (the eye of mind) and, above that, the religion and mysticism of the spiritual realms (the eye of contemplation). Science is relegated to low man on the totem pole, a role that modern science has utterly refused to accept, and in fact will not accept, which is precisely why this traditional epistemological pluralism cannot command the respect—or the cooperation—of modern science.

But in a more sophisticated integration, *each of those levels* (sensory, mental, spiritual) *is also divided according to the differentiations of modernity* (art, morals, and science). Thus—and I must put this very loosely for an introductory statement—there are the art and morals and science of the sensory realm, the art and morals and science of the mental realm, and the art and morals and science of the spiritual realm.

It is exactly this type of synthesis, should it prove sound, that would indeed satisfy *both* the core claim of spirituality (namely, the Great Chain) and the core claim of modernity (namely, the differentiation of the value spheres).

Here science, far from being on the bottom rung, has a hand to play in accessing each of the levels of the Great Chain, from the lowest to the highest (sensory science, mental science, spiritual science). It is not that spirituality takes up where science leaves off, but that they both develop up the Great Chain together. Science is not *under* but *alongside,* and this profoundly reorients the knowledge quest, placing premodernity and modernity hand in hand in the quest for the real, and thus bringing science and religion together in a most intimate embrace.

3

Paradigms

A WRONG TURN

O F ALL THE PREVIOUS ATTEMPTS to integrate science and religion, by far the most influential and infectious, at least among
today's counterculture and a substantial portion of academe, is that of
the postmodern/paradigm—the notion that science is actually governed
by "paradigms," and a paradigm is simply one of many possible interpretations of reality, no more binding than any other. Since, it is said,
paradigms are culturally constructed, not discovered, the authority of
science is dramatically undercut, and this leaves room, it is further said,
for a "new paradigm" that would be compatible with a spiritual or
holistic worldview.

Although the claim is made that this "new-paradigm" approach will
at long last integrate scientific and spiritual realities, in fact it totally
cripples any effective integration of science and religion. To understand
why this is so, we turn to Thomas Kuhn, and to the utterly strange case
of his reception by the counterculture.

Although we will devote Part II to an overview of the previous attempts to integrate science and religion—including the postmodern/par-
adigm approach—it is necessary to address this particular approach
right away, before we go any further, and for the simple reason that it
has overwhelmingly dominated today's discussion on science and spirituality. So much so that as soon as most people hear about "integrating
science and religion," they almost immediately think "new paradigm."

Why that approach is a dead end is the topic of this chapter.

THE MISREADING OF THOMAS KUHN

Thomas Kuhn's *The Structure of Scientific Revolutions* was published in 1962; it soon became, for reasons good and bad, the most influential book on the philosophy of science ever written and the most frequently cited academic book of recent times. For reasons that will become obvious, this book had almost no influence on the *historians* of science; but it dominated discussions on the *philosophy* of science, and—in a great ironic twist—became perhaps the most influential *misunderstood* book of the century. Most of its popularity stemmed from a widespread and massive misunderstanding of its central conclusions, a misunderstanding that, many historians now agree, stemmed in large part from the narcissistic mood of the sixties "Me Generation." How sixties narcissism massively distorted Kuhn is itself a paradigm of our times—and a stunning cautionary tale for anyone stepping into the "science-and-religion" game.

Distortions of Kuhn have now become so common that serious scholars of his work have no trouble reciting the popular misunderstanding of the notion of a "paradigm." Here is Frederick Crews reciting the typical (wrong) view: "Kuhn, we are told, demonstrated that any two would-be paradigms, or regnant major theories, will be incommensurable; that is, they will represent different universes of perception and explanation. Hence no common ground can exist for testing their merits, and one theory will prevail for strictly sociological, never empirical, reasons. The winning theory will be the one that better suits the emergent temper or interests of the hour [ideology, class, prejudice, gender, race, power, etc.—in other words, androcentric, ethnocentric, phallocentric, eurocentric, anthropocentric, and so forth]. It follows that intellectuals who once trembled before the disapproving gaze of positivism can now propose sweeping 'Kuhnian revolutionary paradigms' of their own, defying whatever disciplinary consensus they find antipathetic. . . ."

That is indeed the typical interpretation of Kuhn. Crews calls that interpretation "theoreticism," because it is a view lost in mere abstract theory divorced from actual *evidence.* He then points out the obvious: "One can gauge the emotional force of theoreticism by the remoteness of this interpretation from what Kuhn actually said."

The idea was that, since "paradigms" govern science, if you don't like the worldview of science, then simply think up a new paradigm for yourself (this, we will see, is where "narcissism" starts to creep into the picture). Since paradigms are allegedly not anchored in actual facts and evidence (but instead create them), you needn't be tied to the authority of science in any fundamental way. Indeed, science becomes merely one of numerous different readings of the text of the world, with no more actual authority than poetry, astrology, or palmistry: all are equally legitimate interpretations of the blooming buzzing confusion of experience.

This popular (mis)understanding of Kuhn—this "theoreticism"—also meant that science was allegedly *arbitrary* (it is the result not of actual evidence but of imposed power structures), *relative* (it reveals nothing that is actually constant in reality but simply things that are relative to the scientific imposition of power), *socially constructed* (it is not a map corresponding to any actual reality but a construction based on social conventions), *interpretive* (it does not reveal anything fundamental about reality but is simply one of many interpretations of the world text), *power-laden* (it is not grounded in neutral facts; it is not dominated by facts; it simply dominates people, usually for ethnocentric and androcentric reasons), and *nonprogressive* (since science proceeds by ruptures or breaks, there can be no cumulative progress in any of the sciences).

Kuhn maintained none of those views. Indeed, he vehemently argued against most of them. But what Crews so unerringly called *the emotional force* of the misunderstood idea had already taken root: imagine, we can abandon the straitjacket of science and evidence by merely thinking up a new paradigm ("merely thinking up" = "theoreticism"; and this itself, as Crews himself points out, was grounded in a rampant sixties narcissism).

A small list of claimants to the "new paradigm" included neoastrology, ecofeminism, deep ecology, altered states of consciousness, the quantum self, the quantum society, systems theory, process philosophy, nonordinary states of consciousness, holistic health, global ecological consciousness, postmodern poststructuralism, quantum psychotherapy, deconstruction, neo-Jungian psychology, channeling, premodern indigenous tribal consciousness, neopaganism, Wicca, palmistry, and the Internet.

Kuhn himself watched all of this with growing alarm, and made a series of vigorous statements meant to curtail the damage, but to absolutely no avail. Most people using the term "paradigm" and citing Kuhn didn't even know that he had abandoned the term. Is science actually relative, arbitrary, and nonprogressive? Kuhn in exasperation: "Later scientific theories are better than earlier ones for solving puzzles in the quite often different environments to which they are applied. This is not a relativist's position, and it displays the sense in which I am a convinced believer in scientific progress." Obviously, we cannot have real scientific *progress* if paradigms are arbitrary, incommensurable, or relative, with none of them intrinsically better than another.

What, then, did Kuhn mean by "paradigm," and what was the "structure" of scientific revolutions? Nothing nearly as dramatic as postmodern theoreticism proclaimed. To begin with, Kuhn outlined not three or four paradigm shifts in the history of modern science, but *several hundred*. As Ian Hacking summarizes the actual view: *The Structure of Scientific Revolutions* "is about hundreds of revolutions, which are supposed to occur in many disciplines, and which typically involve the research work (in the first instance) of at most a hundred or so investigators. Lavoisier's chemical revolution counts as one, but so does Roentgen's discovery of X-rays, the voltaic cell or battery of 1800, the first quantization of energy, and numerous developments in the history of thermodynamics."

In other words, almost any new experiment generating new data was a new paradigm, which is why a battery was a new paradigm. "Paradigm" itself carried two broad components, which we might call "practical" and "social." Kuhn "used the word [paradigm] to denote both the established and admired solutions that serve as models of how to practice the science [this is the practical component, a set of exemplars or experiments or injunctions], and also for the local social structure that keeps those standards in place by teaching, rewards, and the like [the social component, which is also a set of injunctions or social practices]. The word was mysteriously launched or rather catapulted into prominence, and now seems a standard item in the vocabulary of everyone who writes about science—except Kuhn himself, who has disavowed it. . . . It is at present a dead metaphor."

REAL PARADIGMS

What is not dead—and what Kuhn did not disavow—is that science is grounded in *injunctions,* exemplars, and social practices. Science is not merely an innocent reflection on a pregiven world, but rather discloses data through injunctions or exemplars ("exemplar" is a word Kuhn used interchangeably with "paradigm"). Both components of the paradigm (practical and social) are *grounded in injunctions,* in actual practices, which is why almost any novel experiment that actually produced new data was viewed as a revolution or "new paradigm." This is why Kuhn counted hundreds of revolutions or new paradigms, including X-rays and the battery.

But not one of those new paradigms was merely theoretical (that would be "theoreticism"). Rather, they were all grounded in *evidence* that could be brought forth and reproduced with the given exemplar, paradigm, or injunction. This is why Kuhn's most common use of "paradigm" was "retooling operations with important consequences for research practice"—in other words, specific concrete injunctions. And this is exactly why science can and does show real *progress:* the injunctions or exemplars or paradigms disclose actual evidence, they do not fabricate it based on mere conventions. As Crews notes, "Kuhn happens to be a fervent believer in scientific progress, which, he argues, can occur only after a given specialty has gotten past the stage of what he calls 'theory proliferation' and 'incessant criticism and continual striving for a fresh start.' By incommensurability Kuhn never meant that competing theories are incomparable but only that the choice between them cannot be entirely consigned to the verdict of theory-neutral rules and data. Transitions between paradigms—which in any case are mere *problem solutions, not broad theories* . . . —must indeed be made . . . through 'gestalt switches,' but the rationality of science is not thereby impaired. As Kuhn asked, and as he has continued to insist with mounting astonishment at his irrationalist fan club, 'What better criterion than the decision of the scientific group could there be?' "

To which "new-paradigm" theoreticians of every conceivable sort, astonishingly citing Kuhn, replied, "My new paradigm." This blatant misreading of Kuhn erased evidence from the scene of truth, and into that vacuum rushed every egocentric project imaginable. Science was reduced to rubble, or, more precisely, poetry. As Howard Felperin typically put it—and as one can find echoed in thousands of "new-paradigm," "new age," "transformational" theories—"Science itself is recognizing that its own methods are ultimately no more objective than those of the arts." Science and poetry stand on exactly the same epistemic footing, and this allows us to deconstruct the authority of science right at the start, thus making room for whatever religion we want.

THE POSTMODERN SCENE: NIHILISM AND NARCISSISM

Once this massive distortion of Kuhn was in place, "new paradigm" thinkers in America began to connect this mis-Kuhnian notion with every sort of French parlor game, and this unholy mixture of mis-Kuhn and postmodern poststructuralism has come to dominate everything from the new historicism to premodern tribal revivals to postmodern ecophilosophies to "the new holistic paradigm" to cultural studies in general. Since grounding in facts and evidence is no longer required, slogans are treated as facts, as one critic forcefully noted: "In the human studies today, it is widely assumed that the positions declared by . . . poststructuralism are permanently valuable discoveries that require no further interrogation. Thus one frequently comes upon statements of the type: 'Deconstruction has shown us that we can never exit from the play of signifiers'; 'Lacan demonstrates that the unconscious is structured like a language'; 'After Althusser, we all understand that the most ideological stance is the one that tries to fix limits beyond which ideology does not apply'; 'There can be no turning back to naive pre-Foucauldian distinctions between truth and power.' Such servility constitutes an ironic counterpart of positivism—a heaping up, not of factual nuggets, but of movement slogans that are treated as fact."

All of which horrified Kuhn. And yet, as Crews points out, "Nothing Kuhn can say, however, will make a dent in theoreticism, which is less a specific position than a mood of antinomian rebellion and self-indulgence." Time and again Crews hits the notion of self-indulgence and narcissism, and he is by no means alone. He points to "theoreticism, whose purest impulse is toward positing ineluctable constraints on the perceptiveness and adaptability of everyone but the theorist himself." Such self-indulgence, he says, "comes down to us from the later Sixties."

Historian Ernest Gellner, among many others, has made a similar point, namely, that where evidence is erased, narcissism flourishes. The *demand for evidence*—or validity claims—which has always anchored genuine and progressive science, simply means that one's own ego cannot impose on the universe a view of reality that finds no support from the universe itself. The validity claims and evidence are the ways in which we attune ourselves to the Kosmos. The validity claims force us to confront reality; they curb our egoic fantasies and self-centered ways; they demand evidence from the rest of the Kosmos; they force us outside of ourselves! They are the checks and balances in the Kosmic Constitution.

But it was exactly these checks and balances, these curbs on narcissism, that the mis-Kuhnian "new-paradigm" thinkers of almost every variety implicitly or explicitly attempted to erase. And behind it all lay, in part, the "culture of narcissism." Philosopher David Couzens Hoy points out that "freeing [theory] from its object"—that is, erasing the demand for evidence—"may open it up to all the possibilities of rich imaginations; yet if there is now no truth of the matter, then nothing keeps it from succumbing to the sickness of the modern imagination's obsessive self-consciousness." Theory thus becomes "only the critic's own ego-gratification." The culture of narcissism. "Then a sheer struggle for power ensues, and criticism becomes not latent but blatant aggression," part of "the emergent nihilism of recent times."

From the notion that "We are in the midst of a world-transforming paradigm shift" to the idea that "You create your own reality"—the many permutations of "self-indulgent theoreticism": ideas disconnected from the demand for evidence, science reduced to poetry, narcissism and nihilism joined in a postmodern tag team from hell.

These critics are not saying that all of the poetry/paradigm stance is merely or even especially due to narcissism. They are simply saying— and I agree—that the vaunted narcissism of the Me Generation *predisposed* many individuals to seize upon a profound *misreading* of Thomas Kuhn, a misreading that allowed them arbitrarily to deconstruct any reality that happened not to suit them and then insert their own "revolutionary new paradigm" into the scene, imagining that they were somehow vanguards of a revolutionary transformation that would shake the world to its very foundations, and the keys to which, they now held.

Thus, as historians puzzle over how a *distortion* of Kuhn became one of the most cited and most influential notions of the past three decades, as they puzzle over how an untruth came to be so wildly influential, they are forced to look for other forces driving this avalanche of error, and the "culture of Narcissism"—whether in the new age, in art criticism, in literary theory, in tribal revivals, in the new historicism, in cultural studies, in me-spirituality, in the idea that you create your own reality, in "the holistic new paradigm"—is appearing the ever more likely candidate, infecting a generation that, subtly but insistently, needed to see itself as central to the unfolding of the universe.

THE PERFORMATIVE CONTRADICTION

Whether the "new-paradigm" approaches are indeed shot through with narcissistic self-indulgence is an open question. What is not open to question is the fact that these approaches—and extreme postmodernism in general—are internally self-contradictory. They collapse under their own weight, leaving everything from literary theory to the integration of science and religion *in an even worse state* than when they began.

The moment of truth in the postmodern argument is that, indeed, the world is not an innocent perception. The world is in part a construction, an interpretation. This is one of the enduring truths brought forth by postmodernism in general. (Indeed, Chapter 9 is devoted to an appreciation of many of the important insights of the postmodern movement).

But—and here we must part ways with *extreme* postmodernism—all interpretations are not equally valid: there are better and worse interpretations of every text. *Hamlet* is not about a fun family picnic in Yellowstone Park. That is a very bad interpretation, and it can be thoroughly *rejected* by any community of adequate interpreters. All interpretations are not created equal—and that brings to a crashing halt the major claim of extreme postmodernism.

The difficulty is that, in its totalizing attack on truth ("There is no truth, only different interpretations"), extreme postmodernism *cannot itself claim to be true.* Either it must exempt itself from its own claims (the narcissistic move), or what it says about everybody else is equally true for itself, in which case, what it says is not true, either. As Gellner summarizes the disaster: "So, if true, it is false; so, it is false."

This so-called *performative contradiction* in extreme postmodernism has now been pointed out by numerous scholars, including Jürgen Habermas, Charles Taylor, Karl-Otto Apel, Ernest Gellner, among others. Indeed, there is now something of a consensus among serious scholars that extreme postmodernism is a dead end. It either nihilistically denies truth, including therefore its own; or, attempting to avoid that, it retreats into narcissism, exempting itself from its own claims (this is still the popular "new-paradigm" approach).

But the fact remains that the notion of paradigm *"is at present a dead metaphor."* Thus, in our attempt to integrate science and religion, we will have to look elsewhere for the key.

THE SPIRITUAL CRITIQUE OF "NEW PARADIGMS"

Not only have serious scholars, including Kuhn, abandoned the notion of paradigm (as popularly understood); the great wisdom traditions themselves more often than not find the notion utterly confused.

The perennial core of the wisdom traditions is, recall, the Great Chain of Being and the correlative belief in epistemological pluralism. As Huston Smith summarizes this view, "Reality is graded, and with it, cognition." That is, there are levels of both being and knowing. If we picture the Great Chain as composed of four levels (body, mind, soul, and spirit), there are four correlative modes of knowing (sensory, mental, archetypal, and mystical), which I usually shorten to the three eyes of knowing: the eye of flesh (empiricism), the eye of mind (rationalism), and the eye of contemplation (mysticism).

Empirical science, according to epistemological pluralism, can tell us much about the sensory domain and a little bit about the mental domain, but virtually nothing about the contemplative domain. And no "new paradigm" is going to alter that in any way. Chaos theories, complexity theories, systems theories, quantum theories—none of them requires scientists to take up contemplation or meditation in order to understand those "new paradigms," and thus none of them gives any direct spiritual knowledge at all. They are just more mental ideas hooked to sensory perceptions; they are not transmental contemplation disclosing the Divine.

Worse, the wisdom traditions continue, by presenting these new scientific theories as if they were spiritual realities, these "new paradigms" often discourage people from taking up actual contemplation and thus directly accessing Spirit itself. These "new paradigms" in effect replace the eye of contemplation with the eyes of mind and flesh, thus destroying the only mode that is our salvation. Far from helping integrate science and religion, these approaches devastate the true religious impulse.

TO WHOM AM I SPEAKING?

I am in substantial agreement with that criticism, which can also be put in a more modern light, as follows: the eye of flesh is monological; the eye of mind is dialogical; and the eye of contemplation is translogical.

Monological comes from "monologue," which means a single person talking by him- or herself. Most empirical science is monological, because you can investigate, say, a rock without ever having to talk to it. Empirical science carefully chooses objects of research that it will never have to talk to. Whether those objects are rocks, planets, atoms, cells, geological structures, DNA molecules, brain synapses, kidneys, rivers, atmospheric dynamics, ideal gases, thermodynamic bodies, process patterns, systems interactions, ecosystems, it doesn't matter: you don't have to talk to any of them. This is a monological endeavor, tied to the eye of flesh and the data of the human senses or their instrumental extensions.

Dialogical comes from "dialogue," which means talking with somebody and attempting to understand that person. And whereas the eye of flesh is monological, the eye of mind is, in many important ways, dialogical. As you are now reading these sentences, you are involved in a dialogical mode of knowing. You are attempting to understand what I mean by these symbols. If I were actually present, you might ask me directly, and we would talk. We would be involved in interpretation, in hermeneutics, in symbolic meaning, in mutual understanding. You are not treating me as an *object,* like a rock, which you will stare at monologically; you are treating me as a *subject,* which you will try to understand dialogically.

Translogical means transcending the logical, the rational, or the mental in general. Formless mysticism, disclosed with the eye of contemplation, is translogical: it sees beyond the eye of flesh (and its monological empiricism) and beyond the eye of mind (and its dialogical interpretation), and instead stands open to the radiant Divine (in nondual gnosis). This spiritual opening can be directly accessed by neither the eye of flesh nor the eye of mind, only the eye of contemplation. And the very heart of the great wisdom traditions is a contemplative opening to the spiritual domain, which is not monological, not dialogical, but translogical.

Perhaps we can start to see why even the great wisdom traditions (with their epistemological pluralism) can offer such a devastating critique of the notion that a "new paradigm" in science would, or even could, be equivalent to a spiritual opening. For what is required is not a new monological science or a new dialogical interpretation, but a genuine method for directly opening to translogical contemplation, and no "new scientific paradigm" whatsoever has been able to make that offer.

It is common among the "new-paradigm" thinkers to claim that the basic problem with science is that, under the "Newtonian-Cartesian" worldview, the universe is seen as atomistic, mechanistic, divided, and fragmented, whereas the new sciences (quantum/relativistic and systems/complexity theories) have shown that the world is not a collection of atomistic fragments but an inseparable web of relations. This "web-of-life" view, they claim, is compatible with traditional spiritual worldviews, and thus this "new paradigm" will usher in the new quantum self and quantum society, a holistic and healing worldview disclosed by science itself.

But that approach, according to the great wisdom traditions, completely misses the point. For the real problem with empirical science is *not* that it is atomistic instead of holistic, or that it is Newtonian instead of Einsteinian, or that it is individualistic instead of systems-oriented. The real problem is that *all* of those approaches—atomistic and holistic alike—are monological. They are all empirical and sensorimotor based—evidence supplied by the senses or their instrumental extensions. This is true of Newtonian science and of Einsteinian science. It is true of atomistic science and of systems science. Under no circumstances—and under no paradigm whatsoever—does empirical science show any inclination to deny its empiricism—nor should it.

No, the real problem of our modern fragmentation is not that empirical science is atomistic rather than systems-oriented; the real problem is that *all higher modes of knowing have been brutally collapsed into monological and empirical science.* Both atomism and systems theory are monological/empirical, and *it is the reduction of all knowledge to monological modes that constitutes the disaster of modernity.* The higher modes themselves—mental and supramental, rational and transrational, hermeneutic and translogical, contemplative and spiritual—have all been rudely reduced and utterly collapsed to the eye of flesh and its extensions, and whether that monological madness be atomistic or systems-oriented is quite beside the point.

Has there been a recent revolution in science, a genuine *new paradigm in science itself,* which is holistic rather than atomistic? Yes, definitely. There have been several of them, actually, including various aspects of quantum physics, relativistic physics, cybernetics, dynamical systems theory, autopoiesis, chaos theory, and complexity theory. These are all new revolutions, new paradigms in the true sense, with new modes of research, new social practices supporting them, new types of data, new forms of evidence, and new theories surrounding them.

But they are all, without exception, monological to the core. And thus, as important as they are in their own right, they have little to offer us in terms of actually integrating monological with dialogical and translogical—that is, integrating science and spirituality.

So we can begin to see that, although it is common for "new-paradigm" thinkers to claim that their scientific systems orientation will heal the fragmentation of the modern world, make us feel at home in the universe, save the planet, and reintroduce spirituality into our sick and alienated culture, the fact is that monological science—both atomistic and systems-oriented—is, alas, part of the disease it claims to cure.

SUMMARY

It is not through any sort of "new paradigm" in science that spirituality and modern science will finally find mutual accord. Because, first, "paradigm" as popularly understood "is at present a dead metaphor." Second, even if it were alive—or used in its correct meaning as injunction or social practice—there is still nothing in even the most avant-garde of the empirical sciences (from string theory to hyperspace to chaos theory) that goes beyond its monological/empirical grounding. All of the alleged "new paradigms" would still appear within that monological framework, not outside it, and thus any and all of the "new paradigms" would simply clone the disaster. Third, the entire approach, according to many critics, is heavily infected with a narcissistic disregard for evidence. Fourth, the approach is profoundly self-contradictory (the performative contradiction). Fifth—and worst of all—it is based on a category error, the attempt by the monological eye of flesh and the dialogical eye of mind to see what can be seen only by the translogical eye of spirit. As such, it can profoundly detract from the awakening of a genuine spiritual awareness.

What is required for an integration of science and religion is not an attempt to reduce translogical religion to a new monological paradigm. Rather, we need to take the core of the wisdom traditions—namely, the Great Chain of Being, which includes monological (the eye of flesh) and dialogical (the eye of mind) and translogical (the eye of contemplation)—and expose them to the differentiations of modernity (the differentiation of the value spheres of art, morals, and science).

To do that, we need to understand as clearly as we can the beast called "modernity."

4

Modernity

DIGNITY AND DISASTER

T HE GREAT DIFFICULTY with all of the typical attempts to integrate premodern religion with modern science is, I believe, a failure to grasp either the core of premodernity (the Great Chain) or the core of modernity (the differentiation of the value spheres of art, morals, and science). Since there seems to be less confusion about the core of premodernity—the Great Nest of Being was its heart and soul—perhaps we need to look more carefully at the other side of the equation, the monster known as "modernity."

THE MEANING OF "MODERNITY" AND "POSTMODERNITY"

Modernity, for historians, refers very loosely to the general period that had its roots in the Renaissance, blossomed with the Enlightenment, and continues in many ways to this day. Modernity therefore includes various trends in:

> *Philosophy:* Descartes is considered the first "modern" philosopher; modern philosophy is usually "representational," which means it tries to form a correct representation of the world. This representational view is also called "the mirror of nature," because it was

commonly believed that the ultimate reality was sensory nature and philosophy's job was to picture or mirror this universal reality correctly.

Art: Modern art in the most general sense (from the middle of the eighteenth century forward)—that of Goya, Constable, Courbet, Manet, Monet, Cézanne, van Gogh, Matisse, Kandinsky—is marked at times by an almost total break with traditional themes and modes of composition, and especially a break from depicting merely mythic-religious themes (nature, not myth, comes more to the fore).

Science: Modern science (Kepler, Galileo, Newton, Kelvin, Watt, Faraday, Maxwell) relied in large part on the measurement of empirical-sensory data. The old sciences had *classified* nature, the new sciences *measured* nature; and that was their astonishing and revolutionary strength.

Cultural cognition: This involved a general shift from mythic-membership modes of cognition to mental-rational modes; a shift from conventional to postconventional ethics; a shift from ethnocentric values to universal or global values.

Personal identity: This involved a shift from a role identity, defined by a social hierarchy, to an ego identity, defined by personal autonomy.

Political and civil rights: This included the outlawing of slavery, the institution of women's rights, child labor laws, the rights of humankind (freedom of speech, religion, assembly, fair trial), and equality before the law.

Technology: This refers especially to inventions beginning with the steam engine, as well as industrialization in general.

Politics: This included the rise of the liberal democracies, often through a series of actual revolutions (in, e.g., France and America).

Will and Ariel Durants's description of modernity as *The Age of Reason and Revolution* is as good a summary as any.

While historians basically agree on the general outlines of modernity, *postmodernity* has an extraordinary number of meanings, few of which coincide. "Postmodern" is often given both a narrow or technical meaning, and a broader and more general meaning. The narrow and technical we discussed briefly in the previous chapter—the notion that there is no truth, only interpretation, and all interpretations are socially constructed. This narrow view we also called "extreme postmodernism," because it takes certain very important insights (e.g., many realities are socially constructed) and blows them totally out of proportion (e.g., all realities are socially constructed), which results in nothing but severe performative contradictions.

But in the broader and more general sense, "postmodern" simply means any of the major currents occurring *in the wake of modernity*—as a reaction against modernity, or as counterbalance to modernity, or sometimes as a continuation of modernity by other means. Thus, if industrialization is modern, the information age is postmodern. If Descartes is modern, Derrida is postmodern. If perspectival rationality is modern, aperspectival network-logic is postmodern. If Bauhaus architecture is modern, Frank Gehry is postmodern. If representation is modern, nonrepresentation is postmodern. If the internal combustion engine is modern, the Internet is postmodern. (I will use both of those meanings—the narrow and the more general—as the context will make clear.)

Thus, today's "modern world" actually consists of several different currents, some of which are "modern" in the specific sense (those events set into motion with the Western Enlightenment, as listed above), others of which are carryovers from the premodern world (in particular, remnants of mythic religion, and, more rarely, remnants of tribal magic), and still others of which are postmodern. In short, today's "modern world" actually consists of various premodern, modern, and postmodern currents.

When I refer to *modernity* per se, I mean modernity in the specific sense (the events set into motion with the liberal Enlightenment), whereas "the modern world" simply means today's contemporary world with all of its premodern, modern, and postmodern currents. And it is especially modernity in the specific sense that we wish to understand, because the core claims of modernity must obviously be an essential feature of any genuine integration of modern science and premodern religion.

And, most significantly, the dramatic failure to grasp the actual contours of modernity has crippled more than one attempt to integrate science and spirituality.

The Dignity of Modernity

In many ways, the *governing principles* of the hundred or so democratic nations in today's world are in fact the *principles of modernity*—that is, the values of the liberal Western Enlightenment. These include the values of equality, freedom, and justice; representational and deliberative democracy; the equality of all citizens before the law, regardless of race, sex, or creed; political and civil rights (freedom of speech, religion, assembly, fair trial, etc.). Of course, some of these rights still need to be applied more universally and evenhandedly, but they are nonetheless firmly ensconced as widely held ideals toward which liberal societies ought to strive.

These values and rights existed nowhere in the premodern world on a large scale, and thus these rights have been quite accurately referred to as the *dignity of modernity.* For example, as Gerhard Lenski has documented, every one of the premodern societal types—including tribal, foraging, horticultural, and agrarian—had various degrees of slavery. The only societal types in all of history and prehistory to effectively ban slavery across the board were those that emerged in the wake of modernity. This is simply one example of the many dignities the Enlightenment brought.

To say that no premodern societal type possessed these various dignities is also to say, most damningly, that none of the premodern religions anywhere in the world delivered these dignities and rights on any sort of large scale; in fact, they often did quite the contrary. The battle cry of the Enlightenment—Voltaire's "Remember the cruelties!"—was a call to end the brutal oppression often effected by premodern religion in the name of a chosen God or Goddess. The temples to those Deities were built on the broken backs of millions, who left a trail of blood and tears on the highway to that heaven.

The fact that premodern religion failed to evenhandedly deliver these dignities serves as a sharp reminder that "Godless modernity" was not merely the monster its religious opponents have often claimed. Modernity brought these dignities, so it is to modernity that we will want to look for those factors that supported them. Whatever it was that allowed modernity to bring forth these noble values will be a necessary ingredient in the integration of the best that both epochs have to offer.

MODERNITY AND ITS LEGION OF CRITICS

Almost all of the "new-paradigm" thinkers couple their proposed new paradigm with an aggressive attack on modernity, resorting at times to vicious polemic. Toxic treatise after toxic treatise tears into modernity, with such typically titled books as *My Name is Chellis and I'm in Recovery from Western Civilization* (actual title). Yet, almost without exception, these "new-paradigm" thinkers give little indication that they have grasped or understood the actual nature of modernity itself—its defining characteristics, values, and structures. In particular, they rarely evidence a clear and concise understanding of the dignity of modernity, even though they implicitly and extensively exercise it.

Instead, they often set up a truly pitiful straw man, often centered on poor Newton and Descartes, and then proceed to damn virtually the entire sweep of modernity. The "Newtonian-Cartesian patriarchal alienated fragmented worldview"—which, of course, is now labeled the "old paradigm"—will be replaced with the revolutionary and world-transforming "new paradigm," which these theorists possess and are willing to share with the world in preparation for the coming transformation.

The various "new paradigms" these theorists offer generally fall into one of three broad types (although combinations are common): premodern revivalist, postmodern pandemonium, and global systems. While all of them possess important moments of truth, which need to be fully acknowledged, virtually all of them fail lamentably in their overall grasp of modernity.

The *premodern revivalist* "paradigm" generally maintains that tribal foraging cultures possessed "nondissociated consciousness," whereas the modern world has mostly "dissociated" or "fragmented" consciousness. Alternatively, the premodern world is viewed as matrifocal and holistic, plugged into the Goddess and the unbroken Web of Life, whereas the modern world is patriarchal, analytic, fragmented, and broken. Thus what the modern world needs is a *resurrection* or a *recapturing* of a lost and more "unified" consciousness (a type of U-turn to "original unity"). But, as we will see, these writers tend to drastically misinterpret the premodern consciousness—it was far from "unified" in most instances. Moreover, what none of these theories has been able to satisfactorily explain is why evolution would do something that it has never done in any other living system, namely, make a U-turn right in the middle of its development, rather like every oak tree on the face of the planet suddenly attempting to recapture its acornness.

The *postmodern* "paradigm" ("postmodern" in the narrow and technical sense) is simply the claim that there is no truth, only interpretations, and thus the "sliding nature of all signifiers" means that the authority of science—and therefore modernity itself—can simply be swept under the carpet with not much further ado. We are free of modernity precisely because we are free of the demand for truth and verification in general. The very demand for truth is part of the "old paradigm," which the new paradigm has totally deconstructed. This leaves, as we saw, nothing but one's own ego—one's own narcissism—to impose its will on reality, and this nihilistic narcissism is boldly offered to the world as a revolutionary transformation.

The *global systems* "paradigm" attacks atomism and replaces it with systems thinking, imagining that it has thereby bypassed the central problem of the "Newtonian-Cartesian fragmented worldview." But, as we saw, the specific difficulty with empirical science of *any* variety is not that it is atomistic or holistic, analytic or systems, but rather that it is empirical and monological in the first place. Systems theory does not alter that in the least; it merely continues the monological approach by other means, which, in this case, is all the more insidious because its proponents imagine that they have overcome the problem, whereas they have simply cloned it.

The grave difficulty with all three of these attacks on modernity—other than their own performative contradictions—is that few of them evidence any substantial understanding of the characteristics, let alone the dignity, of modernity. Ironically, most of the decent values that these approaches express are in fact the values of modernity, including equality, freedom, justice, equal opportunity, and egalitarianism before the law. This certainly gives the impression of ungrateful and petulant children not on speaking terms with their parents.

Most egregious, these "new-paradigm" attacks on modernity show no evidence of understanding the difference between *differentiation* and *dissociation*. Yet in that simple but profound distinction lies the key to modernity—and therefore the key to the integration of science and religion in the modern world.

DIFFERENTIATION = DIGNITY

Scholars from Max Weber to Jürgen Habermas have sought a simple way of characterizing the major thrust that was modernity, and they have hit upon what is surely one of the most significant developments in all of human history: as we have briefly seen, modernity was characterized by what Weber called "the differentiation of the cultural value spheres"—that is, *the differentiation of art, morals, and science.* This differentiation is the essence of the dignity of modernity, as a brief glance at premodernity will show.

Many scholars (including Jean Gebser, Habermas, myself, and others) divide the premodern world into archaic, magic, and mythic worldviews (correlated with foraging, horticultural, and agrarian modes of production; these terms will become clearer as we proceed). But none of the premodern worldviews clearly differentiated art-aesthetics, empirical-science, and religion-morals. Although "premodern holists" claim that this was a wonderful state of nondissociated and unified consciousness, it was actually quite the opposite.

The Church during the Middle Ages is a classic example, repeated around the world and in every premodern societal type as variations on a common theme. Because art-aesthetics, empirical-science, and religion-morals were not clearly differentiated, what happened in one sphere could dominate and control what happened in the others. Thus, a scientist such as Galileo could be prevented from pursuing the sphere of science because it clashed with the prevailing sphere of religion-morals. An artist such as Michelangelo was in constant conflict with Pope Julius II about the types of figures he was allowed to represent in his art, because expressive-art and religion-morals were not clearly differentiated, and thus oppression in one sphere was oppression in the other.

Likewise, the state was not yet differentiated from religion—there was no separation of church and state. Accordingly, if you disagreed with the religious authorities, you could be tried for both heresy (a *religious* crime) and treason (a *political* crime). For heresy, you could be eternally damned; for treason, temporally tortured and killed—and those who committed the former usually suffered the latter. Few of the theorists who glowingly eulogize the numerous premodern theocracies (or mythocracies) as "organic and unified" would actually want to live in such a culture, because if your religion did not happen to agree with that of the authorities, you were toast.

This state of affairs was not holistic and integrated, it was simply *predifferentiated*—a huge contrast! That which has not yet been differentiated in the first place cannot be integrated. There were as yet no separate spheres to be brought together into a synthesis or integration; there was simply a fusion of spheres that robbed each of its autonomy and dignity.

But with the rise of modernity, the spheres of art, science, and morals were clearly differentiated, and this marked the *dignity* of modernity because each sphere could now pursue its own truth without violence and domination from the others. You could look through Galileo's telescope without being hauled before the Inquisition. You could paint the human body in a natural setting without being tried for heresy against God and Pope. You could espouse the universal moral rights of humans without being charged with treason against King or Queen.

So here is our first important equation defining modernity: differentiation = dignity. If we are to integrate modern science with premodern religion, that is one of the essential gifts that modernity will bring.

THE GOOD, THE TRUE, AND THE BEAUTIFUL

There is a simple way of referring to these three value spheres of morals, science, and art: they are the Good, the True, and the Beautiful. (These terms were first introduced on a large scale by the Greeks, who were, in this regard, one of the precursors of modernity.)

The Good refers to morals, to justness, to ethics, to how you and I interact in a fair and decent fashion, both with each other and with all other sentient beings. This does not mean that everybody has to agree on a specific type of morality, about which there can be reasonable disagreement. It means, in a general sense, that human beings must discover some way to mutually inhabit the same cultural space, the opposite of which is, quite simply, war.

The True refers, in a very general sense, to objective truth. It means the truth according to dispassionate standards—not merely the truth according to my ego, or my tribe, or my religion. Science, above all, attempts to specialize in objective, empirical, reproducible truth. This does not mean there are no other types of truth; it simply means that science has a deserved reputation for delivering important types of objective truth.

Beauty, it is said, is in the eye of the beholder; it represents the aesthetic and expressive currents of each subjective self. This does not necessarily mean that beauty is "merely subjective" or idiosyncratic; it simply means that beauty is a judgment made by each subject, each "I." This judgment, as Kant pointed out, resides not empirically in an object, but in a discriminating subject. Beauty is (in part) in the "I" of the beholder.

So to say that modernity differentiated morals, science, and art is to say that it differentiated what is good, what is true, and what is beautiful, so that each of the spheres could pursue its own truths and aspirations without domination or violence from the others.

I, WE, AND IT

We now reach a fascinating and important point in this discussion. Each of these spheres—art, morals, and science; or the Beautiful, the Good, and the True—*has a different type of language.* The expressive-aesthetic sphere is described in "I" language. The moral-ethical sphere is described in "we" language. And the objective-science sphere is described in "it" language. *If we are to integrate these various spheres, we must first learn to speak their native tongues.*

Beauty, we just saw, is in the "I" of the beholder. This *subjective* domain represents the self and self-expression, aesthetic judgment, and artistic expression in the most general sense. It also represents the irreducible subjective contents of immediate consciousness (and intentionality), all of which can properly be described in first-person accounts, in "I" language.

Ethics is described in "we" language. It is part of the *intersubjective* domain, the domain of collective interaction and social awareness, the domain of justness, goodness, reciprocity, and mutual understanding, all of which are described in "we" language.

Truth, in the sense of objective truth, is described in "it" language. This is the domain of *objective* realities, realities that can be seen in an empirical and monological fashion, from atoms to brains, from cells to ecosystems, from rocks to solar systems, all of which are described in "it" language.

Thus, when we say that modernity differentiated the spheres of art, morals, and science, this also basically means that modernity differentiated the realms of I, WE, and IT.

Because modernity differentiated the WE and the IT, political or religious tyranny (of the WE) could no longer determine what was objectively true (of the IT). In other words, you could now read Copernicus without being burned at the stake. This differentiation of WE and IT led directly to the rise of the empirical sciences, including the ecological sciences, systems theory, and quantum-relativistic physics. Premodern societies produced none of these empirical sciences, in part because they lacked this crucial differentiation.

Because modernity differentiated the I and the WE, the collective WE could no longer dominate individual I's. That is, each individual I had *rights* that could not be violated by the state, the Church, or the community in general. This differentiation of I and WE contributed directly to the rise of the liberal democracies, where each I was extended the political rights of equality, freedom, and justice. This in turn led to such liberation movements as the abolition of slavery, women's rights, and the freeing of the untouchables.

Because modernity differentiated the I and the IT, individual whim could no longer establish what was objectively true. What the I believed about objective reality now had to be checked against empirical facts, thus curbing the magical and mythical attempts to coerce the Kosmos through egocentric ritual and petition. This contributed directly to everything from the rise of modern medical science to global telecommunications—in other words, if I want something from reality (IT), I am going to have to do something other than merely wish, since the two are not the same. (This also shows us the disasters that occur when both premodern revivalists and postmodern deconstructionists attempt to de-differentiate these realms, thus equating I-art with it-science and immersing themselves in exactly the narcissism that this differentiation overcame.)

And so goes the list of differentiated dignities. Liberal democracy, equality, freedom, feminism, the ecological sciences, the abolition of slavery, extraordinary medical advances, modern physics—all of these rest, in whole or part, on the differentiation of expressive-aesthetics, legal-morals, and empirical-science; the Beautiful, the Good, and the True; I, WE, and IT; self, culture, and nature.

And that is precisely why this series of crucial differentiations is called the "dignity of modernity."

DIFFERENTIATION AND DISSOCIATION

It is this dignity of differentiation that the antimodernity critics so often miss. They do so, I believe, because they confuse *differentiation* with *dissociation*.

Most natural and healthy growth processes proceed by differentiation-and-integration. The clearest example of this is the growth of a complex organism from a single-celled egg: the zygote divides into two cells, then four, then eight, then sixteen, then thirty-two . . . into literally millions of cells. And while this extraordinary *differentiation* is occurring, the different cells are simultaneously being *integrated* into coherent tissues and systems in the overall organism. This differentiation-and-integration process allows a single cell to evolve into a multicellular organism and complex system of exquisite unity and functional integrity.

From a simple acorn to the mighty oak: the extraordinary process of differentiation-and-integration. In this growth process, if something goes wrong with either of those strands of growth—differentiation or integration—the result is *pathology*.

If differentiation fails to occur, the result is *fusion,* fixation, and arrest in general. Growth becomes stuck at a particular stage; there is no further growth because further differentiation fails to occur. To give an example from human psychosexual growth, when we say some people have an oral fixation, it means that they are fixated to an oral impulse that they failed to differentiate from. They remain "fused" to this impulse, which obsessively dominates their awareness.

On the other hand, if differentiation begins but goes too far, the result is *dissociation* or fragmentation. Differentiation gets out of control, and the various subsystems cannot be easily integrated: they fly apart instead of fitting together. The parts don't differentiate, they dissociate, and the result is fragmentation, repression, alienation.

In human growth, for example, the ego and id are supposed to differentiate; but if that differentiation goes too far into dissociation, the ego simply represses and alienates the id, which results in painful neurotic symptoms. Instead of differentiation and integration, there is dissociation and repression.

Now, if we confuse differentiation with dissociation, we will confuse growth with disease. We will confuse dignity with disaster. We will confuse evolution with catastrophe. And that is precisely what so many of the antimodernist critics do.

Of course, differentiation can indeed look like a split, a separation, a breaking, or a fracture. The one-celled egg does indeed divide into two cells, then four, and so on. But that multiplication is how nature creates *higher unities and deeper integrations.* It is easy to unify a hundred items, but try unifying a million. That is exactly why the unity of the oak is infinitely more impressive than that of the acorn: the oak has considerably more *depth* (it has a much greater number of systems that must be vertically integrated in order to function).

Thus, the prior acorn state is not "more unified," it is simply *less differentiated*—and actually, therefore, considerably *less integrated.* The oak is incomparably more unified and integrated than the acorn, and it got that way precisely through the developmental and evolutionary process of differentiation-and-integration.

But the premodern revivalists, looking at the course of humanity's necessary differentiations (on the way to higher integrations), see nothing but a series of fractures, breaks, dissociations, and disasters. When humanity differentiated mind and nature (around the tenth millennium BCE), the premodernists scream dissociation. When humanity differentiated mind and body (around the sixth century BCE), the premodernists scream dissociation. When humanity finally differentiated art and science and morals (with modernity), the premodernists scream dissociation.

And they see nothing but a sinister, malevolent, or even evil agency behind these brutal "ruptures." The oak is somehow a vicious and horrible violation of the acorn. The exact nature of the evil and disruptive agency responsible for humanity's "fragmentation" varies from theorist to theorist. Top contenders include Newton, Descartes, the patriarchy, Plato, analytic reason, farming, cooking, domestication of animals, mathematics, males in general, belief in a transcendent God, and processed foods.

And, for the premodern revivalists, the cure is somehow to recontact and resurrect our acornness. We must get back to a state prior to the "dissociation." But because these theorists tend to confuse differentiation and dissociation, they confuse dignity and disaster, they confuse forward and backward. They would have us heal the dissociations of modernity, which is well and good; but because they do not distinguish between differentiation and dissociation, they keep looking for a previous period in history where there were *no differentiations at all;* this forces them to look further and further back into prehistory, searching for that state of perfect acornness prior to any nasty divisions. They inevitably end up at one of the earliest stages of human evolution— foraging or horticulture—and this simple state of fusion and indissociation is eulogized as being very close to a state of perfect harmony among mind, body, and nature—when in fact those systems were not integrated, they were simply not yet clearly differentiated in the first place.

Thus the recommendations of these theorists often result in nothing but a thinly disguised *regression.* Of course, none of these theorists actually recommends regression, and the stated idea is always to somehow integrate acornness with oakness (whatever that might mean). But precisely because they show so little evidence of understanding the dignity of modernity, they show little insight into the disaster of modernity, either.

Let us see if we can more accurately spot the specific diseases that did indeed plague modernity. This is crucial, because if we are to integrate premodern religion with modern science, we must know what part of modernity was growth, and what part was disease.

DISSOCIATION = DISASTER

Modernity obviously has its own share of horrible problems. In fact, some of modernity's differentiations did indeed go too far, into a specific set of *dissociations*—and those dissociations I refer to as *the disaster of modernity.* Not only did art, morals, and science differentiate—which was necessary and beneficial—they soon began dramatically to dissociate or fly apart, which, as we just saw, is the hallmark of *pathology* in any growing system.

This was indeed a disaster, a pathology, for it very soon allowed a powerful monological science to colonialize and dominate the other spheres (the aesthetic-expressive and the religious-moral), mostly by denying them any real existence at all! If differentiation was the dignity of modernity, dissociation was the disaster.

This dissociation of the cultural value spheres is exactly what began to happen to art, science, and morals. If the modern differentiation began in earnest around the sixteenth and seventeenth centuries, by the end of the eighteenth and the beginning of the nineteenth the differentiation was already drifting into a painful and pathological dissociation. Art and science and morals began going their separate ways, with little or no discourse between these spheres, and this set the stage for a dramatic, triumphant, and altogether frightening invasion of the other spheres by an explosive science. Within a mere century, *monological science*—variously including positivism, empiric-analytic reason, dynamic process theory, systems theory, chaos theory, complexity theory, and technological modes of knowing—would completely dominate serious discourse in the Western world.

Put bluntly, the I and the WE were colonialized by the IT. The Good and the Beautiful were overtaken by a growth in monological Truth that, otherwise admirable, became grandiose in its own conceit and cancerous in its relations to others. Full of itself and flush with stunning victories, empirical science became *scientism,* the belief that there is no reality save that revealed by science, and no truth save that which science delivers. The subjective and interior domains—the I and the WE—were flattened into objective, exterior, empirical processes, either atomistic or systems. Consciousness itself, and the mind and heart and soul of humankind, could not be seen with a microscope, a telescope, a cloud chamber, a photographic plate, and so all were pronounced epiphenomenal at best, illusory at worst.

The entire interior dimensions—of morals, artistic expression, intro-spection, spirituality, contemplative awareness, meaning and value and intentionality—were dismissed by monological science because none of them could be registered by the eye of flesh or empirical instruments. Art and morals and contemplation and spirit were all demolished by the scientific bull in the china shop of consciousness. And there was the disaster of modernity.

FLATLAND

We can also call this disaster "the collapse of the Kosmos," because the three great domains—art, science, and morals—after their heroic differentiation, were rudely collapsed into only one "real" domain, that of empirical and monological science, a world of nothing but meaning-less ITS roaming a one-dimensional flatland. The scientific worldview was of a universe composed entirely of objective processes, all described not in I-language or we-language, but merely in it-language, with no consciousness, no interiors, no values, no meaning, no depth and no Divinity.

And, contrary to what some "new-paradigm" thinkers claim, the worldview of science was, almost from the beginning, a systems or holis-tic view. The Enlightenment philosophers and scientists conceived of nature and humans as one great, interwoven system, with every aspect perfectly intermeshing with every other. This "great interlocking order," as numerous theorists from Charles Taylor to Arthur Lovejoy have care-fully demonstrated, was one of the defining conceptions of the Enlight-enment and of the modern scientific worldview.

The problem, in other words, was not that the scientific worldview was atomistic instead of holistic, because it was basically and generally holistic from the start. No, the problem was that it was a thoroughly *flatland holism.* It was not a holism that actually included all of the interior realms of the I and the WE (including the eye of contemplation).

It was rather a holism, a systems theory, that included nothing but ITS, nothing but objectifiable processes scurrying through information loops, or gravity acting at a distance on objects, or chemical interactions of atomic events, or objective systems interacting with other objective systems, or cybernetic feedback loops, or digital bits running through neuronal circuits. Nowhere in systems theory (or in flatland holism) could you find anything resembling beauty, poetry, value, desire, love, honor, compassion, charity, God or the Goddess, Eros or Agape, moral wisdom, or artistic expression.

In other words, all you found was a holistic system of interwoven ITS. And it was the reduction of all of the value spheres to monological ITS perceived by the eye of flesh that, more than anything else, constituted the disaster of modernity.

THE FACE OF TODAY

It is true that no premodern cultures had this shuddering dissociation and collapse—but only because none had the differentiation of which this dissociation was a pathology. Premodern cultures did not have this disaster precisely because they did not possess the corresponding dignities, either, and thus they cannot serve as role models for the desired integration. The cure for the disaster of modernity is to address the dissociation, not attempt to erase the differentiation!

This dissociation, this disease, this developmental pathology—this collapse of the Kosmos—is of profound significance in attempting to understand what happened to Spirit in the modern world. The Great Chain of Being—the backbone of every human culture prior to modernity—collapsed in the face of unrepentant ITS. All of the higher levels and spheres, including mind and soul, spirit and goodness and beauty, were meticulously scrubbed from the face of the Kosmos, leaving dirt and dust, systems and sand, matter and mass, objects and its. A cold and uncaring wind, monological in its method and calculated in its madness, blew across a flat and faded landscape, the landscape that now contains, as tiny specks in the corner, the faces of you and me.

5

The Four Corners of the Known Universe

E VEN IF WE thoroughly acknowledge the dignity of modernity, we still must address the disaster of modernity. As we saw in the last chapter, the nightmare is not that science is atomistic instead of holistic; the disaster is that science per se—empirical, monological, instrumental, it-language science, in both its atomistic and holistic forms—came to aggressively invade the other value spheres—including interior consciousness, psyche, soul, spirit, value, morals, ethics, and art—thus reducing the entire lot to a colony of science, which itself would pronounce on what was, and what was not, real.

What was real was any objectifiable entity or process that could be described in valueless, empirical, monological, process it-language. These objects, or ITS, all have what Whitehead called *simple location:* you can actually or figuratively put your finger on them, you can see them with your senses (or their extensions). Molecules are real, organisms are real, the brain is real, planets are real, galaxies are real, ecosystems are real. They are all objective, empirical, exterior, positivistic entities: you can put your finger right on them, more or less.

But you cannot put your finger on compassion; it does not have simple location. You cannot put your finger on consciousness; it does not have simple location. You cannot put your finger on honor, valor, love, mercy, justice, morals, vision, or satori—none of the *interior* dimensions of the I and the WE have simple location. They are located in interior spaces, not in exterior spaces. You cannot put your finger on them.

And you certainly cannot put your finger on God. God will not be fingered. Therefore, according to science and its belief in simple location, God does not exist. In fact, according to flatland, none of the interior dimensions and modes of knowing has any substantial reality at all. Only objective ITs are real.

The disaster of modernity, in short, was that all *interior* dimensions (of I and WE) were reduced to *exterior* surfaces (of objective ITs), which, of course, completely destroys the interior dimensions in their own terms. With this collapse of the Kosmos, there is no longer serious room for any interior apprehension whatsoever, and whether that interior vision be of poetry or of God matters not in the least: none of them has any substantial or irreducible reality.

This is why modern science is not impressed with epistemological pluralism. What might make sense to enlightened types like you and me—namely, that other modes of knowing disclose other and equally valid realities, so that science and religion can peacefully coexist—is soundly rejected by science at the very start, simply because the desired integration involves terms that science does not believe are real to begin with. Why, science asks, should we attempt to integrate Santa Claus? Why integrate pathology, illusion, and error? Why a holistic inclusion of nonsense?

Thus we confront what is by far the most important and central issue in the relation of science and spirituality, namely, the actual relation of any *interior realities* to *exterior realities*. When modern empirical science rejected the reality of the interior domains, it in effect *rejected the entire Great Chain of Being,* because all of the levels of the Great Chain except the lowest (the material body) happen to be *interior realities* of the I and the WE, of the subjective and the intersubjective domains. To reject the interiors was to reject the Great Chain, and thus profoundly reject the core of the great spiritual traditions.

We can therefore summarize the entire collapse of the Kosmos—and modernity's rejection of the Great Chain—by saying that all interiors were reduced to exteriors. All subjects were reduced to objects; all depth was reduced to surfaces; all I's and all WE's were reduced to ITs; all quality was reduced to quantity; levels of significance were reduced to levels of size; value was reduced to veneer; all translogical and dialogical were reduced to monological. Gone the eye of contemplation and gone the eye of mind—only data from the eye of the flesh would be accorded primary reality, because only sensory data possessed simple location, here in the desolate world of monochrome flatland.

INTERIOR AND EXTERIOR

Here is the central problem, the major reason modern science rejected religion, and the major reason higher and interior modes were replaced by an exterior and monological monopoly:

In the traditional view of epistemological pluralism, and in the traditional Great Chain of Being—let us use the simple version of body, mind, soul, and spirit—the material body, the lowest rung, was available to science, and it was science's role, limited but important, to investigate this material realm. But the mind, soul, and spirit "transcended" the body, and thus had no major referents in the body itself. In some versions of the Great Chain, the higher levels had no connection to the body whatsoever—and thus, it was maintained, science had nothing to contribute to, or even say about, these higher and more significant realities.

But as modern science (freed from its slavery to religious tenets by the differentiation of the value spheres) began investigating the organic body—the organism itself—it found that many of the "higher" or "transcendent" realities were actually deeply connected to the organic body and its organic brain: they were functions of the overall organism, not functions of some pie-in-the-sky realms. Consciousness, for example, seemed intimately connected with the organic brain, a profound recognition that had been completely lacking in virtually every premodern culture.

Thus, if the higher realm of the "transcendent mind" was actually a function of the organic body (or the overall organism)—and if religion and metaphysics had completely missed this elemental connection—why should any of the other "transcendent realms" be any different? Couldn't all of this "metaphysical otherworldliness" actually involve *functions of the natural organism,* the *this-worldly* organism, best investigated by empirical science, and not relegated to invisible realms manipulated by dubious mystics?

When science discovered that mind and consciousness were anchored in the natural organism—and not merely floating around somewhere in "higher" realms—the Great Chain of Being took a colossal hit from which it never recovered. And unless this hit can be addressed in a straightforward fashion, satisfying the essence of *both* the religious and the scientific claims, the chance of any integration between them is slim indeed.

We have seen that in order to integrate science and religion, we need first to integrate the Great Chain with the claims of modernity. We can now see that a large part of this task is to investigate the relation of *interior* and *exterior* realities. The premodern religions gave a great deal of emphasis to the interior modes of knowing (mental and spiritual), whereas modernity, in both its dignity and disaster, gave an unprecedented emphasis to the exterior modes; with scientific materialism, the exterior *alone* was real. In many ways, then, the battle between premodern and modern is a battle between interior and exterior.

It is my main contention that unless we can find a way for *both* of those claims to be true—the transcendental and the empirical, the interior and the exterior—we will never genuinely integrate science and religion.

THE FOUR QUADRANTS

The Great Chain of Being is, of course, a hierarchy: each higher level transcends but includes its predecessors. As we saw in Chapter 1, it is best pictured not as a ladder but as a series of concentric circles or nests, with each wider nest enveloping or enfolding its juniors. In Plotinus's version, for example, there are matter, life, sensation, perception, impulse, images, concepts, logical faculty, creative reason, world soul, nous, and the One, with each higher *development* being an *envelopment* of its predecessors.

Modern systems science likewise has its own general hierarchy, each term of which also transcends and includes its predecessors: subatomic particles, atoms, molecules, cells, tissue systems, organisms, societies of organisms, biosphere, universe.

It is fascinating that *both premodern religion and modern science have a defining hierarchy,* and both of them are composed of *enveloping nests of increasing embrace* (development that is envelopment). And yet, these two major and extremely influential hierarchies never quite agree with each other. Tantalizingly, they seem to talk about the same thing (a graded series of realities), yet their major terms never really match up. Clearly, if we could find some way that these two hierarchies were genuinely related to each other, we would have taken an important step toward the hoped-for integration of premodern and modern.

In researching this problem, I did an extensive data search of several hundred hierarchies, taken from systems theory, ecological science, Kabbalah, developmental psychology, Yogachara Buddhism, moral development, biological evolution, Vedanta Hinduism, Neo-Confucianism, cosmic and stellar evolution, Hwa Yen, the Neoplatonic corpus—an entire spectrum of premodern, modern, and postmodern nests. After I had collected several hundred hierarchies, I tried grouping them in various ways, and I eventually noticed that, without exception, they all fell into one of four major types.

These four types of hierarchies—which I call *the four quadrants*—are summarized in Figure 5-1 (which is a simple schematic, by no means complete or exhaustive, but only a representative sampling of these major hierarchies). It soon became obvious that these four different types of hierarchies simply deal with the *interior* and the *exterior* of the *individual* and the *collective* (as will soon be explained). The point is

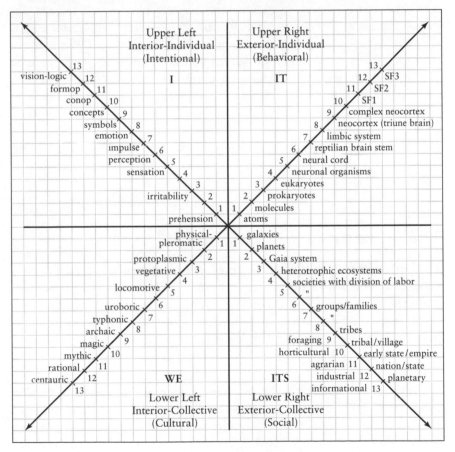

FIGURE 5-1. *The Four Quadrants*

that, while these four major types of hierarchies are indeed different, they are all profoundly interrelated and deeply connected, in what look like intrinsically necessary ways.

But most fascinating of all, I found that the classic hierarchy of traditional religion and the standard hierarchy of modern science are simply two of these four types of hierarchies. As such, they are deeply interconnected with each other, but they are also part of an even larger network of hierarchical patterns. They are actually part of a universal network that involves not just two, but four, major types of hierarchies—yet hierarchies that are interrelated in vital ways.

Now this is an interesting development. What if these quadrants, these four types of hierarchies, are in fact real? Since variations on these four hierarchies show up extensively across cultures and across epochs—premodern, modern, and postmodern—might this indicate that they are actually pointing to certain irreducible realities? What if the four quadrants are an intrinsic aspect of the Kosmos itself? Since they include *both* interior and exterior domains, might the four quadrants provide a series of crucial links in the relation of religion and science? Might they actually contain the secret key to integrating the value spheres themselves?

Perhaps, perhaps not. But it certainly looks encouraging. Let us begin by examining the four quadrants, one at a time, looking more closely at their contours.

THE OUTSIDE OF THE INDIVIDUAL

The Upper-Right quadrant is the standard scientific account of the individual components of the universe: atoms, molecules, single cells (prokaryotes and eukaryotes), multicellular organisms, including (in increasing complexity) organisms with neural cords, reptilian brain stem, paleomammalian limbic system, neocortex, and complex neocortex (with its own higher structure-functions labeled "SF1," "SF2," and "SF3").

This hierarchy shows an *asymmetrical* increase in *holistic* capacity. "Asymmetrical" means "not equivalent": atoms contain neutrons, but neutrons do not contain atoms; molecules contain atoms, but not vice versa; cells contain molecules, but not vice versa. That "not vice versa" establishes an *irreversible hierarchy of increasing wholeness,* increasing holism, increasing unity and integration. This is why all such hierarchies are indeed "higher-archies," containing successively higher or deeper or wider wholes.

Put differently, each successive unit *transcends* but *includes* its predecessors. Each senior element contains or enfolds its juniors as components in its own makeup, but then adds something *emergent,* distinctive, and defining that is not found in the lower level: it transcends and includes.

To put it one last way, each element is a *whole* that is simultaneously a *part* of another whole: a whole atom is part of a whole molecule, a whole molecule is part of a whole cell, a whole cell is part of a whole organism, and so forth. Each element is neither a whole nor a part, but a whole/part.

Arthur Koestler coined the wonderful word *holon* to refer to such "whole/parts." Virtually all natural hierarchies, in any domain, are composed of holons, wholes that are simultaneously parts of other wholes. For exactly this reason, Koestler pointed out that the word *hierarchy* should really be *holarchy.* All natural hierarchies—that is, all natural holarchies—are composed of whole/parts or holons, and they show increasing orders of wholeness, unity, and functional integration.

(Unless, of course, there is a pathology in the holarchy. Holarchies evolve and develop, as we saw, by the process of differentiation-and-integration, and if anything goes wrong with either, a pathology develops. Most antihierarchy critics confuse natural holarchy with pathological holarchy, and catastrophically end up condemning both, an error to avoid. I will use "hierarchy" and "holarchy" interchangeably when referring to their natural and normal forms, and "pathological hierarchy" or "pathological holarchy" for their aberrant displays.)

The fact that each holon is actually a whole/part places it in a profound tension: in order to exist, it must in some sense retain its own identity or its own agency as a relatively autonomous whole; yet it must *also* fit in with the other holons that are an intrinsic part of its environment. Thus, every holon must maintain not only its own *agency,* but its own *communion,* its extensive networks of relationship upon which its own existence fundamentally depends. If any holon profoundly disrupts either its agency (as a whole) or its communion (as a part), it simply ceases to exist.

THE OUTSIDE OF THE COLLECTIVE

The Upper-Right quadrant, then, is the evolutionary unfolding of individual holons according to modern science. If we now look at the *com-*

munities or *societies* of these holons, again according to modern science, we find the Lower-Right quadrant (which I also call the *social*).

At first this quadrant might seem a bit confusing, since in the Upper-Right quadrant each higher level gets *bigger* (e.g., molecules are bigger than atoms because they contain atoms as subholons), but in the Lower-Right quadrant, each higher level gets *smaller*. This has often confused theorists who are trying to correlate various holarchies, because this holarchy seems to be running backward. What is going on here?

Erich Jantsch was one of the first to point out that, in almost any evolutionary or developmental sequence, where the *individual* holons generally get bigger (in comparison with the previous level), their collective or *communal* forms generally get smaller. The reason is twofold: One, since individual holons subsume and contain their predecessors, there will always be fewer holons the higher the level (there will *always* be fewer cells than molecules, fewer molecules than atoms, fewer atoms than quarks, etc.). And two, since there are fewer holons at each higher level, when they are gathered together into their social or collective forms, the collective will be smaller than its predecessor. Thus, as you can see in the Lower-Right quadrant of Figure 5-1, families are smaller than ecosystems, which are smaller than planets, which are smaller than galaxies.

This is generally summarized in the formula: *Evolution produces greater depth, less span.* "Depth" refers to the number of levels in the hierarchy of any holon, and "span" refers to the number of holons on that level. Each higher holon has more depth (it includes more previous holons in its own makeup), but there are fewer holons at that greater depth, and thus the collective becomes smaller and smaller—the so-called *pyramid of development.*

The Lower-Right quadrant, then, is simply a summary of the collective forms of holons as they have evolved, according to modern empirical and systems science.

THE INSIDE OF THE INDIVIDUAL

If we now look to the Upper-Left quadrant, we see yet another holarchy, this time of *interior awareness.* This holarchy moves from simple prehension to irritability (the capacity of protoplasm to respond to outside stimuli), to sensation, perception, impulse, emotion, images and symbols, concepts, concrete rules and operations ("conop"), formal-reflexive cognition ("formop"), and creative vision ("vision-logic").

This hierarchy, too, is a holarchy; it is composed of holons. Each senior holon includes, as components in its own makeup, the earlier and junior holon(s), but then adds a special and emergent capacity not found on the lower levels. Thus, each level is a whole that is part of the whole of the next higher level: each level is a whole/part, a holon, possessing both agency (wholeness) and communion (partness).

This holarchy is, of course, an *interior* holarchy, and for just that reason this entire domain was originally denied and rejected by scientific materialism, behaviorism, and positivism. The modern behavioristic claim was that mental intentionality had no reality apart from its exterior manifestation in specific observable behavior. The "mind" itself was just a "black box," unobservable by empirical science (that is, unobservable by the exterior eye of flesh) and thus not open to scientific investigation (translation: not really real). The collapse of the Kosmos included an aggressive attempt to turn all interior psychology into exterior behaviorism, and only slowly have the psychological domains fought their way back to some sort of recognition.

But for the moment, we are not trying to decide which of these quadrants is "real," or which is "important," or which is most "significant." We are simply looking at the results of a data search based on reputable investigators who have reported their findings from each of these quadrants (and thus we need to "bracket" any attempt at reductionism, if at all, until we finish the survey).

If we look at the research of the investigators of this Upper-Left quadrant, we find that what I have listed in Figure 5-1 is a fairly standard and widely accepted hierarchy, some version of which is presented by most modern developmental psychologists (from Abraham Maslow to Jean Piaget to Lawrence Kohlberg to Carol Gilligan to Jane Loevinger). Moreover, it is a hierarchy that is also quite similar, as far as it goes, to that presented by traditional and classical psychologists from Aristotle to Plotinus to Asanga to Aurobindo (as we will see in greater detail later). What they are all reporting—and generally agreeing on—are some of the basic contours of the interior of the individual, if examined closely and carefully.

Notice the difference between the interior of the individual—such as the mind—and the exterior of the individual—such as the brain. The mind is known by acquaintance; the brain, by objective description. You know your own mind directly, immediately, intimately—all the thoughts and feelings and yearnings and desires that run across your awareness moment to moment. Your brain, on the other hand, even though it is "inside" your organism, is not *interior* in your awareness, like your mind. The brain, rather, is known in an exterior and objectifying fashion; it consists of systems such as the neocortex and neurotransmitters such as dopamine, acetylcholine, and serotonin. But you never directly experience something you identify as dopamine. You do not get up in the morning and exclaim, "Wow, what a dopamine day!" In fact, you cannot even see your brain unless you cut open your skull and get a mirror. But you can see your mind right now.

At the very least, then, the mind and the brain are two different views of your individual awareness, one from within, one from without; one interior, one exterior. Each has a very different phenomenology—they "look" quite different. The brain looks like a crumpled pink grapefruit; the mind looks like . . . all the joys and desires and sorrows and hopes and fears and goals and ideas that fill your awareness from within. No doubt the brain and mind are intimately connected—they are the Right- and Left-Hand aspects of your individual awareness—but they also possess some profound differences that prevent either from being reduced, without remainder, to the other.

For the moment, then, we simply note that those researchers who have investigated the interior aspects of individual holons on their own terms are in general and broad agreement as to the holarchy shown in the Upper-Left quadrant of Figure 5-1.

THE INSIDE OF THE COLLECTIVE

The individual holons of the Upper-Left quadrant exist in communities, as do all holons. When individual and subjective cognitions are shared or exchanged with other individuals, the result is a collective *worldview* or communally shared outlook. As individual cognitive holons develop and evolve—as the awareness in individuals increases in depth from simple sensation to images to concepts to reason (the Upper Left)—so does the collective worldview become deeper and more complex (the Lower Left).

These *collective worldviews* are summarized in the Lower-Left quadrant of Figure 5-1. The meaning of the terms (e.g., "uroboric" means reptilian, "typhonic" means paleomammalian) will become more apparent as we proceed. Where the Upper-Left quadrant represents individual, interior, *subjective* awareness, the Lower Left represents the collective or *intersubjective* forms of awareness, the shared *cultural* meanings, values, and contexts without which individual awareness does not develop or function at all.

This quadrant, too, represents a general consensus of serious scholars in the field who have investigated the evolution of cultural holons on their own terms. In the human realm, for example, the evolution from archaic to magic to mythic to mental has been extensively documented by scholars from the remarkable Jean Gebser to Gerald Heard to Erich Neumann to Robert Bellah to Jürgen Habermas (whom many scholars, myself included, consider the world's greatest living social philosopher).

Note that we will be referring to the inside of the collective as *cultural*, and the outside of the collective as *social*. Both are intrinsic aspects of who and what you are, but one is known from within, the other from without.

THE FOUR FACES OF THE KOSMOS

If we now look at these four quadrants and attempt to ascertain exactly how and why they fit together—what *are* these quadrants and what do they actually mean?—we soon notice that both Right-Hand quadrants represent *objective* or *exterior* realities, and both Left-Hand quadrants represent *subjective* or *interior* realities. In other words, the Right-Hand quadrants are what holons look like *from the outside*, in an objectifying, empirical, scientific type of investigation. The Left-Hand quadrants are what holons look like *from the inside*, from the interior, as part of directly lived awareness and experience.

Likewise, everything on the Right Hand has *simple location*, or location in the sensorimotor and empirical world; but nothing on the Left Hand has simple location at all, because these holons are located not in physical space but in emotional and mental and cognitive spaces (spaces of intention, not simply spaces of extension). Thus, you can point to a rock, a planet, a town, a family, an ecosystem—they all have simple location; but you cannot point to love, envy, pride, joy, or compassion: the former are exterior or Right-Hand realities, the latter are interior or Left-Hand realities.

Where the Right Hand is exterior and the Left Hand is interior, the upper half is individual and the lower half is collective or communal. Putting these all together, the four quadrants represent the exterior and the interior of the individual and the collective. In short: the intentional, behavioral, cultural, and social aspects of holons in general.

Each of these aspects, as you can see on Figure 5-1, has *correlates* with all the others. Each is intimately related to the others, for the simple reason that you cannot have an inside without an outside, or a plural without a singular. The four quadrants, I suggest, might therefore be *intrinsic aspects or features of the Kosmos itself.* Erase any one of the quadrants, and the others disappear, because they are so many sides of any given phenomenon. Exactly what all this means will, I trust, become clearer as we proceed.

As indicated, the interesting thing about all four quadrants is that they are largely uncontested by scholars working in the various fields. The sequence of atoms to molecules to cells to organisms is widely acknowledged by natural scientists. The sequence of sensation, perception, impulse, symbols, and concepts is largely agreed upon by developmental psychologists, ancient and modern. The existence of the exteriors of the collective—whether galaxies and planets or the material forms of techno-economic production (foraging to horticultural to agrarian)—is largely uncontested by serious scholars in the field. And the various worldviews (such as archaic to magic to mythic to mental) have been investigated by several renowned scholars who, despite genuine differences, present a generally similar tale of their sequence in humankind's history.

The problem, we will see, is that many scholars, specializing in only one quadrant, deny importance or even existence to the others. And this, we will see, is a direct result of the collapse of the Kosmos—of the disaster of modernity that denied reality to any of the interior dimensions at all. But if we look at the four quadrants without trying to reduce any to the others, a surprise indeed awaits us.

THE BIG THREE: I, WE, AND IT

We saw that the core of modernity was the widespread differentiation of art, morals, and science (or I, WE, and IT). But if we now look at the four quadrants, we find that they correlate exactly with those domains. The Upper-Left quadrant is described in I-language, the Lower-Left quadrant is described in we-language, and both of the Right-Hand quadrants, because they are objective exteriors, are described in it-language.

And so, in something of a surprise turn, we have arrived back at the "Big Three" cultural values spheres of art, morals, and science; the Beautiful, the Good, and the True; I, WE, and IT. Here are a few aspects of these crucial dimensions:

> *I (Upper Left):* Consciousness, subjectivity, self, and self-expression (including art and aesthetics); truthfulness, sincerity; irreducible and immediate lived awareness; first-person accounts.
>
> *We (Lower Left):* Ethics and morals, worldviews, common context, culture; intersubjective meaning, mutual understanding, appropriateness, justness; second-person accounts.
>
> *It (Right Hand):* Science and technology, objective nature, empirical forms (including brain and social systems); propositional truth (singular and functional fit); objective exteriors of both individuals and systems; third-person accounts.

I refer to these three value spheres as the "Big Three" because they are three of the most significant of modernity's differentiations, destined to play a crucial role in so many areas of life. This is not simply my own idea. The Big Three are recognized by an influential number of scholars. They are Sir Karl Popper's three worlds: subjective (I), cultural (WE), and objective (IT). They are Habermas's three validity claims: subjective sincerity (I), intersubjective justness (WE), and objective truth (IT). They are Plato's Beautiful, Good, and True. They even show up in Buddhism as Buddha, Dharma, and Sangha (the I, the It, and the We of the Real, as will soon become obvious).

And of enormous historical importance, the Big Three showed up in Kant's immensely influential trilogy: *Critique of Pure Reason* (objective science), *Critique of Practical Reason* (morals), and *Critique of Judgment* (aesthetic judgment and art). Dozens of examples could be given, but that is the general picture of the Big Three, which are just a shorthand version of the four quadrants.

The fact that the four quadrants (or simply the Big Three) are the results of an extensive data search across hundreds of holarchies; the fact that they show up cross-culturally and nearly universally; the fact that they recur in philosophers from Plato to Popper; the fact that they strenuously resist being reduced or erased from consideration—ought to tell us something, ought to tell us that they are etched deeply into the Kosmos, that they are the warp and woof of the fabric of the Real, announcing abiding truths about our world, about its insides and outsides, about its individual and communal forms. Ought to tell us, that is, that we are simply looking at the four faces of the Kosmos, the four corners of the known world, and none of them apparently will go away, no matter how tightly we close our eyes.

MODERNITY AND FLATLAND

We now arrive at an absolutely crucial turning point, namely, the point where the *differentiation* of the Big Three (the dignity of modernity) degenerated into the *dissociation* of the Big Three (the disaster of modernity). This dissociation allowed an explosive empirical science, coupled with rampant modes of industrial production—*both of which emphasized solely it-knowledge and it-technology*—to dominate and colonialize the other value spheres, effectively destroying them in their own terms.

Thus, the Left-Hand or *interior* dimensions were reduced to their Right-Hand or *exterior* correlates, which utterly collapsed the Great Chain of Being, and with it, the core claims of the great wisdom traditions.

Left collapsed to Right. There, in four words, is the precise disaster of modernity, the disaster that was the "disenchantment of the world" (Weber), the "colonization of the value spheres by science" (Habermas), the "dawn of the wasteland" (T. S. Eliot), the birth of "one-dimensional man" (Marcuse), the "desacralization of the world" (Schuon), the "disqualified universe" (Mumford).

By any other name, the disaster known as flatland.

PART TWO

PREVIOUS ATTEMPTS AT INTEGRATION

6

The Reenchantment of the World

A MAP OF THE UNIVERSE drawn by the late eighteenth and nineteenth centuries, and continuing down to today in the official mood of empirical and systems science, would essentially be nothing but the Right half of Figure 5-1. Interior holons, such as images, symbols, and concepts, were allowed no substantial reality *on their own;* they were merely *representations* of something in the Right-Hand world, the material world, which now alone was real.

Thus, in the empiricist (and behaviorist) psychology that would seize and freeze the Western soul for almost three centuries (and sophisticated versions of which are still dominant in cognitive science), the mind itself was a *tabula rasa*—a blank slate—filled with nothing but *pictures* of the sensorimotor, empirical, or Right-Hand world. There was nothing in the mind that was not first in the senses, and thus all higher modes of knowing (from the eye of mind to the eye of contemplation) were relentlessly and unsparingly reduced to empirical sensations, which is to say, they were completely destroyed in their own terms.

And so it came about, in this fractured fairy tale, that the interior dimensions of the Kosmos were simply gutted and laid out to dry in the blazing sun of the monological gaze. It is important to realize that *this was not simply or even especially an attack on spiritual realities;* it was an attack on the entire sweep of interior, introspective, lived awareness and consciousness—an attack on the Left-Hand dimensions in toto, whether "low" or "high" didn't matter in the least. *None* of those interior dimensions has simple location in the sensorimotor world, and thus *none* of them was primarily or irreducibly real.

What was real was the world of matter and energy, the world of scientific materialism. The fact that this material reality was usually held to be organized into *holistic systems of dynamically interwoven processes* did not in the least alter the fact that the systems themselves were essentially empirical, objective, positivistic, monological: in short, a flatland holism of interwoven ITS.

This meant, of course, that the entire Great Chain of Being was collapsed to its lowest level, that of empirical or sensorimotor events. For the Great Nest was, above all, the great holarchy of interior consciousness as it developed from matter to sensation to perception to images and symbols and concepts, to rational and higher rational capacities, into trans-rational modes of soul and spirit. (Note: Figure 5-1 represents only overall evolution up to the present, and therefore the higher modes of soul and spirit are not listed in that figure. But the entire point of "the perennial philosophy" or the great wisdom traditions—from Plato to Asanga to Plotinus to Padmasambhava and Lady Tsogyal—is that there are *higher modes of development* beyond rationality [and the eye of mind] that are disclosed in contemplation [and the eye of spirit]. These higher modes in the Upper-Left quadrant were disqualified, not because they were especially singled out, but because the entire Left-Hand dimensions of the Kosmos were equally and thoroughly rejected. We will pursue this important theme of higher development in subsequent chapters.) The point for now is that when the interior dimensions were rejected in toto, the entire Great Chain simply collapsed.

Thus the modern West became the first and only major civilization in the history of humankind to be without the Great Nest of Being. In not much more than a single century, the richly textured and multidimensional Kosmos underwent a shuddering collapse into a flat and faded system of monotonous ITS, utterly devoid of consciousness, care, compassion, concern, values, depth and Divinity.

THE DISQUALIFIED UNIVERSE

This quivering collapse of the Kosmos into nothing but Right-Hand objects and ITS was not, as earlier noted, the result of a Newtonian worldview as opposed to an Einsteinian worldview. In fact, the sciences of both Newton and Einstein (and Bohr and Planck and Heisenberg) contributed equally to this collapse by furthering the cause of monological science at the expense of the subjective and intersubjective domains. The greater the authority of physics and the natural sciences, the less real and less significant appeared the entire sweep of interior apprehensions—moral wisdom, contemplative insights, interpretive knowledge, introspective perceptions, aesthetic-expressive realities—upon which the entire Left-Hand dimensions of the Kosmos rested. The more the world stood in awe of Newton, Einstein, Kelvin, Clausius, Maxwell, Bohr, Planck, and company, the more it looked solely, even desperately, to these men and their monological know-how to deliver real knowledge and hoped-for salvation.

The sweeping success of scientific empiricism—it has dramatically dominated the worldview of modernity (so much so that even the numerous countercultural or countermodernity movements all defined themselves *in reaction to* scientific materialism)—was not due to any sort of evil intent on the part of the natural scientists themselves. By and large they were (and are) decent men and women carefully and laboriously investigating the Right-Hand dimensions of the Kosmos. But they were so stunningly successful that the other approaches—from art to morals to hermeneutics to contemplation—seemed pale and anemic by comparison. It was an embarrassment of riches, a cornucopia of truth, that began through sheer exuberance to crowd out the other, softer voices in the universe.

Make no mistake, these other voices themselves contributed to this hegemony of the hardheaded with their own barely concealed envy and jealousy. That philosophy could produce real knowledge like Newton! That theology could prove Spirit with scientific precision! That God would answer the call of the laboratory! That the Goddess could be seen with a telescope! Kant was merely one of the first in an endless line of theorists to twist philosophy, psychology, and theology into a series of pretzels in order to accommodate the blinding light of Newton and Einstein and Planck and company.

And how understandable this rush to the Right Hand was! After all, every holon in the Kosmos has at least these four aspects or dimensions—behavioral, intentional, cultural, and social. Thus, *every Left-Hand event does indeed have correlates in the Right Hand.* You can see this in Figure 5-1. Wherever we find emotions, we find a limbic system. Wherever we find intentional rationality, we find a neocortex, and so on.

Thus, instead of trying to gain introspective knowledge—which, after all, is a delicate and tricky affair, and often quite hard to pin down with much certainty—let us simply investigate the brain and its empirical processes. Instead of joy, let us examine levels of dopamine. Instead of depression, let us look to serotonin at the synapses. Instead of interior angst, let us look to empirical amounts of acetylcholine in the hippocalamus. These, after all, can be *empirically seen* and *measured* with the eye of flesh. They have simple location and extension. Their results can be repeated in similar experiments. Let us therefore have done with that "introspective" nonsense and turn the entire affair of consciousness over to those variables that can be empirically and scientifically registered. Let us look to the Right-Hand world!

Still, it was not the investigation of the Right-Hand aspects of the Kosmos that caused the modern collapse. Much more than that, it was the growing belief that the entire Left-Hand dimensions were really just poorly understood Right-Hand events. A religious experience was not actually the disclosure of spiritual realities, it was simply a massive discharge of dopamine in the brain. God is not needed or allowed to enter the picture at all. Likewise with compassion and love and awareness and intentionality in general: they are all *really* just Right-Hand events in the biophysical brain. In the stunning move that defined the disaster of modernity, interior states were stripped of their actual contents, because the only "real" referents (or existing entities) were those with simple location, those with Right-Hand credentials, those with an empirical passport, those mindless monological ITs. The *referents* of mental and spiritual propositions were not actual interior realities (perceived by the eye of mind or the eye of contemplation), but merely permutations on sensorimotor ITs perceived by the eye of flesh. (Those empirical correlates are very real and very important; the modern nightmare was the growing belief that those simple sensory correlates were themselves the sum total of reality.)

Thus, all of the Left-Hand and interior domains—including mind, soul, and spirit—were beginning to look more and more like hangovers from the premodern, prescientific ignorance of humankind; and a diligent, thorough, persistent examination of the empirical and positivistic realities of this world, the world of objects and ITs, would yield all the knowledge fit to know and all the salvation reality could offer.

The moment of truth of the scientific approach—a truth utterly lacking in premodern worldviews and among the Great Chain theorists—was that every Left-Hand event does indeed have a Right-Hand correlate. Transcendental events in consciousness do indeed have specific empirical correlates in the brain, a fact noted in none of the world's great religious literature. The mind itself, far from being nothing but an otherworldly soul trapped in a material body, is intimately interwoven with the biomaterial brain (not reducible to it, but not drastically divorced from it either).

Science was bound to find this out sooner or later, and this shocking discovery—Left-Hand consciousness has a Right-Hand correlate—shook to its very foundations the entire "metaphysical" approach to reality that had dominated every premodern worldview without exception. What had been thought for millennia to be radically transcendent and otherworldly was turning out to be much more immanent, this-worldly, empirical, and organic. This monological enterprise therefore made a great deal of sense—initially—because it was indeed disclosing some profound truths about what had previously been mistaken as merely "otherworldly" and "disembodied" and "metaphysical" events.

But as a confident modernity began to erase in earnest the entire Left-Hand dimensions (including the Great Holarchy), it failed to notice that this scientific endeavor was likewise erasing all sense and significance from the Kosmos itself. For there are no values, no intentions, no depths, and no meaning in any of the Right-Hand domains. The Left Hand is the home of *quality*, the Right Hand of *quantity*. The Left is the home of *intention* and thus *meaning;* the Right, of *extension* without purpose or plan. The Left has *levels of significance;* the Right has *levels of magnitude.* The Left has *better* and *worse,* the Right merely *bigger* and *smaller.*

For example, compassion is *better* than murder, but a planet is not better than a galaxy. Health is better than illness, but a mountain is not better than a river. Mutual respect is better than contempt, but an atom is not better than a photon. And thus, as you collapse the Left to the Right—as you collapse compassion to serotonin, joy to dopamine, cultural values to modes of techno-economic production, moral wisdom to technical steering problems, or contemplation to brain waves—you likewise collapse quality to quantity, value to veneer, interior to exterior, depth to surface, dignity to disaster.

The result is what Weber famously called "the disenchanted world" and Mumford so memorably called *the disqualified universe:* a world with no quality or meaning at all, ruled not by spirit or consciousness or purpose or meaning, but merely and always by blind chance or systems necessity, with the blind leading the blind.

THE POSTMODERN REVOLT
AGAINST FLATLAND

In the wake of this *modern* collapse into positivism, empiricism, behaviorism, and systems theory—all monological it-endeavors—there would soon arise a series of *postmodern rebellions,* all fueled, in whole or part, by a resurgence of the interior domains screaming to be heard, acknowledged, realized, honored.

The names of these postmodern rebellions are legion (using "postmodern" in the general sense, meaning any movements occurring in the wake of modernity). Although this is a complex and intricate topic, perhaps we can say that, in a very general sense, they fall into four broad camps: Romantic, Idealist, Postmodern, and Integral.

In this and the next three chapters, we will briefly explore these reactions to flatland, all of which were also *attempts to integrate the Big Three*—which by now had disastrously *dissociated*—and thus "reenchant the world" by bringing science, spirituality, art, and morals into some sort of mutual accord.

These various approaches are not simply historical curiosities. All of them are still with us today, forming the backbone of virtually every attempt to integrate science and religion, from epistemological pluralism to ecophilosophy to postmodern paradigm. Their many successes—and their many failures—are crucial guideposts on our quest for integration.

IMMANUEL KANT AND THE BIG THREE

Immanuel Kant was perhaps the first great philosopher to fight the leveling and deadening of the modern monological collapse, yet the net effect of his work—certainly in the hands of less gifted theorists—was to cement the positivistic hegemony, which, most scholars agree, would have been the very last thing he wanted.

Kant began by convincingly demonstrating that theoretical reason (pure reason, monological rationality, objective it-knowledge) was confined to the categories that organize sense experience. Monological it-rationality, in other words, was limited to categories of the sensorimotor domain (the Right-Hand dimensions in general), and thus pure reason was incapable of grasping, let alone proving, metaphysical or transcendental realities (such as God, freedom, and the timelessness of the soul).

Yet here were the philosophers and theologians all talking about proofs of Spirit's existence, freedom of the will, or immortality of the soul, yet none of these propositions actually had any genuine cognitive validity at all. They were all attempts by reason to step outside the realm in which it is competent, and the result was not actual knowledge, but utter and unprovable nonsense. We might say that scientific reason (it-rationality) cannot grasp God because God is not an empirical object.

Critique of Pure Reason (written in 1781) relentlessly exposed the inadequacies of monological reason to grasp metaphysical truths, and it basically marked the dramatic and historical end of that type of metaphysics. *The death of traditional metaphysics:* this was the virtually unarguable conclusion of Kant's first critique.

But for Kant, this was just the opening act. He demonstrated that monological reason cannot prove the existence of Spirit, freedom, or immortality. *But he also demonstrated that reason could not disprove their existence either.* So science was not allowed to do two things: (1) it could not say that Spirit existed; but (2) it most certainly could not say that Spirit did not exist! Kant's point was that, as he put it, he wanted to demolish knowledge (it-knowledge) in order to make room for faith. Only as objectivistic, positivistic, monological reason stopped trying to get its hands on Spirit, could other types of knowing step in to take up the fight.

Thus, in his second critique (*Critique of Practical Reason,* 1788), Kant attempted to show that where *monological reason* fails to prove (or disprove) Spirit, *dialogical reason* can succeed, at least in certain suggestive ways. For if scientific reason (it-rationality) cannot grasp God, dialogical reason (moral, ethical, practical reason) does tend to show us a type of transcendental and spiritual knowledge. Moral reason (not it-knowledge but we-knowledge) can, he believed, operate only under the assumption that Spirit exists, that freedom makes sense, and that there is a type of immortality to the soul. His argument, basically, is that the interior "ought" of moral reasoning could never get going in the first place without the postulates of a transcendental Spirit: the stomach would not hunger if food did not exist. And where monological it-knowledge can tell us precisely nothing about this spiritual domain, dialogical we-knowledge operates with its postulates all the time!

We can already see that Kant has begun to differentiate clearly the Big Three value spheres (art, morals, and science; I, WE, and IT), and he has dramatically taken spiritual knowledge out of the merely it-domain of science and placed it squarely in the we-domain of moral reasoning and yearning. He wants to limit it-science (and "it-metaphysics"), but only to make room for "we-metaphysics" and dialogical reason and spiritual faith. Morals, not science, point most clearly to God.

What remained to be done was to find some way to integrate this moral we-wisdom with scientific it-knowledge, and in his third great critique (*Critique of Judgment,* 1790), Kant attempts this integration, in part through the expressive-aesthetic dimension (or art in the most general sense). In other words, he wants to introduce the aesthetic I-domain in order to integrate we-morals and it-science. *He wants to integrate the Big Three.*

THE WESTERN WATERSHED

Here we reach an absolutely crucial turning point for the Western world, the very divide between the modern and the postmodern moods. These types of categorizations are always slippery, but it might fairly be said that Kant was either the last of the great modern philosophers or the first of the great postmodern philosophers. He probably was both. But in any event his work is a branch from which stem, in whole or part, virtually all of the four camps: Romantic, Idealistic, Postmodern Poststructuralist, and Integral.

You can easily see that, depending on which of Kant's three critiques you emphasize, you can extract a dramatically different worldview from this great man's work. If you focus on *Critique of Pure Reason,* you could readily become a dedicated positivist and behaviorist: science alone gives cognitive knowledge, "real" knowledge, and all else is nonsensical metaphysics. Let us therefore confine ourselves to the study of sensorimotor phenomena (like Newton!), and relegate everything else to the dustbin of meaningless metaphysics. And indeed, many of the positivistic and antimetaphysical currents in the West trace their lineage directly to Kant's first critique.

But if you focus on the second critique (*Practical Reason*), you will have a very different story to tell. Science delivers genuine it-knowledge, but who cares? The real action is in the moral yearning and ethical reasoning that, if they do not disclose, nonetheless powerfully indicate, spiritual realities. Men and women are not free as *empirical objects*—in the world of ITs, there are only causality and determination (whether strict or statistical). But as *ethical subjects,* men and women are indeed autonomous, or can be if they rise to their own highest occasion and act according to a universal, worldcentric, moral reasoning: not what is right for me and my tribe, or me and my mythic religion, or me and my nation, but what is right and fair for all peoples regardless of race or creed. For when I act in this worldcentric—not egocentric, not ethnocentric, but worldcentric—fashion, I am free in the deepest sense, for I am obeying not an outside force but the interior force of my own ethical reasoning: I am autonomous, I am deeply free.

And that was the exhilarating message of Kant's second critique. It doesn't matter if the world of ITs is a deterministic system, because in the moral stance of worldcentric ethical embrace, I am a free soul, free because those dictates issue from my own deepest being. Numerous religious, spiritual, and especially ethical theories would trace their lineage to this extraordinary second critique. In fact, to this day, many of the great moral theorists from Rawls to Habermas would be described as "Neo-Kantian."

If you focused on the third critique, yet another stunning story would emerge. Granted, science yields genuine knowledge of ITs; and granted, we-morals open us to a spiritual wisdom. But how do we integrate these separate realms? And wouldn't that integration actually be *the* highest and most desirable goal? And if ART is the great bridge between science and morals, is not world salvation in the hands of the artists?

Well, many artists thought so; and in the wake of Kant's third critique (not to mention the French Revolution), the great Romantic *aesthetic-expressive* movements of modernity and postmodernity began, movements that would locate ultimate reality not in the it-domain of science or the we-domain of morals, but in the I-domain, the subjective domain, the domain of art and artistic vision and intense self-expression. Not just Truth, not just Goodness, but above all Beauty, would finally disclose the Divine. And these great aesthetic-expressive movements began in earnest with the Romantics of the late eighteenth century.

The extraordinary attempt to reenchant the world had just begun.

7

Romanticism

RETURN TO THE ORIGIN

K ANT'S FINAL GOAL—to integrate the Big Three of art, morals, and science—ultimately eluded him. Despite his heroic attempts in the third critique to achieve this integration via art and organic telos, most theorists agree that he failed. It is certain that the theorists in his immediate wake believed that he failed, for they took up the task with an astonishing vigor. The simplest way to state this failure is that art could not itself achieve the integration because it was merely one of the three spheres to be integrated, and thus it could not itself accomplish the job.

But that was a fact that the Romantics in general failed to recognize or chose to ignore, and they began an intense effort to make the I-domain, the subjective domain—and especially the domain of aesthetics, sentiment, emotion, heroic self-expression, and feeling—the royal road to Spirit and the Absolute.

THE PRE/TRANS FALLACY

Kant had spotted, and indeed was part of, the extraordinary dignity of modernity, in that he had clearly differentiated the Big Three value spheres of art, morals, and science. But he also realized that the Big Three were starting to fly apart—not just differentiate but dissociate—and that monological it-science was taking advantage of this fragmentation to begin its imperialistic adventures. Kant is *already* trying to beat back it-science "in order to make room for faith." And he is *already* trying to pull the Big Three together in his third critique. But try as he might, he cannot effect the sought-after integration. The Big Three are dissociating; Kant knows it; and he is powerless to prevent the fragmentation or the "diremption," as they were already calling it.

The Romantics took their own approach to this fragmentation and dissociation, but an approach that, it turned out, was in some ways significantly flawed despite the best intentions. As we saw earlier, if you confuse differentiation and dissociation—it's an easy mistake—then you will attempt to cure the dissociation by getting rid of the differentiation itself. You will push back in time, not prior to the dissociation—which is correct—but prior to the differentiation—which is simply wholesale regression. You will try to push back to some sort of prior *fusion* or *undifferentiated* state, some sort of "primal" and "pristine" and "pure" state, prior to the madness of modernity altogether. You will want to get back to nature, back to the noble savage, back to the purity and innocence of a primal past. You will be a retro-Romantic, longing for the "wholeness" and "union" of yesteryear, and ignoring any unpleasantness you might actually find in the halls of premodernity.

Thus, even today, a well-respected reference book such as *The New Columbia Encyclopedia* summarizes the general Romantic movement thus: "The basic aims of romanticism were various: a return to nature and to belief in the goodness of man, most notably expressed by Jean Jacques Rousseau—with the subsequent cult of 'the noble savage,' attention to the 'simple peasant,' and admiration of the violently self-centered 'hero'; the rediscovery of the artist [and aesthetic-expressive self] as a supremely individual creator; the exaltation of the senses and emotions over reason and intellect. In addition, romanticism was a philosophical revolt against rationalism."

Now, if you are in a revolt *against* rationality, it is rather hard to sincerely *integrate* rationality—and thus a genuine integration of the Big Three value spheres will tend to elude you. In fact, the Romantics often fell violent prey to what I have called *the pre/trans fallacy,* namely, the confusion of prerational with transrational simply because both are non-rational.

Granted, spirituality is, in some sense, beyond mere rationality. But there is *trans*-rational, and there is *pre*-rational. Prerationality includes all of the modes leading up to rationality (such as sensation, vital life feeling, bodily emotion, and organic sentiment), and, by its very nature, tends to exclude rationality, no matter what lip service it might give to it. Transrationality, on the other hand, lies on the other side of reason. Once reason has emerged and consolidated, consciousness can continue to grow and develop and evolve, moving into transrational, transpersonal, and supraindividual modes of awareness. Transrationality, unlike prerationality, happily incorporates the rational perspective, and then adds its own defining characteristics; it is thus *never* antireason, but, in a friendly way, transreason.

Assuming, for the moment, that these higher dimensions exist, we can see that the overall arc of consciousness evolution and development moves from prerational to rational to transrational; from subconscious to self-conscious to superconscious; from prepersonal to personal to transpersonal; from id to ego to God.

The pre/trans fallacy occurs when the pre and trans states are confused or equated, and it operates in both directions. For example, Freud tended to take all genuine transrational experiences and reduce them to prerational infantilisms (to primary narcissism, oceanic indissociation, preambivalent oral stage, and so on). Jung, on the other hand, often erred in the opposite direction, taking some very prerational childhood productions and elevating them to transrational glory. Both of these mistakes—*reductionism* and *elevationism*—rest on a prior confusion of pre and trans.

And the Romantics were about to run into the elevationist error with a vengeance, eulogizing the prerational domains with such intensity that they often ended up in blatantly regressive nightmares. Yet it all started so nobly, so understandably, so sincerely. . . .

To Reweave the Web of Life

Prerationality, as we said, includes all of the modes of awareness leading up to formal rationality, such as sensation, emotion, imagery, and intense feeling (all of these are shown in Figure 5-1). As rationality itself then emerges and develops, it ideally transcends and includes, goes beyond but incorporates, the prerational domains (since, as we have seen, "transcend and include" or "differentiate and integrate" is the core dynamic of *all* stages of normal development and evolution).

But if there is a *pathology*—if reason does not just *differentiate*, but instead *dissociates,* from the lower realms—the result is repression and alienation, the suffocation of vital life, feeling, and emotion. Instead of transcend and include, there is deny and repress.

If this pathological dissociation occurs, then reason, with all its rich capacities for dialogue, ethics, mutual recognition, and care, becomes dry and abstract and life-denying in the worst sense. This repression is not something *inherent* in reason and reasonableness; it is a pathological aberration of reason, occurring when its necessary differentiations go too far into morbid dissociations.

But that is exactly what was happening to modernity in general, was it not? The rationality of modernity had admirably differentiated the Big Three of self (I), culture (WE), and nature (IT); but now modernity, hypnotized by a suggestive scientism, was not *integrating* those realms, it was in the process of *dissociating* those realms, with self and culture and nature all at one another's throats, and monological it-science colonializing the entire lot.

And one of the oppressed realms was that of aesthetics, self, and self-expression, including all of the rich feelings, emotions, and vital life that, being part of the Left-Hand or interior domains, had been marginalized from serious discourse—by any other name oppressed, denied, denigrated, devalued. In short: reason was repressing feeling.

(It is no accident that at precisely this point, the likes of Schopenhauer, Nietzsche, and Freud would come forward to point out this epidemic mental repression of instinctual life. It wasn't that this type of repression had not occurred in premodern cultures, for almost any higher level can repress any lower level at any given time; but never had such a powerful rationality so violently clamped down on interior life, which was the essence of a dissociated modernity, itself Dr. Freud's real patient.)

The Romantics were understandably, and rightly, horrified by this repression and dissociation. And the various Romantics—Rousseau, Herder, the Schlegels, Schiller, Novalis, Coleridge, Keats, Wordsworth, Whitman—took it upon themselves to heal this violent fragmentation, not with abstract rationality, but with intense feeling—what Wordsworth called "the spontaneous overflow of powerful feelings." Herder was explicit: "See the whole of nature, behold the great analogy of creation. Everything feels itself and its like, life reverberates with life. . . . Impulse is the driving force of our existence, and it must remain this even in our noblest knowings. Love is the noblest form of knowing, as it is the noblest feeling." As for those who believed that abstract it-rationality was the only true form of knowledge, they must be, said Herder, either "liars or enervated beings."

Moreover, as one scholar of the period summarized the central Romantic aspiration for a *unified feeling of life,* "This feeling cannot stop at the boundary of my self; it has to be open to the great current of life that flows across it. It is this greater current, and not just the current of my own body, which has to be united with higher aspiration . . . if there is to be unity in the self. Thus our self-feeling must be continuous with our feeling for this larger current of life which flows through us and of which we are a part; this current must nourish us not only physically but spiritually as well." That is not some present-day New Age nostrum; it was the precise credo of the general Romantic movement, which began almost two hundred years ago (the New Age movement itself being merely one of its many descendants).

We can see that the Romantics were already trying to integrate the Big Three of self, culture, and nature, to unify that which the disaster of modernity had put asunder. For above all else, the Romantics yearned for *unity* and *wholeness.* As Charles Taylor points out, "There was a passionate demand for unity and wholeness. The [Romantics] bitterly reproached the Enlightenment thinkers for having dissected man and hence distorted the true image of human life in objectifying human nature [reducing it to Right-Hand objects]. All these dichotomies [and dissociations] distorted the true nature of man which had rather to be seen as a single stream of life, or on the model of a work of art [the aesthetic-expressive dimension], in which no part could be defined in abstraction from the others. These distinctions thus were seen as abstractions from reality. But they were more than that, they were mutilations of man. . . . It was a denial of the life of the subject, his communion with nature and his self-expression in his own natural being."

Back to nature, back to some sort of union or communion prior to the modern fragmentation and collapse. As one historian put it, "What they [the Romantics] themselves yearned for was unity with self and communion with nature—that man be *united in communion with nature.*" This was to be accomplished by a "sympathetic insertion into the great stream of life of which we are a part"—a oneness with the great Web of Life.

This extraordinary attempt to integrate the Big Three of self, culture, and nature, and thus introduce some measure of wholeness and unity into a modernity fast becoming sick with its own conceits, was an aspiration as noble as any that can be conceived. This is why, I believe, to this day, we owe the Romantics an undying debt of gratitude. They were the first to spot the disease, more than two hundred years ago. They were the first to react to it with authentic horror. They were the first to attempt to reweave the fragments, heal the wounds, become at home in the universe, be a humble part of life's wondrous web, and not its arrogant master.

THE SLIDE

Alas, in their understandable zeal to get beyond rationality to a genuine spiritual wholeness, the Romantics often ended up recommending *anything nonrational,* including many things that were frankly *prerational,* regressive, egocentric, and narcissistic. They all too often confused prerational impulse with transrational insight; preconventional nature with postconventional spirit; preverbal expression with transverbal awareness; preconventional and egocentric license with postconventional and worldcentric freedom; and predifferentiated fusion with transdifferentiated integration.

In other words, precisely because they confused differentiation with dissociation, they confused prerational with transrational, and they set out to glorify every prerational, preconventional, preconceptual, and "natural" impulse they could find. Put bluntly, the Romantics tended to dedifferentiate, not transdifferentiate. They inadvertently eulogized fusion, not actual integration. They let self-expression slip into self-obsession and "divine egoism." And in this regressive and narcissistic slide into anything preconventional, they imperiled not just the disasters of modernity, but the dignities as well.

No wonder that so many cultural critics, from Robert Bellah to Colin Campbell to Jürgen Habermas, have seen our present-day obsession with self, sentiment, impulsive gratification, "be here now," "lose your mind and come to your senses," the white middle-class consumption of indigenous tribal religions as "pure and innocent and whole," the belief that "you create your own reality," intense sensory gratification, consumerism, self-glorification, and consequent social alienation—as being, in significant ways, direct descendants of Romanticism.

Of course, the more sophisticated Romantics never recommended pure and unadulterated regression. Rather, the idea was that we would somehow recontact and regain the "lost wholeness" but now on a "higher level" or in a "mature form," thus uniting the best of premodernity and modernity. This is assuredly a noble goal, and one that other approaches, including the Integral, would embrace.

But in practice as well as in detailed theory, the Romantics could not actually effect this integration of premodern and modern (or the integration of the Big Three). They had so devalued the rational, conventional, and bourgeois spheres that the promised "integration" of these spheres was, at best, lip service (as the despised spheres themselves were quick to point out). The fact remained that, in confusing differentiation and dissociation—and thus prerational and transrational—the Romantics often ended up with a blanket call for dedifferentiation, a process that, when it occurs in a living system, is called "cancer": a regressive dedifferentiation of cells growing out of control, ending in the death of the system.

Indeed, in this spiraling regressive yearning, you very well might become somewhat dedifferentiated yourself, finding your own ego to be the source and creator of all reality (as preoperational thinking does). Divine egoism will increasingly rear its narcissistic head, and you might be pulled, with every good intention, into the unending drama of your subjective inclinations. The world will become darker and darker, full of malevolent intent; you alone seem pure and clean in a world that does not care. You might become sadder and sadder, sick with the world's sorrow, too beautiful, really, for this wretched world. And if you are a true Romantic, you will nobly end it all with a terribly beautiful suicide. (Many of the great Romantic narratives, and many of the great Romantics themselves, ended in suicide.)

In the meantime, the search was on for the past paradise of wonderful wholeness and pristine purity that modernity had viciously destroyed. The search was for a period not just before the dissociations of modernity but before the differentiations themselves (since the two were thoroughly confused). The oak was somehow a hideous violation of the acorn; and the acorn, not the oak, possessed "more unity"—an utter confusion, to be sure, but the confusion upon which the retro-Romantics, then and now, rested their case.

Thus *the recovery of Origin* became the great theme of this period: a burning desire to find, recontact, resurrect, and embrace a lost and found Beloved, the return of the wondrous God or Goddess, which had once been gloriously present in an actual past era, but had been bruised, banished, burned, or buried by a cruel and uncaring modernity. The attempt to recontact humanity's acornness had just begun.

THE WAY BACK MACHINE

Thus started the search for the period in history or prehistory where the terrible differentiations of modernity had not yet occurred. The Romantics had jumped wholeheartedly aboard the Regress Express, and by far the most popular destination for the early Romantics was ancient Greece.

There are, of course, numerous aspects of classical Greece that deserve much admiration, not the least of which was its precocious embrace of reason and thus its preliminary differentiation of the Good, the True, and the Beautiful (a differentiation that reason alone discloses; this differentiation—and dignity—is lacking in all prerational modes). But precisely because this differentiation was preliminary, none of the massive dissociations of modernity had yet set in; thus there tended to be a marvelous *harmony* among the value spheres in Greek thought. I think this harmony is what many people, to this day, find so attractive about classical Greece, and it certainly attracted the early Romantics.

But had the Greeks actually and fully differentiated the Big Three, they would have evidenced its fruits: they would have banished slavery (one out of every three people in this "democracy" was a slave), and they would have set into motion the apparatus for women's rights, among other dignities. To eulogize a society where many people were slaves, and women and children might as well have been, evidences, to put it mildly, a warped sense of values.

Modern-day Romantics have realized this, and almost to a one they have abandoned ancient Greece (often with horror) and pushed back even further into prehistory in search of their primal paradise—with the result, of course, that they make Greece itself the beginning of the modern disaster, and heap upon it a scorn that the early Romantics would have found incomprehensible.

For the ecofeminists, the especially hallowed period is that immediately preceding agrarian Greece, namely, the horticultural societies that flourished from roughly 10,000 B.C.E. to 4000 B.C.E., before the rise of the early empires and the agrarian "patriarchy" in general.

In *horticultural* societies, the major means of production is a simple digging stick or handheld hoe, whereas in *agrarian* societies (such as Greece), it is the heavy animal-drawn plow. Pregnant women can easily handle a hoe, whereas if they participate in heavy plowing they suffer a significantly higher rate of miscarriage. Thus, in horticultural societies, women were usually a crucial segment of the productive force. Indeed,

up to 80 percent of foodstuffs in these societies were produced by females, and the social relations and mythic divinities of these cultures
appropriately reflected that fact. About one third of these societies had
female-only deities and about another third had male-and-female deities
(and about a third, male-only deities).

It is easy to see the attraction these horticultural societies have for
ecofeminists, which is perhaps why they studiously overlook the fact
that 44 percent of these societies engaged in frequent warfare and more
than 50 percent in intermittent warfare (so much for the peace-loving
Great Mother societies); that 61 percent had private property rights (so
much for communal sharing); that 14 percent had slavery (so much for
slavery's being introduced by patriarchy); and that 45 percent had bride-
price (so much for equal rights). These horticultural societies were anything but "pure and pristine," and if they were in touch with nature, it
was a nature whose values no ecofeminist today would actually defend.

Leave it to the ecomasculinists (deep ecologists) to push back even
further into prehistory, to the previous stage of *foraging,* beyond which
one cannot go (prior to foraging were apes). This *must* be the pure and
pristine and "nondissociated" state, because there is no further destination left on the Regress Express.

The ecofeminists have embraced horticultural matrifocal cultures as
the pure and pristine state, "one with nature" in the seasonal cycles of
the moon, planting, and harvesting, and consequently *condemned* the
rise of patriarchal agrarian societies (e.g., classical Greece) as the fall
of humanity in general. Just so, when the ecomasculinists *pushed back
even further* into foraging, they *condemned* horticultural societies—the
heaven of the ecofeminists—as being the first great rape of the land and
the destruction of paradise. For, according to the ecomasculinists, *farming itself* is an attempt to control and dominate the purity and spontane-
ity of nature. Foraging, gathering, occasionally hunting what nature
offered—now *that* is pure and pristine. Humankind's woes all began
when a woman first took up a hoe.

And let us ignore the data that show that 10 percent of these foraging
societies had slavery, 37 percent had bride-price, and 58 percent engaged
in frequent or intermittent warfare. This *must* be the pure and pristine
state, because there is nowhere further back to go!

Thus we can begin to see what so many of the retro-Romantic, eco-
holistic, back-to-nature, recovery-of-Origin approaches have in common: what might be called the "pick-and-choose" approach to history.
Pick those things you admire about a premodern epoch and studiously

ignore everything else, as if pieces of the fabric of culture could be cut and pasted onto the modern world to effect the desired "integration." Compare the best of yesterday with the worst of today, and scream, "Devolution!"

Even Foucault—no great fan of modernity—was horrified at this pick-and-choose paradise: "I think that there is a widespread and facile tendency, which one should combat, to designate that which has just occurred [i.e., modernity] as the primary enemy, as if this were always the principal form of oppression from which one had to liberate oneself. Now this simple attitude entails a number of dangerous consequences: first, an inclination to seek out some cheap form of archaism or some imaginary past forms of happiness that people did not, in fact, have at all. There is in this hatred of the present [modernity] a dangerous tendency to invoke a completely mythical past."

As we will see, numerous points in the Romantic orientation are in fact quite valuable and should definitely be brought to the integrative table. We do indeed need to recontact and integrate nature, which was, horrifyingly, one of the casualties of the modern dissociation.

But premodern societies did not actually integrate self, culture, and nature; they simply had not yet fully differentiated them in the first place. They were largely *pre* differentiated, not *trans*-differentiated, and therefore they *cannot serve as cogent models for the integration of the Big Three.* This differentiation (and its possible integration) is an *emergent,* something new and novel in the evolutionary stream. It *never* existed before (consciously or unconsciously), and therefore no amount of "return to historical Origin" will help with this novel emergent. To return to Origin forever is to miss the point forever.

Thus, just as the acorn does not actually integrate the leaves and branches and roots—for those have not yet emerged—so premodern cultures did not integrate the modern value spheres, for those had not yet fully differentiated. As with the acorn, these premodern states actually had less differentiation, less integration, less unity, less wholeness; they lacked many of the diseases of modernity because they lacked the differentiations as well. If we fail to grasp that elemental distinction, fusion is confused with integration, and the regressive slide is under way.

It is to tomorrow, not yesterday, that our vision must be turned. And Idealism began in part with exactly that realization, and exactly that attack on Romanticism. The God of tomorrow, not the God of yesterday, comes to announce our liberation.

8

Idealism

THE GOD THAT IS TO COME

O NE OF THE MOST ASTONISHING and radical differences between premodern and modern cultures is the *direction* in which the universe is said to be unfolding. In most premodern religions, the tale is told of the "time before time," the time of creation, where a Great Spirit of one sort or another created the world out of itself, or out of some *prima materia,* or out of nothing. In the immediate wake of this genesis, men and women, as part of that remarkable creation, lived in peace and harmony with themselves and with all other creatures. Living close to Source, close to Spirit, close to God and Goddess, humans bathed in that primordial delight and radiated goodness in all directions.

But then, it is said, through a series of strange events, either this God began slowly to withdraw from humans, or humans withdrew from this God. Either gradually or suddenly, but always and terribly, humans lost touch with the primal Eden.

In the Hindu version, the world then devolved through four yugas, or cosmic epochs, with each one becoming increasingly dark, alienated, fractured, and painful. These epochs are likened to gold, silver, bronze, and iron, leading from pure dharma (spiritual Truth) to complete adharma (spiritual wasteland); and today we are living in the corrupt iron, or Kali, yuga, farthest from the Source.

Scholars of this almost universal tale in premodern cultures summarize what it tells us about the basic form of the universe's direction: from the Age of Myth to the Age of Heroes to the Age of Men to the Age of

Chaos, a steady and dismal downhill slide. Once again, we of today live in the Age of Chaos, farthest from the Source and Origin.

In all these tales, the overall direction of the universe's unfolding is unmistakable: as if following some second law of religious thermodynamics, the spiritual universe is running down. In the actual unfolding of the universe's history, we humans (and all creatures) were once close to Spirit, one with Spirit, immersed in Spirit, right here on earth. But through a series of separations, dualisms, sins, or contractions, Spirit became less and less available, less and less obvious, less and less present. *Deus abscondus:* history itself is the story of spiritual abandonment, with each era becoming darker and more sinister and less spiritual. For premodern cultures, in short, history is devolution.

But sometime in the modern era—it is almost impossible to pinpoint exactly—the idea of history as devolution (or a fall from God) was slowly replaced by the idea of history as evolution (or a growth toward God). We see it explicitly in Friedrich Schelling (1775–1854); Georg Hegel (1770–1831) propounded the doctrine with a genius rarely equaled; Herbert Spencer (1820–1903) made evolution a universal law; and his friend Charles Darwin (1809–1882) applied it to biology. We then find it appearing in Sri Aurobindo (1872–1950), who gave perhaps its most accurate and profound spiritual context, and Pierre Teilhard de Chardin (1881–1955), who made it famous in the West.

Suddenly, within the span of a mere century or so, serious minds were entertaining a notion that premodern cultures, for the most part, had never even once considered, namely that—like all other living systems—we humans are in the process of *growing toward our own highest potential,* and if that highest potential is God, then we are growing toward our own Godhood.

And, this extraordinary view continued, *evolution* in general is nothing but the growth and development toward that consummate potential, that *summum bonum,* that *ens perfectissimus,* that highest Ground and Goal of our own deepest nature. Evolution is simply Spirit-in-action, God in the making, and that making is destined to carry all of us straight to the Divine.

THE RISE OF IDEALISM

This idea—cosmic and human history is most profoundly the evolution and development of Spirit—occurred immediately in the wake of Kant, and was one of the great announcements of the Idealists. This was during that extraordinary period when the Big Three (art, morals, and science) had been clearly differentiated (around the end of the eighteenth century), but before their massive dissociation and eventual collapse (around the end of the nineteenth century). As such, this was a truly fertile period for the value spheres to enrich one another. Although the spheres had not yet been fully integrated (a task that still eludes the West), nonetheless they were all on speaking terms, perhaps the last time in Western history that such fruitful exchange occurred. Out of that astonishingly rich soil, grew Idealism.

As usual, it began with Immanuel Kant, who had famously maintained that we can never know "the thing in itself," only the appearance or phenomenon that results when the thing in itself is acted on by the categories of the human mind. German Idealism began, in a sense, with that notion, the notion that the world is not merely *perceived* but *constructed*. Not naïve empiricism, but mental idealism, has a hand in the perception of the world.

Johann Fichte, a contemporary of Kant, pointed out that if you cannot know anything at all about the thing in itself, you cannot know it exists, either. It is an utterly useless notion. At the same time, Kant had shown that phenomena are constructed by the mind. If we get rid of the impossible notion of the thing in itself, the result is that the entire perceived universe is the product of mind. Yet this obviously cannot be an *individual* mind or self—Mrs. Smith of Boise, Idaho, is obviously not producing the entire Kosmos. It must be a mind beyond you or me or any particular individual: it must be a *supraindividual* and absolute Self producing the entire universe.

This absolute Self Fichte proposed as the first principle of philosophy, and from this transpersonal Self he would attempt to derive the entire manifest universe (and in a fashion strikingly similar to the great Vedanta Hinduism of the East. For both of them, out of the absolute Self's creative imagination issues forth the finite world, and in reaction to the finite world grows the finite self. For both of them, liberation consists in rediscovering the absolute Self of which the finite self and finite world are but a manifestation).

Because all forms of knowledge (including it-science and we-morals) issued forth from this absolute Self, all forms of knowledge could, Fichte believed, be seamlessly integrated in this Self awareness, and this integration would heal the "diremption" or fragmentation of modernity, which was already beginning to rear its pathological head.

In other words, it comes as no surprise that Fichte, too, wants to integrate the Big Three. This integration, we have seen, is actually the single greatest task confronting the postmodern world. What modernity put asunder, postmodernity must heal. And the great theorists in the wake of Kant can all be situated in relation to that burning question: Now that we have successfully differentiated the Big Three, how can they be integrated? (Romanticism tried to do so by regression and dedifferentiation, a suicidal dead end. Idealism would attempt to do so by heading in the opposite direction: higher development.)

Because the absolute Self (which is Spirit itself) gives rise to the entire manifest world, Fichte maintained that part of the task of philosophy was to reconstruct what he called the "pragmatic history of consciousness"—that is, to reconstruct the actual path that consciousness has taken in its creative unfolding of the universe. Fichte was thus one of the very first to introduce the absolutely crucial and historically world-shaking notion of *development* (or evolution). The world is not static and pregiven; it develops, it evolves, it takes on different forms as Spirit unfolds the universe.

And, the Idealists maintained, understanding this unfolding or development is the secret key to understanding Spirit itself.

EVOLUTION AS SPIRIT-IN-ACTION

Friedrich Schelling took that initial developmental insight and worked it into a profound philosophy of spiritual unfolding, and Georg Hegel hammered out its details in a series of brilliantly difficult treatises. The general points may be summarized as follows.

Absolute Spirit is the fundamental reality. But in order to create the world, the Absolute manifests itself, or goes out of itself—in a sense, the Absolute forgets itself and empties itself into creation (although never really ceasing to be itself). Thus the world is created as a "falling away" from Spirit, as a "self-alienation" of Spirit, although the Fall is never anything but a play of Spirit itself.

Having "fallen" into the manifest and material world, Spirit begins the process of returning to itself, and this process of the return of Spirit to Spirit is simply development or evolution itself. The original "descent" (or involution) is a forgetting, a fall, a *self-alienation* of Spirit; and the reverse movement of "ascent" (or evolution) is thus the self-remembering and *self-actualization* of Spirit. And yet, the Idealists emphasized, all of Spirit is fully present at each and every stage of evolution as the *process* of evolution itself.

When Spirit first goes out of itself to create the manifest universe, the result is Nature, which Schelling calls "slumbering Spirit" and Hegel calls "God in its otherness." Nature is a direct manifestation of Spirit, and thus Nature is sacred to the core; but it is *slumbering* Spirit, simply because Nature is not yet self-reflexively aware. It is the lowest form of Spirit, but a form of Spirit nonetheless. It is Spirit in its *objective* manifestation, what Plato had called "a visible God" (or visible Goddess).

In the second major stage of development, Spirit evolves from objective Nature to subjective Mind. Thus, Spirit has now developed from *subconscious* to *self-conscious* (or prepersonal to personal, or prerational to rational), and thus begins to reflect on its own existence. Where Nature was *objective Spirit,* Mind is *subjective Spirit,* and thus we see increasingly more conscious forms of Spirit's own self-actualization and return to itself.

But it is at this point that the subject and the object, or Mind and Nature, can not just differentiate but dissociate, and thus this stage is often marked by a rampant dualism—a "spiritual pathology," according to Schelling; the "unhappy consciousness," as Hegel put it. This unhappiness is not present in the previous stage of Nature, but only because Nature is slumbering; yet with the self-conscious awakening of Mind, these painful divisions become all too obvious.

Here the Idealists—especially Fichte and Hegel—veered sharply away from the Romantics, who by and large wanted to heal the painful unhappy consciousness by a "return to Nature." But this return, the Idealists pointed out, is based on a series of profound confusions. Indeed, some of the earliest, most venomous, most polemical—and altogether most accurate—critiques of retro-Romanticism came from the Idealists, who quickly crawled out of that bed and for good measure set it on fire. Fichte and Hegel rail against the Romantic regression to sentiments, feeling, antirationalism, and organic immersion, pointing out, quite correctly, that the Romantics were headed in precisely the wrong direction.

What the Idealists understood—and what I have called the "pre/trans fallacy"—is that prerational modes can appear to be transrational simply because both are nonrational. And, as we saw, in their understandable rush to go transrational, the Romantics often ended up glorifying *anything* that was nonrational, including states that were frankly regressive, narcissistic, indissociated, and dedifferentiated, all of which thoroughly erased not just the disasters of modernity but the dignities as well. This regressive catastrophe set Fichte and Hegel and occasionally Schelling on polemical fire, and rightly so. That these Idealists were witness to this regressive nightmare as it actually unfolded makes their polemics all the more cogent—and applicable to similar regressive slides now widely occurring under the guise of a "new age" and a "new paradigm."

Fichte, Schelling, and Hegel were united: there is no going back to recontact a lost Spirit—for in the "backward" direction there is only *slumbering* Spirit, which is *already* self-alienated. (This is simply another way of pointing out that the earlier stages of human development, whether phylogenetic or ontogenetic, offer no substantial models for the healing of the dissociations of modernity.)

No, it is not by a "return to Nature" that humans can end their alienation and unhappy consciousness, but rather by moving forward to the third great stage of development and evolution, that of nondual Spirit. Thus, for both Schelling and Hegel, Spirit goes out of itself to produce objective Nature, awakens to itself in subjective Mind, then recovers itself in pure nondual Spirit, where subject and object are one pure act of nondual consciousness that unifies both Nature and Mind in realized Spirit.

Thus, Spirit knows itself objectively as Nature; knows itself subjectively as Mind; and knows itself absolutely as Spirit—the Source, the Summit, the Ground, and the Process of the entire ordeal.

Note, then, the overall sequence of development: from nature to humanity to divinity; from subconscious to self-conscious to superconscious; from prepersonal to personal to transpersonal; from id to ego to God. But Spirit is nonetheless fully present at each and every stage as the *evolutionary process itself*: Spirit is the process of its own self-actualization and self-unfolding; its being is its own becoming; its Goal is the Path itself.

Thus, humans can end their alienated and unhappy consciousness, not primarily by going back to Nature but by going forward to nondual Spirit. Not preconventional Nature but postconventional Spirit holds the key to overcoming alienation and dissociation, and that Spirit is contacted, not by spiraling regression to preconventional slumber, but by evolutionary progression to a radiant Nonduality.

(Of course, when the Mind emerges, it can indeed repress Nature, precisely because Mind is a higher-order holon that can arrogantly usurp its role in the normal holarchy by oppressing its junior holons, including Nature—a suicidal repression in that these are elements of its own being, which is why the ecological crisis is indeed suicidal. Likewise, internally, the ego can repress the id, the same dissociation as Mind repressing Nature. Under this pathological twist, the Mind must recontact Nature and befriend Nature, just as, internally, there must be "regression in service of the ego." That "befriending" is well and good, and mandatory for healing. But that is just the first step. For Mind and Nature to be genuinely integrated and unified, a third term is required, above both Nature and Mind and reducible to neither; that term, of course, is Spirit. Thus, the great integration can never be achieved by Nature alone, or by Mind alone, or by any combination of the two. Only Spirit itself, which is beyond any feelings of Nature and beyond any thoughts of Mind, can effect this radical unity. Spirit alone transcends and includes Mind and Nature. Under the pre/trans fallacy, the Romantics all too often confused preconventional Nature with postconventional Spirit, and thought that *a simple union of prerational Nature with rational Mind would be the same as transrational Spirit,* and therein was their Waterloo. For prerational Nature can be seen with the eye of flesh, and rational Mind can be seen with the eye of reason, but transrational Spirit can be seen only with the eye of contemplation, and contemplation is definitely not feelings plus thoughts: it is the absence of both in formless intuition, which, being formless, can easily integrate the forms of Nature and of Mind, something that either or both together could never do for themselves. This was Schelling's great insight about the formless and the "indifference," the great Abyss or Emptiness from which Mind and Nature both issue, an Abyss alone that can ultimately heal. And this is why the Idealists sharply criticized the Romantics as being hopelessly lost and confused regarding this integration.)

THE GLORY OF THE VISION

This, truly, was a stunning vision, the likes of which humankind has rarely seen: evolution as Spirit's temporal unfolding of its own timeless potentials. Grounded in the pragmatic facts and actual history of consciousness, yet at the same time wedded to an all-pervading spiritual reality glorious in its grace and grand in its splendor, this Idealist vision brought Heaven down to awaken the Earth and brought Earth up to exalt its Heaven.

Idealism came very close to integrating the Big Three. There was abundant room for art, morals, and science, and they were carefully seen as important and cherished moments in the overall process of Spirit itself. Moreover, the Idealist vision was alive to the currents of development (or evolution). It was the first philosophy ever to come to terms with—and fully embrace—the sweeping implications of all-encompassing *development,* especially in religion and spirituality. Moreover, Idealism integrated Spirit and evolution in perhaps the only convincing way, namely, by recognizing that evolution is simply Spirit-in-action, or "God in the making."

Thus evolution, far from being an antispiritual movement—as so many Romantics and antimodernists and virtually all premodern cultures imagined—is actually the concrete unfolding, holarchical integration, and self-actualization of Spirit itself. Evolution is the mode and manner of Spirit's creation of the entire manifest world, not one item of which is left untouched by its all-encompassing embrace.

Henceforth, any spirituality that did *not* embrace evolution was doomed to extinction. Modern science, after the collapse, would reject the spiritual nature of evolution but retain the notion of evolution itself. Modern science, that is, would give us the exteriors of evolution—its surfaces and forms—but not its interiors—including Spirit itself. But even science would realize that evolution is universal, touching everything in existence, and, as Daniel Dennett put it, "like 'universal acid,' evolution eats through every other explanation for life, mind, and culture." How could it not, when it is actually Spirit-in-action, and Spirit embraces all?

Even though modern science has rejected the interiors of evolution while retaining the exterior surfaces, nonetheless science has amassed so much evidence for the existence of evolution in general that, to this day, any religion that attempts to reject evolution seals its own fate in the modern world. Even Pope John Paul II finally conceded that "evolution is more than a hypothesis."

One of the crucial ingredients in any integration of science and religion is the integration of empirical evolution with transcendental Spirit. The Idealists hit upon what very well might be the only conceivable way that this particular requirement can be met, namely, by seeing evolution as Spirit-in-action, thus accounting not only for the *what* and *when* of evolution (the empirical forms and Right-Hand surfaces accepted by modern science) but the *why* and *how* as well (the Left-Hand depths and interior intentionality of Spirit-in-action).

This extraordinary insight is to Idealism's everlasting credit. This lustrous vision saw the entire universe—atoms to cells to organisms to societies, cultures, minds, and souls—as the radiant unfolding of a luminous Spirit, bright and brilliant in its way, never-ending in its liberating grace. For, as Hegel put it, "Everything that from eternity has happened in heaven and earth, the life of God and all the deeds of time simply are the struggles for Spirit to know itself, to find itself, be for itself, and finally unite itself to itself; it is alienated and divided, but only so as to be able thus to find itself and return to itself." Involution is the story of that alienation, and evolution is the story of that extraordinary return.

THE LIMITATIONS OF IDEALISM

And yet, and yet . . . There was at least one crippling inadequacy in Idealism, along with one major and devastating current in the modern world, that together brought Idealism tumbling down (although many of its core insights remain quite valid).

The inadequacy was that it possessed no yoga—that is, no tried and tested practice for *reliably reproducing* the transpersonal and superconscious insights that formed the very core of the great Idealist vision. Either these insights came spontaneously (and thus could not easily be reproduced), or they were the result of interior injunctions that were not anchored in dependable and *sustained* practice (and thus could not easily be reproduced).

Fichte, for example, used to perform this interior experiment with his students: "Be aware of the wall. Now be aware of that which is aware of the wall. Now be aware of that which is aware of that which is aware. . . ." In other words, this was a genuine if somewhat clumsy attempt to push back to the pure Witness, the absolute subjectivity that can never be seen as an object because it is the pure and formless Seer. Fichte wanted his students to contact what he called "the absolute Self," and you can begin to do so by inquiring within, asking "Who am I?" or "What is it that is now aware?" This radical Self, according to Fichte, is the source of the entire manifest world.

This, of course, is virtually identical to the great Vedanta notion of the identity of Atman (the pure Self in the individual) and Brahman (the Self of the Kosmos). Similar types of interior experiments were used by Vedanta, among others, to contact this pure Witness, with one major exception: these interior experiments or injunctions—known as yoga—were what we might call industrial-strength. They were not simply short exercises performed in the classroom to give students a glimpse of the divine Self; they were intense practices often pursued for hours, days, months, even years at a time, in virtually unbroken practice sessions.

In Zen, for example, if the koan (or meditation theme) is "Who am I?" or "Who chants the name of the Buddha?," it takes an average of *six years,* according to Yasutani Roshi, for the successful student to have the first profound satori, or genuine breakthrough to the True Self (which is the True World as well). It is through that *sustained and intense practice* that actual transpersonal awareness of nondual Spirit is awakened, deepened, sustained, and transmitted from master to student.

The Idealists had none of this profound and sustained spiritual practice or yoga. Thus their transpersonal insights, profound as they were, came haphazardly and randomly; worse, they had no means of reliably reproducing these insights in others. Either you stumbled onto this transpersonal and superconscious experience, or you did not. If you did, you found that the Idealists spoke directly to you; if you did not, you found them completely confused and lost in metaphysical rubbish.

Lacking a genuine means of reproducible injunctions (or yoga), the Idealists' "transpersonal knowledge" was thus dismissed as "mere metaphysics," which, in the wake of Kant, was enough to doom any philosophy. And in a sense, precisely because the Idealists lacked a genuine spiritual injunction (practice, exemplar, paradigm), they were indeed, at least in this respect, caught in "mere metaphysics." For metaphysics in the "bad" sense is *any thought system without means of verification* (without validity claims or means of gathering actual data and evidence). Lacking the means of reproducibly generating actual and direct experiential evidence—*lacking the means of consistently delivering direct spiritual experience*—Idealism in this regard degenerated into abstract speculations without the means of experiential confirmation or rejection.

Thus, within a few decades of Hegel's death, the word was out: the Idealists did not in fact deliver the long-sought integration of the Big Three. They *talked* about it, but they did not seem to be able to *actually deliver* the experiential goods for other people. The modern dissociation had not been healed—if anything, it continued to accelerate—and the Idealists had been powerless to stop it.

In less than a century, the great Idealist vision had, for all practical purposes, come and gone. This glorious spiritual flower, perhaps the finest the modern West has ever known, saw its petals wither and fall, blown carelessly across a landscape increasingly flat and faded, the bleak and brave new world of the coming wasteland.

THE REIGN OF THE IT

The major interior deficiency of Idealism was the lack of a genuine yoga; the major exterior current in the modern (and soon-to-be postmodern) world that contributed to the devastation of the Idealist vision was simply the continuing collapse of the Kosmos.

Under the reign of it-science (quickly moving into its most powerful and imperial form as systems science, which saw the world as a holistic web of interwoven ITs) combined with it-industrialization (which objectified and commodified all human and intersubjective exchange, turning "I" and "we" into commercial "its" to be bought and sold in the marketplace)—under those combined forces, the Left-Hand and interior dimensions were being rapidly colonialized and enslaved by the aggressive Right-Hand domains. The value spheres of art and morals and spirituality, of interior consciousness and introspection and contemplation, of meaning and value and depth—in short, the Big Three—were rudely collapsed into the Big One of material monism.

We thus arrive at the official modern Western worldview—namely, *flatland holism*: atoms are parts of molecules which are parts of cells which are parts of organisms which are parts of societies of organisms which are parts of the biosphere which is part of the cosmos at large. However true the elements of that holarchy might be, they all have simple location and thus they all, without exception, are described in it-language and known in an empirical fashion.

This *subtle reductionism* simply reduces every holon in the Left Hand to its corresponding aspects in the Right Hand, thus gutting the interior dimensions and reducing them to empirical systems of ITs. This Right-Hand or flatland holism is a marvelously interwoven and coherent system. It acknowledges holarchies and systems and interwoven processes; it allows the brain and the organism and wonderfully complex ecosystems; it sees relationship upon relationship in never-ending process, all united in the wonderful Web of Life. It simply lacks, in irreducible terms, any actual consciousness, awareness, intentionality, feeling, introspection, contemplation, intuition, value, poetry, meaning, depth or Divinity.

Disenchanted, in other words, was fast becoming disemboweled. And against this flatland holism of scientific materialism, which both Romanticism and Idealism had failed to curb, came the first specifically post-modern revolts, in the more narrow and technical sense of postmodern poststructuralism. Since science arrogantly refused to take its place in a graceful integration with the other equally important value spheres, then let us simply crucify science, deconstruct science, right at its very foundations.

Having slain the Goliath of science, David and his fellow poets, artists, literary theorists, new-paradigm thinkers, and visionaries of every variety could now run free on the gloriously open field. A new age, surely, was about to dawn.

9

Postmodernism

TO DECONSTRUCT THE WORLD

I F WE USE "POSTMODERN" in the broad sense of any development
occurring in the wake of modernity, then both Romanticism and Idealism can be taken as the first great postmodern revolts against the dissociations and disasters of flatland modernity. But with the continuing collapse of the Kosmos—the denial of any substantive reality to any interior or Left-Hand domain—neither Romanticism nor Idealism could breathe; they slowly, inexorably suffocated to death, and by the end of the nineteenth century they were basically ineffectual as any sort of widespread cultural movements with a *serious* chance of challenging scientific monism and flatland holism.

And thus, from *within* the collapsed and postmodern Kosmos, there arose the first great attempt to unseat science, not by arguing for higher modes of knowing (as both Romanticism and Idealism had done), but by *attempting to undermine science in its own foundations*. There arose, that is, postmodernism in the narrow and specific sense (postmodern poststructuralism), generally associated with a list of names stretching from Nietzsche to Heidegger to Bataille, Foucault, Lacan, Deleuze, Derrida, Lyotard, and company (with a dose of late Wittgenstein thrown in for good measure).

There is no way to understand postmodernism without grasping the intrinsic role that *interpretation* plays in human understanding. Postmodernism, in fact, may be credited with making interpretation central to both epistemology and ontology, to both knowing and being. Interpretation, the postmodernists all maintained in their own ways, is not only crucial for understanding the Kosmos, it is an aspect of its very structure. *Interpretation is an intrinsic feature of the fabric of the universe;* and there, in a sentence, is the enduring truth at the heart of the great postmodern movements.

WHAT DOES THAT MEAN?

Many people are initially confused as to why, and how, interpretation is intrinsic to the universe. Interpretation is for things like language and literature, right? Yes, but language and literature are just the tip of the iceberg, an iceberg that extends to the very depths of the Kosmos itself. We might explain it like this:

All Right-Hand events—all sensorimotor objects and empirical processes and ITs—can be seen with the monological gaze, with the eye of flesh. You simply look at the rock, the town, the clouds, the mountain, the railroad tracks, the airplane, the flower, the car, the tree. All these Right-Hand objects and ITs can be *seen* by the senses or their extensions (microscopes to telescopes). They all have simple location; you can actually point to most of them.

But Left-Hand or interior holons cannot be seen in that fashion. You cannot see love, envy, wonder, compassion, insight, intentionality, value, or meaning running around out there in the empirical world. Interior events are not seen in an *exterior* or *objective* manner, they are seen by *introspection* and *interpretation*. Not merely the eye of flesh, but the eye of mind (not to mention the eye of contemplation).

Thus, if you want to study *Macbeth* empirically, you can get a copy of the play and subject it to various scientific tests: it weighs so many grams, it has so many molecules of ink, it has so many pages composed of such-and-such organic compounds, and so on. That is all you can know about *Macbeth* empirically. Those are its Right-Hand, objective, exterior aspects.

But if you want to know the *meaning* of the play, you will have to read it and enter into its interiority, its meaning, its intentions, its depths. The only way you can do that is by *interpretation*: What does this sentence *mean?* Here empirical science is virtually worthless, because we are entering interior domains and symbolic depths, which cannot be accessed by exterior empiricism but only by introspection and interpretation. Not just objective, but intersubjective. Not just monological, but dialogical.

Thus, you might see me coming down the street, a frown on my face. You can see that. But what does that exterior frown actually mean? How will you find out? You will ask me. You will talk to me. You can see my surfaces, but in order to understand my interior, my depths, you will have to enter into the interpretive circle. You, as a subject, will not merely stare at me as an object (of the monological gaze); rather, you, as a subject, will attempt to understand me, as a subject—as a person, as a self, as a bearer of intentionality and meaning. You will talk to me, and interpret what I say; and I will do the same with you. We are not subjects staring at objects; we are subjects trying to understand subjects—we are in the intersubjective circle, the dialogical dance. Monological is to describe; dialogical is to understand.

This is true not only for humans, but for all sentient beings as such. If you want to understand your dog—is he happy, or perhaps hungry, or wants to go for a walk?—you will have to *interpret* the signals he is giving you. And your dog, to the extent that he can, does the same with you. In other words, the *interior* of a holon can *only* be accessed by interpretation.

Thus, to put it bluntly, exterior surfaces can be *seen,* but interior depth must be *interpreted.* And precisely because this depth is an intrinsic part of the Kosmos—it is the Left-Hand dimension of every holon— interpretation itself is an intrinsic feature of the Kosmos. Interpretation is not something added onto the Kosmos as an afterthought; it is the very opening of the interiors themselves. And since the depth of the Kosmos goes "all the way down," then, as Heidegger famously put it, "Interpretation goes all the way down."

Perhaps we can now see why one of the great and noble aims of postmodernism was to *introduce interpretation as an intrinsic aspect of the Kosmos.* As I would put it, every holon has a Left- and a Right-Hand dimension, and therefore every holon without exception has an objective (Right) and an interpretive (Left) component.

The disaster of modernity was that it reduced all introspective and interpretive knowledge to exterior and empirical flatland: it attempted to erase the richness of interpretation from the script of the world. (In postmodernese: Modernity marginalized the multivalent epistemic modes via an aggressive hegemony of the myth of the given that hierarchically inverted hermeneutic inscriptions due to the phallologocentrism of patriarchal signifiers. Translation: it collapsed Left to Right.)

Perhaps we can begin to see that the attempt by postmodernism to reintroduce interpretation into the very structure and fabric of the Kosmos was yet another attempt to escape flatland, to resurrect the gutted interiors and interpretive modes of knowing. The postmodern emphasis on interpretation—starting most notably with Nietzsche and running through Dilthey's *Geist* sciences to Heidegger's hermeneutic ontology to Derrida's "There is nothing outside the text [interpretation]"—is at bottom nothing but the Left-Hand domains screaming to be released from the crushing oblivion of the monological gaze of scientific monism and flatland holism. It was the bold reassertion of the I and the WE in the face of faceless ITS.

EXTREME POSTMODERNISM

Yet, as is so often the case with postmodernism, this moment of truth—every actual occasion has an interpretive component—was taken to absurd and self-defeating extremes: There is *nothing but* interpretation, and thus we can *dispense with the objective component of truth altogether* (in which case this theory cannot itself claim to be true: "So, if true, it is false. So, it is false." This, as we saw, is the performative contradiction hidden in all extreme postmodern "theoreticism," at which point this approach often hooks up with a mis-Kuhnian "new-paradigm" maneuver).

This extreme denial of any sort of objective truth amounts to a *denial of the Right-Hand quadrants altogether,* precisely the *reverse disaster* of modernity: all Right-Hand objects reduced to Left-Hand interpretations. And thus, all truth reduced to interpretive whim. Yet supposedly this reverse disaster will relieve modernity of its fragmented madness.

Since modern science had, in effect, killed two of the three value spheres (I-aesthetics and we-morals), postmodernism would simply attempt *to kill science as well,* and thus, in its own bizarre fashion, attempt an "integration" or "equal valuing" of all three spheres because all three of them were now equally dead, so to speak. Three walking corpses would heal the dissociations of modernity. Into the postmodern wasteland walked the zombie squad, and the wonder of it all is that they managed to convince a fair number of academics that this was a viable solution to modernity's ills.

Nonetheless, (extreme) postmodernism is now by far the most prevalent mood of academia, literary theory, the new historicism, a great deal of political theory, and (whether their proponents realize it or not) virtually all of the "new-paradigm" approaches to integrating science and religion. It thus behooves us to understand both its important truths and its extremist distortions.

MOMENTS OF TRUTH IN POSTMODERNISM

Postmodern philosophy is a complex cluster of notions that are defined almost entirely by what its proponents *reject*. They reject foundationalism, essentialism, and transcendentalism. They reject rationality, truth as correspondence, and representational knowledge. They reject grand narratives, metanarratives, and big pictures of any variety. They reject realism, final vocabularies, and canonical description.

Incoherent as the postmodern theories often sound (and often are), most of these "rejections" stem from three core assumptions:

1. Reality is not in all ways pregiven, but in some significant ways is a construction, an interpretation (this view is often called "constructivism"); the belief that reality is simply given, and not also partly constructed, is referred to as "the myth of the given."
2. Meaning is context-dependent, and contexts are boundless (this is often called "contextualism").
3. Cognition must therefore privilege no single perspective (this is called "integral-aperspectival").

I believe all three of those postmodern assumptions are quite accurate (and need to be honored and incorporated in any integral view). Moreover, each tells us something very important with regard to any conceivable integration of science and religion, and thus they need to be studied with care. But each of those assumptions has also been blown radically out of proportion by the extremist wing of postmodernism, and the result is a totally deconstructed world that takes the deconstructionists with it.

Let us review those important truths—and their extremist contortions—one at a time.

THE MYTH OF THE GIVEN

We have already seen that Kant provided convincing arguments that much of what we take to be innocently given to us by the senses is actually a construction of the mind. For example, we say that we can easily see that our fingers are different from one another. But where is that difference located? Can you actually point to it? Can you see it? You can see the individual fingers, but can you actually *see* the difference between them?

The fact is, "difference" is a mental concept that we superimpose on certain raw sensations. Nowhere in those sensations do we actually experience or see "difference"—we *construct* it, *impose* it, *interpret* it; we never actually *perceive* it. In other words, much of what we take to be *perceptions* are actually *conceptions,* mental and not empirical.

Thus, when many empiricists demand sensory evidence, they are actually demanding mental interpretations without realizing it. The Idealists, recall, took this fact and moved in a very "mental" direction: *Everything* we see is the product of mind (but a supraindividual and transpersonal mind or spirit). The postmodern poststructuralists took this notion and moved in a similar but much less spiritual and much more chaotic direction: The world given to us is not a perception but an interpretation, and thus there are no foundations, spiritual or otherwise, to ground anything.

It is exactly at that point that much of postmodernism starts to go extreme. It does not just emphasize the Left-Hand (or interpretive) aspects of all holons, *it attempts to completely deny reality to the Right-Hand (or objective) facets.* The important features of the Kosmos that are interpretive are made the *only* features in existence. Objective truth itself disappears into arbitrary interpretations, themselves imposed by power, gender, race, ideology, anthropocentrism, androcentrism, speciesism, imperialism, logocentrism, phallocentrism, phallologocentrism, or other varieties of utter unpleasantness (except for the claims of the theoreticists themselves, which are miraculously exempted from the charges of prejudice that are supposedly present in all claims—the performative contradiction).

But the fact that all holons have an interpretive as well as objective component does *not* deny the objective component, it merely situates it. Even Wilfrid Sellars, generally regarded as the most persuasive opponent of "the myth of the given"—the myth of direct realism and naive empiricism, the myth that reality is simply given to us—maintains that, even though the manifest image of an object is in part a mental construction, it is *guided* in important ways by *intrinsic features* of sense experience, which is exactly why, as Kuhn knew, science can make *real* progress.

Thus, all Right-Hand exteriors, even if we superimpose conceptions upon them, nonetheless have various intrinsic features that are regis-tered by the senses or their extensions, and in that general sense, all Right-Hand holons have some sort of objective reality. The "difference" between your fingers might be a mental construct, but the fingers them-selves in some sense preexist your conceptualization of them; they are not totally or merely a product of mental constructions (which is exactly why a dog, a preconceptual infant, and a camera—all lacking a concep-tual mind to do any constructing—will still register them). A diamond will cut a piece of glass, no matter what cultural words or concepts we use for "diamond," "cut," and "glass," and no amount of cultural constructivism will change that simple objective fact.

So it is one thing to point out the partial but crucial role that interpre-tation plays in our perception of the world (so that we can indeed deny the myth of the given). But to go to extremes and deny any moment of objective truth at all (and any form of correspondence theory or service-able representation) is simply to render the discussion unintelligible.

No wonder John Searle had to beat this approach back in his wonder-ful book *The Construction of Social Reality*—as opposed to "the social construction of reality"—the idea being that cultural realities are con-structed on a base of correspondence truth that grounds the construction itself, without which no construction could get under way at all. Once again, we can accept the partial truths of postmodernism—interpretation and constructivism are crucial ingredients of the Kosmos, all the way down—without going overboard and attempting to reduce all other quadrants and all other truths to that partial glimpse.

MEANING IS CONTEXT-DEPENDENT

The same caution applies to the second important truth of postmodern-ism, namely, that meaning is context-dependent. The word "bark," for example, means something entirely different in the phrases "the bark of a dog" and "the bark of a tree"—in other words, meaning is in many important ways dependent upon the context in which it finds itself. Moreover, these contexts are in principle *endless* or *boundless,* and thus there is no way finally to master and control meaning once and for all (because one can always imagine a further context that would alter the present meaning).

As I would put it, contexts are indeed boundless precisely because reality is composed of holons within holons within holons *indefinitely,* with no discernible bottom or top. Even the entire present universe is simply a part of the next moment's universe. Every whole is always a part, endlessly. And therefore every conceivable context is boundless. To say that the Kosmos is holonic is to say it is contextual, all the way up and down.

But that postmodern moment of truth has, once again, been deformed and pressed into self-contradictory duty by extreme postmodernists (particularly the branch known as "deconstruction," and especially its American proponents), who use it to deny that any sort of meaning actually exists or can be conveyed at all. Anytime science or traditional philosophy attempts to make a statement about the objective world, deconstruction will simply find a context that renders the statement absurd or self-contradictory, thus "deconstructing" the attempt. Since such a context can *always* be found (they are limitless), any and all meaning can be aggressively exploded and deconstructed right at the start. No wonder even Foucault referred to this extreme postmodernism as "terrorism." (Critics noted that these terrorists did not, however, attempt to deconstruct the meaning of "tenure," "pay raise," "promotion," or "salary"; these, apparently, are all very meaningful.)

But again, if that is a meaningful theory, its own meaning is meaningless. If it is so, then it isn't; so, it isn't. Contextualism, yes; extreme contextualism, no.

The Linguistic Turn

The importance of contextualism, interpretation, and hermeneutics in general came to the fore historically with what has been called *the linguistic turn* in philosophy—the general realization that language is not simply a representation of a pregiven world, but has a hand in the creation and construction of that world. With the linguistic turn, which began roughly in the nineteenth century, philosophers stopped using language to describe the world, and instead started looking at language itself.

Suddenly, language was no longer a simple and trusted tool. Metaphysics in general was replaced with linguistic analysis, because it was becoming increasingly obvious that language is not a clear window through which we innocently look at a given world; it is more like a slide projector throwing images against the screen of what we finally see. Language helps to create my world, and, as Wittgenstein would put it, the limits of my language are the limits of my world.

In many ways, "the linguistic turn" is just another name for the great transition from modernity to postmodernity. Where both premodern and modern cultures simply and naively used their language to approach the world, the postmodern mind spun on its heels and began to look at language itself. In the entire history of human beings, this, more or less, had never happened before. Some altogether startling findings were to result.

If we are to integrate the wisdom of yesterday with the knowledge of today—and that means, in the broadest sweep, the best of premodern, modern, and postmodern—we will have to look carefully at what the postmodern linguistic turn brought to our understanding of the Kosmos. For the integration of science and religion is a camel that, one way or another, must be able to pass through the eye of the postmodern needle: constructivism, contextualism, and integral-aperspectival—all of which came to the fore with the linguistic turn.

LANGUAGE SPEAKS

Most forms of postmodern poststructuralism trace their lineage to the work of the brilliant and pioneering linguist Ferdinand de Saussure. Saussure's work, and especially his *Course in General Linguistics* (1916), was the basis of much of modern linguistics, semiology (semiotics), structuralism, and hence poststructuralism, and his essential insights are as cogent today as they were when he first advanced them almost a century ago.

According to Saussure, a linguistic *sign* is composed of a material *signifier* (the written word, the spoken word, the marks on this page) and a conceptual *signified* (what comes to mind when you see the signifier), both of which are different from the actual *referent*. For example, if you see a tree, the actual tree is the referent; the written word "tree" is the signifier; and what comes to mind (the image, the thought, the mental picture or concept) when you read the word "tree" is the signified. The signifier and the signified together constitute the overall sign.

But what is it, Saussure asked, that allows a sign to mean something, to actually *carry meaning*? For example, bark of a dog, bark of a tree. As we saw, the word "bark" has meaning, in each case, because of its place in the phrase (a different phrase gives the same word a totally different meaning). Each phrase likewise has meaning because of its place in the larger sentence and, eventually, in the total linguistic structure. Any given word in itself is basically *meaningless* because the same word can have different meanings depending on the context or the structure in which it is placed.

Thus, Saussure pointed out, it is the *relationship among all of the words themselves* that stabilizes meaning (and not merely some simple pointing to an object, because that pointing cannot even be communicated without a total structure that holds each word in meaningful place). So—and this was Saussure's great insight—*a meaningless element becomes meaningful only by virtue of the total structure.* (This is the beginning of *structuralism,* virtually all schools of which trace their lineage in whole or part to Saussure. Present-day descendants include aspects of the work of Lévi-Strauss, Jakobson, Piaget, Lacan, Barthes, Foucault, Derrida, Habermas, Loevinger, Kohlberg, Gilligan . . . it was a truly stunning discovery.)

In other words—and no surprise—every sign is a holon, a context within contexts within contexts in the overall network. And this means, said Saussure, that the entire language is instrumental in conferring meaning on an individual word.

Now, the standard Enlightenment (and flatland) notion was that a word gains meaning simply because it *points to* or *represents* an object. It is a purely monological and empirical affair. The isolated subject looks at an equally isolated object (such as a tree), and then simply chooses a word to represent the sensory object. *This, it was thought, is the basis of all genuine knowledge.* Even with complex scientific theories, each theory is simply a *map* that *represents* the objective territory. If the correspondence is accurate, the map is true; if the correspondence is inaccurate, the map is false. Science—and all true knowledge, it was believed—is a straightforward case of *accurate representation,* accurate mapmaking. "We make pictures of the empirical world," as Wittgenstein would soon put it, and if the pictures match, we have the truth.

This is the so-called *representation paradigm,* which is also known as the *fundamental Enlightenment paradigm,* because it was the general theory of knowledge shared by most of the influential philosophers of the Enlightenment, and thus modernity in general. (Recall that in Chapter 4 I actually listed that as one of the defining aspects of modernity: "Modern philosophy is usually 'representational,' which means it tries to form a correct representation of the world. This representational view is also called 'the mirror of nature,' because it was commonly believed that the ultimate reality was sensory nature and philosophy's job was to picture or mirror this reality correctly.")

It was not the existence or the usefulness of representation that was the problem; representational knowledge is a perfectly appropriate form of knowing for many purposes. Rather, it was the aggressive and violent attempt to reduce all knowledge to empirical representation that constituted the disaster of modernity—the reduction of translogical spirit and dialogical mind to monological sensory knowing: the collapse of the Kosmos to nothing but Right-Hand representation.

Saussure, with his early structuralism, gave one of the first, and still one of the most accurate and devastating, critiques of empirical theories of knowing, which, he pointed out, cannot even account for the simple case of "the bark of a tree." The meaning comes not merely from *objective* pointing but from *intersubjective* structures that *cannot themselves be objectively pointed to*! Yet without them, there would, and could, be no objective representation at all!

So what I, as a proper Enlightenment philosopher, took to be a simple "representation" is not so simple after all. I thought that I, the autonomous subject, the isolated and independent self, could simply choose a word (such as "bark") and then say what object I wanted it to point to, to represent. So I imagine that I am utterly prior to this creation of meaning—I am the proud and autonomous subject that creates all this meaning by simply pointing to the objects that I mean.

The reality is pretty much the opposite: Meaning is created for me by vast networks of background contexts about which I consciously know very little. I do not fashion this meaning; this meaning fashions me. I am part of a vast background of cultural signs, and in many cases I have no clue as to where it all came from.

In other words, every subjective intentionality (Upper Left) is *situated* in vast networks of intersubjective or cultural contexts (Lower Left) that are instrumental in the creation and interpretation of meaning itself. Meaning is not merely *objective* pointing but *intersubjective* networks; not simply *monological* but *dialogical;* not just *empirical* but *structural;* not just *representational* images but systemic *networks*—and the meaning is as much a result of the network as of the referent. This is precisely why meaning is indeed context-dependent, and why the bark of a dog is different from the bark of a tree.

In the wake of this extraordinary linguistic turn, philosophers would never again look at language in a simple, trusting way. Language does not merely report the world, represent the world, describe the world.

Rather, language creates worlds, and in that creation is power. Language creates, distorts, carries, discloses, hides, allows, oppresses, enriches, enthralls. For good or ill, language itself is something of a demigod, and philosophers henceforth would focus much of their attention on that powerful force. From linguistic analysis to language games, from structuralism to poststructuralism, from semiology to semiotics, from linguistic intentionality to speech act theory, postmodern philosophy has been in large measure *the philosophy of language,* and it pointed out—quite rightly—that if we are to use language as a tool to understand reality, we had better start by looking very closely at that tool.

LANGUAGE GROANS

The postmodern poststructuralists took many of these profound and indispensable notions and, in carrying them to extremes, rendered them virtually useless. They did not just *situate* individual intentionality in background cultural contexts, they tried to *erase* the individual subject altogether: "the death of man," "the death of the author," "the death of the subject"—all were naked attempts to reduce the subject (Upper Left) to nothing but intersubjective structures (Lower Left). "Language" replaced "humans" as the *agent* of history. It is not I, the subject, who is now speaking, it is nothing but impersonal language and linguistic structure speaking through me.

Thus, as only one of innumerable examples, Foucault would proclaim that "Lacan's importance comes from the fact that he showed how it is the structures, the very system of language, that speak through the patient's discourse and the symptoms of his neurosis—not the subject." Upper Left reduced to Lower Left, to what Foucault famously called "this anonymous system without a subject."

Thus I, Ken Wilber, am not writing these words, nor am I in any way primarily responsible for them; language is actually doing all the work (although this did not prevent I, Roland Barthes, or I, Michel Foucault, from accepting the royalty checks written to the author that supposedly did not exist).

Put simply, the fact that each "I" is always situated in a background "We" was perverted into the notion that there is no "I" at all, but only an all-pervading "We"—no individual subjects, only vast networks of intersubjective and linguistic structures. (Buddhists, take note: this was in no way the notion of *anatta,* or no-self, because the "I" was replaced, not with Emptiness, but with finite linguistic structures of the "We," thus multiplying, not transcending, the actual problem.)

Foucault eventually rejected the extremism of his early stance, a fact studiously ignored by extreme postmodernists. Among other hilarious spectacles, postmodernist biographers began trying to write biographies of subjects that supposedly did not exist in the first place, thus producing books that were about as interesting as dinner without food.

For Saussure, the signifier and signified were an integrated unit (a holon); but the postmodern poststructuralists—and this was one of their most defining moves—shattered this unity by attempting to place almost exclusive emphasis on sliding chains of *signifiers* alone. The signifiers—the actual material or written marks—were given virtually exclusive priority. They were thus severed from both their signifieds and their referents, and these chains of sliding or "free-floating" signifiers were therefore said to be anchored in nothing but power, prejudice, or ideology. (We see again the extreme constructivism so characteristic of postmodernism: signifiers are not anchored in any truth or reality outside of themselves, but simply create or construct all realities.)

Sliding chains of signifiers: this is the essential postmodern poststructuralist move. It is postSTRUCTURAL, because it starts with Saussure's insights into the networklike structure of linguistic signs, which partially construct as well as partially represent; but POSTstructural, because the signifiers are cut loose from any sort of anchoring at all. There is no objective truth (only interpretations), and thus, according to extreme postmodernists, signifiers are grounded in nothing but power, prejudice, ideology, gender, race, colonialism, speciesism, and so on (a performative contradiction that would mean that this theory itself must also be anchored in nothing but power, prejudice, etc., in which case it is just as vile as the theories it despises).

This is exactly where the postmodern agenda would often hook up with the mis-Kuhnian notion of "paradigm." It was a marriage made in interpretive heaven for all those who wished to "deconstruct" the "old paradigm" and replace it with the "new paradigm," which itself lacked any genuine exemplars or injunctions and thus, according to Kuhn's actual notion of paradigm, was no such thing at all, but merely ideology dressed up as cultural studies, narcissism and nihilism in transformational drag.

INTEGRAL-APERSPECTIVAL

The fact that meaning is context-dependent—the second important truth of postmodernism, also called "contextualism"—means that a multiperspective approach to reality is called for. Any single perspective is likely to be partial, limited, perhaps even distorted, and only by taking multiple perspectives and pluralistic contexts can the knowledge quest be fruitfully advanced. That "diversity" and "pluralism" is the third important truth of general postmodernism.

Jean Gebser, whom we have seen in connection with worldviews, coined the term *integral-aperspectival* to refer to this pluralistic or multiple-perspectives view, which I also refer to as *vision-logic* or *network-logic*. "Aperspectival" means that no single perspective is unduly privileged, and thus, in order to gain a more holistic or *integral* view, we need an *aperspectival* approach, which is exactly why Gebser usually hyphenated them: integral-aperspectival.

Gebser contrasted integral-aperspectival cognition with formal rationality, or what he called "perspectival reason," which tends to take a single, monological perspective and view all of reality through that narrow lens. Where perspectival reason privileges the exclusive perspective of the particular subject, vision-logic *adds up all the perspectives,* privileging none, and thus attempts to grasp the integral, the whole, the multiple contexts within contexts that endlessly disclose the Kosmos, not in a rigid or absolutist fashion, but in a fluidly holonic and multidimensional tapestry.

This parallels almost exactly the Idealists' great emphasis on the difference between a reason that is merely monological, representational, or empiric-analytic, and a reason that is dialogical, dialectical, and network-oriented (vision-logic). They called the former *Verstand* and the latter *Vernunft*. And they saw *Vernunft* or vision-logic as being a higher evolutionary development than mere *Verstand* or formal rationality. In fact, they tended to view monological or perspectival rationality as a "monster of arrested development"—and that monological monster was, of course, the mode of knowing that largely defined the Enlightenment, which is why the Idealists' critique of the Enlightenment (and flatland modernity) is still one of the most powerful and cogent ever advanced.

Gebser, too, believed that vision-logic was an evolutionary development beyond monological rationality. Nor are Gebser and the Idealists alone. Many schools of transpersonal psychology and sociology, not to mention important conventional theorists from Jürgen Habermas to Carol Gilligan, see dialectical vision-logic as a higher and more embracing mode of reason. (This is shown in Figure 5-1, where "formop" is formal rationality and "vision-logic" is integral-aperspectival. Vision-logic is not yet transrational but, we might say, lies on the border between the rational and the transrational, and thus partakes of some of the best of both.)

This vision-logic not only can spot massive interrelationships, it is itself an intrinsic part of the interrelated Kosmos, which is why vision-logic does not just *represent* the Kosmos, but is a *performance of* the Kosmos. Of course, all modes of genuine knowing are such performances; but vision-logic is the first that can self-consciously realize this and articulate it. Hegel did so in the first extensive and pioneering fashion—vision-logic evolutionarily became conscious of itself in Hegel—and Saussure did exactly the same thing with linguistics. Saussure took vision-logic and applied it to language, thus disclosing, for the first time in history, its network structure. The linguistic turn is, at bottom, vision-logic looking at language itself.

This same vision-logic would give rise to the extensively elaborated versions of systems theory in the natural sciences; it would stand as well behind the postmodernists' recognition that meaning is context-dependent and contexts are boundless. In all these movements and more, we see the radiant hand of vision-logic announcing the endless networks of holonic interconnection that constitute the very fabric of the Kosmos itself.

This is why I believe that the recognition of the importance of integral-aperspectival cognition is the third great (and valid) message of postmodernism in general. This is likewise why one of the ways we can date the beginning of the general postmodern mood is with the great Idealists (note that Derrida does exactly that; Hegel, he says, is the last of the old or the first of the new).

LANGUAGE COLLAPSES

All of which is well and good. But it is not enough, we have seen, to be "holistic" instead of "atomistic," or to be network-oriented instead of analytic and divisive. Because the alarming fact is that *any mode of knowing can be collapsed* and confined merely to surfaces, to exteriors, to Right-Hand occasions. And, in fact, almost as soon as vision-logic had heroically emerged in evolution, it was crushed by the flatland madness sweeping the modern world.

Indeed, as we have repeatedly seen, the systems sciences themselves did exactly that. The systems sciences denied any substantial reality to the I and the WE domains (in their own terms), and reduced all of them to nothing but interwoven ITs in a dynamical system of network processes. This was vision-logic at work, but a crippled vision-logic, hobbled and chained to the bed of exterior processes and empirical ITs. This was a holism, but merely an exterior holism that perfectly gutted the interiors and denied any sort of validity to the extensive realms of Left-Hand holism (of the I and the WE). The shackles were no longer atomistic; the shackles—and don't we all feel better?—were now holistically interwoven chains of degradation.

Precisely the same fate awaited so much of the general postmodern agenda. Starting from the admirable reliance on vision-logic and integral-aperspectival awareness—yet still unable to escape the collapse of the Kosmos—these postmodern movements ended up subtly embodying and even extending the reductionistic nightmare. They all became a new and higher form of reason, yes, but *reason still trapped in flatland.* They were perfectly, but perfectly, another twist on flatland holism, material monism, monological madness. They still succumbed to the disaster of modernity even as they loudly announced they had overcome it, subverted it, inverted it, deconstructed it, exploded it.

There is nothing but *sliding chains of signifiers:* you see, the only reality is sliding chains *of material marks*—in other words, sliding chains of ITs. For all the emphasis on interpretation and interior validation, postmodern poststructuralism all comes down to sliding chains of material ITs. Gone are the actual signifieds—the actual interior domains of the I and the WE disclosed in their own terms—and what we have left, as with systems theory, are holistic chains of interwoven ITs, holistic surfaces, all utterly lacking any genuine depth whatsoever, and thus utterly incapable of curing the dissociations of modernity. And so it came about that extreme postmodernism was simply part of the insidious disease for which it loudly claimed to be the cure.

DEPTH TAKES A VACATION

In fact, most postmodernists would go to extraordinary lengths to deny depth in general. It is as if, suffering under the onslaught of flatland aggression, postmodernism identified with the aggressor. Postmodernism came to embrace surfaces, champion surfaces, glorify surfaces and surfaces alone. There are only sliding chains of signifiers; everything is a material text; there is nothing under the surface; there is only the surface. As Bret Easton Ellis put it in *The Informers:* "Nothing was affirmative, the term 'generosity of spirit' applied to nothing, was a cliche, was some kind of bad joke. . . . Reflection is useless, the world is senseless. Surface, surface, surface was all that anyone found meaningful . . . this was civilization as I saw it, colossal and jagged."

Robert Alter, reviewing William H. Gass's *The Tunnel*—a book claimed by many to be the ultimate postmodern novel—points out that the defining strategy of this postmodern masterpiece is that "everything is deliberately reduced to the flattest surface." It does so by "denying the possibility of making consequential distinctions between, or meaningful rankings of, moral or aesthetic values. There is no within: murderer and victim, lover and onanist, altruist and bigot, dissolve into the same ineluctable slime"—the same sliding chains of equally meaningless signifiers.

Everything reduced to the flattest surface. . . . *There is no within*—a perfect description of flatland, a flatland that, beginning with modernity, was actually amplified and glorified with extreme postmodernity: "surface, surface, surface was all that anyone found."

Alter is exactly right that behind it all is the inability or refusal to make "consequential distinctions between, or meaningful rankings of, moral or aesthetic values." In this wasteland where Right-Hand signifiers and surfaces alone exist, there are no value, no meaning, and no qualitative distinctions of any sort, for those exist only in the Left-Hand domains. To collapse the Kosmos to Right-Hand signifiers is to step out of the real world and into the twilight zone known as the disqualified universe. Here there are no interior holarchies, no meaningful rankings of the I and the WE, no qualitative distinctions of any sort and no gradations of depth, so that fact and fiction, truth and lies, murderer and victim, as Alter said, are all reduced to equivalent surfaces.

"Subvert all hierarchies!"—one of the battle cries of extreme postmodernism—actually means "Destroy all value, kill all quality, massacre all meaning." Extreme postmodernism went from the noble insight that all perspectives need to be given a fair hearing, to the utterly self-contradictory belief that no perspective whatsoever is better than any other (self-contradictory because their own belief is held to be much better than the alternatives).

Thus, under the intense gravity of flatland, integral-aperspectival awareness became simply *aperspectival madness*—the contradictory belief that no belief is better than any other—a total paralysis of thought, will, and action in the face of a million perspectives all given exactly the same depth, namely, zero.

At one point in *The Tunnel*, Gass himself, the author of this postmodern masterpiece, describes the *perfect postmodern form*, which serves "to raunchify, to suburp [*sic*] everything, to pollute the pollutants, explode the exploded, trash the trash. . . . It is all surface. . . . There's no inside however long or far you travel on it, no within, no deep."

No within, no deep. That may serve as a perfect credo for extreme postmodernism in general. And it is into this modern and postmodern wasteland—and against its dominant and domineering mood—that we wish to introduce the within, the deep, the interiors of the Kosmos, the contours of the Divine.

PART THREE

A RECONCILIATION

10

The Within

A VIEW OF THE DEEP

T HE MODERN and postmodern world is still living in the grips of flatland, of surfaces, of exteriors devoid of interior anything: "no within, no deep." The only large-scale alternatives are an exuberant embrace of shallowness (as with extreme postmodernism), or a *regression* to the *interiors* of *premodern* modes, from mythic religion to tribal magic to narcissistic new age. A modern and postmodern spirituality has continued to elude us, primarily because the *irreversible* differentiations of modernity have placed difficult but unavoidable demands on the sought-after integration: spirituality must be able to stand up to scientific authority, not by aping the monological madness but by announcing its own means and modes, data and evidence, validities and verifications. Spirituality must be able to integrate the Big Three value spheres of self, culture, and nature, not merely attempt to dedifferentiate them in a premodern slide or deconstruct them in a postmodern blast.

We have seen that historically the three most important attempts to introduce Spirit into the modern and postmodern world were Romanticism, Idealism, and some schools of Postmodernism. And we saw why each ultimately failed. The Romantics, caught in the pre/trans fallacy, often ended up recommending dedifferentiation instead of genuine integration (no matter what lip service they paid to the latter). The Idealists avoided regression but had no yoga, no transpersonal injunctions to reproduce their spiritual intuitions in others (so that Idealism degenerated into "mere metaphysics," or thought without actual evidence). And the Postmodernists, unanchored in any conception of truth, had nothing left but their own dispositions: narcissism and nihilism as a postmodern tag team from hell. Coupled with a mis-Kuhnian notion of "paradigm," egocentrism rushed in to announce the dawn of the glorious world transformation, gleefully giddy at the thought of how central its own ego was to the entire global show.

With the dominance of flatland, two major types of attempts *to break the hold of scientific monism* arose: Romanticism and Idealism attempted a type of epistemological pluralism, while postmodernism opted for "theoreticism." In the former, science is seen as one of several valid modes of knowing, so that science and religion can coexist as different but equally important aspects of the Real. In the latter, all modes of knowing are deconstructed, leaving an *extremely* level playing field, which, it is hoped, will be liberating due to a subverting of the dominator hierarchies.

All of them ultimately failed. Epistemological pluralism had been embraced in various forms by classical religion, Romanticism, and Idealism. But none of those forms could withstand the assault of an aggressive modern scientific monism (or epidemic systems IT-ism). Modern science simply discovered that too many items that were supposed to be completely transcendent actually had very real, very immanent, and very natural anchors in the empirical brain and organism—nothing "otherworldly" about them, and thus no other modes of knowing that needed to be acknowledged. Epistemological pluralism collapsed with the rest of the Kosmos: there are only Right-Hand occasions accessed by monological and empirical modes of knowing. Science alone rules, the epidemic reign of the omnipresent It.

Postmodern theoreticism (science as poetry/paradigm) also collapsed, this time under the weight of its own absurdities and performative self-contradictions. Science and religion were placed on equal footing by killing them both, and the wasteland of endless surfaces was proclaimed the only real, a proclamation that, if true, is false.

Nonetheless, each of those approaches—Romanticism, Idealism, Postmodernism—has moments of truth that need to be honored and incorporated in a more integrative embrace. This, indeed, is one of the aims of a truly Integral approach, which this book is attempting to express.

If a genuine integration of science and religion is to be a reality, it will have to include an integration of the Big Three (of art, morals, and science), not by *deforming* any of them to fit some sort of pet scheme, but by taking each of them more or less exactly as they are. There is no need to force science into some sort of "new paradigm" that will then supposedly be compatible with spirituality. The very attempt is a massive category error, a profound confusion about the nature and role of monological science, dialogical philosophy, and translogical spirituality. These are to be integrated as we find them, not as we deform them in a monological leveling that erases the very differences that are supposed to be integrated in the first place.

The Integral approach, therefore, attempts just that—an integration, just as they are, of the Big Three of art (aesthetic-expressive, self and self-expression, subjective phenomenology), morals (intersubjective justness, ethical goodness, cultural communion), and science (objective nature, the empirical world, concrete occasions). Nothing spectacular has to be done to any of these three value spheres (or four quadrants); we take them more or less as we find them. All that is required is that each begin to harbor the suspicion that its truth is not the only truth in the Kosmos.

Nonetheless, exactly there is the difficulty. All of the past forms of epistemological pluralism *failed the test of modernity* because science itself did not and would not fundamentally doubt its own competence to reveal all important forms of truth. With the collapse of the Kosmos, the integration of the Big Three was no longer even perceived to be a problem. It was not a problem because there was no Big Three, only the Big One of scientific materialism and flatland holism: no integration was needed, none was sought.

In order to proceed effectively on our quest, we therefore need to back up prior to the collapse of the Kosmos. Not prior to the differentiations of modernity, but merely prior to the dissociations—and begin our reconstruction at that fateful point, that point of fragmentation, alienation, separation, and collapse.

And that was the point that *any and all interior dimensions lost legitimacy.* Modernity did not reject Spirit per se. Modernity rejected *interiors* per se, and Spirit was simply one of the numerous casualties. The within itself—from the lowest to the highest, from prepersonal to personal to transpersonal—the interiors themselves were objectified, turned into objects of the monological gaze, forced under the instrumental scope of scientific materialism: subjective mind reduced to material brain, intersubjective values reduced to technical steering problems, intentionality reduced to behavioral conditioning, Spirit (if it survived at all) reduced to the empirical Web of Life and econature (flatland holism), cultural worldviews reduced to material modes of production, compassion reduced to serotonin, consciousness reduced to digital bits—in short, and in all ways, I and we reduced to scurrying ITs.

Granted, Spirit did not survive this modern collapse. But the point is, neither did any other interior dimension, including the simplest feelings, perceptions, and affects—not to mention intentionality in general, the mental domains as irreducible realities with their own ontological weight, and, yes, the spiritual and transpersonal realms as well. Flatland accepts no interior domain whatsoever, and reintroducing Spirit is the least of our worries.

Thus our task is not specifically to reintroduce spirituality and somehow attempt to show that modern science is becoming compatible with God. That approach, which is taken by most of the integrative attempts, does not go nearly deep enough in diagnosing the disease, and thus, in my opinion, never really addresses the crucial issues.

Rather, it is the rehabilitation of the *interior in general* that opens the possibility of reconciling science and religion, integrating the Big Three, overcoming the dissociations and disasters of modernity, and fulfilling the brighter promises of postmodernity. Not Spirit, but *the within,* is the corpse we must first revive.

THE OBJECTIONS OF EMPIRICAL SCIENCE

All of the typical attempts to integrate science and religion have consistently failed because empirical science rejects the interior dimensions. It does so for two major reasons:

1. The allegedly "interior," "higher," "transcendental," "otherworldly," or "mystical" modes of consciousness all seem to be thoroughly embedded in natural, objective, empirical processes in the brain. Thus they are not higher in any genuine sense, but merely different types of biomaterial events in the biomaterial brain. No higher levels of reality, beyond the sensorimotor, are needed to explain any of these states.

    Thus there are no irreducible interior domains that can be studied by different modes of knowing; there are only objective ITs (atomistic or holistic) studied best by science. In short, interior domains have no reality of their own; thus there are no "interior" modes of knowing that cannot be explained away, literally.

2. Even if there were other modes of knowing than the sensory-

empirical, they would have no means of validation and thus could not be taken seriously. They are, at best, merely personal or subjective tastes and idiosyncratic displays, useful perhaps as emotional preferences but with no cognitive validity at all.

I believe, of course, that both of those objections—there are no interiors, and even if there are, they cannot be verified—are profoundly incorrect. Yet they stand like a reinforced brick wall across the road to the marriage of science and religion. If you find my responses to these two objections satisfactory, fine; if not, perhaps they will help you think of better ones. But unless and until these two objections are directly met and countered, there will be precisely zero integration of science and religion, and approaches not directly addressing them will be largely irrelevant, I believe.

Here is a brief overview of my responses, which I trust will come more alive as we proceed.

I believe that objection number 1 (there are no real interiors) can be answered by the compelling evidence for the existence of all four quadrants, which themselves have an enormous amount of data—empirical, phenomenological, cross-cultural, and contemplative—supporting their existence. The sometimes staggering weight of this evidence places what many would see as a frightful burden on would-be reductionists, who would have to work relentlessly to erase it all to their satisfaction.

More to the point, if empirical science rejects the validity of any and all forms of interior apprehension and knowledge, then it rejects its own validity as well, a great deal of which rests on interior structures and apprehensions that are *not* delivered by the senses or confirmable by the senses (such as logic and mathematics, to name only two).

If science acknowledges these interior apprehensions, upon which its own operations depend, then *it cannot object to interior knowledge per se.* It cannot toss *all* interiors into the garbage can without tossing itself with it. (As we will see, most of the philosophers of science have *already* conceded this point.) This undermines objection number 1, leaving science to resort solely to objection number 2 in order to disqualify the other modes of knowing and maintain its hegemony.

I will then argue that objection number 2 can be answered by showing that the scientific method, in general, consists of three basic strands of knowing (injunction, apprehension, confirmation/rejection). If it can be shown that *the genuine interior modes of knowing also follow these same three strands,* then objection number 2—that these alternative modes have no legitimate validity claims—would be substantially re-futed.

With the two major scientific objections to the interior domains un-done, the door would be open to a genuine reconciliation of science and religion (and the Big Three in general). We will attempt to demonstrate to science, *not* that it is wrong, old paradigm, a product of dissociated consciousness, patriarchal, divisive, or sick to the core, but rather that it is correct but partial. Science, quite rightly, will accept none of the former critiques; if it will budge at all, it will have to be here.

THE RESURRECTION OF THE INTERIOR

As we have seen, empiricists (and positivists and behaviorists and scien-ticians in general) deny irreducible reality to virtually all Left-Hand di-mensions; only the Right Hand is real. All Left-Hand occasions are at best reflections or representations of the sensorimotor world, the world of simple location, the world of ITs, detected by the human senses or their extensions (or, in general, by some sort of objectifying activity).

In other words, they all subscribe to the myth of the given, the myth that the sensorimotor world is simply given to us in direct experience and that science carefully and systematically reports what it there finds. But this view is indeed a myth, and even most orthodox philosophers of science now concede this elemental point, so much so that it is already regarded as something of a settled issue.

We already saw that the myth of the given has been blown out of proportion by extreme postmodernists and then used to deny any objec-tive truth whatsoever. This is an extremism we certainly wish to avoid. There are indeed what Wilfrid Sellars calls *intrinsic features* of the senso-rimotor world that prevent the total dissolution of objective truth and allow science to make *real* progress.

But by the same token, a naive empiricism—that science simply and innocently reports to us the unshakable givens of experience—is likewise an extreme and untenable view. It is the myth of the given.

We do not, for example, perceive a tree. What we actually see, what is given in our experience, is simply a bunch of colored patches. On this, empiricists, rationalists, and Idealists all agree. The traditional empiri-cist then attempts to ground all knowledge in these sensory "givens"— *the colored patches.* But it is now widely acknowledged that you cannot derive knowledge solely from patches. Classical empiricism has run aground on just this impossibility.

Thus, even *The Cambridge Dictionary of Philosophy,* long a bastion of the orthodox and consensus view, soberly points out that "Epistemologies postulating [simple] givenness require a single entity-type to explain the sensorial nature of perception and to provide immediate epistemic foundations for empirical knowledge. *This requirement is now widely regarded as impossible to satisfy;* hence Wilfrid Sellars describes the discredited view as the myth of the given. . . . Concluding that the doctrine of the given is false, he maintains that classical empiricism is a myth" (my italics).

And not just Sellars. As the dictionary itself points out, the requirements of classical empiricism are "now widely regarded as impossible to satisfy . . . classical empiricism is a myth." This parallels nicely John Passmore's summary of the state of positivism, the official philosophy of scientism: "Logical positivism, then, is dead, or as dead as a philosophical movement ever becomes."

This can all be put fairly simply: science approaches the empirical world with a massive conceptual apparatus containing everything from tensor calculus to imaginary numbers to extensive intersubjective linguistic signs to differential equations—virtually all of which are *nonempirical* structures found *only* in interior spaces—and then it astonishingly claims it is simply "reporting" what it "finds" out there in the "given" world—when, in fact, all that is given is colored patches.

For science to acknowledge the massive interior structures that it brings to the party is *not* to deny the objective intrinsic features of the exterior world; it is simply to recognize as well the reality and importance of the subjective and intersubjective domains responsible for generating so much of the knowledge.

Thus there are indeed preexisting intrinsic features in the sensorimotor world that constrain our perceptions—for example, if you drop the colored patch called an apple, it always falls to the colored patch called the ground. These intrinsic features *anchor* the objective component of truth (in any domain).

At the same time, these objective features are differentiated, conceptualized, organized, and given much of their actual form and content by conceptual structures that themselves exist *in nonempirical and nonsensory spaces.* These *interior structures* include not only deeply background cultural contexts, intersubjective linguistic structures, and consensus ethical norms, but also most of the specific conceptual tools that scientists use as they analyze their objective data, tools such as logic, statistical displays, and all forms of mathematics, from algebra to Boolean algebra to calculus to complex numbers to imaginary numbers. *None of these structures can be seen or found anywhere in the exterior, empirical, sensory world.* They are all, all of them, subjective and intersubjective occasions, interior occasions, Left-Hand occasions. And nobody has ever found any way whatsoever to reduce this knowledge to colored patches.

To Investigate the Interiors

Of course, empirical science is free to go on its merry way without stopping to look at the interior tools it uses in its assault on the world. What it is not allowed to do, without self-obliteration, is deny the existence or the importance of these tools. Yet that is exactly what happens when science degenerates into scientism and rejects in toto the existence of the interior dimensions, simply because none of them is a colored patch.

Empirical science depends upon these interior domains (subjective and intersubjective) for its own objective operation. But because they *cannot be accessed* by simple monological and objective and sensorimotor methods, empirical science, in its more brutish forms, has simply rejected these interiors altogether, interiors that not only allow its own operations, but also contain the within of the Kosmos.

This self-obliterating reductionism is not genuine science, it is simply science the village idiot. And, as everybody knows, it takes a village to raise a complete idiot—the village of collapsed modernity, in this case. Science becomes imperial scientism and falls into the simpleminded myth of the given, naively ascribing to its colored patches a great deal of what is found only in its conceptual apparatus, whose existence it has just denied.

But the crucial point is that these interior spaces and structures—from linguistics to mathematics to interpretive modes to logic—*can be investigated in their own right.* Scientists already do this with logic and mathematics. Nobody has ever seen imaginary numbers (such as the square root of negative one) running around in the sensory world, but mathematical scientists use them all the time, and they do so by investigating *the interior structures and patterns* that string various, nonempirical symbols together. The same can be said for most forms of logic, *n*-dimensional theories, tensor calculus . . . the list is almost endless.

We already saw the same approach applied to linguistics, where Saussure, in a historically groundbreaking move, rejected the myth of the given (simple empirical representation) and demonstrated that the meaning of a word comes not simply from its pointing to a colored patch, but also from its being part of a vast intersubjective network of nonempirical signs (none of which are merely colored patches).

Behaviorist theories of language can investigate only the simple pointing (and thus, as Chomsky notes, have never been able to explain language acquisition at all!). But *semiotics* (the study of signs in their intersubjective settings) and *hermeneutics* (the study of interpretation based on grasping the entire network of meaning) have made stunning advances in our understanding of linguistics, precisely by denying the myth of the given, the myth that the monological sensory world alone is the sole irreducible reality.

The conclusion is straightforward: the interior spaces not only structure empirical knowledge but constitute an interior domain that itself contains a vast store of other types of structures, patterns, knowledge, values, and contents—ranging from logic to mathematics to ethics to linguistics. Empirical-sensory science cannot investigate these domains with its exterior tools; but it would indeed take a village idiot to deny their existence or to deny that other modes of investigation might give access to these extraordinary domains.

An Opening to the Deep

Objection number 1—the belief that interior domains have no irreducible reality of their own, and that only sensory-empirical objects are fundamentally real—is actually a notion that few philosophers of science, and few scientists themselves, really believe. Any scientist who uses mathematics already knows that reality is not just sensory. The vast majority of scientists already reject the myth of the given, and all that is required is to keep pointing it out.

The myth of the given is really the myth of exteriors untouched by interiors, of mere objects untouched by subjective and intersubjective structures. It is the myth that there are less than four quadrants to the Kosmos, the myth of the Big One instead of the Big Three. It is the myth at the very core of classical empiricism, positivism, behaviorism, collapsed modernity, and scientism. It is the myth of objects without subjects, of surfaces without depth, of quantity without quality, of veneers without value—the utterly rancid myth that *the Right-Hand world alone is real*. But it is indeed a myth, and the myth is decidedly dead.

Once the myth of the given is exploded, the first major objection of empirical science to interior knowledge is likewise exploded. Science cannot reject a mode of knowing merely because it is interior. That being so, science is then forced to get, shall we say, picky. It must attempt to reject *some* interior modes—such as the contemplative and spiritual—and it can do so *only* by resorting to objection number 2, namely, that these other interior modes have no valid means of verification.

Well, let us see.

11

What Is Science?

W E HAVE SEEN that the philosophers of science are in widespread
agreement that empirical science depends for its operation upon
subjective and intersubjective structures that allow objective knowledge
to emerge and stabilize in the first place. Put bluntly, knowledge of sensory exteriors depends upon nonsensory interiors, interiors that are just
as real and just as important as the exteriors themselves. You don't get
a message on the telephone, claim the message is real but the phone is
illusory. To discredit one is to discredit the other.

If sensory-oriented science is not equipped to investigate these interior
domains, it nonetheless cannot deny their existence without denying its
own operations. It can no longer claim that the exteriors alone are real.
And that, very simply, completely undercuts what we called objection
number 1 (the belief that interior domains have no reality of their own).
Precisely because empirical science is forced to acknowledge interiors, it
cannot dismiss Spirit merely on the basis that Spirit is interior. The first
major objection falls.

Thus, if science wishes to continue to deny Spirit, it is forced to retreat
to objection number 2 and attempt to deny, not all interiors, but only
certain types of interiors, because, it is claimed, these other and "dis-
reputable" interiors—such as spiritual experience—cannot be verified.
They are at best merely private modes of knowing; at worst, hallucina-
tions.

Traditionally, what has spooked empirical and positivistic science
about these "interiors" is that they cannot be objectified and thus nailed
with a sensorimotor hammer, whether that hammer be a telescope, mi-

croscope, photographic plate, or whatnot. Thus traditionally, empirical science tended to a simple confusion: it claimed that its basic *methodology* covered all of the real *dimensions* of existence, whereas these are two entirely separate considerations. Once we tease apart the scientific *method* from its application to a particular *domain,* we might find that a certain spirit of scientific inquiry, honesty, and fallibilism can indeed be carried into the interior domains (which science *already* does with its own mathematics and logic). We might find that "science" in the broadest sense does not have to be confined to sensory patches, but might include a science of sensory experience, a science of mental experience, and a science of spiritual experience.

If this were so, it might go a long way to help "unspook" the interiors and set them on a much more reassuring epistemological footing. To do this, we must look a little more closely at what we mean by "science."

THE SCIENTIFIC METHOD

The notion that there exists a single, straightforward "scientific method" has long been discredited. It is almost unanimously acknowledged that there is no algorithm (no set method) for generating theories from data; the very notion was part of the myth of the given. Nonetheless, most philosophers—and certainly most working scientists—have a clear enough idea of what "doing science" actually means; enough, anyway, to differentiate scientific knowledge from poetry, faith, dogma, superstition, and nonverifiable proclamations. The scientific method might be slippery, but it still manages to get a lot of work done—it can, after all, plop a person on the moon, which presumably it could not do if it had no method at all. I believe we can in fact state some of the general ingredients in the scientific method, and I will attempt do so in a moment.

But one of the most interesting things about the scientific method is that nothing in it says that it must be applied *only* to sensory domains or to sensory experience alone. After all, we tend to think of vector analysis, logic, tensor calculus, imaginary numbers, Boolean algebra, and so on as being "scientific" in the broad sense, yet none of those are primarily empirical-sensory. Clearly, "sensory" and "scientific" are not the same thing at all.

Thus, when we look for the defining characteristics of the scientific method, we cannot make "sensory empiricism" one of them. The defining patterns of scientific knowledge must be able to embrace both biology and mathematics, both geology and anthropology, both physics and logic—some of which are sensory-empirical, some of which are not.

Part of the confusion in this area comes from the fact that, historically, "empirical" has been given two broad but quite different meanings. And, I believe, it is an understanding of these two types of empiricism that holds the key to the scientific method.

TWO TYPES OF EMPIRICISM

On the one hand, "empirical" has meant *experiential* in the broadest sense. To say that we have empirical verification simply means that we have some sort of direct experiential evidence, data, or confirmation. To be an "empiricist" in this broad sense simply means to demand *evidence* for assertions, and not merely to rely on dogma, faith, or nonverifiable conjectures.

I have a great deal of sympathy for that position. In fact, using "empirical" in the broad sense of "demand for experiential evidence," I count myself a staunch empiricist. For the fact is, there is sensory experience, mental experience, and spiritual experience—and empiricism in the very broadest sense means that we always resort to *experience* to ground our assertions about any of those domains (sensory, mental, spiritual).

Thus, there is *sensory empiricism* (of the sensorimotor world), *mental empiricism* (including logic, mathematics, semiotics, phenomenology, and hermeneutics), and *spiritual empiricism* (experiential mysticism, spiritual experiences).

In other words, there is evidence seen by the *eye of flesh* (e.g., intrinsic features of the sensorimotor world), evidence seen by the *eye of mind* (e.g., mathematics and logic and symbolic interpretations), and evidence seen by the *eye of contemplation* (e.g., satori, nirvikalpa samadhi, gnosis).

As we will see, the experiential evidence in each of these modes is actually quite *public* or shared, because each of them can be trained or educated with the help of a teacher, and an educated eye is a shared eye (or else it could not be educated in the first place). In all of these ways and more, empiricism in the broadest sense is the surest way to anchor the objective component of truth and the demand for evidence (whether of the exteriors or interiors or both), and thus *empiricism in the broadest sense* will be a crucial aspect of our validity procedures for any domain.

On the other hand, empiricism has also historically been given an extremely narrow meaning, not of experience in general, but of sensory experience alone. Moving from the profoundly important notion that all knowledge must be ultimately grounded in experience, many classical empiricists collapsed this to the absurd notion that all knowledge must be reduced to, and derived from, colored patches. The myth of the given, the brain-dead flatland stare, the monological gaze, the modern nightmare: with this impoverished empiricism, we can have little sympathy.

This dual meaning of "empiricism"—very broad and very narrow—is actually reflected in the extensive confusion about the scientific method itself, and whether it must be "empirical" or not. For the enduring strength of science—the reason it can indeed plop a person on the moon—is that it always attempts, as best it can, to rest its assertions on *evidence* and *experience*. But sensory experience is only one of several different but equally legitimate types of experience, which is precisely why mathematics—seen only inwardly, with the mind's eye—is still considered scientific (in fact, is usually considered extremely scientific!).

When we "do mathematics," we *inwardly perceive,* with the mind's eye, a whole series of symbolic and imaginative events. These are not "mere abstractions"; as any mathematician will attest, they are part of an incredibly rich stream of often quite beautiful images, patterns, scenes, and interior landscapes, which follow what seem at times to be almost divine patterns, exquisitely unfolding before the mind's eye. More astonishingly, many of the patterns in the exterior and sensorimotor world—from the motion of the planets to the speed of falling objects—happen to follow quite precisely these interior mathematical patterns. These are no mere abstractions but profound patterns embedded in the Kosmos itself, yet seen only with the mind's inward eye!

This interior mathematical *experience* is part of the essential ground of mathematical knowledge. We run the equations "through our head" and see if they *make sense*—not sensory sense but mental sense, logical sense (following any number of logics, from Boolean to n-dimensional, none of which can be seen with the eye of flesh). In mathematical proofs, we follow a *mental empiricism,* a mental experience, a mental phenomenology, and we see if the patterns connect correctly. We then *check our interior experience with others* who have run the same interior experiment, in order to see if they experienced the same result. If the majority of people who are qualified report the same interior experience, we generally call this a "mathematical proof," and we consider it a case of genuine knowledge.

Thus, a direct, interior, mental *experience* (or empiricism in the broad sense) has guided our every move through the mathematical domain, and these inwardly experiential moves can be checked—confirmed or rejected—by those who have *performed the same interior experiment* (run the proof through their minds).

So the confusion about whether "the scientific method" must be empirical depends entirely on what we mean by "empirical." Do we mean in the broad sense (experience in general), or the narrow sense (sensory experience only, the eye of flesh alone)? My point is that *science cannot mean empiricism in the narrow sense,* because that would rule out mathematics, logic, and most of the conceptual tools of science itself (not to mention psychology, history, anthropology, and sociology).

With all that in mind, let us see if we can abstract the essentials of the scientific method *in the broad sense,* which would be based on *empiricism in the broad sense.* If we can do this—and then further show that this scientific method in the broad sense is applicable to the interior domains in general (as it already is in the case of mathematics and logic)—we will have gone quite a distance in legitimating the interiors themselves (and defusing objection number 2).

We would indeed then have a science of sensory experience, a science of mental experience, and a science of spiritual experience—a monological science, a dialogical science, and a translogical science—a science of the eye of flesh, a science of the eye of mind, and a science of the eye of contemplation—with the traditional concerns of religion joining hands with the assurances of modern science.

THE THREE STRANDS OF VALID KNOWLEDGE

We begin with what appear to be some of the essentials of the scientific method in general. Having extracted these ingredients, the hope is that we will find them equally applicable to the interior domains, thus giving us a methodology that could legitimate the interiors with as much confidence as the exteriors. And the further hope is that, hidden somewhere in those newly legitimated interiors, awaits the awareness of a radiant God.

Here are what I believe are three of the essential aspects of scientific inquiry—what I will also call the "three strands of valid knowing":

1. *Practical injunction.* This is an actual practice, an exemplar, a paradigm, an experiment, an ordinance. It is always of the form "If you want to know this, do this."

2. *Direct apprehension.* This is an immediate experience of the domain brought forth by the injunction; that is, a direct experience or apprehension of data (even if the data is mediated, at the moment of experience it is immediately apprehended). William James pointed out that one of the meanings of "data" is direct and immediate experience, and science anchors all of its concrete assertions in such data.

3. *Communal confirmation (or rejection).* This is a checking of the results—the data, the evidence—with others who have adequately completed the injunctive and apprehensive strands.

To take them one a time:

In order to see the moons of Jupiter, you need a telescope. In order to understand *Hamlet,* you need to learn to read. In order to see the truth of the Pythagorean theorem, you must learn geometry. If you want to know if a cell has a nucleus, you must learn to take histological sections, learn to stain cells, learn to use a microscope, and then look. In other words, all of those forms of knowing have, as one of their significant components, an *injunction:* If you want to *know* this, you must *do* this.

This is obviously true in the sensory sciences, such as biology, but it is true as well in the mental sciences, such as mathematics. As G. Spencer Brown, in his famous *Laws of Form,* pointed out: "The primary form of mathematical communication is not description, but injunction. In this respect it is comparable with practical art forms like cookery, in which the taste of a cake, although literally indescribable, can be conveyed to a reader in the form of a set of injunctions called a recipe. . . . Even natural science [sensory-empirical] appears to be dependent on injunctions. The professional initiation of the man of science consists not so much in reading the proper textbooks [although that is also an injunction], as in obeying injunctions such as 'look down that microscope' [strand 1]. But it is not out of order for men of science, having looked down the microscope [and apprehended the data, strand 2], now to describe to each other, and to discuss among themselves, what they have seen [strand 3]. Similarly, it is not out of order for mathematicians, each having obeyed a set of injunctions [e.g., imagine two parallel lines meeting at infinity; picture the cross-section of a trapezoid; take the square of the hypotenuse], to describe to each other, and to discuss among themselves, what they have seen [with the eye of mind], and to write textbooks describing it. But in each case, the description is dependent upon, and secondary to, *the set of injunctions having been obeyed first. . . ."* (my italics).

The injunctive strand of knowledge leads to an *experience, apprehension,* or *illumination,* a direct disclosing of the data or referents in the worldspace brought forth by the injunction. Thus, if you want to know if it is raining outside, go to the window and look (the injunction). With this looking or experiencing, there is a direct apprehension ("I see the rain"). This is the immediate data, the direct experience, the intuitive or nonmediated grasp of the moment's appearance. It does not matter in the least if the *immediate* data themselves are actually embedded in chains of *mediated* events (such as culturally molded contexts), because at the moment of apprehension, even mediated events are immediately experienced (or else there would be no experience whatsoever, just endless mediation).

Thus an injunction brings forth or discloses an illumination, experience, or data, and these data are a crucial anchor of genuine knowledge. This also implies that if other competent individuals faithfully repeat the injunction or the experiment ("Go to the window and look"), they will experience roughly the same thing, the same data ("Yes, it is raining outside"). In other words, the illumination or apprehension is then *checked* (confirmed or refuted) by all those who have adequately performed the injunction and thus disclosed the data.

Science, of course, usually includes the formation of hypotheses and the testing of these hypotheses against further data accumulation, but each of those steps also follows the same three strands. The hypothesis is a mental experience that is used to represent various intrinsic features of sensory experience, and both of those—the mental map and the sensory territory—are checked for validity by following the three strands applied to their own domain. The map is thus checked against other maps for coherence, and against other sensory data for correspondence. Each of these checking procedures follows the three strands.

Evidence, Kuhn, and Popper

Those three strands, I believe, are the essential ingredients of the scientific method (and all valid modes of knowing in general, as I will try to show). This conclusion is bolstered by the fact that, of the three major schools of the philosophy of science that are most influential today—namely, empiricism, Thomas Kuhn, and Sir Karl Popper—this approach explicitly incorporates the essentials of each of them. To take them in that order.

The strength of empiricism is its demand that all knowledge be grounded in experiential evidence, and I agree entirely with that demand. But, as we saw, not only is there sensory experience, there is mental experience and spiritual experience (direct data or direct experience delivered by the eye of flesh, the eye of mind, and the eye of contemplation). Thus, if we use "experience" in its proper sense as direct apprehension, we can firmly honor the empiricists' demand that *all genuine knowledge be grounded in experience,* in data, in evidence. The empiricists, in other words, are highlighting the importance of the apprehensive or *illuminative strand* in all valid knowledge.

But evidence and data are not simply lying around waiting to be perceived by all and sundry, which is where Thomas Kuhn enters the picture.

Kuhn, as we saw, pointed out that normal science proceeds most fundamentally by way of *paradigms* or *exemplars.* A paradigm is not merely a concept, it is an actual practice, *an injunction,* a technique taken as an exemplar for generating data. And Kuhn's point is that genuine scientific knowledge is grounded in paradigms, exemplars, or injunctions. New injunctions disclose new data (new experiences), and this is why Kuhn maintained *both* that science is progressive and cumulative, and that it shows certain breaks or discontinuities (new injunctions bring forth new data). Kuhn, in other words, is highlighting the importance of the *injunctive strand* in the knowledge quest, namely, that data are not simply lying around waiting for anybody to see, but rather are brought forth by valid injunctions.

The knowledge brought forth by valid injunctions is indeed genuine knowledge precisely because, contrary to extreme postmodernism, paradigms disclose data, they do not merely invent it. (The data itself may have been given or constructed, but the disclosure itself is not merely a construction.) The validity of these data is demonstrated by the fact that *bad data can indeed be rebuffed,* which is where Popper enters the picture.

Sir Karl Popper's approach emphasizes the importance of falsifiability: genuine knowledge must be open to disproof, or else it is simply dogma in disguise. Popper, in other words, is highlighting the importance of the *confirmation/rejection strand* in all valid knowledge; and, as we will see, this falsifiability principle is operative *in every domain,* sensory to mental to spiritual.

Thus this overall approach acknowledges and incorporates the moments of truth in each of those important contributions to the quest for knowledge (evidence, Kuhn, and Popper), *but without the need to reduce those truths to sensory patches.* The mistake of the narrow empiricists is their failure to see that, in addition to sensory experience, there is mental and spiritual experience. The mistake of the Kuhnians is their failure to see that injunctions apply to all forms of valid knowledge, not just sensorimotor science. And the mistake of the Popperians is their attempt to restrict falsifiability to sensory data and thus make "falsifiable by sensory data" the criterion for mental and spiritual knowledge—thus implicitly and illegitimately rejecting those modes right at the start—whereas bad data in those domains *are indeed falsifiable,* but only by further data *in those domains,* not by data from lower domains!

For example, a bad interpretation of *Hamlet* is falsifiable, not by sensory data, but by further mental data, further interpretations—not monological data but dialogical data—generated in a community of interpreters. *Hamlet* is not about the search for a sunken treasure buried in the Pacific. That is a bad interpretation, a false interpretation, and this *falsifiability* can easily be demonstrated by any community of researchers who have adequately completed the first two strands (read the play and apprehend its various meanings).

As it is now, the Popperian falsifiability principle has one widespread and altogether perverted use: it is implicitly restricted *only to sensory data,* which, in an incredibly hidden and sneaky fashion, *automatically bars all mental and spiritual experience from the status of genuine knowledge.* This unwarranted restriction of the falsifiability principle claims to separate genuine knowledge from the dogmatic, but all it actually accomplishes, in this shrunken form, is a silent but vicious reductionism.

On the other hand, when we free the falsifiability principle from its restriction to sensory data, and set it free to police the domains of mental and spiritual data as well, it becomes an important aspect of the knowledge quest in all domains, sensory to mental to spiritual. And in each of those domains, it does indeed help us to separate the true from the false, the demonstrable from the dogmatic.

These three strands, then, will be our guide through the delicate world of the deep interiors, the within of the Kosmos, the data of the Divine, where they will help us, as they do with the exteriors, to separate the dependable from the bogus.

TO GIVE A LITTLE

If science and religion are to be integrated, each must give at least a little, without, however, deforming themselves beyond recognition. We have asked science to do nothing more than expand from narrow empiricism (sensory experience only) to broad empiricism (direct experience in general), which it already does anyway with its own conceptual operations, from logic to mathematics.

But religion, too, must give a little. And in this case, religion must open its truth claims to direct verification—or rejection—by experiential evidence. Religion, like science, will have to engage the three strands of all valid knowledge and anchor its claims in direct experience.

In this chapter, we have looked at "real science." In the next, we will look at "real religion." And perhaps we will find that, just as science can, by its own admission, expand its scope from a narrow empiricism to a broad empiricism, so religion can, as it were, restrict its scope from dogmatic proclamations to direct spiritual experience. In this move, with both parties surrendering an aspect of their traditional baggage that in fact serves neither of them well, science and religion would fast be approaching a common grounding in experiential data that finds the existence of rocks, mathematics, and Spirit equally demonstrable.

12

What Is Religion?

"RELIGION," of course, has many meanings, definitions, and proposed functions. The term has been applied to everything from dogmatic beliefs to mystical experience, from mythology to fundamentalism, from firmly held ideals to passionate faith. Moreover, scholars tend to separate the content of religion (such as belief in angels) from the function of religion (such as maintaining social cohesion), arriving at the awkward conclusion that even when the content may be dubious, the function may be beneficial. We will examine many of these definitions and proposed functions of religion as we proceed.

In the meantime, it will escape no one's attention that in referring to authentic spirituality I am largely excluding the mythological and mythopoetic themes—such as the virgin birth, the bodily ascension, the parting of the Red Sea, the birth of Lao Tzu as a nine-hundred-year-old man, the earth resting on a divine Hindu serpent, the goddess as mythic Gaia—that have formed the substance of the vast majority of the world's religious systems, whether existing in the premodern world or carrying over into the modern.

I am not claiming that these beliefs are unimportant or that they serve no function at all. In fact, they serve a very important developmental or evolutionary function; but as we will see, with the irreversible differentiations of modernity, most of those premodern beliefs and functions of religion are no longer legitimate and can no longer be sustained in modern consciousness (except among those who remain at a premodern level in their own development).

I am therefore claiming that when it comes to a modern science of spirituality (a science of direct spiritual experience and data), those mythological themes—and mythology itself—will form no essential part of authentic spirituality. Isn't this rather drastic? And how many religions would agree with this claim?

As we began to see in the previous chapter, if science and religion are to be integrated, each of them will obviously have to give a little—and yet, I maintain, not so much as to deform them and make them unrecognizable to themselves. We saw that science needs to recognize that its own method rests, not on empiricism in the narrow sense (sensory experience), but on empiricism in the broad sense (experience in general), and this is not a very difficult stretch because virtually all of science's own conceptual apparatus (from logic to mathematics) is *already* empirical in the broad sense.

We simply ask science *to form a more accurate self-image:* to surrender its narrower and inaccurate conception of itself for a broader and more accurate (and already implicitly accepted) conception of itself. Most philosophers of science have already done so, as we saw: "Classical empiricism is a myth."

Likewise, we must ask religion to accept *a more authentic self-image* of its own possibilities. Particularly in the wake of the irreversible differentiations of modernity, religion must seriously ask itself: What is the actual cognitive content and validity of its claims? Did Moses really part the Red Sea? Was Jesus actually borne by a virgin? Does the earth really rest on a divine serpent? Did creation really occur in six days? Was Lao Tzu actually nine hundred years old when he was born?

If those proclamations are quietly put aside, what is left of religion that it can call its own? And would it still indeed recognize itself?

MYTHOLOGY AND POWER

Religious *mythological* proclamations are clearly *dogmatic,* which means that when they are taken to be literal truths, they are simply asserted without any supporting evidence. As such, they fail the test of the three strands of valid knowledge. At one time, those beliefs performed various important cultural functions, such as maintaining social cohesion, because they formed the basis of a legitimate (or consensual) intersubjective worldview. But with the differentiations and increased depth of the dignity of modernity, a more sophisticated truth disclosure placed these mythological claims in irreversible doubt.

With each developmental unfolding, the truths of the higher domain place the truths of the lower domains into a profoundly different context, a context that, because it transcends and includes its juniors, also *preserves* and *negates* various features of its predecessors. Modernity *preserved* many of the aspirations, ideals, and values expressed in the best of mythology (such as retribution and justice) but *negated* most of its literal contents (such as the notion that we all actually descended from Adam and Eve).

This is why I depart from most modern sociologists, who generally maintain that mythology has no cognitive value at all (its claims are bogus), yet it nonetheless forms an indispensable social glue and cohesive force for many cultures. This is an incoherent position. Humans cannot live on cognitive falsity alone. Mythology is true enough in its own worldspace; it's just that perspectival reason is "more true": more developed, more differentiated-and-integrated, and more sophisticated in its capacity to disclose verifiable knowledge.

Thus the higher truths of rationality pass judgment on the lower truths of mythology, and for the most part mythology simply does not survive those more sophisticated tests. Moses did not part the Red Sea, and Jesus was not borne by a biological virgin. Those claims, in the light of a higher reason, are indeed bogus.

Of course, premodern revivalists often read deeply metaphorical meanings into mythology (e.g., the virgin birth is really a metaphor for the pure and "immaculate" nature of our higher Self), claiming that it communicates and delivers truths that are higher than reason. This is a double duplicity: first, because this approach actually uses reason to explain some deep truth for which mythology is supposed to be superior, and second, because it then reads this truth into mythology in a way that believers in the myth do not accept at all. For a true believer, the virgin birth is absolutely *not* a metaphor but a concrete, literal, historical fact (one the premodern revivalist actually denies!). The premodern revivalist simply uses the higher powers of reason to read deeper truths into a mythic symbol that itself rarely if ever carried any such meaning for its actual believers, and thus the premodern revivalist, attempting to elevate myth above reason, conceals two deceptions in every utterance: reason is robbed of its actual contribution while mythology is given credit for what it does not possess. This double lie is offered to humanity as a source of spiritual transformation.

But the fact remains: the concrete-literal forms of mythology cannot withstand—and have not withstood—the tests of modernity: those concrete claims are indeed bogus. And *if religion is to survive in a viable form in the modern world, it must be willing to jettison its bogus claims,* just as narrow science must be willing to jettison its reductionistic imperialism.

The real problem is that the mythic, mythological, and mythopoetic approaches to spirituality all involve various types of *mental* forms attempting to explain *transmental* and *spiritual* domains, and however phase-specifically appropriate those approaches might have been for the premodern mythic era, they will no longer work on a collective or even individual level. Mythology will not stand up to the irreversible differentiations of modernity; it confuses prerational with transrational; it fosters regressive ethical and cognitive modes; it hides from any sort of validity claims and actual evidence; and thus avoiding truth, is left only with power as one of its prime motives.

Because evidence undoes mythology, mythology intrinsically hides from evidence. Thus mythology is—and historically has been—a massive source of personal and social oppression. This is why the Enlightenment, as Habermas points out, always understood itself as a *counterforce to mythology.* The clarion call of the Enlightenment was for *evidence,* not for myths, because these myths, despite the lovely halo given them by today's premodern revivalists, were in fact a source of brutal social hierarchies, gender oppression, wholesale slavery, and barbaric torture. "Remember the cruelties!" was indeed the battle cry of the Enlightenment, and for precisely that reason.

The Enlightenment thus maintained that those who come to you with mythology come with hidden (or not so hidden) power drives. Those who attempt to wield these forms of myth hide from evidence, understandably: *to expose their claims to evidence would rob those claims of their power*—and thus rob the owners of those claims of their power, too. Thus hidden from truth and seated in power, they seek to enclose others in that same darkness, usually in the name of their God or Goddess. It is no accident that wars fought in whole or part in the name of a particular mythic Deity have historically killed more human beings than any other intentional force on the planet. The Enlightenment pointed out—quite rightly—that religious claims hiding from evidence are not the voice of God or Goddess, but merely the voice of men or women, who usually come with big guns and bigger egos. Power, not truth, drives claims that hide from evidence.

THE CONTEMPLATIVE CORE

Authentic spirituality, then, can no longer be merely mythic, imaginal, mythological, or mythopoetic: it must be based on actual evidence. In other words, it must be, at its core, a series of direct mystical, transcendental, meditative, contemplative, or yogic experiences—*not sensory* and *not mental,* but supramental, transpersonal, transcendental consciousness—data seen not merely with the eye of flesh or with the eye of mind, but with the eye of contemplation.

Authentic spirituality, in short, must be based on direct spiritual experience, and this must be rigorously subjected to the three strands of valid knowledge: injunction, apprehension, and confirmation/rejection—or exemplar, data, and falsifiability.

With the differentiations of modernity, premodern religions of every variety faced an unprecedented situation: precisely because modernity differentiated the value spheres and let them proceed unencumbered and with their own dignity, these newly liberated spheres quickly outpaced in most ways anything the premodern religions could offer. When it came to the world of sensory facts, the answers given by premodern religion (e.g., the earth was created in six days) now faced modern empirical science, and it was simply no contest. When it came to the mental sphere and its operations, religion faced modern developments in mathematics, logic, critical philosophy, philology, and hermeneutics (including the *real* sources of the biblical narratives), and once again premodern religion was no match for the differentiations of modernity.

It is only when religion emphasizes its heart and soul and essence—namely, direct mystical experience and transcendental consciousness, which is disclosed not by the eye of flesh (give that to science) nor by the eye of mind (give that to philosophy) but rather by the eye of contemplation—that religion can both stand up to modernity and offer something for which modernity has desperate need: a genuine, verifiable, repeatable injunction to bring forth the spiritual domain.

Religion in the modern and postmodern world will rest on its unique strength—namely, contemplation—or it will serve merely to support a premodern, predifferentiated level of development in its own adherents: not an engine of growth and transformation, but a regressive, antiliberal, reactionary force of lesser engagements.

But the thorny question remains: Can religion recognize itself if it brackets (or temporarily sets aside) its mythic baggage? For an answer,

I suggest we look at the example, not of the followers, but of the founders, of the major religions themselves.

REAL AND BOGUS

The first thing we can't help but notice is that the founders of the great traditions, almost without exception, underwent a series of profound *spiritual experiences*. Their revelations, *their direct spiritual experiences,* were *not* mythological proclamations about the parting of the Red Sea or about how to make the beans grow, but rather direct apprehensions of the Divine (Spirit, Emptiness, Deity, the Absolute). At their peak, these apprehensions were about the direct union or even identity of the individual and Spirit, a union that is not to be thought as a mental belief but lived as a direct experience, the very *summum bonum* of existence, the *direct realization of which* confers a great liberation, rebirth, metanoia, or enlightenment on the soul fortunate enough to be immersed in that extraordinary union, a union that is the ground, the goal, the source, and the salvation of the entire world.

And what each of those spiritual pioneers gave to their disciples was *not* a series of mythological or dogmatic beliefs but a series of practices, injunctions, or exemplars: "Do this in remembrance of me." The "do this"—the injunctions—included specific types of contemplative prayer, extensive instructions for yoga, specific meditation practices, and actual interior exemplars: if you want to *know* this Divine union, you must *do* this.

These injunctions reproduced in the disciples the spiritual experiences or the spiritual data of the evolutionary pioneers. In the course of subsequent interior experiments (over the decades and sometimes centuries), these injunctions and data were often refined and sophisticated, with initial or preliminary methods and data polished in the direction of more astute observations. Of numerous examples: the growth and evolution of Hinayana Buddhism into Mahayana Buddhism, which grew and evolved into the magnificent Vajrayana; the exquisite growth of Jewish mysticism through Hasidim and Kabbalah; the great Hindu flowering from the early Vedas to the extraordinary Shankara to the unsurpassed Ramana Maharshi; the six centuries of refinement from Plato to Plotinus.

On the other hand, the moment that any particular spiritual lineage stopped this exploratory and experimental process—that is, the moment it ceased to employ all three strands in the spiritual quest—it began to harden into mere dogma or mythological proclamations, devoid of direct evidence and experience or the power to transform, and it then served merely to translatively console isolated egos in their immortality projects, instead of transcending the ego in the great liberation of a radiant and spiritual splendor.

The conclusion seems obvious: when the eye of contemplation is abandoned, religion is left only with the eye of mind—where it is sliced to shreds by modern philosophy—and the eye of flesh—where it is crucified by modern science. If religion possesses something that is *uniquely* its own, it is contemplation. Moreover, it is the eye of contemplation, adequately employed, that follows all three strands of valid knowing. Thus religion's great, enduring, and unique strength is that, at its core, *it is a science of spiritual experience* (using "science" in the broad sense as direct experience, in any domain, that submits to the three strands of injunction, data, and confirmation).

Thus, if science can surrender its narrow empiricism for a broader empiricism (which it *already* does anyway), and if religion can surrender its bogus mythic claims in favor of authentic spiritual experience (which its founders uniformly did anyway), then suddenly, very suddenly, science and religion begin to look more like fraternal twins than centuries-old enemies.

For it then becomes perfectly obvious that the real battle is not between science, which is "real," and religion, which is "bogus," but rather between real science and religion, on the one hand, and bogus science and religion, on the other. *Both* real science and real religion follow the three strands of valid knowledge accumulation, while both bogus science (pseudoscience) and bogus religion (mythic and dogmatic) fail that test miserably. Thus, real science and real religion are actually *allied* against the bogus and the dogmatic and the nonverifiable and the nonfalsifiable in their respective spheres.

If we are to effect a genuine integration of science and religion, it will have to be an integration of real science and real religion, not bogus science and bogus religion. And that means each camp must jettison its narrow and/or dogmatic remnants, and thus accept a more accurate self-concept, a more accurate image of its own estate.

THE EYE OF CONTEMPLATION

We have seen that all valid forms of knowledge have an injunction, an illumination, and a confirmation; this is true whether we are looking at the moons of Jupiter, the Pythagorean theorem, the meaning of *Hamlet,* or . . . the existence of Spirit.

And where the moons of Jupiter can be disclosed by the eye of flesh or its extensions (sensory data), and the Pythagorean theorem can be disclosed by the eye of mind and its inward apprehensions (mental data), the nature of Spirit can be disclosed only by the *eye of contemplation* and its directly disclosed referents: the direct experiences, apprehensions, and data of the spiritual domain.

But in order to gain access to any of these valid modes of knowing, I must be *adequate* to the injunction—I must successfully complete the injunctive strand, I must follow the exemplar. This is true in the physical sciences, the mental sciences, and the spiritual sciences. And where the exemplar in the physical sciences might be a telescope, and in the mental sciences might be linguistic interpretation, in the spiritual sciences the exemplar, the injunction, the paradigm, the practice is: meditation or contemplation. It too has its injunctions, its illuminations, and its confirmations, all of which are repeatable—verifiable or falsifiable—and all of which therefore constitute a perfectly valid mode of knowledge acquisition.

But in all cases, we must engage the injunction. We must take up the exemplary practice, and this is certainly true for the spiritual sciences as well. If we do not take up the injunctive practice, we will not have a genuine paradigm, and therefore we will never see the data of the spiritual domain. We will in effect be no different from the churchmen who refused to follow Galileo's injunction and look through the telescope itself.

Let us examine more closely what this spiritual injunction might mean, and why it might indeed constitute a spiritual science.

TRAINING IN SPIRITUAL SCIENCE

Zen Buddhism has a reputation as a "no-nonsense" school of spiritual discipline. It therefore serves well as a classic example of a science of spiritual experience. The following points can as easily be made with Vedanta, Christian contemplation, meditative Taoism, Neo-Confucianism, or Sufi meditation, to name a few. But Zen's "hardheadedness" might make it easier for scientists who are getting the religion tour for the first time and worrying considerably where Mr. Toad's Wild Ride is leading.

A typical Zen story begins with the student earnestly asking the Master a deeply troubling question, such as what is the meaning of life, why am I here, what or where is Buddha, and so on. The Master in turn might ask a counterquestion, some of which might be very straightforward ("Who is it that wants to know?"), but some of which are famously nonsensical ("What is the sound of one hand clapping?"). In a sense, these are all variations on "Show me your spiritual understanding right now! Show me your Buddha nature, right now!"

The Zen Master, of course, will reject every imaginable intellectual response. A clever student might say, "We are all strands in the great Web of Life." That is exactly a wrong answer, because it is a *mental* response, not a directly transmental, transconceptual, or spiritual response. A more advanced student might yawn, jump up and down, or slap the floor. This is at least getting closer, in that the action is direct and immediate, not some sort of mental chatter. But the Zen Master, in all cases, wants to see direct evidence of immediate realization apprehended with the eye of contemplation, not some sort of intellectual philosophy seen with the eye of mind. Any intellectual response will be radically rejected, no matter what its content!

Rather, the new student, in order to gain this spiritual knowledge, must take up an *injunction,* a paradigm, an exemplar, a practice, which in this case is *zazen,* sitting meditation. And—to make a very long and complex story brutally short—after an average of five or six years of this exemplary training, the student may begin to have a series of profound illuminations. And it's very hard to believe that over the years hundreds of thousands of students would go through this extended hell in order to be rewarded only with an epileptic fit or a schizophrenic hallucination.

No, this is Ph.D. training in the realm of spiritual data. And once this injunctive training begins to bear fruit, a series of illuminations or apprehensions—commonly called "kensho" or "satori"—begin to flash forth into direct and immediate awareness, and this data is then checked (confirmed or rejected) by the community of those who have completed the injunctive and the illuminative strands. At this point, the answer to the question "What or where is Buddha nature (or Godhead or Spirit)?" will become extremely clear and straightforward.

When the Zen Master then asks you where Buddha is, you will directly and immediately give the answer, and if it springs from a deep and spontaneous realization, the Master will recognize it immediately. The answer is not coming merely from some colored sensory patches, nor from some mental symbols or myths or rational abstractions, but directly from a contemplative realization that is so utterly simple and obvious that Zen says it is just like having a glass of cold water thrown in your face.

But the point is, the actual *answer* to the question "Does Spirit exist?"—the technically correct and precise answer is: satori. The technically correct answer is: Take up the injunction, perform the experiment, gather the data (the experiences), and check them with a community of the similarly adequate.

We cannot mentally *state* what the answer is other than that, because if we did, we would have merely words without injunctions, and they would indeed be utterly meaningless. As G. Spencer Brown said, it's very like baking a pie: you follow the recipe (the injunctions), you bake the pie, and then you actually taste it. To the question "What does the pie taste like?," we can only give the recipe to those who inquire and let them bake it and taste it themselves.

Likewise with the existence of Spirit: we *cannot* theoretically or verbally or philosophically or rationally or mentally describe the answer in any other ultimately satisfactory fashion except to say: *engage the injunction*. If you want to *know* this, you must *do* this. Any other approach and we would be trying to use the eye of mind to see or state that which can be seen only with the eye of contemplation, and thus we would have nothing but metaphysics in the very worst sense—statements without evidence.

Thus: take up the injunction or paradigm of meditation; practice and polish that cognitive tool until awareness learns to discern the incredibly subtle phenomena of spiritual data; check your observations with others who have done so, much as mathematicians will check their interior proofs with others who have completed the injunctions; and thus confirm or reject your results. And in the verification of that transcendental data, the existence of Spirit will become radically clear—at least as clear as rocks are to the eye of flesh and geometry is to the eye of mind.

PROOF OF GOD'S EXISTENCE

We have seen that authentic spirituality is not the product of the eye of flesh and its sensory empiricism, nor the eye of mind and its rational empiricism, but only, finally, the eye of contemplation and its spiritual empiricism (religious experience, spiritual illumination, or satori, by whatever name).

In the West, since Kant—and since the differentiations of modernity—religion (and metaphysics in general) has fallen on hard times. I maintain that it has done so precisely because it attempted to do with the eye of mind that which can be done only with the eye of contemplation. Because the mind could not actually deliver the metaphysical goods, and yet kept loudly claiming that it could, somebody was bound to blow the whistle and demand real evidence. Kant made the demand, and metaphysics collapsed—and rightly so, in its typical form.

Neither sensory empiricism, nor pure reason, nor practical reason, nor any combination thereof can see into the realm of Spirit. In the smoking ruins left by Kant, the only possible conclusion is that all future metaphysics and *authentic spirituality* must offer *direct experiential evidence*. And that means, in addition to *sensory experience* and its empiricism (scientific and pragmatic) and *mental experience* and its rationalism (pure and practical), there must be added *spiritual experience* and its mysticism (spiritual practice and its experiential data).

The possibility of the direct apprehension of sensory experience, mental experience, and spiritual experience radically defuses the Kantian objections and sets the knowledge quest firmly on the road of evidence, with each of its truth claims guided by the three strands of all valid knowledge (injunction, apprehension, confirmation; or exemplars, data, falsifiability) *applied at every level* (sensory, mental, spiritual—or across the entire spectrum of consciousness, however many levels we wish to invoke). Guided by the three strands, the truth claims of real science and real religion can indeed be redeemed. They carry cash value. And the cash is experiential evidence, sensory to mental to spiritual.

With this approach, religion regains its proper warrant, which is not sensory or mythic or mental but finally contemplative. The great and secret message of the experimental mystics the world over is that, with the eye of contemplation, Spirit can be seen. With the eye of contemplation, God can be seen. With the eye of contemplation, the great Within radiantly unfolds.

And in all cases, the eye with which you see God is the same eye with which God sees you: the eye of contemplation.

13

The Stunning Display of Spirit

I F THERE IS INDEED a genuine spiritual science, what does it disclose? What does it tell us? And can it really be verified?

NARROW SCIENCE AND BROAD SCIENCE

We have seen that both "empiricism" and "science" have a narrow and a broad meaning (or shallow and deep, depending on your metaphor). Broad empiricism is experience in general (sensory, mental, spiritual), whereas narrow empiricism is sensory experience only. Science per se, or the scientific method, consists of the three strands of valid knowing (exemplar, experience, validation). *Narrow science* confines its use of the three strands to sensory experience only (it follows narrow empiricism), whereas *broad science* applies the three strands to any and all direct experience, evidence, and data (it follows broad empiricism).

Modern empirical science tended to reject the interiors because they (mistakenly) appeared opaque to the scientific method. But, as we have seen, the interiors themselves are in fact accessible, not to narrow science, but to broad science, because the interiors of the I and WE can be experientially explored, investigated, reported, confirmed or rejected using the three strands of all valid knowledge accumulation—using, that is, broad science or deep science.

Thus, we are aiming for a broad science of all four quadrants, not a narrow science of the Right-Hand quadrants only. We are looking for a deep science that includes not just the exteriors of ITs but the interiors of I and WE. We are looking for a deep science of self and self-expression and aesthetics; of morals and ethics and values and meaning; as well as of objects and ITS and processes and systems.

Thus, the Big Three—art, objective science, and morals—can be brought together under one roof using the core methodology of deep empiricism and deep science (the three strands of all valid knowledge). *The I and the WE are finally put on an equal footing with the IT,* NOT by reducing the I and the WE to ITS (whether interwoven or holistic or "new paradigm" or otherwise), but by seeing that all three, just as they are, can be equally accessed using the same general methodology: the three strands of broad science. Broad science (or deep science or deep empiricism) can in fact guide our search in each domain, without the necessity to deform one domain to make it "compatible" with the others. The three strands of deep science *separate the valid from the bogus in each quadrant* (or simply in each of the Big Three), helping us to separate not only true propositions from false propositions, but also authentic self-expression from lying, beauty from degradation, and moral aspirations from deceit and deception.

This move *simultaneously* gives to empirical science its nonnegotiable demand that the scientific method be employed for truth accumulation, yet also relieves narrow science from its imperialism by pointing out that the scientific method can apply as fully and as fruitfully to broad empiricism as to narrow empiricism. This brings broad science to the interior domains of direct mental and spiritual experience: shallow science opens to deep science.

With this move, science is both *satisfied* that its central method is still the epistemological cornerstone of all inquiry (without which it will accept no proposed integration whatsoever), yet also *limited* in its imperialism by the recognition that its own narrow empiricism of ITS can gracefully exist alongside the broad empiricism of I's and WE's, since all are equally and confidently covered by broad science.

The four quadrants (or simply the Big Three) can thus be genuinely united, joined, and integrated under the auspices of a deep science that is as operative in profound mystical experience as in geology, as applicable to moral aspirations as to biology, as dependable in hermeneutics as in physics. None of these domains need to be reduced to the others, tortured to fit some "new paradigm," or twisted beyond recognition in order to "fit" some integrative scheme. Each domain, just as it is, is allowed its own dignity, its own logic, its own architecture, its own form and structure and content—yet each is joined and united by the thread of direct experience and evidence, a deep empiricism that grounds all knowledge in experience and all claims in verifiability.

A BROAD SCIENCE OF EACH QUADRANT

This integration promises to be a genuine unity-in-diversity. The domains are importantly different and are allowed to be so, but their access follows a similar pattern of disclosure and verification or rejection—namely, the three strands of deep science. This unity-in-diversity is like one flashlight investigating different caves: the light is the same, but the actual form of the investigation will take on different contours in each cave. The same light will disclose different territories, as it should be.

Thus, when we apply the three strands of deep science to the Upper-Right quadrant, this gives us the sciences of the *exteriors* of *individual* holons: physics, chemistry, geology, biology, neurology, medicine, behaviorism, and so forth. I have listed these in Figure 13-1, along with some recognized pioneers in these fields.

Applying the three strands of deep science to the Lower-Right quadrant gives us the sciences of the *exteriors* of *communal* holons: ecology, systems theory, exterior holism, sociology, and so on. In humans, these "exterior sociological" approaches have included those of such notables as Auguste Comte, Karl Marx, Talcott Parsons, and Niklas Luhmann.

A deep science of the Upper-Left quadrant gives us the terrain, the data, the contours of the *interiors* of *individual* holons. In the human realm, this includes not only the more formal structures that are disclosed inwardly to the mind's eye—such as logic and mathematics—but also the more personal contours disclosed by introspective psychology and depth psychology. This is likewise the domain of self and self-expression, art and aesthetics, and mental phenomenology in general.

Moreover, as we will see in a moment, with the *higher stages of interior development,* genuinely spiritual or mystical experiences begin to unfold, and these, too, can be investigated and validated with the three strands of deep science applied to the advanced stages of the Upper-Left quadrant (I did not list any of these higher stages in Figure 5-1, because that figure covers only average evolution up to this point; it does not include higher evolution, which will be discussed in a moment). Pioneers in this quadrant have included Sigmund Freud, C. G. Jung, Alfred Adler, Jean Piaget, St. John of the Cross, St. Teresa of Ávila, Ralph Waldo Emerson, Plotinus, Shankara, Chih-I, and Gautama Buddha.

INTERIOR	EXTERIOR
· Interpretive	· Monological
· Hermeneutic	· Empirical, positivistic
· Consciousness	· Form

	INTERIOR	EXTERIOR
INDIVIDUAL	Sigmund Freud C. G. Jung Jean Piaget Sri Aurobindo Plotinus Gautama Buddha	B. F. Skinner John Watson John Locke Empiricism Behaviorism Physics, biology, neurology, etc.
COLLECTIVE	Thomas Kuhn Wilhelm Dilthey Jean Gebser Max Weber Hans-Georg Gadamer	Systems Theory Talcott Parsons Auguste Comte Karl Marx Gerhard Lenski

FIGURE 13-1. *Broad Sciences of the Four Quadrants*

A broad science of the Lower-Left quadrant reveals the *interiors* of *communal* holons, the intersubjective signs, values, shared cultural meanings and worldviews of a given culture. Unlike the social sciences of the Lower Right, which tend to focus on exterior systems and the monological data of a society (its birthrates, population size, dietary patterns, forces of techno-economic production, types of monetary exchange, information flowcharts, feedback loops, and so on, all of which can be described in it-language), *cultural studies* focus on the shared meanings and intersubjective values that act as the interior glue for members of the society (all of which are significantly described in we-language, and therefore must be studied as a "participant observer").

Thus, social system sciences ask, "What does it do?" or "How does it work?," whereas interpretive and cultural sciences ask instead, "What does it mean?" They approach a culture not from the outside, in an objectifying and distancing stance, but rather from the inside, from the within, in a stance of mutual understanding and recognition. Both approaches are useful and necessary, the one investigating the communal holon from the outside (Right Hand), the other from the inside (Left Hand). Pioneers in cultural hermeneutics include Friederich Schleiermacher, Wilhelm Dilthey, Martin Heidegger, Jean Gebser, Hans-Georg Gadamer, Thomas Kuhn, Mary Douglas, Peter Berger, and Charles Taylor.

We can start to see that although the three strands of deep science (or valid knowledge accumulation) guide our research in each of the quadrants—thus giving us a methodological integrity capable of integrating all four quadrants (or simply the Big Three)—nonetheless, because the quadrants each have very different contours and types of data, we find different "types of truth" in each of the quadrants, and these differences need to be acknowledged and honored. They are the "diversity" part of the unity-in-diversity, and this diversity is every bit as important as the unity.

These different types of equally important truths are referred to as *validity claims*. Each time the same broad science is applied to a different quadrant, it generates a different type of truth: objective truth (behavioral), subjective truth (intentional), interobjective truth (social systems), and intersubjective truth (cultural justness). One method, many truths, each therefore equally dependable.

The Spiritual Domains

But if that is so, where does Spirit fit into this scheme?

As I began to suggest in the last chapter, there *already* exist numerous spiritual disciplines that carefully follow the three strands of valid knowledge accumulation, disciplines that are therefore, in effect, authentic spiritual sciences (not exterior sciences but interior sciences, following not narrow empiricism but deep empiricism). These spiritual sciences include the contemplative and meditative traditions of a collective humanity, East and West, North and South, traditions that have been carefully collecting interior spiritual data for at least three thousand years, and traditions that, in deep structure analysis, show a surprising unanimity as to the basic architecture of the higher or spiritual stages of human development.

Moreover, the modern discipline known as *transpersonal psychology and psychiatry* has taken, as one of its tasks, the scientific investigation of these higher stages of human and spiritual development, and it, too, has discovered a striking similarity of these higher stages, across individuals and across cultures. (If you are interested in pursuing the details of these discoveries, excellent transpersonal anthologies include *Paths Beyond Ego*, edited by Roger Walsh and Frances Vaughan; *Textbook of Transpersonal Psychiatry and Psychology*, edited by Bruce Scotton, Allan Chinen, and John Battista; *What Really Matters—Searching for Wisdom in America*, by Tony Schwartz.)

What transpersonal psychology has discovered, and what the contemplative traditions themselves disclose, is that beyond the typical rational-egoic stages of development ("formop" and "vision-logic" in Figure 5-1), there appear to be at least *four higher stages of consciousness development.*

These higher stages have been given many different names; I refer to them as the psychic, the subtle, the causal, and the nondual. Each of these stages appears to have a quite different type of direct spiritual experience associated with it: nature mysticism, deity mysticism, formless mysticism, and nondual mysticism. (For a detailed discussion of these findings, see *Transformations of Consciousness, A Brief History of Everything,* and *Integral Psychology.*)

Now those particular names and experiences are not so important. What is important is that the transpersonal domains themselves appear to consist of at least four major stages of spiritual development, with different types of data and experiences disclosed at each of those verifiable stages.

Here is the point: if, with reference to the Upper-Left quadrant, we take the stages of human development as carefully outlined by modern developmental psychology (and summarized in Figure 5-1, sensation to vision-logic), and if we *add* the four higher and transpersonal stages (psychic to nondual), *the result is exactly the traditional Great Chain of Being* (as shown, for example, in Table 2-1).

THE MEETING OF PREMODERN AND MODERN

This is fascinating. The deep sciences of the Upper-Left quadrant (from modern developmental psychology to the contemplative sciences) converge on the traditional Great Chain of Being, exactly as disclosed in the core of the premodern religions. The Great Chain, in this regard, receives a stunning vindication by deep science.

But look at what this also means: for each and every one of the wisdom traditions, the Great Chain of Being covered the whole of reality. But we have just seen that, in the light of the differentiations of modernity (the differentiation of the Big Three, or the four quadrants in general), *the Great Chain, apart from its lowest level, actually covers only the Upper-Left quadrant.* It is far from the whole of reality; it is, as it were, merely one fourth of reality!

And that is exactly why the traditional Great Chain did not, and could not, survive the differentiations of modernity. Because the Great Chain, in effect, covered only "one fourth" of the overall Kosmos— namely, the interior dimensions of the individual from prepersonal to personal to transpersonal—it had no conception of, and thus no way to answer, the stunning discoveries in the other three quadrants, including the amazing discoveries about the brain and consciousness (Upper Right), or about how cultural worldviews affect individuals' perceptions (Lower Left), or about how the social conditions of a culture shape the values of its people (the Lower Right). All of those quadrants were either lumped together as "matter" (the Upper Right and Lower Right) or ignored altogether (the Lower Left)—*precisely because, in the premodern view, these were still largely undifferentiated.*

Every one of those quadrants thus launched a series of devastating attacks against the Great Chain, and, for the most part, those attacks were altogether correct. The modern and differentiated disciplines of physics, chemistry, biology, linguistics, hermeneutics, systems theory, philology, semiotics, anthropology, and sociology tore into the premodern and predifferentiated worldview with a vengeance, and neither the Great Chain, nor the spiritual worldviews associated with it, ever recovered.

Just as egregious, the Great Chain theorists, to the extent they acknowledged the Right-Hand quadrants, placed all of them on the lowest rung in the Great Chain, namely, the material level. All of the higher levels (including vital body and mind) were thus "transcendent" to the material body. But the differentiations of modernity disclosed that the "material" domains are not so much the lowest rung on the great hierarchy as they are the exterior forms of *each and every rung* on the hierarchy.

(You can easily see this in Figure 5-1. The Right-Hand or material components are not the lowest level of the hierarchy, they are simply the objective correlates of each and every Left-Hand component. They are not lower and higher, but outer and inner. The material neocortex, for example, is not on the lowest level; it is the correlative, exterior form of advanced self-reflexive consciousness and is intimately interwoven with it. The Right Hand is not lower than the Left: they are the exterior and the interior of any given level of existence. This, with few exceptions, the Great Chain theorists missed entirely, so that the Great Chain remained largely an Upper-Left quadrant affair, accurate as far as it went.)

Thus, with the differentiations of modernity, we can clearly see that the traditional Great Chain occupies, as it were, not all of reality, but one fourth. In other words, *the Great Chain is now firmly situated within the differentiations of modernity,* something that had never happened in any premodern culture. The Great Chain is vindicated in its essential contours, but it is basically situated in the Upper-Left quadrant, taking its place alongside the other three—and equally important— quadrants, each of which brings its own irreducible truths to bear on the overall picture.

But this is exactly what we set out to do in the beginning of this book, namely, to find some scheme that could accommodate both premodern and modern worldviews, and thus integrate religion and science. Since the core of premodern religion was the Great Chain, and since the essence of modernity was the differentiation of the value spheres (the Big Three or the four quadrants), then *in order to integrate religion and science, we sought to integrate the Great Chain with the four quadrants.* We have just done so.

Should this integration prove to be sound, as I believe it will, the Great Chain of Being can take its rightful place within the differentiations of modernity. The massive amounts of data from the traditional spiritual sciences can then be correlated and integrated with the equally massive amounts of data from the modern objective sciences (such as biology, neurology, and medicine), the cultural sciences (such as hermeneutics, semiotics, and political theory), and the social sciences (such as systems analysis, ecology, and sociology).

Since these quadrants are all interrelated and mutually interdependent, the Great Chain itself could not exist without them. And it is only by acknowledging, honoring, and including all four quadrants that the long-sought integration of premodern religion and modern science might finally become a reality.

We are now ready to explore exactly how this extensive integration might occur.

PART FOUR

THE PATH AHEAD

14

The Great Holarchy in the Postmodern World

THIS IS WHAT we have seen. The Great Chain of Being—from gross body to conceptual mind to subtle soul to causal spirit, with each expanding sphere enveloping its juniors—was the essential core of the world's great wisdom traditions. No major culture in history was without grounding in some version of this Great Holarchy.

Until, that is, the rise of the modern West. In the wake of the Enlightenment, the modern West became the first significant culture to radically deny the Great Nest of Being—or, more specifically, to deny all but its lowest sphere, matter. Gone the mind, gone the soul, gone the spirit, and in their place, the unending nightmare of monochrome surfaces, the disqualified universe of flatland holism, the great and utterly meaningless system of dynamically interwoven ITS. Bertrand Russell was unerringly accurate when he reported that "Blind to good and evil, reckless of destruction, omnipotent matter rolls on its relentless way. All these things, if not beyond dispute, are yet so nearly certain that *no philosophy that rejects them can hope to stand*" (my italics).

Matter, energy, and information—whether atomistic or systems-oriented, whether static or dynamic processes, whether classical thermodynamics or order-out-of-chaos complexity theories—*are all ITS*, and this epidemic "IT-ism" (with no room for the I or the WE in their own terms) was the final mark of official modernity, the strange and distorted legacy of the Western Enlightenment. Thus, to put it mildly, the attempt to integrate premodern religion and modern science has been more than a little daunting, since scientific materialism seems so utterly uncompromising, and "no philosophy that rejects [it] can possibly hope to stand."

It is therefore routine, in virtually all of today's attempts to integrate science and spirituality, to claim that the rise of modern science contributed directly to, or even caused, the "disenchantment of the world." The common and widespread view is that the modern West with its modern science, more or less in one major step, massively rejected Spirit, God and Goddess, sacred nature and immortal soul—and left us with the modern wasteland.

The claim that modernity itself, in one very bad move, rejected the spiritual, now dominates most discourse in this area. This is a typical claim: "The desacrimentalization or devaluation of nature that was begun by the scientific revolution was completed by what is called 'the enlightenment.' " That claim has likewise been made by deep ecologists, neopagans, ecofeminists, radical feminists, wiccans, neoastrologers, theosophists, retro-Romantics, and virtually all of the "new-paradigm" theorists.

Yet we have seen that modernity's rejection of the spiritual actually involved not one but two quite different moves, one of which was very good and one of which was very bad. By teasing apart these two steps, we were able to distinguish between the dignity and the disaster of modernity, and this allowed us the first genuine foothold in the sought-for integration.

For, as we saw, the rise of modernity in the West was marked most essentially by the widespread differentiation of the cultural values spheres (of art, morals, and science), spheres that, in premodern cultures, tended to be fused, undifferentiated, or indissociated, so that violence or oppression in one sphere tended to bleed into the others. But with the rise of modernity and the differentiation of the spheres, you could look through Galileo's telescope without being burned at the stake, and you could paint nature without the image of a patriarchal God if that was your desire.

But within a century or so, this differentiation of the spheres—which was the enduring dignity of modernity—began to drift into a dramatic dissociation—which was the horrifying disaster of modernity. The Big Three (of art, morals, and science) splintered and fragmented, and this epidemic *alienation* began to invade and corrupt every corner of modernity itself.

Most egregious of all, sensory-empirical and systems science, in league with industrialization—*since both of them were aggressive "it" endeavors*—began to assault and dominate the other spheres. The colonialization and commodification of the I and the WE by the rampant IT came to define the disaster of modernity. The interior domains altogether—consciousness, soul, spirit, mind, values, virtue, meaning—were all reduced to frisky dust, to order-out-of-chaos process ITs. And so, in this fractured fairy tale, the modern West became the first major culture in all of history to deny the Great Holarchy of Being—and in its place, omnipotent matter, atomistic or systemic or informational ITs, the reign of the unending surface.

Precisely because we can now see that this historic denial occurred, not in one but in two steps, we can more accurately see what of modernity must be treasured—*and therefore integrated*—and what can be discarded. What needs to be integrated is not the dissociations but the differentiations of modernity, for not only do these define the dignity of modernity, they are an *irreversible* part of the evolutionary process of differentiation-and-integration. Modernity has *already* given us these irreversible differentiations—we couldn't undo them even if we tried. What is now required is their *integration,* or the inclusion of all three value spheres (or all four quadrants) in a more encompassing embrace. It is not necessary to attempt to integrate spirituality with the collapsed Kosmos or with the disaster of modernity; it is necessary only to integrate spirituality with the differentiated Kosmos or the dignity of modernity.

Thus, precisely because the essence of the premodern religions was the Great Chain, and because the essence of modernity was the differentiation of the value spheres (the four quadrants, or simply the Big Three), then in order to integrate modern science and premodern religion it is necessary to *integrate the Great Chain with the four quadrants.*

We did exactly that in the last chapter. Here are some of the implications of what we found.

LEVEL AND DIMENSION

Using the three strands of all valid knowledge (paradigm, experience, confirmation), we were able to suggest a way to integrate the four quadrants with the traditional Great Holarchy of Being. In doing so, we found that each level in the traditional Great Chain is not a single, uniform, monolithic plane (as was traditionally thought), but rather, *each level of the Great Chain actually consists of at least four dimensions or four quadrants.* Each level has a subjective, objective, intersubjective, and interobjective dimension—intentional (Upper Left), behavioral (Upper Right), cultural (Lower Left), and social (Lower Right).

The words "level" and "dimension" are deliberately chosen. In a five-story building, each of its floors is a level, with some floors being higher or lower than others. But the length and width of each floor are its dimensions; neither length nor width is better than the other, and both dimensions are equally present and equally important—you can't have one without the other.

Thus, if we picture the Great Chain as body, mind, soul, and spirit, then *each of those levels* has an intentional, behavioral, cultural, and social dimension. You can see many of these in Figure 5-1, which covers evolution up to the mental levels, and I will give examples of the higher levels as we proceed.

One of our scales therefore involves vertical levels (the traditional Great Chain), and one involves the horizontal dimensions present on each and every level (the four quadrants). In integrating these two scales, we therefore look for the four quadrants (or simply the Big Three) on each of the levels of the traditional Great Holarchy of Being (but *only* to the extent that those levels themselves pass the test of deep science; any "levels" that do not pass the test of deep science, we are not obliged to integrate, for we then have no guarantees that they are real or genuine, and we are not interested in integrating dogma).

Thus, if we continue to use the simple version of the Great Chain—body, mind, soul, and spirit—and if, also for convenience, we shorten the four quadrants to the Big Three (of art, morals, and objective science), then we would have four levels with three dimensions each: the art, morals, and science of the sensory realm; the art, morals, and science of the mental realm; the art, morals, and science of the soul realm; and the art, morals, and science of the spirit realm.

What remains is to give some concrete examples of each of those twelve domains. I am going to give several specific details, some of which you might agree with, some of which you might not; I would ask that you simply take this as a series of examples of how we might proceed in this multidimensional endeavor. If you wish to use other details, or different ones altogether, fine. Don't let my particular details detract from the general procedure. Also, I am going to make these examples deliberately brief and sketchy, so as to not crowd the reader with my own version of events.

LEVELS OF ART

The four levels we are using, in this simplified account, are the sensorimotor, the mental, the subtle soul, and the causal spirit. Each level, as always, transcends and includes its predecessors, so there is nothing mutually exclusive about any of these levels. It is simply that each senior level possesses emergent qualities not found in its juniors, and the art of each level often takes these new, emergent, and defining characteristics as the topic for aesthetic appreciation, *thus giving each level of art a very distinctive stamp* (precisely the same is true for the levels of morals and of science, as we will see). I will use the visual arts, but any will do.

The art of the sensorimotor world takes as its content or referent the sensory world itself, as perceived with the eye of flesh, from realistic impressions to landscapes to portraiture. This is "objective" art or representational art, and whether the art objects are bowls of fruit, landscapes, industrial towns, nudes, railroad tracks, mountains, or rivers, they are all sensorimotor objects. Typical examples include the realists, the Impressionists, and the entire tradition of naturalism.

The art of the mental domain takes as its referent the actual contents of the psyche itself, as interiorly perceived with the eye of mind. The Surrealists are the most obvious; but conceptual art, abstract art, and abstract expressionism are also typical examples. Marcel Duchamp summarized the general point: "I wanted to get away from the physical aspect of painting. I was much more interested in recreating *ideas* in painting. I wanted to put painting once again at the service of the mind"—and not simply the eye of flesh.

But this is not "mental abstraction" in the dry sense. The inward empiricism of the eye of mind—from mathematics to mental art—is actually experience in some of its deepest, richest, most intense textures. As Constantin Brancusi almost screamed out, "They are imbeciles who call my work abstract; that which they call abstract is the most realist, because what is real is not the exterior form but the idea, the essence of things." Mental art attempts to give visual expression to just those ideas and essences.

The art of the subtle level takes as its content or referent various illuminations, visions, and archetypal forms, as inwardly and directly perceived with the beginning eye of contemplation (or transpersonal awareness by whatever name). It is, we might say, *soul art*, as František Kupka stated, "Yes, [this] painting means clothing the processes of the human soul in plastic forms."

This means, of course, that the artists themselves must have evolved or developed into the subtle domain, as Wassily Kandinsky knew: "Only with higher development does the circle of experience of different beings and objects grow wider. Construction on a purely spiritual basis is a slow business. The artist must train not only his mind *but also his soul*" (my italics).

In the Eastern traditions, one of the main functions of this soul art is to serve as a support for contemplation. In the extraordinary tradition of Tibetan *thangka* painting, for example, the buddhas and bodhisattvas that are depicted are not symbolic or metaphoric or allegorical, but rather direct representations of one's own subtle-level potentials. By visualizing these subtle forms in meditation, one opens oneself to those corresponding potentials in one's own being.

The point is that soul art, of any variety, is not metaphoric or allegorical; *it is a direct depiction of the direct experience of the subtle level*. It is not a painting of sensory objects seen with the eye of flesh, and it is not a painting of conceptual objects seen with the eye of mind; it is a painting of subtle objects seen with the eye of contemplation.

That means that artist and critic and viewer alike must be alive to that higher domain in order to participate in this art. As Brancusi reminded us, "Look at my works until you see them. Those who are closer to God have seen them." As Kandinsky put it, the aim is to "proclaim the reign of Spirit . . . to proclaim light from light, the flowing light of the Godhead," all seen, not with the eye of flesh or the eye of mind, but with the eye of contemplation, and then rendered into artistic material form as a reminder of, and a call to, that extraordinary vision.

As the eye of contemplation deepens, and consciousness evolves from the subtle to the causal (and nondual), subtle forms give way to the formless (e.g., *nirvikalpa, ayin, nirodh*) and eventually to the nondual (*sahaja*), which I will together treat as the domain of pure Spirit. The art of this domain takes no particular referent at all, because it is bound to no realm whatsoever. It might therefore *take its referent from any or all levels*—from the sensorimotor/body level (such as in a Zen landscape) to the subtle and causal levels (such as in Tibetan *thangka*s). What characterizes this art is not its content, but the utter absence of the self-contraction in the artist who paints it, an absence that, in the greatest of this art, can at least temporarily evoke a similar freedom in the viewer (which was Schopenhauer's profound insight about the power of great art: it brings transcendence).

But all we need note is that the aesthetic-expressive dimension—the dimension of subjective intentionality and individual interiors—can express and represent any of the levels of the Great Chain, from gross to subtle to causal to nondual, depending upon which level the artists themselves are alive to.

Art, then, is one of the important dimensions of every level in the Great Holarchy of Being. Art is the Beauty of Spirit as it expresses itself on each and every level of its own manifestation. Art is in the eye of the beholder, in the I of the beholder: Art is the I of Spirit.

LEVELS OF MORALS

Developmental psychologists have charted the major stages of moral development in both men and women, and, although the details vary considerably, there is a widespread and general consensus that moral development moves from stages that are *preconventional* (sensorimotor, hedonistic, egocentric, magic-impulsive) to *conventional* (conformist, sociocentric, mythic-membership) to *postconventional* (worldcentric, rational-centauric, universal). You can see many of these on Figure 5-1. Carol Gilligan has suggested that men progress through this hierarchy with an emphasis on justice and rights, whereas women tend to develop through the same hierarchy with an emphasis on relationship and care (Gilligan's three hierarchical female stages she calls selfish, care, and universal care, which are the preconventional, conventional, and post-conventional stages).

None of these moral structures can be exteriorly seen, of course, because they are interior structures, but structures that nonetheless govern an individual's behavior in the sensory-empirical world. They are, we might say, as real as logic or linguistics or any other authentic interior domain, and they can be studied (and validated) by *a deep science of the intersubjective world*, which is exactly what Piaget, Kohlberg, and Gilligan did (to name a very few).

Both Kohlberg and Gilligan (and, in fact, a now-extensive number of major moral theorists) have suggested that there is a still higher stage of moral development, which Kohlberg called "universal spiritual." Transpersonal researchers, based on an increasing body of evidence collected by a deep science of the interior, have further suggested that what Kohlberg called "one" spiritual stage has at least three or four subdivisions (as we saw). Let us, for this brief example, simply say that the evidence at this point strongly suggests that there are at least two higher stages of moral development, which I will again simply call subtle soul (saint or bodhisattva) and causal spirit (sage or *siddha*).

The morals of the subtle-soul level, the bodhisattva level, typically involve the deep aspiration to gain enlightenment for all sentient beings (literally). This extraordinary aspiration, which arises spontaneously from the depths of the soul, is based on the growing perception that all sentient beings are direct manifestations of the Divine, and thus are to be treated as manifestations of one's own deepest Being and Self.

The morals of the causal-spirit level, the sage level, involve the paradoxical aspiration to free all sentient beings by realizing that all beings are always already and eternally free. This direct realization of the radically self-liberated nature of all manifestation is behind some of the most sublime (and paradoxical) of the spiritual sciences, and stands as a self-confirming testament of Spirit's timelessly free nature.

What all of that tells us, of course, is that there are levels of moral development, and these levels appear to span the Great Chain from body (hedonistic, preconventional) to mind (conventional and postconventional) to subtle (saintly) to causal (sagely).

Morality, in other words, is one of the important dimensions of every level in the Great Holarchy of Being. Morals are the intersubjective form of Spirit, the Good of Spirit, as it expresses itself on each and every level of its own manifestation. Morals are the We of Spirit.

THE NEW ROLE OF SCIENCE

By levels of science I mean levels of objective, exterior, sensory-empirical science. We are not at this point talking about broad science or deep science (the three strands of all valid knowledge wherever they are applied, interior or exterior). We are talking about traditional empirical science. For the crucial point is that sensory-empirical science, although it cannot see into the higher and interior domains on their own terms, can nonetheless register their empirical correlates. The whole point about the differentiations of modernity is that all interior events have exterior correlates (all holons have both a Left- and a Right-Hand dimension), and this dramatically but *dramatically* changes the role of sensory-empirical science itself.

For objective empirical science is no longer relegated to the bottom rung of the hierarchy (which the traditional approach gave it and which contemporary epistemological pluralism still gives it); rather, empirical science is accessing the *exterior* modes of *all of the higher levels as well.* This moves empirical science off of the bottom level of the Great Chain and places it on the exterior side of each level of the Great Chain. (You can see this in Figure 5-1.) Thus, objective empirical science does not give the whole story, but neither does it have nothing to say about the higher domains, which is the untenable stance of both traditional and contemporary epistemological pluralism (and the crushing error that contributed to the collapse of the Great Chain).

Moreover, this allows us to thoroughly "ground" or "embody" metaphysical or transcendental claims, in effect providing a seamless union of transcendental and empirical, otherworldly and this-worldly. For the higher levels themselves are not *above* the natural or empirical or objective, they are *within* the natural and empirical and objective. Not on top of, but alongside of. Spirit does not physically rise above nature (or the Right-Hand world); Spirit is the interior of nature, the within of the Kosmos. We do not look up, we look within.

This union of Left and Right, interior and exterior, is a type of transcendental naturalism or naturalistic transcendentalism—a union of otherworldly and this-worldly, ascending and descending, spiritual and natural—a union that avoids, I believe, the insuperable difficulties of either position taken alone.

We saw that one way to summarize the premodern worldview is that it largely emphasized the interior domains (the Great Chain itself, except for its lowest level, is entirely interior and transcendental), and one way to summarize the modern worldview is that it is largely exterior (naturalistic and Right-Hand-oriented). Thus, a type of transcendental naturalism, uniting Left and Right, interior and exterior, transcendental and empirical, is therefore just another way to summarize the marriage of the best of premodern wisdom and modern knowledge.

LEVELS OF SCIENCE

With that prologue, we can now look at the actual levels of sensory-empirical science. In one sense, of course, there are no levels of sensory-empirical science: it simply registers the facts of the sensorimotor world, period. That is true enough; but these "sensorimotor facts" are the exteriors of interiors that are themselves graded in value and meaning and morals and art, and empirical science is perfectly designed to spot the exterior correlates of these interiors.

Here is a simple example. In 1970, R. K. Wallace published "Physiological Effects of Transcendental Meditation" in the prestigious journal *Science*. Wallace's (and others' subsequent) research demonstrated that people in a meditative state display very real and sometimes very dramatic changes in the body's physiology, including everything from blood chemistry to brain-wave patterns. On the basis of this *repeatable data,* Wallace concluded that the meditative state is a "fourth state of consciousness," as real as the waking, dreaming, and deep sleep states (because, for example, all four states have signature brain patterns as disclosed on an EEG machine).

This research arguably did more to legitimize the meditative state (at least for the Western mind) than all the Upanishads put together. For this research clearly demonstrated that, whatever else meditation is, it is no mere subjective fantasy, ineffectual daydreaming, or inert trance. It produces dramatic and repeatable changes in the entire organism, and most significantly in the electrical patterns of the brain itself, presumably the seat of consciousness.

The question then arises, "But what is the actual meaning of this fourth state? What does it tell us?" And the only possible answer is "Enter that state yourself and find out." For the almost universal consensus of those who do is that this state begins to disclose the Divine.

"Ah," retorts the empirical scientist, "the EEG did not show that the meditators were seeing Spirit or the Divine or some sort of genuinely mystical state. All the EEG showed was that there are empirical differences in the brain waves of the meditative state. You have no right to conclude that the meditative state is a Divine reality, or a higher reality, or that it is in some way more real than the other states."

Correct, but that statement is true for all states on the EEG. When you are in the dream state, perhaps dreaming of seeing a unicorn, the EEG will register a particular pattern. When you wake up, the EEG will register a different pattern. *Subjectively,* you realize that the unicorn of the dream state does not really exist, and so you say the waking state is real and the dream was not real. *But the EEG registers each of them as equally real.* The *objective* machine cannot decide on *subjective* realities, only on the empirical or exterior correlates of those realities.

In other words, the empirical machine gives us the *quantitative* (Right-Hand) but not the *qualitative* (Left-Hand) aspects of these different states. And nothing on the machine says, or can say, that one state is more real or more valuable or more meaningful than another; it can only say that one is different from another. It cannot say that compassion is better than murder, or that truthfulness is better than deceit, or that tolerance is better than bigotry, or that care is better than neglect, only that they are different. The machine can register only changes in size, magnitude, and quantity—all valueless in themselves—whereas the qualitative differences are seen *only* by the inward eye of mind or the inward eye of contemplation, all of which equally register on the neutrally objective machine.

Thus, the empirical scientist is right that the EEG will not say that this fourth state of consciousness is more real (or is disclosing higher realities) than the other states. But neither will the EEG machine say that waking is more real than dreaming or compassion better than murder. If empirical scientists maintain that waking is more real than dreaming, or compassion better than murder, or tolerance better than bigotry, then they will likewise have to hold open the possibility that the meditative state is an opening to the Divine even more real than waking, because that is exactly what is subjectively announced in all of those cases.

And they can actually *check (or refute) that claim using deep science:* namely, take up the injunction or paradigm of meditation; gather the data, the direct experience, the apprehensions that are disclosed by the injunction; compare and contrast the resultant data with that of others who have completed the first two strands. (Those who refuse this injunction are simply not allowed to vote on the truth of the proposition, just as the churchmen who refused to look through Galileo's telescope were not competent to form an opinion about the existence of the moons of Jupiter.)

Of those who do take up the injunction, the strong consensus is that, in this fourth state of consciousness, qualities and insights and freedoms most often characterized as "spiritual" come increasingly to the fore. An expanded sense of self, consciousness, compassion, love, care, responsibility, and concern, tend gradually but insistently to enter awareness. (These claims, too, can—and have—been subjected to empirical and phenomenological tests. See *The Eye of Spirit* for a summary of this research.)

In short, it appears that the very contours of the Divine begin more clearly and more intensely to manifest through this fourth state of consciousness. Subjectively, it is experienced as an increase in precisely those qualities often termed "spiritual" (from awareness to love to compassion), while objectively, it registers in a distinctive set of physiological changes in the organism, including signature brain-wave patterns.

As for the meditative state itself, recent research has begun to reveal numerous levels or sublevels of "the" meditative state, each of which has a distinctive brain-wave pattern (or other empirical correlates). I will, again, simply use two meditative states, traditionally referred to as *"savikalpa samadhi"* and *"nirvikalpa samadhi."*

Savikalpa is "meditation with form," and *nirvikalpa* is "formless meditation." *Savikalpa* produces *subjectively* various displays of archetypal illumination, expansive states of deeply felt love and compassion, and profound motivations to be of service to others; while *objectively* there tends to be brain-hemispheric synchronization (among other things).

Nirvikalpa produces *subjectively* complete cessation of all mental activity, a radically *formless* consciousness that at the same time is experienced as immense (even infinite) freedom and boundless existence, the great Abyss or Emptiness from which all manifestation emerges; while *objectively* there tend to be several rather striking changes in the empirical organism, one of the most stunning of which includes, on occasion, the almost complete cessation of alpha, beta, and theta brain waves, but a large increase in delta waves (usually associated only with deep, dreamless sleep, except that in this case the subject is wide awake and superalert).

Thus, when we talk about *levels of sensory-empirical science,* we mean levels of the interiors (seen with the eye of mind or the eye of contemplation) as they register in the objective and exterior world (seen with the eye of flesh or its extensions—seen, that is, by modern empirical science). We mean the Right-Hand correlates of the Left-Hand worlds (precisely because all holons, without exception, have both Left- and Right-Hand dimensions).

Objective science, then, is one of the important dimensions of every level in the Great Holarchy of Being. Science is the exterior of Spirit, the objective Truth of Spirit, the surface of Spirit, as it expresses itself on each and every level of its own manifestation. Science is the It of Spirit.

THE FACES OF SPIRIT

We have seen that each vertical level of the Great Holarchy has four horizontal dimensions or quadrants—intentional, behavioral, cultural, and social—or simply the Big Three of art, morals, and science; the Beautiful, the Good, and the True; I, WE, and IT.

The Good, the True, and the Beautiful, then, are simply the faces of

Spirit as it shines in this world. Spirit seen subjectively is Beauty, the I of Spirit. Spirit seen intersubjectively is the Good, the We of Spirit. And Spirit seen objectively is the True, the It of Spirit.

From the time before time, from the very beginning, the Good and the True and the Beautiful were Spirit whispering to us from the deepest sources of our own true being, calling to us from the essence of our own estate, a whispering voice that always said, love to infinity and find me there, love to eternity and I will be there, love to the boundless corners of the Kosmos and all will be shown to you.

And whenever we pause, and enter the quiet, and rest in the utter stillness, we can hear that whispering voice calling to us still: never forget the Good, and never forget the True, and never forget the Beautiful, for these are the faces of your own deepest Self, freely shown to you.

15

The Integral Agenda

I F WE HAVE SEEN a way to integrate the Great Holarchy of Being with the differentiations of modernity, thus integrating premodern religion and modern science, the question is, what next?

THE PRENUPTIAL AGREEMENT

We have seen that the three strands of deep science (injunction, apprehension, confirmation; or paradigm, data, verification) apply not only to exterior experience; they are the means whereby we decide if a particular interior experience carries genuine knowledge and cognitive content, or whether it is merely hallucinatory, dogmatic, bogus, idiosyncratic, or personal preference. Any interior experience that passes the test of deep science may be provisionally regarded as *genuine knowledge*—that is, it tells us something *real,* something *actual,* about the contours of the Kosmos.

Although many of the claims of the premodern religions cannot pass the test of deep science—and therefore must, at this point, be considered dogmatic, nonverifiable, or bogus—nonetheless the esoteric core of the premodern religions consists not of a series of mythic and nonfalsifiable beliefs, but a series of contemplative practices, actual interior experiments in consciousness, grounded in direct experience. Yoga, *zazen, shikan-taza, satsang,* contemplative prayer, *zikr, daven,* t'ai chi—these are not beliefs, these are injunctions, exemplars, practices, paradigms.

Thus, the great contemplative traditions (from Zen to Sufism to Kabbalah to mystical Christianity) are, in every sense of the word, a deep science of the spiritual interiors, and they have universally concluded that there are *levels of interior experience.* These levels of consciousness are, of course, the Great Chain of Being. Specific mythic beliefs vary dramatically from religion to religion, and it is virtually impossible to construct a universal theology based on these often wildly differing myths. But the Great Holarchy, in one form or another, is the single common framework found in virtually all of the major religions, and thus it is the Great Chain itself that must be included in the long-sought integration.

It is exactly here that the various religions must carefully focus their concerns and make their own modest compromises. Religions the world over will have to *bracket their mythic beliefs,* beliefs such as Moses parting the Red Sea or Lao Tzu being nine hundred years old at birth. I am not asking the more fundamentally oriented faithful to reject those beliefs, merely to set them aside for a moment. For it is abundantly clear that we cannot have any sort of integration of modern science with those specific mythic beliefs. In fact, we cannot have any sort of common ground among the world's religions themselves based on mythic beliefs. For, as we were saying, the myths differ so much in details and content that if one of the ten thousand myths is right, 9,999 are dead wrong. This is no way to build a consensus.

Instead, each religion needs to focus on those aspects of its tradition that were disclosed by its own deep science of the interiors, whether the contemplative prayer of St. Teresa of Ávila, the yoga of Patanjali, the vision quest of tundra shamanism, the *zikr* of Rumi, the self-inquiry of Sri Ramana Maharshi, the *shikan-taza* of Bodhidharma, the contemplation of Isaac of Akko, or the meditation of Lady Tsogyal and Padmasambhava, to name a very few. We have been summarizing all of those interior sciences by saying that they universally point to the Great Nest of Being, body to mind to subtle soul to causal spirit, by whatever names.

Each religion can, with modest discomfort, look to the Great Chain in its own tradition, and temporarily bracket its specific, exclusive, proprietary, dogmatic, mythic beliefs. Those beliefs may be true, they may not be true—but so far, they have dramatically failed to pass the test of deep science. Therefore they are not something that science itself (narrow or deep) will accept as valid knowledge, and thus they are not going to be a part of any marriage that science will accept.

But the deep sciences of the interior domains, disclosed by direct experiential evidence and data, evoked by repeatable injunctions, and open to confirmation or rejection by a community of the adequate—those deep sciences are the core of the great wisdom traditions and the core of the Great Chain, and those deep sciences of the spiritual interiors are precisely the genuine knowledge that religion, holding its head high, can bring to the integrative table.

The Great Holarchy itself is more than enough to get the conversation started, and more than enough to serve as a frame to anchor any ongoing integration. *Coupled with the differentiations of modernity and submitted to the tests of deep science,* the Great Chain and its newfound validity ought to be enough foundation for any religion, and on that frame proponents can hang whatever mythic beliefs they want, as long as they do not expect any form of science or any other religion to acknowledge them.

At the same time, this does not mean that we will lose all religious differences and local color and fall into a uniform mush of homogenized New-Age spirituality. The Great Chain is simply the skeleton of any individual's approach to the Divine, and on that skeleton each individual, and each religion, will bring appropriate flesh and bones and guts and glory. Most religions will continue to offer sacraments, solace, and myths (and other translative or horizontal consolations), in addition to the genuinely transformative practices of vertical contemplation. None of that necessarily needs to change dramatically for any religion, although it will be set in a larger context that no longer demands that its myths be the only myths in the world.

EVOLUTION

Religion will also have to adjust its attitude toward evolution in general. I maintain that, contrary to all appearances, this is a *modest* adjustment, because the Great Chain itself is already fully compatible with an evolutionary view. As has often been pointed out, evolution is actually not much more than the Great Chain *temporalized.* That is, if you look at the traditional Great Holarchy as presented by, say, Plotinus or Aurobindo (Table 2-1), it becomes obvious that the *levels of the Great Chain* are actually some of the *major stages of evolution.* As you can see in Figure 5-1, science tells us that the universe has evolved from matter to sensations (in neuronal organisms) to perceptions (with the emergence of the neural cord) to impulses (in reptiles) to images (in mammals) to concepts (in humans). And those are exactly the beginning levels of the Great Chain itself. As the Idealists pointed out, the Great Chain is not given all at once, it unfolds (or evolves) over time; and the stages of evolution given by science closely match the corresponding stages given by the Great Chain theorists.

Thus, to the extent religions bracket their mythic beliefs and focus on their esoteric core (the Great Chain), an acceptance of evolution is a modest adjustment indeed. In fact, Aurobindo has already brought Vedanta (and the entire sweep of Indian philosophy) into an evolutionary accord. Abraham Isaac Kook has already pointed out that "The theory of evolution accords with the secrets of Kabbalah better than any other theory." The great Idealists have already cleared the way for an evolutionary spirituality. And has not the Pope himself finally declared that "evolution is more than a hypothesis"?

What makes it especially hard for some religions to come to terms with evolution is not only their reliance on dogmatic mythic beliefs, but also their commitment to a retro-Romantic view. This view tends to confuse the differentiations (and dignity) of modernity with the dissociations (and disaster) of modernity, and thus it tends to see in modernity nothing but an antispiritual, antireligious desacralization of the world, with the modern West being akin to the Great Satan.

But, as we saw, the modern West is actually an intense combination of good news, bad news. The self or *subject* of rationality was *deeper* than the subject or self of mythology (i.e., the mental-egoic self has *more depth* than the mythic-membership self, because it transcends and includes the essentials of its predecessor). However—solely because of the collapse of the Kosmos—the *object* of rationality (which was confined to sensorimotor flatland) was much less deep than the object of mythology (which was the Divine order, however crudely or anthropomorphically depicted). Thus, *a much deeper subject confined its attention to a much shallower object.* And there, in a nutshell, the combination of dignity and disaster that is the paradox of modernity: a deeper subject in a shallower world.

But retro-Romanticism of every variety imagines that the mythological era itself contained deeper subjects that were subsequently lost and must be regained (in a "mature" form), and that profound error at the very heart of Romanticism guarantees that it and its allies, failing to see that there is no future in the past, will forever be at odds with the general thrust of evolution itself. To the extent that a religion pledges allegiance to a mythic Eden in any actual sense, it will have insuperable difficulty participating in the integration of modern science and spirituality.

The evolutionary or developmental view does not simply praise one epoch and condemn another. Rather, each epoch, each era, each stage of cultural evolution brings with it important truths, valuable insights, and profound revelations. The general evolutionary or developmental view, precisely because it transcends and includes the important truths of each and every one of its stages, takes all important truths with it, enfolded in its own ongoing embrace, and thus honors and includes more truths than any of the alternatives. This means that an evolutionary view is the most viable chariot for a truly integrative stance, extending an embrace that, by any other name, is genuinely compassionate. And if pathology is to be avoided, these truths must be taken up and included in subsequent stages of evolution. Each stage is true, each succeeding stage is "more true": it contains the previous truths and then adds its own, emergent, novel truths, thus both including and transcending its predecessors.

This is not elitist, and it offers no reason for any epoch (even ours) to picture itself as privileged, because it, too, is destined to pass, to be transcended and included in tomorrow's greater embrace. We are, all of us, tomorrow's food. Thus, not only does a developmental or evolutionary view generously give to each period its own important truths, it gives to the present its own appropriate humility.

DEEP SCIENCE RESEARCH

One of the most pressing agendas for this integral view is what might be called an "all-level, all-quadrant" approach to research. This research would *attempt to investigate the various phenomena in each of the four quadrants*—subjective states, objective behavior, intersubjective structures, and interobjective systems—*and correlate each with the others*, without trying to reduce them to the others. This integral approach is a harmonization of the broad sciences of all of the levels in each of the quadrants: thus, "all-level, all-quadrant." Let me give two or three quick examples, relating specifically to psychological and spiritual growth, to show what might be involved.

I mentioned earlier that evolution in general is not much more than the Great Chain temporalized. If we again take Plotinus and Aurobindo as representative examples (see Table 2-1), we can see that evolution so far has unfolded about the first three fourths of the Great Chain, from matter to life function to sensation to perception to emotions to images to concepts to formop to vision-logic. But what about the highest fourth, the stages beyond reason? What about the subtle and causal, the Overmind and the Supermind? If evolution unfolded the first three fourths, is not there every reason to suppose that it will eventually unfold the highest fourth as well? And that, therefore, the levels of soul and Spirit, Overmind and Supermind, lie not in our collective past but in our collective future? And that true religion, far from being a reactionary force yearning for a lost yesteryear, would become, for the first time in history, the vanguard of a progressive, liberal, and evolutionary force?

That, of course, was one of the basic insights of Idealism, and, as far as it goes, there are good reasons to suppose it might indeed be true. This, no doubt, was also one of the great appeals of Father Pierre Teilhard de Chardin, whose notion of the Omega point (of Christ consciousness) as a future attractor for present evolution—a notion borrowed from Schelling and Hegel—freed many Christians from the impossible mythic belief in a literal Garden of Eden and a morbid fixation (a Romantic death wish) to the long-deceased past. This idea is likewise behind the extraordinary integral yoga of Sri Aurobindo, arguably the greatest spiritual-evolutionary theorist.

Should it prove to be the case that future evolution is in the process of collectively unfolding the yet higher stages of the Great Chain, as it has already unfolded the lower, it would give real religion—genuine spirituality and the deep sciences of the interior—an unprecedented role as the vanguard of evolution, the growing tip of the universal organism, growing toward its own highest potentials, namely, the ever-unfolding realization and actualization of Spirit.

Those, of course, are grand themes. Although there is considerable evidence to suggest that those themes are at least a genuine possibility (see *Up from Eden*), I would here like to focus on *individual* growth and evolution, because we can *already* do some profound and direct research on just this possibility. That is, we can already do extensive research on *the higher stages of individual growth and development*—the higher stages of moral growth, cognitive growth, affective growth, and interpersonal growth—using, of course, the deep science of the Upper-Left quadrant.

In fact, a good deal of orthodox research has already been done in each of those domains, evidenced in such groundbreaking research reports as *Higher Stages of Human Development* (Alexander and Langer),

Transcendence and Mature Thought in Adulthood (Miller and Cook-Greuter), *The Future of the Body* (Michael Murphy), and *Beyond Formal Operations* (Commons, Richards, and Armon), and summarized in *A Brief History of Everything* [and *Integral Psychology.*]

The conclusion of all of this research is that, as we briefly saw in the last chapter, there are indeed several major stages of development beyond the formal-rational stage—higher stages of cognitive, affective, and moral development, among others. What we have here, in other words, is *the deep science of the higher stages of development or evolution in the Upper-Left quadrant.*

What remains to be done is to begin correlating this data with the simultaneous and corresponding *changes in the other quadrants,* thus generating an "all-level, all-quadrant" integral view. For example, what happens to brain physiology, neurotransmitter levels, and the organic body itself when individuals move through these higher developmental stages? What types of worldviews are generated from these higher stages? How might these higher worldviews affect our political, social, and cultural institutions? If these higher spiritual stages are in fact stages of our own greater potentials, what types of integral techniques could facilitate this evolutionary growth? How will higher stages of growth affect our democratic institutions, our educational policies, and our economics? How will higher development alter the practice of medicine? law? government? politics?

In short, *how will these stages of our own higher evolution manifest in all four quadrants?* What higher art and science and morals await us? And what should we do about it now?

Political Awareness

Those are simply a few of the questions that we can ask, and perhaps begin to answer, with a truly integrative view. What I want to emphasize here is that this "all-level, all-quadrant" or *integral approach* is the direct result of the harmonization of premodern religion (all-level) with the differentiations of modernity (all-quadrant). And this integral approach forces us, as it were, to realize that any integration of science and religion is going to be much more than just that.

For example, what tends to be missing in most of the attempts to integrate science and religion is a deep discussion of its political dimensions. For modern science is part and parcel of the liberal Enlightenment and the differentiations of modernity, differentiations that brought with them the rise of the representative democracies, universal human rights, and the ideas of freedom and equality of all individuals, which in turn gave rise to everything from the abolition of slavery to feminism. Modern science was an integral part of this differentiated worldspace, in which those freedoms, values, and rights arose, and thus to talk genuinely and deeply of the integration of science and religion is to talk, sooner or later, of politics.

The core of the liberal Enlightenment was the assertion that *the state does not have the right to legislate or promote any particular version of the good life.* This can be put in several different ways: the state cannot legislate morality; there is a separation of church and state; the individual has the right to decide what constitutes his or her own happiness, as long as it does not violate the rights of others; the state may not unduly infringe on an individual's private life. These extraordinary freedoms— the product of differentiating the I and the WE—were part of the great dignity of modernity, of which modern science was an *inseparable* aspect.

This is why so much of the "new-paradigm" talk is profoundly off the mark. In the retro-Romantic versions, the dedifferentiation that is recommended would, if actually pressed into service, erase these freedoms and dignities. In the complexity theory versions, the political dimension is simply ignored (because monological science deals only with ITs, not with I's and WE's, and thus these "new paradigms" have nothing substantial to contribute to politics). In the "quantum society" versions, the political and dialogical are rudely reduced to the monological, thus devastating precisely that which is claimed to be healed.

No, if there is to be a genuine integration of modern science and premodern religion, it will have political dimensions sewn into its very fabric. And just as the integration of modern science and premodern religion actually involved the integration of the differentiations of modernity with the Great Chain of Being, so the political integration of modernity and premodernity would involve the integration of the Enlightenment of the West with the Enlightenment of the East.

By the Enlightenment of the East I simply mean *any genuine spiritual experience,* whether of East or West. It is simply that the Eastern traditions have demonstrated, on balance, a somewhat more widespread reliance on a deep science of the interior, made most famous in Gautama Buddha's enlightenment under the Bodhi tree around the sixth century B.C.E. But any direct spiritual realization—East or West, North or

South—conforming to the tenets of deep science could just as well serve as an example (Plotinus, Eckhart, Catherine of Siena, al-Hallaj, St. Teresa, Boehme, Rumi, St. Augustine, Origen, Hildegard, Baal Shem Tov, Dame Julian, etc.).

This spiritual Enlightenment is, by the virtually unanimous consensus of the higher sciences, the *summum bonum* of the Good life. And yet, by the tenets of the Enlightenment of the West, which must also be preserved, the state cannot in any way advocate or legislate in favor of this spiritual Enlightenment. The state must stay out of the business of publicly legislating the Good life, which belongs to the private sphere of each individual's own choice.

The only possible way to integrate these two demands is to realize that the *summum bonum* of the Good life lies not on this, but on the other, side of the political liberalism of the Enlightenment. That is, spiritual or transrational awareness is *trans*liberal awareness, not *pre*liberal awareness. It is *not reactionary* and *regressive*, it is *evolutionary* and *progressive* ("progressive" being one of the common terms for "liberal").

Thus, genuine spiritual experience (or spiritual Enlightenment) as it displays itself in the political arena is not prerational mythic belief—which almost always wishes to coerce others to that belief, whether the belief be in God or Goddess, patriarchy or matriarchy, Gaia or otherwise—but rather transrational awareness, which, *building on the gains of liberal rationality and political liberalism,* extends those freedoms from the political to the spiritual sphere.

Thus, spiritual or transrational awareness accepts the general tenets of rational political liberalism (not prerational mythic reactionism), but then, within those freedoms, pursues spiritual Enlightenment in its own case; and, through the powers of advocacy and example, encourages others to use their liberal freedom—the Enlightenment of the West—in order to pursue spiritual freedom—the Enlightenment of the East.

The result, we might say, is a liberal Spirit, a liberal God, a liberal Goddess. Or, more accurately, postliberal or transliberal, in that it transcends and includes the best of both liberalism and conservatism. In common with *traditional liberalism,* this stance agrees that the state shall not legislate the Good life. But with *traditional conservatism,* this stance places Spirit—and all its manifestations—at the very heart of the Good life, a Good life that therefore includes relationships in all domains, from family to community to nation to globe to Kosmos to the Heart of the Kosmos itself, by any other name, God.

(Traditional conservatism is in many important ways anchored in premodern worldviews—from mythic religion to civic humanism—whereas liberalism is largely anchored in the rational differentiations of modernity. Thus, the integration of premodern religion with the differentiations of modernity would open up the possibility of a significant reconciliation of conservative and liberal views. See *The Eye of Spirit* [and the Introduction to this volume] for further discussion of this theme.)

This is a "politics of meaning," to be sure, but a transliberal, not a preliberal, meaning. It does not come from the reactionary and regressive attempt to tell others what kind of mythology they must pursue. It does not claim that world transformation rests on accepting their paradigm. It does not attempt to heal the fragments by killing the contenders. It does not ask the state in any way to support or advocate on its behalf. It pursues none of those preliberal avenues.

Rather, standing *within* the political freedom—the liberal freedom—offered by the Enlightenment of the West, transrational awareness then moves into its own higher estate by pursuing spiritual Enlightenment, which it then offers, within that same political freedom, to any and all who desire to be released from the chains of space and time, self and suffering, hope and fear, death and wonder. In its own spiritual realization it is thoroughly transliberal, bringing together the Enlightenment of the East with the Enlightenment of the West.

Surely, both Enlightenments must be preserved. Both Enlightenments offer freedoms that took evolution billions of years to unfold. Both Enlightenments speak to the kindest heart and highest soul and deepest destiny of a common humanity. Both Enlightenments cry out to the best that we are and the noblest that we might yet become. Both Enlightenments taken together point to the liberation of all beings, both in the temporal realm (the Enlightenment of the West) and the timeless realm (the Enlightenment of the East), weaving together political freedom and spiritual freedom as the warp and woof of a culture that cares.

Could we really speak of world peace without both of these freedoms made available to all? Could any of us be deeply happy without these freedoms shining from the faces of all of Spirit's children? Could any of us truly sleep at night without all souls being liberated in this vast expanse? Could we dare begin to pray for ourselves without praying for one and all? And could any of us be truly free until all beings without exception swim equally in this ocean of emancipation?

And perhaps, political freedom joined with spiritual freedom, time joined with the timeless, space joined with infinity, we will come finally to rest, finally to peace, finally to a home that structures care into the Kosmos and compassion into the world, that touches each and every soul with grace and goodness and goodwill, and lights each being with a glory that never fades or falters. And we are called, you and I, by the voice of the Good, and the voice of the True, and the voice of the Beautiful, called exactly in those terms, to witness the liberation of all sentient beings without exception.

And on the distant, silent, lost horizon, gentle as fog, quiet as tears, the voice continues to call.

Further Reading

If you would like to pursue the topics raised in this volume, you might start with my books *A Brief History of Everything* and *Integral Psychology*. These books contain numerous references to other significant works in this area, and interested readers can begin following these leads as they wish.

SOURCES

Chapter 3: F. Crews, "In the Big House of Theory," *The New York Review of Books,* May 29, 1986. T. Kuhn, *The Structure of Scientific Revolutions,* 2d ed. I. Hacking, "Science Turned Upside Down," *The New York Review of Books,* Feb. 27, 1986. B. Barnes, *T. S. Kuhn and Social Science* (New York: Macmillan). D. Hoy, *The Critical Circle* (Berkeley: University of California Press, 1978). E. Gellner, "The Paradox in Paradigms," *Times Literary Supplement,* April 23, 1982.

Chapter 7: All quotes from C. Taylor, *Hegel* (Cambridge, Mass.: Harvard University Press, 1975). (See *Sex, Ecology, Spirituality* for an extensive discussion).

Chapter 9: R. Alter, "Review of *The Tunnel* by William H. Gass," *The New Republic,* March 27, 1995.

Chapter 14: All quotes from R. Lipsey, *An Art of Our Own* (Boston: Shambhala, 1988). For an extensive discussion of art and literary theory from an integral perspective, see *The Eye of Spirit,* Chapters 4 and 5.

Chapter 15: D. Matt, *The Essential Kabbalah* (San Francisco: HarperSanFrancisco, 1995). For a detailed discussion of an "all-level, all-quadrant" research agenda—and for my suggested answers to the questions raised in the section "Deep Science Research"—see *A Brief History of Everything* and *The Eye of Spirit.*

Foreword to

THE SPIRIT OF GEN-X

edited by Steve Dinan

I WROTE MY FIRST BOOK when I was twenty-three; I have been writing ever since, more or less. I am now fifty—not very old, I suppose, although when I was twenty-three, it seemed an eternity. And anyway, my generation had already announced that "I hope I die before I get old"—another of our many maxims put with a thundering assurance that was inversely proportional to its believability. Have you seen Mick Jagger, who is now one hundred and seven years old, singing and gyrating on stage? Can we be ridiculous, or what?

Well, I am not here to bad-mouth my generation; not too much, anyway. I am here to say hello to yours. But I can't help noticing that generations define themselves in part by trying to distance themselves from what went before. The baby boomers—a funny phrase, but somehow appropriate—have been notorious for a fiery rebellion against their parents: "Down with the system! Question all authority! Do your own thing!" We never saw a conventional truth that we didn't want to tear down. "Transgress, subvert, deconstruct!"

It has been a mixed blessing. On the one hand, some critics saw our rebelliousness as an inability to grow up (not just baby boomers, but *baby* boomers), an inability to surrender a certain childish narcissism. There is some truth to that; we were not named "the Me Generation" for nothing. Most boomers approached a problem as if nobody had ever thought about it before, and the self-absorption of the Me Generation became notorious, not to mention suffocating. (If I had a boomer for a parent, why, I just might have killed myself by age three, just to get a little breathing room.)

On the other hand, it was precisely this rambunctious spirit that broke down many ugly barriers and opened many important truths. From civil rights to ecological concern, the boomers managed to grasp a bit of genuine idealism here and there, and, on a good day, might be remembered for just that. But there is something else, I think, that is less well known, less widespread, but more important about my generation, and it relates directly to yours. It has to do with the word "integral."

I am sometimes asked what I think the greatest impact of World War II was. (I am asked a lot of strange things.) Obviously there were many profound effects, humanitarian to geopolitical, but I always say: it brought Zen to the West. Seems a very narrow answer, doesn't it? Still, what I mean is simply that world cultures became inextricably mixed the day Hitler invaded Poland, and the day we dropped an Einsteinian nightmare on Nagasaki. Every cultural egg was broken in those years, and the world omelet called today was the result.

It seems unimaginable to us that, for humanity's entire stay on this planet—for some million years up to the present—a person was born into a culture that knew virtually nothing about any other. You were, for example, born a Chinese, were raised a Chinese, married a Chinese, and followed a Chinese religion—often living in the same hut for your entire life, on a spot of land that your ancestors settled for centuries. Every now and then this cultural isolation was interrupted by a strange and grotesque form of Eros known as war, where cultures were thrown together violently, through brutally ravishing means, yet the secret outcome was always a type of erotic cultural intercourse. The cultures got to know each other, even in a biblical sense—a hiddenly blissful sado-masochism that drove history to its present global village. From isolated tribes and bands, to small farming villages, to ancient nations, to conquering feudal empires, to international corporate states, to global village: many, many eggs were broken to make this extraordinary world omelet, as the cunning of Eros worked its many wonders.

The boomers were the first generation to be raised in this global village, and Gen-X is the first generation to make it their own. This is something you and I share, this global consciousness. This is something that has never existed before on this planet. This is something you and I will leave the world. And how we handle it will be the tale that future generations will speak of quietly, in those times when the past times are remembered.

The global village is an integral village; or rather, it can be an integral village. Every major cultural treasure, every profound cultural wisdom, every form of human transformation ever conceived on this planet, is to some degree available in this global village—and it spans the spectrum of goods, from very low to very high: hookers in Bangkok to Zen to Kyoto; hashish in Marrakech to Vedanta in Arunachala.

The global village is, at this time, mostly a global heap. What converts heaps to wholes is *vision*. Only by seeing how the parts fit together can the parts become parts of wholes. Only by expanding our own consciousness to embrace, quite literally, the global scale can our vision rise to greet this new dawn. It is our vision that will convert heapism to holism, fragmentation to belonging, alienation to compassion, despair to exultation, as our own consciousness spans the spectrum from dust to Deity. And this is where, I believe, your generation enters the picture: this vision is now up to you.

This is the message and the hope of *The Spirit of Gen-X*. Steve Dinan, who assembled this extraordinary collection, has written: "My generation is remarkably savvy in many ways but most of my confreres feel thwarted in their drive to create a better world. However, in the last few years, I have befriended a series of remarkable 'youngsters,' afire with the Divine, willing to use a variety of tools from sacred and secular traditions in the service of transformation, and eager to manifest the fruits of their practice in the world. I believe that these individuals are part of the vanguard of a truly integral, global culture that is yet to emerge, a society in which both spiritual and mundane life are engaged with equal parts passion, intelligence, and whimsy."

Indeed. An integral culture that has yet to emerge. This vision is now up to you. To contribute to this integral culture and this integral vision, you do not necessarily have to think of the big picture specifically; you do not have to write large ponderous tomes explaining all the details of what an integral picture might look like. As my own writings have demonstrated, any idiot can do that. (Well, not just any idiot; any idiot with a really nifty keyboard.) What is especially required, it seems to me, is to live your own vision with sincerity, with genuineness, with authenticity—with *you-ness*. And that is what I see, with a tinge of heartfelt envy, in every contribution to this book. Approached with sincerity, Spirit is everywhere, as these chapters show: Kabbalah crossed with Aikido; the patterns of Authentic Movement; kids in juvenile hall;

the secrets of the body; quiet prayer circles in the evening; the simplest African violets. Why, I even have it on good authority that strange wisdom drifts through the mists of dimly lit cigarettes in the roadside cafés of Virginia. So Eros will carry on, it seems.

My own writing went through several phases, which critics now refer to as phases 1, 2, 3, and 4 (proving that I couldn't get it right the first time, or the second, or . . .). These are really just the phases of carrying on the work of those who went before me. Steve Dinan, who has appreciated my work and also appropriately criticized it, wrote of my latest phase, "Wilber-4 may be more encompassing than any previous intellectual edifice, but that does not mean there won't be a Wilber-5 and still more complete visions further down the road." But Steve is wrong; there might be a Wilber-5, but it will be called Dinan-1, or Davis-1, or Jordan-1, or all of them and hundreds more, and so that particular story will go. Eros, indeed, will carry on. . . .

There follow twenty tales of the Spirit of Generation-X, tales of the Spirit carrying on in the most amazing ways. They are brilliant stories, crackling insights, songs of the heart that speak to us in terms too tender to repeat. Radical authenticity, as one contributor puts it, is what it is all about, and radical authenticity is what speaks to us most clearly from each and every page of this book. This is a lesson that my generation, and every generation hence, can learn from the contributors to this volume. And into the hands of this radical authenticity the integral vision goes.

ONE TASTE

The Journals of Ken Wilber

A Note to the Reader

IN THE PAST I have strenuously resisted going public. I am not a private person, in the sense of secretive; I'm just not a public person, in the sense of seeking the limelight. Nonetheless, as one who has written extensively about the interior life, it seemed appropriate, at some point, to share mine. The following pages therefore contain a fair amount of what would ordinarily be considered private material. Still, in the last analysis, this is a philosophical more than personal journal: it deals primarily with ideas, and especially those ideas that orbit the sun of the perennial philosophy (or the common core of the world's great wisdom traditions). In one area, however, this is a very personal journal: extensive descriptions of meditation practice and various mystical states, based on my own experience. (Those who wish a more personal account in other areas might consult *Grace and Grit*.)

Because this book is idea-focused, I have taken a few liberties with the order of the entries. Some theoretical pieces were moved up, because other entries don't make sense without them. Dates are generally accurate, but in a few cases they might be off because I sometimes made notes without dating them, so I entered these wherever it seemed appropriate. Some Naropa seminars originally occurred within a few days of each other; I have spread these out (otherwise, too much academic talk in one place); the dates are therefore not always accurate, but the excerpts themselves are. In any event, it should be remembered that these journals were not primarily meant to be a record of the details of my personal life, but rather a record of further attempts to convey the perennial philosophy.

Because the theoretical entries are fairly brief and self-contained—a page or two, usually, a dozen pages at most—the ideas themselves come in bite-size chunks. If you hit an entry that doesn't interest you—one on politics, perhaps, or business, or art—you can easily skip to the next

entry. If, however, you are reading these pages for the theoretical information, you should know that each entry builds on its predecessors, so
skipping around is not the best idea.

If there is a theme to this journal it is that body, mind, and soul are
not mutually exclusive. The desires of the flesh, the ideas of the mind,
and the luminosities of the soul—all are perfect expressions of the radiant Spirit that alone inhabits the universe, sublime gestures of that Great
Perfection that alone outshines the world. There is only One Taste in the
entire Kosmos, and that taste is Divine, whether it appears in the flesh,
in the mind, in the soul. Resting in that One Taste, transported beyond
the mundane, the world arises in the purest Freedom and radiant Release, happy to infinity, lost in all eternity, and hopeless in the original
face of the unrelenting mystery. From One Taste all things issue, to One
Taste all things return—and in between, which is the story of this moment, there is only the dream, and sometimes the nightmare, from which
we would do well to awaken.

K.W.
Boulder, Colorado
Spring 1998

January

You could not discover the limits of the soul, even if you traveled by every path in order to do so; such is the depth of its meaning.

—HERACLITUS

Thursday, January 2, 1997

Worked all morning, research and reading, while watching the sunlight play through the falling snow. The sun is not yellow today, it is white, like the snow, so I am surrounded by white on white, alone on alone. Sheer Emptiness, soft clear light, is what it all looks like, shimmering to itself in melancholy murmurs. I am released into that Emptiness, and all is radiant on this clear light day.

Friday, January 3

A while ago—somewhere around Thanksgiving—I started writing *The Integration of Science and Religion: The Union of Ancient Wisdom and Modern Knowledge.*[1] The book is now done, and I'm wondering just what to do with it. I wrote it with a specific audience in mind—namely, the orthodox, conventional, mainstream world, not the new-age, new-paradigm, countercultural crowd. I have no idea if I succeeded, and I'm not sure exactly what my next step should be.

I need to figure out a way to do this type of intense work and still

---

1. Published as *The Marriage of Sense and Soul: Integrating Science and Religion.*

have some sort of social life. Every time Balzac had an orgasm, he used to say, "There goes another book." I seem to have it exactly backwards.

After Treya's death—it's been eight years this month—I didn't date for a year or so. I've since had a few very nice relationships, but nothing quite right. I wonder . . .

Saturday, January 4

Some students have invited me to a "rave"—an all-night dance party with techno music and—ahem—certain illegal substances. The kids—and these really are kids, twentysomethings—use small amounts of Ecstasy, a drug that enhances empathy and group rapport. The atmosphere is communal, asexual or perhaps androgynous, and gentle but intense—with, for lack of a better term, a type of spiritual background. The music (e.g., Moby and Prodigy) generally lacks words—that is, lacks a referential nature, so the symbolic mind is not engaged—and this allows, on occasion, little glimmers of the supramental, not to mention huge doses of the inframental.

Well, whatever disapproving parents may say about all that, I find it infinitely preferable to what we used to do at our dances, which was, basically, drink a six-pack of beer and throw up on your date. And as for baby-boomer parents cluck-clucking about illegal substances, ah, gimme me a break.

Still, I think I'll pass on the rave. But more power to 'em, I say.

Tuesday, January 7

This weekend is the "Ken Wilber Conference" in San Francisco. I'm told it's sold out and they're looking for a bigger place to hold it. I'm not sure whether that's good or bad.

Roger [Walsh][2] will be one of the main presenters. I wonder if he will tell his Neil Armstrong joke, which seems to be the funniest thing anybody can ever remember hearing:

When Neil Armstrong set foot on the moon, his first words were, "One small step for a man, one giant leap for mankind." The next thing he said was, "Good luck, Mr. Gorsky." The little-known story behind those words: When Armstrong was a young boy, he overheard a heated

---

2. All bracketed interpolations were added for publication; all parentheses are in the original journals. All footnotes were added for publication.

argument coming from the neighbor's bedroom window. Mrs. Gorsky screamed at Mr. Gorsky, "You'll get oral sex when that little boy next door walks on the moon."

Wednesday, January 8

Got another letter from a woman who read my foreword to Frances's book [*Shadows of the Sacred: Seeing Through Spiritual Illusions*, by Frances Vaughan]. I've received so many letters from women who relate directly to the issues raised in it.

The foreword begins, "Frances Vaughan is the wisest of the Wise Women I know. Such a wonderful concept: the woman who is wise, the woman who has more wisdom, perhaps, than you or I, the woman who brings a special knowledge, a graceful touch, a healing presence, to her every encounter, for whom beauty is a mode of knowing and openness a special strength—a woman who sees so much more, and touches so much more, and reaches out with care, and tells us that it will be all right, this woman who is wise, this woman who sees more.

"Frances is such a one: the woman who brings wisdom into the world, and does not simply flee the world for wisdom somewhere else. The woman who teaches individuality, but set in its larger and deeper contexts of communion: communion with others, with body, with Spirit, with one's own higher Self: the Spirit that manifests its very being in relationships. And that is how I think of Frances most often: the wise woman who teaches sane and sincere relationship, the woman who sets us in our deeper contexts, this wise woman whom I am proud to know."

Today's letter (from a woman therapist) talks at length about the historical tradition of the Wise Woman, and the importance of uniting psychotherapy with spirituality. I couldn't agree more. From the last part of the foreword:

"In the type of practice that Frances (and a handful of others) are attempting to forge, we see the emergence of what is so crucial: some sense of the spiritual and transpersonal, some sense of the Mystery of the Deep, some context beyond the isolated me, that touches each and every one of us, and lifts us from our troubled and mortal selves, this contracted coil, and delivers us into the hands of the timeless and very Divine, and gracefully releases us from ourselves: where openness melts defenses and relationship grounds sanity, where compassion outpaces the hardened heart and care outshines despair, this opening to the Divine that Frances teaches each of us.

"One of Frances's clients once told her that she (Frances) had helped to midwife her soul, deliver her soul. I think that somehow says it all. To midwife the Divine—already present in each, but perhaps not shining brightly; already given to each, but perhaps not noticed well; already caring for the world, but perhaps forgotten in all the rush: this opening to the Divine that Frances teaches each of us.

"Let us both, you and I, take the hand of the Wise Woman, and walk with her through the land of our own soul, and listen quietly to the tale she has to tell. And know that a surer pair of hands we are not likely to find in this lifetime."

Thursday, January 9

Fame in this country is a religion that demands human sacrifice, a religion to which I do not wish to belong. You start to take yourself so seriously—I saw it happening to me, after I had written my first book at the age of 23. I'd give lectures or seminars, people would tell me how amazingly great I was, and sooner or later, *you believe them*. You end up exactly with what Oscar Levant said to George Gershwin: "Tell me, George, if you had it to do all over again, would you still fall in love with yourself?"

After about a year of that, I decided I could either teach what I had written yesterday, or write something new. So I stopped going to conferences, I stopped teaching, I stopped giving interviews.

For the next twenty years, I stuck to that plan with virtually no exceptions. And yet here I am, thinking about taking *Science and Religion* straight to the biggest mainstream publishers and really going for it. I think I am seriously deranged.

Tuesday, January 14

Frank Visser, my Dutch translator, has come from the Netherlands to say hi, after stopping by the kw conference in San Francisco. Frank translated *The Atman Project* and *A Brief History of Everything*. I hear he's very good.

"In this field, what's the hot topic in Europe?"

"How *regressive* so many of the American approaches to spirituality are. The schools that confuse bodily feeling with spiritual awareness, bioenergetics, experiential this and that, ecopsychology, feelings and more feelings, the regressive therapies, the whole lot. I have written a paper about it. Don't you agree that you Americans are insane for regression?"

"I'm afraid so. Mostly because it's something *anybody* can do—growth is hard, regression is easy."

"It's your pre/trans fallacy all over the place."

Frank is referring to an essay I wrote, almost two decades ago, called "The Pre/Trans Fallacy." The idea is simple: since both *pre*-rational and *trans*-rational are *non*-rational, they are easily confused. And then one of two very unpleasant things happens: either you *reduce* genuine, transrational, spiritual realities to infantile, prerational states; or you *elevate* childish, prerational sentiments to transcendental glory. In the first case you deny spiritual realities altogether, since you think they are all infantile rubbish. In the second case, you end up glorifying childish myth and preverbal impulse. You are so intent on transcending rationality, which is fine, that you go overboard and champion *anything* that is not rational, including much that is frankly prerational, regressive, downhill.

And Frank is right; much of what is being called a "spiritual renaissance" in this country is really a prerational slide—narcissistic, self-centered, self-glorifying, self-promoting.

"We Europeans find it alarming."

Wednesday, January 15

Read all morning, part of the seemingly unending research for volume 2 of the Kosmos trilogy (*Sex, God, and Gender*).[3] The relation between men and women: the agony and the ecstasy. And it tends to drive both sides insane. I expect to see a Bret Harte update: *The Outcasts of Testosterone Flat*. Take Aldous Huxley's quip: "It's a law of nature. Man minus woman equals pig. Woman minus man equals lunatic." Or Gloria Steinem: "A woman without a man is like a fish without a bicycle." Woody Allen: "God gave males a penis and a brain, but only enough blood to operate one at a time." Billy Crystal: "A woman needs a reason to make love, a man needs a place."

Volume 1 was eight hundred pages, so will be volume 2. "Another damned thick square book! Always scribble, scribble, scribble, eh, Mr. Gibbon?"

---

3. Volume 1 is *Sex, Ecology, Spirituality* (Shambhala, 1995); volume 2 is tentatively titled *Sex, God, and Gender: The Ecology of Men and Women*, which I am now working on; volume 3 is outlined, and is tentatively subtitled *The Spirit of Post/Modernity*.

Friday, January 17

Got a letter from Alex Grey, whose book *Sacred Mirrors: The Visionary Art of Alex Grey* I wrote a foreword for. In the letter, Alex reminds me of the conversation we had at my house, when we were talking about the nature of genuine art: "The purpose of truly transcendent art is to express something you are not yet, but that you can become."

The foreword I did for Alex's book stresses the theme that all of us possess the eye of flesh, the eye of mind, and the eye of spirit. We can classify art in terms of which eye it mostly relies on. Realism and naturalism, for example, rely mostly on the eye of flesh; abstract, conceptual, and surrealistic art rely mostly on the eye of mind; and certain great works of spiritual art—Tibetan thangkas, for example—rely on the eye of contemplation, the eye of spirit.

Each of these eyes sees a different world—the world of material objects, of mental ideas, of spiritual realities. And each eye can paint what it sees. The higher the eye, the deeper the art.

Alex is representative of those rare artists who paint with the eye of contemplation, the eye of spirit. This type of art is not symbolic or metaphorical; it is a direct depiction of realities, but realities that cannot be seen with the eye of flesh or the eye of mind, only with the eye of spirit. And the point of this art is not simple viewing but *transformation*: it represents higher or deeper realities available to all of us if we continue to grow and evolve. And *that* is why "the purpose of truly transcendent art is to express something you are not yet, but that you can become."

Wednesday, January 22

Going mainstream. This is all Tony Schwartz's fault.

I first met Tony when he was doing *What Really Matters: Searching for Wisdom in America.* Tony's is one of the great stories: an accomplished journalist—he had worked for the *New York Times*, *New York* magazine, had done almost a dozen *Newsweek* cover stories—and he had just finished coauthoring Donald Trump's *The Art of the Deal*, which promptly perched on top of the *Times* bestseller list and tossed Tony into the big time of megabucks, glamour, and glitz. Being immersed in Trump's extravagant world let Tony know that, even if he had all that material wealth, it somehow wouldn't touch the really important issues in life. So, with the money he made on the Trump book, Tony spent the next five years on his own search for wisdom, crisscrossing this country and talking to over 200 psychologists, philosophers, mystics, gurus, therapists, and teachers of all sorts. He devoted a chapter in his book to my work, and we became best of friends.

After Tony finished *What Really Matters*, and having a family to support, he took on the co-writing of Michael Eisner's autobiography, essentially doing the same job for the head of Disney that he had done for the Donald. But there the similarities ended. As Tony explains it, Trump is simply Trump: what you see is what you get; the book was fairly straightforward, if demanding. But Michael Eisner is a considerably different story, involving the entire Walt Disney empire—theme parks, movies, books, towns, television—not to mention such sideshows as Jeffrey Katzenberg and Michael Ovitz. Tony has now spent over three years on this project.

What Tony wants to do next is work on an *integral* approach to human growth and transformation, as he summarized it in *What Really Matters* and as he finds outlined in my work (but not only mine). He is determined to take this integral message to a larger audience, and this has made me more sensitive to the fact that, to some degree at least, I need to do the same thing. Yes, this is definitely all Tony's fault.

Thursday, January 23

Finished Christopher Isherwood's thousand-page diary (volume one!), and I have been deeply depressed for almost a week. Many reasons.

Isherwood represents for me several very important strands of life, all rolled into one. First, there is the whole Vedanta Society connection, and that includes, in various ways, Aldous Huxley, Gerald Heard, and Thomas Mann (the latter, loosely, but significantly). Isherwood, working with Swami Prabhavananda (cf. *My Guru and His Disciple*), produced some of the first, and certainly the most readable, translations of the *Bhagavad Gita*, Patanjali's *Yoga Sutras*, and my favorite, Shankara's classic *The Crest Jewel of Discrimination*.

So as early as 1941, Christopher is writing in his diary, "To try to annihilate your ego, to let the Real Self walk about in you, using your legs and arms, your brain and your voice. It's fantastically difficult—and yet, what else is life for?" This would also let him understand something that the purely Descended religions—from ecology to Gaia worship to ecopsychology—often fail to understand: "Whenever a movement has its objectives within time, it *always* resorts to violence." This deeply spiritual strand in Christopher was thankfully given a little spice of biting humor; he was determined to live his life "with passion, with sincere involvement, and with heartfelt hostility."

But Isherwood was always struggling, in his own way, for an integral approach that united spirituality with *this* life, probably because, as he put it, sex and spirit were both very strong in him and yet often apparently antagonistic. I love his honest struggle to stay with both, even in extremes.

Most people know Isherwood, even if they don't realize it, because he was the lead male figure in *Cabaret*, which was based on one of his short stories in *Goodbye to Berlin* ("Sally Bowles," based loosely on singer Jean Ross, whom Isherwood met in 1931 Berlin). Michael York plays Christopher, and Liza Minnelli earned an Oscar for her role as Sally. The writing is brilliant, as Virginia Woolf must have known when she made this entry in her diary: "Isherwood and I met on the doorstep. He is slip of a wild boy. That young man, said W. Maugham, 'holds the future of the English novel in his hands.'"

The story "Sally Bowles" (the last name, incidentally, is from Paul Bowles—musical composer, translator of Sartre—"No Exit" is Bowles—and writer's writer, *The Sheltering Sky* being his most famous; Isherwood admired his work and named Sally after him) was also the basis of the earlier Broadway play *I Am a Camera*, which was made into a movie starring Julie Harris. The title comes from a famous passage in the book, often quoted, usually misunderstood: "I am a camera with its shutter open, quite passive, recording, not thinking. Recording the man shaving at the window opposite and the woman in the kimono washing her hair. Some day, all this will have to be developed, carefully printed, fixed." At this point, Isherwood was only vaguely aware of the great teachings, East and West, about the real Self as pure choiceless Witness, but you can see it shining through (it is quite similar to Emerson's famous "transparent eyeball": "All mean egotism vanishes. I become a transparent eyeball; I am nothing; I see all"). Critics jumped on Isherwood for this detachment, lack of care, etc. But this misses the nature of that state, as Isherwood himself pointed out: "The idea that I was a person very divorced from what was going on around me is quite false." The true Witness allows whatever arises to arise—passion, calm, involvement, detachment, heartfelt hostility, it doesn't matter. But the notion that it is a deathly divorce from life is silly.

Isherwood, anyway, was certainly not divorced. In fact, one of his best friends at the time, and through most of his life, W. H. Auden—already destined to be one of the two or three greatest poets of the century—had gone to Berlin in the late 1920s, mostly in search of the decadent sex, and Auden convinced Christopher to join him there. Both of them were gay, and the famous boy bars—particularly the Cosy Corner—kept Isherwood and Auden bound to Berlin for several years. Wild sex, especially as a young man—well, there's another strand.

(Isherwood has become something of a hero for present-day gays, mostly because of his unflinching acceptance of his homosexuality, an admiration I share. So did E. M. Forster; his very touching, and very gay, novel *Maurice*, which Forster understandably felt reluctant to publish during his life, he left to Christopher. We of today tend to forget that, until just recent times in most countries, "being homosexual" was a crime punishable by imprisonment and sometimes death. England was particularly barbaric in its stance, as the wretched cautionary tale of Alan Turing ought to remind us—Turing, who cracked the Enigma secret code machine of the Nazis and rendered Hitler's every move transparent to the Allies, a stunning display of brilliance that arguably did more to win the war than any other single act, and for which he was awarded, upon discovery of his homosexuality, with imprisonment and forced hormone injections to correct his "disease." He committed suicide shortly thereafter.)

Adolf Hitler made his Munich beer-hall putsch in 1923, was jailed, wrote *Mein Kampf*. By 1929, economic devastation and desperation gave the National Socialists mass support, and, astonishingly, by 1934, with the death of Hindenburg, Hitler united the offices of President and Chancellor to become Führer of all Germany.

Isherwood arrives in Berlin in 1929, and stays until 1933—exactly the hot period for this, probably the most shocking period in Western history, the ascendancy of a lunacy never seen before or since. And he records what he sees. "Here it is rather like living in Hell. Everybody is absolutely at the last gasp, hanging on with their eyelids. We are under martial law. Nobody in England can have even the remotest idea of what it is like. There are wagon-loads of police at every corner to sit on any attempt at a demonstration. You can scarcely get along the street for beggars. . . ."

Germany, the brightest of philosophical lights in the West, heir to Greece, and it had all come to this: a madman disguised as a house painter from Austria. And so now, today, one cannot think of the greats—Kant, Hegel, Spinoza, Marx, Fichte, Freud, Nietzsche, Einstein, Schopenhauer, Leibniz, Schelling—the whole Germanic sphere—without thinking, at some point, of Auschwitz and Treblinka, Sobibor and Dachau, Bergen-Belsen and Chelmno. My God, they have names, as if they were human.

But the causal linking of Germany's transcendental tradition with the death camps, which is quite common in American postmodern cluck-clucking about meta-narratives, is simply cheap and vulgar, not to mention wrong. What happened in Germany is, among a million other causes, a classic case of the pre/trans fallacy. In fact, the entire German tradition is a study in the pre/trans fallacy, producing now a Hegel, now a Hitler. Precisely because the German tradition strove so nobly and so mightily for Geist and Spirit (which is to its everlasting credit), it was open more intensely to confusing prerational bodily and emotional enthusiasms with transrational insight and awareness. Blood and soil, return to nature, and noble savages flourished under the banner of a Romantic return to spirit, a recapture of the lost Ground, a return of the hidden God, a revelation written in blood and etched in the flesh of those who would stand in the way of this ethnic-blood purity, and the gas chambers waited as the silent womb of the Great Mother, who always rules over such proceedings, to receive all of those who corrupted this purity. It was not the rationality or the transrationality of Germany that undid her, but her reactivated prerational impulses that brought the fortress tumbling down.

But that's another strand: God and the Devil together in Berlin in 1933, and Isherwood was there.

Then there's the whole Huxley connection. Aldous Huxley was probably the last—and this is part of my depression—was probably the last author who could write intensely, deeply, and philosophically about mystical and transcendental topics . . . *and be taken seriously* by the intelligentsia, the media, the Manhattan Inc. crowd, the liberal insiders, the avant-garde—the last author who could write about transcendental topics and have it considered hip, hot, happening. Liberals are wary of Spirit, basically, and conservatives think Spirit means their own fundamentalist mythic God—they are both off the mark, and both of them would today find Huxley largely incomprehensible. Who could write *The Perennial Philosophy* now and get it enthusiastically reviewed outside of California? Today's "spirituality" is mostly (1) fundamentalist revivals, (2) new age narcissism, (3) mythic regression, (4) web-of-life subtle reductionism, (5) flatland holism. Huxley and Heard and Isherwood and even Mann would have found the lot of them drearily tiresome.

Gerald Heard (author of several brilliant books, including *The Five*

Ages of Man—which was the basis for Jean Houston's very perceptive *Life-Force*—and himself quite instrumental in the founding and flourishing of the Vedanta Society) introduced Isherwood to Huxley not long after Christopher had settled, more or less permanently, in Los Angeles, earning his living by writing scripts, as Huxley (and Tennessee Williams and William Faulkner and F. Scott Fitzgerald) sometimes did (those were the days!); they remained friends until Huxley's death in 1963. It was in L.A. that the Vedanta Society was formed (in one of whose temples, I believe, Adi Da had his first major breakthrough). It would form one of the three or four major currents by which Eastern wisdom would gain strong entrance to this country.

If Christopher was its literary voice, Huxley provided its sheer brain power. As Isherwood and almost everybody else commented, Aldous was not much of a novelist; his characters are cardboard. I always liked his own explanation for this: "I have almost no ideas about myself and don't like having them—avoid having them—on principle even—and only improvise them, when somebody like you asks to know them. . . ." So he wrote novels about ideas instead, although he was aware of the grave risks involved. "Not only must you write about people who have ideas to express—o.o1 percent of the human race. Hence the real, the congenital novelists don't write such books. But then I never pretended to be a congenital novelist."

Instead, he played with ideas in a dazzling way, bright and brilliant and sometimes breathtaking. And liberating. As Sir Isaiah Berlin put it in his memoirs, "As men of letters—led by Voltaire, the head of the profession—rescued many oppressed human beings in the eighteenth century; as Byron or George Sand, Ibsen, Baudelaire, Nietzsche, Wilde and Gide and perhaps even Wells or Russell have done since, so members of my generation were assisted to find themselves by novelists, poets, and critics concerned with the central problems of their day." Sir Isaiah places Huxley with Ezra Pound and J. B. S. Haldane as among the major emancipators of his time.

Sybille Bedford, one of Huxley's biographers, gives another take on this great emancipatory tradition: it involved "a number of extraordinarily and diversely gifted individuals whose influence . . . had been tremendous. Their common denominator was an intense desire to acquire, to advance, and to disseminate knowledge—a wish to improve the lot as well as the administration of humankind, an assumption of responsibility—*l'intelligence oblige*—and a passion, no tamer word will do, for truth."

This was a time when such things even made sense, let alone mattered. That is to say, this was before my generation, whose humanities professors decided that they could not assist anybody in creating anything, and so devoted themselves, in a fit of *resentiment*, to tearing down instead, leaving only the deconstructionist's Cheshire-cat smile hanging in midair; and they are shocked, *shocked*, that anybody could ever have a passion for truth, since, as they happily misinterpret Foucault, truth is nothing but thinly concealed power—thus attempting to ensure that none of their students seek truth either, lest they actually find it and begin producing real works that shine with depth and glory.

Precisely because Huxley was plugged into the transcendental, his prose had power to liberate. You have to know that there actually is a transcendental something, if you are going to free anybody from anything—if there is no beyond-the-given, there is no freedom from the given, and liberation is futile. Today's postmodern writers, who hug the given, stick to the obvious, cling to the shadows, celebrate the surface, have nowhere else to go, and so emancipation is the last of what they offer . . . or you get.

No wonder that one of Aldous's best friends for several decades was Krishnamurti (the sage on whom I cut my spiritual teeth). Krishnamurti was a supreme liberator, at least on occasion, and in books such as *Freedom from the Known*, this extraordinary sage pointed to the power of nondual choiceless awareness to liberate one from the binding tortures of space, time, death, and duality. When Huxley's house (and library) burned down, the first books he asked to be replaced were Krishnamurti's *Commentaries on Living*.

Yehudi Menuhin wrote of Aldous: "He was scientist and artist in one—standing for all we most need in a fragmented world where each of us carries a distorting splinter out of some great shattered universal mirror. He made it his mission to restore these fragments and, at least in his presence, men were whole again. To know where each splinter might belong one must have some conception of the whole, and only a mind such as Aldous's, cleansed of personal vanity, noticing and recording everything, and exploiting nothing, could achieve so broad a purpose."

To the Huxley-like emancipators I would add, of course, Thomas Mann, whom I became obsessed with for several years, reading all I could by and about him. He writes his first novel, *Buddenbrooks*, at age 25 and gets the Nobel for it. Who could write *The Magic Mountain* today and even get it published? And is not "Death in Venice" perhaps the most perfect short story ever penned? Mann, too, had contact with the Vedanta Society when he moved to California. Robert Musil, Proust, and Mann are my favorite unrelentingly intelligent authors of this century. "Which remarkably enough, does not get anyone anywhere"— Musil.

Mann first supported the retro-Romantic and reactionary fascist movements in Germany—volkish blood and soil and the "soul" of Germany—and then turned away in shock and disgust to embrace humanistic rational pluralism, become the clearest and loudest anti-Nazi voice coming from a German, and perhaps the greatest humanist novelist of the century. He made a profound study of interior life—Freud, Nietzsche, Schelling, Schopenhauer, mysticism—but precisely because of his previous slide into prerational fascism, he is always at pains to differentiate prerational regression from transrational glory. His is one of the great and precious voices of this century; he belongs so clearly in that pantheon of those who helped to emancipate, to one degree or another, untold numbers of sensitive souls.

So that's another strand: the great tradition of emancipatory writing, of intellectual light in the service of liberation—helping to undo repression, thwart power, and shun shallowness, quaint as all that sounds to this year's ears. Today that noble tradition is reduced to rational scientists, such as the good Carl Sagan, trying to beat back Elvis sightings and UFO abductions, but it is so much nobler than all of that, and speaks to so much that is higher and deeper and truer in us all. That emancipatory tradition died, I fear, with Huxley.

All those strands, rolled into one. So Christopher Isherwood is sort of my "six degrees of Kevin Bacon." You can get from Isherwood to everything that's important in six moves or less.

But lord, it's so sad, because so few want to make those moves. And I am so depressed reading his diaries and being reminded of it daily.

Friday, January 24

Rented *Bound*, which I had already seen in a theatre; it's superb. Jennifer Tilly, Gina Gershon, Joe Pantoliano—two lesbians who do Joe in, but in fingernail-biting (and finger-removing) tension. The movie is shot in a sensual noir fashion, one of my favorite cinematic atmospheres. They're not really that similar, but it made me think of the opening credits to *Seven*, which were brilliantly shot. Several critics snootily dismissed *Seven* beginning to end (well, the entire city did seem to lack overhead lights), so I was glad to see the opening credits get the International Design Award for excellence. The designer, Kyle Cooper, described them as "bleak yet playful bookends for the feel-bad movie of the year."

I have the strangest feeling that the writing and publication of *Science and Religion* will be the bleak yet playful bookends of this year. Whether it's going to be "feel-bad" remains to be seen.

Saturday, January 25

Date with a woman, who shall go nameless, it didn't quite work out. Turns out that most of her relationships are *very* short-lived. One of her marriages lasted only a few months. I mean, I've got food in my refrigerator older than that.

Monday, January 27

Sam [Bercholz] rushed *The Eye of Spirit* out in time for the kw conference. My copies arrived today, a little late; but, as usual, Shambhala has done a beautiful job. In some ways this is one of my favorite books, but I'm not sure how well it will do.

Jack's generous foreword. Jack [Crittenden] and I go back a long way, to the early Lincoln days, when he came to visit me after reading *The Spectrum of Consciousness*. He wanted to start a journal, *ReVision*, and I helped get it up and running. We're no longer associated with that journal, but Jack and I have remained fast friends. He's a brilliant theorist, superb writer. He and Patricia now have three teenage sons, hard to believe. He's published *Beyond Individualism* (Oxford University Press) and is now working, with varying seriousness, on two or three other books, which he's sandwiching in between his teaching chores at Arizona State.

Jack does a great job explaining the meaning of "integral" and the lamentable, fragmented nature of so much of what is called "knowledge" in today's world. I've already received numerous comments on Jack's piece, along the lines of, "Oh, now I see what you're trying to do in all your writing." Thank god somebody can explain it.

[Several subsequent entries refer to Jack's foreword. For reference, a few excerpts:

> Wilber's approach is the opposite of eclecticism. He has provided a coherent and consistent vision that seamlessly weaves

together truth-claims from such fields as physics and biology; the ecosciences; chaos theory and the systems sciences; medicine, neurophysiology, biochemistry; art, poetry, and aesthetics in general; developmental psychology and a spectrum of psychotherapeutic endeavors, from Freud to Jung to Piaget; the Great Chain theorists from Plato and Plotinus in the West to Shankara and Nagarjuna in the East; the modernists from Descartes and Locke to Kant; the Idealists from Schelling to Hegel; the postmodernists from Foucault and Derrida to Taylor and Habermas; the major hermeneutic tradition, Dilthey to Heidegger to Gadamer; the social systems theorists from Comte and Marx to Parsons and Luhmann; the contemplative and mystical schools of the great meditative traditions, East and West, in the world's major religious traditions. All of this is just a sampling. Is it any wonder, then, that those who focus narrowly on one particular field might take offense when that field is not presented as the linchpin of the Kosmos?

In other words, to the critics the stakes are enormous, and it is not choosing sides at this point if I suggest that the critics who have focused on their pet points in Wilber's method are attacking a particular tree in the forest of his presentation. But if we look instead at the forest, and if his approach is generally valid, it honors and incorporates more truth than any other system in history.

How so? What is his actual method? In working with any field, Wilber simply backs up to a level of abstraction at which the various conflicting approaches actually agree with one another. Take, for example, the world's great religious traditions: Do they all agree that Jesus is God? No. So we must jettison that. Do they all agree that there is a God? That depends on the meaning of "God." Do they all agree on God, if by "God" we mean a Spirit that is in many ways *unqualifiable*, from the Buddhists' Emptiness to the Jewish mystery of the Divine? Yes, that works as a generalization—what Wilber calls an "orienting generalization" or "sturdy conclusion."

Wilber likewise approaches all the other fields of human knowledge: art to poetry, empiricism to hermeneutics, psychoanalysis to meditation, evolutionary theory to idealism. In every case he assembles a series of sturdy and reliable, not to say irrefutable, orienting generalizations. He is not worried, nor should his readers be, about whether *other* fields would accept the conclusions of any given field; in short, don't worry, for example, if empiricist conclusions do not match religious conclusions. Instead, simply assemble all the orienting conclusions as if each field had incredibly important truths to tell us. This is exactly Wilber's first step in his integrative method—a type of phenomenology of all human knowledge conducted at the level of orienting generalizations. In other words, assemble all of the truths that each field believes it has to offer humanity. For the moment, simply assume they are indeed true.

Wilber then arranges these truths into chains or networks of interlocking conclusions. At this point Wilber veers sharply from a method of mere eclecticism and into a systematic vision. For the second step in Wilber's method is to take all of the truths or orienting generalizations assembled in the first step and then pose this question: What coherent system would in fact *incorporate the greatest number of these truths*?

The system presented in *Sex, Ecology, Spirituality* (and clearly and simply summarized in the following pages) is, Wilber claims, the system that incorporates the greatest number of orienting generalizations from the greatest number of fields of human inquiry. Thus, if it holds up, Wilber's vision incorporates and honors, it integrates, more truth than any other system in history.

The general idea is straightforward. It is not which theorist is right and which is wrong. His idea is that everyone is basically right, and he wants to figure out how that can be so. "I don't believe," Wilber says, "that any human mind is capable of 100 percent error. So instead of asking which approach is right and which is wrong, we assume each approach is true but partial, and then try to figure out how to fit these partial truths together, how to integrate them—not how to pick one and get rid of the others."

The third step in Wilber's overall approach is the development of a new type of *critical theory*. Once Wilber has the overall scheme that incorporates the greatest number of orienting generalizations, he then uses that scheme to criticize the partiality of narrower approaches, even though he has included the basic truths from those approaches. He criticizes not their truths, but their partial nature.

In his integral vision, therefore, is a clue to both of the extreme reactions to Wilber's work—that is, to the claims that it is some of the most significant work ever published as well as to the chorus of angry indignation and attack. The angry criticisms are coming, almost without exception, from theorists who feel that their own field is the only true field, that their own method is the only valid method. Wilber has not been believably criticized for misunderstanding or misrepresenting any of the fields of knowledge that he includes; he is attacked, instead, for including fields that a particular critic does not believe are important or for goring that critic's own ox (no offense to vegetarians). Freudians have never said that Wilber fails to understand Freud; they say that he shouldn't include mysticism. Structuralists and post-structuralists have never said that Wilber fails to understand their fields; they say that he shouldn't include all those nasty other fields. And so forth. The attack always has the same form: How dare you say my field isn't the only true field!

Regardless of what is decided, the stakes, as I said, are enormous. I asked Wilber how he himself thought of his work. "I'd like to think of it as one of the first believable world philosophies, a genuine embrace of East and West, North and South." Which is interesting, inasmuch Huston Smith (author of *The World's Religions* and subject of Bill Moyers's highly acclaimed television series *The Wisdom of Faith*) recently stated, "No one—not even Jung—has done as much as Wilber to open Western psychology to the durable insights of the world's wisdom traditions. Slowly but surely, book by book, Ken Wilber is laying the foundations for a genuine East/West integration."

At the same time, Ken adds, "People shouldn't take it too seriously. It's just orienting generalizations. It leaves all the details to be filled in any way you like." In short, Wilber is not offering a conceptual straightjacket. Indeed, it is just the opposite: "I hope I'm showing that there is more room in the Kosmos than you might have suspected."

There isn't much room, however, for those who want to preserve their fiefdoms by narrowing the Kosmos to one particular field—to wit, their own—while ignoring the truths from other fields. "You can't honor various methods and fields," Wilber adds, "without showing how they fit together. That is how to make a genuine world philosophy." Wilber is showing exactly that "fit." Otherwise, as he says, we have heaps, not wholes, and we really aren't honoring anything.]

Tuesday, January 28

Dental appointment. All the dentists in Boulder are "holistic." They can't fill a cavity but they're good for your soul. Your teeth rot, but apparently your spirit prospers.

Wednesday, January 29

It dawns on me that, for *Science and Religion,* I am going to have to get an agent, which I haven't had in years. For the past decade I've settled into a comfortable working relationship with Shambhala Publications, run by my long-time friend Sam Bercholz. But Sam understands that I want to go with a more mainstream publisher this time, and so, with his blessings, I am going to head out into the big bad world of commercial publishing.

So where do you find agents, anyway? Agent World? Agents Are Us? We Be Agents?

Thursday, January 30

Tomorrow is my birthday. But it's "Ken Wilber's" birthday, not the birthday of my Original Face, the great Unborn, the vast expanse of Emptiness untouched by date or duration, tense or time. This infinite ocean of Ease, this vast expanse of Freedom, this lucid sea of Stillness, is what I am in the deepest part of me, the infinite intersection where I am not, and Spirit only is.

There is no birthday for the great Unborn, for that which never comes to be, but is the Suchness of all that is, radiant to infinity. There is no celebration for the timeless moment, which is prior to history and its lies, time and its ugly terrors, duration and its drudgery. There are no gifts for the great Uncreate, the Source of all that is, the boundless Sea of Serenity that lines the entire Kosmos. There is no song for Always Already, the infinite Freedom gloriously beyond both birth and death altogether.

For every sentient being can truly say: in essence I am timeless, in essence I am All—the lines in my face are the cracks in the cosmic egg, supernovas swirl in my heart, galaxies pulse through my veins, stars light up the neurons of my night. . . . And who will sing birthday songs to that? Who will celebrate the vast expanse that sings its songs unheralded in the stillness of the night?

February

All the Buddhas and all sentient beings are nothing but
One Spirit, beside which nothing exists. This Spirit, which
is without beginning, is unborn and indestructible. It is not
green or yellow, and has neither form nor appearance. It
does not belong to the categories of things which exist or
do not exist, nor can it be thought of in terms of new or
old. It is neither long nor short, big nor small, for it transcends all limits, measures, names, traces, and comparisons. Only awaken to the One Spirit.

—ZEN MASTER HUANG PO

Saturday, February 1

Worked all morning, went shopping, got groceries. There are two pigeons living under my roof, nestled in a large air vent that comes from
my clothes dryer. I took the screen off the vent so they could get in
during the winter; they like the warm air that comes off the dryer. So
today I notice there are now three of them—they just had a bambino.
People should mate for life, like pigeons, penguins, and Catholics. Except, of course, pigeons never get their marriages miraculously annulled.

Sunday, February 2

Got a copy of Andrew Harvey's *The Essential Gay Mystics*, a book for
which I was glad to write a short blurb ["Andrew Harvey has pulled
together some of the most passionate and touching works in all of mysti-

cal literature, and as it happens, the authors are all gay. But the words speak for themselves: that is, the Divine directly speaks through the words in this volume, words that flowed through gay hearts and gay minds and gay love, but words which speak profoundly, eloquently, gorgeously, to the same Divine in all of us. A mystic is not one who sees God as an object, but one who is immersed in God as an atmosphere, and the works collected here are a radiant testament to that all-encompassing condition. Harvey has given us a cornucopia of mystical wisdom, tender as tears and gentle as fog, but also passionately ablaze with the relentless fire of the very Divine."]

Before he started work on this book (whose author notice states, with characteristic charm, "Andrew attended Oxford, and at age twenty-one received England's highest academic honor, becoming the youngest Fellow of All Soul's College in its history. A prolific writer, Harvey is the author of over ten books, including *Journey to Ladakh*. He collaborated with Sogyal Rinpoche on the best-selling *Tibetan Book of Living and Dying*. Based now in Paris, Harvey is the subject of a 1993 BBC documentary, 'The Making of a Mystic' "), Andrew and his soon-to-be husband, Eryk, stopped by my house, along with Alec Tsoucatos, to say hi. I made them pasta and we ate it out on the balcony, overlooking the Denver plains.

As a Romantic, Andrew is bound to alternate between idealizing and loathing the lost lover, so he has gone through his love-Mother-Meera, hate-Mother-Meera phase, but is now, it seems, quite happily married to Eryk, from whom, he says, he has learned more about true love than from anybody else. I hope this works for him; he seems genuinely happy.

Tuesday, February 4

I'm worried about Huston's health [Huston Smith]. I sometimes feel that he will live another decade or two, then I worry he won't live out the year. Ever since Treya's death, I have tried to tell people how I feel about them before they are gone, before it's too late. Treya and I had the chance to do that, but I saw what it did to those who did not.

The amazing thing about Huston is that he was working on the perennial philosophy long before most people had even heard of it. Years before it became fashionable—multicultural wisdom traditions, the world's religious heritage, the celebration of spiritual diversity and spiritual unity—Huston was doing the work.

His body is almost transparent now, like a thin, beautiful, translucent tissue. The last time I saw him he was very frail and fragile, but radiant. I have the deep suspicion that if you turn off the lights, he might faintly glow.

Dearest Huston,
It was wonderful seeing you. But when you said, when asked about your health, "The citadel is crumbling," it had a profound effect on me, which has lingered to this day. I wanted to write and tell you about it.

The more that Emptiness saturates my being, the more my life takes on a strange "double-entry" type of awareness. On the one hand, everything that happens—every single thing, from the very best to the very worst—is the equal radiance of the Divine. I simply cannot tell the difference between them. It is a mystery, this: that pain and happiness are equal in this awareness, that the most wretched soul and the most divine are equal in this radiance, that the setting sun and the rising sun bring equal joy, that nothing moves at all, in this splendor of the All-pervading. And when, in touch with that all-pervasiveness, I hear that the citadel of dearest Huston is crumbling, it is simply as it is, just so, and all is still right, and all is still well, and all is still good, and all still radiates the unending glory that we all are.

The other side of this Emptiness—the other part of the "double-entry"—is that, in addition to (or alongside of) the constant radiance of this moment, all the little moments are all the more themselves, somehow. Sadness is even sadder; happiness is happier; pleasure is more intense; pain hurts even more. I laugh louder and cry harder. Precisely because it is all the purest Emptiness, each relative phenomenon is allowed to be itself even more intensely, because it no longer contends with the Divine, but simply expresses It.

And on *that* side of the double-entry—where pain is more painful (because it is Empty), and where sadness is much sadder (because it is Empty)—when I hear that the citadel of dearest Huston is crumbling, I am overcome with a sadness that I do not know how to convey.

You have meant so much to so many, you have come with the voices of angels to remind us who we are, you have come with the light of God to shine upon our faces and force us to remember, you have come as a beacon radiating in the darkest night of our confused and wretched souls, you have come as our own deepest being to never let us forget. And you have done this consistently, and with integrity, and with brilliance, and with humility and courage and care, and you have left, and are still leaving, a path in which we all will follow, and we will do so with more gratitude and respect and love than my words will ever be able to convey.

So, you see, I have become a Divine schizophrenic. I am always, simultaneously, of two minds. Steeped in Emptiness, it is all exactly as it should be, a stunning gesture of the Great Perfection. And—at precisely the same time, in precisely the same perception—I am reduced to tears at the thought of you leaving us, and it is simply intolerable, it is radically unacceptable, I will rage against the dying of that light until I can rage no longer, and my voice is ragged with futile screams against the insult of samsara. And yet, just that is nirvana; not theoretically, but just so, like this, right now: Emptiness. Both perceptions are simultaneous; I know I don't have to tell you about this; it is so in your case, I know.

And so, on the side of the double-entry that rages against the crumbling of the citadel, I just wanted to tell you, as deeply as I could, what you have meant to all of us. And to me, specifically, my entire career has marched, step by step, with you never out of the picture. From that glorious letter you wrote to a young 25-year-old, praising his first book, to your agreement to sign on with *ReVision* (I told Jack Crittenden that I wouldn't feel comfortable doing the journal unless Huston came aboard), to giving the eulogy at Treya's ceremony, which reduced me to tears and made me pretty much incoherent. On this side of the double-entry, I know I will not do well when the citadel crumbles.

Now you must forgive me for prematurely burying you, and speaking as if your demise were imminent; God willing, it will be decades before we will all gather together to actually speak out loud these types of words as your ashes return to the cosmic dance and your soul returns to where it never left. But, as I warned you, "the citadel is crumbling" sent such a sadness rushing through me, I wanted to err on the side of getting these words to you now, even if decades too soon. Perhaps because of

Treya, I am more sensitive than most to the "bubble bursting" at just the damnedest times, expected or not.

So do forgive me for delivering my eulogy to you; at the same time, I always liked the derivation of "eulogy"—*eu*: true, *logy*: story—the true story. I send back to you the biggest portion that I can manage of that love that you have freely given to us all and called us all to incarnate. Your own love, God's love—you have taught us that they are the same—I offer back to you, my mentor, my guide, my friend, the man I am least likely ever to forget.

Yours always,
Ken

Sunday, February 9

Right before I began work on *Sex, Ecology, Spirituality* [SES], several teachers at The Naropa Institute in Boulder asked me if I would meet with them and their students. I generally decline offers to lecture or teach, which is too bad, because I enjoy it, but in this case we hit upon a compromise. I would simply invite the students to come to my house—in three or four shifts, thirty to fifty students each shift—and we would discuss any topics they wanted for as long as they wanted. During my three-year hermitage [working on SES] these seminars were canceled, but this year I agreed to start them up again. As long as the students come to my house, I can pretend to keep my "no public teaching" record clean—you know, I'm not lecturing, I'm just having a few students over to chat.

So today we had another seminar. I've agreed to do these seminars perhaps twice a month, more or less indefinitely. Somebody suggested we start videotaping these, and perhaps we will.

Monday, February 10

By last week, the blurbs for *Science and Religion* had all arrived, from some very kind people who took pity on me. I assembled these into a package, with a blustery braggadocio letter, and sent it off to all the agents recommended to me by various friends and publishers. I have now heard back from all of them. The whole idea is funny. I am in effect doing an auction among a half-dozen agents, the winner of which will then auction my book among a half-dozen publishers, the winner of which will then publish the book.

It's also slightly awkward, because several of these agents are involved with flamboyant new-age writers. I appreciate the work of some of these writers, but in too many cases, it seems to me, the spirit offered is prerational and narcissistic, not transrational and divine. These writers, finding God and Goddess absent in the modern world, have decided to take their place. And their agents are anxious to get 15% of God. Already I have the feeling that this is much more than I bargained for.

Tuesday, February 11

A Spirituality That Transforms

Hal Blacker, the editor of *What Is Enlightenment?*, has described the topic of this issue of the magazine in the following way:

> We intend to explore a sensitive question, but one which needs to be addressed—the superficiality which pervades so much of the current spiritual exploration and discourse in the West, particularly in the United States. All too often, in the translation of the mystical traditions from the East (and elsewhere) into the American idiom, their profound depth is flattened out, their radical demand is diluted, and their potential for revolutionary transformation is squelched. How this occurs often seems to be subtle, since the *words* of the teachings are often the same. Yet through an apparent sleight of hand involving, perhaps, their context and therefore ultimately their meaning, the message of the greatest teachings often seems to become transmuted from the roar of the fire of liberation into something more closely resembling the soothing burble of a California hot tub. While there are exceptions, the radical implications of the greatest teachings are thereby often lost. We wish to investigate this dilution of spirituality in the West, and inquire into its causes and consequences.

I would like to take Hal's statement and unpack its basic points, commenting on them as best I can, because taken together, those points highlight the very heart and soul of a crisis in American spirituality.

TRANSLATION VERSUS TRANSFORMATION

In a series of books (e.g., *A Sociable God, Up from Eden, The Eye of Spirit*), I have tried to show that religion itself has always performed two very important, but very different, functions. One, it acts as a way of creating *meaning* for the separate self: it offers myths and stories and tales and narratives and rituals and revivals that, taken together, help the separate self make sense of, and endure, the slings and arrows of outrageous fortune. This function of religion does not usually or necessarily change the level of consciousness in a person; it does not deliver radical transformation. Nor does it deliver a shattering liberation from the separate self altogether. Rather, it consoles the self, fortifies the self, defends the self, promotes the self. As long as the separate self believes the myths, performs the rituals, mouths the prayers, or embraces the dogma, then the self, it is fervently believed, will be "saved"—either now in the glory of being God-saved or Goddess-favored, or in an afterlife that ensures eternal wonderment.

But two, religion has also served—in a usually very, very small minority—the function of radical transformation and liberation. This function of religion does not fortify the separate self, but utterly shatters it—not consolation but devastation, not entrenchment but emptiness, not complacency but explosion, not comfort but revolution—in short, not a conventional bolstering of consciousness but a radical transmutation and transformation at the deepest seat of consciousness itself.

There are several different ways that we can state these two important functions of religion. The first function—that of creating meaning for the self—is a type of *horizontal* movement; the second function—that of transcending the self—is a type of *vertical* movement (higher or deeper, depending on your metaphor). The first I have named *translation;* the second, *transformation.*

With translation, the self is simply given a new way to think or feel about reality. The self is given a new belief—perhaps holistic instead of atomistic, perhaps forgiveness instead of blame, perhaps relational instead of analytic. The self then learns to translate its world and its being in the terms of this new belief or new language or new paradigm, and this new and enchanting translation acts, at least temporarily, to alleviate or diminish the terror inherent in the heart of the separate self.

But with transformation, the very process of translation itself is challenged, witnessed, undermined, and eventually dismantled. With typical *translation,* the self (or subject) is given a new way to think about the world (or objects); but with radical *transformation,* the self itself is inquired into, looked into, grabbed by its throat and literally throttled to death.

Put it one last way: with horizontal translation—which is by far the most prevalent, widespread, and widely shared function of religion—the self is, at least temporarily, made happy in its grasping, made content in its enslavement, made complacent in the face of the screaming terror that is in fact its innermost condition. With translation, the self goes sleepy into the world, stumbles numbed and near-sighted into the nightmare of samsara, is given a map laced with morphine with which to face the world. And this, indeed, is the common condition of a religious humanity, precisely the condition that the radical or transformative spiritual realizers have come to challenge and to finally undo.

For authentic transformation is not a matter of belief but of the death of the believer; not a matter of translating the world but of transforming the world; not a matter of finding solace but of finding infinity on the other side of death. The self is not made content; the self is made toast.

Now, although I have obviously been favoring transformation and belittling translation, the fact is that, on the whole, both of these functions are incredibly important and altogether indispensable. Individuals are not, for the most part, born enlightened. They are born in a world of sin and suffering, hope and fear, desire and despair. They are born as a self ready and eager to contract; a self rife with hunger, thirst, tears, and terror. And they begin, quite early on, to learn various ways to translate their world, to make sense of it, to give meaning to it, and to defend themselves against the terror and the torture never lurking far beneath the happy surface of the separate self.

And as much as we, as you and I, might wish to transcend mere translation and find an authentic transformation, nonetheless translation itself is an absolutely necessary and crucial function for the greater part of our lives. Those who cannot translate adequately, with a fair amount of integrity and accuracy, fall quickly into severe neurosis or even psychosis: the world *ceases to make sense*—the boundaries between the self and the world are not transcended but instead begin to crumble. This is not breakthrough but breakdown; not transcendence but disaster.

But at some point in our maturation process, translation itself, no matter how adequate or confident, simply ceases to console. No new beliefs, no new paradigm, no new myths, no new ideas, will staunch the encroaching anguish. Not a new belief for the self, but the transcendence of the self altogether, is the only path that avails.

Still, the number of individuals who are ready for such a path is, always has been, and likely always will be, a very small minority. For most people, any sort of religious belief will fall instead into the category of consolation: it will be a new horizontal translation that fashions some sort of meaning in the midst of the monstrous world. And religion has always served, for the most part, this first function, and served it well.

I therefore also use the word *legitimacy* to describe this first function (the horizontal translation and creation of meaning for the separate self). And much of religion's important service is to *provide legitimacy* to the self—legitimacy to its beliefs, its paradigms, its worldviews, and its way in the world. This function of religion to provide a legitimacy for the self and its beliefs—no matter how temporary, relative, nontransformative, or illusory—has nonetheless been the single greatest and most important function of the world's religious traditions. The capacity of a religion to provide horizontal meaning, legitimacy, and sanction for the self and its beliefs—*that function of religion has historically been the single greatest "social glue" that any culture has.*

And one does not tamper easily, or lightly, with the basic glue that holds societies together. Because more often than not, when that glue dissolves—when that translation dissolves—the result, as we were saying, is not breakthrough but breakdown, not liberation but social chaos. (We will return to this crucial point in a moment.)

Where translative religion offers *legitimacy*, transformative religion offers *authenticity*. For those few individuals who are ready—that is, sick with the suffering of the separate self, and no longer able to embrace the legitimate worldview—then a transformative opening to true authenticity, true enlightenment, true liberation, calls more and more insistently. And, depending upon your capacity for suffering, you will sooner or later answer the call of authenticity, of transformation, of liberation on the lost horizon of infinity.

Transformative spirituality does not seek to bolster or legitimate any present worldview at all, but rather to provide true authenticity by shattering what the world takes as legitimate. Legitimate consciousness is sanctioned by the consensus, adopted by the herd mentality, embraced by the culture and the counterculture both, promoted by the separate self as *the* way to make sense of this world. But authentic consciousness quickly shakes all of that off its back, and settles instead into a glance that sees only a radiant infinity in the heart of all souls, and breathes into its lungs only the atmosphere of an eternity too simple to believe.

Transformative spirituality, authentic spirituality, is therefore revolutionary. It does not legitimate the world, it breaks the world; it does not console the world, it shatters it. And it does not render the self content, it renders it undone.

And those facts lead to several conclusions.

WHO ACTUALLY WANTS TO TRANSFORM?

It is a fairly common belief that the East is simply awash in transformative and authentic spirituality, but that the West—both historically and in today's "new age"—has nothing much more than various types of horizontal, translative, merely legitimate and therefore tepid spirituality. And while there is some truth to that, the actual situation is much gloomier, for both the East and the West alike.

First, although it is generally true that the East has produced a greater number of authentic realizers, nonetheless, the actual percentage of the Eastern population that is engaged in authentic transformative spirituality is, and always has been, pitifully small. I once asked Katagiri Roshi, with whom I had my first breakthrough (hopefully, not a breakdown), how many truly great Ch'an and Zen masters there have historically been. Without hesitating, he said, "Maybe one thousand altogether." I asked another Zen master how many truly enlightened—deeply enlightened—Japanese Zen masters there were alive today, and he said, "Not more than a dozen."

Let us simply assume, for the sake of argument, that those are vaguely accurate answers. Run the numbers. Even if we say there were only one billion Chinese over the course of history (an extremely low estimate), that still means that only one thousand out of one billion had graduated into an authentic, transformative spirituality. For those of you without a calculator, that's 0.0000001 of the total population. (Even if we say a million instead of a thousand, that is still only 0.001 of the population—a pitiful drop in the bucket.)

And that means, unmistakably, that the rest of the population were (and are) involved in, at best, various types of horizontal, translative, merely legitimate religion: they were involved in magical practices, mythical beliefs, egoic petitionary prayer, magical rituals, and so on—in other words, translative ways to give meaning to the separate self, a translative function that was, as we were saying, the major social glue of the Chinese (and all other) cultures to date.

Thus, without in any way belittling the truly stunning contributions of the glorious Eastern traditions, the point is fairly straightforward: radical transformative spirituality is extremely rare, anywhere in history, and anywhere in the world. (The numbers for the West are even more depressing. I rest my case.)

So, although we can very rightly lament the very small number of individuals in the West who are today involved in a truly authentic and radically transformative spiritual realization, let us not make the false argument of claiming that it has otherwise been *dramatically* different in earlier times or in different cultures. It has on occasion been a *little* better than we see here, now, in the West, but the fact remains: authentic spirituality is an incredibly rare bird, anywhere, at any time, at any place. So let us start from the unarguable fact that vertical, transformative authentic spirituality is one of the most precious jewels in the entire human tradition—precisely because, like all precious jewels, it is incredibly rare.

Second, even though you and I might deeply believe that the most important function we can perform is to offer authentic transformative spirituality, the fact is, much of what we have to do, in our capacity to bring decent spirituality into the world, is actually to offer more *benign and helpful modes of translation.* In other words, even if we ourselves are practicing, or offering, authentic transformative spirituality, nonetheless much of what we must *first* do is provide most people with a more adequate way to translate their condition. *We must start with helpful translations, before we can effectively offer authentic transformations.*

The reason is that if translation is too quickly, or too abruptly, or too ineptly taken away from an individual (or a culture), the result, once again, is not breakthrough but breakdown, not release but collapse. Let me give two quick examples here.

When Chögyam Trungpa Rinpoche, a great (though controversial) Tibetan master, first came to this country, he was renowned for always saying, when asked the meaning of Vajrayana, "There is only Ati." In other words, there is only the enlightened mind wherever you look. The ego, samsara, maya, and illusion—all of them do not have to be gotten rid of, because none of them actually exist: There is only Ati, there is only Spirit, there is only God, there is only nondual Consciousness anywhere in existence.

Virtually nobody got it—nobody was ready for this radical and authentic realization of always-already truth—and so Trungpa eventually introduced a whole series of "lesser" practices leading up to this radical and ultimate "no practice." He introduced the Nine Yanas as the foundation of practice—in other words, he introduced nine stages or levels of practice, culminating in the ultimate "no practice" of always-already Ati.

Many of these practices were simply translative, and some were what we might call "lesser transformative" practices: miniature transformations that made the bodymind more susceptible to radical, already-accomplished enlightenment. These translative and lesser practices issued forth in the "perfect practice" of no-practice—or the radical, instantaneous, authentic realization that, from the very beginning, there is only Ati. So even though ultimate transformation was the prior goal and ever-present ground, Trungpa had to introduce translative and lesser practices in order to prepare people for the obviousness of what is.

Exactly the same thing happened with Adi Da, another influential (and equally controversial) adept (although this time, American-born). He originally taught nothing but "the path of understanding": not a way to attain enlightenment, but an inquiry into why you want to attain enlightenment in the first place. The very desire to seek spiritual enlightenment is in fact nothing but the grasping tendency of the ego itself, and thus the very search for enlightenment prevents it. The "perfect practice" is therefore not to search for enlightenment but to inquire into the motive for seeking itself. You obviously seek in order to avoid the present, and yet the present alone holds the answer: to seek forever is to miss the point forever. You always already *are* enlightened Spirit, and therefore to *seek* Spirit is simply to deny Spirit. You can no more attain Spirit than you can attain your feet or acquire your lungs.

Nobody got it. And so Adi Da, exactly like Trungpa, introduced a whole series of translative and lesser transformative practices—seven stages of practice, in fact—leading up to the point that you could dispense with seeking altogether, there to stand open to the always-already truth of your own eternal and timeless condition, which was completely and totally present from the start, but which was brutally ignored in the frenzied desire to seek.

Now, whatever you might think of those two adepts, the fact remains: they performed perhaps the first two great *experiments* in this country on how to introduce the notion that "There is only Spirit"—and thus seeking Spirit is exactly what prevents realization. And they both found that, however much we might be alive to Spirit, alive to the radical *transformative* truth of this moment, nonetheless *translative* and lesser transformative practices are almost always a prerequisite for that final and ultimate transformation.

My second point, then, is that in addition to offering authentic and radical transformation, we must still be sensitive to, and caring of, the numerous beneficial modes of lesser and translative practices. This more generous stance therefore calls for an "integral approach" to overall transformation, an approach that honors and incorporates many lesser transformative and translative practices—covering the physical, emotional, mental, cultural, and communal aspects of the human being—in preparation for, and as an expression of, the ultimate transformation into the always-already present state.

And so, even as we rightly criticize merely translative religion (and all the lesser forms of transformation), let us also realize that an integral approach to spirituality combines the best of horizontal and vertical, translative and transformative, legitimate and authentic—and thus let us focus our efforts on a balanced and sane overview of the human situation.

WISDOM AND COMPASSION

But isn't this view of mine terribly elitist? Good heavens, I hope so. When you go to a basketball game, do you want to see me or Michael Jordan play basketball? When you listen to pop music, who are you willing to pay money in order to hear? Me or Bruce Springsteen? When you read great literature, who would you rather spend an evening reading, me or Tolstoy? When you pay sixty-four million dollars for a painting, will that be a painting by me or by Van Gogh?

All excellence is elitist. And that includes spiritual excellence as well. But spiritual excellence is an elitism to which all are invited. We go first to the great masters—to Padmasambhava, to Saint Teresa of Ávila, to Gautama Buddha, to Lady Tsogyal, to Emerson, Eckhart, Maimonides, Shankara, Sri Ramana Maharshi, Bodhidharma, Garab Dorje. But their message is *always* the same: let this consciousness be in you which is in me. You start elitist, always; you end up egalitarian, always.

But in between, there is the angry wisdom that shouts from the heart: we must, all of us, keep our eye on the radical and ultimate transformative goal. And so any sort of integral or authentic spirituality will also involve a critical, intense, and occasionally polemical shout from the transformative camp to the merely translative camp.

If we use the percentages of Chinese Ch'an as a simple blanket example, this means that if 0.0000001 of the population is actually involved in genuine or authentic spirituality, then 0.9999999 of the population is involved in nontransformative, nonauthentic, merely translative or horizontal belief systems. And that means, yes, that the vast, vast majority of "spiritual seekers" in this country (as elsewhere) are involved in much less than authentic occasions. It has always been so; it is still so now. This country is no exception.

But in today's America, this is much more disturbing, because this vast majority of horizontal spiritual adherents often claim to be representing the leading edge of spiritual transformation, the "new paradigm" that will change the world, the "great transformation" of which they are the vanguard. But more often than not, they are not deeply transformative at all; they are merely but aggressively translative—they do not offer effective means to utterly dismantle the self, but merely ways for the self to think differently. Not ways to transform, but merely new ways to translate. In fact, what most of them offer is not a practice or a series of practices; not *sadhana* or *satsang* or *shikan-taza* or yoga. What most of them offer is simply the suggestion: read my book on the new paradigm. This is deeply disturbed, and deeply disturbing.

Thus, the authentic spiritual camps have the heart and soul of the great transformative traditions, and yet they will always do two things at once: appreciate and engage the lesser and translative practices (upon which their own successes usually depend), but also issue a thundering shout from the heart that translation alone is not enough.

And therefore, all of those for whom authentic transformation has deeply unseated their souls must, I believe, wrestle with the profound moral obligation to shout from the heart—perhaps quietly and gently, with tears of reluctance; perhaps with fierce fire and angry wisdom; perhaps with slow and careful analysis; perhaps by unshakable public example—but *authenticity* always and absolutely carries a *demand* and *duty*: you must speak out, to the best of your ability, and shake the spiritual tree, and shine your headlights into the eyes of the complacent. You must let that radical realization rumble through your veins and rattle those around you.

Alas, if you fail to do so, you are betraying your own authenticity. You are hiding your true estate. You don't want to upset others because you don't want to upset your self. You are acting in bad faith, the taste of a bad infinity.

Because, you see, the alarming fact is that any realization of depth carries a terrible burden: Those who are allowed to see are simultaneously saddled with the obligation to *communicate* that vision in no uncertain terms: that is the bargain. You were allowed to see the truth under the agreement that you would communicate it to others (that is the ultimate meaning of the bodhisattva vow). And therefore, if you have seen, you simply must speak out. Speak out with compassion, or speak out with angry wisdom, or speak out with skillful means, but speak out you must.

And this is truly a terrible burden, a horrible burden, because in any case there is no room for timidity. The fact that you might be wrong is simply no excuse: You might be right in your communication, and you might be wrong, but that doesn't matter. What does matter, as Kierkegaard so rudely reminded us, is that only by investing and speaking your vision with *passion,* can the truth, one way or another, finally penetrate the reluctance of the world. If you are right, or if you are wrong, it is only your passion that will force either to be discovered. It is your duty to promote that discovery—either way—and therefore it is your duty to speak your truth with whatever passion and courage you can find in your heart. You must shout, in whatever way you can.

The vulgar world is already shouting, and with such a raucous rancor that truer voices can scarcely be heard at all. The materialistic world is already full of advertisements and allure, screams of enticement and cries of commerce, wails of welcome and whoops of come hither. I don't mean to be harsh here, and we must honor all lesser engagements. Nonetheless, you must have noticed that the word "soul" is now the hottest item in the title of book sales—but all "soul" really means, in most of these books, is simply the ego in drag. "Soul" has come to denote, in this feeding frenzy of translative grasping, not that which is timeless in you but that which most loudly thrashes around in time, and thus "care of the soul" incomprehensibly means nothing much more than focusing intensely on your ardently separate self. Likewise, "spiritual" is on everybody's lips, but usually all it really means is any intense egoic feeling, just as "heart" has come to mean any sincere sentiment of the self-contraction.

All of this, truly, is just the same ole translative game, dressed up and gone to town. And even that would be more than acceptable were it not for the alarming fact that all of that translative jockeying is aggressively called "transformation," when all it is, of course, is a new series of frisky translations. In other words, there seems to be, alas, a deep hypocrisy hidden in the game of taking any new translation and calling it the great transformation. And the world at large—East or West, North or South—is, and always has been, for the most part, perfectly deaf to this calamity.

And so: given the measure of your own authentic realization, you were actually thinking about *gently whispering* into the ear of that near-deaf world? No, my friend, you must shout. Shout from the heart of what you have seen, shout however you can.

But not indiscriminately. Let us proceed carefully with this transformative shout. Let small pockets of radically transformative spirituality, authentic spirituality, focus their efforts, and transform their students. And let these pockets slowly, carefully, responsibly, humbly, begin to spread their influence, embracing an *absolute tolerance* for all views, but attempting nonetheless to advocate a true and authentic and integral spirituality—by example, by radiance, by obvious release, by unmistakable liberation. Let those pockets of transformation gently persuade the world and its reluctant selves, and challenge their legitimacy, and challenge their limiting translations, and offer an awakening in the face of the numbness that haunts the world at large.

Let it start right here, right now, with us—with you and with me—and with our commitment to breathe into infinity until infinity alone is the only statement that the world will recognize. Let a radical realization shine from our faces, and roar from our hearts, and thunder from our brains—this simple fact, this obvious fact: that you, in the very immediateness of your present awareness, are in fact the entire world, in all its frost and fever, in all its glories and its grace, in all its triumphs and its tears. You do not see the sun, you are the sun; you do not hear the rain, you are the rain; you do not feel the earth, you are the earth. And in that simple, clear, unmistakable regard, translation has ceased in all domains, and you have transformed into the very Heart of the Kosmos itself—and there, right there, very simply, very quietly, it is all undone.

Wonder and remorse will then be alien to you, and self and others will be alien to you, and outside and inside will have no meaning at all. And in that obvious shock of recognition—where my Master is my Self, and that Self is the Kosmos at large, and the Kosmos is my Soul—you will walk very gently into the fog of this world, and transform it entirely by doing nothing at all.

And then, and then, and only then—you will finally, clearly, carefully and with compassion, write on the tombstone of a self that never even existed: There is only Ati.

Wednesday, February 12

I have finally settled on Kim Witherspoon as an agent (protégée of my old acquaintance John Brockman). We have chosen the top seven "mainstream" publishers we are hoping for: Random House, Simon and Schuster, Doubleday, Bantam, Broadway, Riverhead/Putnam, Harper SanFran. Kim sent the book out to all of them today. So we wait.

Friday, February 14

Well, pretty good news. All seven publishers got back to Kim within forty-eight hours. She says the book is "red hot," but in the publishing world of hype and holler, you have to wonder what that actually means. "Here's what's happening. Ann Godoff, the head editor at Random House—she's our first choice—wants to make a preemptive bid."

"How much?"

"I don't know; I'm guessing around $500,000."

"Good lord. Well, the problem is, I promised the other publishers they could get in on the bidding. I feel kind of odd leaving them out."

"They want in, especially since all fourteen of your books are still in print. It looks like we're headed into an auction, and it could get pretty wild. It would be a good idea for you to come to New York."

"Um, okay."

"Soon."

"Um, okay."

"Like next week."

"Um, okay."

Friday, February 21—Boulder—New York

Early morning, on a plane to New York, rushing to the mainstream. I'm deeply ambivalent: Of course I want the book to do well; I hope it's a mega-best-seller—I just don't want to be a part of it. I'm not even sure if I packed all the right clothes. I need something that won't clash with reluctance.

I will split my stay between Tony Schwartz's house and a downtown hotel. I'm looking forward to seeing Tony and his family—wife Deborah and two adorable daughters, Emily and Kate, just in their teens. But for the auction, I need to be in the thick of it, and a hotel in midtown Manhattan will be best. "Fasten your seatbelts, it's going to be a bumpy night."

Sunday, February 23—New York

Tony and Deborah have the most beautiful house. It's in Riverdale, an anomalously posh section of the Bronx just north of Manhattan. I arrive on Friday, have a few days to relax before the auction, which begins tomorrow. The first night they forgot to show me where the thermostat was, and, this being winter in New York, I was properly freezing to death, and spent most of the night trying to get their two dogs to jump into bed with me for some warmth, Eskimo-style. "Come on, you can do it, you can do it, jump right up, right here, that's a good dog." But the little rats had been totally trained to never get on beds, and the most I could do is get one of them to come halfway on board; she insisted on keeping her hind legs on the floor, thus never technically committing a foul. They must train these dogs with cattle prods.

So, tomorrow it starts.

Tuesday, February 25—New York

Tony pulled some strings and got me into the Four Seasons Hotel—the only hotel in the Western hemisphere, I note, designed by I. M. Pei. It's exquisite.

Meetings all day long yesterday and today. All of the publishers kindly consented to meet me at the restaurant here at the Four Seasons. They each were scheduled for two-hour presentations, starting at ten and going till six. I sat at the same table each day, all day, drinking tomato juice, trying to impress them as they tried to impress me. I hate tomato juice.

Kim and I knew early on that there was a buzz starting about the book, and it continued. Alice Mayhew, grand dame of Simon and Schuster, editor of *All the President's Men*, etc., said she definitely wanted it. Phyllis Grann, head of Putnam, publisher of Tom Clancy, etc., said, "This is the first nonfiction book I really want to publish." I am slightly flabbergasted by these reactions. What's going on? There are larger currents afloat here, I think, and my book is getting caught up in them. By the time Ann Godoff and I meet—she was the last meeting, late today—the first thing she said was, "In my professional career I've never seen a buzz like this on a nonfiction book."

"Good grief." And we talk for an hour or two. What I like about Ann, even more than the nice comment, is that when I say I will do nothing to promote the book, she says, "No problem," whereas the other publishers were visibly appalled at my lack of interest in the marketing end of the deal.

"Listen, Ann, we really do have to see what the other publishers are going to do. But please try to keep Random House in the game."

"Don't worry."

Wednesday, February 26—New York

The auction began this morning, and almost immediately we ran into something of a catastrophe. Kim began reading the various bids to me, over the phone. By one P.M., the bidding was approaching $400,000. Random House's top bid, however, was $200,000, which meant they were definitely out of the running. I was totally taken aback. What's going on here?

What we didn't know was that Harry Evans, head of Random House, looked at the book—just this morning, right as the auction was getting under way—and decided that anything over $200,000 was too much for an academic work. (Personally, I think he's right.)

This meant a difficult decision. Although I could use the money, I have decided—and Kim strongly agrees—that the only house that can really do what I want for this particular book is Random House. In the middle of the proceedings I tell Kim my decision and she immediately calls off the auction, which shocks pretty much everybody.

But I am very glad to have Random House, and very glad to have Ann. Wonder who will tell her.

Thursday, February 27—New York

I meet with Ann in her office. She has just finished ushering James Hillman's *The Soul's Code* to #1 on the *Times* best-seller list, no small feat. And her *Midnight in the Garden of Good and Evil* is the best-seller of the decade. I sent her flowers late yesterday; they're on her desk.

"Harry's around here somewhere. You should meet him."

In comes Harry, short, sharp, bright, and rambling. Harry is a leading contender to get the Eisner book, so it's funny that I'm staying with Tony. Both of our editors might be in this room right now.

"Ken Wilber, it's fine to meet you! Ann, when . . . when . . . when is the last time we've seen a buzz like this on a nonfiction book?"

"Never, Harry."

"That's right, never. We're very happy about this."

We chat for a few moments, and then Harry vanishes as quickly as he had materialized.

Ann and I talk for an hour or two—I like her enormously—and I return to the Four Seasons. Her comment about the book's buzz gave me one of those warm glows, but she probably says that to all the boys.

It has been a swift five months, almost to the day, since I started writing *Science and Religion*. And now, suddenly, it all seems over.

March

Our normal waking consciousness is but one special type of consciousness, while all about it, parted from it by the filmiest of screens, there lie potential forms of consciousness entirely different. We may go through life without suspecting their existence, but apply the requisite stimulus and at a touch they are there in all their completeness. . . . There is a continuum of cosmic consciousness, against which our individuality builds but accidental fences, and into which our several minds plunge as into a mother-sea or reservoir.

No account of the universe in its totality can be final which leaves these other forms of consciousness quite disregarded.

—WILLIAM JAMES

Monday, March 3—New York—Boulder

On the plane, back to Boulder, back to a life that seems somehow far away from itself.

Is this a topic whose time has truly come? The integration of science and religion? Or have I just written a clever book that temporarily impressed a few people and will otherwise go as quickly as it came? Publication date is set for early 1998; we'll find out soon enough.

Tuesday, March 4—Boulder

Worked all morning, went grocery shopping, paid bills, watched two videos. Atom Egoyan's *Family Viewing*, one of his first, and quirkily brilliant. All of Egoyan's films are fascinating; his *Exotica* is a truly stunning film. I keep hoping he'll break out soon. And Hal Hartley's *Amateur*, my favorite of his (also *Simple Men* and *Unbelievable Truth*). Hartley's films are all so slyly funny.

There is light snow falling now, dancing with the sunlight shining off the ground. I feel enfolded in some sort of luminous cosmic blanket, lightly.

Wednesday, March 5

Science and Religion opens with a quick summary of the perennial philosophy, or the common core of the world's great wisdom traditions. They all maintain, in their various ways, that there are different levels or dimensions of existence, stretching from *matter* to living *body* to symbolic *mind* to subtle *soul* to causal and nondual *spirit*. Matter, body, and mind we moderns have no problem accepting; but soul and spirit? Where is the *proof* that soul and spirit actually exist? The answer, it seems, involves direct spiritual experience—repeatable, reproducible, confirmable. This, anyway, is what *Science and Religion* attempts to demonstrate.

[See figure 1. This is the so-called Great Chain of Being, although that is something of a misnomer. Each senior level transcends and includes, or enfolds and embraces, its juniors, so this is really the Great Nest of Being. For this reason it is more accurately called, not a hierarchy, but a *holarchy*, a series of nested spheres.]

The cross-cultural evidence is massive and overwhelming: it appears that human awareness and identity *can span the entire spectrum of consciousness*, from matter to body to mind to soul to spirit. There appears to be an actual development or *evolution of consciousness* along that extraordinary continuum. At each level, what we consider to be our "self" changes dramatically. When consciousness is identified with the vital body, we have the bodyego or bodyself—we are identified with our impulses, our feelings, our immediate bodily sensations. When consciousness identifies with the mind, we have the ego—the conceptual, mental, narrative sense of self, involving the taking of roles and the following of rules. When consciousness identifies with the subtle level, we have the soul—a supra-individual sense of self that begins to breathe an atmosphere beyond the conventional and mundane. And when consciousness evolves even further, and identifies with nondual reality, we have Spirit itself, the Goal and Ground of the entire Nest of Being.

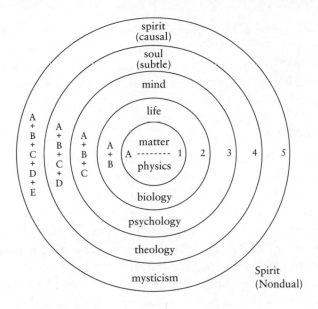

FIGURE 1. *The Great Nest of Being. Spirit is both the highest level (causal) and the nondual Ground of all levels.*

The evidence for this Great Spectrum is grounded at every point in *direct experience* that can be confirmed or rejected by any who adequately follow the interior experiments in consciousness. These experiments, generally known as meditation or contemplation, cannot be dismissed on the ground that they are "merely subjective" or "interior" apprehensions—after all, mathematics is "merely subjective" and "interior," but we don't dismiss that as unreal or illusory or meaningless. Just so, the contemplative sciences have amassed an extraordinary amount of phenomenological data—direct experiences—relating to the subtle and causal, or soul and spirit, levels. And if you want to know if this data is real, all you have to do is follow the experiment—contemplation—and see for yourself. Of those who adequately do so, the majority report a simple conclusion: you are directly introduced to your True Self, your Real Condition, your Original Face, and it is none other than Spirit itself.

Thursday, March 6

Read all morning (new historicism, cultural studies, critical legal studies, new paradigm), most of it very disappointing, and poorly written to boot. I don't mind if most theoretical writers can't turn a phrase like William James. When Whitehead was asked, "Why don't you write more clearly?," he replied, "Because I don't think more clearly." Fine, no problem. It's the sense you get that so few are even trying. . . .

Friday, March 7

Mail bag from Shambhala, containing last month's letters. About one-fourth of the mail I get is still from *Grace and Grit: Spirituality and Healing in the Life and Death of Treya Killam Wilber*; to date I've received over eight hundred letters. Many of these I try to respond to, however briefly, because they are always so deeply moving.[4] When I first wrote *Grace and Grit*, I thought that the intense mail would last for a year or so and then perhaps fade out. But it has been continuous; I get dozens of the most agonizing letters a month. But I have also come to realize that this will be a part of my life indefinitely, and that is fine. So once each month, I go through the letters.

> Dear Ken,
> My name is —— and I just finished reading *Grace and Grit*. I had been diagnosed with Breast Cancer in February and a friend from Zurich sent me and my husband your book. At first I felt it would be too depressing to read, but I became curious about it and began. Sometimes it was too sad for me to read and I would put it down. However, I continued to read it and at some point I no longer felt afraid to read it. On the contrary, I felt supported by it. I appreciated your honesty in sharing what it was like being a support person and I also loved getting to know Treya. She was a remarkable and wonderful role model. I do believe I have learned more about love, compassion and forgiveness from this book than from anything else I have read.

---

4. When it became apparent that I might publish these journals, I thought about deleting these letters—they are so painfully personal. But because they are an indelible part of my life, I decided to leave them in, with one editorial change: I have deleted, from the letters, most of the congratulatory praise for the book's author, simply because publishing that would be more than ordinarily self-serving. It is simply understood that most of the people who write me about G&G are grateful, but it is their stories, not their gratitude, that I hope these letters most convey.

Your book gave me another chance to cry and reconnect with myself. Thank you.

Love,
———

Dear Mr. Wilber,
I want to thank you for your book *Grace and Grit*. I bought it for Christmas 1994, after my wife died in September. She had a terrible Non Hodgin Lymphom.

Over one Year she was in hospital for getting chemo therapie. My wife came from Laos and lived in Thailand since thirty years. About six years I had a wonderful time of marriage with her.

She was a Buddhist.

I stopped my working and stayed with her in hospital. All day and night I was beside her. By this time I didn't know your book. But today I can find a lot of truth in your words.

My wife died in hospital, because she could not leave her bed anymore. I was very sad about this situation, but we were forced to stay. I would be happy if I could bring her back home. But it was impossible.

As she died in the afternoon a great storm and strong rain came up. And I saw a great grey cloud going upstairs from her body and drifting away out of the opened window. After twenty minutes the storm was over.

Then one week later I brought her body back to Thailand. I didn't cremate her in Germany. An inner voice told me—bring her back home—and I did so.

Since last weeks I studied your book nearly six or seven times.

And every time I find something more for my spirit. And I hope many people will read your books and try to change something in their lives.

You have written a great book. It will be one of the important books of my life. I can read it again and again. And for this I must thank you so much.

Greetings,
———

The stories are so moving, they just tear your heart out; that dear man, taking his wife back to Thailand. Here's an easier one from a young man:

Dear Ken,

I have just finished reading *Grace and Grit*. In a way, I feel that I know Treya, or perhaps I should say that I feel her. I would like to share with you my experience on finishing the book.

As I read the last two chapters, I could feel the tears coming. I don't know why I waited to the end to cry but I did. Then, just as I finished the last page, I *really* cried, and my whole body started shaking uncontrollably. I thought to myself, "What's happening here?," and got up and walked around the house, as if movement would somehow give me understanding. About this time, I was also struck with the realization of how precious life is, and I had a strong desire to rush upstairs and awaken my sleeping parents so that I could tell them how much I loved them. Something held me back, perhaps my ego, perhaps the late hour—I do not know—but I do know that I shall not look at them the same way again.

Then I sat down again, and just sat quietly for a few minutes. No tears now, just quiet. And a sense of peace.

I'm very grateful to you, Ken, and to Treya, for sharing your special gift with me. The message of the book, my message, is Life, and Love.

Peace,

————

Dear Ken,

Last August I was diagnosed with breast cancer. I had segmental surgery, lymph node dissection and a three week treatment. I am in constant relationship with cancer on all levels. Several weeks ago a friend told me of your book and I knew I had to read it. It was a scary thought because, after all, I knew the ending.

"But," I thought, "she had some other kind of more serious cancer." How's that for denial? The fact is, I have the same kind of terrible cancer Treya had. The truth is this book has been at moments *terrifying*, but totally *freeing*.

As I read Treya's writings and your reflections I heard my own voice and those of people I know who love me as well. The same self-abuse, the same "I can do it, thank you very much" way of being. And my friends and family puzzled over how I could not see how beautiful I am, how much they love me, and how accomplished they believe me to be. I too have struggled for years with the question of "What's my work, my purpose here?" I too have a willingness to let go and trying to live in the knowing that living is not a reward and death is not a punishment.

I thank you, praise you and bless you for your courage and honesty in writing *Grace and Grit*. I offer the enclosed music a gift back to you. May you continue to be healed and blessed.

Peace,

———

I have received many letters from women who say expressly how much they identified with Treya—that her concerns and issues were exactly the ones they were wrestling with in their own lives. And often people just want to tell their story, share it with me, whether it has anything to do with cancer or not.

Dear Mr. Wilber,
Greetings from Poland.

I have just read your book *Grace and Grit*, and I am still under the influence of it. I have been touched by the book to the bottom of my heart. I haven't experienced similar feelings for many years.

Many years ago I was interested in Freud's theory of psychoanalysis but when I became a mother I had to change my interests. Although I was very busy taking care of my children and working as a teacher, I have always tried to perceive the other people near by me. But I am very unhappy because of my unsuccessful personal life and sometimes I ask the question "Why me?" The answer is "Why not?"—I have found it also in your book. I would like to live the fullness of life, like your Treya, but it is so difficult. Her life was so unusual that it seems to be unreal. Sometimes I feel it was a dream only, not a book written by you.

I have just started looking for my daemon and I think I have to change something in my life. I have made some notes about your other books and also about the other authors and philosophers you wrote about in your book.

At the end of the letter I want to say that the book about your wife, Treya, and you is for me the most beautiful book about love and sacrifice. I am very happy I have read it.

If the letter reached you I would be very pleased.
With best summer wishes from Poland.

Yours sincerely,

————

Dear Mr. Wilber,
I just finished *Grace and Grit*. I identified so much with Treya.
She was struggling with so many of the same things that I have
been struggling with—trying to find her daemon, exploring spirituality and creativity, being vs. doing, masculine vs. feminine,
excessive self-criticism—these are the major issues in my life. I
was completely taken over by the book when I was reading it,
and I don't believe it will ever leave me. Your openness about
your and Treya's feelings was very courageous and poignant.
The admiration I grew to have for both of you, combined with
your openness about your weaknesses, was a good lesson for me
in learning not to be so hard on myself. Thank you. I was impressed with Treya's acceptance and transcendence of her cancer
and its implications. It was an impetus for me to put more energy into my meditation practice. The words that kept coming
into my mind when reading *Grace and Grit* were "devastating"
and "beautiful," it was devastatingly beautiful. I just wanted to
say thanks.

With appreciation and affection,

————

Dear Ken,
My husband and I have been reading the book *Grace and Grit*.
It is so full of love and emotions and also very educational.
When we read the book we get lumps in our throats and can
barely continue reading it with our teary eyes. If I may say, the
love that is expressed is so genuine. My husband's sister is undergoing chemotherapy and it is helping us understand what she
is feeling and experiencing.

Sincerely,

————

It has surprised me how many letters I get from couples who read the
book aloud to each other. I think because I quoted extensively from
Treya's journals—letting her speak for herself—couples like to take

turns reading each part. I didn't expect this would happen, but it is very moving to think of lovers using our experience, and Treya's death, to express their love for each other in life—and not waiting until it's too late to say the dear things that need to be said now.

Dear Ken,
I am writing to you, even though I don't know if you'll receive this or if in fact you do read unsolicited mail, to thank you from the bottom of my heart for writing *Grace and Grit*. I was, and still am some 10 days after finishing it, so moved and touched by your courage and love to write so deeply and honestly about your time together with Treya. How you must miss her physical presence and yet paradoxically how can you miss someone who is so completely with you in that immersion of love?
I, too, know of that love. I met —— in 1988 and a year after we married she was diagnosed with an almost crippling case of Lyme disease. It took me about a year of being a round the clock support person to realize I desperately needed help, which I found in a wonderful therapist who I still see regularly today. Some five years later my wife has recovered from most of her debilitating symptoms except her back pain which still keeps her lying down a good half to two-thirds of her waking hours. We, too, have become very familiar with all the levels that a disease resides in and all the levels of healing that can take place. And likewise our anger and outrage at our new-age–thinking friends who could say such things as "Oh, you have a pain in your back, what are you trying to avoid?" Enough of this, Ken, really all I wanted to say is thank you and God Bless you for sharing with me and the world your incredible and continuing love story. When I finished it I cried like I haven't cried in many, many years with such deep and sad and heart-opening sobs and tears.
                                        With my love and gratitude,
                                        ——

Dear Ken,
With fullest of hearts, I write to you thanks for living your story of *Grace and Grit* with such candor, love, honesty, and acceptance. I have set your book down a few days ago, and the story runs through my being, so powerful, even many years after her passing. The experience for me has been one of those lovely mys-

tical events that opens me up in new and better ways (not without a few floods!), changing me once again. I feel such a kinship with Treya because our life paths have crossed in so many ways, so I could relate to her intimately. Would I choose the same choices? Would a noble soul within me be revealed by such a devastating disease?

Though I never knew her in life, I am so very grateful to you for showing her to me in such clear ways. Her struggle with and eventually accepting the unacceptable, to continue on to her physical death in "passionate equanimity" (a perfect term for me to embrace) mixed with her utter humanity, moved me immeasurably. I feel such a longing for female role models to be inspired by, so many spiritual teachers are male and for me somehow there is a gap in understanding. Treya's story spoke to me in my words, and bless you for allowing her to tell her own story, in her own words, and never once speak for her.

I was also very touched, very moved by your process, your struggle, your acceptance in serving her, totally loving her. Your devotion to her, even after death in those 24 hours—I am really so blown away—tears—I have never known such a love. Though I have always imagined such depth, for whatever luck, karma, destiny or unconscious choices I have not experienced what the two of you found. However, just the fact that you and Treya found that kind of love feels so good to me! I'm not completely crazy! It does exist. Yes. It does.

When you write a book, it's strange that you let so many people into your soul and you may not ever meet them or hear from them. I just wanted you to know that you helped me, affected me by living your story. Thank you with all my heart.

Love,
———

Dear Ken,
Last year I was diagnosed with advanced metastatic breast cancer. A friend of mine said I had to read this book, *Grace and Grit*, but when I asked how it ended, he said, "She died." I was afraid of the book for a long time.

But having finished it, I wanted to thank you and Treya from the bottom of my heart. I know I might die, too, but somehow following Treya's story has made me unafraid. I feel free of fear, for the first time. I had two strong experiences, satori I guess, just from reading your descriptions of higher awareness. When Treya died in the book, I felt like I died, so now I don't have to worry.

Thank you again so very, very, very much. I do think I will die and I do think Treya will be there for me.

Sincerely,

———

I feel I am with these people, and they with me. Suffering is a constant reminder of the pain of being human, but also one of the most elemental ways that we all connect with each other, because we all suffer terribly at some point. Suffering is not just "negative"; it is a bond through which we all touch each other. Suffering, truly, is the first grace.

Dear Ken,
Grace and Grit pretty much stopped my life. I had to finish it, or should I say, consume it before I could do much else. When I read the first few chapters, I sat down and sobbed uncontrollably for quite some time. It is hard for me now to capture the intensity I felt. I was totally overwhelmed as if a torrent of blocked emotion had been released and was flooding my body. You know the kind of sobs that start way down in your gut and rattle your whole being. I was touched so deeply. I found *Grace and Grit* to be the most beautiful love story I have ever read. I sobbed for your joy and for your loss, bliss that I have only glimpsed, pain that I am not sure I can imagine. And, I sobbed for the sense of joy and loss it triggered in me.

My joy sprang from knowing that it is possible to experience the kind of connection you so beautifully reveal, that sacred love is real and not just some crazy fantasy and that a man of your intellectual depth and intensity is capable of such profound emotional connection. I suppose, because of my father, a brilliant man who has never really inhabited his body (pretty much cut off at the neck), I have always separated these things. As sobs racked my body, for the first time in my life I really got in the fabric of my being that it is possible to connect mind and body and heart in a deeply felt connection.

I grieved, for while I have had fleeting glimpses of this type of connection, I have never experienced it with a man who was willing or ab e to maintain that level of intensity beyond the briefest encounter. And, even more so, because it is my deepest heart's desire and I had, after years of holding hope in my heart, stopped believing it was possible.

Once again, your words brought me back to what I knew to be True at the deepest level; that it really is OK for me not to settle for anything less than the depth I desire and that *this is* possible!

I understand that you are something of a recluse, but I hope someday we can meet. With much respect, admiration, and love,

———

Dear Ken Wilber,

I am fourteen years old. Since I was a little girl I have been very afraid of dying. I read Treya's story, and ever since, I have not been afraid to die. I wanted to tell you this.

Sincerely,

———

Treya's journals were truly extraordinary. As I went through them some time after her death, I was struck by one amazing fact: there were no secrets in them. Oh, they were very intimate and very personal, but nothing Treya hadn't shared with me or somebody. She simply had no split between her public and private selves—they were basically identical. With Treya, you knew exactly what she was thinking and feeling—she simply never lied or shaded the truth. This enormous integrity was what people found absolutely compelling, and irresistibly attractive, about her. I think this honesty comes across in the book, and people respond gratefully for getting her uncompromisingly honest account of living—and dying—with a terrible disease. Many of them write to me in an attempt to thank Treya, and that is fine with me; and they say nice things about me, in an attempt to praise Treya, and that's okay, too.

It's funny, though. I had planned to destroy Treya's journals when she died, and I decided that I would not read them first. Even though, as I later found out, there were no secrets in them, Treya cherished her time alone when she wrote in her journal, and I was determined not to violate that by reading them. Curious as I might be, I was very clear about this. Nobody was ever going to see her journals.

And then, twenty-four hours before she died—and right before I carried her up the stairs for the last time—she pointed toward her journals and said, very simply, "You'll need those."

A week earlier she had asked me to write of our ordeal—she was diagnosed with breast cancer ten days after we were married. She hoped, she said, that all the lessons we had learned the hard way would help others. I promised her I would write the book. And so, "You'll need those" meant, you'll need my journals if you are going to give a full account of what transpired. I knew then that I would read them, all of them, first page to last, and I did, with more difficulty than I can record.

The last entry in those journals—ten notebooks in all—the very last entry was: "It takes grace, yes!—and grit."

Saturday, March 8

Joyce Nielsen is the author of *Sex and Gender in Society*, which is probably the single best text on feminism. It is thorough, fair, comprehensive, judicious. Nielsen is one of my favorite feminist writers, along with Janet Chafetz, Carol Gilligan, Martha Nussbaum. . . . It never really dawned on me that she teaches at the University of Colorado, Boulder.

I get home today and there's a message on the machine: "If this is the Ken Wilber who wrote *Sex, Ecology, Spirituality*, and I'm pretty sure it is, I'd like to talk to you. I teach sociology at the University of Colorado, and I use *Sex, Ecology, Spirituality* as a textbook for my advanced graduate seminar. I was wondering if you could come and talk with us. Please call me at. . . ."

I pick up the phone and call her number, get her machine. "If this is the Joyce Nielsen who wrote *Sex and Gender in Society*, and I'm pretty sure it is, I'm a real fan. . . ." I'm hoping she'll call back.

Sunday, March 9

It's taken almost a week for any sort of meditative awareness to return, including lucid dreaming. The entire time I was in New York I lost all access to pure witnessing, and I had no subject permanence during the dream and deep sleep state. That is, I was not conscious during the dreaming and deep sleep state—a consciousness, a kind of current, that has been with me off and on for the last three or four years.

This constant consciousness through all states—waking, dreaming, and sleeping—tends to occur after many years of meditating; in my case, about twenty-five years. The signs are very simple: you are conscious during the waking state, and then, as you fall asleep and start to dream, you still remain conscious of the dreaming. This is similar to lucid dreaming, but with a slight difference: usually, in lucid dreaming, you start to manipulate the dream—you choose to dream of sex orgies or great food or flying over mountains or whatnot. But with constant witnessing consciousness, there is no desire to change anything that arises: you simply and innocently witness it. It's a choiceless awareness, a mirrorlike awareness, which equally and impartially reflects whatever arises. So you remain conscious during the dream state, witnessing it, not changing it (although you can if you want; usually you don't want).[5] Then, as you pass into deep, dreamless sleep, you still remain conscious, but now you are aware of nothing but vast pure emptiness, with no content whatsoever. But "aware of" is not quite right, since there is no duality here. It's more like, there is simply pure consciousness itself, without qualities or contents or subjects or objects, a vast pure emptiness that is not "nothing" but is still unqualifiable.

Then, as you come out of the deep sleep state, you see the mind and the dream state arise and take form. That is, out of causal emptiness there arises the subtle mind (dreams, images, symbols, concepts, visions, forms), and you witness this emergence. The dream state continues for a while, and then, as you begin to wake up, you can see the entire gross realm, the physical realm—your body, the bed, the room, the physical universe, nature—arise directly out of the subtle mind state.

In other words, you have just taken a tour of the Great Chain of Being—gross body to subtle mind to causal spirit—in both its *ascending* and *descending* movements (evolution and involution). As you fall asleep, you pass from gross body (waking) to subtle mind (dreaming) to causal emptiness (deep sleep)—that's evolution or ascent—and then, as you awaken, you move down from causal to subtle to gross—that's involution or descent. (The actual order of states can vary, but the entire cycle is generally present.) Everybody moves through this cycle every twenty-four hours. But with constant consciousness or unbroken witnessing, you remain aware during all these changes of state, even into deep dreamless sleep.

Since the ego exists mostly in the gross state, with a few remnants in

---

5. I call this "pellucid dreaming" to distinguish it from lucid dreaming. Throughout many entries I simply use the well-known term "lucid dreaming." Nonetheless, I almost always mean pellucid dreaming. I also refer to pellucid deep sleep, or tacit witnessing in the deep dreamless state.

the subtle, then once you identify with constant consciousness—or that which exists in all three states—you break the hold of the ego, since it barely exists in the subtle and does not exist at all in causal emptiness (or in the deep sleep state, which is one type of emptiness). You cease identifying with ego, and you identify with pure formless consciousness as such, which is colorless, spaceless, timeless, formless—pure clear emptiness. You identify with nothing in particular, and therefore you can embrace absolutely everything that arises. Gone to the ego, you are one with the All.

You still have complete access to the waking-state ego, but you are no longer *only* that. Rather, the very deepest part of you is one with the entire Kosmos in all its radiant glory. You simply *are* everything that is arising moment to moment. You do not see the sky, you are the sky. You do not touch the earth, you are the earth. You do not hear the rain, you are the rain. You and the universe are what the mystics call "One Taste."

This is not poetry. This is a *direct realization*, as direct as a glass of cold water in the face. As a great Zen Master said upon his enlightenment: "When I heard the sound of the bell ringing, there was no bell and no I, just the ringing." And in that nondual ringing is the entire Kosmos, where subject and object become One Taste and infinity happily surrenders its secrets. As researchers from Aldous Huxley to Huston Smith have reminded us, One Taste or "cosmic consciousness"—the sense of oneness with the Ground of all creation—is the deepest core of the nearly universal consensus of the world's great wisdom traditions. One Taste is not a hallucination, fantasy, or product of a disturbed psyche, but the direct realization and testament of countless yogis, saints, and sages the world over.

It is very simple, very obvious, very clear—concrete, palpable, unmistakable.

Monday, March 10

Aldous Huxley, of course, wrote a famous book, *The Perennial Philosophy*, which is about the universal core of the world's great wisdom traditions. Huston Smith's *Forgotten Truth* is still its best introduction. I wrote an essay for the *Journal of Humanistic Psychology* that begins: "Known as the 'perennial philosophy'—'perennial' precisely because it shows up across cultures and across the ages with essentially similar features—this worldview has, indeed, formed the core not only of the world's great wisdom traditions, from Christianity to Judaism to Buddhism to Taoism, but also the thinking of some of the greatest philosophers, scientists, and psychologists East and West, North and South. So overwhelmingly widespread is the perennial philosophy—the details of which I will explain in a moment—that it is either the single greatest intellectual error ever to appear in humankind's history—an error so colossally widespread as to literally stagger the mind—or it is the single most accurate reflection of reality yet to appear."[6]

So what are the details of this perennial philosophy? Very simple: *the Great Nest of Being, culminating in One Taste*—there, in a nutshell, is the perennial philosophy.

This is not to say that everything about the perennial philosophy is set in concrete or etched in gold. I actually wrote a paper called "The Neo-Perennial Philosophy," pointing out that much of it needed to be updated and modernized.[7] Nonetheless, the core of the world's great wisdom traditions is a framework we ought to consult seriously and reverentially in our own attempts to understand the Kosmos.

And at its heart is the experience of One Taste—clear, obvious, unmistakable, unshakable.

Tuesday, March 11

Well, unshakable with further practice. I'm always curious what will interrupt this nondual current, what will obscure or disrupt constant consciousness, what will throw you out of the All and into the clutches of your separate self, where suffering awaits. Interestingly, in my case, one glass of wine will prevent it (that is, if I have one glass of wine, then that night I am not conscious during the dream and deep sleep state. I'm sure great yogis can drink and still remain conscious through all three states, but not me). Stress usually does not disrupt this constant current. But in New York I drank several glasses of wine most of the days there, so that alone would account for the disruption of witnessing. On the other hand, I was there to do blatant self-promotion, something that I am not good at doing gracefully—I either underdo or overdo it. So it could have been the simple fact that I was in the clutches of the egoic self-contraction for the better part of a week that virtually obliterated stable access to the Witness.

Last night it all seemed to rearrange itself. I was not lucid dreaming

---

6. This essay is included in chapter 1 of *The Eye of Spirit*.
7. This essay is included in chapter 2 of *The Eye of Spirit*.

at first, I was just dreaming: a woman and I are sitting in front of Sri Ramana Maharshi. There is a large audience, but I don't really notice it. The woman is explaining how you practice self-inquiry, which is a practice of inquiring "Who am I?" and attempting to feel into the very source of consciousness; it is an attempt to find the pure and ever-present Witness. For some reason the woman was explaining it all wrong; she was presenting it as the *result* of making an *effort* to be aware. I looked at Ramana and said, No, there's no effort, you simply notice that you are *already* aware, and that awareness—just as it is—is it. No effort at all. Ramana smiled, and my mind and his mind were instantly one. I started lucid dreaming at that point, but more a witnessing. That current of witnessing or constant consciousness has stayed with me now for several days and nights, which is usually the way it has been, off and on, for several years now.

It's a fascinating process. It is pure Emptiness, altogether unbounded, radiant, pure, free, limitless, beyond light and beyond bliss, radically unqualifiable. Ramana called this deep witnessing (or constant consciousness) the I-I, because it is aware of the little I or separate self. Ken Wilber is just a gross-level manifestation of what I-I really am, which is not Ken at all, but simply the All. Ken was born and will die, but I-I never enters the stream of time. I-I am the great Unborn, I-I am the mysterious Undying; the entire Kosmos exists as the simple feeling of my own Being. And every sentient being in the entire universe can make that claim, as long as they stand as the great I-I, which is no I whatsoever.

(Vedanta emphasizes the I-I, Buddhism emphasizes no I, but they are both pointing to pure, nondual, unqualifiable Emptiness—*shunyata* or *nirguna*—which is the simple suchness or thusness or isness of the entire world, and is not other than the pure, natural, spontaneous, ever-present consciousness that is your own true state right now—an unbroken nondual stream that persists through all possible changes of state, waking, dreaming, sleeping. In its pure form the Witness dissolves into everything it witnesses—the mirror-mind is one with its objects, Emptiness is one with all Form. And so, as both Vedanta and Buddhism emphasize, pure consciousness itself is nondual, empty, and finally unqualifiable.)

When meditators first start developing (or rather, noticing) this constant consciousness, they tend to go through a type of split-mind awareness. On the one hand, you are developing a capacity for strong meditative equanimity, a capacity to Witness both pain and pleasure without flinching, without either grasping or avoiding. "The perfect person," said Chuang Tzu, "employs the mind like a mirror: it accepts but does not grasp, it receives but does not keep." As this mirror-mind awareness (or constant consciousness) grows stronger, the gross waking state becomes more and more "dreamlike," in the sense that it loses its power to overwhelm you, to shake you, to make you believe that passing sensations are the only reality. Life starts to look like one great big movie, and you are the unmoved Witness watching the show. Happiness arises, you witness it; joy arises, you witness it; pain arises, you witness it; sorrow arises, you witness it. In all cases, you are the Witness, and not some passing surface wave of silly sound and fury. At the center of the cyclone, you are safe. A deep and inward peace begins to haunt you; you can no longer manufacture turmoil with quite the same conviction.

But that doesn't mean that you can't feel desire, hurt, pain, joy, happiness, suffering, or sorrow. You can still feel all of those; they just don't convince you. Again, it's like being at the movies. Sometimes you get so caught up in what is happening on screen that you forget it's just a movie. At a thriller, you might actually become frightened; at a romance, you might start crying. Then your friend leans over and says, Hey, lighten up, it's just a movie, it's not real! And you snap out of it.

Enlightenment is . . . to snap out of the movie of life. To wake up, to shake it off. You are, and always have been, at the movies, as the Witness. But when you take life seriously—when you think the movie is real—you *forget* you are the pure and free Witness and you *identify* with a little self—the ego—as if you were part of the movie you are actually watching. You identify with somebody on screen. And therefore you get frightened, and therefore you cry, and therefore you suffer altogether.

With meditation, you begin to relax in your seat and just watch the movie of life, without judging it, avoiding it, grasping it, pushing it, or pulling it. You merely Witness it: you employ the mirror-mind, you rest in simple, clear, spontaneous, effortless, ever-present consciousness.

As you persist in noticing (and relaxing into) the choiceless awareness of what is, then this consciousness will begin to extend from the waking state into the dream state—you will simply remain as choiceless awareness, as the mirror-mind, as constant consciousness, even as the dream state arises. You will notice that phenomenologically the gross world—the physical body, the sensorimotor world, and the ego built upon them—all begin to dissolve into the subtle world of imagery and vision. In any event, you remain conscious.

With further practice, that choiceless awareness will extend from the dream state even into deep dreamless sleep. And since "you" are still present (not as ego but as I-I, as pure consciousness without an object), you will find a much deeper and truer identity: you are still tacitly conscious when there are no objects, no subjects, and no contents at all—no suffering, no pain, no pleasure, no desire, no goals, no hope, no fear. There is nothing arising at all, in this pure Formless state—and yet you are, you still exist, but only as pure consciousness. There is no body, there is no ego, there is no mind—and yet you know that you exist, and so you are obviously none of those lesser states. You are only you—that is, there is nothing but pure I AMness, pure nondual Consciousness, which is so radically free, unlimited, unbounded, and unqualifiable, that strictly speaking we can only call it "Emptiness"—and that is what it "feels" like as well: an infinite Absence or Abyss, which is just another name for infinite Freedom.

Thursday, March 13

Just got off the phone with Mike Murphy (our exuberant conversations rarely last less than two hours). He and his friend Sylvia Tompkins are doing a series of projects, including a CD-ROM and a book, focusing on an integral (or balanced) spirituality—an updated, modernized version of the perennial philosophy, which is also sympathetic with my own work. Sylvia thought of putting this integral view on CD-ROM, and she and Mike eventually found themselves hooked up with James Redfield, author of *The Celestine Prophecy* and *The Tenth Insight*, who, because of his extraordinary commercial success (over fifteen million readers), would help these projects reach a much wider audience.

It looks like I will be going to San Francisco to speak to the Fetzer Institute, so I arranged to get together with Mike when I'm out there. Mike is truly amazing. Not only did he cofound Esalen Institute—ushering in the Human Potential Movement—he has remained on the forefront of psychological and spiritual development ever since. He's just finished writing *The Kingdom of Shivas Irons*, the avidly awaited follow-up to his classic *Golf in the Kingdom*. Last I heard, Clint Eastwood was going to make, and star in, the film version of *Golf*, along with Sean Connery. Lord, that will probably ruin Mike's life; he'll never have a quiet moment again.

Friday, March 14—Boulder—San Francisco

Early morning, on a plane, headed to San Francisco. The Fetzer Institute, founded by John Fetzer, is one of the few liberal organizations that will fund genuinely spiritual projects. Liberals and God don't get along too well, so conservatives have cornered the market on God-talk in this country. Both of those facts are unfortunate.

This is why Fetzer is largely unique—a liberal charity not frightened by Spirit. They have, for example, funded Bill Moyers's PBS series on health and meditation. Rob Lehman is now head of Fetzer, although he works closely in conjunction with a Board. My old friend Judith Skutch (publisher of *A Course in Miracles*) has been on the Board for a long time, and she has been instrumental in getting several other good people to join, including Frances Vaughan. Fetzer is in the process of reorganizing, and they asked me to talk with them about various directions for their future development.

So here I am, 36,000 feet above it all, about to abruptly descend into it. The Board is meeting all day Friday and Saturday; I am scheduled to speak each afternoon from around 2 to 5. The format is question and answer. I'll go directly from the plane to the meeting, which starts a few hours from now.

Saturday, March 15—San Francisco

I figured that, in order to describe a comprehensive or integral approach to transformation, I would have to spend the first hour or two outlining my general ideas, as summarized in, say, *A Brief History of Everything*. But when I got to the conference room, they had diagrams from *Brief History* on the wall, and everybody was quite conversant with all the technical terms. Then I think I went too far the other way. During the first break, I passed Roger [Walsh] in the hall—he was there as a consultant—and he whispered "Keep it simple."

Today more meetings, and I again went on in the afternoon. The questions—and my answers, or attempted answers—centered on the nature of a truly integral or holistic or comprehensive vision, and how best to implement it, or simply make it available to individuals and the culture at large.

There are many ways to explain "integral" or "holistic." The most common is that it is an approach that attempts to include and integrate matter, body, mind, soul, and spirit—attempts, that is, to include the entire Great Nest of Being. Thus, physics deals with matter, biology deals with the living body, psychology deals with the mind, theology deals with the soul, and mysticism deals with the direct experience of spirit—so an integral approach to reality would include physics, biology, psychology, theology, and mysticism (to give just a few examples). [See figure 1 on page 319.]

Although that is a good start at defining "integral," what I have tried to do in my writings is make that scheme a little more sophisticated by pointing out that each of those *levels* actually has at least four important aspects or *dimensions*: each level can be looked at from the inside and from the outside in both individual and collective forms.

For example, your consciousness can be looked at from the inside— the subjective side, your own awareness right now—which is experienced in the first person as an "I" (all the images, impulses, concepts, and desires floating through your mind right now). You can also study consciousness in an objective, empirical, scientific fashion, in the third person as an "it" (for example, the brain contains acetylcholine, dopamine, serotonin, etc., all described in objective it-language). And both of those exist not just in singular but in plural forms—not just an "I" or an "it," but a "we." This collective form also has an inside and outside: the cultural values shared from within (e.g., morals, worldviews, cultural meaning), and the exterior concrete social forms seen from without (e.g., modes of production, technology, economic base, social institutions, information systems).

So each level in the Great Chain actually has an *inside* and *outside* in both *individual* and *collective* forms—and that gives us the four dimensions (or "four quadrants") of each level of existence. [Figure 2 gives several details of the four quadrants; the terminology will be explained as the entries proceed.]

Because both of the Right-Hand quadrants are objective it(s), they can be counted as one, so I often simplify the four dimensions to just three: I, we, and it; or first-person, second-person, and third-person. [These are also indicated in figure 2.]

There's an easy way to remember these three basic dimensions. *Beauty* is in the eye of the beholder, the "I" of the beholder. The *Good* refers to moral and ethical actions that occur between you and me, or "we." *Truth* usually refers to objective empirical facts, or "its." So the three basic dimensions of "I," "we," and "it" also refer to the Beautiful, the Good, and the True. Or again, art, morals, and science.

So a truly integral view would not talk just about matter, body, mind, soul, and spirit—because *each* of those levels has a dimension of art, of morals, and of science, and we need explicitly to include all of them. So, for example, we have the art of the matter/body realm (naturalism, realism), the art of the mental realm (surrealistic, conceptual, abstract),

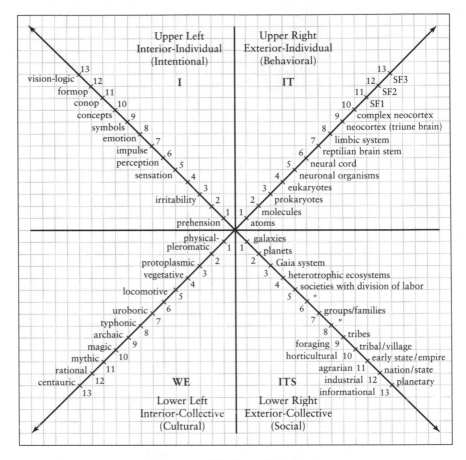

FIGURE 2. *The Four Quadrants*

the art of the soul and spirit realm (contemplative, transformative). Likewise, we have morals that spring from the sensory realm (hedonism), from the mental realm (reciprocity, fairness, justice), and from the spiritual realm (universal love and compassion). And so on.

So putting these three *dimensions* (I, we, and it; or art, morals, and science; or Beauty, Goodness, and Truth) together with the major *levels* of existence (matter, body, mind, soul, and spirit) would give us a much more genuinely integral or holistic approach to reality. [See figure 3. See also *The Marriage of Sense and Soul* for a further discussion of this topic.]

The Fetzer Institute wants to support and promote an integral approach to the world—in education, medicine, spirituality, scientific re-

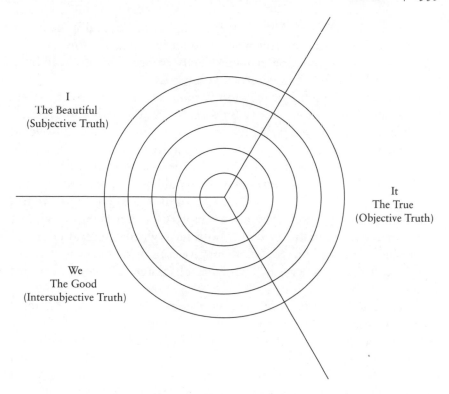

FIGURE 3. *Levels of the Good, the True, and the Beautiful*

search, consciousness studies, and so forth. The Board members found my dimensions/levels to be useful in furthering the discussion, and for several hours the dialogue focused on these issues.

Apparently today I was doing better, since nobody whispered urgent suggestions to me in the hall.

Monday, March 17—San Francisco

Today I moved from the Inn Above Tide, in Sausalito, where Fetzer put us all up (we figured it beat the Inn Below Tide), and into the Hyatt off Union Square in downtown San Francisco. I'm sitting here on the thirty-sixth floor, in a restaurant at the top of the hotel, overlooking the most beautiful city in America. The Golden Gate, on my left, connecting the airiness of the city to the greenness of Marin; the Bay Bridge, on the right, reaching over to unamusing Oakland; the prison Alcatraz, straight ahead, a craggy monument to male aggression.

I love San Francisco. I'd live here if I could afford it, and if the house in Boulder weren't the perfect place to do a lot of work. I'm going to spend a few days wandering around the city before I have to head back to the relentless grind of research on volume 2.

My old friend Mitch Kapor is in town; he's staying across the street at Campton Place, but he's away for a few days at a meditation retreat. Yesterday, on his way out, I asked him to stop by at Frances and Roger's, so I could introduce them. Frances and Roger are the most special couple in my life, and have been for over two decades—all my adult life, really. I still sort of think of us as a trio. My life would be so much less without them; we have all shared our greatest ups and downs, and most things in between. To my mind, they are exemplary human beings in almost every way, caring, bright, brilliant. Both have written several books of surpassing merit, and I have seen them give countless hours of what can only be called selfless service. They both absolutely die when I say this kind of stuff, but there it is.

Mitchell and I met back in the Lincoln days. He had read *The Spectrum of Consciousness* and came out to my house a couple of times to talk. I liked him immediately—Mitch is bitingly brilliant but it's not off-putting; there is something instantly likeable about him. He was then friends with—and the meditation teacher of—Jack Crittenden. Jack and I were in the process of setting up *ReVision Journal*, which we did, and which eventually took me to Boston, where both Jack and Mitch lived. Mitch, in the meantime, went back to graduate school, got a business degree from MIT, then founded Lotus software, the most successful software of its time. He eventually sold Lotus for many millions, cofounded the Electronic Frontier Foundation, and set up Kapor Enterprises. It's always nice to introduce friends, so Mitch and Frances and Roger and I spent an afternoon together, talking about this and that.

Wednesday, March 19—San Francisco

This morning I rented a car and drove out to Muir Beach, to Sam Keen's house, where Treya and I first lived together after we were married (we rented the house from him; nobody was there today). I sat on the porch for an hour, maybe two. It's still with me. She lingers still. The sadness is palpable, part of the misty atmosphere over the beach, making it hard to breathe.

For about two weeks after her death, I was in the same state of glory and grace in which she had passed. There was only radiant awareness, with no subject and no object, but everything arising just as it should, beautifully. We were together, then, I'm sure. And then the self-contraction returned, as is its wont, and I was Ken again, mostly.

I look out over the beach; scenes of our life together emerge from the clouds and come looking for me. In many ways, I always think of Treya and me together in this house. We had a few months here before cancer struck; it was the only cancer-free zone in our entire time together. So it is here that I see her whole and full, breathtakingly beautiful, a radiance that reached right into you and grabbed your soul, and spoke in words too tender too repeat. It was here that we danced and cried, made love and laughter, held on to each other as if to life itself. And it was here that those wretched words, "Terry has cancer," were first spoken by me, over the phone, to family and friends, in that first, horrible, hideous night.

But I don't think of her that much anymore, because she is a part of that which thinks. She runs in my blood and beats in my heart; she is part of me, always, so I don't have to picture her to remember her. She is on this side of my skin, not that, not out there, not away from me. Treya and I grew up together, and died together. We were always two sides of the same person. It will always be so, I think.

Thursday, March 20—San Francisco—Boulder

On the plane, back to Boulder. Had dinner with Mike Murphy and Sylvia the other night. We talked about the Integral Transformative Practice centers that he and George [Leonard] are starting. Mike's got the Stanford Center for Research in Disease Prevention on board to help document the progress and effectiveness of the integral training. This is truly important work, groundbreaking work, I think, and it will help to define an entirely new approach to psychological and spiritual transformation, one that includes the best of ancient wisdom and the brightest of modern knowledge. No surprise that once again Murphy is at the leading edge.

Friday, March 21—Boulder

Glorious morning—Boulder can be beautiful. Went shopping, restocked the refrigerator, started through the piles of mail, 62 phone messages, etc.

Finished reading *The Andy Warhol Diaries*. Well, now we know the speed of shallow. Actually, I came to rather like Warhol. And his art. The fruit of one branch of the tree of Duchamp, Warhol is the consummate artist of flatland. His works are all surface, bright and vigorous, alarming and electric, with absolutely nothing underneath. I don't like flatland, but I like his striking representation of it. "Surface, surface, surface was all that anyone found meaningful." Warhol is really a great forerunner of postmodernism's aggressive, virulent, unyielding shallowness.

Sunday, March 23

Sitting here on the porch, watching the sun go down. Except there is no watcher, just the sun, setting, setting. From purest Emptiness, brilliant clarity shines forth. The sound of the birds, over there. Clouds, a few, right up there. But there is no "up," no "down," no "over," and no "there"—because there is no "me" or "I" for which these directions make sense. There is just *this*. Simple, clear, easy, effortless, ever-present *this*.

I became extremely serious about meditation practice when I read the following line from the illustrious Sri Ramana Maharshi: "That which is not present in deep dreamless sleep is not real."

That is a shocking statement, because basically, there is nothing—literally nothing—in the deep dreamless state. That was his point. Ultimate reality (or Spirit), Ramana said, cannot be something that pops into consciousness and then pops out. It must be something that is constant, permanent, or, more technically, something that, being *timeless*, is *fully present* at every point in time. Therefore, ultimate reality must also be fully present in deep dreamless sleep, and anything that is *not* present in deep dreamless sleep is NOT ultimate reality.

This profoundly disturbed me, because I had had several *kensho* or *satori*-like experiences (glimpses of One Taste), but they were all generally confined to the waking state. Moreover, most of the things I cared for existed in the waking state. And yet clearly the waking state is not permanent. It comes and goes every twenty-four hours. And yet, according to the great sages, there is something in us that is *always conscious*—that is literally conscious or aware at all times and through all states, waking, dreaming, sleeping. And that *ever-present awareness is Spirit in us*. That underlying current of constant consciousness (or nondual awareness) is a direct and unbroken ray of pure Spirit itself. It is our connection with the Goddess, our pipeline straight to God.

Thus, if we want to realize our supreme identity with Spirit, we will have to plug ourselves into this current of constant consciousness, and follow it through all changes of state—waking, dreaming, sleeping—which will (1) strip us of an exclusive identification with any of those states (such the body, the mind, the ego, or the soul); and (2) allow us to recognize and identify with that which is constant—or timeless—through all of those states, namely, Consciousness as Such, by any other name, timeless Spirit.

I had been meditating fairly intensely for around twenty years when I came across that line from Ramana. I had studied Zen with Katagiri and Maezumi; Vajrayana with Kalu and Trungpa; Dzogchen with Pema Norbu and Chagdud; plus I had studied—sometimes briefly, sometimes for extended periods—Vedanta, TM, Kashmir Shaivism, Christian mysticism, Kabbalah, Daism, Sufism . . . , well, it's a long list. When I ran across Ramana's statement, I was on an intensive Dzogchen retreat with my primary Dzogchen teacher, Chagdud Tulku Rinpoche. Rinpoche also stressed the importance of carrying the mirror-mind into the dream and deep sleep states. I began having flashes of this constant nondual awareness, through all states, which Rinpoche confirmed. But it wasn't until a year later, during a very intense eleven-day period—in which the separate self seemed to radically, deeply, thoroughly die—that it all seemed to come to fruition. I slept not at all during those eleven days; or rather, I was conscious for eleven days and nights, even as the body and mind went through waking, dreaming, and sleeping: I was unmoved in the midst of changes; there was no I to be moved; there was only unwavering empty consciousness, the luminous mirror-mind, the witness that was one with everything witnessed. I simply reverted to what I am, and it has been so, more or less, ever since.

The moment this constant nondual consciousness is obvious in your case, a new destiny will awaken in the midst of the manifest world. You will have discovered your own Buddha Mind, your own Godhead, your own formless, spaceless, timeless, infinite Emptiness, your own Atman that is Brahman, your Keter, Christ consciousness, radiant Shekhinah—in so many words, One Taste. It is unmistakably so. And just that is your true identity—pure Emptiness or pure unqualifiable Consciousness as Such—and thus you are released from the terror and the torment that necessarily arise when you identify with a little subject in a world of little objects.

Once you find your formless identity as Buddha-mind, as Atman, as pure Spirit or Godhead, you will take that constant, nondual, ever-present consciousness and reenter the lesser states, subtle mind and gross body, and reanimate them with radiance. You will not remain merely Formless and Empty. You will Empty yourself of Emptiness: you will pour yourself out into the mind and world, and create them in the process, and enter them all equally, but especially and particularly that specific mind and body that is called you (that is called, in my case, Ken Wilber); this lesser self will become the vehicle of the Spirit that you are.

And then all things, including your own little mind and body and feelings and thoughts, will arise in the vast Emptiness that you are, and they will self-liberate into their own true nature just as they arise, precisely because you no longer identify with any one of them, but rather let them play, let them all arise, in the Emptiness and Openness that you now are. You then will awaken as radical Freedom, and sing those songs of radiant release, beam an infinity too obvious to see, and drink an ocean of delight. You will look at the moon as part of your body and bow to the sun as part of your heart, and all of it is just so. For eternally and always, eternally and always, there is only *this*.

But you have not found this Freedom, or in any way *attained* it. It is in fact the same Freedom that has lived in the house of the pure Witness from the very start. You are merely recognizing the pure and empty Self, the radical I-I, that has been your natural awareness from the beginning and all along, but that you didn't notice because you had become lost in the intoxicating movie of life.

Monday, March 24

With the awakening of constant consciousness, you become something of a divine schizophrenic, in the popular sense of "split-minded," because you have access to *both* the Witness and the ego. You are actually "whole-minded," but it sounds like it's split, because you are aware of the constant Witness or Spirit in you, and you are also perfectly aware of the movie of life, the ego and all its ups and downs. So you still feel pain and suffering and sorrow, but they can no longer convince you of their importance—you are no longer the victim of life, but its Witness.

In fact, because you are no longer afraid of your feelings, you can engage them with much greater intensity. The movie of life becomes more vivid and vibrant, precisely because you are no longer grasping or avoiding it, and thus no longer trying to dull or dilute it. You no longer turn the volume down. You might even cry harder, laugh louder, jump higher. Choiceless awareness doesn't mean you cease to feel; it means you feel fully, feel deeply, feel to infinity itself, and laugh and cry and love until it hurts. Life jumps right off the screen, and you are one with all of it, because you don't recoil.

If you are having a dream, and you think it's real, it can get very scary. Say you are dreaming that you are tightrope walking across Niagara Falls. If you fall off, you plunge to your death. So you are walking very slowly, very carefully. Then suppose you start lucid dreaming, and you realize that it's just a dream. What do you do? Become more cautious and careful? No, you start jumping up and down on the tightrope, you do flips, you bounce around, you have a ball—precisely because you know it isn't real. When you realize it's a dream, you can afford to play.

The same thing happens when you realize that ordinary life is just a dream, just a movie, just a play. You don't become more cautious, more timid, more reserved. You start jumping up and down and doing flips, precisely because it's all a dream, it's all pure Emptiness. You don't feel less, you feel more—because you can afford to. You are no longer afraid of dying, and therefore you are not afraid of living. You become radical and wild, intense and vivid, shocking and silly. You let it all come pouring through, because it's all your dream.

Life then assumes its true intensity, its vivid luminosity, its radical effervescence. Pain is more painful and happiness is happier; joy is more joyous and sorrow is even sadder. It all comes radiantly alive to the mirror-mind, the mind that doesn't grasp or avoid, but simply witnesses the play, and therefore can afford to play, even as it watches.

What would motivate you if you saw everything as the dream of your own highest Self? What would actually move you in this playful dream world? Everything in the dream is basically fun, at some deep level, except for this: when you see your friends suffering because they think the dream is real, you want to relieve their suffering, you want them to wake up, too. Watching them suffer is not fun. And so a deep and powerful compassion arises in the heart of the awakened ones, and they seek, above all else, to awaken others—and thus relieve them from the sorrow and the pity, the torment and the pain, the terror and the anguish that comes from taking with dreadful seriousness the passing dream of life.

So you are a divine schizophrenic, you are "split-minded" in the sense that you are simultaneously in touch with both the pure Witness and the world of the ego-film. But that really means you are actually "whole-minded," because these two worlds are really not-two. The ego is just the dream of the Witness, the film that the Witness creates out of its own infinite plenitude, simply so it will have something to watch at the movies.

At that point the entire play arises within your own constant consciousness. There is no inside and no outside, no in here versus out there. The nondual universe of One Taste arises as a spontaneous gesture of your own true nature. You can taste the sun and swallow the moon, and centuries fit in the palm of your hand. The pure I-I, the great I AMness, breathes to infinity and creates a Kosmos as the Song of its very Self, and oceans of compassion fall as tears from your very own Original Face.

Last night I saw the reflection of the moon in a cool clear crystal pond, and nothing else happened at all.

Friday, March 28

A small stream, softly murmuring, runs down behind my house; you can hear it actually singing, if you listen with ears of light. The sun plays on the green leaves, sparkling emeralds each and all, and Spirit speaks in times like these, just a little louder. "I become a transparent eyeball; I am nothing, I see all." There is nothing solid here, all that is hard melts into air, all that is rigid softens to transparency, the world is diaphanous, not in appearance but essence. I disappear into the transparent show, and we are all light in light, images in images, floating effortlessly on a sea of the serene.

Nature is the outer form of Buddha, nature is the corporeal body of Christ. Take, eat, for this is my flesh; take, drink, for this is my blood. Poor dear nature, expression of the Real, impulse of the Infinite, transparent to Eternity, is merely a shining surface on an ocean of unending Spirit, dancing in the daylight of the Divine, hiding in the night of ignorance. For those who do not know the Timeless, nature is all they have; for those who do not taste Infinity, nature serves its last supper. For those in need of redemption, nature tricks you into thinking it alone is real. But for those who have found release, nature is the radiant shell in which a deeper truth resides. So it is—nature, mind, and spirit—Nirmanakaya, Sambhogakaya, and Dharmakaya—gross, subtle, and causal—are an eternal trinity in the folds of the Kosmos, never lost, never found.

Except today, where we are all light in light, and images in images, floating effortlessly on a sea of the serene.

April

Now I shall tell you the nature of this absolute Witness. If you recognize it, you will be freed from the bonds of ignorance, and attain liberation.

There is a self-existent Reality, which is the basis of our consciousness of ego. That Reality is the Witness of the states of ego consciousness and of the body. That Reality is the constant Witness in all three states of consciousness—waking, dreaming, and dreamless sleep. It is your real Self. That Reality pervades the universe. It alone shines. The universe shines with Its reflected light.

Its essence is timeless awareness. It knows all things, Witnesses all things, from the ego to the body. It is the Witness of pleasure and pain and the sense-objects. This is your real Self, the Supreme Being, the Ancient. It never ceases to experience infinite release. It is unwavering. It is Spirit itself.

—SHANKARA

Wednesday, April 2

Resting as the formless Witness brings both a radical liberation and a compelling duty: *liberation*, in that you are free from the bondage to the world of objects, which only live and die and suffer in the process; and *duty*, in that, from this infinite space of release, you feel compelled to help others find the same salvation, which is their own truest Self and deepest Condition—pure Emptiness, pure Spirit, pure Godhead. The ultimate metaphysical secret is that there are no others to save; the problem is, they don't realize that, and this ignorance drives the relentless round of birth and death and untold agony.

"Ignorance," Patanjali reminds us, "is the identification of the Seer with the instruments of seeing." Instead of Witnessing the body, we identify with it. Instead of Witnessing the ego, we identify with it. Instead of Witnessing suffering, we identify with it. And yet inevitably we are controlled by that with which we identify; we are tortured by all that we have not transcended. Thus lashing ourselves to the masts of misery, we suffer the outrages of space and time and terror. As one poet expressed the message of the Buddha:

> Ye suffer from yourselves, none else compels,
> None other holds you that ye live and die
> And whir upon the wheel, and hug and kiss its spokes of agony,
> Its tire of tears, its nave of nothingness.

Thursday, April 10

Alec Tsoucatos is an old friend of Treya's who has become a good friend of mine. He teaches business and economics at various colleges in the area, and every now and then leads a kw study group. He brought his group by the house to say hello, and I invited a few other friends, Kate Olson, a PBS producer, and Phil Jacobson, Director of Continuing Education at Naropa.

At some point in the evening we got into a discussion about meditation and the changes it can produce in brain waves. A young man training to be a psychiatrist asked me to get out a videotape I have of me connected to an EEG machine while I meditate. He believed none of the discussion about how meditation could profoundly alter brain waves, and he wanted "proof."

The tape shows me hooked to an EEG machine; this machine shows alpha, beta, theta, and delta waves in both left and right hemispheres. Alpha is associated with awake but relaxed awareness; beta with intense and analytic thinking; theta is normally produced only in the dream state, and sometimes in states of intense creativity; and delta is normally produced only in deep dreamless sleep. So alpha and beta are associated with the gross realm; theta with the subtle realm; and delta with the causal realm. Or, we could say, alpha and beta tend to be indicative of ego states, theta of soul states, and delta of spirit states. Delta presumably has something to do with the pure Witness, which most people experience only in deep dreamless sleep.

This video starts with me hooked up to the machine; I am in normal waking consciousness, so you can see a lot of alpha and beta activity in both hemispheres. But you can also see a large amount of delta waves; in both hemispheres the delta indicators are at maximum, presumably because of constant or stable witnessing. I then attempt to go into a type of nirvikalpa samadhi—or complete mental cessation—and within four or five seconds, all of the machine's indicators go completely to zero. It looks like whoever this is, is totally brain-dead. There is no alpha, no beta, no theta—but there is still maximum delta.

After several minutes of this, I start doing a type of mantra visualization technique—yidam meditation, which I have always maintained is predominantly a subtle-level practice—and sure enough, large amounts of theta waves immediately show up on the machine, along with maximum delta. The fact that theta, which normally occurs only in dreaming, and delta, which normally occurs only in deep sleep, are both being produced in a wide-awake subject tends to indicate a type of simultaneous presence of gross, subtle, and causal states (e.g., turiyatita). It is, in any event, attention-grabbing.

I dragged the video out and we all watched it. Sam says I make a total ass out of myself by showing this, since it seems so self-serving, so braggadocio. Probably so. But to me it's just an objective event. Too bad the test subject isn't somebody else, because the results are striking to the average viewer. It really gets their attention, and much more than my books do. It also convinced the soon-to-be psychiatrist, as it does virtually every scientific type I show it to.

I had started doing these videos—entering various types of meditation states and videotaping the corresponding brain-wave patterns on the EEG—as part of an integral approach to studying higher states and levels of consciousness (correlating what I would call Upper Left—subjective consciousness—and Upper Right—objective brain). I've found that there really are distinctively different brain-wave patterns for different types and levels of meditation. If nothing else, this could serve as a simple pilot project for more adequate and controlled studies. And, of course, Charles Alexander and the TM people are doing this type of research with much greater sophistication, and I'm a big fan of their work. Most of my friends who have seen this tape—Roger Walsh, Frances Vaughan, Mike Murphy, Tony Schwartz, Lex Hixon—have immediately seen the usefulness of this general type of research.

Anyway, people tend to get very serious after seeing this tape—serious in a good sense, I think, because it shows them that there is truly something profound going on, that primordial awareness is not just an idea you memorize but the result of actual practice that truly changes your very makeup. Some people are discouraged watching this, because they think they can't do it; but most people are encouraged, encouraged to take up an authentic spiritual practice and follow the current of constant consciousness through all three states, waking, dreaming, and deep sleep, thus finding that constant ray of Spirit that speaks to each and all in no uncertain terms.

Saturday, April 12

Sam is coming in tomorrow for a short visit. I've invited Reb Zalman Schachter-Shalomi to stop by with his wife, Eve, to meet Sam. Zalman is radiant, beautiful, blessed, sanctus. He's the spearhead of the Jewish Renewal movement, and a great scholar, especially of Kabbalah and Jewish mysticism. He's also the one who "rabbitized" Michael Lerner. Michael strikes me as a perfect spiritual descendant of Zalman—they both have the same type of twinkle in their eyes. Michael's new book, *The Politics of Meaning*, is a significant attempt to get liberalism and spirituality together (as is his magazine, *Tikkun*). But when Michael was last in Boulder he told me how disappointed he was with the book, because it had to be dramatically edited to make it more "popular" (he's happier with his previous book, *Jewish Renewal*).

Michael's story is a real cautionary tale about what the liberal media in this country will do to anything "spiritual." My own politics can fairly well be described as postconservative, postliberal. I'm working on several books on just this topic. Both liberalism and conservatism have their strengths and weaknesses, and we need to combine the strengths of both and jettison the weaknesses.

The main strength of liberalism is its emphasis on individual human rights. The major weakness is its rabid fear of Spirit. Modern liberalism came into being, during the Enlightenment, largely as a counterforce to mythic religion, which was fine. But liberalism committed a classic pre/trans fallacy: it thought that *all* spirituality was nothing but prerational myth, and thus it tossed any and all transrational spirituality as well, which was absolutely catastrophic. (As Ronald Reagan would say, it tossed the baby with the dishes.) Liberalism attempted to kill God and replace transpersonal Spirit with egoic humanism, and as much as I am a liberal in many of my social values, that is its sorry downside, this horror of all things Divine.

One of the strengths of typical conservatism is its reliance on Spirit; one of its downsides is that this "spirit" is almost always prerational, mythic, fundamentalist, ethnocentric. As such, conservatives are a little too eager to impose their beliefs and their "family values" on you, and since they have God on their side, they feel quite confident in their agenda. Witch hunts are never far behind the more intense conservative smiles.

The trick is to take the best of both—individual rights plus a spiritual orientation—and to do so by finding liberal humanistic values plugged into a *trans*rational, not prerational, Spirit. This spirituality is transliberal, evolutionary, and progressive, not preliberal, reactionary, and regressive.

It is also political, in the very broadest sense, in that its single major motivation—compassion—is pressed into social action. However, a postconservative, postliberal spirituality is *not* pressed into service as a *public* policy (transrational spirituality preserves the rational separation of church and state, as well as the liberal demand that the state shall neither protect nor promote a favorite version of the good life). Those who would "transform" the world by having all of us embrace their new paradigm, or their particular God or Goddess, or their version of Gaia, or their favorite mythology—those are all, by definition, reactionary and regressive in the worst of ways: preliberal, not transliberal, and thus their particular versions of the witch hunt are never far removed from their global agenda. A truly transliberal spirituality exists instead as a cultural encouragement, a background context that neither prevents nor coerces, but rather allows, genuine spirituality to arise. [See December 10 for further discussion of this topic.]

Michael Lerner is working on this most important issue, and I support him strongly. His organization wanted to give *Sex, Ecology, Spirituality* its ethics award, but I don't get out much, so we are trying to work out some way for me to do a column in *Tikkun*. I'm not sure if I can manage it, but it is very tempting.

The cautionary tale. Michael is friends with Bill and Hillary, and his "politics of meaning" was particularly espoused by Hillary. The liberal media found out about it and had a field day. Saint Hillary, Michael was "Hillary's guru," and so on. This was very hard on Michael, and it never really let up until . . . Jean Houston stepped in to take the flack. A simple visualization technique, used by thousands of therapists daily, was turned into Hillary's "channeling" Eleanor Roosevelt, whereas all she was doing was creative visualization. But anything *interior* is so utterly, radically, hideously alien to the liberal media that they could hardly discuss the topic without snickering or choking.

This is why *Science and Religion* is such a test case, at least as I see it. It is written expressly to take into account the fears of liberals, and attempts to hold their hands on what they must see as Mr. Toad's Wild Ride. The last chapter emphasizes the importance of keeping the gains of the liberal Enlightenment, and outlines a trans-liberal, not anti-liberal, view, which calls for the joining of the Enlightenment of the West (or political freedom) with the Enlightenment of the East (or spiritual freedom). Of course, by "Enlightenment of the East" I mean any truly authentic spiritual transformation, whether East or West, North or South. The point is to take the legal, political, and civil liberties of the modern West and, using that as a protective platform, allow transformative spiritual realization—and its compassion—to flourish. So I see *Science and Religion*, which ends on that message, as a test case on how far liberals can move in the direction of a transrational spirituality.

Sunday, April 13

Last night I had a date with a really nice woman, very beautiful, Marci Walters. We went to her favorite restaurant, Mataam Fez (Moroccan)— sat on the floor, ate with our fingers, and I tried not to drool on myself. She's a graduate student at Naropa, while holding down two jobs (working with the developmentally disabled). She's been accepted into the Peace Corps when she finishes school. She's a dedicated meditator, lifts weights, has completed over a dozen marathons and six triathlons. If I get out of line I suspect she will simply beat the crap out of me.

Wednesday, April 16

Back on typical schedule. I awaken between three and five, meditate for one or two hours, go straight to my desk and work till one or two P.M. The type of meditation I do varies, but the basic form is "the practice of the morning," or "ultimate guru yoga," where the true nature of one's own mind is the ultimate guru. The practice is: Upon waking, or upon passing from the dream state to the waking state, look directly into the mind, inquire directly into the source of consciousness itself—inquire "Who am I?" if you like, or practice looking directly into the looker.

Upon inquiring into the self, the self disappears, dissolving back into radiant Emptiness, and consciousness rests as absolute Freedom and Fullness, unbounded and unlimited, unborn and undying, unseen and unknown.

Within that vast Emptiness, the subtle soul arises, but you are not that. Within that vast Emptiness, the gross ego arises, but you are not that. Within that vast Emptiness, the gross body, nature, and matter all arise, but you are not those either. You are the radiant I AMness, prior to all worlds but not other to all worlds, which you embrace with a single glance, and your grace will make the sun rise, and the moon will reflect your glory, and you will not exist at all, in this vast expanse of Emptiness, that only alone is.

Thursday, April 17

In that transcendental state, delta presumably is off the wall, and if you keep some sort of access to that mirror-mind or stable witnessing as you enter the waking state, presumably delta waves would also remain operative. This seems to be the case in the videotape; but it is, at any rate, a fertile field of research.

As you "come out" of the causal or unmanifest state—the state of pure cessation, deep dreamless sleep, nirvikalpa samadhi, ayn, jnana samadhi, or pure consciousness without an object, to name a few variations on a theme—you can directly perceive the subtle and mental realms arise, and it is obvious that these subtle realms are a type of condensation or crystallization or contraction of the causal. That is, the subtle realm *feels* like a *gesture* of causal spirit, much like, if you make a fist, it is a gesture of your hand.

Likewise, if you remain witnessing, and you then come out of the subtle state—savikalpa samadhi, archetypal illumination, the dream state, creative vision, to name a few variations on that theme—you can directly perceive the gross realm arise, the realm of the physical body, matter, nature, and the gross-reflecting ego which arises in that sensorimotor world. These gross realms likewise feel like a gesture of the subtle: they feel like something the subtle *is doing*.

The net result of this involutionary arc—where causal spirit contracts into subtle soul, and subtle soul contracts into the gross world of ego and nature—is that the entire manifest world is a gesture of your own primordial awareness, your own Spirit, your own Godhead, your own Original Face. Each and every thing in the Kosmos is thus a manifestation of the Great Perfection, a manifestation of Primordial Purity in all its infinite delight.

Manifestation is not a sin; getting lost in manifestation is. We think that ego and nature are the only realities in the entire Kosmos, and there is our sin and our suffering. We have become lost in the gross movie of life, forgetting that the projector, the light, and the screen are all nothing but forms of the ultimate One Taste, radiant ripples on luminous Emptiness.

When you reestablish even a modest capacity for the mirror-mind or stable witnessing, and you generate a little bit of continuity between states (so you are not always losing consciousness as you pass from state to state, such as from waking to deep sleep), then it starts to become obvious that all states and levels—high or low, sacred or profane, shallow or deep—are in fact the effervescent manifestation of your own primordial Spirit. And therefore all seemingly "lesser" occasions, which the orthodox would consider "sin," become not *distractions* from Spirit but *celebrations* of Spirit's exuberant, wild, overflowing, ever-present creativity.

This is the whole point of Tantra, of course: each "defilement"—anger, envy, grasping, ignorance, jealousy—*has hidden in its very heart a transcendental wisdom*—clarity, equality, openness, all-accomplishing, discriminating. Tantra is based on one uncompromising insight: There is only God. There is only Spirit. There is only Goddess. There is only Tao. Not metaphorically, but *literally*. As Zen puts it, "That which one can deviate from is not the true Tao." You *cannot deviate* from It because there is *only* It—every "deviation" is still nothing but It. (Which is why the books purporting to tell us how we have deviated from the Goddess, or from Tao, or from the true Way, are miles off the mark.)

This is the experience of One Taste, where every single thing and event in the Kosmos, high or low, sacred or profane, has the same taste, the same flavor, and the flavor is Divine. All are gestures of God, which is to say, gestures of your own primordial Perfection, manifestations of your own radiant Emptiness, waves of your own nondual Consciousness. The entire universe will fit in the palm of your hand, you can hold the moon in two fingers, you can give the sun for Christmas presents, and nothing really happens at all.

Friday, April 18

The sunlight is playing off the remnants of snow, scattered everywhere in patches, snuggling under the dark green pines that cozy up against the house. It all arises in the luminous clearing of Emptiness, the spaciousness of Godhead, the unqualifiable expanse of All Space, which is not other than one's own choiceless awareness, moment to moment. There is *just this*. It blinds me into submission, takes my breath away, forces me to surrender to my own deepest state, where I am totally undone in the Beauty of it all.

That is exactly why *Beauty* takes on such a profound meaning. In that choiceless awareness, in the utter simplicity of One Taste, all realms—from causal formlessness to subtle luminosity to gross body, mind, and nature—take on a painful beauty, a truly painful beauty. Aesthetics takes on an entirely new importance, aesthetics in all domains— the beauty of the body, the beauty of the mind, the beauty of the soul, the beauty of spirit. When all things are seen as perfect expressions of Spirit, just as they are, all things become deeply, painfully beautiful.

Yesterday I sat in a shopping mall for hours, watching people pass by, and they were all as precious as green emeralds. The occasional joy in their voices, but more often the pain in their faces, the sadness in their eyes, the burdenous slowness of their paces—I registered none of that. I saw only the glory of green emeralds, and radiant buddhas walking everywhere, and there was no I to see any of this, but the emeralds were there just the same. The dirt on the sidewalk, the rocks in the street, the cries of the children, here and there—a paradise in a shopping mall, and who would ever have suspected?

Saturday, April 19

Just got a rather extraordinary letter from Joyce Nielsen [author of *Sex and Gender in Society*]. Six pages, single-spaced, and thoughtful from beginning to end. She refers specifically to the chapter entitled "Integral Feminism" in *The Eye of Spirit*. In that chapter, I point out that there are at least a dozen schools of feminism, and the only thing they all agree on is that females exist. Otherwise, they possess widely divergent views about what constitutes feminism (and females, for that matter). Using an "all-quadrant, all-level" approach, I try to show that each of these dozen schools stems from, or emphasizes, a different quadrant/level. As such, they *all* have something important, if limited, to tell us, and the only sane approach is an "integral feminism" that draws upon the strengths of each and jettisons their partialities. So a truly integral feminism would include all four quadrants (intentional, behavioral, social, and cultural)—*each of which* has preconventional, conventional, and postconventional levels, giving us a truly multidimensional feminism—not flatland, not one quadrant only, not one level only. Anyway, I try to spell this out in *The Eye of Spirit*, and Joyce says she is appreciative of (and mostly agrees with) this inclusiveness.

Nonetheless, Joyce feels—and here is the main difference she is writing to tell me about—that biological factors are negligible in explaining gender stratification, and worse, to even entertain such ideas, as I do, can help to bring about exactly the stratification we are trying to avoid. I understand her concern, but I do disagree. Besides, I think she is for emphasis exaggerating the role I place on biological sex differences. They are definitely important, in my opinion (that women get pregnant, for example, has an enormous influence in the productive roles of men and women in agrarian societies—and the fact of pregnancy is not itself a social construction). But I do not think that biology is the only, or even the most important, factor. In addition to the biological differences in the sexes (Upper Right), there are the social forces (Lower Right), individual differences (Upper Left), and background cultural values (Lower Left). Culturally constructed values play a tremendous role in gender stratification—I emphasize that strongly—but I refuse, contra the constructivists, to reduce all other quadrants to that quadrant. All four are equally important.

Perhaps Joyce can be persuaded to look over volume 2 (*Sex, God, and Gender: The Ecology of Men and Women*) when I write it. I'm hoping she can help prevent me from making a total ass of myself, although this will be asking an awful lot of her.

Monday, April 21—Denver

Marci and I spent the weekend in Denver, at the Oxford Hotel, in an area called LoDo (LOwer DOwntown), deliberately modeled on SoHo. I love this place, and love this antiquated hotel. The old Union Railroad Station, eight stories high and half a block long, is right across the street. Around the corner is a branch of the Tattered Cover bookstore, which several news organizations have labeled the finest bookstore on the planet. My friend Dave Query—who was the chef on Malcolm Forbes's yacht for two years—has just opened Jax restaurant next door. There are dozens of art galleries, stores, cafés, bars, restaurants. . . . It really is like a little cross-section of SoHo.

Especially for the last five or six years, I have become fascinated with aesthetics, with beauty in any domain, which I attribute directly to meditative awareness. The great contemplative traditions did not hate this world, they strove mightily to bring beauty into it (along with compassion, clarity, and care). Think of the great Zen gardens, the exquisite illumined manuscripts of medieval mysticism, the stunning architectural beauty of everything from the Taj Mahal to Angkor Wat. The true nondual mystics are not haters of this world, but celebrators of it. Grace, said St. Thomas, perfects nature, it does not obliterate it.

Physical aesthetic beauty is simply one of the ways that Spirit shines in and through the sensorimotor world. And for many people—this was Thomas Mann's point—for many people, seeing something physically beautiful is the closest they will ever get to the Beauty of the Divine. It's a little miniature version, a little reduced version, of the infinite Beauty that is the radiant Face of God. Reduced, yes, but still a ray of the Divine. Plato's *Symposium*, of course, is a reminder that we can start with this ray of physical beauty and use it to climb back to a vision of the Good, the ultimate Beauty itself.

But in this country we have this sad, aggressive, puritanical, merely ascending notion that aesthetic beauty—in architecture, in people, in clothing—is somehow a sin. What a sorry notion.

The other side is equally true, of course. For many people in this country, physical beauty is *all* there is. We know of no higher beauty—the beauty of a mental vision, the stunning beauty of archetypal illumination, the blissful painful excruciating beauty of the true and radiant soul, the beauty beyond beauty that is the infinite unmanifest. And so we worship fashion models. And they all marry rock stars or sports figures—good lord, will the depth never cease?

I like the LoDo precisely because of the aesthetics; it's just beautiful, and therefore a beautiful reminder. Marci and I had a grand time—art galleries, bookstores, carefree cappuccinos, naked bodies in the night. Marci wanted some new makeup, and settled on Dior, so the saleswoman and I struck up a conversation about the Brit John Galliano taking over Dior instead of Jean-Paul Gaultier; I was for Jean-Paul, she for John; but then, she works there. Martinis in the Cruise Bar, huge salads at Jax. When you spend so much time at a desk, these are wonderful pleasures.

Tuesday, April 22—Boulder

Sam called and said Shambhala is planning on bringing out my collected works, starting next year. I believe they are going to release all the volumes at once. Here are the tentative contents at this point:

Sunday, April 27

Another Naropa seminar at my house. These seminars usually last for three or four hours, and follow a Q&A format. Mostly I like to hear the students' confusions, because it gives me clues to issues I need to address in my writing. They also point out problems they have with my work, which helps me clarify it.

This time the students were particularly interested in the Witness. We're videotaping these seminars now; here are a few excerpts:

* * *

I know I've talked about witnessing awareness persisting through waking, dreaming, and deep sleep. But the Witness is *fully* available in *any* state, including your own *present* state of awareness *right now*. So I'm going to talk you into this state, or try to, using what are known as "pointing out instructions." I am *not* going to try to get you into a *different* state of consciousness, or an altered state of consciousness, or a nonordinary state. I am going to simply point out something that is *already* occurring in your own present, ordinary, natural state.

So let's start by just being aware of the world around us. Look out there at the sky, and just relax your mind, let your mind and the sky mingle. Notice the clouds floating by in the sky. Notice that this takes no effort on your part. Your present awareness, in which these clouds are floating, is very simple, very easy, effortless, spontaneous. You simply notice that there is an *effortless awareness* of the clouds. The same is true of those trees, and those birds, and those rocks. You simply and effortlessly witness them.

Look now at the sensations in your own body. You can be aware of whatever bodily feelings are present—perhaps pressure where you are sitting, perhaps warmth in your tummy, maybe tightness in your neck. But even if these feelings are tight and tense, you can easily be aware of them. These feelings arise in your present awareness, and that awareness is very simple, easy, effortless, spontaneous. You simply and effortlessly witness them.

Look at the thoughts arising in your mind. You might notice various images, symbols, concepts, desires, hopes, and fears, all *spontaneously* arising in your awareness. They arise, stay a bit, and pass. These thoughts and feelings arise in your present awareness, and that awareness is very simple, effortless, spontaneous. You simply and effortlessly witness them.

So notice: you can see the clouds float by, because you are *not* those clouds—you are the witness of those clouds. You can feel bodily feelings, because you are *not* those feelings—you are the witness of those feelings. You can see thoughts float by, because you are *not* those thoughts, you are the witness of those thoughts. Spontaneously and naturally, these things all arise, on their own, in your present *effortless* awareness.

So who are you? You are not objects out there, you are not feelings, you are not thoughts—you are effortlessly aware of all those, so you are not those. Who or what are you?

Say it this way to yourself: I *have* feelings, but I am not those feelings. Who am I? I *have* thoughts, but I am not those thoughts. Who am I? I *have* desires, but I am not those desires. Who am I?

So you push back into the source of your own awareness. You push back into the Witness, and you rest in the Witness. I am not objects, not feelings, not desires, not thoughts.

But then people usually make a big mistake. They think that if they rest in the Witness, they are going to see something, or feel something, something really neat and special. But you won't see anything. If you see something, that is just another object—another feeling, another thought, another sensation, another image. But those are all objects; those are what you are *not*.

No, as you rest in the Witness—realizing, I am not objects, I am not feelings, I am not thoughts—all you will notice is a sense of Freedom, a sense of Liberation, a sense of Release—release from the terrible constriction of identifying with these puny little finite objects, your little body and little mind and little ego, all of which are objects that can be seen, and thus are not the true Seer, the real Self, the pure Witness, which is what you really are.

So you won't see anything in particular. Whatever is arising is fine. Clouds float by in the sky, feelings float by in the body, thoughts float by in the mind—and you can effortlessly witness all of them. They *all* spontaneously arise in your own present, easy, effortless awareness. And this witnessing awareness is not itself anything specific you can see. It is just a vast, background sense of Freedom—or *pure Emptiness*—and in that pure Emptiness, which you are, the entire manifest world arises. You *are* that Freedom, Openness, Emptiness—and not any itty bitty thing that arises in it.

Resting in that empty, free, easy, effortless witnessing, notice that the clouds are arising in the vast space of your awareness. The clouds are arising within you—so much so, you can taste the clouds, you are one with the clouds, it is as if they are on this side of your skin, they are so close. The sky and your awareness have become one, and all things in the sky are floating effortlessly through your own awareness. You can kiss the sun, swallow the mountain, they are that close. Zen says "Swallow the Pacific Ocean in a single gulp," and that's the easiest thing in the world, when inside and outside are no longer two, when subject and object are nondual, when the looker and looked at are One Taste. You see?

May

A kind of waking trance I have frequently had, quite up
from my boyhood, when I have been all alone. This has
generally come upon me through repeating my own name
two or three times to myself silently, till all at once, as it
were out of the intensity of the consciousness of individuality, the individuality itself seemed to dissolve and fade
away into boundless being; and this is not a confused state,
but the clearest of the clearest, the surest of the surest . . . ,
utterly beyond words, where death was an almost laugh-
able impossibility, the loss of personality (if so it were)
seeming no extinction, but the only true life.

—ALFRED, LORD TENNYSON

Friday, May 2

The sunlight is playing with the drops of rain, turning each into colored
diamonds, which explode with energy as they fall to earth. They are
talking to each other as they fall, I think, but then, I know better than
that.

The Eye of Spirit was the first time since *Transformations of Consciousness* that I could cover the field of developmental psychology and
spirituality, bringing my work up to date (and comparing it with many
important and recent contributions by others). It was also a chance to
write even more explicitly about my own spiritual life and try to convey,
once again, the radiance of always-already truth. I also included chapters on philosophy, anthropology, epistemology, meditation, and femi-

nism, all from an integral perspective. And finally, a long essay I had written on art and its interpretation, which is perhaps my favorite single piece of all my writings. Its genesis is interesting.

I had for some time been working on "hermeneutics"—the art and science of *interpretation*, or how we discover the *meaning* of a statement, the meaning of last night's dream, the meaning of mathematics, of a work of art, a play, a movie, or anything, really. Even right now, what does this sentence *mean*? Meaning, you know, hermeneutics. And it's not so easy to figure out. A staggering number of factors go into our ability to understand any sort of meaning at all—and therefore to understand life, or God, or literature, or even each other. I had found a way, or so it seemed, to unite signifier (the written word), signified (its interior meaning), syntax (its formal rules), and semantics (its cultural background) into an integral view of symbolic meaning and interpretation.[8] This also led to certain specific conclusions about *art* and *how to interpret it*.

At about the same time, several previously unseen Andrew Wyeth paintings had surfaced from an anonymous art collector—which was something of a big deal—and, concomitant with the international Olympics in Atlanta, a large exhibition was planned. They asked me to write the art essay for the companion volume, and I was glad to oblige.[9] I think they asked me because they were positively sick of the standard postmodernist "theory," which embarrassingly talks about everything but the actual artwork. So I took a strange and novel approach, for an art theorist, and wrote about art.

I first gave a brief historical overview of the major schools of art and its interpretation—including representational, intentional-expressivist, symptomatic, formalist, and reception-and-response. I then tried to show that—using holons,[10] the spectrum of consciousness, and the four

---

8. This integral theory of semiotics is outlined in *The Eye of Spirit*, chap. 5, n. 12.

9. "How Shall We See Art?," in *Andrew Wyeth: America's Painter*, by Martha R. Severens with an essay by Ken Wilber (New York: Hudson Hill Press, 1996). Reprinted in *The Eye of Spirit*, chaps. 4 and 5.

10. A holon is a whole that is also a part of other wholes. The universe is basically composed of holons: a whole atom is part of a molecule, the whole molecule is part of a cell, the whole cell is part of an organism, the whole organism is part of an ecosystem, and so on. Holons are organized holarchically, with each higher holon transcending but including its juniors: organisms contain cells which contain molecules which contain atoms—*but not vice versa*, hence the hierarchy (or holarchy). The Great Nest is also a holarchy composed of holons: spirit transcends but includes soul, which transcends but includes mind,

quadrants—all of these schools could be integrated in a very precise way. Moreover, the interpretive tools of each of them would then have a useful place in the repertoire of the integral interpretation of any piece of art.

And then the conclusion: if science gives us objective Truth, or the "it" of Spirit, and morals give us the Good, or the "we" of Spirit, then Beauty—which is in the "eye" of the beholder—helps open us to the "I" of Spirit. The essay ended:

> Think of the most beautiful person you have ever seen. Think of the exact moment you looked into his or her eyes, and for a fleeting second you were paralyzed: you couldn't take your eyes off that vision. You stared, frozen in time, caught in that beauty. Now imagine that *identical* beauty radiating from every single thing in the entire universe: every rock, every plant, every animal, every cloud, every person, every object, every mountain, every stream—even the garbage dumps and broken dreams— every single one of them, radiating that beauty. You are quietly frozen by the gentle beauty of everything that arises around you. You are released from grasping, released from time, released from avoidance, released altogether into the eye of Spirit, where you contemplate the unending beauty of the Art that is the entire World.
>
> That all-pervading Beauty is not an exercise in creative imagination. It is the actual structure of the universe. That all-pervading Beauty is in truth the very nature of the Kosmos right now. It is not something you have to imagine, because it is the actual structure of perception in all domains. If you remain in the eye of Spirit, every object is an object of radiant Beauty. If the doors of perception are cleansed, the entire Kosmos is your lost and found Beloved, the Original Face of primordial Beauty, forever, and forever, and endlessly forever. And in the face of that stunning Beauty, you will completely swoon into your own death, never to be seen or heard from again, except on those tender nights when the wind gently blows through the hills and the mountains, quietly calling your name.

---

which transcends but includes body. Each senior holon enfolds, envelops, and embraces its juniors, and this is the very nature of whole/parts, holons, and holarchy: nests of increasing wholeness and embrace.

Monday, May 5—Denver

Marci and I spent the weekend in Denver again. Back to LoDo, back to the Oxford, back to some sort of aesthetic wonder.

I tend to follow pop culture closely—music, books, movies, fashion, fads—first, because I enjoy it; second, to spot the zeitgeist, the general cognitive structure serving as a background that organizes average or popular perception—and the only way you can spot this is by following popular culture. The broad trend now is a slow movement from modern rational to postmodern aperspectival, and nowhere can this be seen more clearly than in pop culture, especially fashion.

Giorgio Armani, for example, is pure modernist—sleek, sparse, elegant, beautiful, often in monotones. Versace and Gaultier, on the other hand, are quintessentially postmodern—wild, exuberant, pluralistic, disheveled, diversity on the verge of fragmentation, trying to find a unity, close to falling apart. The central cognitive structure of postmodernity has been called *integral-aperspectival* (which I also call *vision-logic*): "aperspectival," because no particular perspective is privileged, and "integral" because nonetheless some sort of coherence has to be found or the whole thing falls apart. This, for example, is Frank Gehry's brilliance; he is a towering genius of postmodernism; he produces stunning examples of integral-aperspectival vision: his architectural designs are a collection of curving, twisting, pluralistic pieces right on the verge of dissociating and completely flying apart, and yet they are all inevitably, miraculously brought together into an exquisitely whole and unified form—a true integral-aperspectival vision, a true "unity-in-diversity."

The problem with much of postmodernism is that it has initially been so taken with *diversity*, it has forgotten the *unity*, and so it simply falls into fragmented pieces, jerking and choking in their own isolated little worlds. This is simply the *pathological* form of integral-aperspectival, a pathology I call *aperspectival madness*—all diversity, no unity: schizophrenic fragments. And almost all of postmodernism, so far, is not much more than aperspectival madness, awaiting the emergence of the truly great geniuses—like Gehry, but in other fields as well—who will unify the fragments, connect the unconnected, reweave the fabric of a reality ripped to shreds by the mindless diversity movements.

Well, to hell with all that. I think I'm falling in love.

Sunday, May 11—Boulder

Mother's Day, called Mom. She's such a dear, but she's infuriated with Tony Schwartz's chapter on me in *What Really Matters*, because Tony made some passing Freudian Oedipal comments about her. She hopes the book suffers a horrible fate and nobody ever, ever buys it. Otherwise, she's doing fine. After my visit with them last year, both Mom and Dad are now lifting weights—they're in their seventies. I took them to a gym and got them signed up, and they love it.

Got an essay from Michael Zimmerman, the great Heidegger scholar—and a wonderful man, bright, witty, sincere. He spoke at the kw conference in San Francisco last year, and I hear he was the audience favorite. The essay is "Heidegger and Wilber on the Limitations of Spiritual Deep Ecology." Michael is a sympathetic and profound ecological theorist, as evidenced in his book *Radical Ecology*. But he also is cognizant of the major limitations of most forms of "spiritual ecology."

From the essay: "In my opinion, Wilber achieves a great deal in his analysis of modernity, retro-romanticism, and the ecological crisis. He manages to include much of what is worthwhile in Heidegger's views about the transcendent domain, while discarding the anti-modernist sentiments that led Heidegger into such political trouble [collaborating with the Nazis]. Moreover, Wilber's view of the transcendent includes important aspects of spiritual traditions that Heidegger either rejected or adopted in truncated ways. Wilber's contention that modernists and environmentalists alike adopted the materialistic world-system of modern science allows him to conclude that nothing good will come of well-meaning efforts to 're-sacralize' nature, unless the transcendent dimension of nature, humankind, and the divine is first rediscovered and reaffirmed."

Nice as that is, today, anyway, all it does is seem to throw me into doubt and sadness. "I remain convinced that Wilber has made an enormous contribution to the contemporary discussion of the divine, nature, and humanity. In particular, he has something important to say both to modernists and to spiritual deep ecologists: that the way beyond ecological crisis lies in solving the crisis of meaning created by the adoption of a one-dimensional materialist ontology [i.e., flatland]. Wilber makes clear that this crisis cannot be solved by a spasm of life-denying transcendentalism and otherworldly longing, but rather by developing a multi-dimensional [i.e., integral] non-dual ontology that allows room for what has so long been excluded. A truly deep spiritual ecology would acknowledge the depth dimension of reality, rather than maintaining that the material natural system—the 'web-of-life'—exhausts the infinite dimensions of the divine. Wilber is playing an important role in the process of generating such a deeply spiritual ecology."

It just makes me sad. For some reason, all I am thinking about right now is what a slim chance any of this has in making any sort of difference at all. Not just my work, but any of the truly integral writers—Zimmerman's own good work, Roger, Frances, Tony, Jack, Murph, and crew; it's just so empty out there, it seems. I am totally at home in Emptiness, but emptiness just sucks.

Monday, May 12

On the spur of the moment, Marci and I have decided to take a short vacation. I haven't had a real vacation in, well, many years. Manhattan and San Francisco were fun, but they were work, and I did anything but relax. Since I am not specifically writing now, but plowing through research reading, I don't mind, in the least, missing a few days of that.

We need a place that fits several difficult requirements. Marci and I both like sun and sand and beach. But since I spend most of my time working alone, away from people, I also want to be in the middle of a crowd, rubbing elbows and getting jostled. We also both like culture as much as nature, so we'd like an urban center close by. I don't just want to lie in the sun, I want to suck auto fumes and have people yelling at me. What fun is a vacation without a genuine possibility of getting shot at, or at least mugged? And finally, since both Marci and I spend our days studying depth, we want, as a change of pace, something utterly superficial, glitzy, shiny and vapid.

No question about it. We're on our way to South Beach, Miami.

Sunday, May 18—South Beach

Oh, this is glorious. What a riot. In our real lives, South Beach is everything we don't want, and less. Which is to say, it's perfect.

Actually, it's very, very beautiful. South Beach is the southern twenty blocks or so of Miami Beach; it used to be quite run down and dilapidated, but has, in the last decade, undergone a spectacular development, mostly under the influence of the jet set, modeling agencies, movie stars, and megabucks. Madonna owns the restaurant in the Delano Hotel; Sly Stallone owns a dance club; Michael Caine runs the Brasserie; Versace's house on Ocean Drive looks like an embassy. There are over two dozen restored Art Deco hotels, all brightest of neon and softest of pastels, all simply gorgeous. The hotels face the ocean, which is right across the street, which is pure sandy sand with no rocks or shells to tear the feet.

The ocean, unlike most Atlantic Ocean water, is not cold steel gray blue, but beautiful aqua green and turquoise, and it makes me happy just to look. The ocean flickers and floats in transparency, no substance here but scintillation, luminous arising, shimmering ornaments on primordial awareness, the mind and the world are not-two, here on the edge of the earth.

We check into the Cavalier, which is the hip hotel on Ocean Drive, and it is, shall we say, way cool. Everybody in South Beach is gay, or a model, or an actor, or all three. The hotels alternate with superb and adorable restaurants, most of which have sidewalk cafés, so you can sit and watch the half-naked bodies go by. Marci, getting into the swing of things, has her navel pierced. She's now an official Gen-Xer. We alternate stays on the beach with restaurant sampling, bar hopping, boutique shopping, and outright gawking. We are both determined to drink a bottle of wine a day—her, hearty triathlon red; me, sissy dry white. Goodbye Witness, hello cruel world.

Each day we hit the beach around eleven A.M. and stay until around four P.M. This is truly one of the nicest beaches I've ever seen. Besides being pure sand—you can wade out forever and never hit a rock or shell—the water temperature is perfect, somewhere around eighty degrees, so you never get chilled, no matter how long you stay in. And, as a matter of fact, I spend about three hours in the water each day, exactly up to my neck, gently bobbing up and down, tiptoes barely touching the bottom to hold me up. Marci, a champion swimmer, swims circles around me, literally. Where does that woman hide all her muscles? She's too curvaceous to be this athletic. Don't triathlon women have, like, 0% body fat? Actually, aren't they in negative fat space? Don't they like owe the world some fat?

I had fully expected to lose all access to the Witness, given our vino schedule. And for the first night and day this happened. But floating in the water has not only brought back the Witness, it seems to have facilitated the disappearance of the Witness into nondual One Taste, at least on occasion. (The Witness, or pure witnessing awareness, tends to be of the causal, since there is usually a primitive trace of subject/object duality: you equanimously Witness the world as transparent and shimmering object. But with further development, the Witness itself disappears into everything that is witnessed, subject and object become One Taste, or simple Suchness, and this is the nondual estate. In short: ego to soul to pure Witness to One Taste.) So I am utterly, pleasantly surprised, floating here in nature's blood, to be dipped into One Taste, which in this case, is nicely salty.

There is no time in this estate, though time passes through it. Clouds float by in the sky, thoughts float by in the mind, waves float by in the ocean, and I am all of that. I am looking at none of it, for there is no center around which perception is organized. It is simply that everything is arising, moment to moment, and I am all of that. I do not see the sky, I am the sky, which sees itself. I do not feel the ocean, I am the ocean, which feels itself. I do not hear the birds, I am the birds, which hear themselves. There is nothing outside of me, there is nothing inside of me, because there is no me—there is simply all of this, and it has always been so. Nothing pushes me, nothing pulls me, because there is no me—there is simply all of this, and it has always been so.

My ankle hurts from dancing last night, so there is pain, but the pain doesn't hurt me, for there is no me. There is simply pain, and it is arising just like everything else—birds, waves, clouds, thoughts. I am none of them, I am all of them, it's all the same One Taste. This is not a trance, or a lessening of consciousness, but rather an intensification of it—not subconscious but superconscious, not infra-rational but supra-rational. There is a crystal-clear awareness of everything that is arising, moment to moment, it's just not happening to anybody. This is not an out-of-the-body experience; I am not above looking down; I am not looking at all; and I am not above or below anything—I am everything. There is simply all of this, and I am that.

Most of all, One Taste is utter simplicity. With mystical experiences in the subtle and causal, there is often a sense of grandeur, of ominous awesomeness, of numinous overwhelmingness, of light and bliss and beatitude, of gratefulness and tears of joy. But not with One Taste, which is extraordinarily ordinary, and perfectly simple: *just this*.

I stay here, neck deep in water, for three hours. How much of it I spend as ego, as Witness, or as One Taste, I don't know. There is always the sense, with One Taste, that you have never left it, no matter how confused you get, and therefore there is never really the sense that you are entering it or leaving it. It is just so, always and forever, even now, and even unto the ends of the world.

But in this particular now, it is time for early dinner, and for the ugly business of moving this particular bodymind from one place to another. Besides, I'm sure Marci is going to get something else pierced, and no-body—ego, soul, or God—wants to miss that one.

Tuesday, May 20—South Beach

For a change of pace, we move from the Cavalier to the Casa Grande; both are fabulous. The Cavalier is hot and hip, the Casa Grande is elegant. But none of them are mega-hotels like a Hyatt or Four Seasons; they are, like most of the hotels in South Beach, relatively small Art Deco buildings, three or four stories high, at most, and all a type of quaint chic.

Day before we went boutique shopping—we both liked the Nicole Miller shop, but there are a dozen terrific little shops in the area. Heated discussion with the sales folks over who the hottest new designer was—I was championing Tom Ford, who has taken over the stodgy old house of Gucci and is causing a major sensation (especially for an American); his clothes, for both men and women, are stunning, sexy, sleek, and elegant. They, the fools, were for Galliano. Marci likes Isaac Mizrahi, because we saw *Unzipped* and she thought he was adorable (and has "fun fun colors"). It's too bad Hollywood has made Armani a cliché, because there's still nothing like him; he's a modernist genius, bulwark against the goofier elements of postmodernism in La Croix, Gaultier, Versace, Dolce & Gabbana, although many of their designs I definitely like. But postmodernism has yet to produce its genius in fashion, the way it has in architecture with Gehry, although Gaultier verges on it; and who knows, Galliano or McQueen might yet pull it off. Great dinner—some sort of fish, can't remember exactly, why I don't know—oh yes, the wine.

Then last night, we were standing in front of Versace's house, and we met a really nice couple, struck up a conversation, and all went to dinner together. In the course of the evening it became obvious that the woman—these people were very bright and perceptive but somewhat conservative—was going to get a tattoo. The more she drank, the more certain she became.

We went to the same place that pierced Marci's navel. I guess it's sort of an all-purpose body mutilation store. Disfigurations Are Us, I suppose. Marci was hilariously egging the woman on: "Oh look at this great American eagle," pointing to an image the size of a dinner plate. I started getting nervous for the woman. "Oh gee, look at this nice little heart"—about the size of a pea. She settled on the heart, and two minutes later, done.

Monday back on the beach, but this time, no Witness and no One Taste, just a slightly hungover ego. But the water is exquisite, and we eat sandwiches and drink beer and fry in the sun on this largely topless beach. Marci is not only going topless, she is getting more and more into the spirit of South Beach, which is to say, no spirit at all, just bright and shiny and down and dirty. That night, she decides to have both nipples pierced. I give a very serious let's-be-responsible speech, and then we both rush right over to Mutilations Are Us. A hundred dollars later—and a few images I will not soon forget—and Marci's got two nipple rings, which look sorta like two towel holders coming at me. (Every time I tell this to baby boomers, they get alarmed, disgusted, or slightly nauseous; every Gen-Xer says, "Cool!")

We fly back tomorrow, but it's been a scream. And Marci is a wonderful traveling companion. She never gets angry, she's genuinely happy and delighted with life, she's very sincere but not in the least serious. On the plane, looking down, I watch the ocean shimmering in Emptiness, a wonderful dream vacation—literally, a dream.

Sunday, May 25—Boulder

Another Naropa seminar. Topics the students raised included compassion versus idiot compassion, the pre/trans fallacy, meditation and neurosis, the startling anger of several theorists when you try to bring up an integral view. . . . A few excerpts:

STUDENT: I was discussing an integral view with some other students, and they said that because I was making judgments I was showing a real lack of compassion. I didn't think I was.

KW: Yes, there is probably more confusion about this issue than any other in spiritual circles. Basically, most of the trouble comes from confusing compassion with idiot compassion, which are the terms Trungpa Rinpoche used for this crucial distinction. We in this country—and especially in new-age circles—have a type of tepid egalitarianism and political correctness that says no view is really any better than another, and therefore all views are to be cherished equally, as a sign of rich diversity. If we don't make any judgments about better or worse, then we are showing real compassion. So we have judgmental versus compassionate, and that is the common understanding.

But, you see, that stance is a massive self-contradiction. On the one hand, it says that all views are equally part of a rich diversity, and thus no view is better than another. On the other hand, it strongly claims that this view itself is *better* than the alternatives. So this "compassion" states that no view is better than another, *except its own view*, which is *superior* in a world where nothing is supposed to be superior at all. It is a ranking that denies ranking and a judgment that all judgments are bad. So, although it is often truly well-intentioned, it's nonetheless a type of hypocrisy, because it is strongly doing that which it condemns in everybody else.

That hypocrisy has nothing to do with real compassion; in fact, that is idiot compassion. Idiot compassion thinks it is being kind, but it's really being very cruel. If you have an alcoholic friend and you know that one more drink might kill him, and yet he begs you for a drink, does real compassion say that you should give it to him? After all, to be kind you should give him what he wants, right? Who are you to impose your views on him, right? Giving him the drink would therefore show compassion, yes? No. Absolutely not.

Real compassion includes wisdom and so it makes *judgments* of care and concern: it says some things are good, and some things are bad, and I will choose to act only on those things that are informed by wisdom and care. Giving a severe alcoholic a case of whiskey because he wants it and you want to be "kind" is not being kind at all. It is showing idiot compassion, not real compassion.

Zen calls this the difference between "grandmother Zen" and "real Zen." In order to awaken from the dream of samsara, the ego itself must be really kicked around, often severely. Otherwise you will simply continue to play your favorite games. Grandmother Zen doesn't challenge you. In order to be "kind," grandmother Zen will let you sleep a little late if you want, and stop meditating early if you don't like how it's going, and allow you to wallow in you. But real Zen uses a very big stick, and lots of loud yelling, and there are occasionally broken bones and certainly shattered egos. Real compassion kicks butt and takes names, and it is not pleasant on certain days. If you are not ready for this fire, then find a new-age, sweetness-and-light, soft-speaking, perpetually smiling teacher, and learn to relabel your ego with spiritual-sounding terms. But stay away from those who practice real compassion, because they will fry your ass, my friend. What most people mean by "compassion" is: please be nice to my ego. Well, your ego is your own worst enemy, and anybody being nice to it is not being compassionate to you.

Now maybe you and I aren't accomplished masters, and so maybe we don't always know what is real compassion and what is not. But we must *start* to try to learn to exercise real compassion instead of idiot compassion. We need to learn to make *qualitative distinctions*. These are hierarchical judgments that involve the ranking of values. If you don't like hierarchy, well, fine, that is *your* hierarchy: you hierarchically value nonhierarchies more than you value hierarchies. That's fine with me, just be honest enough to correctly label what you are really doing. If you don't like value rankings and want to avoid them, then fine, *that* is your value ranking—you rank nonranking as better than ranking—and that itself is a ranking, *your* ranking. At least be honest about this. The fact is, ranking is unavoidable in values, so at least do it consciously, honestly, and above board, and stop this hypocritical stance that you are being "nonjudgmental," which itself is a colossal judgment.

STUDENT: But isn't choiceless awareness without judgments?

KW: Choiceless awareness accepts absolutely *everything* that arises, including *both* judging and not judging. You see, nonjudgmental is itself a *choice* between two opposites—judging versus not judging—which is why "nonjudgmental" is not at all the same as choiceless awareness. Choiceless awareness is the absolute mirror that effortlessly reflects whatever arises—it does *not* try to choose not-judging versus judging.

Choiceless awareness really refers to what the Buddhists call *absolute* bodhichitta, or Emptiness; whereas making judgments is referred to as *relative* bodhichitta, or compassion. This means real compassion, not idiot compassion, and real compassion uses wisdom to make judgments! *So in neither case*, absolute or relative, is "nonjudgmental" a wise stance. In the absolute, we rest in Emptiness, which doesn't care if we make judgments or not, since both arise equally in pure Emptiness. In the relative, we make judgments based on wisdom and compassion, and that means judgments based on qualitative distinctions, value rankings, and depth.

So when you hear somebody saying they are being "nonranking" and "nonjudgmental," run! We need to learn to *consciously* make qualitative distinctions. We need to make judgments, based on degrees of depth. Idiot compassion has nearly destroyed this field, and made genuine spiritual progress difficult indeed.

STUDENT: These people jumped all over me for making qualitative judgments, and they were really sanctimonious. . . .

KW: Well, you know, there is a big difference between making qualitative judgments and being obnoxious. So my advice, when you run into this, is to first check your own attitude and check your own motivation. It does no good for us to also get sanctimonious. You know, we have the real compassion and those schmucks have the idiot compassion. We can all get caught in this; I know I do. It's judgment bereft of skillful means, and that's just obnoxious. So watch out for that. But you said you were attacked because you were talking about the importance of a more integral view?

STUDENT: Yes.

KW: That's a special problem. A good rule of thumb is that people are not going to expand their present views or outlooks by much more than 5% at any given time. So if you are trying to push a very big picture at them, they are probably going to shut down, and maybe get angry, and then start calling you names—you lack compassion, you're arrogant, etc. If you keep pushing, then at that point it really is your problem. Maybe your ego is enjoying shoving this down their throats. I know I've done that on occasion, and it helps nothing. Anyway, if you are really trying to help—real compassion—then don't put more in the spoon than can be swallowed, yes?

Also, remember that belief systems are not merely beliefs—they are the home of the ego, the home of the self-contraction. Even a holistic belief, like the web-of-life, *always* houses the ego, because beliefs are merely *mental* forms, and if the *supramental* has not been discovered, then any and all mental constructions house a tenacious ego. When you challenge any belief system, the separate-self experiences that as a death threat and a death seizure, and this will engage all its survival instincts. You are not just discussing the truth or falsity of a theory—you are engaged in a life and death struggle. Whenever we do this, we're dealing with a cornered rat—in others and in ourselves, so watch out.

STUDENT: Why is idiot compassion so popular?

KW: Oh, because it does not threaten anything. It's rampant in so many spiritual circles because the ego does not fundamentally want to be challenged. It wants grandmother Zen. So the ego will pay big money for a weekend workshop that will "empower" the ego, tell it that it is really God or Goddess, give it a new concept to think about and call "spirit," plug it into the "web-of-life" and promise ultimate unity from that merely mental idea. In fact, the huge market in spiritual books in this country is basically motivated by one intense drive: the boomers want to be told that their ego is God, their self-contraction is Spirit. The self-contraction is simply relabeled "sacred" and grandmother Zen smiles on all.

But I don't think any of those approaches are bad or mean-spirited or anything like that at all. I just think they are a little bit confused. I think that because they don't have a very comprehensive map of the Kosmos, they get a little sidetracked in their noble search. So the hope is that a more integral view will help clear up some of this confusion.

STUDENT: Why is an integral view so threatening to so many people?

KW: Well, it almost always demands much more than a 5% expansion of beliefs, and few will follow that.

STUDENT: I was shocked at the anger that came up at me.

KW: Yes, that's unfortunate. I used to think that if you took approach A, approach B, and approach C, and showed how all of them are *equally important*, they would all be very grateful and thank you profusely. In fact, A and B and C all tend to get very annoyed with you, because you have just demonstrated that their field is not the only important field in existence. As soon as you show that Freud, Piaget, and Buddha are all important for understanding consciousness, Buddhists will say, Why are you trashing Buddhism? As soon as you show that gross-realm nature, subtle-level soul, and transcendental spirit are all important, ecologists will say, Why do you hate nature?

Of course, let me add, some people might react negatively to an integral view because it's wrong! I mean, it's possible that those of us who believe in a more integral view might simply be mistaken, and so of course sane and rational people will react negatively to it. So we always have to keep that possibility in mind. It's not automatic that they are threatened because we're right and they're wrong—it could be the other way around.

Tuesday, May 27

Worked all morning, reading, reading, reading. Marci and I went grocery shopping and then worked out together. The family that pumps iron together . . . stays together? Ends up in the emergency room together?

Wednesday, May 28

The tenth anniversary issue of the *Noetic Sciences Review* recently came out. For it, they asked me to write a summary and overview of the last decade of consciousness studies. They followed this with responses by Alwyn Scott, Duane Elgin, Jeanne Achterberg, Peter Russell, and Will Keepin. The responses were all very thoughtful and perceptive, and I think the entire issue was quite well done, thanks largely to the efforts of the executive editor, Barbara McNeill, and managing/associate editors David Johnson, Carol Guion, Christian de Quincey, and Keith Thompson.

The editors introduce the discussion: "In a special overview of the field of consciousness studies for our tenth anniversary Review, Wilber outlines 12 key components of a truly integral approach to this most challenging topic of our times." And, well, that's more or less what I tried to do—outline a dozen different fields of consciousness studies, all of which need to be brought together in an integral view. I summarized the twelve main schools: cognitive science, introspectionism, neuropsychology, individual psychotherapy, social psychology, clinical psychiatry, developmental psychology, psychosomatic medicine, nonordinary states of consciousness, Eastern and contemplative traditions, quantum consciousness approaches, and subtle energies research. The point was:

"What I have observed in the field of consciousness studies (as elsewhere), is that consciousness researchers tend to choose one or two of those approaches very early in their careers, usually under the influence of a significant mentor, organization, or academic department. And, human nature being what it is, it is then extremely difficult for them to embrace, or sometimes even acknowledge, the existence of the other approaches. Evidence that supports their position is avidly accumulated; evidence that does not is ignored, devalued, or explained away.

"But what if, instead, we make the following assumption: the human mind is incapable of producing 100 percent error. In other words, nobody is smart enough to be wrong all the time.

"That would mean, very simply, that each of those dozen approaches cannot contain only error; put positively, each of them has something extremely important and valuable to say. And that means, inescapably, that we will measure our progress toward a truly integral orientation based precisely on our capacity to include, synthesize, and integrate all twelve of those important approaches. It is clearly a daunting challenge; but it is equally clear that anything less than that simply cannot claim the adjective 'integral.' "

After a long discussion of that theme, the essay concludes:

"How far down this integral path are we? In the last decade, although there have been some significant exceptions, we have mostly had twelve pieces all claiming to be the whole pie.

"In a series of books (particularly *The Eye of Spirit* [and *Integral Psychology*]), I have attempted to outline one version of an integral theory of consciousness that explicitly includes those twelve major approaches. But what is important is not my particular version of an integral view, but rather that we all begin to enter into this extraordinary dialogue about the possibility of an integral approach in general, an approach that—we can say this in several different ways—integrates the hard-headed with the soft-hearted, the natural sciences with the noetic sciences, objective realities with subjective realities, the empirical with the transcendental.

"And so let us hope that a decade from now somebody might spot a great mega-trend in consciousness studies—namely, the truly integral—and let it start right now with all of us who share this concern for holism, for embrace, for synthesizing, for integrating: let this outreach start with us, right here, right now.

"Is a genuinely integral theory of consciousness even possible? Well, that would be my question to you all, and that would be my challenge. How big is our umbrella? How wide and how deep can we throw our net of good will? How many voices will we allow in this chorus of consciousness? How many faces of the Divine will smile on our endeavor? How many colors will we genuinely acknowledge in our rainbow coalition?

"And when we pause from all this research, and put theory temporarily to rest, and when we relax into the primordial ground of our own intrinsic awareness, what will we find therein? When the joy of the robin sings on a clear morning dawn, where is our consciousness then? When the sunlight beams from the glory of a snow-capped mountain, where is consciousness then? In the place that time forgot, in this eternal moment without date or duration, in the secret cave of the heart where time touches eternity and space cries out for infinity, when the raindrop pulses on the temple roof, and announces the beauty of the Divine with every single beat, when the moonlight reflects in a simple dewdrop to remind us who and what we are, and when in the entire universe there is nothing but the sound of a lonely waterfall somewhere in the mists gently calling your name—where is consciousness then?"

Thursday, May 29

The world arises quietly this morning, shimmering on a radiant sea of transparent Emptiness. There is only *this*, vast, open, empty, clear, nakedly luminous. All questions dissolve in this single Answer, all doubts resolve in this single Shout, all worries are a ripple on this Sea of equanimity.

This One Taste is compatible with any and all worlds, but, paradoxically, it is happiest when it sings of holistic embrace. Which is why the whole point of an *integral theory of consciousness* is to include and integrate all levels in all quadrants—or simply all levels in the Big Three of I, we, and it; or first-person, second-person, and third-person accounts of consciousness.

We have a huge war now raging between the *first-person* or introspective accounts (which emphasize the immediate introspection of the mind's contents as they display themselves to your own awareness) and the *third-person* or objective/scientific accounts (which seek to translate all of consciousness into objective entities or "its" disclosed by empirical science). Both of them overlook the importance of *second-person* accounts—the *intersubjective* domain of linguistic structures, moral contexts, shared semantics, and cultural backgrounds, without which neither "I" nor "it" can be recognized in the first place. On the other hand, the humanities and cultural studies emphasize *nothing but* cultural backgrounds, as they attempt to reduce all subjective awareness (of "I") and all objective knowledge (of "its") to nothing but cultural constructions (of "we").

All three of those approaches are wrong, because all three are right—partially right, that is, and all three need to be brought *equally* to the integrative table. I am aware of nobody taking a similar integral approach (embracing equally first-, second-, and third-person realms), except, of course, the smartest man on the face of the planet, Jürgen Habermas. But Habermas doesn't allow for any of the transrational, transpersonal domains, so he is all-quadrant but not all-level, or so it seems to me.

At any rate, I specifically spelled out this approach in *The Eye of Spirit* and more technically in "An Integral Theory of Consciousness," which was published by the *Journal of Consciousness Studies*. This is an exceptional journal, only been out four years, and yet it has already become the central focal point for these important discussions, involving luminaries such as John Searle, Daniel Dennett, Francisco Varela, John Eccles, Roger Penrose, David Chalmers, the Churchlands, etc. The front cover of this particular issue says: "Taxonomy or Taxidermy?," which is very clever: is consciousness to be accepted and categorized as real (taxonomy) or is it dead meat (fit only for taxidermy)?

Saturday, May 31

In meditation this morning, instead of resting in choiceless, clear, ever-present awareness—a standard "nonpractice"—I did an old yabyum tantra visualization (technically, anuttaratantra yoga)—"old," because I used to do this a lot—which involves the transformation of sexual energy into radiant bliss and compassionate embrace. These are all mostly subtle-level practices (they start at psychic, lead to subtle, and occasionally dissolve into causal. Rarely do they reach nondual One Taste or *sahaja*, but they are exemplary exercises for the development of the psychic-to-subtle domains). The standard core of this type of practice is summarized as "Bliss cognizing Emptiness arises as compassion."

It goes something like this. In meditation, you visualize yourself in sexual union with your consort. You visualize yourself and your consort as a god or goddess, angel or bodhisattva, buddha or saint—whatever works as a symbol of your deepest or highest nature. But you must visualize very intensely and very clearly you and your consort as transparent radiant divinities, making love. You actually become sexually aroused, and you coordinate this with breathing: on the in-breath, you breathe Light down the front of the body to the genitals, seat of Life; on the out-breath, you breathe Life up the back of the body—up the spine—into Light at and above the crown of the head. (This is just another version of involution/evolution, or the higher entering into the lower, and then the lower returning to the higher, forming a great circle of descending and ascending energy. If you are doing this with an actual partner, you can coordinate breathing.)

Any pleasure that is generated in the genital region is, with the out-breath, directed up the spine and released into the Light at the crown of the head—you simply breathe any pleasure from the body directly into and above the crown of the head, the home of infinite Light and Release. Then, on the in-breath, you directly breathe Light down and into the body—especially down the frontal line of the body, face to throat to chest to stomach to the base of the genitals. And so the cycle goes, bringing heavenly Light down and into earthly Life, and then returning Life to Light—thus uniting downward Agape and upward Eros, Descending and Ascending, Compassion and Wisdom, with every breath you take.

As your entire bodymind becomes full with circulating pleasure-bliss, you simply but directly take any bliss that is present and use it to meditate on Emptiness—or on the absolute Mystery of existence, or on the simple Transparency of the world, or on God as unqualifiable expanse—whatever works for you. In practice, a simple way to do this is to rest as I-I—rest as the great Seer which cannot itself be seen, the pure Witness that is completely open and empty. And then, resting as I-I, allow bliss to expand into that open and empty space that you now are—allow bliss to expand and fill the infinity of the I-I that you are. The sky of your awareness becomes filled with the bliss of the divine union that you are.

When you are in this state of the spacious bliss of I AMness, and you are full to infinity, with no desires and no wants, allow a gentle, small, ripple of a thought to arise: I vow to liberate all sentient beings into this free and open space. And with that, a ripple of compassion arises out of this vast ocean of bliss. That compassion is literally *composed of* this *infinite empty bliss*, it is made of it, as waves are of the ocean. Compassion is infinite empty bliss in action.

And so: bliss cognizing emptiness arises as compassion—in other words, bliss recognizing and reconnecting with its own divine ground (spirit or emptiness) is moved to extend this liberating and ecstatic grace to all beings, and so it arises as compassion in the service of others.

June

Why are you unhappy?
Because 99.9 percent
Of everything you think
And of everything you do,
Is for yourself—
And there isn't one.
                    —WEI WU WEI

Sunday, June 1

T George Harris and Kate Olson just stopped by. Kate, a producer for
the "Jim Lehrer News Hour" on PBS, is largely responsible for getting
some very good spiritual segments on the air, such as those on Father
Thomas Keating, the Dalai Lama, etc. Kate is a wonderful person—very
bright, attractive, dedicated to spiritual practice—so we hang out whenever we can.

T George is in the process of trying to start up a national magazine
on spirituality. I suppose if anybody can do it, he can. He was responsible for starting *Psychology Today*, which, as long as he was running it,
was an extraordinary publication. It seemed that everybody was reading
it; it was a real lifeline to so many of us. That was twenty years ago; I
still have many of my copies. George then started *American Health* magazine, and now he's working on *Spirituality and Health*. He's in his
seventies, and, like Huston Smith, a real role model for not letting age
intimidate you.

We sit out on the balcony, overlooking the plains, and begin to nibble
lunch. The standard discussion that T George and I have is about how

to make the magazine accessible and popular, but also include some real depth and sophistication. It's a standard commercial dilemma—the more depth in the product, the smaller the audience, usually. My lame contribution is to layer the magazine, with many departments simple and accessible, but several that are advanced and demanding. Lame, because how do you actually do that? Anyway, George is still working on getting funding; he says right now he's negotiating with Time Warner. I hope something comes of it, because we really need a national forum for an authentic spirituality.

So we have a long discussion focused on the pre/trans fallacy. The pre/trans fallacy—which was introduced in *The Atman Project* and elaborated in an essay called "The Pre/Trans Fallacy" (included in *Eye to Eye*)—is a simple concept. It says that because both *pre*-rational and *trans*-rational are *non*-rational, they are easily confused. And then one of two very unfortunate things happens: either mature, spiritual, transrational states get *reduced* to infantile, prerational states; or infantile, narcissistic, prerational states get *elevated* to transrational glory. Reductionism and elevationism. Freud was a typical reductionist, who tried to reduce profound nondual mystical states to primary narcissism and infantile oceanic fusion: *The Future of an Illusion*. And Jung was a typical elevationist, who often took prerational myth and elevated it to transcendental greatness.

(A myth is a story that, for the most part, is always taken to be literally and concretely true by its believers: Moses really did part the Red Sea, Jesus really was born of a biological virgin, etc. When, on the other hand, myth is consciously used in an allegorical, symbolic, or interpretive fashion, it is actually drawing on higher cognitive faculties, reason to vision-logic, and, in that mode, occasionally stands open to transpersonal glimmers. Unless otherwise specified, when I refer to myth, I mean concrete-literal myths, which are generally prerational.)

It used to be that the real threats to genuine spiritual studies were the reductionists, but an even greater threat has surfaced from the new-age movement, namely, the elevationists. These folks, with many good and decent intentions, nonetheless take some rather infantile, childish, egocentric states and, simply because they are "nonrational," relabel them "sacred" or "spiritual," which is definitely a problem.

Real growth generally moves from prerational to rational to transrational; from subconscious to self-conscious to superconscious; from preconventional to conventional to postconventional; from prepersonal to personal to transpersonal; from id to ego to God. But under confusion of the pre/trans fallacy, pre is often getting elevated to trans, and a narcissistic immersion is taking the place of the demanding process of genuine growth and transformation.

Alas, it seems to me, much of the "spiritual renaissance" supposedly sweeping this country is really a case of prerational regression, not transrational growth. This is deeply worrisome. Prerational acting out is being confused with transrational awareness; preverbal feeling and impulse are being elevated to transverbal insight; premoral ego-license is confused with transmoral Self; preconventional nature is promoted to postconventional Spirit; prerational id is confused with transrational God.

This entire package of "spirit" is being sold by publishers and book clubs at an astonishing rate. But the notion that we are entering a genuinely "integral culture" or a "spiritual renewal" is a little bit dubious, I'm afraid. William Irwin Thompson estimated that about 80% of this "spiritual" renaissance was prerational, and less than 20% was transrational. I tend to agree, but it's really much worse than that. My own analysis indicates that the truly transrational is less than 1% of the population.[11] Studies consistently show that the percentage of those reaching the highest stages of *personal* development is less than 5%—imagine how fewer there are that go *even further* into the realms of *transpersonal* development!

In any event, this is a marketing nightmare, and this is what T George and Kate and I discuss. If the majority of the "spiritual market" is drawn to prerational magic and myth, how do you reach the small group who are involved in genuine, laborious, demanding, transrational spiritual practice? This is very difficult, because both markets are referred to as "spiritual," but these two camps really don't get along very well—one is mostly translative, the other is mostly transformative, and they generally disapprove of each other—so how do you put them into one magazine without alienating them both? More than that, a large portion of those involved in prerational pursuits genuinely wish to open themselves to authentic, transpersonal, transrational states, so it's very important to make room for everybody. T George is alive to this issue, which is good, because this is going to be *the* marketing difficulty for boomer spirituality.

---

11. See *The Eye of Spirit*, chapters 9 and 10, for an extended discussion of this theme. [See also *Integral Psychology* and especially the introduction to Volume Seven of the *Collected Works*.]

Monday, June 2

Early morning, the orange sun is slowly rising, shining forth in empty luminous clarity. The mind and the sky are one, the sun is rising in the vast space of primordial awareness, and there is *just this*. Yasutani Roshi once said, speaking of satori, that it was the most precious realization in the world, because all the great philosophers had tried to understand ultimate reality but had failed to do so, yet with satori or awakening all of your deepest questions are finally answered: it's *just this*.

Tuesday, June 3

And we worry about the state of art in the postmodern world? From the magazine *5280*:

"When '60 Minutes' aired a report on the ridiculous world of postmodern art, Morely Safer noted an eight-foot ashtray—filled with real cigarette and cigar butts—as one of the most outrageous examples of what passes for art these days. As a postscript, Safer noted that the piece was recently purchased by the Denver Art Museum for $60,000."

And we worry about business ethics in today's world? Reported in *Men's Health*:

"Quality to Exhibit at Work: *Best*: Loyalty. In a recent survey of chief executives, 86 percent of them said they valued that attribute the most in their subordinates. *Worst*: Integrity. Only 3 percent valued that the most."

Wednesday, June 4

Worked all morning; decided to go jogging down behind my house. If you remain as the Witness while you run, you don't move, the ground does. You, as the Witness, are immobile—more precisely, you have no qualities at all, no traits, no motion and no commotion, as you rest in the vast Emptiness that you are. You are aware of movement, therefore you as the Witness are not movement. So when you run, it actually feels as if you are not moving at all—the Witness is free of motion *and* stillness—so the ground simply moves along. It's like you're sitting in a movie theater, never moving from your seat, and yet seeing the entire scenery move around you.

(This is easy to do when you're driving down the highway. You can simply sit back, relax, and *pretend* that you are not moving, only the scenery is. This is often enough to flip people into the actual Witness, at which point you will simply rest as choiceless awareness, watching the world go by, and you won't move at all. This *motionless* center of your own pure awareness is in fact the *center* of the *entire* Kosmos, the eye or I-I of the Kosmic cyclone. This motionless center—there is only one in the entire world and it is identical in all beings, the circle whose center is everywhere and whose circumference, nowhere—is also the center of gravity of your soul.)

This is why Zen will say, "A man in New York drinks vodka, a man in Los Angeles gets drunk." The *same* Big Mind is timelessly, spacelessly, present in both places. So drinking in New York and getting drunk in L.A. are the same to the motionless, *spaceless* Witness. This is why Zen will say, "Without moving, go to New York." The answer: "I'm already there."

As the Witness, I-I do not move through time, time moves through me. Just as clouds float through the sky, time floats through the open space of my primordial awareness, and I-I remain untouched by time and space and their complaints. Eternity does not mean living forever in time—a rather horrible notion—but living in the *timeless* moment, prior to time and its turmoils altogether. Likewise, infinity does not mean a really big space, it means completely *spaceless*. As the Witness, I-I am spaceless; as the Witness, I-I am timeless. I-I live in eternity and inhabit infinity, simply because the Witness is free of time and space. And *that* is why I can drink vodka in New York and get drunk in L.A.

So this morning I went jogging, and nothing moved at all, except the scenery in the movie of my life.

Thursday, June 5

As scholars from Ananda Coomaraswamy to Huston Smith have pointed out, the core of the perennial philosophy is the Great Chain of Being, the Great Nest of Being. But it is now apparent that there are at least four major inadequacies to the Great Chain as it was traditionally conceived, and in order to bring it into the modern and postmodern world—and develop a truly *integral* approach—these shortcomings need to be carefully addressed.

The Great Chain is traditionally given as matter, body, mind, soul, and spirit [figure 1, page 319]. Many traditions subdivide this considerably. For example, the soul is often divided into *psychic* and *subtle* levels, and spirit into *causal* and *nondual*. An expanded Great Nest would therefore include: matter, body, mind, soul (psychic and subtle), and spirit (causal and nondual).

That is fine. But those levels are supposed to include *all of reality*. Yet as stated, they mostly apply to just the Upper-Left quadrant (the spectrum of interior consciousness)—and that's the first inadequacy. Thus, as I have often tried to point out, each of the *vertical levels* of the Great Chain needs to be differentiated into four *horizontal dimensions* (the four quadrants). So in addition to the subjective spectrum of consciousness, we need to add objective correlates (the Upper-Right quadrant), intersubjective cultural backgrounds (Lower-Left quadrant), and collective social systems (Lower-Right) [see figures 1, 2, and 3]. Otherwise the Great Chain *cannot* withstand the blistering critiques that modernity has (correctly) leveled at it.

For example, the great traditions rarely understood that states of consciousness (UL) have correlates in the organic brain (UR), a fact that has revolutionized our understanding of psychopharmacology, psychiatry, and consciousness studies. Likewise, the traditions evidenced little understanding that individual awareness (UL) is profoundly molded by both its background cultural worldviews (LL) and the modes of techno-economic production (LR) in which it finds itself. This left the Great Nest open to devastating critiques from modern biological science, from Marxists, and from cultural and historical studies, among others, all of which demonstrated that consciousness is not merely a disembodied, transcendental noumenon, but is deeply embedded in contexts of objective facts, cultural backgrounds, and social structures. The Great Chain theorists had no believable response to these charges, precisely because they were deficient in these areas. Only as body, mind, soul, and spirit are differentiated into the four quadrants (or simply the Big Three), can these objections be handled.[12]

The second inadequacy is that the *level of mind itself* needs to be *subdivided* in the light of its *early development*. Here the contributions of Western psychology are decisive. To put it in a nutshell, the mind itself has at least four major stages of growth: *magic* (2–5 yrs), *mythic* (6–11 yrs), *rational* (11 onward), and integral-aperspectival or *vision-logic* (adulthood, if then).

If we put all this evidence together, drawing on the East and West alike, then a more complete Great Nest of Being would include these ten

---

12. See *The Marriage of Sense and Soul* for a discussion of this topic.

spheres, each of which enfolds its predecessor(s) in a development that is envelopment:

1. *Sensorimotor*—the physical body, the material level, the physiosphere.
2. *Emotional-sexual*—biological drives, sensations, perceptions, feelings; life energy, élan vital, libido, prana, bioenergy.
3. *Magic*—the early form of the mind ("preop," or early symbols and concepts), where subject and object are poorly differentiated. It is marked by egocentrism, artificialism, animism, anthropocentrism, and word magic. Because inside and outside are poorly differentiated, physical objects are imbued with human egoic intentions. Likewise, the narcissistic ego believes that it can directly and magically alter the world (Saturday morning children's cartoons are largely of the magical structure: superheroes can move mountains just by a glance; they can fly, melt steel, zap enemies, and otherwise push the world around by sheer magical power). In short, because subject and object are not yet clearly differentiated, the magical ego treats the world as an extension of itself and imbues the world with its own egoic traits. Narcissism and egocentrism rule.
4. *Mythic*—an intermediate level of mind ("conop," or the concrete rule/role mind), where magical power is shifted from the ego to a host of mythic gods and goddesses; if the ego cannot miraculously alter the world at will, the gods and goddesses can. In magic, the ego *itself* always has the power to perform miracles; in myth, the power to perform miracles is always possessed by a great Other, in a very *concrete-literal* way (e.g., Jehovah really did part the Red Sea). Thus magic uses *rituals* to display its own miraculous power; myth uses *prayer* in an attempt to get the god or goddess to perform the miracle for it. Myth is nonetheless the beginning realization that the ego cannot itself magically push the world around; it is thus a lessening of narcissism, a diminution of egocentrism.
5. *Rational*—a highly differentiated function of the mind ("formop," or formal reflexive) that dispenses with concrete-literal myths and attempts instead to secure its needs through evidence and understanding. Neither egocentric magic nor mythic god figures are going to miraculously intervene in the course of Kosmic events just to satisfy your egoic desires. If you want some-

thing from the Kosmos, you are going to have to understand it on its own terms, following its own evidence; the birth of a truly scientific attitude, another lessening of narcissism.

6. *Vision-logic*—the highest function of the gross-realm mind; a synthesizing, unifying mode of cognition. Vision-logic does not achieve unity by ignoring differences but embracing them—it is integral-aperspectival—it finds universal pluralism and unity-in-diversity.

7. *Psychic*—the beginning of the transpersonal, supra-individual, or spiritual realms. This level is often marked by an intense mystical union with the entire gross realm—the realm of nature, Gaia, the World Soul. The home of *nature mysticism*.

8. *Subtle*—the subtle realm proper is the home, not of gross-realm mythological god and goddess figures focused on your ego, but of directly cognized, vividly intense, and ontologically real Forms of your own Divinity. The home of genuine *deity mysticism*.

9. *Causal*—the causal realm per se, the formless unmanifest, nirvikalpa, nirvana, pure Emptiness, the Abyss, ayn. The root of the Witness. The home of *formless mysticism*.

10. *Nondual*—this is both the highest *Goal* of all stages, and the ever-present *Ground* of all stages. The union of Emptiness and Form, Spirit and World, Nirvana and Samsara—One Taste, sahaja samadhi, turiyatita. The home of integral or *nondual mysticism*.

That is a much more complete Great Chain or spectrum of consciousness (a more complete Upper-Left quadrant).[13] Each of those levels actually has four dimensions or four quadrants, but even on its own, this more complete Great Nest allows us to do several important things at once:

---

13. For this simplified account, I am not distinguishing between basic structures, transition structures (such as worldviews), or self-fulcrums. See the November 16 entry for a short overview, and *The Eye of Spirit* [and especially *Integral Psychology*] for a detailed presentation. At the same time, this simple summary is more than adequate for the following discussion. Incidentally, the levels themselves are defined by the basic structures of each level (sensorimotor, rule/role cognition, formal reflexive, vision-logic, etc.). Each of those levels has a particular worldview (magic, mythic, rational, existential, etc.), and I often use those more accessible terms to describe the level itself. But basic structures and worldviews should not be confused. See November 16.

- Stop elevating magic and mythic to psychic and subtle. This elevation of magical narcissism to transcendental awareness is perhaps the single defining characteristic of much of the new-age movement, however well intentioned it often is.
- Stop confusing mythological stories with direct and immediate transpersonal awareness. This elevation of myth to subtle illumination is common in countercultural spirituality.
- Stop confusing magical indissociation with holistic vision-logic. This elevation of magical cognition, which *confuses* whole and part, to the status of vision-logic, which *integrates* whole and part, is prevalent in eco-primitivism (or the belief that foraging tribes integrated self, culture, and nature, whereas—as theorists from Lenski to Habermas to Gebser have pointed out—they actually failed to clearly differentiate them in the first place).
- Stop confusing the biosphere, bioenergy, and prana (level 2) with the World Soul (level 7). This elevation of ecology to World Soul is often one of the defining characteristics of ecopsychology, ecofeminism, and deep ecology. (It often joins the previous confusion—that of magic with vision-logic—to recommend a retro-embrace of foraging or horticultural worldviews).

Those examples could be multiplied almost indefinitely. Suffice it to say that, with a more complete Great Holarchy of Being, we can more easily recognize whether a movement is progressive or regressive. Thus the great wisdom traditions, when complemented by Western psychology, help us to move forward, not backward.

Here is the problem, correctable by Western developmental psychology: In the *traditional* depiction of the Great Chain (e.g., matter, body, mind, psychic, subtle, causal, and nondual), the "mind" level almost always meant the logical or rational faculty, and anything nonrational *had* to be placed on the higher, transrational levels because the early *prerational* stages of development were poorly understood. These early, prerational levels can be grasped only by an intense investigation of infant and child development, an almost exclusive contribution of the modern West.

In other words, the *traditional* Great Nest (in Christianity, Hinduism, Buddhism, Sufism, Taoism, paganism, Goddess worship, etc.) is open to massive pre/trans fallacies, because it has no way to differentiate magic and mythic from psychic and subtle—they *all* get placed in the transpersonal/transrational domain. This unfortunate confusion was responsible, in no small measure, for the Western Enlightenment's complete and total rejection of spirituality, since so much of it (and the Great Chain) was obviously full of dogmatic magic and myth. The West officially tossed the bathwater of prerationality, but it also, unfortunately, tossed the transrational baby with it.

The third inadequacy: Because the traditional Great Chain theorists had a poor understanding of the early, infantile, prerational stages of human development, they likewise failed to grasp the types of *psychopathologies* that often stem from complications at these early stages. In particular, psychosis can often stem from problems at stages 1–2; borderline and narcissistic disorders, stages 2–3; and psychoneurosis, stages 3–4.[14]

Western depth psychology has amassed compelling evidence for these pathologies and their genesis, and the Great Chain needs desperately to be supplemented with these findings. As it is, every time the Great Chain theorists were confronted with a case of mental madness—and lacking an understanding of the prerational stages—they were forced to assume it was a wild descent of transrational God, whereas it was, more often than not, a frightening resurgence of prerational id. These poor deranged people were rarely God-intoxicated, they were borderline basket cases. Treating them as God-realized is right up there with sacred cows—and did *nothing* to assuage modernity's suspicion that *all* of spirituality is a nut case. If babbling idiots and cows are enlightened, why listen to Eckhart and Teresa and Rumi, either?

The fourth inadequacy in the traditional Great Chain is its lack of understanding of evolution, an understanding that is also a rather exclusive contribution of the modern West. The funny thing—as many theorists have pointed out—is that if you tilt the Great Chain on its side and let it unfold in time—instead of being statically given all at once, as traditionally thought—you have the outlines of evolution itself. Plotinus temporalized = evolution.

In other words, evolution to date—starting with the Big Bang—has unfolded approximately three-fifths of the Great Chain, in precisely the order predicted—insentient matter to living bodies to conceptual mind (or physiosphere to biosphere to noosphere). All that is required is to see that the Great Chain does not exist fully given and statically unchanging, but rather evolves or develops over great periods of time, with

---

14. See *Transformations of Consciousness* for a discussion of the spectrum of psychopathology. See September 10, note 17, for the role of neurophysiology.

each of the higher levels emerging through (not from) the lower. And the fact is, despite the bluff of western biologists, nobody really understands how higher stages emerge in evolution—*unless* we assume it is via Eros, or Spirit-in-action.

Evolution in the *cultural* domain is, of course, a politically incorrect topic, which almost certainly means it is true. Numerous theorists have come around to this view. In recent times, cultural evolution has been championed, in various ways, by Jürgen Habermas, Gerald Heard, Michael Murphy, W. G. Runciman, Sisirkumar Ghose, Alastair Taylor, Gerhard Lenski, Jean Houston, Duane Elgin, Jay Earley, Daniel Dennett, Robert Bellah, Ervin Laszlo, Kishore Gandhi, and Jean Gebser, to name a few. The pioneering work of Jean Gebser is paradigmatic for the lot: he sees cultural worldviews evolving—to use his words—from *archaic* to *magic* to *mythic* to *mental* to *integral*. Sound familiar?

The point is that, once the Great Chain is plugged into an *evolutionary* and *developmental* view, it can happily coexist with much of the God of the modern West, namely, evolution.[15] Moreover, it raises the stunning possibility: if evolution has thus far unfolded the first three-fifths of the Great Chain, isn't it likely that it will continue in the coming years and unfold the higher two-fifths? If that is so, God lies down the road, not up it; Spirit is found by going forward, not backward; the Garden of Eden lies in our future, not our past.

Those are four inadequacies of the Great Chain of Being that have thoroughly prevented it from being accepted by modernity (it doesn't cover the four quadrants; doesn't take early, prerational development into account, and thus is open to massive pre/trans fallacies; doesn't understand early pathologies; doesn't grasp evolution). Conversely, repairing those deficiencies can—and I believe will—make the Great Holarchy fully compatible with modern research, evidence, and information, thus uniting the best of ancient wisdom with the brightest of modern knowledge—and this is precisely the essence of the integral approach.

I can't help but think of Huston here. The Great Chain is his legacy, the one idea that he has fought the hardest to introduce into the modern world. But if the Great Chain is indeed to survive, it will have to be in this refurbished and reconstructed and integral form.

---

15. For an extensive discussion of this theme, see *The Marriage of Sense and Soul.*

Friday, June 6

Outlining the Great Nest [in the above entry], it dawns on me, yet again, how tiresome it is to write of the levels of consciousness in third-person it-language. Useful (and necessary) as that is, it is rather beside the point. I'm going to write a piece—I think I'll call it "Anamnesis"—where each level is described from within, in first-person I-language: not what each level looks like, but what the world looks like from each level.

Saturday, June 7

Worked all morning, went grocery shopping, lifted weights. Back at my desk, and I see my little fox friend. He has taken to living under my porch, so I toss him eggs every now and then. A few months ago I found out he has a girlfriend, because I was working and they both came up and sat down outside my window—I looked up and they were staring at me. They were adorable; they looked like twins. I haven't seen her lately, though, I wonder where she is.

Sunday, June 8

This morning, only vast Emptiness.
I-I is only, alone with the Alone, all in All.
Fullness pushes me out of existence,
radiance blinds me to the things of this world,
I see only infinite Freedom,
which means I see nothing at all.
There is a struggle to reanimate the soul,
to crank consciousness down and into the subtle,
to pull it down into ego and body,
and thus get out of bed at all.
But the Freedom is still there,
in this little twilight dawn,
and Release inhabits even
the smallest moves to make manifest
this glorious Estate.

Thursday, June 12

Interview with Scott Warren. Scott is a graduate student with Michael Mahoney, author of the superb *Human Change Process* (and literally

hundreds of other publications of exceptional merit). Scott is also a dedicated Zen practitioner and transpersonal psychologist, so I agreed to
meet with him. A few excerpts:

sw: What's your typical day like? What's your schedule?

kw: I wake up around three or four A.M., meditate for one or two
hours, and I'm at my desk around five or six. I work pretty much non-
stop until around two P.M. Then I lift weights for an hour or so. I run
errands, and eat dinner around five. I then go out, usually to a movie,
or watch a movie at home, hang out with friends, meet with visitors, or
do correspondence and light reading, make phone calls, go to bed
around ten. If I'm seeing somebody, we spend evenings together.

sw: When you say work until two, what is the work like?

kw: Well, this depends on whether I'm researching or writing. If I'm
researching, it's plain old-fashioned homework—you just read and read
and read. I usually try to go through two to four books a day, which
means I skim through them very quickly, making a few notes where
necessary. If I find a really important book, then I'll slow down and
spend a week or more with it, taking extensive notes. Really good books
I'll read three or four times.

When I'm writing, it's a little different. I work at a very intense pace,
in some sort of altered state, where I seem to process information at a
frightening rate. I'll sometimes put in fifteen-hour days. In any event it's
truly exhausting, physically exhausting, which is the main reason I took
up weightlifting.

sw: How long does it take to write a book?

kw: My usual pattern of writing is, I read hundreds of books during
the year, and a book forms in my head—I write the book in my head.
Then I sit down and enter it on computer, which usually takes a month
or two, maybe three.

sw: So all these books took a few months to write?

kw: Yes, except *Sex, Ecology, Spirituality*. That book took me three
years, really excruciating years. But the amount of actual writing time
itself was still fairly short, several months.

sw: Why excruciating? What happened?

kw: Well, if you think about a book like *The Spectrum of Consciousness* or *The Atman Project*, those were difficult books to conceive
because you're trying to fit together dozens of different schools of psychology. But those books only covered the Upper-Left quadrant. In SES
I was trying to pull together dozens of disciplines in all four quadrants,

and this was a seemingly unending nightmare. So I really closed in on myself, and for three years I lived exactly the type of life that many people think I live all the time—namely, I really became a hermit. In fact, apart from grocery shopping and such, I saw exactly four people in three years. It turned out to be very close to a traditional three-year silent retreat. It was by far the most difficult voluntary thing I've ever done.

sw: Didn't you go nuts?

kw: The worst part came about seven months into the retreat. I found that what I missed most was not sex, and not talking, but skin contact—simple human touch. I ached for simple touching, I had what I started calling "skin hunger." My whole body seemed to ache with skin hunger, and for about three or four months, each day when I finished work, I would sit down and just start crying. I'd cry for about half an hour. It just really hurt. But what can you do in these cases except witness it? So eventually a type of meditative equanimity started to develop toward this skin hunger, and I found that this very deep need seemed to burn away, at least to some degree, precisely because of the awareness I was forced to give it. After that, my own meditation took a quantum leap forward—it was shortly thereafter that I started having glimpses of constant consciousness, or a mirrorlike awareness that continued into the dream state and the deep sleep state. All of this came about, I think, because I was not allowed to act on this skin hunger, I was forced to be aware of it, to bring consciousness to it, to witness it and not merely act it out. This skin hunger is a very primitive type of grasping, a very deep type of desire, of subjective identity, and by witnessing it, making it an object, I ceased identifying with it, I transcended it to some degree, and that released my own consciousness from this most ancient of biological drives. But it was a very rocky roller-coaster ride for a while.

sw: Okay, some theoretical questions. Based on extensive cross-cultural references, you have divided transpersonal or spiritual development into four higher waves or realms, which you call psychic (which centers on the gross waking state), subtle (which centers on the subtle dream state), causal (which centers on the deep formless state), and nondual (which integrates all of them). This also gives four different types of spiritual experience: nature mysticism, deity mysticism, formless mysticism, and nondual mysticism.

kw: That's generally correct, yes. But the idea is to bring all of them into awareness, so that a basic wakefulness and choiceless awareness pervades all realms of life—waking, dreaming, sleeping—at which point you are known, appropriately enough, as an Awakened One, which really means, very ordinary, just this.

sw: Many of the transpersonal and spiritual therapists I know use your material in a very rational way. They say that the only thing they have to do is memorize your higher stages. They don't think they need to take up a spiritual practice, like Zen or yoga or centering prayer, because you've already given all the results.

kw: They don't practice because of me? Good lord, that is exactly the opposite of what I intended. I constantly emphasize that you have to take up a practice, an injunction, to actually see and understand these higher stages of development. Tell me you're kidding.

sw: Seriously, they think that memorizing your stages is all they need in order to be a good transpersonal therapist.

kw: Well, I couldn't disagree more. That's like saying, I have drawn a nice map of the Bahamas, and so now you don't need to actually go to the Bahamas for your vacation, you can just sit in your living room and look at the map. This is horrible. You cannot be a tour guide of the Bahamas if you have never been there.

sw: The common practice, when you find it, seems to be a type of bodily focusing and sensory awareness. This sensory body awareness seems to be confused with spiritual awareness.

kw: Yes, that's very common, and it is a confusion, as you say. Sensory body awareness is very important, but it is not the same as spiritual awareness. To begin with, nondual or spiritual awareness is "bodymind dropped"—that is, you cease identifying exclusively with the bodymind and its thoughts and feelings. Those are still present and fully functioning, but in addition to those, you find a more expansive identity with all of manifestation—and focusing on your body will definitely *not* cover that.

sw: These therapists say that experiential bodily focusing results in the same state as enlightenment.

kw: Yikes. It's true that meditation often starts with bodily awareness—following the breath, focusing on various bodily sensations and feelings—but it *never* simply stays there. Meditative awareness—the capacity to evenly witness or give bare attention to whatever arises—eventually extends from a few minutes to several hours, and, during intensives, for most of the day. Once you can stabilize witnessing for most of the day, that mirrorlike meditative awareness will then extend into the dream state and something like lucid dreams, and from there it will extend into deep dreamless sleep, so that one will finally discover turiya, the "fourth state," which is the pure Witness above and beyond the three states of waking, dreaming, and sleeping, and then turiyatita— "beyond the fourth," which means One Taste, or the *ever-present awareness* or *constant consciousness* or *basic wakefulness* or *choiceless awareness* that transcends and includes all possible states and is therefore confined to none. This is not a Witness but a Nondual consciousness that is not other than radical Spirit itself. To say that all of this is found in waking, experiential, bodily focusing is considerably off the mark. Likewise, you find none of this constant consciousness in the writings of deep ecology, ecofeminism, neopaganism, Jungian, web-of-life, ecopsychology, or new-paradigm theorists—which means, whatever else they are doing—and I'm a fan of much of their work—they are not dealing with constant consciousness, mirror awareness, or ever-present nondual Spirit.

sw: Well, that's my next question. Another common approach to spiritual therapy is a type of systems theory thinking, or Gaia thinking, or ecopsychology, or web-of-life theories, and so on. The idea is that if you begin to think holistically, you will get better. And the final idea is that Gaia or the web-of-life is Spirit itself.

kw: But, you see, the web-of-life is just a concept, just a thought. Ultimate reality is not that thought, it is the Witness of that thought. Inquire into this Witness. Who is aware of both analytic and holistic concepts? Who or what in you right now is aware of all those theories? The answer, you see, lies in the direction of this Witness, not in the direction of all those objects of thought. Whether they are right or wrong is beside the point. The point is the Self, the Witness, which itself is actually pure Emptiness. If an analytic concept arises, we witness that; if a holistic concept arises, we witness that. The ultimate reality is in the Witness, not in the concepts, right or wrong. As long as you are trying to work at the level of thoughts and concepts and ideas and images, you will never get it.

sw: Pure consciousness is pure Emptiness?

kw: Yes, radical consciousness is unqualifiable, which can be metaphorically indicated by saying that pure consciousness is pure Emptiness. But I repeat, Emptiness is not a concept, it is a simple and direct awareness. Look, right now you can see various colors—that tree is green, the earth over there is red, the sky is blue. You can see color, so your awareness itself is colorless. It's like the cornea of your eye, which is clear—if the cornea were red, you wouldn't be able to see red. You can see red because the cornea is "red-less" or colorless. Just so, your present consciousness sees color and is therefore itself *colorless*. You can see space, so your present consciousness is *spaceless*. You are aware of time, because your consciousness is *timeless*. You see form, your consciousness is *formless*.

So your basic, immediate consciousness—not the objects of consciousness, but consciousness itself, the witnessing awareness—is colorless, formless, spaceless, timeless. In other words, your basic and primordial awareness is unqualifiable. It is *empty* of form, color, space, and time. Your consciousness, right now, is pure Emptiness, and yet an Emptiness in which the entire universe is arising. The blue sky exists in your consciousness, right now. The red earth exists in your consciousness, right now. The form of that tree exists in your consciousness, right now. Time is flowing by in your consciousness, right now.

So the entire world of Form is arising in your own Formless awareness right now. In other words, Emptiness and Form are not-two. They are both One Taste in this moment. And you are That. Truly. Emptiness and Consciousness are just two names for the same reality, which is this vast Openness and Freedom in which the entire universe is arising moment to moment, an Emptiness that is your own primordial Awareness right now, and an Emptiness that by any other name is radical Spirit itself.

And then—as an entirely separate issue—there is the question of what the *manifest* world is actually like. I happen to believe it is an interwoven network of interpenetrating processes or holons, which is indeed a type of holistic model. But we decide the truth of that model—and the truth of the manifest world—by investigating the manifest world. We decide the truth of Spirit by investigating the inward I-I. That they are eventually not-two is correct, but the *only* way you can find that reality is by following the inward I-I, not by running around in the objective world looking for the web-of-life. If you do that, you will miss the mark. If you do that forever, you will miss the mark forever.

sw: So what do you think the role of a spiritual therapist should be? We've talked about the ones that don't seem to work—memorizing the higher stages without practicing them, confusing body sensory awareness with spiritual awareness, confusing web-of-life and ecopsychology theories with direct spiritual consciousness. What would work?

kw: I have what I think is a fantastic idea, [laughing] so of course I can't get anybody interested in it. In medicine we have the wonderful concept of a General Practitioner or GP. These are your basic family doctors. They are trained in general medicine, but not in specialized medicine. They can't do brain surgery, or make intricate differential diagnoses, or perform lab work—but they know specialists who can, and they are trained to refer you to these specialists should you need it.

I think a spiritual therapist should be like a GP of the spirit. They should have at least a theoretical familiarity with all levels of the spectrum of consciousness—*matter, body, mind* (magic, mythic, rational, and integral-aperspectival), *soul* (psychic and subtle), and *spirit* (causal and nondual). They should be familiar with the types of pathologies that can occur at each of those levels. They should be trained in the general lower techniques of bodily focusing and mental interpretation. They should know how to deal with persona, shadow, and ego problems. And they should themselves have a specific higher or contemplative practice. But they should also be trained to spot specific pathologies from the entire spectrum of consciousness, low to high—and for the ones that they cannot handle themselves, *they should refer their clients to specialists*—maybe in Zen, vipassana, t'ai chi, Vedanta, TM, Christian centering prayer, Sufi zikr, Jewish hitbodedut, the Diamond Approach, yoga—at the upper end—and at the lower end, weightlifting, aerobics, nutritional counseling, Rolfing, bioenergetics, whatever. The point is, they wouldn't try to do the brain surgery themselves. Their primary responsibilities are: first, to practice general psychotherapy and some transpersonal therapy with the client; second, to recommend specialists if needed; and third, to help *coordinate all of the client's various tools of transformation.* But they can't actually do all the therapies themselves. As it is now, too many transpersonal and spiritual therapists think they can and should do it all themselves, which is unfortunate for their clients. So that's my stupid idea, which nobody seems to like.

Friday, June 13

Went to see *Children of the Revolution*, mostly because of Judy Davis, who is quite amazing. She was hysterical in Woody Allen's *Husbands and Wives*, brilliant as Madame George Sand in *Impromptu*—to name a few. *Children of the Revolution* is a black comedy that succeeds modestly, despite an uneven style that veers between *Strictly Ballroom* and *Daniel.* But Davis is riveting. What I like about the script is the way it captures the fact that Marxism/Leninism was a religion, a fundamentalist bible-thumping religion, for millions and millions of people around the world. It was, in fact, the first truly great *modern* religion—that is, a religion that tried to make scientific materialism, gross-realm natural-ism, and flatland holism into an emancipatory God. The God of the Right-Hand world, the God and Goddess of Flatland. In this regard, it was a forerunner of many purely Descended and flatland religious movements in today's world, including much of deep ecology, ecofemin-ism, Gaia worship, neopaganism, and web-of-life revivals [see May 11]. There are many wonderful aspects about all of those movements, but they do tend to be very flatland—and the flatter the religion, the more intense the fanaticism.

Saturday, June 14

"My problems start when the smarter bears and the dumber visitors intersect."—Yosemite Park official Steve Thompson.

Sunday, June 15

Random House asked for a literary title for *Science and Religion* (and could I use the words "soul" or "spirit" or some such?). Oh well. Think-ing of Oscar Wilde's great quote ["There is nothing that will cure the senses but the soul, and nothing that will cure the soul but the senses"], I suggested several variations on *Sense and Soul*, and they finally settled on *The Marriage of Sense and Soul: Integrating Science and Religion*. So there it is. So much for my diatribes against the commodification of the words "soul" and "spirit"—I'm now guilty as charged.

Oh well. I think I'll take the afternoon off and heal my inner child.

Tuesday, June 17

For almost twenty years, I've done hatha yoga as my main physical exer-cise. Five years ago, I also began weightlifting, which has been an ex-traordinary help in writing, meditation, and immune system health—a true testament to integral practice. I'm forty-eight, and I don't ever re-member being this comfortable in the body.

Which makes it all the easier to transcend. That is, my experience is that when the bodymind is strong and healthy—not ascetically starved and despised—it is all the easier to drop it, transcend it, let it go. Pre-cisely because the bodymind is running smoothly, with no distracting glitches, it doesn't hold awareness obsessively circling around it. You can more easily forget it and slip into Witnessing or even One Taste.

Of course, neither the ego nor the body is left behind in higher states. They are still present, still functioning, still serving their conventional purposes. If somebody calls your name, you will respond. You know where your body starts and where it stops—this is not borderline or psychotic indissociation. It's just that your identity is no longer exclusively confined to these lesser vehicles. When these vehicles are functioning smoothly, and not being the squeaky wheel that demands the oil of your awareness, your awareness is free to settle into deeper and higher domains. Of course, you can do this under almost any circumstances, but a strong glitch-free bodymind makes it all the easier to drop, and thus find it floating on the ocean of infinity that is its true abode.

Wednesday, June 18

Speaking of integral practice, this is certain to be the "next big thing" on the spiritual circuit; but this "fad," for one, is going to last, at least among that 1% who are serious about transformation.

There are many ways to talk about integral practice. "Integral yoga" was a term first used by Aurobindo (and his student Chaudhuri), where it specifically meant a practice that unites both the ascending and descending currents in the human being—not just a transformation of consciousness, but of the body as well. (Which makes it all the sadder that the California Institute of Integral Studies, founded by Chaudhuri, today has little if any integral practice, which is why I cannot, at this time, recommend CIIS to students.) Mike Murphy's *Future of the Body* is an excellent compendium of an integral view, as is Tony Schwartz's *What Really Matters*. I outline my own integral approach in *The Eye of Spirit*. Murphy and Leonard's *The Life We Are Given* is a practical guide to one type of integral practice, and is highly recommended.

But anybody can put together their own integral practice. The idea is to simultaneously exercise all the major *levels* and *dimensions* of the human bodymind—physical, emotional, mental, social, cultural, spiritual. To give several examples, going around the quadrants, we have the following levels and capacities, with some representative practices from each:

UPPER-RIGHT QUADRANT
(INDIVIDUAL, OBJECTIVE, BEHAVIORAL)

Physical
　DIET: Pritikin, Ornish, Eades, Atkins; vitamins, hormones

STRUCTURAL: weightlifting, aerobics, hiking, Rolfing, etc.

Neurological

PHARMACOLOGICAL: various medications/drugs, where appropriate

BRAIN/MIND MACHINES: to help induce theta and delta states of consciousness

UPPER-LEFT QUADRANT
(INDIVIDUAL, SUBJECTIVE, INTENTIONAL)

Emotional

BREATH: t'ai chi, yoga, bioenergetics, circulation of prana or feeling-energy, qi gong

SEX: tantric sexual communion, self-transcending whole-bodied sexuality

Mental

THERAPY: psychotherapy, cognitive therapy, shadow work

VISION: adopting a conscious philosophy of life, visualization, affirmations

Spiritual

PSYCHIC (shaman/yogi): shamanic, nature mysticism, beginning tantric

SUBTLE (saint): deity yoga, yidam, contemplative prayer, advanced tantric

CAUSAL (sage): vipassana, self-inquiry, bare attention, witnessing

NONDUAL (siddha): Dzogchen, Mahamudra, Kabbalah, Zen, Eckhart, etc.

LOWER-RIGHT QUADRANT
(SOCIAL, INTEROBJECTIVE)

Systems: exercising responsibilities to Gaia, nature, biosphere, and geopolitical infrastructures at all levels

Institutional: exercising educational, political, and civic duties to family, town, state, nation, world

LOWER-LEFT QUADRANT
(CULTURAL, INTERSUBJECTIVE)

Relationships: with family, friends, sentient beings in general; making relationships part of one's growth, decentering the self

Community Service: volunteer work, homeless shelters, hospice, etc.

Morals: engaging the intersubjective world of the Good, practicing compassion in relation to all sentient beings

The general idea of integral practice is clear enough: Pick a basic practice from each category, or from as many categories as pragmatically possible, and practice them concurrently—"all-level, all-quadrant." In short, *exercise body, mind, soul, and spirit in self, culture, and nature.* "Body, mind, soul, and spirit" are the levels; and "self, culture, and nature" are the quadrants (or simply the Big Three of I, we, and it). The more categories engaged, the more effective they all become (because they are all intimately related as aspects of your own being). Practice them diligently, and coordinate your integral efforts to unfold the various potentials of the bodymind—until the bodymind itself unfolds in Emptiness, and the entire journey is a misty memory from a trip that never even occurred.

Friday, June 20

Books, just out, by friends, keep arriving. M. Scott Peck—everybody calls him "Scotty"—sends *Denial of the Soul.* "I don't pick up too many causes," his letter says, "but the euthanasia or assisted suicide issue is of great concern to me." His point is that the euthanasia movement sometimes hides a glib denial of the lessons that can be learned from conscious death and dying. He's a supporter of the hospice movement, as am I, where the standard procedure is to almost completely eliminate pain (with medication that does not dull the mind), so the individual can face death consciously, with family and loved ones present. I strongly agree. (At the same time, in cases of truly intractable pain, I support euthanasia.)

Michael Crichton has signed his novel *Airframe*: "For the next time you want some airplane reading." This is very funny, and has its genesis here: after I read his *Travels,* where he ends one chapter by saying that he sat on the beach in Hawaii and read Wilber, I sent him a copy of SES, that 800-page monster, inscribed "For the next time you're on the beach." About the only thing that two-ton book would be good for on the beach is beating a shark to death should one attack, and reading it there would be about as much fun as . . . reading *Airframe* while flying, hence the inscription. (*Airframe* is about the literally one-million ways a plane can fall out of the sky.)

A pre-pub copy of Mike Murphy's *The Kingdom of Shivas Irons* arrives. It's wonderful, a rip-roaring read. I can't believe Murphy is slipping this massive amount of mysticism into the golf section of every Barnes and Noble bookstore in the country—not just a little hint every now and then, but page after page of it. John Updike called *Golf in the Kingdom* "A golf classic if any exists in our day," and it looks like *Shivas Irons* is going to pick right up where that left off. I'm really happy for him. All of this helps to break up the topsoil of the rocky inhospitality of pragmatic America to transcendental concerns.

Surya Das's *Awakening the Buddha Within*, and it's really quite good. Those of us who followed its writing were a little worried that it was a bit disconnected, but Surya really pulled it together.

It's been a while since I've seen Surya. He, Sharon Salzberg, Mitch Kapor, and Mitch's son, Adam, stayed at my house last summer for a four-day visit. I have a lot of respect for what Surya is trying to do—make Tibetan Dzogchen accessible to American culture, which upsets both most Americans and most Tibetans.

It looks like the book is off to a great start, with everybody from Richard Gere to Alan Dershowitz lining up behind it. One Spirit Book Club and Tommy Boy Records are co-sponsoring some of its promotion. Tommy Boy was founded by Tom Silverman when he was still a boy (hence the name), but now we call him Tommy Man. He and his girl Friday, Susan Pivar (a meditation student of Sam's), stopped by the house recently for an afternoon; Tom and I spent much of our time trading weightlifting training tips. He's set up a branch of Tommy Boy—Upaya—to help get a spiritual orientation out to a larger pop audience. He's the one getting Deepak on MTV, Andrew Weil on tape, etc. This got him featured in *W*'s "The God Rush: Is the new spirituality in New York and Hollywood a godsend—or just divine madness?" Tom and Susan know I'm skeptical about the possibility of doing "pop spirituality" without its becoming thin and diluted, but it's certainly worth a try, and it can always serve to whet the appetite in a large and hungry audience.

Tuesday, June 24

There are four or five major obstacles to an integral orientation and integral practice. I'm not talking about mainstream—atheistic liberals and fundamentalist conservatives—both of whom will ignore integral spirituality anyway. I'm talking about threats from within the avant-garde, countercultural, alternative spiritual community itself.

The first obstacle, as I see it anyway, is from the merely translative camps, who focus on new ideas or new paradigms about reality. Some of these concepts and ideas are truly important, and I often agree with them; but learning a new concept will not get you to nondual constant consciousness; only intense and prolonged practice will. This translative camp includes many aspects of systems theory, ecopsychology, ecofeminism, the web-of-life theorists, neopaganism, astrology and neo-astrology, deep ecology, and Goddess/Gaia worship. There are some wonderful exceptions, but most of those approaches are largely trapped in the gross sensorimotor world, the descended world of flatland, and they simply offer new ways to *translate* that world, not ways to *transform* consciousness into subtle, causal, and nondual domains. At best they access the psychic level of nature mysticism and the World Soul, which is truly wonderful, but is nonetheless only the beginning of the transpersonal realms.

Of course, they often say that these higher realms deny and repress the earth, but that only applies to *pathologies* of the higher states; the normal higher states *transcend and include* the lower, so that Spirit transcends and includes nature, not denies it. It is true, however, that certain spiritual paths do in fact repress the lower domains, and those paths constitute the *second* major obstacle to a balanced or integral practice. This threat can be introduced in the following way.

During the great *axial period* (roughly sixth century BCE), the growing tip of an evolving humanity made·a monumental breakthrough: certain pioneering sages—Parmenides, Krishna, Jesus of Nazareth, Gautama Buddha, Lao Tzu—found that they could follow consciousness *to its source*, at which point a psychic-level *communion* with Spirit and a subtle-level *union* with Spirit gives way to a causal-level *identity* with Spirit: the Atman that is Brahman, I and the Father are One, the separate self dissolves in Emptiness, consciousness finds the unqualifiable One. This breakthrough—from the highest *Forms* of consciousness (subtle level) to pure *Formless* consciousness (causal level)—was a stunning achievement, the greatest mutation in consciousness up to that time, and the power of which set in motion virtually every one of the world's major wisdom traditions that still flourish to this day.

(It only confuses things to bring gender politics into this particular issue. The causal level is a genuine state attainable by either sex; it is itself *gender-neutral*. The cornering of this state by males during the axial period was unfortunate by today's standards and unavoidable by yesterday's. The agrarian structure itself selects the male value sphere, on average, for non-home enterprises, including intense religious re-treats, where most of these breakthroughs occurred. We of the industrial and postindustrial social structure, which does not necessitate this type of gender stratification, can begin to equalize access to these domains without having to call men dirty names as a prelude.)

The great *downside* of these axial discoveries was that, in their rush to find the Formless beyond the world of Form, they generally came to despise the entire world of Form itself. The aim was to find a nirvana divorced from samsara, a heaven that is not of this earth, a kingdom that is not of this world, a One that excludes the Many. The paradigm, the exemplar, of these axial approaches was nirvikalpa samadhi, ayn, nirodh—in other words, pure cessation, pure formless absorption. The goal, in short, was the causal or unmanifest state. The path was purely Ascending and otherworldly, and almost everything identified with "this world"—sex, money, nature, flesh, desire—was pronounced sin, igno-rance, illusion.

In a sense, there is a fair amount of truth to that. If you are *only* after the things of this sensory world, then you will not discover higher or deeper realities. But if you go overboard and deny or repress this world, you will never find the Nondual, the radical estate that includes *both* the One and the Many, otherworldly and this-worldly, Ascending and Descending, Emptiness and Form, Nirvana and Samsara, as equal ges-tures of One Taste.

The great axial age began around the sixth century BCE in both East and West. The advanced religions of that period were all dominated by yogic withdrawal, purely ascending practices, life-denial, asceticism, bodily renunciation, and the "way up." They were, almost without ex-ception, deeply dualistic: spirit divorced from body, nirvana separate from samsara, formless at war with form. But by the second century CE, the limitations of a causal and dualistic nirvana were becoming quite apparent, and the growing-tip (or most-advanced) consciousness began a great movement beyond the causal unmanifest, a movement that would transcend yet include the causal Abyss. Spirit, in other words, began to recognize its own pure Nondual condition, and it first did so, most especially, in two extraordinary souls, Nagarjuna in the East and Plotinus in the West.

"That which is Form is not other than Emptiness, that which is Emp-tiness is not other than Form," is perhaps the most famous summary of this Nondual breakthrough (the quote is from *The Heart Sutra*, said to summarize the entire essence of Mahayana Buddhism, a revolution set in motion largely by Nagarjuna). Nirvana and Samsara, the One and the Many, Ascending and Descending, Wisdom and Compassion, the Witness and everything witnessed—these are all not-two or nondual. But that nonduality is *not* an idea or a concept; it is a *direct realization*. If it is made into a concept, or something merely believed in, then all you get is a sharp whack from the Zen master's stick. For this reason, nonduality is often referred to as "not-two, not-one" (just to make sure we don't turn it into a merely conceptual monism, web-of-life theory, or flatland holism).

The point was clear enough: what was taken by the merely Ascending paths to be defilements, sins, or illusions were now seen as radiant gestures of Spirit itself. As Plotinus put it, the Many are not apart from One, the Many are a manifestation of the One (not as a theory you think about with the eye of mind, but as something you directly perceive with the eye of contemplation). Thus one's spiritual practice was not to deny all things manifest, but rather to "bring everything to the path." According to Tantra, another flower of the Nondual revolution, even the worst sin contains, hidden in its depths, the radiance of its own wisdom and salvation. In the center of anger is clarity; in the middle of lust is compassion; in the heart of fear is freedom.

It all rested on a simple principle: the higher transcends and includes the lower, not transcends and denies it. Spirit transcends and includes soul, which transcends and includes mind, which transcends and includes body, which transcends and includes matter. And therefore all levels are to be included, transformed, taken up and embraced in the true spiritual path. This is essentially the same Great Chain of the ascending schools, but now it was understood, not as a map of the escape route from the prison of the flesh, but as the diagram of the eternal embrace of all manifestation by the Spirit from whence it issued.

So began the extraordinary Nondual revolution. In the West, the great Neoplatonic tradition would carry it bravely forward, but it was everywhere resisted by the Church, which had officially pledged allegiance to the Ascending path, for my kingdom is not of this world, and render unto Caesar. . . . But for those with eyes to see and souls to hear, the Neoplatonic current blazed a trail of Nonduality across the first and second millennia. When it was realized that the Great Nest actually unfolded or *developed* in time, the Neoplatonic tradition directly fueled the great Idealist vision of Fichte, Schelling, and Hegel (which saw the entire universe as a product of Spiritual development and evolutionary unfolding—a product of Spirit-in-action), although all that remains today of that stunning vision is the scientific theory of evolution, a true but pale and anemic and sickly little child of its towering parents.

In the East, the Nondual revolution gave rise to Mahayana Buddhism, Vedanta, neo-Confucianism, Kashmir Shaivism, and Vajrayana Buddhism—all of which can loosely be summarized as "Tantra." The great flowering of the nondual Tantra especially occurred from the eighth to the eleventh centuries in India, and from there it spread (beginning as early as the sixth) to Tibet, China, Korea, and Japan. When it was also understood in the East that the Great Chain did indeed unfold or evolve over time, the great Aurobindo expounded the notion with an unequaled genius.

We are today at an auspicious moment in history, where these two great Nondual currents, in their evolutionary and integral form, are starting to come together. The Neoplatonic and Idealist currents of the West, appropriately combined with the West's scientific understanding of evolution, are being integrated with the East's great Nondual and Tantric schools, also with their own strong developmental orientation.

The result is the general *integral approach*, now involving, in its various forms, hundreds of researchers around the world. To this mix the modern integral approach also brings a commitment to depth psychology—a virtually exclusive discovery of the modern West—and a desire to allow excellence to shine from every level, every dimension, every quadrant, every domain in the human and divine estate. This integral approach is in its infancy, but growing at an exhilarating rate.

If the first obstacle to the integral approach is flatland (or the merely Descended schools), the second obstacle, as I started to say, is the reverse error, the merely Ascending path. That approach—remnant from the axial age—includes Theravadin Buddhism, some forms of Vedanta (that rest in nirvikalpa or jnana samadhi, and don't push through to sahaja), many forms of asthanga and hatha yoga (when they aim only for mental cessation). Again, it's not that these approaches are wrong; they simply need to be supplemented with the Path of Descent in order to take a more Nondual stance.

A third obstacle is the "spiritual bypass" school, which imagines that if you find Spirit or Goddess or your Higher Self, everything else will magically take care of itself. Job, work, relationships, family, community, money, food, and sex will all cease their annoying habits. The despairingly sad thing is, it usually takes ten or twenty years to discover that this is definitely not the case, and then, where has your life gone?

So the first half of your life is spent somewhat misguided, the second, bitter.

This spiritual bypass approach can be very tricky, especially—and ironically—if you are dealing with the very highest Nondual schools. One Taste is an *ever-present* consciousness (it is the natural and spontaneous mind in its present state: if you are aware of this page right now, you have 100% of this ultimate consciousness fully present). Precisely because One Taste is "always already" present, many people can gain a quick but extremely powerful glimpse of this ultimate state if an accomplished teacher carefully points it out to them. And, in fact, many of the great Nondual schools, such as Dzogchen and Vedanta, have entire texts devoted to these "pointing out instructions" [see April 27 for an example].

Once students get a strong hit of this always-already awareness, certain unfortunate things can happen. On the one hand, they are, in some profound ways, liberated from the binding nature of the lower levels of the bodymind. On the other hand, that doesn't mean these lower levels cease to have their own needs or problems, relative though they may be. You can be in One Taste consciousness and still get cancer, still fail at a marriage, still lose a job, still be a jerk. Reaching a higher stage in development does *not* mean the lower levels go away (Buddhas still have to eat), nor do you automatically master the lower levels (enlightenment will not automatically let you run a four-minute mile). In fact, it often means the opposite, because you might start to neglect or even ignore the lower levels, imagining that they are now no longer necessary for your well-being, whereas in fact they are the means of expression of your well-being and the vehicles of Spirit that you now are. Neglecting these vehicles is "spiritocide"—you are neglecting to death your own sacred manifestations.

It gets worse. In order to pass through the oral stage of psychosexual development, you don't have to become a great chef. In order to discover the transverbal, you do not have to be Shakespeare. In other words, you absolutely do *not* have to develop perfect mastery of a lower stage before you can move to a higher stage—all that is required is a certain vague competence. But this means that you can arrive at some very high stages of development and *still have all sorts of problems at various lower stages*. And simply plugging into the higher stage is *not* necessarily going to make those lower problems go away.[16]

---

16. For further discussion of this topic, see the entries for November 16 and December 18 [and see *Integral Psychology*, chap. 8].

This becomes a bit of a nightmare with the always-already schools, because once you get a strong glimpse of One Taste, you can lose all motivation to fix those holes in your psychological basement. You might have a deep and painful neurosis, but you no longer care, because you are no longer identified with the bodymind. There is a certain truth to that. But that attitude, nonetheless, is a profound violation of the bodhisattva vow, the vow to communicate One Taste to sentient beings in a way that can liberate all. You might be happy not to work on your neurotic garbage, but everybody around you can see that you are a neurotic jerk, and therefore when you announce you are really in One Taste, all they will remember is to avoid that state at all costs. You might be happy in your One Taste, but you are failing miserably to communicate it in any form that can be heard, precisely because you have not worked on all the lesser vehicles *through which* you must communicate your understanding. Of course, it is one thing if you are being offensive because you are engaged in angry wisdom or dharma combat, quite another if you are simply being a neurotic creep. One Taste does not communicate with anything, because it is everything. Rather, it is your soul and mind and body, your words and actions and deeds, that will communicate your Estate, and if those are messed up, lots of luck.

Again, it's not that the One-Taste or sahaja schools are wrong. They are plugged into the highest estate imaginable, but they need to be complemented with an understanding that work also needs to be done on the lower levels and lesser stages (including psychotherapy, diet and exercise, relationships, livelihood, etc.) in order for a truly *integral* orientation to emerge. In this way only can a person communicate One Taste to all sentient beings, who themselves live mostly on lower domains and respond most readily to *healthy* messages addressed to those domains, not higher messages strained through neurotic and fractured lower realms.

The last major obstacle to an integral approach, as I see it, is the new-age epidemic, which . . . oh, well. Elevates magic and myth to psychic and subtle, confuses ego and Self, glorifies prerational as transrational, confuses preconventional wish-fulfillment with postconventional wisdom, grabs its self and calls it God. I wish them well, but . . . May they get their wishes quickly granted, so they can find out how truly unsatisfying they really are.

So those are the major obstacles to a nondual integral approach, as I see them: Descended flatland and its merely translative schools; the solely Ascending paths with their distaste for this world; spiritual bypassing; One-Taste sufficiency that leaves schmucks as it finds them; and new-age elevationism. If we add the conventional world at large—both liberal atheists and conservative mythic fundamentalists—that's a half-dozen roadblocks to integral self-realization, which only means, Spirit has certainly not yet tired of this round of the Kosmic Game of Hide and Seek, for it is content to continue hiding in just the damnedest places.

Thursday, June 26

Ram Dass is doing better, and there is hope that a fair amount of recovery will occur. The last time I saw him was at Roger's fiftieth birthday party. Frances and I had planned this party as our present to Roger on his half-century milestone. We thought the best thing we could give him was a gathering of those who love him dearly. Roger is eminently lovable. Huston Smith, Stan and Christina Grof, Jack Kornfield, Jim Fadiman, Miles Vich, Bryan Wittine, John O'Neil, Robert McDermott, Keith Thompson, Philip Moffet, Ram Dass . . . over fifty people, and we held it at Campton Place, off Union Square in San Francisco.

Ram Dass and I sat together with Roger and Frances, and he was full of life, full of spirit. Then, when I was in New York, Frances leaves a message on Tony's machine: Ram Dass has had a major stroke; his body is almost completely paralyzed; he can't move or speak. Frances is audibly shaken; she and Roger and Ram Dass had become especially close in the last few years. But Ram Dass is now speaking some, and with two years or so of therapy, might make a reasonable recovery. I'm praying he can indeed make this grist for the mill. I also know, from painful experience, that no matter how strong and seemingly unshakable one's spiritual realization, life can yank the rug right out from under you when you're not looking, and, more embarrassingly, when you are.

Saturday, June 28—Denver

Dinner in Denver with two of my best friends in the area, Warren Bellows and Willy Kent, and I'm sad that they are moving. To Sonoma County, right north of San Francisco. I met Warren through Treya; they had met at Findhorn. I describe Warren in *Grace and Grit*; he was the only non–family member present at Treya's death. It was really Warren and I who took care of her those last few weeks, and he was an absolute godsend. His longtime lover, Willy, is a gifted physician; I love them both. Warren tends to be more spiritually oriented, especially in his acupuncture practice, and Willy is more the skeptical scientist; I have strong affinities with both camps, so we've always enjoyed hanging out together. I've never had a homosexual experience, but I've always been comfortable in gay culture, probably because of the aesthetics. Straight males are, on average, aesthetically challenged.

"You really are sad they're leaving, aren't you?" Marci asked.

"Yes, of course. Why would you even ask that?"

"Well, you know, I thought you'd just make your brainwaves go to zero and not worry about it."

"Emptiness means you care more, not less. I'm very sad."

"Yes, I know. I'm glad."

Monday, June 30

Emptiness alone, only and all, with an edge of extremely faint yet luminous bliss. That is how the subtle feels when it emerges from the causal. So it was early this morning. As the gross body then emerges from this subtle luminous bliss, it's hard to tell, at first, exactly where its boundaries are. You have a body, you know that, but the body seems like the entire material universe. Then the bedroom solidifies, and slowly, very slowly, your awareness accepts the conventions of the gross realm, which dictate that *this* body is *inside* this room. And so it is. And so you get up. And so goes involution, yet again.

But the Emptiness remains, always.

July

See! I am God; see! I am in all things; see! I do all things; see! I never lift mine hands off my work, nor ever shall, without end; see! I lead all things to the end I ordained it to from without beginning, by the same Might, Wisdom, and Love whereby I made it. How should anything be amiss?

—DAME JULIAN OF NORWICH

Tuesday, July 1

ANAMNESIS, OR THE PSYCHOANALYSIS OF GOD

1

Push pull crash . . . push pull crash . . .

2

  Yearning, yearning.
  Hunger, thirst, hunger here.

Swallowing, to swallow.
Must have, must have, must have.
Move toward, run away.
Fear, fear, fear, here.
Anger, rage, explode, swallow, grasping hard, terror.

3

I see, hear, feel. I am not alone. There are others here, of my blood, and we are one, against the others.

Nature sleeps with us, and rises with us, and we are sometimes bright, sometimes frightened, by this power over us. Our strong desire is not strong enough, many times. Earth, air, fire, water, follow no course, sometimes they help, many times they hurt.

Life is short, following the way of all blood on earth. There are others here, some are bright, some are dark. Those of my blood are with me. Those who are not, are not. Death is with us, and we put death on those who are not.

Family is of blood, and is with us. I am four in this family. Eighteen suns have brought me here. Now the moon is putting death on me. The moon, the snake, the water, they are one.

All things touch all things. There is no separation here on earth. To touch a thing is to be that thing; to eat a thing is to be that thing. We do not touch that of the other, we do not eat that of the other. Life is on this side, of our blood. Death is on that side, of the other. We do not touch the other, we do not eat that of the other. Now the moon is putting death on me, because the snake, the moon, and the water are one. When the snake bit, the moon entered me, and now death is entering me.

I have learned these things, from those who know. My family goes on, our blood mixed with this earth.

4

Boy and girl together are killed, we roast them and eat them carefully, for they are of the Mother. Blood is of the Mother, and we offer blood to Her, which comes back as our food.

I am Tiamat, of the fifth house, planter of the seeds that were brought to us by ancestors in the days before time began. My blood is of the Mother, my bones are of the Mother, my heart beats with the time calling us to Mother. My body mixes with earth, which is the Mother.

Few understand Mother. She is Life, her blood makes life. We offer her blood, the boy and girl are killed together, which we eat for the Mother, or else the seeds will not bring forth. Each four moon season, we sacrifice for Mother, which comes back as our food. If we do not sacrifice, we all will perish. I, Tiamat, know this, from the ancestors who brought us the seeds, in the days before time began.

5

My father's father descended from the Creator, whose abode is not here, but Heaven, and His ways we cannot know. In our city, the priests have means to contact our Father, but my family does not understand them. My father's father understood the Father, for they were kin, but we have forgotten. It does not matter, our lives are in His hands. There are many gods and goddesses, and He is just the leader of them all, though we do not know how.

The priests tell us that there was a time that our ancestors walked with the Creator, but then something terrible happened. We pray twice daily to be returned to before the mistake. I pray very hard, but the last time I prayed hard, my sister died anyway. My uncle said I must pray harder, so something must be wrong with me.

I am being trained to be a potter, because I am very good with my hands, and I see things about making. My brother was a potter; my other brother plows. One of my sisters died; they will not tell me what happened to my other sister.

We are fortunate, for we have a strong house. This is because my father's father was descended from the Creator. Also, in the blood fight that took this city from the others, our family fought well, and so we have this house.

The day of sacrifice is the best day, because everything comes from the Creator and we must give some of it back. My family sacrifices beautiful birds, which we raise for this. There are dark rumors about what goes on in the Temple, but I don't believe them. We see the sacrifices here, with the birds. The blood of the bird returns to the earth. Blood is the life we are given, so we give it back. To eat a thing is to be that thing, so after the bird is blessed by the priest, we eat it, because now it is food of the gods, and the gods are in it. So in this way we become strong, and the elements leave us alone. And yet, the last time I prayed for my sister, she died anyway, so there must be something wrong with me.

6

This world makes sense, obviously. And I am constantly struggling with those who want to hide the light of rationality under some obscure basket of deceit. UFOs, astrology, alchemy, astral travel, Eastern mysticism. . . . What a mess.

Most of these people, however well intentioned, don't seem to realize that they are living in a relatively safe and protected world precisely because of rational science and its fruits of medicine, dentistry, physics, economic production and abundance, the extension of average life span from thirty years to seventy years. The critics condemn that which shelters them. I've been an electrical engineer for over three decades, because it works, it is verifiable, it betters human lives. There is a real world out there, with real truth in it, and real hard work required to dig it out. You can't just contemplate your navel and hope to find out anything worth anything.

The fortress of science, is how I think of it. It will stand forever, constantly updated. That is, as long as the antirational inmates don't take over the hospital.

Perhaps I shouldn't get angry, but I do. Ever since my son died last year in an automobile accident, things have been a little rough. But running to a pie-in-the-sky God does no good at all. We human beings, for good or ill, are the only gods in existence, the only force of rational intention and good will. And we will save ourselves if we can be saved at all. The Bible is right about one thing: the truth will set you free. And science is the only path of discovering truth. What else could there be?

I'm not worried, anyway. Oh, once in a while, I can't sleep, you know. I lie awake and stare into the darkness, and wonder.

7

All things are related to all things. When I first had that realization, perhaps when I was a young girl, maybe fourteen or so, it completely changed my life! I would later learn names for this—holism and so on— but at the time, all I knew was that all things were related to, connected to, all things. Twenty years, two husbands, no kids, three jobs, and one National Book Award later, I still believe this firmly!

My book, *To Re-weave the Web*, is a detailed account of this holistic view, based not only on all the late-breaking scientific discoveries—and oh there are so many! from chaos theory to quantum physics to complexity theories and systems theory, my head just spins, it's so exciting!—but also we have the holism of the indigenous peoples the world over, who knew all this stuff way before modern science stumbled onto it. The Great Goddess returns! Gaia is alive! All things are related to all things.

This is wondrous, isn't it? Now that science is catching up with this holistic interwoven view—why, I was writing about this years ago!—I am looked upon as something of a forerunner. So I have become a heroine, imagine that! I've been asked to be on this board and that, serve on this journal and that, go to this conference and that. Me! Imagine that!

Oh, I forgot. Not just the indigenous beliefs, but Eastern mysticism, too. All saying the same thing, about the web-of-life, all things and all things and all of that and so on. So I don't see why those Zen people keep annoying me and asking if I meditate. What difference does it make?, I keep asking them. If you believe that everything is connected to everything, what else is there? You do it your way, which is meditation, and I do it my way, which is called holistic thinking. They said, that was just an idea and could I show them this oneness right now? And that made no sense to me at all. They're just being obnoxious, I think, like they know it all. Imagine that!

8

The hike through the mountain with my fiancé was everything I wanted. Madly in love, slightly crazed, we both were babbling fools. More like children, but it didn't matter. For an hour John had dutifully carried the picnic basket on his back, kidding all the time that it was only fitting that he should carry the food of the CEO of Digital Data Corporation, and I said, No, it's only fitting for a love slave, and that would be you. And I wasn't even finished with the sentence when suddenly I disappeared, and there was only the vista in front of me, and John, and this body . . . but no me, or no I, or . . . well, I'm not sure. I was one with all of this scenery, one with the mountain, one with the sky, it was exhilarating, a little scary, but mostly completely peaceful, like coming home. I've never really told anyone about it, because on Monday I was back at the office, running Digital, and who would have believed me anyway?

It never happened again. I sometimes read about things like this, oneness and whatnot, cosmic consciousness, but none of the words sound right for what happened to me. I hear that some people can stay in this state constantly, but I don't see how, I really doubt it. You'd lose all sense of orientation, I think. Anyway, it came and went. The more I think about it, the more I think it might have been something like a small seizure. It didn't seem like it at the time, but now it does. After all, what else could it be, seriously?

9

It was just the other day, I can still remember it as if it's happening right now, vivid, electric, weird. I was sitting alone, at home, and it's late, around midnight maybe. I have the distinct feeling that somebody or something is in the house—you know that feeling? Well at first it really scared me, I was really scared. I finally got up the nerve to go through the house, checked it really well. I sit back down and it happens.

This really intense fireball, I don't know what else to call it, simply materialized right there in front of me, right there in the living room. I know this sounds crazy, but this has never happened to me before, I don't see things, you know? But it wasn't just an electrical thing. I know this sounds crazy, but it was alive. Well, I'll just say it: it was Love. It was a living fire of Love and Light. I know this as sure as I'm sitting here. It sort of moved from in front of me to on top of my head, then back in front of me, then on top of my head. When it sits on top of my head my whole spine begins to vibrate, and shooting currents run up it, right to the top. Pretty crazy, huh? And then as soon as I knew that this was Love, it just disappeared, just like that. It just went away, but it scared the daylights out of me. But then it didn't, I mean it didn't scare me. It made me feel completely safe, I've never really felt like that.

I've heard about, you know, that light at the end of the tunnel? Except I wasn't dead. But I know what I know, and I know that Love is somewhere out there. My entire body feels different somehow. My spine hurts, like somebody plugged it into the wall socket, I don't know exactly. But the truth is out there. I know that. Oh, and I know I've started praying, just to say thanks.

10

Nature retreats before its God, Light finds it own Abode. That's all I keep thinking as I enter into this extraordinary vastness. I am going in and up, in and up, in and up, and I have ceased to have any bodily feelings at all. In fact, I don't even know where my body is, or if I even have one. I know only shimmering sheaths of luminous bliss, each giving way to the next, each softer and yet stronger, brighter and yet fainter, more intense yet harder to see.

Above all, I am Full. I am full to infinity, in this ocean of light. I am full to infinity, in this ocean of bliss. I am full to infinity, in this ocean of love. I cannot conceive of wanting something, desiring something, grasping after anything. I can contain no more than is already here, full to infinity. I am beyond myself, beyond this world, beyond pain and suffering and self and same, and I know this is the home of God, and I know that I am in God's Presence. I am one with Presence, it is obvious. I am one with God, it is certain. I am one with Spirit, it is given. I shall never want again, for Grace abounds, here in the luminous mist of infinity.

Around the edges of this love-bliss there are tender tears, the faint reminders that I have so wanted this, so longed for this, so desperately yearned for this—to be saturated to the ends of the universe, to be full and free and final. All the years, all the lifetimes, searching for only this, searching and suffering and screaming for only this. And so the tender tears stand at the edge of my infinity, reminding me.

Out of this Light and Love, all things issue forth, of this I am now certain, for this I have seen with the eye of my own true soul. Into this Light and Love, all things will return, of this I am now certain, for this I have seen with the eye of my own true soul. And I have returned with a message: Peace be unto you, my human brothers and sisters; and peace be unto you, my animal brothers and sisters; and peace be unto you, my inanimate brothers and sisters—for all is well, and all is well, and all manner of things shall be well. We are all of the same Light and Love, of this I am now certain, for this I have seen with the eye of my own true soul.

11

Exactly how long I was Light, I cannot say. How long Form existed, I cannot say. How long I have been neither, I cannot say.

On the other side of Light, the Abyss. On the other side of Love, the Abyss. How long, I cannot say.

I once was a rock, I remember that, and push pull crash, I remember that. I roamed the universe of myself in slumbering abandon, and truth be told, it was humorous, always.

I once was a plant, then an animal, and thirst and hunger, I remember that. I ran toward, and ran away from, the forms of my own lust. I wandered driven, starving, dying. But truth be told, it was humorous, always.

I once awoke as human beings, and entered into the school of my own becoming. I first worshipped myself in the form of my other, I worshipped my slumbering self. I moved toward my own skin, dear nature, and I approached me now with wonder, now with terror, and did unending trembling and ritual pleading to deal with the terror I induced by my own sleep. But truth be told, it was humorous, always.

I once awoke as human beings in search of me as heavenly other, in my own form as misty mythic mystery, still asleep, but barely. I sacrificed aspects of my still slumbering self in order to appease the terror that my own twilight still evoked. But to awaken all at once, you see, would have ended the game right there. And truth be told, it was humorous, always, even as I cut into myself.

I soon awoke as human beings who, in striving to be a light unto themselves, were dimly on the trail of the Light that I am, even in my otherness. In one great move I stopped looking for me out there. In one great move, I awoke to a consciousness of light. In one great move, I turned within, or began to, and I could sense that this game was getting old, because I was now on the trail of I. Truth be told, it was humorous, even as it was starting to end.

And then one day, sitting alone as my otherness, I saw myself as a ball of Light and Love, and knew the Great Awakening was upon me.

In the next move in the school of myself, I entered into Me, as that Love and Light itself, and I was with I to infinity. And this I recognized altogether, in a whisper of breath that embraced all space, and a flash of Light that contained all time.

And then, the Abyss beyond all beyonds. Some would call it radical Freedom, infinite Release, ultimate Liberation, the great Redemption, boundless Being. I wouldn't know, for there is no I to know, in any form, sacred or profane, and so there is only this radical Formlessness, which remains its own remark. It is not bliss, it is not God, it is not love. It is not holistic, it is not Goddess, it is not interwoven anything. It is not infinite, it is not eternal, it is not any conception or object or state whatsoever. I-I am not light, am not love, am not spirit, am not bliss. I-I am not bound, am not free, am not ignorant, am not liberated.

But this much can be said: where there is not this Emptiness, there is only suffering.

All this I remember, in the school of myself. All this I have seen, in the history of my own discovery. All this I sing of now, to the audience of myself. All this I promise to others, who are the forms of my own slumbering. All this others will also see, as they awaken from their otherness and return their slumbering selves to the Wakefulness that has always existed, undiminished and untorn, in the heart of what they are.

Exactly how long I was Light, I cannot say. How long Form existed, I cannot say. How long I have been neither, I cannot say.

On the other side of Light, the Abyss. On the other side of Love, the Abyss. How long, I cannot say.

But I know I will empty even this Emptiness, and therefore create a Kosmos, and therefore incarnate as the world of Form, and enter with Wakefulness the children of my own Awareness.

12

Around the sea of Emptiness, a faint edge of bliss.
From the sea of Emptiness, a flicker of compassion.
Subtle illuminations fill the space of awareness,
As radiant forms coalesce in consciousness.
A world is taking shape,
A universe is being born.
I-I breathe out the subtlest patterns,
Which crystallize into the densest forms,
With physical colors, things, objects, processes,
That rush upon awareness in the darkness of its night,
To arise as glorious sun, radiant reminder of its source,
And slumbering earth, abode of the offspring of Spirit.

13

The phone rings and I run to pick it up. "Yes?"

"Hi, it's Marci."

"Hi, sweetie. What's up?"

"I think we should go on a vacation, spur of the moment. Just do it."

"Um, well, I've got all this work, you know, it's sorta . . ."

"Come on, it won't kill you to take a few days off."

"Okay, okay. We've never been to South Beach, and we wanted to give it a try, so we might as well do it now, yes?"

"Yes!"

Two weeks later, here we are, in South Beach, Miami, of all places.

And resting in the ocean, dipped into the sea, I find glimmers of One Taste everywhere.

Emptiness, clarity, and care, are the names of this present moment, exactly as it is arising, now and now and now. The bodies of Buddha, the hands of Christ, the faces of Krishna, the breasts of the Goddess, the aspects of this very moment. I know that all of that is somehow tied to a pledge that I have made, deep in the heart of my very soul, how or where or when exactly, does not really matter. It is just that, for those who remember the course of their own consciousness—from mineral to plant to animal, from magic to mythic to mental to supramental, from body to ego to soul to Emptiness to radical One Taste—there is an extra duty asked of them, and that is to communicate what they have seen, and what they have remembered, and what they have found—what each I has found in the school of I as it returns to itself, shining and free, empty and bright, called and caring, just so, and again, just so.

And truth be told, it was humorous, always.

14

Marci is swimming. I finish my Coke and my sandwich. It is noon. The sky is clear, the ocean is blue, the waves surge freely on the beach, wetting the soft white sand.

Wednesday, July 2

Read all morning, answered a few urgent phone messages, spent an hour unpacking and shelving the weekly shipment of books that arrived. Books, really, who needs them? People think that being awakened means you understand everything, but it really means the opposite. It means you don't understand anything. It is, all of it, a total Mystery, a baffling babbling of unending nonsense.

Enlightenment is *not* "omniscience" but "ascience"—not all-knowing but not-knowing—the utter release from the cramp of knowledge, which is always of the world of form, when all you are in truth is formless. Not the cloud of knowing, but the cloud of unknowing. Not divine knowledge, but divine ignorance. The Seer *cannot* be seen; the Knower *cannot* be known; the Witness *cannot* be witnessed. What you are, therefore, is just a free fall in divine ignorance, a vast Freedom from all things known and seen and heard and felt, an infinity of Freedom on the other side of knowledge, an eternity of Release on the other side of time.

Knowledge is mandatory in the conventional, relative world, and I am glad to unpack those particular books and try to communicate through them, because of certain vows and duties that operate in that world. But all of it, truly, is just a series of ornaments on primordial awareness, a pattern of reflections in the empty mirror. Ken Wilber is just a scab on my Original Face, and this morning I flick it off like a tiny insect, and disappear back into the infinite space that is my true abode.

But that infinite space is impulsive. It sings its songs of manifestation, it dances the dance of creation. Out of sheerest purest gossamer nothingness, now and now and forever now, this majestic world arises, a wink and a nod from the radiant Abyss. So I finish unpacking the books, and go on about the morning's business.

Friday, July 4

Got a copy of the Association for Transpersonal Psychology Newsletter, and find this notice: "The American Medical Writers Association of New England has given its Award in Excellence in Medical Communication to the *Textbook of Transpersonal Psychiatry and Psychology* (Basic Books, 1996) by psychiatrists Bruce Scotton, Allan Chinen, and John Battista."

They deserve it; they did an absolutely first-rate job on that book. They asked me to do a foreword for it, and I was glad to, with an added bonus for all of us: I sat down to write the piece, got carried away, and fifty pages later had what I thought was a terrific article—but a horrible foreword, massively too long. No way they could use it. So I then wrote a properly short, four-page foreword—which worked just fine—and the long essay became one of my favorite pieces, called "The Integral Vision," which is now the Introduction to *The Eye of Spirit.* So everybody got something out of my ineptitude.

But more than that, to have the very conservative New England medical establishment give an award to a book on spiritual and transpersonal psychiatry is extraordinary, truly amazing. In what amounts to a *political* act, medical psychiatry in this country *determines* which states of consciousness are "real" and which are "pathological," "sick," "illusory." And what do you know, it looks like God is no longer a mental disease.

Saturday, July 5

Perhaps a few explanatory notes to "Anamnesis." In it, I tried to describe what each major level of consciousness looks like from within, from the inside, from the first-person or "I" point of view. Since, in academic writing, you are always forced to speak in objective it-language, I wanted to speak, for a change, in I-language. Of course, one of the main reasons academic religious writers stick to objective it-language is that it relieves them of the burden of having to transform consciousness (the I) in order to see any of this. Instead of going to Bermuda, they read books about Bermuda and *discuss the books*! Very strange.

For the lower levels (up through section 9), I created short stories to represent what the world looks like at each level. Starting with section 10, the entries are phenomenological: entering the various states, recording the experience. I ended up rather arbitrarily with 14 sections to "Anamnesis," and since I usually use ten major levels of consciousness, the correlations are as follows:

• Section 1 is the *sensorimotor* world (level 1), the world of matter and physics. My treatment is not very imaginative, but there it is.

• Section 2 is the pranic or *emotional-sexual* world (level 2). Also not that imaginative, but obvious enough.

• Section 3 is the *magical* world (level 3). In magical-animistic cognition, subjects with similar predicates are often equated, and wholes are conflated with parts, so that condensation and displacement rule. Still, it is in its own way one of the more beautiful worldviews, and its laws of metaphor (equating items with similar agency) and metonym (equating items with similar communion) are important roots of language and still expressly inhabit poetry; it's easy to see how Romantics get confused about its actual contours.

• Sections 4 and 5 are the *mythic* world (level 4), divided into *horticultural* mythology (section 4), which is often matrifocal, and *agrarian* mythology (section 5), which is almost always patrifocal (patriarchal). Historically, the shift from the previous magical/foraging to mythological/horticultural occurred when *planting* was discovered. In horticultural societies, planting is done with a simple digging stick or hand-held hoe; because the physical demands are modest, pregnant women can participate, and up to 80% of foodstuffs in horticultural societies were produced by females. Consequently, around one-third of all horticultural societies had female-only deities (the Great Mother); about one-third had male and female deities; and about one-third, male-only deities. (With a few maritime exceptions, wherever you find a Great Mother society, it has a horticultural base.) When it was discovered that an animal could pull a large and heavy plow, much more planting could be done, but the work was physically harsh and demanding (women who participate in heavy physical plowing have a significantly higher rate of miscarriage; it is to their Darwinian advantage not to plow). Consequently, almost the entire food production was done by males, and—accordingly—over 90% of agrarian societies have predominantly male deities.

What was particularly striking about the matrifocal horticultural societies was the sporadic practice of human sacrifice. The Great Earth Mother demanded blood to bring forth new crops, and, as scholars such as Joseph Campbell have documented, "a fury for sacrifice" marked the rise of many matrifocal horticultural societies around the world (starting around 10,000 BCE). Although sacrifice in some cases intensified in later cultures, it appears certain to have begun here. I have used a particularly graphic and well-documented example from Campbell, where a young boy and girl are killed while copulating, their bodies roasted and eaten. This blood-and-body earth worship is typical of Great Mother religion.

The rise of patrifocal agrarian societies was often marked by a sharp break with human sacrifice, but a retention of many of its themes in symbolic or reduced form (as in the Catholic Mass—"Take, eat, this is my body; take, drink, this is my blood"). The patriarchal mythic religions saw themselves as more ethical than the previous earth-worshipping pagan religions, largely because of the banning of human sacrifice.

This overall mythic level is one that Jungian psychology often confuses with transrational spiritual domains. It has its own haunting beauty, but it is prerational, not transrational. Nonetheless, we still have a type of access to all of these early levels, and, when properly subsumed, they offer a great deal of vitality and imaginative richness. But my overall point is that neither horticultural nor agrarian mythology—nor mythology in general—can serve as genuine, transrational, spiritual guides for the modern and postmodern world.

· Section 6 is the *rational* world (level 5). The capacity for rational-perspectivism and pluralism brings such an increase in the good, the true, and the beautiful—brings such an increase in the light of understanding—no wonder they almost immediately called it "the Enlightenment." But there is also much hubris with rationality; only occasionally, with tragedy, do wonder and remorse break through.

· Section 7 is *vision-logic* or the integral-aperspectival world (level 6). In this story I went a little bit overboard; I was playing off the typical new-age new-paradigm exuberance, which takes the important truths of vision-logic and holism, but then injects them with a number of confusions: systems theory is not disclosing the same "web of life" that the magical world sees (systems theorists do not think that the volcano is exploding because it is personally mad at them); holistic thinking is not the same as Eastern contemplation (the former is mental, the latter is supramental); Gaia is not the same as the Goddess (the former is finite, the latter, infinite). In general, the woman in this story is falling prey to the fallacies that often dog the new-age new-paradigm agenda. [I call this the "415 Paradigm," since its epicenter is the Bay Area and such institutions as CIIS. I have been a sharp critic of the 415 Paradigm, and many of its believers have responded with vehemence. See September 23 for an elaboration and critique of this view.] But the higher truth concealed in all this is indeed that of vision-logic and the integral-aperspectival view.

• Section 8 is one type of experience at the *psychic* level (level 7); specifically, this is a classic example of cosmic consciousness, or the temporary feeling of oneness with the entire gross realm. Notice that it is not permanent, and it does not involve the higher subtle or causal realms—in other words, it is a classic case of *nature mysticism*. This is the highest type of mysticism generally recognized by deep ecologists, ecopsychologists, neopagans, ecofeminists, Gaiasophists, and Great Mother worshippers, although it is the lowest of the mystical spheres, that of the World Soul or Eco-Noetic Self. Nonetheless, it is a profound and powerful dimension of consciousness, one glimpse of which can alter a life irrevocably.

The *tone* of experience at the psychic level (of nature mysticism) is almost always one of complete *reverence*; a sense of the *awesomeness* of existence; and a sense of the *insignificance* of humans in general and me in particular.

• Section 9 is another type of experience at the *psychic* level (level 7), pursued on *the path of shaman/yogis*, namely, the awakening of the psychic currents known as kundalini. These currents begin with the etheric body (the emotional-sexual body), but usually become conscious at the psychic level (as in this story) and persist into the subtle. This person has a kundalini awakening and, unable to contain it, sees it as an external other, which only slowly returns to the currents of his own bodymind. These types of psychic experiences are often the gateway to the next level, the subtle; and in kundalini yoga, the practitioner rides these bodily currents to their source in the sahasrara, the radiance of light at and beyond the crown of the head (epitome of the high subtle).

The *tone* of these experiences often starts reverential (when the sacred force is externalized as a Great Other), but eventually becomes one of *power* and *empowerment* (when the sacred force is realized to be an internal current of one's own bodymind). Traditionally, it is said that at this level the power can easily be misused, a type of Darth Vader, Castaneda move.

• Section 10 is a typical experience at the *subtle* level (level 8), pursued on *the path of saints*. The gross realm is temporarily left behind, so much so that it is often not even recognized. The energy currents of the bodymind return to their origin in the subtle (and especially the sahasrara, the infinity of Light and Bliss that is Above all gross orientation, a "saintly" stance often symbolized as a halo of light around the head). In these types of meditation, the sensation is always "in and up," in a literal, not metaphorical, sense. The Light and Bliss that is infinitely Above is directly experienced as such; this is the Form of Deity, which is one's own deepest Structure. This is the Sambhogakaya, the home of *deity mysticism*, the *union* of God and soul.

The *tone* of these experiences is usually *ecstatic, visionary, apocalyptic, peaceful*, and *prophetic*.

• Section 11 is the *causal* level (level 9), pursued on *the path of sages*. This is the home (the root source) of the Witness, of consciousness without an object, of pure cessation, classical nirvana and nirvikalpa, ayn, the unmanifest, the Formless, the great Unborn, Godhead, Urgrund, Dharmakaya, pure Emptiness. Where the psychic involves the *communion* of soul and God, and the subtle involves the *union* of soul and God, the causal is the *identity* of soul and God in prior Godhead. That is, when consciousness ascends to the infinity of subtle Light and Bliss Above (which is the subtle realm), at some point it "falls" into the causal Heart, and the separate-self sense is finally undone in radical Emptiness, nirguna Brahman, or unqualifiable Godhead. (The causal Heart, on the right, is not to be confused with the heart chakra, which is a subtle-level energy center of love on the central meridian; the former is pure Emptiness or absolute bodhichitta, the latter is compassion, or relative bodhichitta; cf. Sri Ramana Maharshi.)

With all lesser mystical states, there is always the sense of *entering* or *leaving* the state, always the sense of *something different* happening (seeing Light, feeling Love, knowing Deity, finding peace, etc.). But at some point in those ascending or descending currents—which are all gross or subtle experiences—there comes a sudden Witnessing of anything and everything that arises, and one no longer is moved to search for experiences of any variety at all. One moves off the line of ascent and descent (which, in itself, is samsara), and stands Free as the Witnessing Heart. Instead of chasing after objects—sacred or profane, high or low, earthly or heavenly—one simply rests as the mirror-mind in which all objects are equally and impartially reflected. One is no longer moving up to the infinite Light above, or down to the vital Life below—one is simply Witnessing any and all movements. This is a *stepping off* of the Great Circle of Ascent (Eros) and Descent (Agape), and, although both those movements are perfectly embraced by the Witness, they no longer motivate consciousness itself. As consciousness—as the empty Witness—one is the Unmoved Mover.

The centers of the gross-vital Life below (i.e., the lower chakras) are themselves a condensation of the subtle Light above (the higher chakras), and the highest chakra itself (the sahasrara) is simply the manifest *reflection* of the Unmanifest—it *shines* by the power of the causal Heart, even though the causal Heart is not itself Light (or any other manifest quality). In other words, all ascending and descending currents have their ultimate root source in the causal Heart, which itself is none of those currents—which is why the Witness can impartially witness all of manifestation, itself being free of the entire show.

(The Witness itself, however, inherently possesses the last remnant of separation, self, and duality, present as the tension between the Witness and everything witnessed, the tension—and the separation—between the unmanifest and the manifest, nirvana and samsara, emptiness and form; this final duality will dissolve when the causal Witness itself dissolves into nondual One Taste, where Emptiness embraces all Form, nirvana and samsara are not-two, and the Witness is everything witnessed).

I chose, in this section, to include a recollection of past stages of growth. Just as an individual with a near-death experience might "see" a review of his or her entire life, so upon causal death, one might "see" a review of the entire sweep of cosmic history, which is the history of the unfolding of one's deepest Self. (Such an experience, when I was twenty-seven, was the basis of *Up from Eden*). This "review" does not itself take place in the causal—*nothing* exists in the causal—but rather, on either side of it (going in or coming out).

The *tone* of the causal is stone. It is unmoved and unmovable; a great mountain of the unmanifest; but also a sense of *vastness, freedom, spaciousness, release, liberation*. Also—and this is rather hard to convey—*none* of those "tones" has a sense of being an experience. Experiences come and go, but the empty Mirror is the vast space in which all experiences come and go, and is not itself experiential in the least.

· Section 12 is the *descent* from the causal to the subtle, or the beginning of involution, emanation, or manifestation itself. Sections 1–11 are the story of the *ascent* or *evolution* of consciousness, from matter to body to mind to soul to causal spirit. But once consciousness returns to its root source in the causal Heart, then descent or involution can *consciously* begin, moving from spirit to soul to mind to body to matter. Of course, variations on this cycle are occurring constantly, and it's a thoroughly nested affair (evolution and involution are occurring with each breath, and even with each microsecond. It's just that, at the point of return to the causal Heart, the entire cycle can be investigated consciously and deliberately, thus penetrating and undoing its power to fascinate.) Sections 12–14 are a very short version of the involution story, told from the perspective of this particular bodymind (i.e., kw).

Most people "experience" this transition each night when they move from deep sleep (one version of the causal) to the dream state (one version of the subtle), but they can't remember it. One of the aims of meditation is to render all these transitions conscious and thus become transparent to Source of the movement itself.

· Section 13 is the continuation of descent, moving from the subtle to the gross, completing the circle of evolution and involution (what Plotinus called reflux and efflux). When there is continuity of consciousness through all three major realms or states (causal, subtle, gross), in ascending and descending arcs, then the One Condition and One Taste of all realms becomes shockingly, simply obvious.

The *tone* of One Taste—and *the path of the siddhas*—is traditionally described in one of two ways, both of which tend to confuse people. The first is a tone of utter *boredom*, a great big yawn in the face of the entire world. The reason is that, because One Taste is the taste of absolutely everything in existence, then tasting One Taste, you have tasted it all. Been there, seen That. And thus it is traditional in, for example, Dzogchen Buddhism, to picture the Adept as looking infinitely bored.

The second is a tone that is *flippant*, almost wise-ass, and certainly irreverent. When Bodhidharma was asked the nature of reality, he said, "Vast Emptiness, nothing holy, nothing sacred." Nothing, in other words, that can't be made fun of. When *all* things are seen to be *equally* Spirit, there is no room for piety. Where the psychic shaman/yogi embodies great power, where the subtle saint embodies peaceful radiance, where the causal sage embodies stony equanimity, the nondual siddha embodies limitless humor. A great laughter returns, a lightness surrounds all acts. Needless to say, not everybody with a sense of humor is established in One Taste; humor is usually egoically driven. It's just that, when nothing is sacred, everything is taken lightly.

· What both of those tones have in common is a relentless ordinariness, nothing special. It is *just this*, nothing more (section 14).

Sunday, July 6

Phil Jacobson—his full name is Philip Rubinov-Jacobson, an old and honorable Russian Jewish name—has just returned from a month in Vienna with Ernst Fuchs, founder of the Vienna School of Fantastic Realism and major heir of Salvador Dali. Because I've written fairly extensively on art and aesthetics, I have often been contacted by artists from around the world, who send me their material and ask for help in getting it promoted. So I have for some time been trying to think of how to help with this situation. It seemed that a good place to start would be to create a type of clearinghouse—a modern museum—for transpersonal or spiritual art. It turns out that Phil had been thinking along similar lines for a very long time. I thought Phil would make a good project coordinator for this museum, and he agreed. The question has been where to locate it, and how to fund it.

Off Phil goes to Vienna. Fuchs, it turns out, has *also* been thinking about a museum for spiritual art, and when Phil mentions our similar idea, Fuchs gets so excited that they go into Vienna and Fuchs buys a building to house it! Fuchs is now looking for a castle to buy in which the artists themselves could actually work, while the Vienna building will house the archives, information exchange network, etc. Right now, it looks like Phil will spend about six months in Vienna getting the museum up and running, and then he will return to the States, set up a branch outlet here, and divide his time between the States and Europe.

The house in Vienna is actually a baroque palace, apparently quite beautiful, very large. And the castle—they are now in the process of buying it—is Franz Josef's summer castle. This is astonishing. If it works out—and the devil, of course, is in the details—this could be a real boon to transpersonal artists around the world.[17]

---

17. As of this writing, the Transpersonal and Spiritual Art Museum is still going forward. Those interested can contact Phil Jacobson in care of Shambhala Publications.

Tuesday, July 8

Raindrops are beating, a large puddle is forming, there on the balcony. It all floats in Emptiness, in purest Transparency, with no one here to watch it. If there is an I, it is all that is arising, right now and right now and right now. My lungs are the sky; those mountains are my teeth; the soft clouds are my skin; the thunder is my heart beating time to the timeless; the rain itself, the tears of our collective estate, here where nothing is really happening at all.

Wednesday, July 9

Sam and his daughter, Sara, arrived. It's always wonderful to see a little girl that you have known all her life suddenly show up a young woman. Sara is now eighteen, and simply beautiful. She's very bright, with a sharp and keen intellect, and she wants to get her degree in, of all things, philosophy.

"Sara wanted to talk to you about where to go to college."

"Yes," she said, "whether here, at a place like Sarah Lawrence or Brown, or perhaps in Canada, or somewhere else."

"The problem with a humanities education in the States is that my generation has made it a very dicey game, I'm ashamed to say. Extreme postmodernism is the mood, and the problem with extreme postmodernism is that in many ways it's driven by nihilism and narcissism. In other words, it believes in nothing but itself. Too many present-day treatises in the humanities are simply boomers attempting to demonstrate their moral superiority by condemning all previous works of art, science, literature, and philosophy. So cultural studies have often been turned into, basically, self-esteem therapy for boomers, a way to promote themselves at the expense of all who came before."

Harsh words, but I recalled a recent article in *lingua franca: The Review of Academic Life*, by Professor Frank Lentricchia, where he exposes the epidemic of nihilism and narcissism now parading as literary and cultural studies in American universities. It "stems from the sense that one is morally superior to the writers that one is supposedly describing. This posturing of superiority," he says, treats everything that came before it as "a cesspool that literary critics will expose for mankind's benefit." Then he nails it: "The fundamental message is self-righteous, and it takes this form: 'T. S. Eliot is a homophobe and I am not. Therefore, I am a better person than Eliot.' To which the proper response is: 'But T. S. Eliot could really write, and you can't.' " No wonder Lentricchia concludes his survey of the present state of humanities in America: "It is impossible, this much is clear, to exaggerate the heroic self-inflation of academic literary and cultural criticism." Ouch.

"Are there any good points about the postmodern movements?" Sara wondered.

"Oh, definitely. I'm criticizing the extremists. But postmodernism in general has introduced what I think are three very important truths: constructivism, contextualism, and pluralism. *Constructivism* means that the world we perceive is not simply *given* to us, it is partially *constructed* by us. Many—not all—of the things we thought were universal givens are really socially and historically constructed, and thus they vary from culture to culture. *Contextualism* points out that meaning is context-dependent. For example, the 'bark of a dog' and the 'bark of a tree'—the word 'bark' means something entirely different in each phrase—the context determines the meaning. This gives interpretation (also called hermeneutics) a central place in our understanding of the world, because we do not simply perceive the world, we interpret it. And *pluralism* means that, precisely because meaning and interpretation are context-dependent—and there are *always* multiple contexts—then we should privilege no single context in our quest for understanding. (This is also referred to as integral-aperspectival, vision-logic, or network-logic.)

"So those three truths are the core of the various postmodern movements, and I strongly support those core truths. In that sense, I am definitely a postmodernist. The problem is, as with any movement, you can take these truths and blow them all out of proportion, at which point they become self-contradictory and self-defeating. So the *extreme* postmodernists do not just say that *some* truths are socially constructed and relative, they say *all* truths are, so there is no such thing as universal truth. But they are claiming that *their* truth is in fact universal. So they exempt themselves from the charges they level at everybody else—and again we see the narcissism underlying their nihilism."

"I see," Sara said, "so it's not so much postmodernism as extreme postmodernism we want to avoid."

"In my opinion, yes. Unfortunately, the extremists have a dominant hand in the humanities departments of most American universities today." Another recollection from a recent article, this one by Richard A. Posner in *The New Republic*: "The postmodern left is defined by its opposition to the values, the beliefs, and the culture of the 'West,' the 'West' being conceived as the domain of nondisabled heterosexual white males of European extraction and their east Asian and west Asian 'imitators,' such as the Japanese (Hitler's 'honorary Aryans') and the Jews. The postmodern left is radically multiculturalist, but it is more, for the 'West' that it denigrates is not historically specific; it encompasses liberalism, capitalism, individualism, the Enlightenment, logic, science, the values associated with the Judeo-Christian tradition, the concept of personal merit, and the possibility of objective knowledge." In other words, a nihilistic rejection of everything except its own worth: nihilism, narcissism. And the melancholy conclusion: "The postmodern left is well ensconced in American universities."

"So where can you get a good humanities education?" Sara asked, naturally concerned.

"Well, one good professor can turn almost any university into a worthwhile experience. There are plenty in the States, so shop around."

"I've thought about several universities in Canada, such as Victoria."

Sam jumped back in. "There's always Cambridge and Oxford."

"What do you think, Sara?"

"I'm visiting London this year, so maybe I'll check them out."

"The great advantage of a place like Oxford or Cambridge is that you can help to design and create your own curriculum, so you can turn it into a genuine multicultural education, studying the best of both West and East, North and South, without getting caught up in massive ideological agendas and the silliness of extreme postmodernism. We're slowly moving in this direction in the States, but in the meantime . . ."

Thursday, July 10

Sam is putting together a project that sounds exceptional; I've signed on as a consultant. It's a documentary called *Pilgrimage*, consisting of six one-hour segments. Each segment is by, and about, one person making a pilgrimage to a major religious site. So far the six are: Sri Lanka for Hinduism, Bodhgaya for Buddhism, Greenland for Inuit, Konya for Islamic dervishes, Australia for the Aboriginal tradition, and Jerusalem for Christianity/Judaism/Islam. This film will be distributed all over the world, through various television, satellite, cable, and theater outlets.

Rudy Wurlitzer is the main screenwriter, and Philip Glass has signed on to do the music. The idea of the series is to avoid the "anthropological tourism" of a National Geographic special, and aim instead for a combination of *subjective* journey with *objective* pilgrimage site. Each person will share their own hopes, fears, desires, worries, as they make their way to the particular shrine. So it will combine a rich, luscious photography of the objective site with a very personal account of spiritual seeking. And above all, the idea is to show each of the great traditions, not as a relic of the diminished past, but as an invitation to take up a genuine spiritual practice and thus open oneself to the glory of a greater tomorrow.

Friday, July 11

Party for Alex Grey at my house, with Marci, Sam, Sara, Tami Simon (of Sounds True), Kate, Phil, etc. Alex is a remarkable person. It's not just that he's a brilliant and pioneering painter. He has a heart of gold and a gentleness that indicates not weakness but great strength. He also has the capacity to offer almost ecstatic praise of others, which is painfully rare in our culture of irony.

I had known that Alex had, for quite some time, been working on a book about art; he surprised me by pulling out a first draft. An accompanying volume contained dozens of his stunning artworks. Sam made an offer to publish both volumes, and Alex was simply stupefied. He could hardly talk.

I'm so glad for Alex. I think he's right on the verge of major international recognition. If only all parties could be this fun *and* this rewarding.

Saturday, July 12

There is an ecopsychology conference coming up at Naropa. Ecopsychology has some wonderful points to recommend it. Among other things, it attempts to heal the dissociation between the knowing human subject and objective nature known; it seeks to end a certain arrogant anthropocentrism; it wishes to protect the environment, not as an "Other" but as part of our deepest Self; it sees human neurosis embedded in the (avoidable) fragmentation of organism and environment; it seeks to cure many of our major ills by healing this (arrogant) split between human and nature.

All of that is to ecopsychology's great credit. But my concern is that ecopsychology, in attempting to be a truly holistic approach, actually falls into the merely Descended world of flatland (or "flatland holism"), which is exactly the charge leveled by Michael Zimmerman [see May 11]. Here are my concerns (and this really applies to virtually all forms of eco-philosophy—deep ecology, ecofeminism, neopaganism, neo-astrology, ecopsychology):

1. At its best, ecopsychology deals beautifully with the World Soul, Gaia, or the Eco-Noetic Self, by whatever name (level 7). In other words, at its best it is a genuine nature mysticism of the gross realm. But it tends to leave out and completely ignore the deity mysticism of the subtle realm, the formless mysticism of the causal realm, and the integral mysticism of the nondual. (Some Buddhists seem drawn to ecopsychology, but they should realize that it deals only with the Nirmanakaya, and leaves out the Sambhogakaya, the Dharmakaya, and the Svabhavika-kaya.)

2. Although at its best it aims for the World Soul or Eco-Noetic Self, the bulk of ecopsychology, under a pre/trans fallacy, confuses the biosphere (level 2) with the World Soul (level 7). It doesn't appear to understand that the World Soul is that which *transcends* the physiosphere (matter), the biosphere (life), and the noosphere (mind)—and therefore can *include* and *integrate* all of them. Instead, it tends to reduce everything to the biosphere (what many critics have called eco-fascism).

3. Even those ecopsychologists who grasp the actual nature of the World Soul generally lack an interior technology of transformation—that is, they lack any sort of injunction, exemplar, or paradigm for genuinely transforming consciousness to the level of the World Soul. They champion a goal without a path. Lacking such, ecopsychology, even at its best, tends to degenerate into flatland maps and systems theory—mere *mental* concepts without the power to take you to the *transmental*.

4. The magical structure of foraging tribes is often confused with, and elevated to, the holistic embrace of vision-logic, and thus a regressive eco-primitivism is coupled with flatland systems theory, and this is often presented as a "new paradigm," which is, let us say, problematic.

In short, only a few of the ecopsychology approaches seem to grasp the nature of the World Soul or Eco-Noetic Self, and of those that do, few have a reproducible technique for actually getting you there. Almost all ecopsychology, under the pre/trans fallacy, confuses the biosphere with the World Soul, which collapses the interior dimensions of consciousness, prevents people from taking up truly transformative practices, fosters regression to mere sensory-vital life, and champions a descended and flatland view, which itself is a prime contributor to ecological despoliation.

The major reason I mention this is that ecopsychology, as a profound attempt to grasp the World Soul, could—if it pursued its venture more consistently—take its worthy spiritual project even deeper, into the genuinely transpersonal domains of subtle, causal, and nondual occasions. But in order to do so it must relinquish its grasp on the gross sensorimotor world as if that were the only major reality in the Kosmos. There are deeper domains, higher affairs, wider perceptions—gross to subtle to causal to nondual—awaiting those who penetrate the World Soul and find its Witness, and from there, One Taste.

At that point, the glorious promise of the eco-philosophies could be fulfilled and completed, resting in the One Taste that has often been their own admirable intuition from the start.

Tuesday, July 15

Good lord, Gianni Versace was shot to death early this morning, right outside his house in South Beach. At first it was thought that it might be due to his alleged connections with the Mafia—it's been rumored for years that he was laundering money for the mob. But now it looks like it was Andrew Cunanan, a serial gay murderer.

In the world of pop culture, this is a great loss, and it's sad he had to die so senselessly. There are no happy deaths; but many are redeemed in a moment of transcendence, or clarity, or care, or suffering carried with grace. But poor Versace, two bullets to the head, no grace, no glory, just sudden darkness.

It's especially sad because Versace—in addition to his electrifying effect on fashion—was instrumental in the renovation of South Beach. So much so that, as one TV commentator put it, Versace's house had become "the most famous house on the most famous drive in the most famous vacation spot in the world." Well, a little hyperbole never hurt anybody. But Versace managed to unite the worlds of entertainment and fashion—"frock and roll"—and his loss is truly lamentable.

At the same time, I can't help but be reminded how shallow pop culture is, was, and probably always will be. When gross-realm aesthetics are consciously plugged into subtle or causal depth, then sensory display in fashion and form becomes a rich expression of Spirit instead of a pitiful substitute for it. But such is popular culture—a sea of substitute gratifications, attempts to wring a pleasure from the body that can be found only in the fullness of Spirit—a sea of desires yearning for infinity, an ocean of itches eager for the All, finding instead a pathetic trickle of passing temporal release—an orgasm here, fifteen minutes of fame there, a sleek fashion here, a sneeze of cocaine there, all packaged by the purveyors of glossy glitzy shiny surfaces, one of whom was brutally murdered today.

It's very eerie watching the coverage on TV, because Versace was shot on exactly the place Marci and I stood to admire his house—directly on the steps outside of the iron gate. The place where we were standing is now a small puddle of blood.

Saturday, July 19

Roger and Frances arrived for a few days' visit, on their way to Fetzer, where Frances has organized a conference on "Spiritual Intelligence." Tony is coming tomorrow, to decompress from Eisner and Aspen, so it's a bit crowded around here, but pleasantly so.

Monday, July 21

Roger and Frances left for Fetzer, leaving Tony and me. For several years Tony has been a practitioner and an advocate of the Diamond Approach, a method of psychospiritual growth founded by Hameed Ali. In fact, Tony gave the Diamond Approach one of his highest ratings in *What Really Matters*. But it now appears that, while he continues to appreciate that approach, he is also having a few second thoughts.

(I wrote a thirteen-page critique of the Diamond Approach in *The Eye of Spirit* [chapter 11, note 11]. I believe that the approach is very important and a major step forward in the integration of psychology and spirituality. But it also contains several pre/trans fallacies that render it dangerously unstable, and I said so strongly in the critique. Tony has come to a similar position.)

To put it in a very simplified form, the Diamond Approach maintains that we all start out, as infants, basically in touch with our spiritual Essence, but the process of growing up represses or chokes off this Essence. This repression of Essence leaves us with various 'holes' in our being—various symptoms and defenses and distresses. Using *psychological* techniques to undo this repression allows us to recontact the lost Essence, and thus bring a *spiritual* awareness into our lives. The Diamond Approach therefore seeks to unite psychotherapy and spirituality in one system. It is now enjoying a surging popularity.

"But you think that the Diamond Approach is caught in a pre/trans fallacy," Tony said.

"Yes, definitely. It confuses pre-egoic impulse with trans-egoic Essence, just because both are non-egoic. That's a classic mistake."

"But they would say something like this. You can tell by watching young children when they play that they are really in touch with Essential Joy. They are spontaneous, alive, vibrant, and glowing with pure joy. But then as they grow up, they start to lose touch with that pure joy, they . . ."

"Just a second. You've already loaded the argument by using the word 'pure' in front of 'joy.' Who says this is *pure* joy, meaning pure spiritual joy? It's not pure, and it's not spiritual. It's just impulsive. There is a big difference."

"Why?"

"As you know, a crucial watershed in psychological development occurs somewhere around ages five to seven, when young children learn to *take the role of other*. There is a series of famous experiments that show this. If you take a ball colored green on one side and red on the other, put the green side facing the child, and ask him, 'What color are *you* looking at?,' he will correctly say green. But if you ask him, 'What color am *I* looking at?,' he will say green, even though you are looking at red. He cannot put himself in your shoes, he cannot take the role of other."

"Yes, I know. And around age seven, children will get the answer right. They can start to take the role of other."

"Yes, meaning that the child has moved from an *egocentric* to a *sociocentric* capacity—from *me* to *we*—from narcissism to social sharing, to taking the role of others and including others. This is a huge transformation in consciousness—also known as the shift from *preconventional* to *conventional* awareness. And then finally, around adolescence, there occurs a shift from conventional to *postconventional* awareness, which means that awareness is no longer trapped and limited to my group or my tribe or my nation, but rather opens to a universal, global, *worldcentric* awareness, where all people are treated with justice and fairness, regardless of race, sex, religion, or creed. And, as you know, in my system this global worldcentric awareness is the gateway to genuine spiritual states."

"Yes," said Tony. "So how does this apply to the Diamond Approach?"

"Well, to use your example, the Diamond Approach confuses preconventional, narcissistic, egocentric joy with postconventional, worldcentric, spiritual joy. It confuses pre and trans."

"But what exactly is the difference?" Tony asked.

"Joy is not *spiritual* joy until it can take the joy of *others* into account. Joy that is confined solely to your own ego may be joy, but it is not spiritual joy or essence of joy or anything like that at all. It is self-centered, self-absorbed, self-glorifying—and if that is your idea of Spirit, somebody is in deep trouble."

"So joy would what? develop into higher forms?"

"Yes, that's right. Like most traits, joy grows and evolves—or develops—from preconventional to conventional to postconventional to spiritual forms."

"What would joy at the conventional level look like?"

"When most people are happy, it's not really fun until you can share it with someone, especially someone you love, a mate or a friend. It's the joy not just of 'me' but of 'we'—not egocentric but sociocentric. You aren't happy if just you are happy—you want your family and friends to be happy, and you suffer if they aren't. In fact, at this level, if your joy remains locked in the self-absorbed mode, there is probably some deep pathology."

"And joy at the postconventional level?"

"As your consciousness grows and evolves into global and worldcentric modes, you can no longer be truly happy without at least the thought of extending this happiness and joy to *all* others. You become idealistic in the best sense of the word, wishing to relieve the suffering of—and extend happiness to—*all people*—not just your family, or your friends, or your tribe, your religion, your nation (those are all sociocentric and ethnocentric), but rather to *all peoples*, regardless of race or sex or creed. At least to some degree, you realize that you are not deeply and truly happy if somebody, somewhere, is suffering. The thought of others suffering starts to disturb your awareness, just a little at first, then a lot—a nagging thought that rains on your parade and keeps you from rejoicing, and you begin to act, to whatever degree you are moved, to try to better the lot of humankind, with whatever talents and resources you have. Your happiness is not truly happy until all others can share in that joy."

"Using your words," said Tony, "that would begin to open to the genuine spiritual modes of happiness, extended to all sentient beings. Like the bodhisattva vow."

"Yes, I think so. And *that* is where we start to see Essential Joy, or true spiritual Joy—and *not* at the narcissistic and egocentric stage! Confusing these two is a nightmare, really, and is itself deeply narcissistic. It is a travesty that these narcissistic modes are being elevated to spiritual glory."

"Okay. But you do acknowledge that the young child's joy can be repressed and choked off?"

"Oh, definitely, absolutely. Of course you can seal out the joy of childhood, but it's a preconventional joy, not a postconventional joy."

"And your point has always been that sealing out the former makes it less likely the latter will emerge," Tony added.

"Exactly. If you step on an acorn, you are going to damage it, and it will have a hard time growing into the oak that it might be. But what you are hurting and repressing is the acorn—you are *not* repressing or stepping on the oak, because that hasn't emerged yet—there aren't any leaves, branches, roots, etc., to step on. So you can definitely repress or damage joy at *any* of its stages of growth, and this will make it less likely that Essential Joy will emerge later in development. But that Essence is an *emergent* that comes down, not a *recontacted* infantile state coming back up. It is God descending, not id arising."

"Yes, I agree," he said. "But the proponents of the Diamond Approach would say that they have the experiential data to prove they are right. When you do the Diamond work, you start by feeling or experiencing any 'hole' that you might have—any empty feeling, bored feeling, agitated feeling, whatever. When you relax your defenses and simply feel into this hole, then sooner or later the corresponding Essence will emerge, and the hole will 'fill up' with a positive warmth and wisdom. That shows, they say, that you are *recontacting* the Essence that was repressed while growing up."

"It shows nothing of the sort. There are two very different things going on here, and they have thoroughly confused them. To begin with, if you repress a preconventional impulse—say, early joy—then that repression is a wall that seals off not only the lower impulses trying to come up, but the higher impulses trying to come down. In other words, a strong repression against id will also tend to block out God, simply because both id and God can threaten the ego, and a defense against one helps defend against the other. Thus, if you relax the wall of repression—a repression first created against a *lower* impulse when you were perhaps two or three years old—you can simultaneously open yourself to the descent of a *higher* impulse, which itself was *never* repressed in the past but is now *emerging* for the first time. Essence is an emergent, not an infantile regurgitation. There is a timeless feeling about Essence, which gives it a sense of being recontacted, which is true enough, but it is a recontacting of the depth of the timeless present, not a dredging up of an infantile past. By relaxing and disarming the repression against preconventional impulses, you can more easily open yourself to postconventional and spiritual modes. But to confuse the two is a classic pre/trans fallacy."

Tuesday, July 22

"I still think," Tony picked up the conversation, "that the Diamond Approach is a useful path, but it definitely seems caught in these pre/trans fallacies. I've also begun to worry that for all its talk of healing early childhood traumas, it doesn't go very far in *actually* reaching these early traumas, let alone healing them. And this problem applies to virtually all spiritual approaches to growth, as far as I can tell."

"How so?" I asked.

"You were saying that relaxing the defenses meant to keep the id from coming up can allow Spirit to come down."

"Yes. There are other, separate defenses that are often put up against Spirit, and they need to be addressed on their own. But yes, the early defenses against a lower impulse also tend to seal out the higher, and regression in service of transcendence is then necessary."

"Going back and undoing these early defenses so higher growth can proceed. I totally agree. The problem is that very few approaches go back far enough, or efficiently enough, to genuinely relax and undo these primitive defenses and repressions. I don't think the Diamond Approach does. And most forms of spiritual growth don't even address this issue, so they don't either."

"True. About the only schools that deal effectively with these early traumas are object relations—such as Kernberg—and self psychology—such as Kohut—and the similar approaches of Masterson, Stone, and so on. The Diamond Approach draws on these sources for theoretical understanding, which is great, but it doesn't really use any of the powerful tools of these approaches, which is too bad."

"That's right. So the loosening of early defenses that occurs is very short-lived. I once finished an intense period of Diamond work, and I was in a state of essential Joy for two hours—it was wonderful. Then it faded. Never happened since. It's like you open the doors, and they snap back like a rubber band. The Diamond Approach is powerful enough to stretch the rubber band for a short period, but it always snaps back," Tony concluded.

"And just as you said, Tony, virtually all forms of spiritual growth don't even address this issue—don't even try to understand and undo these early defenses—and so they don't stretch the rubber band at all. The result is that your own individual bodymind cannot really become a spacious vehicle for Spirit. Your being is too tight, too enclosed, too defended, too sealed off to open fully to the Divine."

"In your system," Tony said, "the Diamond Approach deals with mostly levels 7 and 8, the soul levels."

"Yes, I think so. Which itself is pretty impressive. And Hameed at least takes into account the extensive theoretical work that has been done on levels 1, 2, and 3—the early object relations and primitive defenses. But, as we were saying, the Diamond Approach doesn't seem to have the tools to actually reach and repair these early lesions in awareness. But I'm very encouraged that they are aware of the extensive research that has been done on the early levels, and I applaud this in my review."

I then told Tony about my idea of "spiritual GPs"—full-spectrum therapists who, even if they can't themselves perform all types of therapy, are trained to spot problems coming from any and all levels of the spectrum of consciousness, and can therefore refer their clients to therapists, spiritual teachers, analysts, yogis, psychotherapists, etc., who focus on the particular level(s) where the client is having a problem.

Tony responded with a typical Tonyism: "I once asked Hameed what he did when students in the Diamond Approach really needed psychotherapy, and he said, 'Oh, when they need it, we recommend a therapist.' I said, 'But they *all* need it.' And they do."

Wednesday, July 23

Got an e-mail from Leo Burke in Beijing. Leo heads the team at Motorola responsible for the development of some twenty thousand managers worldwide. Business management is one of the last areas that I have addressed, and Leo helped spark this interest when, two years ago, he sent an arresting fax, brilliant in its analysis of the state of business in the world today. They're using *Sex, Ecology, Spirituality* in their courses at Motorola University. Since Leo's fax, I have been more open to the correspondence coming to me from business people around the world, and I expect that interest will accelerate with the publication of volume

2, which deals specifically with the techno-economic base of social evolution—"business" in the broad sense.

Leo writes that "My own journey at this point is interesting. At a meeting on Friday at the Santa Fe Institute I posed the questions, 'What role do institutions of commerce, especially multinational corporations, play in the evolution of our species? And what potential, if any, does business have to support a vision of humanity that integrates spirit, mind, and body on individual, organizational, and societal levels?' There were no answers forthcoming, but asking the questions in a business context is a small step forward. Yet any exercise of considering such questions is quite limp without the questioners having a fundamental commitment to their own transformation. Ultimately, of course, this is a commitment not to incremental self-improvement, but to genuine self-transcendence."

Amen.

Tuesday, July 29

Roger is now involved in a national debate on astrology. I'm loving this, because so far I've been the only one to draw intense fire from the new-age new-paradigm crowd, and now Roger is going to get both barrels. This is great.

Bless their hearts, but what so many new-agers do not seem to understand is that there are not *two* major groups in this country—the rational (which they distrust) versus the nonrational (which they champion). Rather, there are *three* major groups—the prerational, the rational, and the transrational. And, again bless their hearts, the vast majority of new-age approaches tend to slide into the prerational camp. To make matters worse, the transrational camp—including Roger—actually has more in common with the rational than with the prerational (although the aim, of course, is to integrate all three).

So the new-age coterie is surprised, hurt, and angered when a genuine transrational mystic—such as Roger—starts criticizing them, because all us "nonrational mystics" are supposed to be in the same boat, fighting the rational, conventional, antispiritual types. But the *trans*-rational mystics are fighting, most strongly, *pre*-rational regression, and then mere rationality, attempting to open both to a genuine transrational approach.

Well, Roger has now stepped directly in the line of fire. He's going public with his attack on astrology. Roger maintains that he has come to his conclusion—namely, that virtually all of traditional astrology is somewhere in the neighborhood of bunk—by systematically reviewing the massive amount of carefully controlled studies done on the topic. He wants to write a book with the title *The Scam of the Century* or *The Rip-Off of the Ages* or something like that [but has since decided against it].

So *Noetic Sciences Review* has invited Roger and Will Keepin to debate this topic in its pages. Will is a very intelligent writer, with a felicitous style and thoughtful presentation. Trained as a physicist and originally viewing astrology as totally bonkers, he came late to a strong belief in its validity, based on the same claim Roger makes: the evidence itself led him to this conclusion. So eloquent is Will on this topic, he is the feature theorist in *Life* magazine's cover story on astrology, where he convinced the journalist of its truth. This promises to be a *great* match. Really, this is the closest thing this field gets to a thrilla in Manila.

I'm getting the papers as they're written, and here's where it stands so far. Roger opened round 1 with a summary of research to date: "Most people are surprised to learn just how much experimental research has been conducted on astrology. Well over one hundred studies are available, some of them done by astrologers or in collaboration with astrologers. Taken together they constitute a body of research of sufficient quality and quantity to provide a powerful assessment of the validity of astrological claims."

What has been found? Roger asks. Quoting from his paper:

> Researchers have studied five capacities that astrologers claim are essential if astrology is to be considered legitimate.
> · The first group of studies examined the degree of agreement between astrologers in judging the same birth charts. The results are striking! *There is virtually no agreement whatsoever between different astrologers' interpretations of the same chart.* This was a consistent finding across studies, including those using expert astrologers, those run by astrologers themselves, and those run by astrologers and scientists in collaboration.
> · This finding alone is devastating and virtually destroys any claim for reliability or validity of astrological readings. As one critic concluded, "If astrologers can't even agree on what a birth chart *means* then their entire practice is reduced to absurdity."
> · Subjects of astrological readings are unable to pick their own readings from other randomly chosen profiles. In other

words, subjects are just as likely to think that another person's profile is as accurate a description of them as their own.

· Studies of over 3,000 astrological predictions showed that they fared no better than chance or guesses.

· Over three dozen studies show that astrologers' readings do not match or correlate at better than chance levels with well-validated psychometric tests of personality. This failure occurred even when the astrologers were highly esteemed experts, helped design the study, regarded the study as good measures of their skills, and rated their confidence in their readings as high.

· Astrologers usually claim that whole chart readings are more accurate than individual factors. However, the research finds no support for the accuracy of either individual factors or whole chart readings.

"In short," Roger concludes, "research finds no support whatsoever for the reliability or validity of astrological readings."

Oooooooh, great opening shots! Some skull-crunching punches. We might have had a total knockout were it not for the rather extraordinary Gauquelin studies. Starting in the 1950s, French researcher Michel Gauquelin began a several-decades-long exhaustive analysis of statistical data relating to astrology. "To his surprise," Roger points out, "analysis did reveal small but significant correlations between eminence in various professional fields and the position of certain planets at birth. For example, eminent scientists, journalists, and athletes were likely to have the planets Saturn, Jupiter, and Mars, respectively, just over the horizon or at the zenith of the sky at the time of their birth."

Oooooh, a big opening here, and Will moves right in. He begins by pointing out that several skeptical scientific organizations have tried to refute the Gauquelin studies, to no avail. Hans Eysenck, the highly respected statistical psychologist, has summarized what this means: "Emotionally, I would prefer the Gauquelin results not to hold, but rationally, I must accept that they do. . . . We can find no valid major criticism of their conclusions, methods, or statistics. They cannot be wished away because they are unpalatable or not in accord with the laws of present-day science. . . . Perhaps the time has come to state quite unequivocally that a new science is in the process of being born."

Wow! Great left hook, as round 1 closes. Astonishingly, Roger doesn't even blink. He opens round 2 by straightforwardly accepting the general results of the Gauquelin studies. But it's all in the interpretation, he says:

"First, Gauquelin's patterns do not fit traditional astrological patterns." In other words, if this is true, and since the Gauquelin study is the only major study that has shown validity, then if we are to agree with its findings, we must also jettison most of traditional astrology, because there was little if any support found for that. "Second, Gauquelin's findings apply *only* to eminent people. People who do not attain eminence—in other words, the vast majority of us—show no correlation with planetary birth position." Again, traditional astrology takes a huge hit. "Third, the correlations are *extremely* small, about 0.05, meaning that they account for less than 1% of variability." This means that, for example, eminent athletes are only 5% more likely to have Mars in position. Whatever the effect, it is clearly very weak. Roger maintains that "this is far, far too small to be of any value whatsoever for astrological readings or predictions."

Ooooooh. This is where it stands at the end of round 2. Whatever else may be said, traditional astrology has taken a very bad beating. The only studies either side can come up with that unequivocally command respect are Gauquelin's. But according to those results, a good deal of traditional astrological claims do not hold up at all. Will maintains that *some* of them do, although both agree that sun-sign astrology and newspaper astrology are kaput. But Roger comes back with a strong right jab: "You [Will] imply that Gauquelin's findings support traditional Western-applied astrology, whereas I argue for several reasons that his findings offer no comfort whatsoever to the specific claims of traditional astrology. Indeed, apart from a few very general principles, which you quote him to support (e.g., the meridian is important), Gauquelin himself was very clear that his findings did *not* fit traditional astrological patterns." Roger then makes what is probably a safe conclusion, at least at this point: "I emphasize the absolute necessity of differentiating clearly between Gauquelin findings and traditional astrology"—because there is strong evidence for the former, little for the latter.

But even the Gauquelin astral associations that hold are very, very weak. According to Roger, fatally so. But Will maintains that, even if small, these influences *are a fact*, which Roger does not contest, and so they *must be explained*. Drawing on a few of my ideas, Will suggests a way to do so. "The implications [of the Gauquelin studies] are dumbfounding. Borrowing on Wilber's concepts, astrology points toward a vast 'holarchy' which not only unifies the physiosphere, biosphere, and noosphere, as Wilber calls for, but does so in a larger celestial context that 'transcends but includes' the Gaian system. By going deeper within, we indeed discover a wider beyond: a living 'Kosmic' holarchy in which the Earth is but one among many higher planetary 'superholons.' Astrological transits correspond to the effects of these celestial superholons as they 'limit the indeterminacy' of their junior holons, i.e., they modify the probability structures of terrestrial events. The entire process is not mechanistically causal, but is more likely a unitive process that unfolds holographically at multiple holonic levels simultaneously—thereby giving rise to observed temporal correlations."

Will uses each of my terms accurately, which is impressive; and I find his theory plausible. However, I think there is another explanation, within the same "wilber" framework, that makes more sense.

The question is, are we working with upward or downward causation? That is, are these weak astral influences generated at the level of the World Soul ("celestial superholons"), and then imposed on the junior holons of individual human beings—by "downward causation" or "downward influence"—as Will maintains? Or are they operating merely at the physical level—exerted by physical planets on the physical human body—and from there have a mild "upward influence" on the emergence of higher levels, including the emotions and the mind? I strongly suspect the latter, for several reasons.

First, these influences, as both Roger and Will note, are very, very weak. This is often a tip-off to upward influence, not downward influence. Downward influence is often very strong, almost causal. For example, when the senior-holon "I" decides to move my junior-holon arm, all of the molecules in my arm get right up and move. Five percent of them don't move, they *all* bloody well move.

Second, there is that fascinating point that Gauquelin's astral associations do not hold with Caesarean or induced deliveries. Any Kosmic superholon that can't override a C-section is not much of a superholon.

Third, these astral associations occur only for people of eminence. This is extremely telling—and, I think, the crucial point—and it is very hard to account for if the influences are stemming from the level of the World Soul. If the World Soul or Kosmic superholon is happily modifying the probability of the lower holons, why does it do so only for the prominent and powerful and famous?

But these astral associations with eminence make sense if they are emanating from the physical level and exerting their relatively weak upward influence on the higher levels of emotion and mind (and character traits), because only the *strongest* of these already weak forces would be expected to have any observable influence at all. That is, only the really strong influences manage to persist through the dampening that occurs with upward influence: the lower has to struggle very hard to override—or decisively influence—the higher. For the average person, who is presumably not getting a huge dose of what are already very weak astral forces, these tepid influences would wash out entirely.

At the close of round 3, I'd have to say that Roger has delivered a devastating blow to most of typical astrology. I myself, who have remained agnostic on this topic for quite some time, find many of his arguments compelling. And Will agrees that sun-sign astrology, newspaper astrology, and outer planet astrology are dead meat. So it's a clean knockout to all those forms of typical astrology.

Both agree, however, that Gauquelin astral associations are real, but very weak: 0.05 is simply not much to write home about. However, as Will (and Eysenck) point out, this anomaly is devastating to any worldview that cannot accommodate it. Both Will and I agree that, at least at this point, only some sort of holonic (or holarchical) conception can do so. I used to think that this explanation would come from the level of the World Soul (or psychic-level superholon), but I now think that the most likely explanation involves physical-level interaction—merely physical planets on physical human bodies—and this is carried, via upward influence *during development*, to the higher levels of emotion and mind (possibly through gravitational/hormonal interaction, or geomagnetic/neuronal interaction, or some combination thereof), with only the strongest of the relatively weak forces surviving in observable forms as eminence in various fields.

My sun sign is Aquarius, although I'm trying to have it legally changed. Let's see what my horoscope says for today. "The beautiful creature I'm spying on seems to be turning into a bliss addict. The ambiance here is lush and sensual. The air is saturated with juicy pheromones. Yet there's also an unmistakably *sacred* feeling. It's not out of the question to speculate that Aquarius is poised to break all previous records for Spiritual Growth While under the Influence of Lust."

I take it back, I believe everything about sun signs.

August

What is the world? An eternal poem,
out of which the spirit of Godhead shines and glows,
the wine of wisdom foams and sparkles,
the sound of love speaks to us.
—HUGO VON HOFMANNSTHAL

The new spirit, as it becomes more conscious, is increasingly capable of transforming the moments of contemplation into one moment, into a permanent vision.
—PIET MONDRIAN

Saturday, August 2

"Hi Ken, it's Frances."

"Oh, hi, Frances. Now that Roger is off to his month-long meditation retreat, are you enjoying your breathing space?"

"Things are too busy around here. I just got back from the annual Association for Transpersonal Psychology conference."

"They asked you to give the closing address."

"Yes. I arrived the day before and mingled with old friends, which was nice, very nostalgic. My first conference there was thirty-two years ago! It was a big event in my life; it really changed my life. Huston Smith, Jim Fadiman, the original crew. Anyway, one person came up to me and I was so glad to meet her after all these years. It was Laura Huxley."

"You're kidding."

"She must be in her eighties, very small and petite, but very lively. She told me how much she liked my work, I told her how much I admired hers, it was very nice."

"How'd the speech go?"

"I did it on creativity, it was fine."

"I'll bet it was better than fine."

"Creativity can be a way for people to connect with their own spiritual intelligence, so I talked about that. It was fine."

"How's the World Forum coming along?"

The State of the World Forum is a rather remarkable organization founded by James Garrison and Mikhail Gorbachev, and has included Desmond Tutu, Elie Wiesel, James Baker, Jehan Sadat, Ted Turner, among hundreds of others. This year's Forum will be held November 4–9 in San Francisco. Frances was asked to put together the session on "Intelligence and Evolution," which she divided into three subsessions: Human Intelligence and Evolution, Practice and Inner Work, and Legacy of Wisdom. She has assembled a stellar cast of participants for the first two, but the last one—which was meant to be a panel of elders discussing the importance of tradition and legacy—is not proceeding smoothly.

"Everything is going fine except the Legacy of Wisdom. Some of the participants, like Ram Dass, are ill, and others, like Huston, are wisely choosing not to come. They have too much wisdom to be part of a show on wisdom, so I'm stuck!"

Frances will pull it off, though, she always does.

Sunday, August 3

People typically feel trapped by life, trapped by the universe, because they imagine that they are actually *in* the universe, and therefore the universe can squish them like a bug. This is not true. You are not in the universe; the universe is in you.

The typical orientation is this: my consciousness is in my body (mostly in my head); my body is in this room; this room is in the surrounding space, the universe itself. That is true from the viewpoint of the ego, but utterly false from the viewpoint of the Self.

If I rest as the Witness, the formless I-I, it becomes obvious that, right now, I am not in my body, my body is IN my awareness. I am aware of my body, therefore I am not my body. I am the pure Witness in which my body is now arising. I am not in my body, my body is in my consciousness. Therefore, *be* consciousness.

If I rest as the Witness, the formless I-I, it becomes obvious that, right now, I am not in this house, this house is IN my awareness. I am the pure Witness in which this house is now arising. I am not in this house, this house is in my consciousness. Therefore, *be* consciousness.

If I look outside this house, to the surrounding area—perhaps a large stretch of earth, a big patch of sky, other houses, roads and cars—if I look, in short, at the universe in front of me—and if I rest as the Witness, the formless I-I, it becomes obvious that, right now, I am not in the universe, the universe is IN my awareness. I am the pure Witness in which this universe is now arising. I am not in the universe, the universe is in my consciousness. Therefore, *be* consciousness.

It is true that the physical matter of your body is inside the matter of the house, and the matter of the house is inside the matter of the universe. But you are not merely matter or physicality. You are also Consciousness as Such, of which matter is merely the outer skin. The ego adopts the viewpoint of matter, and therefore is constantly trapped by matter—trapped and tortured by the physics of pain. But pain, too, arises in your consciousness, and you can either be in pain, or find pain in you, so that you surround pain, are bigger than pain, transcend pain, as you rest in the vast expanse of pure Emptiness that you deeply and truly are.

So what do I see? If I contract as ego, it appears that I am confined in the body, which is confined in the house, which is confined in the large universe around it. But if I rest as the Witness—the vast, open, empty consciousness—it becomes obvious that I am not in the body, the body is in me; I am not in this house, the house is in me; I am not in the universe, the universe is in me. All of them are arising in the vast, open, empty, pure, luminous Space of primordial Consciousness, right now and right now and forever right now.

Therefore, *be* Consciousness.

Monday, August 4

Mitch [Kapor] is just back from the Spiritual Intelligence conference, organized by Frances, held at Fetzer. He thought it was interesting and useful in many ways, but could have benefited from a little more critical and skeptical attitude. Frances knew that Mitch—our glorious skeptic, as Kate Olson calls him—felt this way, so on the last day she invited him to voice his concerns.

"So how did it go?" I asked over the phone.

"Stan Grof was there. He was talking about his latest book, *The Cosmic Game*. He said you helped with it."

"Not really. Only a little. He sent me the manuscript, and it became apparent that there were really two books mixed together in it, so I suggested separating them, which works much better, I think. He did so, and now SUNY is publishing the first one. It's really an exceptionally important work, and yet another version of the Great Chain of Being, this time developed with modern techniques. Anyway, how did the last day go, with your skepticism and all?"

"A few of us got on the topic of UFO abductions, and some people simply did not want to have their beliefs questioned. One person said, 'There are over ten thousand reported abductions each year. Do you think all of these people are just making this up?' 'Well, sure,' I replied. It didn't go over too well."

"I can imagine."

"I'm sometimes too skeptical, but some of these people seem to lack the capacity entirely. It's too bad, because this field is crazy enough without UFO abductions getting tossed in. And if you don't believe them, they think you are sick, or antispiritual, or whatever. But the fact that ten thousand people claim to have been abducted is the last place you would look for corroborating evidence."

"I agree," I said. "Last year alone there were a reported fifteen hundred Elvis sightings. So I suppose that means Elvis is alive and well and making all these visits. This is *not* evidence."

Mitch and I said goodbye, after making some plans for his visit.

UFO abductions. I saw John Mack on a talk show with several "abductees." It was painfully obvious what was happening. These people had all been "abducted," given a physical exam, subjected to the ubiquitous anal probe, and had sperm or ovum collected from them. And then—this was the primal scene, the dark heart of the hallucination—they had been shown their sons and daughters, produced by a cross-fertilization between their sperm/ovum and the aliens'. These people, in other words, were the fathers and mothers of the new race that would populate the earth. And right there the staggering narcissism becomes perhaps too obvious. I really don't mean to be cruel, but all you keep thinking is, if these folks are the parents of the new race, we're in deep trouble. Sort of like your parents being first cousins.

When people have a memory or an experience of being "abducted," I don't doubt the experience seems absolutely real to them (most would pass a lie detector test). And it *is* real, as an experience, as phenomenology, but *not* as ontology, not as an objective reality. So there's the *phenomenology* (or the experience itself), and there is how you *interpret* the experience. And for that interpretation—as with all interpretation—you need to draw on the total web of available evidence, which is exactly what the believers in these experiences are *not* doing.

Do any UFO experiences represent higher realities? It's theoretically possible that some of these experiences are stemming from the psychic or subtle level of consciousness (levels 7 and 8), and that, precisely because these people do not directly grow and evolve into these levels, they experience them as an "other." Instead of their own deeper and higher luminous nature, they project it outwardly as an alien form. Even if that is true, these people are still in the grips of a dissociative pathology. In either case, this is nothing to brag about.

The giveaway, as usual, is the narcissism. The comedian Dennis Miller nailed it: "Only man is a narcissistic enough species to think that a highly evolved alien life force would travel across billions and billions of light-years—a group of aliens so intelligent, so insouciant, so utterly above it all, they feel no need whatsoever to equip their spacecraft with windows so that they can gaze out on all that celestial beauty—but then immediately upon landing, their first impulse is to get in some hick's ass with a flashlight."

What do people really want when they think about UFOs? What are they yearning for at the thought of something extraterrestrial? Why, they want something bigger than themselves. They want to know that, in the entire, wild, extraordinary Kosmos, there is something other than their meager egos.

Well, there is.

Tuesday, August 5

Just this greets me this morning; just this, its own remark; just this, there is no other; just this, the sound of one hand clapping—the sound, that is, of One Taste. The subtle and causal can be so overwhelmingly numinous and holy; One Taste is so pitifully obvious and simple.

Maureen Silos sent me her doctoral dissertation, "Economics Education and the Politics of Knowledge in the Caribbean"—she just got her Ph.D. from UCLA. Maureen and I began corresponding last year, when she wrote that she was applying my work "to issues of Third World development." I put her in touch with, among others, Michael McDermott, who is doing similar work in Swaziland. Maureen was born and raised in the Caribbean; as a black woman she is uniquely situated to address these difficult, delicate, seemingly intractable problems. She had originally contacted me in mild exasperation at the anti-evolutionary, implicitly reactionary stance of her supposedly "liberal" and "progressive" advisory committee—a stance that is, in fact, the norm in postmodern flatland, and especially in its universities, where an allegiance to a dogmatic egalitarianism (maintained only by an intellectual elite!) actually has the effect of discouraging interior consciousness development, individual as well as cultural, which alone can alleviate so many of these distresses.

Maureen tackles these issues head on, based in part on my work, but going quite beyond that with her own additions and applications. The results are impressive. She begins by pointing out that "Evolution is taboo in anthropology and progressive circles of the social sciences, [due to] a particular reaction within progressive circles in the West to social Darwinism, colonialism, racism, the holocaust, and assorted ideas that rank human beings as essentially inferior or superior. Even though the reaction is understandable, the result is disastrous for social theory because we now face a massive hostility to cultural evolution."

I'll say. She continues: "The social origins of the wholesale rejection of the notion of cultural evolution by Western progressive social theorists is something that Caribbean and other Third World scholars have to be aware of when we adopt these ideas, because this position, even though very well intended, creates 'the extremely bizarre situation of driving a virulent wedge right through the middle of the Kosmos: everything nonhuman operates by evolution; everything human does not.' What I try to do therefore is to distinguish between the valid and invalid aspects of the notion of cultural evolution, because this is the only approach that offers me the opportunity to understand the *nature* of the clash between worldviews in the Caribbean *and* to argue for a vertical dimension of cultural and consciousness development based on the evolutionary model of the contemplative traditions of both the East and the West."

Excellent. Maureen continues: "The idea of the evolution of cultures, consciousness, and worldviews is necessary because without it there seems to be no alternative to the idea that with the emergence of liberal democratic industrialized Western societies humankind has reached the end of history. And that is unacceptable to me. Is there something better possible and how do we get from here to there?" Touché. Her point is that, contrary to the prevailing flatland postmodern view, not only is cultural evolution *not* an ethnocentric or eurocentric notion, it is the only way out of the hidden ethnocentrism of most "progressive" circles of Western social science, which in fact discourage the cultural evolution that alone would transcend the ethnocentrism. In other words, although they nobly desire to alleviate oppression, the anti-cultural-evolutionists are part of the very disease they so aggressively denounce.

But we must distinguish between *valid* and *invalid* theories of cultural evolution, and here Maureen outlines some of my work: "So to make the case for cultural evolution, for ways of being in the world and ways of knowing in the world that are higher and better than the current hegemonic model, we need 'a set of tenets that can explain *both* advance and regression, good news and bad news, the ups and downs of an evolutionary thrust that is nonetheless as active in humans as it is in the rest of the Kosmos.' Wilber discusses five of these tenets in his book *The Eye of Spirit*. These are: the dialectic of progress, the distinction between differentiation and dissociation, the difference between transcendence and repression, the difference between natural hierarchy and pathological hierarchy, and the fact that higher structures can be hijacked by lower impulses."

Maureen then proceeds through a smart, occasionally brilliant analysis of the cultural conditions and future of the Caribbean. She says that "This quarter I am teaching two courses at UCLA, one on the 'Sociology of Education' and one on 'Identity, Agency, and Social Transformation in the African Diaspora.' The latter is based on your work. The students really like it. But some have a problem with the fact that you hardly mention Islam or African philosophy. The emphasis on Eastern religions is a bit frustrating. . . ."

Good point. I need to emphasize more explicitly that I have drawn on African and Islamic religion, especially Sufism and core African shamanism. My tendency in the past has been to simplify by presenting "the best of the West"—summarized mostly by the Neoplatonists—and "the best of the East"—summarized mostly by India (Hinduism and Buddhism). But it clearly wouldn't hurt to be more specific about the many different sources I have in fact drawn upon.

"I have set myself the task to place African thought within your schema in such a way that it does not reinforce racism nor lapse into romanticizing pre-colonial Africa"—in other words, steering between *repression*, on the one hand, and *regression*, on the other—how to avoid both of those is a major theme of my work. "My first attempt to do this publicly is a lecture that I will give entitled 'Religion, Spirituality, and

Social Transformation in the African Diaspora.' I am a bit nervous about it because it is going to be very critical of attempts to ground an African-American identity in ancient Egyptian thought. I will also argue for an evolutionary view of consciousness and spirituality and how this relates to social transformation." That is one brave soul.

"My next project is a postdoctoral fellowship with the UCLA Center for Pacific Rim Studies, where I will replicate my Caribbean project for the emerging economies of East Asia, in an ongoing attempt to theorize the complex relationship between cultural context (consciousness) and economic prowess. I hope to visit Indonesia, Taiwan, and Malaysia in 1998 to interview faculty in the departments of economics, businessmen/women, and policy makers."

Godspeed, Maureen Silos.

Wednesday, August 6

William S. Burroughs died. With his death, the Beat triumvirate—Kerouac, Ginsberg, Burroughs—is no more.

Ginsberg ended up a student of Trungpa Rinpoche; we ran into each other every now and then, particularly in connection with Naropa, whose new library building was named after him. Every time he saw me he would ask if he could rub my shaved head; I always said yes, he always rubbed away happily. What I liked most about Allen was not his poetry—blasphemy, I realize—but watching him read his poetry, which was an unending delight. He was a contorting vortex of playful energy; bliss packaged, bound, and offered to the audience, generously.

What I loved about the Beats was not their writing but their theater—the theater of themselves, of course, but done with a bravura unusual even for the sixties. Their lives were an unending drama of sometimes hilarious, sometimes grotesque, performance art—starting most conspicuously with Burroughs accidentally killing his wife while attempting to shoot a glass off her head; running through Kerouac's hideous death agony as a wasted alcoholic; ending with Ginsberg's embrace of a religion whose central aim is to undermine egoic performance, and which, if successfully practiced, would erase his raison d'être.

It was a show the likes of which we will not again soon see. Along with the death of Timothy Leary—and Ram Dass's stroke—I fear my generation is now officially beginning its death watch. The last few years have seen a rash of fiftieth birthdays—and the beginning wave of deaths. It's now a long, slow glide path to that final exit, at least for this time around. And will we find the great Unborn, the womb of saints and sages and bodhisattvas, or we will find only ourselves?

Sunday, August 10

Very early in the morning, maybe 3 A.M. Surfing the subtle—riding the boundary between the causal formless of deep sleep and the subtle form of the dream state. Out of pure, infinite, formless blackness—yet alive, and tacitly conscious, a radiantly clear emptiness—arises the most subtle form, sometimes a luminous blue-white billowing cloud, sometimes an infinite impulse of faintest bliss. Strange that such bliss is actually a step down. At the same time, it simply coexists with Emptiness; it is the Form of Emptiness at that point.

But behind it all, and all along, there is *just this*.

Tuesday, August 12

Naropa seminar. This time the dominant theme, raised by several students, was the rampant anti-intellectualism that you usually find at many spiritual and countercultural institutions. "Experiential" is contrasted to "intellectual"; the former is valued, the latter, denigrated. If you start to give an intellectual explanation of anything, you are, as one student put it, "nearly crucified on the spot." This is because you are supposed to be *experiential*, not intellectual, abstract, or conceptual. You are supposed to come from the heart, not from the head; you are supposed to center in the body, not in the mind. Experiential is spiritual, which is good; intellectual is the ego, which is analytic and divisive and "like way totally bad."

All of which, I responded, is an unfortunate misunderstanding of both experiential and spiritual. A few excerpts:

KW: We were talking about experiential. Experience is basically just another word for *awareness*. If I experience my body, it means I am aware of my body. You can indeed be aware of your body, but you can also be aware of your mind—you can right now notice all the thoughts and ideas and images floating in front of the mind's inward eye. You can, in other words, *experience your mind*, be aware of your mind. And it's very important to be able to experience your mind directly, cleanly, intensely, because only by bringing awareness to the mind can you begin to transcend the mind and be free of its limitations. When that begins to happen, usually in meditation or contemplation, you can have even higher experiences, spiritual experiences, mystical experiences—satori, kensho, samadhi, unio mystica, and so on. You can, we might say, be aware of spirit, experience spirit, although in a more nondual manner.

So you can *experience* body, mind, and spirit. All of those are *experiential*. So perhaps you can begin to understand why it is a grave error to reduce experiential to *just the body*, to just bodily sensations, feelings, emotions, impulses, and so on. This is a very unfortunate reductionism. It denies the higher experiential realities of the mind and spirit: it denies intellect and buddhi, higher mental vision and imagery and dreams, higher rational discrimination and perspectivism and moral depth, higher formless awareness and deeply contemplative states—all are denied or reduced.

The body, you see, is basically narcissistic and egocentric. Bodily feelings are just about *your* body, period. The body's sensations cannot take the role of other—that's a *mental* capacity—and therefore the body's sensory awareness cannot enter into care and compassion and ethical discourse and I-thou spirituality—all of those demand a cognitive, mental, intellectual awareness. To the extent you "stay in your body" and are "anti-intellectual," then you stay in the orbit of your own narcissism.

So that's the first mistake in this "experiential versus intellectual" prejudice—all of the experiential modes are reduced to bodily experiences only, which is the essence of egocentrism. The second mistake is to then reduce spiritual experiences to bodily experiences. The idea is that if you stay focused in your body, focused in your feelings, that these are the direct door to spirituality, because they transcend the mind. But bodily sensations and feelings and emotions are not transrational, they are prerational. By staying only in the body, you are not beyond the mind, you are beneath it. You are not transcending, you are regressing—becoming more and more narcissistic and egocentric, focusing on your own feelings. And this, if anything, prevents actual spiritual experiences, because genuine spirituality is "bodymind dropped"—that is, you cease identifying exclusively with both the feelings of the body and the thoughts of the mind, and this you cannot do if you merely "stay in the body."

So anytime you hear somebody tell you to be "experiential" instead of "intellectual," you can almost be certain they are making these two simple but crucial mistakes. They are taking the experiences of body, mind, and spirit and claiming that only the body experiences are real—the lowest of the experiential domains!—and then they are reducing spiritual experiences to bodily experiences. Both are extremely unfortunate.

But the thing is, it's even worse than that. Although we can accurately speak of bodily, mental, and spiritual experiences, the fact is, the *very highest spiritual states are not even experiences.* Experiences, by their very nature, are temporary; they come, stay a bit, and pass. But the Witness is not an experience. It is aware of experiences, but is not itself experiential in the least. The Witness is the vast openness and freedom in which experiences arise, and through which experiences pass. But the Witness itself never enters the stream of time—it is aware of time—and thus it never enters the stream of experiences.

So even here, to say that Spirit is experiential (versus intellectual) is still to profoundly distort Spirit, because Spirit is not a passing experience but the formless Witness of all experience. To remain stuck in experiences is to remain ignorant of Spirit.

STUDENT: But the body does contain "felt meanings" that are important.

KW: Oh, definitely, and they need to be *integrated* with the mind and spirit. But to call those bodily sensations alone "spirituality" is a travesty.

STUDENT: Why is that so popular?

KW: Because everybody already has that bodily capacity available. You've had access to body awareness since you were a child. Anybody can experience the body, so you have a high success rate with "body focusing work." But if you were giving a workshop on "Let's contact nirvikalpa samadhi"—a true spiritual state—that takes the average person five years or more. That's not going to be a popular weekend workshop! So you can't easily market these genuine transpersonal realms, you can only market quick altered states that come and go, or simple bodily experiences that everybody can already tap into fairly easily.

Likewise, if you are an institution that relies on student money to survive, you are not going to make much money if you specialize in genuine subtle and causal and nondual states of consciousness—you can't afford to wait five and ten years for these things to come to fruition and you get paid! So there is a hidden but intense economic pressure to offer these lesser, even regressive states, call that "spirituality," and plug ahead. With this approach, you have a chance of close to a 100% success rate, because pretty much everybody can locate some sort of feeling or bodily emotion or bodily awareness, whereas very few can demonstrate satori on the spot. So everybody feels good, everybody is being "experiential" and "coming from the heart" and "not coming from the nasty intellect" and so everybody is being "spiritual." Oy vey.

STUDENT: Is there no use for bodily awareness?

KW: Oh, I don't want to give that impression. There is a very important role in contacting the body, which perhaps we can explain this way. In the course of human growth and development, consciousness begins identified largely with the body—with the vital and sensorimotor domain. Starting around age 2 or 3, the mind begins to emerge, and by age 6 or 7, consciousness begins to identify with the expanded perspective offered by the mind. The sensory body, recall, is preconventional and egocentric, because it cannot take the role of other. But with the emergence of the mind, consciousness can switch from *egocentric* to *sociocentric* modes of awareness—that is, evolve from *me* to *we*. The mind transcends and includes the body, so the mind can be aware of *both* "me" and "we."

But if there is *pathology*—and here Freud's contributions are pivotal—then the mind does not just *transcend and include* the body, it *represses* the body, denies the body, alienates and dissociates the body. More specifically, some mental concept or idea or superego represses or denies some bodily feeling, impulse, or instinct, often sex or aggression, or sometimes just bodily vitality in general. And that *repression* of the body by the mind produces various types of neurosis, emotional illness, bodily alienation, and life numbness.

So one of the first things you do in therapy—in "uncovering therapies"—is to relax the repression barrier and allow yourself to feel your body, feel your feelings, feel your emotions, and try to understand why you repressed them in the first place. You then *befriend* these lost feelings and reintegrate them with the mental-ego to form a more wholesome and accurate self-image.

Now the fact that you have *recontacted* the body and its feelings, and this has made you feel alive, vibrant, radiant—this is terrific, this is what is supposed to happen. You are recontacting your organic roots, your élan vital. But many people then erroneously conclude that the bodily feelings themselves are somehow a *higher* reality than the mental-ego, which is absolutely incorrect. They believe this because they feel so much better after having recontacted the body. But we need to recontact the body, not because it is a higher reality, but because it is a lower one being terribly mistreated by a higher. So we temporarily regress to the bodily sensations that were alienated—"regression" simply means moving to a lower level in the hierarchy of consciousness—and we reintegrate those lost feelings. This is regression in the service of a higher growth.

So the result of that higher growth is then the *integration* of the mind and the body—I call that the *centaur*, where human mind and animal body are one. But many body therapists confuse this integrated mind-and-body union with *just* the body itself. You find this confusion in writers like Alexander Lowen and Ida Rolf and Stanley Keleman. They frequently elevate the body to the status of the centaur (or mind-and-body integrated unit), and you can tell they do this because there is virtually no discussion of the mind per se, the mind as mind—no discussion of rational ethics, of perspectivism, of postconventional morality, of mutual understanding, and so on. What they call the bodymind union is really just a bunch of deep bodily sensations. This is a miniature pre/trans fallacy—it confuses postconventional centaur with preconventional body—and this confusion marks many of the body therapy schools.

At any rate, both therapy and meditation often *begin with the body* and with body awareness, because most people are indeed out of touch with their roots. But neither effective therapy nor authentic meditation *remains* at the level of bodily awareness. In effective therapy, you eventually must move to *cognitive* and *mental* experience and begin to understand why you repressed the body and certain of its feelings in the first place. It is only as you cease to act out your alienated impulses on a bodily level and convert them into mental insight that therapy advances.

Likewise with genuine meditation. Although it often *starts* with bodily awareness—focusing on the breath, on bodily sensations, and so on—it soon moves to an investigation of *mental experience* and the mind stream itself. It moves from the gross body and sensorimotor world to the mental and subtle world. It is only by investigating the subtle contractions in the mind stream—and especially the subtle contraction known as the separate-self sense—that one's identity can expand from the bodymind to Spirit itself. One's personal identity with the organism is subsumed by an identity with the All.

So the body is never left behind. It is transcended and included by the mind, which is transcended and included by Spirit. The body is the foundation and the roots and the starting point. But if you merely stay there, you will totally sabotage mind and Spirit. You will get the Nirmanakaya (form body), but not the Sambhogakaya (subtle realm) and not the Dharmakaya (causal Emptiness) and not the Svabhavikakaya (nondual Suchness). But once you plug the body into these higher stages and realms, they tend to reach down and literally transfigure the physical body itself. Why, who knows, you might even begin to glow in the dark. The body will take on a strange and haunting beauty, and in any event the body will be the transparent vehicle of the primordial Spirit that you eternally are.

Friday, August 15

Richard G. Young, one of the directors of The Center for Contemplative Christianity and the publisher of *Pathways: A Magazine of Psychological and Spiritual Transformation*, wrote a review of *The Eye of Spirit* for that magazine. It's very funny. In the middle is this: "Why am I such a devotee of this elusive iconoclast who never gives lectures or leads retreats, rarely grants interviews, and goes out of his way to discourage anyone from considering him a spiritual teacher? Simple. I'm hoping to *guilt* him into granting us an interview for *Pathways*."

I faxed *Pathways*—"Okay, okay."

Saturday, August 16—Denver

Marci and I spent the day in Denver, wandering around, shopping for some shoes for her, enjoying the ease of existence. Marci is an adorable, extraordinary soul. She works daily with developmentally challenged people; I have seen her interact with these innocents, who are loving and direct, but who do not know enough to know the terrible ways of civilized folks, and therefore need supervision. They slobber on her, they clutch at her, they demand her attention, they cry and shout and yell— and she never turns away, she never recoils. She holds them, and says it will be okay, and they believe her, they reach out to her, they trust her, and for very good reason: she is always there for them, and they know it.

She's been accepted for the Peace Corps, which she is due to enter this coming February. But she is having second thoughts, in part, no doubt, because of our relationship; but also, and just as decisive, she has been promoted to head of marketing for the organization that runs several care centers where she works. This was unexpected, and a superb opportunity. She would still be working in a service organization, which is what she wants, but this one will also allow her to pay off her student loans, etc. That means our relationship won't have to end in February; I'm selfishly delighted.

Love for a specific person is radiant when it arises in Emptiness. It is still love, it is still intensely personal, it is still very specific; but it is a wave that arises from an ocean of infinity. It is as if a great sea of love brings forth a wave, and that wave carries the force and thrill of the entire sea in its every breaking crest. The sensation is like watching an early morning sunrise in the desert: a vast open clear blue spaciousness, within which there arises, on the horizon, an intense red-yellow fire. You are the infinite sky of Love, in which a particular fire-ball of personal love arises.

One thing is certain: infinite love and personal love are not mutually exclusive—the latter is just an individual wave of an infinite ocean. When I lie awake, next to her, early in the morning, doing meditation, nothing really changes in the contemplation except this: there is a whole-body bliss, paradoxically faint but intense, that edges my awareness. It is sexual energy reconnected to its source in the subtle regions of the bodymind. I will often touch her lightly as I meditate; it definitely completes an energy circuit, and she can feel it, too.

But that is what men and women (as well as "butch/femme" pairings across sexual orientations) can do for each other, and that is the core claim of Tantra as well: in a very concrete, visceral way, the union of male and female is the union of Eros and Agape, Ascending and Descending, Emptiness and Form, Wisdom and Compassion. Not theoretically but concretely, in the actual distribution of prana or energy currents in the body itself. And this is why, in the very highest Tantric teachings (anuttaratantrayoga), the mere visualization of sexual congress with the divine consort is not enough for final enlightenment. Rather, for ultimate enlightenment, one must take an actual partner—real sex—in order to complete the circuits conducive to recognizing the already-enlightened mind.

Monday, August 18—Boulder

Just got off the phone with Professor Sara Bates, who is using *Brief History* and *Eye of Spirit* as texts for her classes on art and native cultures. She teaches at Florida State but is now visiting lecturer at San Francisco University, from which she phoned me. Sara is Cherokee Indian; she and two of her friends—one a Hopi, one a Mojave—have formed a discussion group concerned with issues of cultural studies, religion, art, and native societies. They are using my work, she says, because of its cross-cultural and integral nature.

"What do you think of this new interest in Native American spirituality?" she asked.

"I think that middle-class white people do some very strange things with Native beliefs."

"I'll say. This whole romanticizing of Native belief is sad. Because that romantic view just doesn't exist; certainly not now, and maybe not ever. But a lot of Indians now go along with it."

"Yes, it's strange. Many Natives are buying the white man's version of the Natives' spirituality. It's weird."

"I've had this experience," Sara said, "of communing directly and immediately with an inner Light. This is a common type of spiritual experience in my tradition. One of my colleagues said, 'Do you think you have to be a Cherokee in order to have this experience?' He thought, of course, that I would say 'Yes,' but I said, 'No, of course not!' "

Sara is referring to the fact that extreme postmodernism has now slipped into a rather sad essentialism: you have to be a woman to know *anything* about women; you have to be an Indian to say anything about Indians; you have to be gay before you can explain anything about homosexuality. In other words, there is a regression from worldcentric to ethnocentric—*identity politics* alone rule, and extreme pluralism means none of us have anything in common anymore.

In this regressive atmosphere, as David Berreby puts it, writing in *The Sciences*, "Americans have a standard playbook for creating a political-cultural identity. You start with the conviction that being a member of your group is a distinct experience, separating you from people who are not in it (even close friends and relatives) and uniting you with other members of the group (even if you have never met them). Second, you assume that your own personal struggles and humiliations and triumphs in wrestling with your trait are a version of the struggles of the group in society. The personal is political. Third, you maintain that your group has interests that are being neglected or acted against, and so it must take action—changing how the group is seen by those outside it, for instance."

It's not that such action is bad. It's just that, taken in and by itself, it is alienating and fragmenting, a type of *pathological pluralism* that astonishingly believes that acceptance of my group can be accomplished by aggressively blaming and condemning exactly the group from which I seek the acceptance.

True pluralism, on the other hand, is always *universal pluralism* (or integral-aperspectival): you start with the *commonalities* and *deep struc-*

tures that *unite* human beings—we all suffer and triumph, laugh and cry, feel pleasure and pain, wonder and remorse; we all have the capacity to form images, symbols, concepts, and rules; we all have 208 bones, two kidneys, and one heart; we are all open to a Divine Ground, by whatever name. And *then* you add all the wonderful differences, surface structures, culturally constructed variants, and so on, that make various groups—and various individuals—all different, special, and unique. But if you start with the differences and the pluralism, and never make it to the universal, then you have only the aperspectival, not also the integral—you have, that is, pathological pluralism, aperspectival madness, ethnocentric revivals, regressive catastrophes.

Of course it is fine to highlight any group that you feel is important. But it's becoming impossible to define that group as "oppressed," because now *every* group claims to be oppressed, and none admit they are oppressors. White males used to be the bad guys, but now even they have caught the fever. White males are no longer a single group that can be blamed for oppression, because most of them now claim to belong to an oppressed or marginalized group themselves: they are drug addicts, physically handicapped, alcoholics, were sexually abused as a child, victims of an absent father, abducted by aliens, or turned into "success objects" by women. They can't oppress anybody because they are too busy being oppressed themselves.

Besides, according to essentialism, you can't say anything about white males unless you are a white male. So we can ignore everything feminists say about white males, and ask the white males themselves if they are oppressors. They say no. So there it is: we are a nation of brutally oppressed groups, but without a single oppressing group. This is a nifty trick.

It is, of course, simply another name for narcissism. Whatever my problems, they do not stem from me. They stem from the Other, who is the Bad Guy always. The real travesty here is that the cases of true oppression—a genuine case of a woman, a gay, a black, an Indian, a white male, getting held back due *solely* to *ethnocentric* or *group* prejudice—those cases lose all their urgency because they are drowned out by a thousand other voices all screaming oppression to explain even the most trivial and often unavoidable disappointments of life.

So here is Sara taking the course of universal pluralism—not ethnocentric pluralism—and it is refreshing beyond belief.

"So I told him, 'No, I do not think you have to be a Cherokee to have this type of interior illumination.' I definitely do not think these inner experiences are culturally constructed, do you?"

"Not totally, no. Cultural construction is, at best, only one of the four quadrants [the Lower Left]. What I try to do is highlight the universal or *deep features* in these experiences—seeing an interior illumination, for example—which appear to be fairly similar wherever they appear. But they all have various *surface features* that do in fact vary from culture to culture, so some cultural construction is indeed present, but not nearly what the extreme postmodernists say."

"But are those cultural surface structures present even at the point of the direct communion with this interior being of Light?"

"To some degree, yes, I think so. For example, when these experiences occur in the Tibetan tradition, the inner being never looks like Jesus of Nazareth. Likewise, if this experience occurs to a Christian, the inner being rarely has four arms, which is quite common with the Tibetan version, like Chenrezi."

"I see, so even at the moment of direct experience, the cultural background is playing some sort of role."

"Yes, right up to complete cessation, but, as you say, you don't have to be a Cherokee to have these types of experiences. The fact that they are *partially* molded by culture does not mean they are *merely* a product of your culture or your group background. This extreme constructivist view is a terrible distortion of religious experience. It reduces all spiritual realities to nothing but human-created symbols. Humans do not create Spirit, Spirit creates humans! I think these people have it a little backwards. Anyway, I think it's useful to highlight the universal or deep features of these experiences, as well as the cultural surface features and local variations. They are both very important."

"Well, that's what my friends and I are doing. We want to explain our traditions, but we want to fit them with other traditions as well."

And so the discussion went. Sara had some sharp criticism for ecopsychology ("it really does leave out the interior dimensions"), for art theory that actually ignores art ("they talk about everything except art"), for the sad state of extreme postmodernism ("fragments everywhere"), and for the devaluation of aesthetics in favor of it-language ("anthropology over art"). She is going to send me some of her writing in aesthetic theory, as well as some of her art. I really like her; am glad we have connected.

Tuesday, August 19

Inner Directions is bringing out a new edition of *Talks with Sri Ramana Maharshi*, which is the main source of the teachings of this extraordinary Realizer. They asked to me write a foreword, and I agreed. I don't think we could say that Ramana was an exemplary representative of an integral view; but his own Self-realization—or the recognition of the always-already truth of the Witness and its ever-present ground in One Taste—was unsurpassed.

In the foreword, I incorporated a few pointing-out instructions that I had given in one of the Naropa seminars, and somehow this seemed appropriate enough. The Naropa Institute was named after the renowned Indian teacher and mahasiddha Naropa (eleventh century CE), who was a central figure in the university of Nalanda—which at one time had over ten thousand students and was one of the truly great learning centers of the world. This was also the period—from the eighth to the eleventh centuries CE in India—during which occurred the greatest flowering of the Nondual tradition the world has ever seen. That Nondual vision—in the form of Vedanta, Shaivism, Mahayana and Vajrayana Buddhism—is the precious gift of India to the world, and it found its purest, most elegant, most brilliant expression in the simple sage of Arunachala.

THE SAGE OF THE CENTURY

I am often asked, "If you were stranded on a desert island and had only one book, what would it be?" The book you are now holding in your hands—*Talks with Sri Ramana Maharshi*—is one of the two or three I always mention. And the *Talks* tops the list in this regard: they are the living voice of the greatest sage of this century and, arguably, the greatest spiritual realization of this or any time.

One of the many astonishing things about these *Talks* is how remarkably unwavering is the tone and style, the voice itself—not in the sense that it is fixed and rigid, but rather that it speaks with a full-blown maturity from the first word to the last. It is as if—no, it is certainly the case that—Ramana's realization came to him fully formed—or perhaps we should say, fully formless—and therefore it needed no further growth. He simply speaks from and as the absolute, the Self, the purest Emptiness that is the goal and ground of the entire manifest world, and is not other to that world. Ramana, echoing Shankara, used to say:

The world is illusory;
Brahman alone is real;
Brahman is the world.

This profound realization is what separates Ramana's genuine en-lightenment from today's many pretenders to the throne—deep ecology, ecofeminism, Gaia revivals, Goddess worship, ecopsychology, systems theory, web-of-life notions—none of which have grasped the first two lines, and therefore, contrary to their sweet pronouncements, do not really understand the third. And it is exactly for all of those who are thus in love merely with the manifest world—from capitalists to social-ists, from green polluters to green peacers, from egocentrics to ecocen-trists—that Ramana's message needs so desperately to be heard.

What and where is this Self? How do I abide as That? There is no doubt how Ramana would answer those—and virtually all other—questions: Who wants to know? What in you, right now, is aware of this page? Who is the Knower that knows the world but cannot itself be known? Who is the Hearer that hears the birds but cannot itself be heard? Who is the Seer that sees the clouds but cannot itself be seen?

And so arises *self-inquiry*, Ramana's special gift to the world. I *have* feelings, but I am not those feelings. Who am I? I *have* thoughts, but I am not those thoughts. Who am I? I *have* desires, but I am not those desires. Who am I?

So you push back into the source of your own awareness—what Ra-mana often called the "I-I," since it is aware of the normal I or ego. You push back into the Witness, the I-I, and you rest as That. I am not ob-jects, not feelings, not desires, not thoughts.

But then people usually make a rather unfortunate mistake in this self-inquiry. They think that if they rest in the Self or Witness, they are going to see something, or feel something, something really amazing, special, spiritual. But you won't see anything. If you see something, that is just another object—another feeling, another thought, another sen-sation, another image. But those are all objects; those are what you are *not*.

No, as you rest in the Witness—realizing, I am not objects, I am not feelings, I am not thoughts—all you will notice is a sense of Freedom, a sense of Liberation, a sense of Release—release from the terrible con-striction of identifying with these little finite objects, the little body and little mind and little ego, all of which are objects that can be seen, and thus are not the true Seer, the real Self, the pure Witness, which is what you really are.

So you won't see anything in particular. Whatever is arising is fine. Clouds float by in the sky, feelings float by in the body, thoughts float by in the mind—and you can effortlessly witness all of them. They *all* spontaneously arise in your own present, easy, effortless awareness. And this witnessing awareness is not itself anything specific you can see. It is just a vast, background sense of Freedom—or *pure Emptiness*—and in that pure Emptiness, which you are, the entire manifest world arises. You *are* that Freedom, Openness, Emptiness—and not any little finite thing that arises in it.

Resting in that empty, free, easy, effortless witnessing, notice that the clouds are arising in the vast space of your awareness. The clouds are arising within you—so much so, you can taste the clouds, you are one with the clouds, it is as if they are on this side of your skin, they are so close. The sky and your awareness have become one, and all things in the sky are floating effortlessly through your own awareness. You can kiss the sun, swallow the mountain, they are that close. Zen says "Swallow the Pacific Ocean in a single gulp," and that's the easiest thing in the world, when inside and outside are no longer two, when subject and object are nondual, when the looker and looked at are One Taste. And so:

The world is illusory, which means you are not any object at all— nothing that can be seen is ultimately real. You are *neti, neti*, not this, not that. And under no circumstances should you base your salvation on that which is finite, temporal, passing, illusory, suffering-enhancing and agony-inducing.

Brahman alone is real, the Self (unqualifiable Brahman-Atman) alone is real—the pure Witness, the timeless Unborn, the formless Seer, the radical I-I, radiant Emptiness—is what is real and all that is real. It is your condition, your nature, your essence, your present and your future, your desire and your destiny, and yet it is always ever-present as pure Presence, the alone that is Alone.

Brahman is the world, Emptiness and Form are not-two. *After* you realize that the manifest world is illusory, and *after* you realize that Brahman alone is real, *then* you can see that the absolute and the relative are not-two or nondual, then you can see that nirvana and samsara are not-two, then you can realize that the Seer and everything seen are not-two, Brahman and the world are not-two—all of which really means, the sound of those birds singing! The entire world of Form exists nowhere but in your own present Formless Awareness: you can drink the Pacific in a single gulp, because the entire world literally exists in your pure Self, the ever-present great I-I.

Finally, and most important, Ramana would remind us that the pure Self—and therefore the great Liberation—*cannot be attained*, any more than you can attain your feet or acquire your lungs. You are *already* aware of the sky, you *already* hear the sounds around you, you *already* witness this world. One hundred percent of the enlightened mind or pure Self is present right now—not ninety-nine percent, but one hundred percent. As Ramana constantly pointed out, if the Self (or knowledge of the Self) is something that comes into existence—if your realization has a beginning in time—then that is merely another object, another passing, finite, temporal state. There is no reaching the Self—the Self is reading this page. There is no looking for the Self—it is looking out of your eyes right now. There is no attaining the Self—it is reading these words. You simply, absolutely, cannot attain that which you have never lost. And if you do attain something, Ramana would say, that's very nice, but that's not the Self.

So, if I may suggest, as you read the following words from the world's greatest sage: if you think you don't understand Self or Spirit, then rest in that which doesn't understand, and just that is Spirit. If you think you don't quite "get" the Self or Spirit, then rest in that which doesn't quite get it, and just that is Spirit.

Thus, if you think you understand Spirit, that is Spirit. If you think you don't, that is Spirit. And so we can leave with Ramana's greatest and most secret message: the enlightened mind is not hard to attain but impossible to avoid. In the dear Master's words:

> There is neither creation nor destruction,
> Neither destiny nor free-will;
> Neither path nor achievement;
> This is the final truth.

Wednesday, August 20

Got up a little earlier than usual so I could get the day's reading done before Mitch and his new love Freada arrive. For volume 2 specifically, I've now gone through around five hundred books, with as many more to go—on anthropology, ecology, feminism, postmodernism, cultural studies, postcolonial studies—and the vast majority of them are, alas, drudgery. To add insult to injury, the style is ponderously indecipherable; you can read entire chapters possessing not a single understandable sentence; the prose suffocates you with insignificance. The best it gets up to is a type of rancid torpor, where the prose drags its belly across the gray page, always on the verge of a near-life experience.

Thursday, August 21

Freada is a real sweetie. Attractive, very bright, very open, very perceptive. Mitchell just lights up around her, which makes me quite happy. We threw a party for Mitch Wednesday night; several people wanted to meet him and several others wanted to meet me, so I just invited them all, thus killing several birds with one party.

And now they are off. It was great seeing them together. I'm guessing it will last. Shiva and Shakti always find each other, and who would ever suspect?

Monday, August 25

Sara Bates called and left a message, inviting me to participate in a conference being sponsored by the San Francisco Art Commission and the Society for American Indian Studies. She said the nicest thing: "You are the only person I have read recently who really has a complete understanding of cross-cultural integrative vision." Even better, she sent me some of her art, and it is deeply beautiful. The photos show large (twelve-foot) mandalas, lying on the ground, which Sara has constructed out of hundreds of different types of objects and materials, both natural and manmade. Her art is a type of integration and inclusion of modernist themes (abstract patterns), postmodern themes (multiperspectival), and traditional themes (in her case, Native American).

The Cherokee Nation has seven clans—Wolf Clan, Deer Clan, Red Pain Clan, Bird Clan, Twisters Clan, Blue Clan, and Wild Potato Clan. Sara is Wolf Clan, so she includes elements of this in her art. But what attracts me to her work is the way she embraces elements representative of a collective and interconnected humanity—again, not ethnocentric pluralism but universal pluralism.

From one of her brochures: "Many artists draw from history to tell a story of their particular reality as an American Indian or a woman or an artist within the milieu of art history. They go to great pains to describe what sets them apart from other individuals [group-identity or ethnocentric pluralism]. Bates has chosen instead to use the history and philosophy of her heritage as an American Indian and, more particularly, a member of the Cherokee Nation to talk about how similar we are and to describe our *interconnectedness*"—worldcentric or universal pluralism. Lord, this makes my heart so happy! This is such balm for our fragmented souls, for the nightmare of identity politics, the politics of narcissism, the politics of self-pity. That Sara is expressing universal pluralism in her art—and fighting the fashionable but brutal trends of ethnocentric pluralism and extremist diversity—is absolutely wonderful.

Friday, August 29

There is a superb rock group called Līve; its lead singer is Ed Kowalczyk. Their CD *Throwing Copper* sold over five million copies and is one of my favorites. They are giving a concert in the area and Ed called and wanted to know if he could drop by—*Brief History* apparently meant a lot to him. I said fine, come on over.

Ed is twenty-six, very bright, handsome, and actually quite sweet. He has a strong spiritually devotional side to him and wants increasingly to write music reflecting this. Both he and his fiancée, Erin, are altogether likeable, genuine people. The three of us spent the evening together, and I promised to follow his progress as he heads into more spiritual music.

Marci is visiting her folks in Pennsylvania, and as much as she said she was going to miss me, she was *really* upset she couldn't meet Ed.

Sunday, August 31

A TICKET TO ATHENS

PATHWAYS: Why does Spirit bother to manifest at all, especially when that manifestation is necessarily painful and requires that It become amnesiac to Its true identity? Why does God incarnate?

KW: Oh, I see you're starting with the easy questions. Well, I'll give you a few theoretical answers that have been offered over the years, and then I'll give you my personal experience, such as it is.

I have actually asked this same question of several spiritual teachers, and one of them gave a quick, classic answer: "It's no fun having dinner alone."

That's sort of flip or flippant, I suppose, but the more you think about it, the more it starts to make sense. What if, just for the fun of it, we pretend—you and I blasphemously pretend, just for a moment—that we are Spirit, that Tat Tvam Asi? Why would you, if you were God Almighty, why would *you* manifest a world? A world that, as you say, is *necessarily* one of separation and turmoil and pain? Why would you, as the One, ever give rise to the Many?

PATHWAYS: It's no fun having dinner alone?

KW: Doesn't that start to make sense? Here you are, the One and Only, the Alone and the Infinite. What are you going to do next? You bathe in your own glory for all eternity, you bask in your own delight for ages upon ages, and then what? Sooner or later, you might decide that it would be fun—just *fun*—to pretend that you were not you. I mean, what else are you going to do? What else *can* you do?

PATHWAYS: Manifest a world.

KW: Don't you think? But then it starts to get interesting. When I was a child, I used to try to play checkers with myself. You ever tried that?

PATHWAYS: Yes, I remember doing something like that.

KW: Does it work?

PATHWAYS: Not exactly, because I always knew what my "opponent's" move was going to be. I was playing both sides, so I couldn't "surprise" myself. I always knew what I was going to do on both sides, so it wasn't much of a game. You need somebody "else" to play the game.

KW: Yes, exactly, that's the problem. You need an "other." So if you are the only Being in all existence, and you want to *play*—you want to play any sort of game—you have to take the role of the other, and then *forget* that you are playing both sides. Otherwise the game is no fun, as you say. You have to pretend you are the other player with such conviction that you forget that you are playing all the roles. If you don't forget, then you got no game, it's just no fun.

PATHWAYS: So if you want to play—I think the Eastern term is *lila*—then you have to forget who you are. Amnesis.

KW: Yes, I think so. And that is exactly the core of the answer given by the mystics the world over. If you are the One, and—out of sheer exuberance, plenitude, superabundance—you want to play, to rejoice, to have fun, then you must first, manifest the Many, and then second, forget it is you who are the Many. Otherwise, no game. Manifestation, incarnation, is the great Game of the One playing at being the Many, for the sheer sport and fun of it.

PATHWAYS: But it's not always fun.

KW: Well, yes and no. The manifest world is a world of opposites—of pleasure versus pain, up versus down, good versus evil, subject versus object, light versus shadow. But if you are going to play the great cosmic Game, that is what you yourself set into motion. How else can you do it? If there are no parts and no players and no suffering and no Many, then you simply remain as the One and Only, Alone and Aloof. But it's no fun having dinner alone.

PATHWAYS: So to start the game of manifestation is to start the world of suffering.

KW: It starts to look like that, doesn't it? And the mystics seem to agree. But there is a way out of that suffering, a way to be free of the opposites, and that involves the overwhelming and direct realization that Spirit is not good versus evil, or pleasure versus pain, or light versus dark, or life versus death, or whole versus part, or holistic versus analytic. Spirit is the great Player that gives rise to *all* those opposites equally—"I the Lord make the Light to fall on the good and the bad alike; I the Lord do all these things"—and the mystics the world over agree. Spirit is not the good half of the opposites, but the ground of *all* the opposites, and our "salvation," as it were, is not to find the good half of the dualism but to find the Source of both halves of the dualism, for that is what we are in truth. We are both sides in the great Game of Life, because we—you and I, in the deepest recesses of our very Self—have created *both* of these opposites in order to have a grand game of cosmic checkers.

That, anyway, is the "theoretical" answer that the mystics almost always give. "Nonduality" means, as the *Upanishads* put it, "to be freed of the pairs." That is, the great liberation consists in being freed of the pairs of opposites, freed of duality—and finding instead the nondual One Taste that gives rise to both. This is *liberation* because we cease the impossible, painful dream of spending our entire lives trying to find an up without a down, an inside without an outside, a good without an evil, a pleasure without its inevitable pain.

PATHWAYS: You said that you had a more personal response as well.

KW: Yes, such as it is. When I first experienced, however haltingly, *nirvikalpa samadhi*—which means meditative absorption in the formless One—I remember having the vague feeling—very subtle, very faint—that I didn't want to be alone in this wonderful expanse. I remember feeling, very diffusely but very insistently, that I wanted to share this with somebody. So what would one do in that state of loneliness?

PATHWAYS: Manifest the world.

KW: That's how it seems to me. And I knew, however amateurishly, that if I came out of that formless Oneness and recognized the world of the Many, that I would then *suffer*, because the Many always hurt each other, as well as help each other. And you know what? I was glad to surrender the peace of the One even though it meant the pain of the Many. Now this is just a little tongue taste of what the great mystics have seen, but my limited experience seems to conform to their great pronouncement: You are the One freely giving rise to the Many—to pain and pleasure and all the opposites—because you choose not to abide as the exquisite loneliness of Infinity, and because you don't want to have dinner alone.

PATHWAYS: And the pain that is involved?

KW: Is *freely* chosen as part of the necessary Game of Life. You cannot have a manifest world without all the opposites of pleasure and pain. And to get rid of the pain—the sin, the suffering, the *duhkha*—you must *remember* who and what you really are. This remembrance, this recollection, this anamnesis—"Do this in Remembrance of Me"— means, "Do this in Remembrance of the Self that You Are"—Tat Tvam Asi. The great mystical religions the world over consist of a series of profound practices to quiet the small self that we pretend we are—which *causes* the pain and suffering that you feel—and awaken as the Great Self that is our own true ground and goal and destiny—"Let this consciousness be in you which was in Christ Jesus."

PATHWAYS: Is this realization an all-or-nothing affair?

KW: Not usually. It's often a series of glimpses of One Taste— glimpses of the fact that you are one with absolutely all manifestation, in its good and bad aspects, in all its frost and fever, its wonder and its pain. You are the Kosmos, *literally*. But you tend to understand this ultimate fact in increasing glimpses of the infinity that you are, and you realize exactly why you started this wonderful, horrible Game of Life. But it is absolutely not a cruel Game, not ultimately, because you, and you alone, instigated this Drama, this Lila, this Kenosis.

PATHWAYS: But what about the notion that these experiences of "One Taste" or "Kosmic Consciousness" are just a by-product of meditation, and therefore aren't "really real"?

KW: Well, that can be said of any type of knowledge that depends on an instrument. "Kosmic consciousness" often depends on the instrument of meditation. So what? Seeing the nucleus of a cell depends on a microscope. Do we then say that the cell nucleus isn't real because it's only a by-product of a microscope? Do we say the moons of Jupiter aren't real because they depend on a telescope? The people who raise this objection are almost always people who don't want to look through the instrument of meditation, just as the Churchmen refused to look through Galileo's telescope and thus acknowledge the moons of Jupiter. Let them live with their refusal. But let us—to the best of our ability, and hopefully driven by the best of charity or compassion—try to convince them to look, just once, and see for themselves. Not coerce them, just invite them. I suspect a different world might open for them, a world that has been abundantly verified by all who look through the telescope, and microscope, of meditation.

PATHWAYS: Could you tell us. . . .

KW: If I could interrupt, do you mind if I give you one of my favorite quotes from Aldous Huxley?

PATHWAYS: Please.

KW: This is from *After Many a Summer Dies the Swan*:

> "I like the words I use to bear some relation to facts. That's why I'm interested in eternity—psychological eternity. Because it's a fact."
>
> "For you perhaps," said Jeremy.
>
> "For anyone who chooses to fulfill the conditions under which it can be experienced."
>
> "And why should anyone wish to fulfill them?"
>
> "Why should anyone choose to go to Athens to see the Parthenon? Because it's worth the bother. And the same is true of eternity. The experience of timeless good is worth all the trouble it involved."
>
> "Timeless good," Jeremy repeated with distaste. "I don't know what the words mean."
>
> "Why should you?" said Mr. Propter. "You've never bought your ticket for Athens."

PATHWAYS: So contemplation is the ticket to Athens?

KW: Don't you think?

PATHWAYS: Definitely. I wonder, could you tell us a little bit about your own ticket to Athens? Could you tell us a little about the history of your own experiences with meditation? And what is "integral practice" and what does it offer the modern spiritual seeker?

KW: Well, as for my own history, I'm not sure I can say anything meaningful in a short space. I've been meditating for twenty-five years, and I suspect my experiences are not terribly different from many who have tread a similar path. But I will try to say a few things about "integral practice," because I suspect it might be the wave of the future. The idea is fairly simple, and Tony Schwartz, author of *What Really Matters: Searching for Wisdom in America*, summarized it as the attempt to "marry Freud and Buddha." But that really just means, the attempt to integrate the contributions of Western "depth psychology" with the great wisdom traditions of "height psychology"—the attempt to integrate id and Spirit, shadow and God, libido and Brahman, instinct and Goddess, lower and higher—whatever terms you wish, the idea is clear enough, I suspect.

PATHWAYS: As an actual practice?

KW: Yes, the actual practice is based on something like this: Given the Great Nest of Being—ranging from matter to body to mind to soul to spirit—how can we acknowledge, honor, and *exercise* all of those levels in our own being? And if we do so—if we engage all of the levels of our own potential—won't that *better* help us to remember the Source of the great Game of Life, which is not other than our own deepest Self? If Spirit is the Ground and Goal of all of these levels, and if we are Spirit in truth, won't the whole-hearted engagement of all of these levels help us remember who and what we really are?

Well, that is the theory, which I realize I have put in rather dry terms. The idea, concretely, is this: Take a practice (or practices) from *each* of those levels, and engage whole-heartedly in all of those practices. For the physical level, you might include physical yoga, weightlifting, vitamins, nutrition, jogging, etc. For the emotional/body level, you might try tantric sexuality, therapy that helps you contact the feeling side of your being, bioenergetics, t'ai chi, etc. For the mental level, cognitive therapy, narrative therapy, talking therapy, psychodynamic therapy, etc. For the soul level, contemplative meditation, deity yoga, subtle contemplation, centering prayer, and so on. And for the spirit level, the more nondual practices, such as Zen, Dzogchen, Advaita Vedanta, Kashmir Shaivism, formless Christian mysticism, and so forth.

I hesitate to give that list, because, as you know, there are literally thousands of wonderful practices for all of those levels, and I shudder at excluding any of them. But please just focus on the general idea: take one or more practices from each of the levels of your own being—matter to body to mind to soul to spirit—and exercise *all of them* to the best of your ability, individually and collectively. Not only will you, on a mundane level, simply start to feel better, you will dramatically increase your chances of falling into your own radical Estate, which is Spirit itself, your own deepest identity and impulse.

PATHWAYS: Are there any teachers who are now doing this type of integral practice?

KW: Well, unfortunately, there are not many teachers, at this early time, who are doing this. In part, this type of integral practice is a union of East and West, and they have just recently been introduced to each other. But there are many *superb* teachers dealing with one or more of the many levels in your own being—and therefore, at this time, you simply have to "mix and match"—or choose the best teachers for you at each of the levels. Find a good physical exercise that works for you, and a decent nutritional program. Try to engage in a good psychotherapeutic practice—it could be as simple as writing down your dreams, or belonging to a discussion group. Try a good meditation practice, and engage in community service. I don't want to make this sound like it's a horrible fascist type of thing—but just try, as best you can, to engage all of you in order to awaken all of you.

PATHWAYS: Are there any teachers who are at least moving toward this integral practice?

KW: Yes. There are a few writers who today emphasize the importance of an integral approach, and although all of them are very preliminary, they are a good place to start. You might try Michael Murphy and George Leonard's *The Life We Are Given*; Tony Schwartz's *What Really Matters*; Roger Walsh and Frances Vaughan's *Paths Beyond Ego*; and my *The Eye of Spirit*.

But the idea is simple enough: practicing on only one level of your being will not enlighten all of you. If you *just* meditate, your psychodynamic "junk" will not automatically go away. If you *just* meditate, your job or your relationship with your spouse will not automatically get better. On the other hand, if you *only* do psychotherapy, do not think that you will be relieved from the burden of death and terror. Render unto Freud what is Freud's, and render unto Buddha what is Buddha's. And best of all, render unto the Divine all of yourself, by engaging all that you are.

Good grief, I sound like a commercial for the Marines: "Be all that you can be." But the point, really, is that the more of your own dimensions you engage in the quest to find the Source of this Game of Life, the more likely you are to discover the stunning fact that you are its one and only Author. And that's not a theoretical proposition, it is the very best chance we have to get our ticket to Athens.

September

Universal truth, the Way of heaven and earth, in other words the experience of the absolute and infinite, or in spiritual terms the Tao—the great mistake is to think of getting it in some heaven or world on the other side. We never leave the Tao for a moment. What we can leave is not the Tao.

—AMAKUKI SESSAN

Tuesday, September 2

When bodymind drops, when I am nowhere to be found, there is such an infinite Emptiness, a radical Fullness, endlessly laced with luminosity. I-I open as the Kosmos, here where no object corrupts primordial Purity, here where concepts are too embarrassed to speak, here where duality hides its face in shame, and suffering cannot even remember its name. Nothing ever happens here, in the fullness of infinity, singing self-existing bliss, alive with self-liberating gestures, always happy to be home. Infinite gratitude meets utter simplicity in the openness of this moment, for there is *just this*, forever and forever and hopelessly forever.

Saturday, September 6

Both Princess Diana and Mother Teresa are dead. The two most famous women in the world, gone within a week. (The world's response to their deaths was a striking example of the pyramid of development—the greater the depth, the less the span.)

Diana, by all accounts, was a good person, caring, loving, and devoted; but more to the point, she was stunningly beautiful and glamorous. She really was the world's Princess. And in our flat and faded postmodern world, where everything is supposed to be drearily equal, a true Princess was promise that there can be more. In her own way, she was royally, divinely beautiful, and millions of people around the world loved her deeply and sincerely, because she evoked the beauty hidden in all of them as well. She was a ray of something more, and the world responded with adoration—it went quite beyond anything Diana was in person; but it was still through her person, and no other, that this wonderful ray shone forth. Watching her two sons, William and Harry, walk behind her funeral carriage, I began crying, like millions of others.

Mother Teresa was much closer to that divine ray, and practiced it more diligently, and without the glamour. She was less a person than an opening of Kosmic compassion—unrelenting, fiercely devoted, frighteningly dedicated.

I, anyway, appreciated them both very much, for quite different reasons, and there is considerably less light in the world this morning than there was yesterday.

Wednesday, September 10

Kate Olson and T George came over for dinner last night with Marci and me. T George is pretty amazing. He's what? Seventy-two years old? And still vital and alert and impressive. It's almost impossible to create a successful magazine—nine out of ten quickly fail—and yet T George has started two of them—*Psychology Today* and *American Health*, both still going strong. I'm convinced he'll make it three, with *Spirituality and Health*, but the odds are rather steep this time, because "spirituality" means so many things to so many people that it's hard to focus efforts and rally others to the cause.

The difficulty is exacerbated, of course, by the pre/trans fallacy: much of what people call "spiritual" is not transrational awareness but prerational feeling, and this is a real problem—which we spent much of the evening discussing. I used the diagram in figure 4 to suggest a few points.

Human growth and development generally unfolds from body to mind to soul to spirit—not as a linear ladder, but as nested waves, with each wave enveloping its predecessor(s)—*if* all goes well. But at almost any stage, the higher *can repress* the lower. Instead of enfold and em-

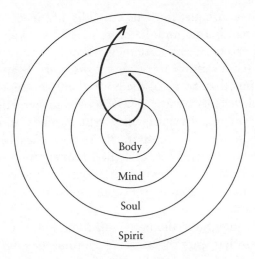

Body

Mind

Soul

Spirit

FIGURE 4. *The Curative Spiral*

brace, there is deny and reject. Instead of transcend and include, there is alienate and repress.

This is especially true of the relation between the mind and body. The first few years of life are basically sensorimotor, preverbal, and largely premental—the self is all body, feelings, and organic impulse. But starting around age 2, the symbolic and conceptual mind begins to emerge, and by age 6 or 7, the concrete operational mind emerges. Ideally the mind transcends and includes the previous bodily sensations, feelings, impulses, and drives. But more often than not—and this is Freud's great province—the mind (the ego-mind) represses or denies some previous bodily feeling, often sex or aggression. This repressed feeling does not simply go away, but rather reappears, in disguised forms, as painful neurotic symptoms.[18]

Thus, by the time most people reach young adulthood, they suffer various forms of mind/body dissociation: *they are out of touch with their bodies*, their feelings, their organic richness, their élan vital. This

---

18. This is not to deny the importance of brain neurochemistry and developmental neurobiology in the genesis of psychopathology. Every Upper-Left (or psychological) event has an Upper-Right (or material) correlate—in fact, all four quadrants have an interactive hand in every psychopathology. In this discussion I am simply focusing on the Upper-Left component—the inner dissociation of conceptual mind and felt body. [See *Integral Psychology* for further discussion.]

has two specific consequences: one, it dulls life itself; two, it makes *higher* development harder and therefore much less likely to occur.

Thus, in order to both revitalize the present and allow higher growth to occur, it is often necessary to *recontact the body*. Many therapies are designed to do just this. Some of the body therapies approach the body directly (through sensory awareness, Rolfing, bioenergetics, etc.), while other therapies will actually engage in a type of regression to the awareness of early childhood. We temporarily regress back to the preverbal body, recontact and befriend it, and then reintegrate it with the mind (this is classically called "regression in service of the ego"). But in all these cases, the ultimate goal is to become fully in touch with *both* the body and the mind.

Once we have integrated the body and the mind, it is much easier—and more likely—that growth can then continue *beyond* the body and mind, into the realms of soul and spirit. In the diagram, these two general movements—regression in service of the ego, and then progression in transcendence of the ego—are indicated by the large spiral, which, for the typical adult, first moves down (regression) and then up (transcendence).

In the regressive part of this spiral, we are *not*, as maintained by the Romantics, recontacting a higher Ground that was lost, but simply a lower bodily feeling that was repressed.[19] We are not recapturing a transrational awareness that we had as an infant but then lost, but rather a prerational impulse that we unfortunately repressed. That repression is nonetheless painful and deleterious, and it can only be cured by recontacting and befriending the alienated impulses and bodily feelings (regression in service of ego, as a prelude to progression in transcendence of ego).

Now the problem with many forms of therapy, and most forms of alternative spirituality, is that we start along this healing spiral and then we get stuck at the prerational, sensory, bodily stage. We regress back to feelings, emotions, sensations, bodily awareness—which itself is fine, and is the first leg of the journey—but then we simply *stop* there and call that transrational spirit, whereas it is nothing of the sort. Trying to go transrational, we end up prerational, and this is called liberation. This is a bit of nightmare.

---

19. Michael Washburn also speaks of a spiral in development, but we disagree on almost all aspects of this spiral movement. See *The Eye of Spirit*, chapter 6, for a full discussion of this topic.

Both T George and Kate seemed to agree with this analysis, and Kate jumped in. "I agree with that, but you are not saying that *all* feelings are prerational or egocentric, are you?"

"No, not at all. There are, as it were, levels of feeling, or levels of affect—moving from egocentric feelings to sociocentric feelings to worldcentric feelings to spiritual feelings—roughly, body to mind to soul to spirit."

"But how can you tell which feeling is which?" Marci wondered.

"If you are sitting around trying to get in touch with *your feelings*—if you are using sensory awareness, felt meaning, bodily focusing, somatic therapy, bioenergetics—then you are at the egocentric stage. This in itself is not bad. As a matter of fact, it is the *foundation* of all further practice. But if you *stay* there, you are in fact deeply regressed to a preconventional mode of awareness. Of course it feels good—*initially*—because you have abdicated the rigors of sociocentric awareness and mutual understanding. You are simply wallowing in you—constantly 'processing' your feelings and prodding your impulses—and this feels great for a little while, until—as Kierkegaard pointed out—it inevitably turns into *despair*, because you are cut off from the circle of sharing that exists outside of yourself."

"That circle of sharing is the next stage," T George pointed out.

"Yes, I think so. You move from egocentric feelings to sociocentric feelings—from Me to We—when you take your feelings and relate them to others in a dialogue aimed at mutual understanding, concern, and care. This is true for both men and women—Kohlberg called this moving from self-oriented to reciprocity, and Gilligan called it moving from the 'selfish stage' to the 'care stage.' Your feelings now expand to include a circle of sharing, caring, and mutual understanding. You are at least as concerned with how others feel as with how you feel. You have expanded from self to group."

"So what's the stage after group?" Kate wondered.

"*All* groups," said T George.

"Yes, worldcentric. You go from egocentric to sociocentric to worldcentric, from me to us to all of us. You are concerned not just with your tribe, your nation, your group—but instead with all groups, all peoples, everywhere, regardless of race, sex, or creed. And you *feel* this; it is not an abstraction. You ache for the world, silly as that sounds."

"I know exactly that feeling," said Kate. "It sometimes comes up when I am doing centering prayer. It's like the bodhisattva vow."

"Yes, and I think that is actually the next stage—worldcentric feelings give way to truly spiritual feelings, because all sentient beings as such are taken into account. But the wonder of this is that we *can* feel a deeply worldcentric/spiritual feeling of universal care and compassion. Schopenhauer said the *only* way we could feel this feeling is if we are all ultimately One Self, and I think that is definitely the case."

"But," Marci pointed out, "all of that universal compassion gets lost when all you do is try to contact your feelings, or stay in your body, or process your emotions. That happens at Naropa all the time. Everybody is trying to remain in their feelings—they call that 'spiritual'!—and so nobody transcends anything."

"Very true," I agreed, "but by no means confined to Naropa. In fact, being fixated to sensory or bodily modes is called *bodyism*, and bodyism is actually a hallmark of the modern and postmodern world. Bodyism is just another term for *flatland*, for the belief that only gross, sensory, empirical realities are real. And both the mainstream culture *and* the counterculture are *equally* dominated by bodyism, by flatland. We all recognize that scientific materialism is the dominant worldview of the mainstream. But look at the countercultural views: ecopsychology, deep ecology, body therapies, ecofeminism, the web of life, Great Mother religions, immanent spirituality, somatic therapy—they all have one thing in common: ultimate reality is the gross sensory world. In other words, *bodyism*—the same bodyism subscribed to by the mainstream. Welcome to flatland, to the purely Descended world of the modern and postmodern era."

Both T George and Kate were curious as to why this bodyism has become so rampant. I suggested it was part of the downside of modernity.[20] For over a thousand years, the West was dominated by an Ascending ideal—God was purely otherworldly, merely transcendent, and his Kingdom was not of this world. But then, beginning with the Renaissance and culminating with the Enlightenment, this Ascending ideal was violently rejected, so much so that the baby of transcendental truth was tossed with tons of bathwater. The result was that the modern West ended up embracing a purely Descended worldview—gross, sensorimotor, empirical bodyism—in other words, flatland.

And so now, even when the countercultural movements claim that

---

20. For a fuller account of the historical rise of bodyism and flatland, see *A Brief History of Everything*. Bodyism is simply another term for subtle reductionism, for the belief that only entities with simple location are real, the belief that only Right-Hand realities are real.

they are overthrowing or transgressing the old Enlightenment paradigm, they are, for the most part, still firmly caught in it. They are trapped in the purely Descended grid, with its intense bodyism and flatland holism and avid embrace of the merely gross realm, exactly like the "old paradigm" they so vocally condemn.

(I was also thinking of Joan Brumberg's *The Body Project*, which tracks girls and their bodies over the last two centuries. A typical diary entry in the late eighteen hundreds ran: "To work seriously. To be dignified. Interest myself in others." A typical entry today reads: "I will lose weight. Get new lenses, good makeup, new clothes and accessories." Brumberg comments: "Before the twentieth century, girls simply did not organize their thinking around their bodies. Today they believe that the body is the ultimate expression of the self." Brumberg, of course, tries to make this bodyism a feminist issue, when it is nothing of the sort; it is simply one of the definitions of flatland, affecting men and women equally—a regressive, narcissistic, leveling pull in consciousness—we have tried to cure *repression* of the body with *regression* to the body—we no longer deny the body, we are obsessed with it and totally fixated to it—and the result is a purely Descended, sensorimotor world.)

The idea, of course, is to integrate *both* the Ascending movement (from body to mind to soul to spirit) and the Descending movement (from spirit to soul to mind to body). But so far, all we really have are a few merely Ascending transcendental religions, and tons of totally Descended, flatland, bodyism movements. We are still awaiting a truly integral, nondual worldview, and although several people are working in this direction, there is still much work to do.

Friday, September 12

The galleys arrived for *Sense and Soul*; minor corrections and sent them back; we're close to the end.

When I was in New York, at the Four Seasons, during that two-day auction, talking to the various publishers, I always ended up saying the same thing, and I am convinced more than ever of its truth: There are *two major dialogues* in the modern world that I believe must take place, one between science and religion, and then one between religion and liberalism. Spirituality must *first* get through the eye of the needle of modern science—and showing how that might happen was a main theme of *Sense and Soul*. But once that happens, spirituality must *then* get through the eye of the needle of liberalism (and that is a main theme of the planned follow-up book to *Sense and Soul*).

The way it is now, the modern world really is divided into two major and warring camps—science and liberalism, on the one hand, and religion and conservatism, on the other. And the key to getting these two camps together is *first*, to get religion past science, and then *second*, to get religion past liberalism, because both science and liberalism are deeply antispiritual. And it must occur in that order, because liberalism won't even listen to spirituality unless it has first passed the scientific test.

In one sense, of course, science and liberalism are right to be antispiritual, because most of what has historically served as "spirituality" is now prerational—magic or mythic, implicitly ethnocentric, fundamentalist dogma. Liberalism traditionally came into existence to fight the tyranny of prerational myth—to fight traditional, parochial, ethnocentric religion—and that is one of its enduring and noble strengths (namely, the freedom, liberty, and equality of individuals in the face of the often hostile or coercive collective). And this is why liberalism was always allied with rational science as against fundamentalist, mythic, prerational religion (and the conservative politics that usually hung on to that religion).

But neither science nor liberalism is aware that, in addition to prerational myth, there is transrational awareness. There are not two camps here: mythic religion versus liberalism. There are three: mythic religion, rational liberalism, and transrational spirituality. Liberalism can be rightfully distrustful of prerational myth, and yet still open itself to transrational awareness. Its objections to mythic forms do not apply to formless awareness, and thus liberalism and authentic spirituality can walk hand in hand into a greater tomorrow. If this can be demonstrated to them *using terms they both find acceptable*, then we would have, I believe for the first time, the possibility of a *postliberal spirituality*, which combines the strengths of conservatism and liberalism, but moves beyond both in a transrational, transpersonal integration. I believe *Sense and Soul* is at least a good start for the first dialogue, and my hope is to follow that up with the second dialogue (spirituality and liberalism) within five years or so.

But one thing is absolutely certain: all the talk of a "new spirituality" in America is a complete waste of time unless those two central dialogues are engaged and answered. Unless spirituality can pass through the gate of science, then of liberalism, it will never be a significant force in the modern world, but will remain merely as the organizing power for the prerational levels of development around the world.

Monday, September 15

"What's a pandit?" Her name was Pritam. Tami had brought Pritam and Matthew over for a long talk about several pressing matters. (Tami Simon is the founder of Sounds True, one of the most successful audio-tape companies in America, located here in Boulder. Tami tapes everybody, from Thich Nhat Hanh to Carolyn Myss to the Dalai Lama. Her favorites she drags up to my house and we all have dinner.) Matthew, an assistant at Sounds True, and Tami were editing the most recent book of Gangaji, an American woman spiritual teacher in the lineage of Vedanta. Pritam wanted to ask me questions about my work, and Tami and Matthew were full of questions about Gangaji.

"I am a pandit, not a guru." And with that line, which I have used a hundred times in my life, the conversation moved, yet again, to this most difficult topic. "In India they make that important distinction. The main difference is that a guru accepts devotees, a pandit does not. Also, pandits are usually scholars of a particular tradition—in America we call them 'pundits'—whereas a guru may, or may not, be very knowledgeable about the tradition."

"So why does a pandit refuse to take disciples or devotees?"

"It's an entirely different profession, as it were. For a guru or master to take on a devotee is a very serious affair—almost like a psychotherapist taking on a client. This is nothing that either party should do lightly, because it means years, even decades, of the most personal, intimate, and intense work between them. Gurus have to wrestle, often in public, with the karma or conditioning of all those who come to them. This is a severe and demanding task."

"So pandits don't do that."

"No, they don't. A particular pandit may be more, or less, enlightened than a particular guru, but in any event, pandits usually confine their understanding to writing, or teaching (at say, a university), or in other fairly ordinary pursuits. But they do not usually engage in spiritual therapy with people. That's an entirely different ballgame."

"So how does the guru actually work?" wondered Tami.

"Well, it depends on the guru. But there is a common thread among *good* gurus, and this is the basis of Guru Yoga. Namely, the guru eats the karma (or conditioning) of the devotee. This occurs when the *com-*

passion of the guru meets the *devotion* of the student. That, anyway, is how it is traditionally stated. Let's use a fairly noncontroversial example here, say Sri Ramana Maharshi. (Ramana is arguably the greatest guru who ever lived, just as Plotinus was probably the greatest pandit.) You've seen pictures of Ramana, and although he is not what you would call handsome, he is incredibly beautiful. You can't take your eyes off him. He is radiating the Beauty of the Divine, which is not other than his own condition, and you are natively drawn to that condition. You want to be in its presence. The guru—the authentic guru—radiates the attractiveness of the Divine, and this helps to awaken you to your own inherent Beauty, your own spiritual essence."

"Can't pandits do that?"

"Many do. But the second part of Guru Yoga is, there is an intense bond formed between the guru and the devotee—like between therapist and client, only more so—and that bond is an important part of the devotee's transformation and awakening. I suppose it's some sort of subtle transference process at work. In classical Freudian transference, the client transfers or projects past relationships onto the therapist, and it is then through an analysis of this projection that the client comes to understand—and hopefully be relieved of—the neurosis.

"The same thing, but on a higher level, seems to go on in authentic Guru Yoga. You, the devotee, project not merely your shadow but your own True Self onto the guru. You see the guru, but not yourself, as possessing the Divine Reality. And this is why the devotee is absolutely fascinated with the guru, drawn to the guru, wants always to be with the guru. You fall in love with your own True Self, as projected onto the figure of the guru.

"Now an accomplished guru will use this transference to awaken devotees to their own True Self, their own true Godhood or Buddha-nature. Traditionally, there are two ways that this can occur. One is through an actual transmission from the guru, and one is through a meditative practice on the part of the student or devotee. In the first, you completely submit to the guru and that submission will reduce the ego, allowing the True Self to shine forth; in the second, you inquire into the source of the ego, and it will revert to its ground in the True Self. Either way will work—submission or inquiry—but the first depends upon how genuine and how potent the guru is."

"Okay, okay, one at a time," said Tami. "In the first, the transmission route, is there actually something that is transmitted, like a force?"

"In my experience of this, yes, definitely. When a person is fairly enlightened, they can transmit—actually transmit—that enlightened awareness through a touch, a look, a gesture, or even through the written word. It's not as weird as it sounds. We are all 'transmitting' our present state to each other all the time. If you are depressed, it can be 'contagious,' depressing others around you. When you are happy, others tend to get happy. Just so with the higher states. In the presence of a psychic-level yogi, you tend to feel power. In the presence of a subtle-level saint, you tend to feel great peace. In the presence of a causal-level sage, you tend to feel massive equanimity. In the presence of a nondual siddha—these are often very ordinary people—you simply find yourself smiling a lot."

"But pandits can do that, too."

"*Anybody* can do that. We are *all* transmitting our own level of awareness all the time. What a *guru* does that nobody else does, is take a particular person as a devotee—as a 'client'—and work with them personally. And, since you were asking, that is something that I myself do not wish to do."

"Can that even be done in America?" asked Matthew.

"Well, that's a good point. I happen to believe that, when it is done right, Guru Yoga is the most powerful yoga there is. But in today's world it is almost impossible to do it right, for at least two reasons. One, Guru Yoga was invented in agrarian-feudal times. To completely submit to the guru—your money, your possessions, your body and mind and soul— was, if not exactly easy, nonetheless acceptable. But in today's democratic societies, this surrender is viewed as alarming, or even as a sign of pathology. Which is the second problem. In our egalitarian culture, where nobody is supposed to have any more depth than anybody else, the whole notion of the guru is frowned on. The thought that anybody is better than anybody else is profoundly offensive and officially taboo. We are a society of deeply entrenched egos, and if you threaten the ego with thoughts of submission or transcendence, you will be run out of town on a rail.

"So for all these reasons, doing Guru Yoga in this country is probably not a good idea, which is too bad. On the other hand, Guru Yoga, precisely because it is so strong, has more problems than . . ."

"Wait," said Tami. "Why is it so strong?"

"Have you ever tried learning a foreign language? It's really quite hard to do, and takes a very long time, especially if you want to be proficient at it. But I have been told by many people that if you have a lover who speaks a foreign language, you can learn it much more quickly. Makes sense, doesn't it?, because the learning is driven by love. The same is true with Guru Yoga. With Guru Yoga, you fall in love— deeply and desperately in love—and that love is the vehicle through which you can much more quickly learn the language of your own True Self. Precisely because this learning is driven by love, it happens more rapidly than sitting alone, in the corner, on your meditation mat, count- ing your breaths."

"I see. But that opens it to much abuse."

"Yes, that's what I was about to say. Precisely because Guru Yoga is so strong, it can also cause the most damage. The abuses are legion, and we hear about a new one almost every day. In any event, I honestly do not think that Guru Yoga—for some very good reasons, and for some truly pathetic reasons—can flourish in this country."

"So that is why you don't want to be a guru?"

"No, I don't want to be a guru because I do not want to enter into a therapist/client relationship with people. Whatever understanding I have I try to put into my writing—the transmission is in the written word— and you can use that transmission as you wish, and judge for yourself whether it is true or not. But whenever I feel myself going down anything that even vaguely resembles a guru path, such as intentionally transmit- ting in person, I simply stop it. It's *not* that I think the guru principle is bad. It's just that there are no karmas in me to do this. I am not qualified to wrestle with people over their spiritual destinies. I have no desire to interfere with the course of anybody's life—whereas, if you are a thera- pist or a guru, you most certainly are going to interfere in the course of people's lives, even or especially if you are being nondirective. I totally applaud therapists, spiritual teachers, and good gurus—we need them all desperately—but they are not my calling."

"So you will never have any students?"

"Traditionally there is a gradation of increasing involvement with any teacher: student, disciple, and devotee. If you study any of my books, you are already a *student* of my work, and that's fine. I accept that particular teacher/student relationship. But because I have no plans to get involved with anybody's personal transformation, it looks like I will never have disciples, let alone devotees."

"So there are students of your *work*. Will there be any students of *yours*? I mean, you teach seminars every now and then. Will you do more of that?"

"In a seminar I can reach perhaps a hundred people. With a book, a hundred thousand. I really feel I have to concentrate on writing. On the other hand, I've always said that when I retire from academic writing, I'd like to teach, travel, and write bad novels. So who knows."

They all leave, and I am alone with the Alone, the simple Mystery of this moment, and this moment, and this.

Wednesday, September 17

Wonderful! Sara [Bates] was awarded the 1997 Foreman Institute of the Creative Arts Award. I'm so happy for her. But then some bad news: at a conference at Hartwick College, Sara fell and broke her leg in two places. "However, being strong in Spirit, I was able to a create a twelve foot Honoring circle [the type of art Sara specializes in] by rolling around on a mechanics creeper on the floor with a cast on my leg. The students were amazed and so was I. I didn't take any pain medication because I was afraid I wouldn't be able to focus. It took 48 hours of very focused work, but I think it is one of the most beautiful pieces I have ever made."

Now there is strong in Spirit.

Thursday, September 18

Had lunch with Nancy Levine, a wonderful woman, bright, beautiful, vivacious, who worked at Naropa until a few months ago, when she became the conference organizer for *New Age* magazine. She said that she and her staff read "A Spirituality That Transforms" and it really hit them hard, because "almost everything we do at *New Age* is merely translative." But we both agreed that translative spirituality has an important role to play, but it is, at best, introductory. My basic suggestion was, at the very least, don't lie about what you are doing. Don't present translative beliefs and label them as transformative. If *New Age* would simply start telling the truth about what it is doing, that in itself would be a move toward transformation.

Saturday, September 20

Early morning, Emptiness shines, the bodymind is the smallest ripple on this infinitely beautiful sea, the sea of *just this*. And now the sun, usurper of the throne of Luminosity, rises to shine its derivative light on a pitiful little Gaia, a small green speck on an infinite sea of unending tranquillity.

The great Zen Master Yasutani: "Now look. The whole phenomenal world is entirely oneself. Therefore the clouds, the mountains, and the flowers; the sound of a fart and the smell of urine; earthquakes, thunder, and fire are all the Original Self. Reading sutras and holding services, telling a pack of lies, slander and idle talk, ugliness and cuteness, everything altogether is supreme enlightenment. Everything is your Original Self that is perfectly without lack and is completely fulfilled in itself. Don't be surprised."

There is One Taste. There is the Big Self, and it *includes* "farts, the smell of urine, a pack of lies and slander." And likewise, until the ecologists understand that the ozone hole, pollution, and toxic wastes are all completely part of the Original Self, they will never gain enlightened awareness, which alone knows how to proceed with these pressing problems.

At the same time, the entire world can disappear—which it does in nirvikalpa—and the Original Self is still itself, full and complete, spaceless and therefore infinite, timeless and therefore eternal. This is not a doctrine of popular pantheism, which simply equates the manifest world with Spirit. The manifest world is not Spirit, it is a gesture of Spirit, as the waves are a gesture of the ocean. But the wetness of individual waves is *identical* to the wetness of the entire ocean—there is only One Taste to every wave, and that taste is Spirit itself. Spirit is the wetness of every wave in the entire universe, including, as Yasutani said, farts and lies and everything else, ozone hole and all.

We want to fix the ozone hole, not because it is hurting Spirit (or the Goddess), but because it is killing us. A true spiritual ecology does not equate the biosphere with Spirit—a horrible confusion of relative and absolute, finite and infinite, temporal and timeless (and itself just another version of bodyism)—but it does see the biosphere as a glorious manifestation of Spirit, and thus treats it with the respect that all God's children deserve, knowing, too, that these children are the manifestation of one's own deepest Self. You weep at the destruction of the biosphere, not because your God is dying, but because your children are.

Sunday, September 21

There is such a strange and radically paradoxical thing about One Taste: you never really enter or leave it. You have always known One Taste—literally, for fifteen billion years you have known this, and one day, sooner or later, you will admit it, and the Great Search will be undone. And then you will see that any state that can be entered is not One Taste.

Emptiness through all eternity, Fullness to all infinity. And it's just this, only *this*. It cannot be any more obvious, which is why it usually takes lifetimes to see. Too close to be grasped, too effortless to be reached, too present to be attained. The Buddhas never attained this; sentient beings never lost it. Who will believe this?

Monday, September 22

The International Cosmos Prize is an annual award given by a well-known Japanese foundation (Expo '90). It is known as the "Japanese Nobel Prize" or sometimes the "Asian Nobel Prize." Its brochure states that "Its purpose is to honor those individuals who have, through their work, applied and realized a total context and stressed the need to understand our world as a single interdependent entity." The amount of the award is $500,000.

One can certainly applaud the aims of the Cosmos Prize; as their brochure puts it: "Of vital importance for research conducted now and in the future is the need to understand the character of the interdependent relationship among all things. The answers, however, cannot fully be attained with analytical and divisive methods that have served the mainstream science of the past. The necessity for new paradigms formed through *integrative* and *inclusive* approaches has been realized.

"The Foundation recognizes the importance of a holistic global perspective and wishes to extend its support to those dedicated to this approach. Therefore, it has decided to reward the endeavors of researchers and scientists all over the world who have shown their dedication in this respect, thus giving them the recognition they so greatly deserve. By so doing, not only are the ideals of the Foundation upheld, but also it is hoped that a new tide of values is promoted and its fruits shared with all of mankind."

They write that they would like to give me the Cosmos Prize. Before they do so, I must attend a few conferences, etc. This is very interesting, because all of its recipients so far have been Right-Hand-only theorists— that is, systems theorists or eco-theorists working mostly in third-person it-language, thus ignoring and devaluing the first and second (I and we) dimensions. In other words, they have been honoring *exterior holism* (Right Hand) but not *interior holism* (Left Hand), the world of consciousness, lived experience, rich awareness, interior illuminations, spiritual revelations.

This attempt to reduce interior to exterior (or Left to Right) is not gross reductionism, but *subtle reductionism* (flatland holism, systems theory, the empirical web of life, etc.—the reduction of I and we to systems of interactive its). This subtle reductionism or flatland holism—the reduction of art and morals to science—is the dominant mood of modernity, and taken in and by itself, this Right-Hand approach is actually very reductionistic and divisive, despite its vocal pronouncements. As I have often said (paraphrasing Karl Krauss), systems theory is the disease for which it claims to be the cure.

Nonetheless, subtle reductionism (reducing all interwoven I's and we's to interwoven its) is infinitely preferable to gross reductionism (going even further and reducing all interwoven its to atomistic its). So the Expo Foundation has been doing a great service in at least rewarding a holistic approach, even if the holism has been exterior only.

But now, for them to nod in this direction means, I believe, that they recognize that a true holism must include *both* interior holism and exterior holism (i.e., all four quadrants). I think this means that "all-level, all-quadrant" might be an idea whose time has finally come. One can at least hope that it signals the end of a mere flatland holism, a world of meaningless "its" roaming a network world possessing no depth, no within, no soul, no spirit.

Tuesday, September 23

THE NEW PERSON-CENTERED CIVIL RELIGION

Two sociological reports recently surfaced that have caused quite a stir. One is Paul Ray's "The Rise of Integral Culture," the other is Robert Forman's "Report on Grassroots Spirituality." Taken together they purport to show an extraordinary cultural revolution now underway, centered largely on the baby boomers. Paul Ray's conclusion is that a new, higher, more transformative culture—which he calls "Integral Culture," inhabited by what he calls "Cultural Creatives"—is now on the rise, and that it well might be one of the most significant cultural transformations of the last thousand years. In many ways these reports are not much different from the early boomer manifestos, *The Aquarian Conspiracy*, *The Making of a Counter-Culture*, *The Turning Point*, and *The Greening of America*. What sets them apart is an attempt at data collection and sociological methodology: they are presented as something of a social scientific conclusion, however preliminary. And the gist of both reports is that the presently occurring revolution is a deeply *spiritual* revolution. According to Paul Ray, the Cultural Creatives comprise 24% of the adult American population, or a staggering forty-four million people.

At the same time, it seems obvious that forty-four million mostly middle-class and upper-middle-class baby boomers are not undergoing profound transformative spiritual realization, even though at least half of them seem to be *claiming* that they are. What on earth is going on here?

What we have, I think, is a truly fascinating cultural phenomenon, which involves not primarily a new mode of transformative spirituality, but the emergence of a relatively new mode of translative spirituality. Not a new authenticity—or way to find actual transcendence of the self—but a new legitimacy—or way to give meaning to the self. Not a new and profound growth in consciousness, but a new way to feel good at one's present stage. Herein lies a tale.

In the late 1950s, a number of serious scholars (including Talcott Parsons, Edward Shils, and Robert Bellah) put forth the notion of *civil religion*. The idea was that many Americans had transferred a sense of the *sacred* from institutional religion (Church religion) to certain aspects of their own *civil* society. The result—a civil religion—tended to view certain American characteristics and historical events as being sacred, divine, or divinely inspired. The immigration to America was a new Exodus and Americans were the new Chosen People, meant to carry a spiritual epiphany to the rest of the world.

This civil religion was clearly translative, not transformative; it did not transcend the self, but it did connect the self to a sense of something bigger. It thus gave many Americans a sense of meaning and legitimacy to their lives. *Meaning*, because they were linked to something larger than themselves; *legitimacy*, because their lives were sanctioned by what they took to be sacred. And that is indeed what all translative spirituality does for the individual. Correlatively, for the society at large, legitimation is a crucial ingredient in cultural meaning and social cohesion. And the point that these scholars made was that the civil religion was now performing many of these crucial tasks (emotional expression and social cohesion) that the Churches were failing to do. Thus, many civil and *secular* institutions were imbued with a sense of the sacred that the Churches were not adequately offering, but always with the understanding that this sacredness was part of a special mission that these Americans were shouldering.

However, in the late 1960s, the secular and civil religion—along with many other American institutions—underwent a *legitimation crisis*. In

A Sociable God, I discussed this legitimation crisis at length and concluded that three general outcomes were likely. As conventional legitimacy fragmented, individuals (and society itself) could: (1) avail themselves of the opportunity to grow in more postconventional directions, including, for a few, genuinely transpersonal, transrational, and spiritual modes; (2) regress to preconventional and egocentric modes; or (3) find a new civil religion, or comparable legitimating belief system, that would take the ordinary translations of the separate self and call them sacred.

It appears, in almost all ways, that the Integral Culture described by Ray is the new civil religion. There is little evidence that post-postconventional modes are operative in many of the Cultural Creatives, although there is a fair amount of regressive narcissism. But what we see mostly is a new and novel form of translative legitimacy and translative spirituality, which operates not to transcend the separate self but to give it meaning, consolation, sanction, and promise.

Largely boomer driven, this new religion—which I will call Person-Centered Civil Religion—has all the characteristics of the general postmodern post-structuralist agenda that still dominates boomer academia. Namely, with a few exceptions, it is: antihierarchical, anti-institutional, anti-authority, antiscience, antirationality, and deeply subjectivistic [see November 23 for a discussion of these trends]. This is in sharp contrast to much of the old civil religion. However, like the old civil religion, the new believers no longer find the Church to be dispensing enough sacredness ("grassroots spirituality," according to Forman, believes in ABC: Anything But the Church). And also like the old civil religion, they generally believe they are the vanguard of a new spiritual realization, or, at the least, a new paradigm; and many further believe that it will save or transform the world, heal the planet, heal America, etc.

The specific contents of the new Person-Centered Civil Religion (PCCR) can be traced to several influences, in my opinion. First and foremost is Romanticism—an emphasis on feeling instead of reason, on sentimental connection with others, and on the sacredness of nature *as opposed* to culture (the largest subset of the Cultural Creatives, according to Ray, are the Green Cultural Creatives). The second is the self-experiential therapies made popular in the sixties (Cultural Creatives, according to Ray, are the prime consumers of experiential workshops). The third is new-age religion (which is one of the main ingredients of Integral Culture religion, according to Ray, even though many object to the name). The fourth is anything holistic (or, as Ray puts it, "holistic everything"—although, self-contradictorily, the actual details of this holism are never spelled out, since that would be "too controlling"—it's a holism with few specifics, although it sometimes relies on flatland systems theory). The fifth is globalism, or an intent to see their values shared by the rest of the world. The sixth is feminism and women's spirituality (60% of Cultural Creatives are women).

The emphasis on women's spirituality is interesting, I believe, and is a key to much of Person-Centered Civil Religion, both in positive and negative ways. Much of women's spirituality takes its cue from Deborah Tannen's and Carol Gilligan's research, which showed that females tend to emphasize communion, relationship, and care, whereas males tend to emphasize agency, rights, and justice. The former tend to be *heterarchical* (which means no position is privileged, but all perspectives are linked and joined); the latter tend to be *hierarchical* (which means wider and deeper perspectives are ranked). Women's spirituality has therefore taken *a very strong antihierarchical stance* and, indeed, tends to vociferously define itself that way.

What this unfortunately overlooks is Gilligan's actual findings, which is that women (like men) go through three major *hierarchical* (her word) stages of growth, which she calls *selfish* (egocentric or preconventional), *care* (sociocentric or conventional), and *universal care* (worldcentric or postconventional). *Both males and females develop through that same hierarchy*, but males do so with an emphasis on agency, women on communion. (And remember, hierarchy in its healthy sense really means holarchy, because each higher stage transcends but includes—or envelops and nests—its juniors: a development that is envelopment, and this is true for both men and women.)

The fact that so much of women's spirituality, cultural creatives, and grassroots spirituality all aggressively deny a developmental hierarchy is probably one of the main reasons that so few of those movements seem to be genuinely transformative. Transformation means holarchical growth, but if you deny holarchy in the first place, you have no compass, no way to find your direction, no way to find authenticity and transformation, and so you must settle for legitimacy and translation instead. And that is what the new Person-Centered Civil Religion does. In my opinion, this anti-hierarchy stance is very likely destined to keep the PCCR a largely translative, not transformative, movement.

As Roger Walsh, reviewing movements such as the Integral Culture, concluded: "These movements are generally antithetical toward hierarchies. Yet the reality is that spiritual development does occur through levels and some people are more developed than others. Failure to recognize this can lead to such problems as an unwillingness to make essential discernments, a lack of critical thinking, and a pseudo-egalitarianism. To put it bluntly, the central question is to what extent integral culture or grassroots spirituality is actually fostering spiritual maturation and to what extent they are simply making people feel good. Much of what passes for spirituality at the present time seems to consist merely of intense feelings." [See July 5 for the "415 Paradigm," one of the most prominent versions of the PCCR.][21]

Still, there are many good things that can be said about Person-Centered Civil Religion as a translative, legitimate spirituality. It is the first translative religion to take ecological concerns seriously. It includes many previously marginalized groups, including most especially women (however, it is a largely white, middle- and upper-middle-class religion). It has a guarded but infectious social optimism. It highly values education, neighborhood building, and especially dialogue and small group discussion ("civil" means associations that lie between the family and the state; the PCCR values small, civic associations, but still focused on the person, hence the title). These are all quite positive, it seems to me, at least in a translative sense. And, of course, *anybody at virtually any stage of growth can have a temporary peak experience*—an authentic spiritual experience—and this certainly includes members of Person-Centered Civil Religion, so they are not without access to genuine glimpses of the Divine (but the same is true for all people, so this is nothing that sets the PCCR apart).

Tossed into that mix is an intense consumerism; a love of tourism (especially if labeled eco or spiritual); an obsessive interest in food and food consumption; the highest attendee rate at feeling-experiential workshops. They are the innovators for boutique beers, and are more

---

21. Robert Forman is a gifted theorist and a superb editor; his research is not necessarily agreeing with the contents of his respondents, but simply reporting them. In Forman's excellent *The Problem of Pure Consciousness,* he advances the hypothesis that the state of formless absorption (or unmanifest cessation) is a near universal of profound mystical spirituality. I agree. So perhaps in his next round of research, Robert might pointedly ask all of his respondents, "Have you had a direct and prolonged experience of pure formless cessation? If so, please describe it." This would give Robert a better idea of the percentage of grassroots spirituality that is accessing this profound dimension, and, by subtraction, the percentage that is involved in lesser or merely translative spirituality (such as Person-Centered Civil Religion).

likely to have at least five flavors of vinegar. They generally despise TV (which definitely leaves me out of the new Integral Culture; but then, I have always thought that if these authors watched more TV, they would never write books like *The Aquarian Conspiracy* or *The Greening of America*, because they would see what is actually going on out there).

In my opinion, 24% of the population is not engaged in deeply transformative, transpersonal spirituality. About 1% is—*which is still several million people!*—but not nearly the numbers claimed by the Aquarian Conspiracy or the Integral Culture. [See the introduction to Volume Seven of the *Collected Works* for an in-depth discussion of this topic.]

Aside from that 1%, the rest of the population seek their *legitimacy* through (1) traditional mythic (biblical) religion, which is still a huge force in this culture; (2) traditional republicanism or civic humanism, closely allied, in America, with biblical mythic religion; (3) secular science, the religion of the educational elites; (4) political liberalism, closely allied with science; (5) regressive new-age movements; and (6) Person-Centered Civil Religion.

Whatever we might think about the Cultural Creatives, there is one item I especially appreciate about them (which means, about my generation): we were the first generation to take seriously, on a very wide scale, the notion of transformative, authentic, spiritual liberation. We brought Eastern mysticism here in an unprecedented fashion; we insisted on Christianity and Judaism going back to their mystical roots (in everything from the Gnostics to Eckhart to Luria and Kabbalah); we demanded direct spiritual experience, not mere dogma. We were a generation almost defined by *Be Here Now*. We had all of that as at least an *idea* of greater possibilities. We would, in the best and truest sense, subvert and transgress all conventions and thereby find a freedom that previous generations could only dream of.

Alas, all of that remained pretty much an idea only. It was one thing to drink coffee, smoke cigarettes, and talk endlessly about the Zen of this and the Zen of that, the Tao of this and the Tao of that. It was quite another to actually practice Zen, to spend at least six years in grueling meditation practice in order to truly transgress the world and subvert samsara. And thus, in the coming decades, we indeed dropped out, not of conventionality, but of true transgression, true transformative practice, and, with the help of Person-Centered Civil Religion, we reentered the marketplace, not from the tenth of the Zen Ox-Herding Pictures, but from the first. We in fact became yuppies, and carried out our self-obsession with a capitalistic fury; or we confined our spiritual impulses to the gross realm alone, turning poor Gaia into the only God we could find. In general, we took to Romanticism—a horizontal obsession with self—and abandoned real Idealism—a vertical transcendence of self. And with the help of the PCCR, we could rationalize the entire charade, and get on about the dirty business of nursing this self obsession through the long days and lonely nights.

But what I appreciate is the fact that, from that 24% of the population, which at least still has the *idea* that true transcendence is possible, comes most of the 1% of the population that is *actually* transcending, actually engaged not just in translative spirituality or the occasional peak experience, but in authentic practice, plateau experience, and permanent realization. The fact remains that 1% of a population—several million people—actually practicing authentic transcendence and compassionate embrace is extremely rare in any culture, and this just might turn out to be one of the true gifts my generation gives to the world.

At the same time, this sets an important educational agenda: how can we reach out and educate people as to the difference between mere translative beliefs and genuine transformative practices? How can we help turn that 1% into five, ten, twenty percent? As Jack Crittenden says, this is an elitism, but an elitism to which everyone is invited.

Wednesday, September 24

I'm a fan of the art of Anselm Kiefer; it is profoundly significant and moving. In one of those funny synchronicities, today I get the following letter from Marian Goodman, owner of the Marian Goodman Gallery in New York: "I have an art gallery representing a large group of some of the leading contemporary artists. One among them is an artist named Anselm Kiefer, who has had many major one-man museum shows world-wide. I think it is safe to say that he is one of the most important contemporary artists working today, and probably the major European painter of his generation.

"Anselm Kiefer is German, born in 1945, with all the sense of struggle for meaning, so critical to his post-war generation. The subject of his work has evolved over time from the questioning of sources of the German catastrophe, through mythology, history, etc., to a wider reflection on man's capacity for good and evil. In recent years his work has taken an inward, more spiritual and transcendental turn.

"We will be giving a large exhibition of his paintings in mid-November. For this occasion we are planning to publish a book." She says that Anselm would like me to write the text for the book. I'll be glad to.

I was trying to remember where I had last read a review of Anselm's work. It was in Suzi Gablik's wonderful *Has Modernism Failed?*, a brilliant indictment of extreme postmodernism. (I also thoroughly enjoyed her *Progress in Art*, which demonstrates that art does indeed evolve or develop.) Gablik: "If the eclectic image-plundering of the Americans Julian Schnabel and David Salle never quite coalesce into commitment or meaning—and therefore seem more like a symptom of alienation than a cure—there are others, like the German Anselm Kiefer, whose imagery is engaged and even suggests a willingness to believe again. Kiefer, it seems to me, is one of the few artists working today who opens up the vision and ideal of apocalyptic renovation and makes the effort to regain the spiritual dignity of art. It is as if he were opening up the fenestra aeternitatis—the window onto eternity and spiritual clairvoyance—which in our society has been closed for a long time."

Friday, September 26

Roger and Frances are here for two days, hanging out with Marci and me. Frances, representing the Fetzer Foundation, will soon give a speech to the Arizona Center for the Study of Consciousness, which is heavily supported by Fetzer. I had written a long paper (for their associated journal, the *Journal of Consciousness Studies*), called "An Integral Theory of Consciousness," which stressed the need for an "all-level, all-quadrant" approach. The conclusion, put simply, is that we need to combine first-person ("I"), second-person ("we"), and third-person ("it") approaches to the study of consciousness: what we might call a *1-2-3 approach*.

But Roger and Frances and I noticed, as we surveyed the field of consciousness studies, that almost everybody is still in their favorite quadrant, pushing one approach to the exclusion of others, and it's truly depressing. So Frances thought she might call the talk "The 1-2-3 of Consciousness Studies," and encourage a more integral approach. Roger had a fantastic idea, which he calls 20/20: *each quadrant* should have at least a 20% representation in the Center's activities. The chances of that are probably slim, but it's a fine notion, perhaps applicable elsewhere.

Monday, September 29

"It is not what a person says, but the level from which they say it, that determines the truth of a spiritual statement." He was a young professor, from a local college, and I had agreed to chat with him for an hour or so, late this afternoon.

"How do you mean that?" he asked.

"Well, anybody can say, 'All things are One,' 'All sentient beings possess Spirit,' 'All things are part of a great unified Web of Life,' or 'Subject and object are nondual.' *Anybody* can say those things. The question is, do you directly and actually realize that? Are you speaking with any sort of awakened authority, or are these just words to you?"

"What if they are just words? What does it matter?"

"Well, *spiritual realities* involve not merely statements about the objective world, but also statements of *subjective facts*, interior facts—and for those statements to be *true* when they come from your mouth, *you* must be directly in touch with those higher, interior facts, or else you are not being truthful, no matter how 'correct' the words might sound. It is the subjective state of the speaker, and not the objective content of the words, that determines the truth of the utterance."

"Yes, I see. But could you give some examples?" He was furiously scribbling, but I was not sure if he was taking notes or recording his own thoughts.

"Okay. Anybody can say 'All things are One,' so you have to determine the subjective state of consciousness—or the level of consciousness—of the person making the statement in order to judge its actual truth value, its truthfulness. We need to know the level of consciousness of the speaker in order to know what he or she actually means by 'All things.' Do they mean all gross-level things are one? All subtle-level things are one? All causal realities are one? Do they mean all of those taken together? You see, the simple statement 'All things are One' actually has a number of quite different meanings, and those meanings depend, *not* on the objective content of the words—which are the same in each case—but on the subjective level of consciousness of the speaker, which varies dramatically. You might be one with *everything* on a given level, but what if there are higher and deeper levels that you don't know about? You're *not* one with those, you see?"

"Yes. So how can you tell?"

"There are several tip-offs. Most of the books written about systems theory, Gaia, the Great Mother, ecopsychology, the new paradigm, and so on, are all written with reference to the gross, waking state. You can easily tell this because they never mention any of the subtle realm phenomena—nothing about the various meditative states, samadhis, interior illuminations, the extraordinary states of dream yoga, transcendental awareness, and so on. Nor do they mention the even higher states of causal formlessness. So when they claim to be 'holistic' and 'nondual,' they really aren't, not in any full sense. At best, they are at the level of nature mysticism, where consciousness is confined to union with the gross, waking state. This is fine as far as it goes, it just doesn't go very far. It is the shallowest of the spheres of mystical Oneness in the Great Nest of Spirit."

"How can you tell if their consciousness extends beyond the gross realm?"

"Once consciousness becomes strong enough to persist from the waking state into the dream state—once you start to lucid dream, for example, or once you enter into various types of savikalpa samadhi (meditation with form)—an entirely new realm becomes available to you—namely, the subtle realm—and this is unmistakably reflected in your life, your writing, your theorizing, your spiritual practice. You are no longer confined to thinking about the gross sensorimotor realm—your god is no longer merely green—but rather an extraordinary interior landscape opens to the mind's eye. If you are a painter, you are no longer confined to painting bowls of fruit, nature landscapes, or nudes. You can paint the subtle interior scenes, as with Surrealism and Fantastic Realism, or the interior meditation objects, as with Tibetan thangka painting. But none of those subtle objects can be seen with the eye of flesh."

"So when somebody at that subtle level says 'All things are One,' they mean something different than when the gross-realm theorist says that."

"Yes, quite different. Usually, when someone whose access consciousness is confined to the gross realm says 'All things are One,' they mean something like systems theory or ecopsychology—they mean all empirical phenomena are aspects of a unified process. But when someone *also* has access to subtle-realm consciousness, they mean all empirical *and* all subtle phenomena are aspects of a unified process. This is a much deeper and wider realization, which transcends and includes the gross realm."

"So their consciousness is actually stronger."

"In a sense, yes. Their awareness does not blank out at the threshold of the dream state. Because of their own development and evolution of consciousness, they can remain 'awake' even as the dream arises—or they can enter profound states of savikalpa samadhi and not go blank. And this 'strength' of consciousness becomes even greater at the causal stage of development, because you reach a type of 'constant consciousness' or 'constant witnessing capacity,' which means you are 'awake' or conscious through all three major states—waking, dreaming, and deep sleep. So consciousness becomes stronger and stronger, persisting through more and more changes of state, and this is reflected unmistakably in your life, your work, your theorizing, and so on. These signs are hard to miss."

"Yes, I can see that. So if you are at the subtle stage, you have access . . . ?"

"At the subtle stage you have access to a variety of forms of deity mysticism—interior illuminations, nada, shabd, various samadhis or meditative states, saguna Brahman (Deity with Form), prayer of the heart, dream yoga, most of the bardo realms, and so on. This is the subtle realm of *deity mysticism*. Because the subtle-soul transcends but includes the gross-sensorimotor realm, at the level of deity mysticism you *also* have access to nature mysticism, so those are not exclusive. But the lower, nature mystics tend to think you're nuts."

"And the causal . . ."

"Is the home of *formless mysticism*—pure Emptiness, the Abyss, the Unborn, ayn, nirodh, nirvikalpa, jnana samadhi, classical Nirvana or cessation. This experience (or 'nonexperience') of cessation is unmistakable and indelible. And when somebody has *directly* experienced that state, and they are writing spiritual books, believe me, they will write about that! And you will intuitively feel that they know what they're talking about."

"You also mention the nondual."

"Yes, once you push through causal formlessness—which is the home of the pure Witness—then the Witness itself *collapses* into *everything* that is witnessed *through all three states*. Vedanta calls this sahaja, which means the spontaneous union of nirvana (emptiness) and samsara (form); the Tibetans call it One Taste, because all things, in all states, have the same flavor, namely, Divine; the Taoists call it tzu-jan, which means 'of itself so,' or perfectly spontaneous. So when a person here says 'All things are One,' they mean every single thing in the gross and in the subtle and in the causal has the same One Taste. And that is *very* different from somebody awake only in the gross realm saying 'All things are One.' "

"I see, yes. That's why you said that"—he glanced at his notes—"it is the subjective state of the speaker and not the objective content of the words that determines the truth of the utterance."

"Yes, that's right."

"So we have a type of Oneness at the psychic level, at the subtle, at the causal, and at the nondual."

"Basically, yes. And those cover just the transpersonal, transrational types of Oneness or Union. There are also the primitive, prerational, prepersonal forms of 'oneness' or fusion. There is archaic or *pleromatic* fusion, or oneness with the physical world (which is typical of the first year of life). There is *magical* animism, or the indissociation of emotional subject and object, a type of vital-level oneness (which is typical of 1–4 yrs). And there is *mythic* syncretism, or the oneness of symbolic fusions (typical of 4–8 yrs). Of course, as Jean Gebser emphasized, these primitive types of cognition—archaic, magic, and mythic—are still available to all of us, although nested by deeper developments. And then we reach the *rational* forms of Oneness, such as systems theory, which are achieved by mature reason (or vision-logic)."

"Could you just list them all?"

"Pleromatic fusion, magical animism, mythic syncretism, rational systems theory, psychic or nature mysticism, subtle or deity mysticism, formless or causal mysticism, and nondual One Taste."

"And all of those," he said, "can make statements like 'All things are One,' and yet they all mean something totally different."

"That's it."

"Yes, I see, I see." He continued scribbling.

"Look, here's the point," I suggested. "There have recently been a plethora of books about how all things are part of a unified whole, we are all strands in the web of life, all things are aspects of a great unified process, the world is an organic living system, and so on—all of which are variations on 'All things are One.' But that statement in itself is perfectly meaningless, as we have just seen. Its truth depends entirely on the level of consciousness of the person making the statement.

"And that means two things: First, when you read these books, try to judge as best you can the actual depth of the writer—anybody can say 'All things are One.' Most of the books written about 'oneness with the world' are written from, and about, magical animism, mythic syncretism, or, at best, a type of rational systems theory. So try to find a writer addressing the transrational, not just the rational or prerational, levels of awareness. And second, the writer should be giving you, first and foremost, *practices* to help you awaken to a higher level of Oneness in yourself. Not just a new objective description of the world—that's worthless in this regard—but a series of subjective practices to change the level of your own consciousness.

"So these writers should be awakened to a higher Oneness—psychic or subtle or causal or nondual—and they should be giving you practices to help you awaken as well. At the very least, these writers should be giving you, not merely new ways to translate the world, but new ways to transform your own consciousness. And if they don't directly give you these practices, they should make it clear how centrally important they are."

I made him a cup of green tea, and we silently watched the light slowly fade as the sun disappeared behind the mountains. He seemed lost in intense thought, as if wearing an invisible Walkman receiving a song only he could hear. "Thank you," he finally said, and I walked him to the door.

October

And then there is the sense that *in spite of Everything*—I suppose this is the Ultimate Mystical conviction—in spite of Pain, in spite of Death, in spite of Horror, the universe is in some way All Right, capital A, capital R. . . .

—Aldous Huxley

There is no reaching the Self. If Self were to be reached, it would mean that the Self is not here and now but that it is yet to be obtained. What is got afresh will also be lost. So it will be impermanent. What is not permanent is not worth striving for. So I say that the Self is not reached. You *are* the Self; you are already That.

—Sri Ramana Maharshi

Wednesday, October 1

I went to have dinner with Marci, stopping to pick her up at the developmental disabilities apartment where she works. One of the residents, Richard, is what, in a less sensitive time, would be called "retarded." But by whatever name, Richard is, nonetheless, awfully perceptive. He also has a big crush on Marci, so when we started dating, he wanted to know who this interloper was. Marci told him I was a writer, and showed him a few of my books. So today when I arrive, Richard is conspicuously walking around with a copy of *Transformations of Consciousness*.

"I can understand this book, you know. I read at a fourth-grade level."

505

Thursday, October 2

After twenty-five years of meditating in the lotus posture, I now often meditate in the yogic "corpse pose," which is on your back, feet together, arms slightly out at your sides, which is how I also sleep. So when I wake up and start meditation, there is often no movement at all. "But I can tell when you start to meditate," Marci said this morning. "How's that?" "Your breathing changes, becoming very regular but very subtle, sometimes stopping. And when you meditate all night long"—she means, when constant consciousness is present through all three states—"you breathe exactly like that all night long. I like it; it beats snoring."

Started writing the essay for Anselm's art book. It's called "To See a World—Art and the I of the Artist." Speaking of the corpse pose, in some of Anselm's recent paintings, there is a man depicted in the foreground, lying immobile on his back, in exactly the corpse pose—"corpse," because it represents the death of the ego, the death of the separate-self sense, and thus an opening to the transpersonal and superconscious. Art of the superconscious—there is the art of the future.

Friday, October 3

DEVELOPMENT AND REGRESSION
[Phone Conversation with a Study Group]

QUESTION: Since you are presenting a type of integral holism, why do you criticize so many other views, since everything is part of the whole. Shouldn't everything be accepted? Wouldn't a real holism embrace everything instead of criticizing so much of it?

KW: Well, that's exactly the central question for any type of holism, isn't it? You can read in the "new-paradigm" books—books on Gaia, systems theory, and ecology—that "everything is connected to everything else" and that "we are all equally inseparable parts of the web of life." So if *everything* is equally part of the inseparable whole, does that mean that we are to embrace the views of the Nazis? Aren't they equally part of the whole? Are we to make the Ku Klux Klan part of our inseparable whole? Are we to give equal weight to Mother Teresa and Jack the Ripper? I'm not talking about the absolute view, where all things in their suchness are perfect manifestations of Emptiness and all things are equally Divine; I'm talking about the relative, finite, manifest world, where this holism and web of life are supposed to apply. You see the problem?

QUESTION: Not exactly. In the manifest world, if everything is equally part of the whole, why shouldn't we embrace everything?

KW: Everything is not equally part of the whole. Everything is part of a holarchy, and a holarchy is a *ranking* of degrees of wholeness—some things are *more whole* than others. Atoms are contained in molecules, which are contained in cells, which are contained in organisms. The wholeness of an atom is an amazing thing, but a molecule contains *all* of that wholeness *plus* its own more complex wholeness. And that molecule's wholeness, extraordinary as it is, is completely contained in the wholeness of a living cell. And so on up the Great Holarchy or Great Nest of manifest existence. Each senior level has more wholeness—is *higher*—precisely because it *transcends* but *includes* its juniors.

And notice, it is not vice versa. Molecules contain atoms, but atoms do *not* contain molecules. Each senior level embraces and includes its junior, *but not vice versa*—there is a *ranking* of wholeness here—and this ranking is *intrinsic* in the nature of holism. The only way you can get a holism is via a holarchy—otherwise you have heaps, not wholes.

QUESTION: So how do the Nazis and KKK fit in here?

KW: The Nazis and the KKK are indeed part of the holarchy of human development, but they are a particularly pathological version of a rather low level in it. Of course they are "part of everything," but they occupy a very low-level slot in that hierarchical "everything," and as such, they sabotage higher and deeper moral responses to the Kosmos.

QUESTION: But if they are so bad, why do they even exist? What possible part do they play in any sort of holarchy?

KW: Oh, *everybody* goes through some version of these lower and early stages—they are, so to speak, the atoms and molecules of moral development, upon which the higher cells and organisms are built. The Nazis and the KKK have a bad case of arrested development. They are at a lower level of wholeness. In the overall *moral holarchy* or moral sequence of growth—which moves from preconventional and egocentric, to conventional and ethnocentric, to postconventional and world-centric, to post-postconventional and spiritual—the KKK and the Nazis have a twisted case of arrested development at the *ethnocentric* stage: their race, their group, their religion, their extended tribe is superior to all others, who deserve slaughter. The KKK and the Nazis are part of the Web of Life, all right, but a part we must *resist*, precisely because it is a *lower order* of wholeness, and therefore *less* moral.

QUESTION: So a true holism is actually very critical.

KW: Yes, that's right. And that's the important point. A true holism is based on holarchy—a ranking of *increasing* wholeness, inclusion, embrace, and care. A true holism involves levels of love, as it were, and in both directions: Eros reaching up and Agape reaching down. But a love that is, therefore, a "tough love," a true compassion, not an idiot compassion that "avoids ranking." In other words, a true holism contains an explicit *critical theory*.

QUESTION: That's why you're worried about regression in this country.

KW: Yes. We are seeing various trends that want to surrender the postconventional, worldcentric, liberal gains of the Enlightenment and regress to sociocentric and ethnocentric revivals, identity politics, racial essentialism, gender essentialism, blood and soil volkish movements, ecofascism, tribal glorification, and the politics of self-pity. (Not to mention even further regression to egocentric and narcissistic me-ism!) We are seeing, in short, a type of retribalization occurring not only around the world, where nations are disintegrating along racial/tribal lines, but also, most ominously, in this country, where we see back-to-the-noble-savage, back-to-nature, back-to-tribal revivals, all of which are bolstered by a flatland holism—"we're all equally inseparable parts of the great web"—which is not really holism but heapism. It encourages just this type of retribalization and fragmentation, precisely because it refuses to judge degrees of depth, since "everything is equally part of the whole."

This regressive disintegration is also, alas, rampant in academia—it is behind much of postmodernism and the extreme diversity and multicultural movements, where every cultural wiggle is included as part of the "rich diversity" of existence. Well, if we really want diversity, then by all means let us include the Nazis. If we want true multiculturalism, then we must include the KKK.

QUESTION: That's a failure to engage in judgment based on degrees of depth.

KW: Yes, that's right. Compassionate judgment is based on degrees of depth.

QUESTION: Is there anything beneficial in the diversity and multicultural movements?

KW: Oh, definitely. Those liberal movements are *trying* to express a non-ethnocentric or worldcentric stance, which is *universal pluralism*. The problem is that, in their understandable zeal, they emphasize the pluralism and forget the universal. But it is only from a postconventional, universal, worldcentric stance that we *can* embrace true pluralism and *reject* lesser stances, such as Nazism. And that means, if we really want to be genuinely *pluralistic*, we must support and encourage moral *development* as it moves from egocentric to ethnocentric to worldcentric. We must *not* sit back and say, Gee, all views are equally okay because we're celebrating rich diversity.

To the extent liberalism/postmodernism embraces that mindless diversity, it shoots itself in the foot. It undermines, even destroys, its own foundations. Liberalism is a very high, postconventional developmental stance which then turns around and says, Gosh, all stances are to be equally cherished, which completely eats away its own basis.

In other words, liberalism is now encouraging those positions which will destroy liberalism. Precisely because it refuses to make the moral judgment that not all stances are equal, that worldcentric is *better* than both ethnocentric and egocentric, then it ends up, by default, encouraging retribalization, regression to lesser stances, and a feeding frenzy of hyper-individual egocentric rights, all of which are tearing liberalism apart—and ripping the fabric of this society into almost unrecognizable shreds.

So that's the inherent contradiction—and self-destroying stance—of extreme liberalism and postmodernism. I'm obviously sympathetic with many of their goals—particularly universal pluralism—but I'm criticizing the self-defeating ways they are going at it.

QUESTION: So they need to embrace a real holarchy, which is a moral ranking that leads to universal pluralism, but it would be critical of lower moral stances.

KW: Yes. Everybody talks about holism, about the web of life, about being *more inclusive*, about compassion and embrace. But as soon as you really carry it through—and not just give some nebulous notion of the "web of life" and "equal diversity"—you will find that the real world, in all four quadrants, is holarchical (a nested hierarchy)—which is a *ranking* of value and depth and wholeness—and therefore *critical* in the best sense. A new critical theory is the call of a true holism.

STUDENT: Is that why you are sometimes polemical?

KW: No, you can be critical without being polemical. I am occasionally polemical for other reasons.

STUDENT: What?

KW: Well, too often in this field we have a type of sanctimonious stance—you know, we have the new paradigm that will transform the world, or a new spirituality that will save the planet, and so on. You all know how smug and self-righteous this can get. We see it all the time, yes? Well, polemic is an old and honorable way to deflate some of the pomposity, and to really rattle the cage. So I think a good dose of polemic every now and then is sorely needed, especially in this field, which, bless its heart, takes itself altogether too seriously.

Sunday, October 5—Denver

It's 86 degrees today, a record high for this time of year, so after a long morning's work, Marci and I head out to Denver to wander the air-conditioned malls. I feel slightly disconnected from it all. There is such a sharp difference between Witnessing and depersonalization. In the former you are nonattached; in the latter, detached. In the former, you have a ground of equanimity from which you engage passionately in everything that arises; in the latter, you are numb, unable to feel passion for anything. In the former, you see everything with intense clarity and bright luminosity; in the latter, it's like you are looking at the world through the wrong end of a telescope. I have an unusual dose of the latter, the latter, and the latter.

But enter the emptiness, and find Emptiness.

Monday, October 6—Boulder

His name is John; he is staying in one of the care facilities for which Marci does marketing and management. John is dying of AIDS, as did his wife recently. Over his bed—it is a small bed, in a small room, with four other small beds, each with nothing but a thin curtain to mark the space called mine—is a picture of him and his wife, the way they once were, healthy and strong, smiling and happy, both very handsome people. This photograph is all John has left of the life he once knew. The staff have given him perhaps two weeks to live, and John knows it.

"You said I would like this place, and I hate it," he says to Marci, who had arranged for him to be admitted to this facility. The sad fact is, this is by far the best of the options that John has available to him, and he's fortunate Marci got him in. But in times like this, it's hard to remember.

"I hate it! I hate it! I hate it! Look at me!" John pulls up his gown, and there are sticks where his legs used to be, white bones wrapped in parchment paper. "You lied to me, you lied to me. I'm dying, I only have a few weeks left, and look at me. I hate this place! And I hate the food, I especially hate the food. I don't want to die like this."

"John, listen to me. What kind of food do you like?"

And John begins a list of food that he says he wants, but is in fact a list of foods he used to want. He eats nothing now, no matter what.

"And especially I love Mexican burritos and a Coke."

Marci got up early this morning, and got him a burrito and Coke, and put it beside his bed, in his tiny little room, where he is dying.

Tuesday, October 7

Thinking of John, and it dawns on me, yet again, that all spiritual practice is a rehearsal—and at its best, an enactment—of death. As the mystics put it, "If you die before you die, then when you die, you won't die." In other words, if *right now* you die to the separate-self sense, and discover instead your real Self which is the entire Kosmos at large, then the death of this particular bodymind is but a leaf falling from the eternal tree that you are.

Meditation is to practice that death right now, and right now, and right now, by resting in the timeless Witness and dis-identifying with the finite, objective, mortal self that can be seen as an object. In the empty Witness, in the great Unborn, there is no death—not because you live forever in time—you will not—but because you discover the timelessness of this eternal moment, which never enters the stream of time in the first place. When you are resting in the great Unborn, standing free as the empty Witness, death changes nothing essential.

Still, every death is so very sad in its own way.

Wednesday, October 8—Denver

Dinner with Leo and our good friends Paul and Cel Gerstenberger at Morton's in the LoDo. Leo is an awfully nice person, very bright and gentle. Motorola is the only company to get into China without being forced to have the communist government as a partner; there are now 67,000 Motorola workers in China. Leo was just recently in Beijing, and Paul and Cel are headed over there on business for the last three weeks in November, so they traded travel tips.

Business obviously involves the production and selling of goods and services. But these Right-Hand products are originally created by Left-Hand consciousness, and so, as Leo pointed out, much of his job involves the *interior development* of managers—that's what originally put him on to my work. And this is why the three hot areas for the application of consciousness studies are education, political theory, and business.

It was an early evening, since Leo had to fly out at 8 P.M. Paul and Cel returned home, and Marci and I—we had earlier checked in at the Brown Palace—sat in the Roosevelt Room, had a martini, and disappeared in a romantic mist.

Friday, October 10—Boulder

Sam is back from France, where he taught meditation for a month, and Roger just left for a month's meditation retreat. As Frances's son, Bob, puts it, "In order to advance, Roger retreats."

Sunday, October 12

Marilyn Schlitz is in Boulder and came by for dinner with Marci and me, and the three of us just hung out. Marilyn is as bright as they come—she's on various directorial boards at Harvard, Stanford, National Institutes of Health, Arizona Center for Consciousness Studies, Esalen, IONS. . . . And most of all, she's a real sweetie. She's married to Keith Thompson; I like both of them a lot. Keith and I go back a long way. A protégé of Mike Murphy, Keith has written or edited several books; he has a beautiful writing style, very literate and elegant (which is extremely rare in this field, for some reason). Keith is now an editor at the Institute of Noetic Sciences (IONS), where Marilyn is director of research.

Marilyn is particularly interested, at this point, in researching the wisdom of indigenous cultures, but without the Romanticism that marks too much of that research (as she says, referring to one tribe, "Let's not forget these people are head-hunters"). This even-handed approach—acknowledging both wisdom and wretchedness—is one I wholeheartedly support.

Tuesday, October 14

Ever since the publication of *Sex, Ecology, Spirituality*—and particularly *A Brief History of Everything*—there has been increasing interest in my work in very conventional and orthodox areas, particularly politics, business, and education. The reasons for this are very interesting, I think.

The earlier phases of my work (what I described, in *The Eye of Spirit*, as phase-1, phase-2, and phase-3) involve indelibly transpersonal and spiritual realms. If you want to use these models, you pretty much need to include the higher and transcendental levels. This severely limits the use of these models in the real world because few people are actually interested in, or evolved to, those higher levels. Few were the applications to business and education.

But with phase-4 (the four quadrants, each with a dozen or so levels), there is an almost instant applicability to most endeavors, because the four quadrants cover a multitude of ordinary events. You do not have to include, or even believe in, the higher and transpersonal levels of each quadrant in order to find the quadrants themselves useful. And the quadrants *are* useful precisely because they give a simple, easily understood way to fight the flatland reductionism so prevalent in the modern and postmodern world. Since unmitigated reductionism is simply *false*, this reductionism will adversely affect or even cripple your efforts in any and all fields, from business to politics to education—and thus the four quadrants give you an immediate way to avoid this crippling. And *that* will pay off in everything from more responsible politics to more efficient education to increased profits.

I believe that is why this model is now being applied in so many different areas, theoretical as well as practical. A few examples:

Bill Godfrey, head of Greenhills School (levels 6–12) in Ann Arbor, Michigan, sent a long summary of "the application of the quadrant theory to our curriculum design process as well as our entire school model." It's a very impressive document, mapping out the overall goals and means of education using the four quadrants (and their developmental levels); these are now being implemented at Greenhills. Similarly, Ed McManis writes that the Denver Academy, a school for kids with learning disabilities, "has already implemented many of these ideas in our curriculum." I've received several dozen similar letters from educational facilities around the world.

Jeb Bush's people in Florida called and wanted to discuss these ideas in politics—an example from the conservative side—and Michael Lerner and his Politics of Meaning organization find them useful from the liberal (or postliberal) side, something that simply did not—and could not—happen when I was focusing mostly on "the further reaches of human nature." The four quadrants operate with the lower and middle reaches as well—which is where most of the action is in the real world.

Dr. Kenneth Cox, of NASA, sent "A Futurist Perspective for Space," which uses this model to outline future directions for NASA and space research. The report outlines the twenty tenets, the nature of holons, their four characteristics, etc., and concludes "Earth/Space is a holon and evolutionary patterns can be developed by investigating its whole/parts characteristics." I'd love to see NASA try to get funding from Congress by explaining the nature of holons. "Sorry, Colonel, but we're due back on planet earth."

Ron Cacioppe, business expert from Australia, is writing a text on business management using these ideas, and I am increasingly getting mail from business and organizational people (such as Leo Burke at Motorola). Daryl Paulson, founder of BioScience Laboratories, has written a paper on business management that is particularly striking. Daryl points out that there are four major theories of business management—Theory X (individual behavior), Theory Y (individual understanding), Systems Management (organization structure and function), and Cultural Management (management of shared values). These are, of course, precisely the four quadrants. This understanding, which Daryl develops and documents at length, allows us not only to integrate these four important management styles, but also plug business into a much larger "big picture" that gives meaning and substance to the endeavor itself.

This understanding is not merely theoretical or pie-in-the-sky; it has very specific applications. Daryl published "Developing Effective Topical Antimicrobials" (i.e., antibacterial soap), which opens: "Because the goal is to introduce products into the market which will be successful, manufacturers must develop a product from a multidimensional perspective." Good point. "The holonic quadrant model states that at least four perspectives should be addressed: social, cultural, personal subjective, and personal objective. Let us look at the quadrant model in greater detail." He then proceeds to outline why and how the four quadrants offer a much better grasp of market requirements and successful market placement. (My work used to reach those interested in satori; now it reaches those interested in soap.)

Susan Campbell, who worked extensively with John Robbins (*Diet for a New America*), is interested in diet and overall well-being, especially for kids. She wrote *The Healthy School Lunch*, a critically acclaimed book on just that, and is now working on her second book, which uses the four quadrants to design a national nutrition program.

Dr. Thom Gehring (an authority in prison education) and his wife, Carolyn Eggleston, are "writing a book on the history of correctional education (prison education, education for inmates), describing the progress made in our field in each quadrant, by historical period." Thom makes a very interesting point: "I take the 'all quadrants, all levels' advice seriously, but I am currently unable to make the leap to the 'all levels' part of that advice in my presentation. I am therefore seeking to move from a beginner's 'all quadrant' understanding to a more mature 'all level' understanding. Does this strategy seem reasonable and workable?" Indeed it does, and that is rather my point: it is so much easier to start with the four quadrants, since they apply to virtually all endeavors, and *then* move to an "all-level" orientation that includes the higher, transpersonal realms.

Anyway, I've received several hundred examples now of what I take to be an increasingly widespread revolt against flatland reductionism. I'm glad my work has been a catalyst for some of this, but the deeper interest is in integrative and holistic approaches in general, which is very encouraging.

Wednesday, October 15

DEVELOPMENT AND REGRESSION
[Phone Conference, Continued]

QUESTION: You often say that each stage is adequate, but the next stage is more adequate. What does that mean?

KW: Well, you see, if you are going to have a genuinely *holistic* view, you have to find some way to fit *all* views into the holistic picture, but not all views are, or can be, *equally* significant. So you have to figure out some way to rank the importance of views, or else, as we were saying, you have to put Mother Teresa and Jack the Ripper on equal footing, and you have to invite Nazis to the multicultural banquet, since supposedly they are "all inseparable parts of the richly interwoven web." That's a real problem, yes?

This is where the idea of *development* becomes so crucial. Development supplies the key—or certainly, a key—to this extremely difficult problem. Because in virtually all types of development that we are aware of, each succeeding stage *transcends but includes* its predecessor(s), and this gives us a natural, inherent, intrinsic ranking—a ranking of wholeness and depth. We already saw the simple example of atoms to molecules to cells to organisms—each of those stages is whole, but each succeeding stage is "more whole." And this *developmental unfolding* of increasing wholeness and depth gives us a crucial key for understanding how *all* views can fit into the big picture, but some views are *better* than others because they have more depth.

QUESTION: Could you give some examples in human development?

KW: Let's use moral development, since we are already talking about that. Kohlberg's moral stages have now been tested in over forty different cultures—including Third World—and no major exceptions to his scheme have been found. Carol Gilligan suggested that women move through Kohlberg's stages "in a different voice" (namely, relationally rather than agentically), but she did *not* contest the three major stages themselves, which move from *preconventional* (what I want is what is right—egocentric) to *conventional* (what the group wants is right—sociocentric) to *postconventional* (what is right for all people, regardless of race, sex, or creed—worldcentric). So those are good examples to use.

The point is, we all start out at the preconventional stages, then develop the conventional, and then, with luck, the postconventional. None of those stages can be skipped or bypassed. Each succeeding stage builds upon certain features gained in the previous stage, then adds its own unique and emergent elements—just as, for example, you must have letters before you can have words, and words before sentences, and sentences before paragraphs. Nobody has ever gone from letters to sentences and skipped words.

This means that the lower stages are not simply wrong, or stupid, or misguided. The preconventional stages are the *most moral* you *can* be at those early stages. You can't yet take the role of other, you can't participate in mutual understanding, your worldview is magical and narcissistic, and so of course your moral stance is egocentric and preconventional. But because that is the *best* you can possibly be under those circumstances, those early moral stages are *adequate* enough; they are phase-specific and phase-appropriate.

But with the emergence of conventional morality, you learn to take the role of other, you can put yourself in another person's shoes, and so of course your moral response *expands* and *deepens* from *me* to *we*. This is a *more adequate* moral response, because it takes others into account. Of course, your moral response is then *trapped* in the view of the group—this stage is also called *conformist*—but again, the point is, you have no choice at this stage. This is the *best* that you can do with the limited equipment you have at that point. So it is also phase-specific, phase-appropriate, phase-adequate.

With the emergence of postconventional morality, you attempt to decide what is good and right, not just for my group or my tribe or my religion, but for all peoples, regardless of creed or sex or color. Your moral response once again *expands* and *deepens* to encompass more people—it is a *greater wholeness*—and therefore, *even more adequate*. And most of you know that, in my system, this is the gateway to a spiritual morality, which includes all sentient beings as such.

QUESTION: So that's adequate, more adequate, even more adequate. . . .

KW: Yes, that's right. Each stage is adequate, each succeeding stage is more adequate. And that's important because, again, it lets us fit *all* views into the big picture, but *without* giving all views equal weight.

QUESTION: Is the same thing true with worldviews?

KW: Oh, I think so, definitely. As most of you know, I trace several developmental worldviews, which move from archaic to magic to mythic to rational to existential to psychic to subtle to causal to nondual. Each of those views is important and adequate; each succeeding view is more important and more adequate.

The difficulty comes with *regression*, because then you are moving back to a view that was once phase-appropriate but is now outmoded. The magical worldview, for example, is not a sickness or a disease; it is the phase-appropriate and completely adequate worldview of the four-year-old. Age four is not a disease. Moreover, even for adults, magical cognition can play an important, if subsumed, role in various situations. But if you are an adult in a rational-pluralistic culture, and you *regress* to nothing but egocentric magic, then you have a real problem, you have an "emotional illness." In order to regress, several higher and complex structures have to come unglued, and this is catastrophic and very painful. The tectonic plates of your psyche separate and you fall through the cracks.

QUESTION: One last question, if you don't mind. You said that liberalism is based on a high developmental achievement, namely, the worldcentric stance of universal pluralism.

KW: Yes.

QUESTION: How can liberalism encourage that stance without imposing its beliefs on others?

KW: Are you in college?

QUESTION: Yes.

KW: Political theory by any chance?

QUESTION: Yes.

KW: I thought as much, because you just hit on *the* central problem for liberalism. Liberalism is dedicated to the proposition that *the State cannot impose any notion of the Good life on its citizens.* Individuals should be free to choose their own religion, their own beliefs, and their own paths to happiness (as long as they don't harm others or infringe on their rights). The liberal State, in other words, has its moral foundations in postconventional, universal pluralism, and these worldcentric principles are embedded in its laws and institutions so as to prevent egocentric and ethnocentric responses from taking over.

But in democracies, laws are ultimately made and supported by the people, and this means that the liberal State *depends for its existence* on at least a good portion of its population *developing to the postconventional level.* It is only *from* the postconventional level that "rich diversity" can be tolerated, and yet if you *only* encourage rich diversity, you will undermine the need to develop to the postconventional level in the first place (because every response, including egocentric and ethnocentric, is to be "equally cherished," thus removing social incentives to moral growth).

So there's the dilemma: how can the State encourage people to develop to a postconventional stance of universal pluralism, without *imposing* this on people? If liberalism doesn't figure out a way to do this, liberalism and true multiculturalism will die.

QUESTION: That's my question.

KW: Well, here is one short response. It is true that individuals have the right to "life, liberty, and the pursuit of happiness," but the State has certain rights, too. And one of those rights is the right to demand of its citizens certain basic skills necessary for the cohesion and survival of the society. This is why we have long recognized that the State has the right to wage war, to draft people to fight war, to demand that children receive vaccinations against contagious diseases, and—especially important here—the State has the right to demand compulsory education up to a certain level of competence (barring disabilities).

Now traditionally, you see, a *liberal education* was exactly how the liberal State in effect sneaked in the demand to grow, and imposed on its citizens the demand to develop. Citizens *must* complete a certain level of education. And the hope was, in being exposed to a liberal education, the conditions would be set for the growth of a liberal morality—which is to say, a postconventional, worldcentric, universal pluralism—by whatever name.

I happen to think that is a fine idea. Since you cannot *force* plants or people to grow, all you can really do is *set the conditions* that best allow the growth to occur (like water the plant). The State cannot demand the growth, but it can demand the conditions, and this it has traditionally done in the widely accepted demand for compulsory education.

QUESTION: So that puts a large part of the burden on the educational process.

KW: Definitely. Which is why the state of education in this country today is rather disturbing. Education today is often dominated by many extreme postmodern agendas—and therefore it often has some frighteningly regressive tendencies. On the one hand, the diversity and multicultural movements have enormously helped to ensure that universal pluralism is *genuinely* pluralistic by expanding the canon to include many previously marginalized groups. This is simply the culmination of the liberal doctrine of equal access for all, regardless of sex, color, creed—the culmination of worldcentric or universal pluralism—and in that regard I am an ardent fan of those postmodern movements, particularly in education.

But, as we were saying, they have, in their zeal, often gone to self-contradictory and self-defeating extremes. The whole point of a liberal/multicultural education is to provide certain basic skills and conditions within which moral development might, of its own accord, grow from egocentric to ethnocentric/sociocentric to worldcentric/pluralistic. But the New Left agenda has taken that to extremes and totally sabotaged its own higher goals. Middle and higher education in this country now actually *encourages* ethnocentric identity politics, gender essentialism, racial identity, and the politics of self-pity—all part of "rich diversity." History is being taught as self-esteem therapy: not what happened where and when, but what immoral slugs they all were compared to you. Using the values of the liberal Enlightenment, you condemn all previous history, including the liberal Enlightenment.

Even worse, it's not just that education often encourages regression from worldcentric to ethnocentric, it has astonishingly managed, on occasion, to encourage even further regression from ethnocentric to egocentric. Get rid of those nasty grades and give everybody a gold star. There is no better or worse in others, which also means, there is no better or worse in yourself—development is completely undercut. This prepares the child for the future the same way the beggars in India used to prepare their children for a job: by breaking their legs, they gave them a reason and a means to beg.

So once again, liberalism—this time in education—is pursuing self-defeating goals. By emphasizing this flatland notion—this "equal diversity"—and by refusing to make judgments based on degrees of depth, liberal education is encouraging those trends which will destroy liberal education.

QUESTION: Is it your sense that education will correct itself?

KW: Well, the amazing thing about growth and evolution is that there is an Eros to the Kosmos, an intrinsic push to unfold higher and deeper wholes. The regressive trends—which I believe are driven by Thanatos, a type of death wish—sooner or later run into their own inherent painfulness. Across this country, in the last few years, we have seen a backlash, in the good sense, against these regressive agendas, and a call for some enforceable education standards. So, on balance, I'm cautiously optimistic.

All we're really talking about here is the traditional liberal education as an *unfolding of one's deepest and highest potentials*. And that means, in addition to self-esteem and accepting yourself the way you are now, you *also* need to meet yourself with real challenges and real demands— with real wisdom and real compassion—and therefore vow to grow, develop, and evolve into your own highest Estate. But we are not going to do that in lower, middle, or higher education if we meet ourselves with idiot compassion instead of real compassion.

Friday, October 17

Mike [Murphy] is in the middle of a book tour for *The Kingdom of Shivas Irons*, which took him through Denver and Boulder, and he made arrangements to stop by. Mike's book *The Life We Are Given* (coauthored with his friend George Leonard) outlines an excellent version of an integral transformative practice (ITP), and Mike reports that there are now around forty ITP groups that have sprung up around the country, which is good news indeed. There are now the same number of kw study groups around the country, so we discussed ways of perhaps getting them together. When Mike left, Marci said, "He sparkles. What exactly does 'endearing' mean?" "Adorably lovable." "Mike is adorably lovable."

Tony is, at this very moment, flying to Italy, because some Italian foundation or other has selected *What Really Matters* for some sort of big Italian award. It's a huge media event; Tony will give a speech (he wrote a quite impressive twelve-page statement of an integral approach to health and well-being, an approach that most of the time he actually follows) and get his picture in all the papers. Then he will spend a week in Italy, eating and drinking and—at least for this week—not practicing everything in his speech.

Tuesday, October 21

TO SEE A WORLD:
ART AND THE I OF THE BEHOLDER

It is not the object expressed, but the depth of the subject expressing it, that most defines art. And this shifts art and art criticism from irony to authenticity—a rather unnerving move, at least to today's eyes. Can art and art criticism survive the loss of irony, the loss of inauthenticity, as its central source? And if today's art abandons sardonic surfaces, where will it finally reside?

· · ·

We do not live in a pregiven world. One of the more remarkable tenets of the postmodern revolution in philosophy, psychology, and sociology is that *different worldviews exist*—different ways of categorizing, presenting, representing, and organizing our experiences. There is not a single, monolithic world with a single, privileged representation, but rather multiple worlds with pluralistic interpretations. Moreover, these worldviews often—indeed, almost always—change from epoch to epoch, and from culture to culture.

This insight need not be taken to extremes—there are plenty of common features in our various interpretations to prevent the world from falling apart. Indeed, scholars have discovered that there are at least some (and often many) universals in languages, in affects, in cognitive structures, and in color perception, to name a few. But these universal ingredients are woven together and organized in a rich variety of ways, resulting in a tapestry of multiple worldviews.

Although there are, in theory, an almost infinite number of worldviews, in the course of human history on this planet, there seem to be about a dozen that have had, or are still having, a widespread and significant influence. Investigated by scholars such as Jean Gebser, Gerald Heard, Jürgen Habermas, Michel Foucault, Robert Bellah, Peter Berger, and others, these major worldviews include: sensorimotor, archaic, magic, mythic, mental, existential, psychic, subtle, causal, and nondual. (The exact meaning of those terms will become more obvious as we proceed.)

It is not a matter of which of these worldviews is right and which is wrong; they are all adequate for their time and place. It is more a matter of simply cataloging, as carefully as possible, the very general characteristics that define each worldview, and "bracketing" (or setting aside), for the moment, whether or not they are "true"—we simply describe all of them as if they were true.

The *magic-animistic* worldview, for example, is marked by a partial overlap of subject and object, so that "inanimate objects" like rocks and rivers are directly felt to be alive or even to possess souls or subjective spirits. The *mythic* worldview is marked by a plethora of gods and goddesses, not as abstract entities but as deeply felt powers, each having a rather direct hand in the affairs of earthly men and women. The *mental* worldview—of which the "rational worldview" is the best known subset—is marked by a belief that the subjective realm is fundamentally set apart from the objective realm of nature, and how to relate these two realms becomes one of the most pressing problems in this worldview. The *existential* worldview possesses an understanding that multiple perspectives are built into the universe, so that not only are there no privileged perspectives, individuals must carve for themselves some sort of meaning from that frightening multitude of possibilities. The *subtle* worldview is marked by an apprehension of subtle forms and transcendental archetypes, primordial patterns of manifestation which are usually felt (and claimed) to be Divine. The *causal* worldview is marked by the direct realization of a vast unmanifest realm—variously known as emptiness, cessation, the Abyss, the Unborn, ayn, the *Ursprung*—a vast Formlessness from which all manifestation springs. And the *nondual* represents a radical union of the Formless with the entire world of Form.

Those various worldviews present a truly dizzying array of the many ways that our experiences can be organized and interpreted. Those are by no means the only worldviews, nor is the list fixed or predetermined—it is constantly unfolding with new possibilities. But without some sort of worldview, we remain lost in the blooming buzzing confusion of experience, as William James put it.

In other words, all of our individual perceptions are, to some extent, embedded in particular worldviews. Within those worldviews, we still possess abundant freedom of choice; but worldviews generally constrain what we will even consider choosing. We moderns do not, for example, often get out of bed with the thought, "Time to kill the bear." Each worldview, with its distinctive characteristics, stamps itself all over those born within it, and most individuals do not know, or even suspect, that their perceptions are occurring within the horizons of a given and rather specific worldview. Each worldview, operating for the most part collectively and unconsciously, simply presents the world as if it were the case. Few question the worldview in which they find themselves, just as a fish is unaware it is wet.

Nonetheless—and here the story takes a decidedly fascinating turn—research in both individual psychology and cross-cultural anthropology demonstrates rather convincingly that, under various circumstances, individuals have available to them *the entire spectrum of worldviews.* The human mind, it appears, comes with all of these worldviews—archaic to magic to mythic to mental to subtle to causal—as potentials in its own makeup, ready to emerge when various factors conspire to allow them to do so, rather like a seed awaiting water, soil, and sun to unfold.

So, even though certain epochs were especially marked by a particular worldview—foraging, by magic; agrarian, by mythic; and industrial, by mental-rational, for example—nonetheless, all of these major modes of interpreting our experience seem to be potentials of the human organism, and any of them can be brought forth in any individual under the right circumstances. To the question, "Which worldviews are available to us now?," the answer appears to be, "All of them."

Still, at any given time, and in any given culture, most adults tend to inhabit the landscape of one particular worldview. The reason is simple enough: each worldview is, indeed, a person's world. To lose that world is to experience a type of death-seizure. To surrender a worldview is a psychological earthquake somewhere around 7.0 on the internal Richter scale, and most people avoid this at all costs.

But sometimes, under exceptional circumstances . . . or in exceptional artists . . . higher or deeper worldviews break through the crust of our ordinary perceptions, and the world is somehow never quite the same again.

. . .

Artists express worldviews. Paleolithic artists, for example, painted the magical worldspace—objects overlapping each other, little perspectivism, animistic symbols, few constraints of space and time, wholes interchangeable with their parts. Medieval artists painted the mythic worldspace—an entire pantheon of angels, archangels, a God, a Son of that God, the Mother of that God, Moses parting the Red Sea—the themes were the endless possibilities of the mythic worldspace, all depicted, not as symbols, but as realities (precisely because, as we saw, all worldviews present themselves as simply true). With the rise of the very general movement of Modernity in the West—riding as it did on the mental worldview, with its separation of subjective mind from objective nature—we see a gradual replacement of mythic themes with themes dominated by nature, by realism, by impressionism, by subjective expressionism, and by abstract expressionism. And with the general rise of Postmodernism, we see those trends carried even further into the existential worldspace, where multiple perspectives, at first a source of endless creativity, soon became a paralyzing nightmare of infinite jest, met with infinite irony.

The existential worldview is called "integral-aperspectival" by Gebser—"aperspectival" because it presents multiple perspectives, none of which are privileged; and "integral" because nonetheless some sort of unity, coherence, or meaning has to be fashioned in the midst of multiplicity. In the previous worldview—the mental-rational, which Gebser also called "perspectival"—the single, rational subject tended to take up a single, fixed interpretation of the world, and this was evidenced in everything from science (Newton) to philosophy (Descartes) to portraiture (Van Eyck) to perspectivism (starting with Renaissance painting, especially Brunelleschi, Alberti, Donatello, Leonardo, Giotto). But with the shift to integral-aperspectival, the subject itself becomes part of the objective scene—the camera becomes part of the movie, the author's stream of thought becomes part of the novel, the painter's own operations show up conspicuously on the canvas. Multiple perspectives draw the subject into the world of objects, making it one object among many others, all lost in a dizzying regress of self-reflexivity, from which there is no escape.

Every worldview has its pathological expressions. The rational worldview's most notorious is "Cartesian dualism"—subject split from object, mind divorced from nature—a dualism against which, it seems, every thinking person of the last three hundred years has vocally declared war. But the postmodern, integral-aperspectival stance is not without its own major aberration, known generally as "aperspectival madness," the insane view that no view is better than another. Starting with the noble proposition that all of the multiple perspectives are to be treated fairly and impartially ("pluralism and rich diversity"), postmodernism slides,

in its extreme forms, into the insidious notion that no perspective whatsoever is better than another, a confusion that results in complete paralysis of will, thought, and action. Madness it is indeed: it claims no view
is better than another, except its own view, which is superior in a world
where nothing is supposed to be superior at all. And worse: if no view
is better than another, then the Nazis and the KKK are on the same
moral footing as, say, art critics.

"Aperspectival madness" might fairly well describe much of the last
two decades of art, art criticism, lit crit, and cultural studies. Irony is
one of the few places you can hide in a world of aperspectival madness—
say one thing, mean another, therefore don't get caught in the embarrassment of taking a stand. (Since, allegedly, no stand is better than
another, one simply *must not commit*—sincerity is death). So skip sincerity, opt for sardonic. Don't construct, deconstruct; don't look for
depth, just hug the surfaces; avoid content, offer noise—"surfaces, surfaces, surfaces is all they ever found," as Bret Easton Ellis summarized
the scene. No wonder that David Foster Wallace, in a recent essay that
received much attention, lamented the pervasiveness of the art of
"trendy, sardonic exhaustion" and "reflexive irony," art that is "sophisticated and extremely shallow."

But if we do abandon irony and seek to make sincere statements,
where do we begin? If we do surrender surfaces and look also for the
depths, what exactly does that mean? And where are these "depths" to
be found?

Wallace suggests that, instead of "reflexive irony," art should provide
"insights and guides to value." A fine sentiment, but let us note immediately that *specific values exist only in specific worldviews*. The mythic
worldview, for example, valued duty to a rigid social hierarchy, which
few moderns find appealing. The mythic worldview also valued male
dominance and female subordination, which most enlightened moderns
regard as ignorant. All values exist in particular worldviews, and if
trendy sardonic exhaustion is actually the exhaustion of the existential
worldview, then the only possible conclusion is that we will have to look
to other worldviews altogether if we are to escape aperspectival madness
and its relentless insincerity.

· · ·

The reason that art in the postmodern, existential world has reached
something of a cul-de-sac is not that art itself is exhausted, but that the
existential worldview is. Just as rational modernity previously exhausted

its forms and gave way to aperspectival postmodernity, so now the post-modern itself is on a morbid death watch, with nothing but infinitely mirrored irony to hold its hand, casting flowers where they will not be missed. The skull of postmodernity grins on the near horizon, and in the meantime, we are between two worldviews, one slowly dying, one not yet born.

Whatever we may think about it—and volumes have been delivered—perhaps the best that can be said of the avant-garde is that it always implicitly understood itself to be riding the crest of the breaking wave of evolving worldviews. The avant-garde was the leading edge, the growing tip, of an evolving humanity. It would herald the new, an-nounce the forthcoming. It would first spot, then depict, new ways of seeing, new modes of being, new forms of cognition, new heights or depths of feeling, and in all cases, new modes of perception. It would spot, and depict, the coming worldview, while breaking decisively with the old.

The story is familiar. Jacques-Louis David's art was part of the early rise of modernity (reason and revolution) that violently broke with the remnants of the mythic, aristocratic, hierarchical, rococo past. From neoclassicism to abstract expressionism, each succeeding growing tip became in turn the conventional, accepted norm, only to see its own form challenged by the next avant-garde. Even postmodernism, with its aperspectival madness, which first attempted to deconstruct the avant-garde altogether, intimately depended upon it for something to decon-struct; thus, as Donald Kuspit points out in *The Cult of the Avant-Garde Artist*, a type of "neo-avant-garde" art inevitably dogged postmodern-ism from the start.

Like huge successive waves crashing ashore, worldviews succeed one another, and the avant-garde, at its best, were the great surfers of these waves. And now that the postmodern wave is washing on the shore of its own demise, what new waves are forthcoming? What new world-views surge from the ocean of the soul to announce a new perception? Where are we to look for the *contents* of the sincere artistic statements that will supplant irony and aperspectival madness? Standing on tiptoe, looking through the mist, can the vague outline of the face of tomor-row's art—and therefore, tomorrow's world—even be seen?

· · ·

What worldviews, from those available, might carry the contours of tomorrow's art? Of course, some aspects of the coming landscape will be entirely new and original. "Creative advance into novelty," according to Whitehead, is the basic feature of the universe. But we also know, from extensive psychological and sociological research, that certain basic features of the dozen or so major worldviews, briefly summarized above, are potentials *already* available to the human organism, and instead of starting entirely from scratch, nature usually reworks what is at hand, before adding the finishing touches of novelty.

We know the worldviews that have been tried, toiled, worked, and exhausted: archaic, magic, mythic, mental-rational (modern), and existential-aperspectival (postmodern). The postmodern, of course, will continue its major influence for decades to come, on the way to its final resting place. It is simply that artistic productions, as canaries in the cultural mine shaft, are dropping dead in alarming numbers as the rotting gas of postmodernity first starts wafting down that tunnel. So the art world, more quickly than the sturdier herd mentality, seeks out new horizons; and thus, as we earlier noted, the dead-end of today's art is really the future endgame of the postmodern worldview in general. So what other horizons are available *right now*?

Three, at least. We already named them: subtle, causal, and nondual. The phenomenologists of worldviews (those who research and describe the contours of available worldviews) describe these three worldviews as being *transrational* or *transpersonal*, and they contrast them with the earlier worldviews, some of which are *prerational* or *prepersonal* (archaic, magic, and mythic), and some of which are *rational* or *personal* (mental and existential). This gives men and women, as potentials in their own organisms, a spectrum of available worldviews, ranging from prerational to rational to transrational, from prepersonal to personal to transpersonal, from subconscious to self-conscious to superconscious. Supposing that we have exhausted the dizzying rhetorical regress of self-reflexivity, there are only two ways to go: back into subconsciousness, or forward into superconsciousness—back to the infrarational, or beyond to the suprarational.

The distinction is important, because the transrational, transpersonal worldviews are what might be called "spiritual," yet they bear little relation to the traditional religious worldviews of the magic and mythic spheres. The transrational realms have nothing to do with external gods and goddesses, and everything to do with an interior awareness that plumbs the depths of the psyche. Nothing to do with petitionary prayer and ritual, and everything to do with expanding and clarifying awareness. Nothing to do with dogma and belief, everything to do with cleansing perception. Not everlasting life for the ego, but transcending the ego altogether.

When one exhausts the personal, there is left the transpersonal. There is, right now, simply nowhere else to go.

. . .

Not just different values, but different objects, exist in different world-views. And artists can paint, depict, or express their particular perceptions of the objects in any of these realms, *depending on whether or not they are themselves alive to these realms.*

The *sensorimotor* world is familiar enough—those objects that can be seen with the senses: rocks, birds, bowls of fruit, nudes, landscapes. Artists can, and doggedly have, painted those objects, in everything from a glaringly realistic fashion to the softer tones of impressionism. The *magical* worldview is one of plastic displacement and condensation, the world of the dream, full of its own very real objects (when dreaming— when actually in that worldview—it appears absolutely real, as all worldviews do). Artists can paint those objects, as the Surrealists, among others, have demonstrated. The *mythic* worldview is full of gods and goddesses, angels and elves, disembodied souls, figures kind and cruel, helpful and malevolent. Artists can paint those objects, and, indeed, most artists around the world, from 10,000 BCE to 1500 CE, painted *nothing but* those objects. The *mental* worldview is crowded with concepts and ideas, rational perspectivism and abstract forms. Artists not only can represent those contents (conceptual art, abstract art), they can express them as well (abstract expressionism). The *existential* (aperspectival) worldview involves, among other things, the terror of the isolated subject confronting an alien world bereft of mythic consolations and rational pretensions. Artists in every medium have depicted this state of affairs, often overpoweringly (e.g., Edvard Munch, *The Scream*). But the aperspectival worldview is also, at its limits, a subject looking at itself as it tries to look at the world. Artists have attempted to depict this self-reflexive regress in a variety of ways, from deconstruction to ironic reflexivity to doubling (including the artist as part of the art)—all a dicey game, all headed eventually for self-strangulation.

Which leaves the transpersonal worldspaces with their contents, themes, and perceptions. All of these realms are, indeed, transpersonal, which simply means those realities that include, but go beyond, the personal and the individual—wider currents that sweep across the skin-encapsulated ego and touch other beings, touch the cosmos, touch spirit, touch patterns and places kept secret to those who hug the surfaces and surround themselves with themselves.

That these transpersonal worldspaces are available to us as great, potential houses does not mean they come with all the furniture. We supply that ourselves. We build, create, add, model, fashion, mold, bring forth, and compose, and here artists in every medium have traditionally led the way, avant-garde in the best and truest sense. So, on the one hand, we might look to the past for those rare occasions where a subculture plugged into the transpersonal realm and brought it forth in art and architecture, poetry and painting, crafts and compositions—the influence of Zen on Japanese aesthetics, for example. But we can look to the past only for hints, because the house of our tomorrow can only be decorated by those standing now on the threshold of that unfolding.

What will these furnishings look like? We are standing now in the open clearing, between two worlds, awaiting exactly that birth. But one thing is certain: it will come from the consciousness of men and women who stand open to the transpersonal in their own case, who bring forth, from the depths of the heart and spirit, those radiant realities that speak to us in unmistakable terms. For one thing we have seen: all of the major worldviews are available as potentials in the human bodymind. The deeper the awareness of individuals, the more worldspaces they can plumb. And that is why ultimately, profoundly, inescapably, it is the depth of the subject that provides the objects of art.

We have seen sensory objects, magic objects, mythic objects, mental objects, and aperspectival objects . . . and we have seen them all exhaust the play of their own significance. Who will show us now the objects of the transpersonal landscape? Who will open themselves to such depths that they can scale these new heights, and return to tell those of us silently waiting what they have seen? Who can stand so far aside from self and same, ego and shame, hope and fear, that the transpersonal comes pouring through them with such a force it rattles the world? Who will paint what reality looks like when the ego is subsumed, when settling into the corpse pose, it dies to its own wonderment and beholds the world anew? Who will paint that rising landscape? Who will show us that?

Saturday, October 25

Great rock groups of the last few years: Elastica, Pulp, The Crystal Method, Artificial Joy Club, the Chemical Brothers, No Doubt, Garbage, Fluffy, La Bouche, Lush, Rancid, Texas, Klover, the Muffs, Fast-backs, 60 Ft. Dolls, Belly, One Dove, Dance Hall Crashers, Superdrag, En Vogue, Republica, Blackhawk, Goo Goo Dolls, the Fugees, NIN, The Goops, Nitzer Ebb, Sleeper, Bluetones, Offspring, De La Soul, Echo Belly, Midnight Oil, the Mavericks, Līve, Wallflowers, Sleater-Kinney, London Suede.

Marc Jacobs at Louis Vuitton. It's really amazing the number of Anglo-Saxons taking over major Continental design houses—Galliano at Dior, McQueen at Givenchy, McCarthy at Chloe, Marc Jacobs at Vuitton, Rebecca Moses at Genny, and still my favorite, for women anyway, Tom Ford at Gucci.

Robert Isabell's bedroom: my idea of perfection in interior decorating, a type of Zen minimalist aesthetic, beautifully conceived.

I hear Atom Egoyan's *The Sweet Hereafter* won at Cannes, so it looks like he might finally break out.

L. A. Confidential is the best crafted film I've seen this year; it is brilliantly executed in every way by Curtis Hanson, and, so far, gets my vote for Oscar. The Japanese film *Shall We Dance?* is the most touching film I've seen in years. I'm still not sure exactly why it works, except for the deeply nuanced performance of Koji Yakusho; I sat teary-eyed for half the movie, laughed the other half. The African-American film *Love Jones* is probably the most literate film this year—a real sleeper. And Polish-born director Agnieszka Holland has turned in another exquisite effort, Henry James's *Washington Square* (in a world that denies consciousness, a novelist that dwells on it is a freakish relief. What did somebody say about the brothers William and Henry? Something like, William James is a novelist disguised as a psychologist, and Henry James is a psychologist disguised as a novelist). Agnieszka's previous *Europa, Europa* is one of my all-time favorite films, deeply engrossing on several levels, beautifully wrought (and wasn't it one of Julie Delphy's first roles? Isn't that enough?).

The hippest film? *Grosse Pointe Blank*. John and sister Joan are two of my favorites, and Minnie is adorable. New music by Joe Strummer, so no surprise to see a Clash poster on Minnie's wall. Cusack plays a professional hit man, on his way to his tenth-year high-school reunion. Alan Arkin is Cusack's therapist, who is basically scared witless that if he screws up, Cusack will whack him. His standard advice is, "Have a good time, don't kill anybody." Cusack is worried that he won't have anything in common with anybody at the reunion. "What do I say? By the way, I killed the president of Paraguay with a fork. How have you been?" The reunion goes fine, except for that body they have to dispose of in the school's basement incinerator. And so on. But what makes the film work is the sizzling intelligence of the script. Along with *Leaving Las Vegas* (the Zen of self-destruction: when drinking, just drink), *Shallow Grave, Trainspotting, Swingers, Bound, Flirting with Disaster, Kicking and Screaming,* and a few others, it's one of my favorite recent releases.

And yet, I am constantly asked, why pay any attention to any of that? Isn't this middle-brow culture somehow not really spiritual? I hear the same thing about TV all the time: really serious scholars, let alone spiritual practitioners, shouldn't find any of it interesting.

What a small God, that. All forms are one with Emptiness, no exceptions. Why avoid those particular forms, or look down on them? Are they not equally manifestations of Spirit's ultimate delight, splashing in the effervescent waters of its own exuberance? Are they not equally ripples in the waterfall of One Taste, flavors of the very Divine, playing here and there? Must I worship the God of special interests only?

Sunday, October 26

The effects that different types of music have is fascinating. Rock music, no question, hits the lower chakras (perhaps 2 to 3, sex and power.)[22] Rap music is often street survival music (chakra 1). The best of jazz (say, Charlie Parker, Miles, Wynton) is 3 to 4.

The great romantic composers (Chopin, Mahler) are quintessential 4th chakra, all heart emotion, sometimes drippingly. Haydn, Bach, Mozart, later Beethoven, push into 5th to 6th, music of the spheres, or so it seems to me. You can actually feel your attention gravitate to various bodily centers (gut, heart, head) as these musical types play.

I find whenever I am writing about, say, Plotinus, Eckhart, or Emerson, the only music that doesn't disturb thought is Mozart and the later Beethoven, some of Haydn. But when I'm doing the drudge work of bibliography, footnotes, etc., gimme rock and roll any day.

---

22. The seven chakras of kundalini yoga are the archetypal presentation of the Great Chain, consisting of seven basic levels of consciousness, each correlated with a bodily location (because, as I would put it, every Left-Hand or consciousness component has a Right-Hand or objective-bodily correlate). The seven range from the lower chakras (in the gut), to the middle chakras (in the chest/heart), to the upper chakras (crown of the head and beyond).

But the crucial point of kundalini yoga and the seven chakras is: all seven, without exception, are radiant forms of Shakti, the energy of the Goddess, in an eternal embrace with Shiva, the pure formless Witness. All Forms are one with Emptiness: Shakti and Shiva are eternally making love, bound to each other with a fierce devotion that time, turmoil, death, and destiny can never begin to touch.

In Dzogchen Buddhism, the same idea is expressed in the thangka of the Adi-Buddha (or the very highest Buddha), Samantabhadra, and his consort, Samantabhadri. Samantabhadra is depicted as a deep blue/ black figure, naked, seated in the lotus posture. On his lap, facing him, in sexual congress, is Samantabhadri, also naked, but a luminous bright white. Samantabhadra represents the Dharmakaya or radical Emptiness, which is completely formless and therefore "black" (as in deep dream- less sleep). Samantabhadri represents the Rupakaya, the entire world of Form, which is a brilliant white luminous display. Emptiness and Form, Consciousness and Matter, Spirit and the World. But the point is, they are making love; they are one in the ecstatic embrace of each other; they are united through all eternity by the unbreakable bond of a Love that is invincible. They are, to each other, One Taste.

This thangka, of Samantabhadra and Samantabhadri (Purusha and Prakriti, Shiva and Shakti, Emptiness and Form, Wisdom and Compas- sion, Eros and Agape, Ascending and Descending), is not merely a sym- bol. It is a depiction of a direct realization. When you settle back as I-I, and rest as the formless Witness, you literally are Samantabhadra, you are the great Unborn, the radically unqualifiable Godhead. You are a great black Emptiness of infinite release. And yet, in the space of that Emptiness that you are, the entire universe is arising moment to mo- ment: the clouds are floating through your awareness, those trees are arising in your awareness, those singing birds are one with you. You, as formless Witness (Samantabhadra), are one with the entire World of Form (Samantabhadri), and it is forever an erotic union. You are literally making love to the entire world as it arises. The brutal, torturous gap between subject and object has collapsed, and you and the world have entered an intimate, sexual, ecstatic union, edged with bliss, radiant in release, the thunder and lightning of only One Taste.

It has always been so.

Monday, October 27

Marci is working hard to finish her master's thesis, which is on internal management in business. Leo Burke, the head of management training at Motorola, is coming to visit us this Wednesday, and I think Marci is really looking forward to the discussion. It's nice to have a business expert around to help stop me from making an idiot of myself, though I'm not sure even Marci is up to that task.

Friday, October 31

People make two common mistakes on the way to One Taste. The first occurs in contacting the Witness, the second occurs in moving from the Witness to One Taste itself.

The first mistake: In trying to contact the Witness (or I-I), people imagine that they will *see something*. But you don't see anything, you simply rest as the Witness of all that arises—you are the pure and empty Seer, *not anything that can be seen*. Attempting to see the Seer as a special light, a great bliss, a sudden vision—those are all *objects*, they are not the Witness that you are. Eventually, of course, with One Taste, you will be *everything* that you see, but you cannot *start* trying to do that—trying to see the Truth—because that is what blocks it. You have to start with "neti, neti": I am not this, I am not that.

So the first mistake is that people sabotage the Witness by trying to make it an object that can be grasped, whereas it is simply the Seer of all objects that arise, and it is "felt" only as a great background sense of Freedom and Release *from* all objects.

Resting in that Freedom and Emptiness—and impartially witnessing all that arises—you will notice that the *separate-self* (or ego) simply arises in consciousness *like everything else*. You can actually *feel* the self-contraction, just like you can feel your legs, or feel a table, or feel a rock, or feel your feet. The self-contraction is a feeling of interior tension, often localized behind the eyes, and anchored in a slight muscle tension throughout the bodymind. It is an effort and a sensation of contracting in the face of the world. It is a subtle whole-body tension. Simply notice this tension.

Once people have become comfortable resting as the empty Witness, and once they notice the tension that is the self-contraction, they imagine that to finally move from the Witness to One Taste, they have to get rid of the self-contraction (or get rid of the ego). Just that is the second mistake, because it actually locks the self-contraction firmly into place.

We assume that the self-contraction hides or obstructs Spirit, whereas in fact it is simply a radiant manifestation of Spirit itself, like absolutely every other Form in the universe. All Forms are not other than Emptiness, including the form of the ego. Moreover, the only thing that *wants* to get rid of the ego is the ego. Spirit loves everything that arises, just as it is. The Witness loves everything that arises, just as it is. The Witness loves the ego, because the Witness is the impartial *mirror-mind* that equally reflects and perfectly embraces *everything* that arises.

But the ego, convinced that it can become even more entrenched, decides to play the game of getting rid of itself—simply because, *as long as it is playing that game*, it obviously continues to exist (who else is playing the game?). As Chuang Tzu pointed out long ago, "Is not the desire to get rid of the ego itself a manifestation of ego?"

The ego is not a thing but a subtle *effort*, and you cannot use effort to get rid of effort—you end up with two efforts instead of one. The ego itself is a perfect manifestation of the Divine, and it is best handled by resting in Freedom, not by trying to get rid of ego, which simply increases the effort of ego itself.

And so, the practice? When you rest in the Witness, or rest in I-I, or rest in Emptiness, simply notice the self-contraction. Rest in the Witness, and feel the self-contraction. When you *feel* the self-contraction, you are *already* free of it—you are already *looking at it*, instead of identifying with it. You are looking at it from the position of the Witness, which is always already free of all objects in any case.

So rest as the Witness, and feel the self-contraction—just as you can feel the chair under you, and feel the earth, and feel the clouds floating by in the sky. Thoughts float by in the mind, sensations float by in the body, the self-contraction hovers in awareness—and you effortlessly and spontaneously witness them all, equally and impartially.

In that simple, easy, effortless state—while you are *not* trying to get rid of the self-contraction but simply feeling it—and while you are therefore resting as the great Witness or Emptiness that you are—One Taste might more easily flash forth. There is nothing that you can do to bring about (or cause) One Taste—it is always already fully present, it is not the result of temporal actions, and you have never lost it anyway.

The most you can do, by way of temporal effort, is to avoid these two major mistakes (don't try to see the Witness as an object, just rest in the Witness as Seer; don't try to get rid of the ego, just feel it), and that will bring you to the edge, to the very precipice, of your own Original Face. At that point it is, in every way, out of your hands.

Rest as the Witness, feel the self-contraction: that is exactly the space in which One Taste can most easily flash forth. Don't do this as a strategic effort, but randomly and spontaneously throughout the day and into the night, standing thus always on the edge of your own shocking recognition.

So here are the steps:

Rest as the Witness, feel the self-contraction. As you do so, notice that the Witness is *not* the self-contraction—it is aware of it. The Witness is *free* of the self-contraction—and *you are the Witness.*

As the Witness, you are free of the self-contraction. *Rest in that Freedom*, Openness, Emptiness, Release. Feel the self-contraction, *and let it be*, just as you let all other sensations be. You don't try to get rid of the clouds, the trees, or the ego—just let them all be, and relax in the space of Freedom that you are.

From that space of Freedom—and at some unbidden point—you may notice that the *feeling* of Freedom has no inside and no outside, no center and no surround. Thoughts are floating in this Freedom, the sky is floating in this Freedom, the world is arising in this Freedom, and you are That. The sky is your head, the air is your breath, the earth is your body—it is all that close, and closer. You are the world, as long as you rest in this Freedom, which is infinite Fullness.

This is the world of One Taste, with no inside and no outside, no subject and no object, no in here versus out there—without beginning and without end, without ways and without means, without path and without goal. And this, as Ramana said, is the final truth.

That is what might be called a "capping exercise." Do it, not instead of, *but in addition to*, whatever other practice you are doing—centering prayer, vipassana, prayer of the heart, zikr, zazen, yoga, etc. All of these other practices train you to enter a specific state of consciousness, *but One Taste is not a specific state*—it is compatible with any and all states, just as wetness is fully present in each and every wave of the ocean. One wave may be bigger than another wave, but it is not wetter. One Taste is the wetness of the water, not any particular wave, and therefore specific practices, such as prayer or vipassana or yoga, are *powerless* to introduce you to One Taste. All specific practices are designed to get you to a particular wave—usually a Really Big Wave—and that is fine. But One Taste is the wetness of even the smallest wave, so any wave of awareness you have right now is fine. Rest with that wave, feel the self-contraction, and stand Free.

But continue your other practices, first, because they will introduce you to specific and important waves of your own awareness (psychic, subtle, and causal), which are all important vehicles of your full manifestation as Spirit. Second, precisely because One Taste is too simple to believe and too easy to reach by effort, most people will never notice that the wave they are now on is wet. They will never notice the Suchness of their own present state. They will instead dedicate their lives to wave hopping, always looking for a Bigger and Better wave to ride—and frankly, that is fine.

Those typical spiritual practices, precisely by introducing you to subtler and subtler *experiences*, will inadvertently help you *tire of experience altogether*. When you tire of wave jumping, you will stand open to the wetness or Suchness of whatever wave you are on. The pure Witness itself is *not an experience*, but the opening or clearing in which all experiences come and go, and as long as you are chasing experiences, including spiritual experiences, you will never rest as the Witness, let alone fall into the ever-present ocean of One Taste. But tiring of experiences, you will rest as the Witness, and it is as the Witness that you can notice Wetness (One Taste).

And then the wind will be your breath, the stars the neurons in your brain, the sun the taste of the morning, the earth the way your body feels. The Heart will open to the All, the Kosmos will rush into your soul, you will arise as countless galaxies and swirl for all eternity. There is only self-existing Fullness left in all the world, there is only self-seen Radiance here in Emptiness—etched on the wall of infinity, preserved for all eternity, the one and only truth: there is *just this*, snap your fingers, nothing more.

November

The mystics are channels through which a little knowledge of reality filters down into our human universe of ignorance and illusion. A totally unmystical world would be a world totally blind and insane.

—*Grey Eminence,* ALDOUS HUXLEY

Sunday, November 2

Tony flew in today at noon. Marci picked him up at the airport, then went off to work on her thesis. Joyce Nielsen dropped by to say hello (it was the first time we had met). Then Marci joined us, and we all had dinner together. I cooked my world-famous vegetarian chili, of which nobody took seconds.

Tuesday, November 4

Charles "Skip" Alexander sent his latest dream/meditation research; it is as I expected it would be, and it confirms my little experiments on myself with an EEG machine. Namely, advanced meditators, during sleep, show "theta-alpha activity simultaneously with delta activity." The subjects report being "conscious" during sleep, and the EEG seems to support this, in that alpha (waking), theta (dreaming), and delta (deep sleep) patterns are *all simultaneously present*—this is "constant consciousness" through all three states.

What is so exciting about this type of research is that it gives us yet another empirical correlate of higher, transcendental states. There are several immediate applications. One, individuals could use this to help monitor their own progress in consciousness transformation. Spiritual growth would be less of a hit and miss affair. Two, this gives us one way to test the effectiveness of different "transformative practices." Divide students into various groups—let one group spend two years reading books like *Ecopsychology*, *Return of the Goddess*, and *You Can Heal Your Life*; let another group meditate; let another do shamanic drumming, another yoga, another contemplative prayer, etc., and measure the actual changes in brain wave patterns as a correlate of consciousness transformation.

The point, in other words, is *practice*, and this type of research is so important because it encourages people to practice diligently, not merely to think differently. Thinking (and reading) will only alter alpha and beta states (the gross realm); but profound meditative practice will take you into theta (the subtle realm) and delta (the causal), and then allow all three to be present simultaneously—constant consciousness through all three states, whereupon the Ground of all three states—nondual Spirit itself—will become as obvious as a glass of cold water thrown in your Original Face.

This is yet another call to let merely translative spirituality—which is well over 90% of the market—give way to genuinely transformative spirituality, which rewires your soul and plugs it directly into God.

Friday, November 7

UNITAS MULTIPLEX

Rented *Nowhere*, the last of Gregg Araki's nihilism trilogy (along with *Doom Generation*, which was even bleaker, and *Totally Fucked Up*, even stranger). It's appropriately named. The postmodern world has always found nihilism (and it's cousin skepticism) to be very cool, very hip, very "in." Nihilism is supposed to reflect accurately the relativism of cultural values, the socially constructed nature of all reality, the sliding nature of all signifiers, the deconstruction of moral guideposts, and the inherent uncertainty of all beliefs. The only "way cool" stance in the face of the real world is nihilism and a yawn.

But the joke is on the nihilists. They belabor the point that there is nothing to believe in. They accept no value system; embrace no vision; believe no tenets. Yet they eat three times a day, so clearly they believe in food. They sleep at night, so they believe in resting. They seek out water, shelter, and warmth, so they deeply believe in physiological needs. Most of them certainly believe in sex. So here, in fact, are their major beliefs: food, shelter, physiological needs, sex. In other words, they do not lack values, they simply believe in a set of values that are shared with rabbits, rats, and weasels.

So much for nihilism. It's not just that the stance itself is deeply hypocritical—claiming no values, but in fact entrenched in the lowest (and as such, reduced to a value system shared by crustaceans)—but that the only "fun" of nihilism is tearing down somebody else's beliefs—this, after all, was the thrill that the boomers found in deconstruction. But if somebody else doesn't construct first, you can't deconstruct. No more fun, and so you have nothing else to do but go on about your life of ratty, weasel values. And truly, how fun can that be?

But, in just the last two or three years, I sense a real turning against this extreme postmodern nihilism—against *extreme* relativism, contextualism, and constructivism. As Jerome Bruner has pointed out, unitas multiplex is still the rule: there are various *universal* or deep features to human existence, as well as various *local* or surface features, and we have to honor *both*, instead of losing ourselves merely in the relative, constructed, diverse, and different.

Bruner: "Languages differ, but there are linguistic universals that make access into any language easy for any child. Cultures differ, but they too have universals that speak to the generality of mind and probably to some general features of its development. *Unitas multiplex* may still be the best motto."

This issue—the validity of unitas multiplex (or universal pluralism)—is crucial, not only for cultural studies in general, but for spirituality in particular. The standard argument of the constructivists—David Katz, for example—is that there can be no perennial philosophy, no transcendental Reality, no universal Spirit, because there is no universal anything, period. (Except, of course, for his own claim, which he maintains is *universally* true—the performative contradiction.)

I've gone through seemingly endless books for volume 2, and I decided not to discuss any of them in these pages, or else this would turn into nothing but a gigantic book review. But what I've noticed in all these books, across dozens of fields, in a stronger and stronger way, is an unmistakable revolt against relativity and constructivism. Scholars are increasingly recognizing that behind extreme relativism is nihilism, and behind nihilism is narcissism. If I see one more really good book nailing these issues (I have seen at least a dozen so far), I am going to declare my own personal national holiday.

Tuesday, November 11

Constant consciousness all last night; spontaneous wakefulness through the dream and deep sleep state, one with whatever arises. There is no I, but simply a primordial awareness or basic wakefulness—a very, very subtle awareness—that neither comes nor goes, but somehow is timelessly so, One Taste in the dream and dream sleep state. When this occurs, morning meditation is no different from what went on during the night. There is simply One-Taste awareness in the causal itself (during deep formless sleep), and this tacit nondual awareness continues as the subtle arises out of the causal (and the dreaming state begins), and then the gross arises out of the subtle (with normal waking). Thus, when the gross state manifests (around three A.M.), there is no major change in primordial awareness or constant consciousness—there simply occurs within it a perception of the gross body, the bed, and the room. That is, the gross realm arises in the One Taste that I-I timelessly am. There is then nothing specifically called "meditation," since it is already inherent in this nondual awareness or very subtle constant consciousness.

Should constant consciousness not be noticed during the night, then when the gross realm arises, I specifically take up several meditative or contemplative practices, starting always with ultimate guru yoga, which is self-inquiry, or looking directly into the nature of the mind (e.g., "Who am I? What is this pure Empty Witness?"). The way I practice this is generally indistinguishable from the "capping exercise" [October 31]. As I wake up, I contemplate or *feel* the rise of the separate-self sense (i.e., I feel the tiny interior tension in awareness that is the separate self), and rest in the prior Emptiness of which the self-contraction is an unnecessary gesture. If this capping exercise is successful—that is, if it is done with no thought of success—then the separate-self sense relaxes into pure Emptiness, vast Openness, infinite Freedom—which is itself constant, timeless, nondual consciousness, or Infinite Spaciousness. The self uncoils in Emptiness, and I return to what I-I timelessly am. Then kw simply arises as a gesture of what I-I am, and to a great degree (which still varies considerably) I am not particularly identified with that one—kw is simply one among a billion vehicles of Spirit and its everlasting song, and I-I am that Song, not any particular note.

In any event, around four or five A.M. I do one or two hours of more typical meditative and contemplative practices. Even if constant consciousness is present, I try to do these practices, because they exercise and express that Song more beautifully than anything else I know. (Suzuki Roshi, when asked why we should meditate, always said the same thing: We do not meditate to *attain* Buddha-nature—because, being ever-present, it is literally unattainable—rather, we meditate to *express* the Buddha-nature that we always already are.) Although I have been meditating for around twenty-five years—and have tried dozens of different spiritual practices—most of those that I do at this time were received at the Longchen Nyingthig given by His Holiness Pema Norbu (Penor) Rinpoche, now head of the Nyingma school of Tibetan Buddhism. These especially include tigle gyachen and the shi tro (elaborate practices that include togyal and trekchod, the two major practices of Dzogchen or Maha-Ati Buddhism). Many of these practices were also initiated by my primary Dzogchen teacher, Chagdud Tulku Rinpoche.

I end this formal meditation with the practice known as tonglen, "taking and sending," which I also practice randomly throughout the day (probably more than any other practice). The basic form of tonglen is: you breathe in the suffering of the world, you breathe out whatever peace and happiness you possess—you take in suffering, you send out release. This profound practice undercuts the dualism between self and other, enemy and friend, subject and object, and constantly re-introduces you to your own primordial nature, pure Emptiness, pure Spirit.

The general outline of these various practices can be found in *Grace and Grit*. Although they are basically Buddhist, I honestly think I could be just as happy with any number of subtle, causal, and nondual practices, from any of the world's great nondual traditions, East or West, North or South. The whole point of authentic contemplation is simply to accelerate the growth, development, or evolution from the subconscious to the self-conscious to the superconscious dimensions of your own Being. *We now have abundant evidence that meditation does not alter or change the basic stages of the development of consciousness, but it does remarkably accelerate that development.*[23] Meditation speeds up evolution. It accelerates the remembering and the re-discovery of the Spirit that you eternally are. Meditation quickens the rate that acorns grow into oaks, that humans grow into God.

The zikr of Sufism, shikan-taza of Zen, devekut of Judaism, the Prayer of the Heart, vision quest of shamanism, self-inquiry of Ramana,

---

23. See *The Eye of Spirit* for an in-depth discussion of this topic.

vipassana of Theravada, chih-kuan of T'ien T'ai, centering prayer—the raja, jnana, hatha, karma, and kundalini yogas—the vast and stunning panoply of the contemplative practices of the world's great wisdom traditions—the whole point is to re-member, re-collect, and re-discover that which you always already are. And in that shattering realization, you will reawaken to a world where the Kosmos is your soul, the clouds your lungs, the raindrops the beat of your heart.

Thursday, November 13

Stuart Davis is a singer/songwriter, twenty-six years old, internationally recognized (*The Dresdener News*, Germany: "At the forefront of the talented young songwriters from the United States, Stuart Davis offers an insightful, painfully honest look into the social and personal components of life. A truly captivating performer with an equally powerful poetry"). But more than that, he has an outrageous sense of humor. His notes from his latest CD: "At the age of twenty-six, with five albums released in sixteen countries, Stuart Davis has earned an international reputation for his daring command of language and a knack for using it to conquer difficult subjects. On his latest release, *Kid Mystic*, he surveys nothing less than creation, the evolution of consciousness/spirit, and death (all in twelve catchy pop nuggets). Finally a collection of singable, danceable tracks that blend lyrical genius with topics like the direct apprehension of God, alien abduction, and suicide! Davis has put mysticism where it belonged all along, in the hook of a three-minute single."

Stuart wanted to drop by the house—he dedicated *Kid Mystic* to me—so I said sure. Marci got us Chinese takeout and we all spent the evening together. Stuart felt that he was at something of a crossroad in his life, moving more and more into transpersonal and spiritual dimensions (he's already meditating twice daily; I urged him to strengthen that practice). We talked at length about art and its capacity—at its best—to evoke higher realities; I showed him some of Anselm's work, and Alex's. Stuart was absolutely stunned, almost speechless, by Alex's art. This type of transpersonal message could be done in music as well, and since almost nobody is doing this, why shouldn't Stuart be one of the first?

We were then treated to a thirty-minute performance, Stuart singing the most beautiful and touching songs (Marci started crying at one point). He's performing tomorrow night at Mars lounge in Boulder; we've decided to go.

Friday, November 14

We were going to Stuart's performance, but we decided to dye Marci's hair as a prelude, and things went, um, well, slightly wrong.

I'm not sure "wrong" is the right word; depending on your tastes, it could be described as anything from "way cool" to "horrifyingly awful." Marci wanted to dye her hair platinum white, so we hit a local drugstore, realized that dark hair took at least two strong agents to dye white, bought both of them, and gave it a try.

Her hair turned bright orange.

I am now dating Ronald McDonald.

We did not go see Stuart perform.

Saturday, November 15

Marci made emergency calls to every hair salon in the area, begging them to get her in on short notice. I happen to like her hair—it's wild—but she'd like it toned down from outrageous orange to merely shocking white, and she finally found a place that would take her.

It worked fine; pure white hair; I'm no longer dating Ronald McDonald, I'm dating a Q-tip.

Sunday, November 16

Brant Cortright's *Psychotherapy and Spirit* just arrived, and it is quite disappointing, not least of which for the way it badly misrepresents my work. (I am sometimes accused of claiming too often that certain writers distort my work. You decide:)

In *The Eye of Spirit*, I divide my work into four main phases: wilber-1 was Romantic; wilber-2 was basically the Great Chain understood in developmental terms (a model first presented in *The Atman Project*); wilber-3 goes considerably further and suggests that there are numerous different developmental lines that progress relatively independently through the various levels of the Great Chain (a model first presented in *Transformations of Consciousness* and fleshed out in *The Eye of Spirit*); and wilber-4 sets those levels and lines in the context of the four quadrants (the psychological component of wilber-3 and wilber-4 are essentially the same, so I often refer to my latest psychological model as wilber-3, with the understanding that it is simply the Upper-Left quadrant of wilber-4).

Cortright is still dealing mostly with wilber-2, not wilber-3 (let alone wilber-4), which is unfortunate. He anachronistically insists on seeing my position as a monolithic, single spectrum model, a clunky stepladder affair where you have to complete psychological development before spiritual development can occur. This misperception is so common—and inaccurate—that it led Donald Rothberg to go out of his way to emphasize, when summarizing my present (wilber-3) model: "Development doesn't somehow proceed in some simple way through a series of a few comprehensive stages which unify all aspects of growth. . . . The [different] developmental lines may be in tension with each other at times, and some of them do not show evidence, Wilber believes, of coherent stages. . . . There might be a high level of development cognitively, a medium level interpersonally or morally, and a low level emotionally. These disparities of development seem especially conditioned by general cultural values and styles." In other words, through the *levels* of the Great Chain, various developmental *lines* proceed relatively independently, so that you can be at a high level of development in some lines, medium in others, and low in still others.

The central inadequacy of Cortright's book is that he doesn't seem to grasp the basic issues of psychological and spiritual development. First of all, I make it very clear in *The Eye of Spirit* that you can think of these as two separate lines of development—the psychological and the spiritual—so that spiritual development can indeed occur *alongside* of psychological development (as I will explain in a moment). Cortright fully acknowledges that I say this, and then proceeds to completely ignore it. His discussion makes it clear that he has failed to grasp the central, haunting issue: even if spiritual development is a separate line (or lines), *how can you define it?* If spiritual development is a separate line of development (in addition to other lines, such as cognitive, moral, motivational, kinesthetic, affective, etc.), then you must be able to define the spiritual line in terms that do *not* include cognitive insight, morals, motivations, needs, ethical commitments, or affective love and compassion—*because all of those already have their own separate lines of development*. If "spirituality" is a *separate* line of development, you have to be able to describe it in specific, distinctive terms, which Cortright does not credibly do—a defect that cripples his entire approach. I happen to believe that some aspects of spiritual development refer to higher stages of various lines (such as higher affects or transpersonal love, higher cognition or transrational awareness, etc.), and that some aspects of spiritual development are themselves a separate, distinct line (such as concern and openness)—but you must spell these out carefully before you make grand pronouncements about "spiritual" development.

For example, *even if* we say that the higher stages of the various developmental lines are "spiritual," and the lower stages are "personal" or "psychological"—which many transpersonalists do—nonetheless, in my model (wilber-3), the various lines themselves develop relatively independently, and therefore a transpersonal or spiritual stage of development in one line (say, cognition) can occur *simultaneously* with a personal or psychological stage in another line (say, morality)—so that "spiritual" and "psychological" growth, in the various developmental lines, are occurring *alongside of each other*, and not stacked on top of each other like so many bricks (which Cortright maintains is my view). The idea that any of these lines must be fully completed before another can begin is silly—not even wilber-2 maintained that rigid a schedule.

Cortright, in a truly odd section of the book, says that my "middle levels" of development—concrete operational, formal operational, and vision-logic, as they have their own correlative self-pathologies—simply do not exist. If I understand him correctly, he thinks they can all be reduced to one level. Yikes. The evidence for the existence of these stages is massive, and all I have done is to suggest that wherever there is a real stage, there is something that can go wrong at that stage—hence the levels of pathology through these very real stages of development. Cortright ignores all of this evidence, and then moves into a politically correct broadside at my suggestion—following a vast amount of clinical evidence—that many forms of psychosis have a developmental (and/or genetic) lesion in the earliest stages of development. In a cookie-cutter fashion, I am lambasted for my moral insensitivity, as the author preens and prompts us to remember how wonderfully high-minded and moral he is. This is by far the most unbecoming section of the book.

Cortright's understanding of the world's great wisdom traditions seems pale, sometimes completely lacking; and the fact that he clearly misrepresents some of these traditions bodes poorly for the book as a whole. A few examples: Cortright says that the stage conception I present doesn't work for meditative development—e.g., "The Buddhist literature is full of many, many examples of people directly realizing the impersonal emptiness of the nondual." In fact, there are virtually no cases of such. He might have in mind the Zen mondos, where, after a brief and pithy exchange with a Zen Master, a student gets "total satori." But as any Zen teacher will tell you, that exchange occurred after an average of six years of intensive meditation, which itself proceeds through stages (e.g., the Ten Ox-Herding Pictures).

Cortright tries to give several examples to support his case, and they are all demonstrably inaccurate. "Ramana Maharshi, whom Wilber holds out as an exemplar of nondual realization, emerged directly into the nondual experience without 'passing through' either the psychic or subtle stages." In fact, Ramana's awakening was, as he clearly reported, a three-day ordeal, culminating in a thirty-minute climax, in which he passed through savikalpa samadhi (psychic and subtle forms) and nirvikalpa and jnana samadhi (causal formlessness), only then to awaken to sahaja (pure One Taste or nondual Suchness). That Cortright so confidently and cavalierly misreports this crucial event is typical, I'm afraid, of his reporting in general. He similarly misreports Aurobindo's model, and that of Vajrayana. He mentions Aurobindo as an "exemplar of this tradition," the tradition that, according to Cortright, does not believe in a specific sequence of spiritual development, overlooking Aurobindo's explicit statement that "The spiritual evolution obeys the logic of a successive unfolding; it can take a new decisive main step only when the previous main step has been sufficiently conquered: even if certain minor stages can be swallowed up or leaped over by a rapid and brusque ascension, the consciousness has to turn back to assure itself that the ground passed over is securely annexed to the new condition; a greater or concentrated speed [which is indeed possible] does not eliminate the steps themselves or the necessity of their successive surmounting" (Aurobindo, *The Life Divine*, II, 26).

Cortright likewise implies that Vajrayana Buddhism doesn't acknowledge these inherent developmental dimensions, thus overlooking the only in-depth study ever done on this topic—that by Daniel P. Brown, who carefully analyzed over a dozen major texts of Mahamudra meditation, only to find that they all, *without exception*, subscribe to a specific-stage model of development (stages that fit rather precisely what I have defined as psychic, subtle, causal, and nondual, as demonstrated in *Transformations of Consciousness*). Brown and Engler then tested this stage-conception against the typical Chinese meditative tradition, the vipassana tradition, and Patanjali's *Yoga Sutras,* and found that, in every case, it held up consistently. Cortright cheerfully ignores all of this evidence.

When it comes time to summarize the field of transpersonal therapy, Cortright incredibly sets up wilber-2 as the "old paradigm," and then presents wilber-3 as the "new-paradigm," while identifying my model as wilber-2 only. Well, what can I say?

Cortright gives the new-paradigm as follows: "All of this points to a view where psychological and spiritual development are composed of multiple, complex developmental pathways that sometimes intermingle, interpenetrate, and overlap, while other times remain discrete and more obviously separate. Sometimes growth is psychological, sometimes growth is spiritual, and at other times both are occurring together." That is precisely the wilber-3 model, as I just explained. Wilber-3 identifies over a dozen separate developmental lines, such as cognitive, moral, affective, love, concern, attention, self-identity, defenses, interpersonal, artistic, and kinesthetic—some of which themselves are spiritual, and some of whose higher stages are spiritual—which allows us to track these various overlapping developments, all of them organized and coordinated by the self.[24] Cortright triumphantly presents a watered-down version of this wilber-3 model as the new breakthrough paradigm. But the version he offers lacks a real grasp of the developmental evidence, and especially lacks a sensitivity as to how we are honestly going to define "spirituality" in terms that do not merely repeat other developmental lines. (He likewise completely ignores the work of Jenny Wade, gives a strangely skewed interpretation of Hameed Ali, etc.)

Cortright fully embraces Huston Smith's Great Chain of Being, yet he rejects the so-called "monolithic" spectrum of consciousness, failing, apparently, to realize that they are basically identical. But what I have tried to do, with reference to the Great Chain, is go one step further and suggest that there are different developmental lines (or streams) that unfold independently through the different levels (or waves) of the Great Chain, and that only by recognizing that fact—levels and lines—can we integrate Eastern wisdom with Western knowledge. The four quadrants—or simply the Big Three of I, we, and it—are some of the most basic lines or streams, *each of which* develops through the levels or

---

24. Perhaps the dominant theory in cognitive science at this moment is that of *modules*—the idea that the brain/mind is composed of numerous, independent, evolutionary modules, from linguistic to cognitive to moral. These modules are, in many ways, quite similar to what I mean by relatively independent developmental lines or streams. The major difference is that the module theorists vehemently deny that there is any sort of transcendental self or unity of consciousness. And yet, according to their own theory and data, individuals are capable of being aware of these modules, and can in fact override them on occasion. If you can override a module, you are not just a module. QED.

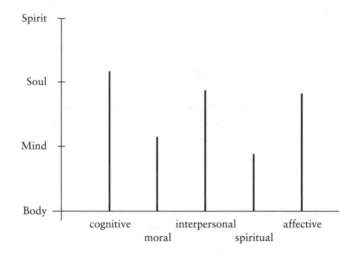

FIGURE 5. *The Integral Psychograph*

waves of the Great Chain [see figure 3, page 339]. Cortright thinks that this "levels and lines" concept terribly complicates the picture, whereas in fact it enormously simplifies a massive amount of data; and he thinks it confuses and weakens the Great Chain, whereas in fact it salvages it.

Here is a simple way to picture wilber-3, which involves the integration of the *levels* of the Great Chain with various developmental *lines* moving through those levels (or streams through those waves). Let's use a simple version of the Great Chain, with only four levels (body, mind, soul, and spirit); let's use only five lines (there are almost two dozen); and let's make spirituality *both* the highest development in each line *and* a separate line of its own, to cover both common definitions (see figure 5).[25]

Since "hierarchy" upsets many people, let's also draw that hierarchy in the way that it is actually defined, namely, as a holarchy (see figure 6). This is the identical concept, but some people are more comfortable with nice feminine circles (I prefer them myself, because they so clearly show the "transcend and include" nature of the Great Nest of Being).

The point of both of those diagrams—what I call an "integral psychograph"—is that you can track the different developmental lines (or

25. For a refined view of this model, see "Two Patterns of Transcendence," *Journal of Humanistic Psychology*, 30, no. 3 (Summer 1990) 113–36. [See especially *Integral Psychology*.]

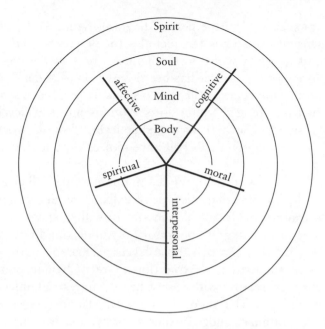

FIGURE 6. *The Integral Psychograph as a Holarchy*

streams) as they move through the various levels (or waves) of the Great Nest. You can be at a higher, transpersonal, or "spiritual" level in several lines, and at a lower, personal, or "psychological" level in others, so that both spiritual and psychological development overlap—and the separate spiritual line(s) can be relatively high or low as well.

All of these streams and waves are navigated by the self (or the self system), which has to balance all of them and find some sort of harmony in the midst of this mélange. Moreover, something can go wrong in any stream at any of its waves (or stages), and therefore we can map various types of pathologies wherever they occur in the psychograph—different types of pathologies occur at different levels or waves in each of the lines.

Even though we can say, based on massive evidence (clinical, phenomenological, and contemplative), that many of these developmental streams proceed through the waves in a stagelike fashion, nonetheless *overall* self development does *not* proceed in a specific, stagelike manner, simply because the self is an amalgam of all the various lines, and the possible number of permutations and combinations of those is virtually infinite. Overall individual growth, in other words, follows no set sequence whatsoever.

Finally, as suggested in the nested diagram (figure 6), because each senior dimension transcends but includes (or nests) the junior dimension, to be at a higher wave does not mean the lower waves are left behind. This is not (and never has been) based on a ladder, but on the model of: atoms, molecules, cells, and organisms, with each senior level enfolding or enveloping the junior—as Plotinus put it, a development that is envelopment. So even at a higher level, "lower" work is still occurring simultaneously—cells still have molecules, Buddhas still have to eat.

That's wilber-3 in a nutshell. While I'm on that topic, I'll give one last example of why I believe that this type of wilber-3 model is an improvement on the traditional Great Chain model (or wilber-2), which contains the various *levels* of Being but does not fully understand how and why different *lines* develop through those levels.[26] Huston Smith, we have seen, accurately summarizes the traditional Great Chain as body, mind, soul, and spirit (correlative with realms he calls terrestrial, intermediate, celestial, and infinite). That model is fine as far as it goes, but the trouble is, it starts to fall apart under further scrutiny, and it completely collapses under the avalanche of modern psychological research.

To begin with, the traditional Great Chain tends to confuse the levels of Being and the types of self-sense associated with each level. For example, mind is a *level* of the Great Chain, but the ego is the *self* generated when consciousness *identifies* with that level (i.e., identifies with mind). The subtle is a level of the Great Chain, the soul is the self generated when consciousness identifies with the subtle. The causal/spirit is a level in the Great Chain, the True Self is the "self" associated with that level, and so on. So the sequence of levels in the Great Chain should be body, mind, subtle, and causal/spirit, with the correlative self stages of body-ego, ego, soul, and Self—to use the very simplified version. Although I often use the traditional terminology (body, mind, soul, spirit), I always have in mind the difference between the actual levels (body, mind, subtle, causal) and the self at those levels (bodyego, ego, soul, Self).

Here is where some of these distinctions start to pay off (and the usefulness of the move from wilber-2 to wilber-3 becomes more obvious). The traditions generally maintain that men and women have two major personality systems, as it were: the *frontal* and the *deeper psychic*. The traditional Great Chain theorists (and wilber-2) would simply say

---

26. [For the relation of wilber-3 to the traditional Great Chain, see *Integral Psychology*.]

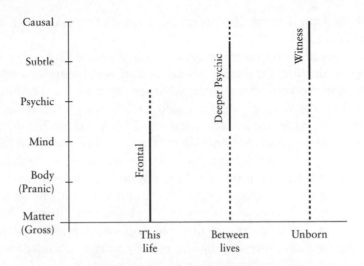

FIGURE 7. *The Development of the Frontal (or Ego), the Deeper Psychic (or Soul), and the Witness (or Self)*

that the frontal is the self associated with the body and mind, and the deeper psychic is associated with the soul, which would indeed be a type of ladder arrangement. But the frontal and the deeper psychic seem much more flexible than that; they seem to be, not different levels, but separate lines, of development, so that their development occurs alongside of, not on top of, each other. We can graph this as shown in figure 7 (for which I have reverted to a more accurate six levels.)[27]

The frontal being is the *gross-oriented personality*—in the widest sense, what we mean by "ego," or the personality that is oriented outwardly to the sensorimotor world. The frontal being begins its developmental line or stream with material conception, continues through the emotional-sexual or pranic stages, into the mental stages, and fades out at the psychic. *Frontal development* represents the evolution of the self

---

27. In Vedanta—the most traditional of the Great Chain models—there are five *levels* (matter, *prana*, *manomayakosha* or lower mind, *vijnanamayakosha* or higher mind, and *anandamayakosha* or bliss mind), divided into three major *realms* (gross, subtle, and causal). Matter is the gross realm, the bliss mind is the causal realm, and the three middle levels (body/*prana*, lower mind, and higher mind) are *all* the subtle realm. When I speak generally and simply of the three realms (gross, subtle, causal), I agree with that correlation. But I also use "the subtle" to mean the *highest* of the three subtle realms (the *anandamayakosha*). Context will indicate which is meant.

(or self-identity) through the lower-to-intermediate waves of the Great Nest of Being.

According to the traditions, while the frontal personality is that which develops in this life, the deeper psychic is that which develops between lives. It is, in the very widest sense, what we mean by the word "soul." At any rate, the deeper psychic is said to be present sometime from conception to midterm; in fact, some research suggests that prenatal, perinatal, and neonatal memories do in fact exist, and since these cannot be carried by the frontal personality and the gross brain (since they have not developed), the traditions would maintain that these memories are being carried by the deeper psychic being and are later lost as frontal development gets under way and submerges the early psychic being.[28] Likewise, past-life memories, if they are genuine, would be carried by the deeper psychic. Nonetheless, it is not necessary to believe in either prenatal memory or past lives in order to acknowledge the deeper psychic self, which is *primarily* defined by its access to higher consciousness, not by its access to past lives.

Although the deeper psychic is present from birth (or mid-prenatal), it plays a modest role until the *necessary* frontal development finishes its task of orienting (and adapting) consciousness to the gross realm. As the frontal personality begins to fade, the deeper psychic being comes increasingly to the fore. Just as the frontal personality orients consciousness to the gross realm, the deeper psychic orients consciousness to the subtle realm. And, as we saw, the self associated with the subtle realm is the "soul," which is why "deeper psychic" and "soul" are generally synonymous. But the deeper psychic, even though its roots are in the subtle realm per se, nonetheless has a development that reaches down to some of the earliest stages, culminates in the subtle, and disappears at the causal.

Already we can begin to see the advantage of making the frontal and the deeper psychic not discrete levels but overlapping lines; not different waves but often parallel streams. We can go one step further and note that there is a last major "personality," that of the Self, associated with the causal, but also, like the others, having developments that reach down into earlier stages. In other words, we can usefully treat the Self as a separate line or stream of development, even though its basic orientation is the causal.

---

28. In this case, in fig. 7 the lowest quarter inch of the "Deeper Psychic" line would also be solid. See *The Eye of Spirit* for a full discussion.

The Self, or the transpersonal Witness, is not—like the ego or the soul—a "personality," since it has no specific characteristics whatsoever (it is pure Emptiness and the great Unborn), except for the fact that it is an Emptiness still separate from Form, a Witness still divorced from that which is witnessed. As such, the Self or Witness is the seat of attention, the root of the separate-self sense, and the home of the last and subtlest duality, namely, that between the Seer and the seen. It is both the highest Self, and the final barrier, to nondual One Taste.

Nonetheless, the power of Witnessing is the power of liberation from all lower domains, and the Witness itself is present, even if latently, at all previous stages. Each developmental stage "transcends and includes" its predecessor, and the "transcend" aspect, in every case, is the power of the higher to be aware of the lower (the soul is aware of the mind, the mind is aware of the body, the body is aware of matter). And in each case, the "is aware of" is simply the power of the Witness shining through at that stage.

Although the Witness is present as the power of transcendental growth at every stage, it comes to its own fruition in the causal realm. *As the ego orients consciousness to the gross, and the soul orients consciousness to the subtle, the Self orients consciousness to the causal.* While all of them have their root dispositions in specific realms or waves of the Great Nest, they also have their own lines or streams of development, so they often overlap each other, as indicated in figure 6. And this is what I think so many meditation teachers and transpersonal therapists see in themselves and their clients, namely, that *ego and soul and Spirit can in many ways coexist and develop together,* because they are relatively separate streams flowing through the waves in the Great Nest of Being. And there can be, on occasion, rather uneven development in between these streams.[29]

We all know fairly enlightened teachers (alive to the Unborn) who nonetheless still have "big egos," in the sense of strong, forceful, powerful personalities. But the presence of the ego is not a problem; it all depends upon whether the person is *also* alive to higher and deeper dimensions. As Hubert Benoit said, it is not the identification with the ego that is the problem, but the exclusive nature of that identification. When

---

29. This is why some early cultures apparently showed advanced psychic capacities but rather poor frontal development. This is why, whatever else their merits, they were not exemplars of integral culture, although we can admire much of their wisdom.

our self-identity expands beyond the ego, into the deeper psychic, then even into the Unborn and One Taste, the ego is simply taken up and subsumed in a grander identity. But the ego itself remains as the functional self in the gross realm, and it might even appropriately be intensified and made more powerful, simply because it is now plugged into the entire Kosmos. Many of the great enlightened teachers had a big ego, a big deeper psychic, and a very big Self, all at once, simply because these are the three functional vehicles of the gross, subtle, and causal domains, and all three vehicles were appropriately intensified in the great awakened ones.

Finally—and this is what tends to confuse people—although the various developmental lines often overlap each other, and in no specific sequence, *the individual lines or streams themselves usually have their own invariant, universal, developmental sequence*—namely, to the extent that they unfold into consciousness, they must negotiate the levels or waves in the Great Nest, and in an order that is given by the Nest itself. For example, we have substantial evidence that cognition, morals, affects, kinesthetic skills, and interpersonal capacity, to name a few, all develop through preconventional, conventional, and postconventional waves.[30] In other words, the various streams seem to move through the levels in the Great Nest in a fashion that is determined by the universal Great Nest itself. Although all sorts of regressions and temporary leaps forward are possible, the empirical fact remains as Aurobindo said: individual streams obey the law of a successive unfolding (undulating through the waves of the Great Nest itself).

At the same time, I repeat: even though all developmental lines (including the frontal, the deeper psychic, and the capacity for witnessing) follow their own stages, the *overall* mixture of lines does not. The "overall self" is a juggling of some two dozen different developmental lines, and thus each individual's unfolding will be a radically unique affair.

Monday, November 17

Precisely because the ego, the soul, and the Self can all be present simultaneously, we can better understand the real meaning of "egolessness," a notion that has caused an inordinate amount of confusion. But egolessness does not mean the absence of a functional self (that's a psy-

---

30. See *The Eye of Spirit* [and *Integral Psychology*] for a summary of this extensive research.

chotic, not a sage); it means that one is no longer *exclusively* identified with that self.

One of the many reasons we have trouble with the notion of "egoless" is that people want their "egoless sages" to fulfill all their fantasies of "saintly" or "spiritual," which usually means dead from the neck down, without fleshy wants or desires, gently smiling all the time. All of the things that people typically have trouble with—money, food, sex, relationships, desire—they want their saints to be without. "Egoless sages" are "above all that," is what people want. Talking heads, is what they want. Religion, they believe, will simply get rid of all baser instincts, drives, and relationships, and hence they look to religion, not for advice on how to live life with enthusiasm, but on how to avoid it, repress it, deny it, escape it.

In other words, the typical person wants the spiritual sage to be "less than a person," somehow devoid of all the messy, juicy, complex, pulsating, desiring, urging forces that drive most human beings. We expect our sages to be an *absence* of all that drives *us*! All the things that frighten us, confuse us, torment us, confound us: we want our sages to be untouched by them altogether. And that absence, that vacancy, that "less than personal," is what we often mean by "egoless."

But "egoless" does not mean "*less* than personal," it means "*more* than personal." Not personal minus, but personal plus—all the normal personal qualities, *plus* some transpersonal ones. Think of the great yogis, saints, and sages—from Moses to Christ to Padmasambhava. They were not feeble-mannered milquetoasts, but fierce movers and shakers—from wielding bullwhips in the Temple to subduing entire countries. They rattled the world on its own terms, not in some pie-in-the-sky piety; many of them instigated massive social revolutions that have continued for thousands of years. And they did so, not because they avoided the physical, emotional, and mental dimensions of humanness, and the ego that is their vehicle, but because they engaged them with a drive and intensity that shook the world to its very foundations. No doubt, they were also plugged into the soul (deeper psychic) and spirit (formless Self)—the ultimate source of their power—but they expressed that power, and gave it concrete results, precisely because they dramatically engaged the lower dimensions through which that power could speak in terms that could be heard by all.

These great movers and shakers were not small egos; they were, in the very best sense of the term, big egos, precisely because the ego (the functional vehicle of the gross realm) can and does exist alongside the soul (the vehicle of the subtle) and the Self (vehicle of the causal). To the extent these great teachers *moved the gross realm*, they did so with their egos, because the ego is the functional vehicle of that realm. They were not, however, identified merely with their egos (that's a narcissist), they simply found their egos plugged into a radiant Kosmic source. The great yogis, saints, and sages accomplished so much precisely because they were not timid little toadies but great big egos, plugged into the dynamic Ground and Goal of the Kosmos itself, plugged into their own higher Self, alive to the pure Atman (the pure I-I) that is one with Brahman; they opened their mouths and the world trembled, fell to its knees, and confronted its radiant God.

Saint Teresa was a great contemplative? Yes, *and* Saint Teresa is the only woman ever to have reformed an entire Catholic monastic tradition (think about it). Gautama Buddha shook India to its foundations. Rumi, Plotinus, Bodhidharma, Lady Tsogyal, Lao Tzu, Plato, the Baal Shem Tov—these men and women started revolutions in the gross realm that lasted hundreds, sometimes thousands, of years, something neither Marx nor Lenin nor Locke nor Jefferson can yet claim. And they did not do so because they were dead from the neck down. No, they were monumentally, gloriously, divinely big egos, plugged into a deeper psychic, which was plugged straight into God.

There is certainly a type of truth to the notion of *transcending ego*: it doesn't mean destroy the ego, it means plug it into something bigger. (As Nagarjuna put it, in the relative world, atman is real; in the absolute, neither atman nor anatman is real. Thus, in neither case is anatta a correct description of reality.)[31] The small ego does not evaporate; it remains as the functional center of activity in the conventional realm. As I said, to lose that ego is to become a psychotic, not a sage.

"Transcending the ego" thus actually means to *transcend but include* the ego in a deeper and higher embrace, first in the soul or deeper psychic, then with the Witness or primordial Self, then with all of them taken up, enfolded, included, and embraced in the radiance of One Taste. And that means we do not "get rid" of the small ego, but rather, we inhabit it fully, live it with verve, use it as the necessary vehicle through which higher truths are communicated. Soul and Spirit include body, emotions, and mind, they do not erase them.

Put bluntly, the ego is not an obstruction to Spirit, but a radiant mani-

---

31. See *Sex, Ecology, Spirituality*, chap. 14, n. 1, for an in-depth discussion of this topic.

festation of Spirit. All Forms are not other than Emptiness, including the form of the ego. It is not necessary to get rid of the ego, but simply to live it with a certain exuberance. When identification spills out of the ego and into the Kosmos at large, the ego discovers that the individual Atman is in fact all of a piece with Brahman. The big Self is indeed *no small ego*, and thus, to the extent you are stuck in your small ego, a death and transcendence is required. Narcissists are simply people whose egos are not yet big enough to embrace the entire Kosmos, and so they try to be central to the Kosmos instead.

But we do not want our sages to have big egos; we do not even want them to display a manifest dimension at all. Anytime a sage displays humanness—in regard to money, food, sex, relationships—we are shocked, *shocked*, because we are planning to escape life altogether, not live it, and the sage who lives life offends us. We want out, we want to ascend, we want to escape, and the sage who engages life with gusto, lives it to the hilt, grabs each wave of life and surfs it to the end—this deeply, profoundly disturbs us, frightens us, because it means that we, too, might have to engage life, with gusto, on all levels, and not merely escape it in a cloud of luminous ether. We do not want our sages to have bodies, egos, drives, vitality, sex, money, relationships, or life, because those are what habitually torture us, and we want out. We do not want to surf the waves of life, we want the waves to go away. We want vapor-ware spirituality.

The integral sage, the nondual sage, is here to show us otherwise. Known generally as "Tantric," these sages insist on transcending life by living it. They insist on finding release by engagement, finding nirvana in the midst of samsara, finding total liberation by complete immersion. They enter with awareness the nine rings of hell, for nowhere else are the nine heavens found. Nothing is alien to them, for there is nothing that is not One Taste.

Indeed, the whole point is to be fully at home in the body and its desires, the mind and its ideas, the spirit and its light. To embrace them fully, evenly, simultaneously, since all are equally gestures of the One and Only Taste. To inhabit lust and watch it play; to enter ideas and follow their brilliance; to be swallowed by Spirit and awaken to a glory that time forgot to name. Body and mind and spirit, all contained, equally contained, in the ever-present awareness that grounds the entire display.

In the stillness of the night, the Goddess whispers. In the brightness of the day, dear God roars. Life pulses, mind imagines, emotions wave, thoughts wander. What are all these but the endless movements of One Taste, forever at play with its own gestures, whispering quietly to all who would listen: is this not you yourself? When the thunder roars, do you not hear your Self? When the lightning cracks, do you not see your Self? When clouds float quietly across the sky, is this not your very own limitless Being, waving back at you?

Tuesday, November 18

Marci has been driving my Jeep for many months, because she doesn't really have a working car. She parked it in front of the Spearly Center, where she works, and it was stolen.

The police told us that there was about a 0% chance of getting it back, so yesterday I went out and bought a new Jeep. This morning I get a call: they recovered the Jeep. Apparently my poor ole Jeep—it's been around awhile—foiled its own theft by blowing a tire one block away, whereupon it was immediately abandoned.

But I don't need two Jeeps, so I gave the new one to Marci. She is major ecstatic. But, of course, "This too will pass," as all things do. Paraphrasing Buddha's last words, "Things that are put together fall apart. Work out your salvation with care." In other words, can you find the great Unborn, which, not being made of form, will never be stolen?

Wednesday, November 19

It's not quite right to describe One Taste as a "consciousness" or an "awareness," because that's a little too heady, too cognitive. It's more like the simple Feeling of Being. You *already* feel this simple Feeling of Being: it is the simple, present feeling of existence.

But it's quite different from all other feelings or experiences, because this simple Feeling of Being does not come or go. It is not in time at all, though time flows through it, as one of the many textures of its own sensation. The simple Feeling of Being is not an experience—it is a vast Openness in which all experiences come and go, an infinite Spaciousness in which all perceptions move, a great Spirit in which the forms of its own play arise, remain a bit, and pass. It is your own I-I as your little-I uncoils in the vast expanse of All Space. The simple Feeling of Being, which is the simple feeling of existence, is the simple Feeling of One Taste.

Is this not obvious? Aren't you *already* aware of existing? Don't you *already* feel the simple Feeling of Being? Don't you *already* possess this immediate gateway to ultimate Spirit, which is nothing other than the simple Feeling of Being? You have this simple Feeling now, don't you? And you have it now, don't you? And now, yes?

And don't you already realize that this Feeling is Spirit itself? God-head itself? Emptiness itself? Spirit does not pop into existence: it is the *only* thing that is *constant* in your experience—and that is the simple Feeling of Being itself, a subtle, constant, background awareness that, if you look very closely, very carefully, you will realize you have had ever since the Big Bang and before—not because *you* existed way back when, but because you truly exist *prior* to time, in *this* timeless moment, whose *feeling* is the simple Feeling of Being: now, and now, and always and forever now.

You feel the simple Feeling of Being? Who is not *already* enlightened?

Thursday, November 20

Ah, but we humans don't just want Spirit, we want agitation as well. We don't just want the simple Feeling of Being, we want to feel . . . *something*. Something *special*. We want to feel rich, or we want to feel famous, or we want to feel important; we want to stand out, make a mark, be a somebody. And so we divide up the simple Feeling of Being—we qualify it, categorize it, name it, separate it. We do not want to impartially *witness* the world as I-I and then *be* the world in the Feeling of One Taste. And so, instead of being the world, we want to be somebody. We want, that is, to suffer the lacerations of finite limitation, and this we do, horribly, when we become a somebody. Abandoning the simple Feeling of Being—where I-I am the world—we identify with a little body in a pitifully small space, and we want this little body to rise up over all other bodies and triumph: we will be somebody, by god.

But if I remain in the simple Feeling of Being, what does it matter if a friend gets a new house and I do not? Her joy is my joy, in the simple Feeling of One Taste. What does it matter if a colleague receives acco-lades and I do not? His happiness is my happiness, in the simple Feeling of One Taste. When there is but one Self looking out through all eyes, do I not rejoice in good fortune wherever it occurs, since it is the good fortune of my own deepest Self? And when suffering occurs anywhere in the universe, do I not also suffer, since it is the suffering of my own deepest Self? When one young child cries from hunger, do I not suffer?

When one young husband delights in seeing his wife come home, do I not rejoice?

Traherne got it exactly: "The streets were mine, the temple was mine, the people were mine. The skies were mine, and so were the sun and moon and stars, and all the world was mine, and I the only Spectator [Witness] and enjoyer of it. I knew no churlish proprieties, nor bounds, nor divisions; but all proprieties and divisions were mine; all treasures and the possessors of them. So that with much ado I was corrupted and made to learn the dirty devices of the world, which I now unlearn. . . ."

In the simple Feeling of Being, where I-I am the world, jealousy and envy can find no purchase; all happiness is my happiness, all sadness is my sadness—and therefore, paradoxically, suffering ceases. Tears do not cease, nor do smiles—just the insane notion that I am somebody in the face of my own display. To cease being somebody—when "bodymind drops"—when I-I rests in Emptiness and embraces the entire world of Form: all of this is given in the simple Feeling of Being, the simple Feeling of One Taste. I simply feel Existence, pure Presence, nondual Isness, simple Suchness, present Thusness. I simply feel Being, I do not feel being this or being that—I am free of being this or being that, which are merely forms of suffering. But as I rest in the simple, present, effortless sensation of existence, all is given unto me.

You *already* possess the simple Feeling of Being. And so, again, please tell me: Who is not *already* enlightened?

Friday, November 21

Paul called from mainland China; he and Cel are having a wonderful trip, but they were taken aback by two things in Beijing: the horrible pollution, and the fact that everybody seems to smoke. Paul said the pollution is so bad they're probably using the cigarettes to filter the air.

Roger has finished his *Seven Practices* book—at least for this draft—and is now in the process of letting his agent shop it around. This is such a profound idea for a book—seven practices that the world's great wisdom traditions all share—but I fear for its fate in the marketplace, simply because *practice* seems to be the last thing people want to do when it comes to spirituality. We want simply to be told that we are the Goddess, or God, or one with eco-Gaia, read a few books, translate a little differently: but years of transformative practice? Well, Roger has written a book for people who are serious about awakening, which is to his everlasting credit, and the good fortune of those few who will engage such a liberating demand.

Saturday, November 22

Ann has been made the president of Random House.

"Is it a little crazy around there?"

"Hell's a poppin'. But it's fine now. It just happened very fast."

I couldn't be happier for her. *Entertainment Weekly* came out with its list of the hundred most powerful people in the entertainment business, and only two editors were on the list: Sonny Mehta and Ann Godoff. I suspect she just moved up several notches. But aside from all that, I simply like her enormously, and am very glad for her.

Sunday, November 23

Just read yet another book that dismantles the relativists, constructivists, and extreme postmodernists, so I am indeed going to declare my own personal national holiday.

The book is Thomas Nagel's *The Last Word*, and, in conjunction with so many other books (I've seen over a dozen), it really does look like the almost three-decades-long reign of the narcissists and nihilists (relativists and constructivists) has finally come to a close. There are some very important truths in postmodernism—which I have gone out of my way to champion and embrace, and will continue to do so—but the extremists have blown them all out of proportion in an attempt to deny any universal truths, any transcendental realities, and any common human ground, and they have done so in a tone that is often vicious, cranky, and mean-spirited.

The extreme relativists and constructivists—who maintain, for example, that all of reality is socially constructed, and thus relative from culture to culture—have already had their tenets decisively deflated by the likes of Jürgen Habermas and Karl Otto-Apel (who both show the performative self-contradiction hidden in the very center of the constructivists' claims), John Searle (who demonstrated that socially constructed realities must rest on objective truths or the construction can never get under way in the first place), Peter Berger (who relativized the relativizers, thus defeating their own claims), Charles Taylor (who showed that the relativists' antiranking was itself a ranking), among others. Nobody has taken these extremists seriously for many years—except the boomers and their "new paradigms," which will "subvert" the old paradigms and replace them with new ones, which is possible because all realities are "socially constructed" and therefore capable of being "deconstructed." All of those notions, however well intentioned, are deeply confused, and Thomas Nagel is simply the last in a long line of theorists to demonstrate why.

Just as significant is the review of Nagel's book by Colin McGinn carried in *The New Republic*.[32] As a bastion of liberalism, TNR has itself often championed the extreme diversity, constructivism, and relativism that is part and parcel of the narcissism and nihilism of postmodernity. To have TNR come out so strongly in favor of Nagel's position is most illuminating.

McGinn starts by summarizing the extreme postmodernist conception of rationality. "According to this conception, human reason is inherently local, culture-relative, rooted in the variable facts of human nature and history, a matter of divergent 'practices' and 'forms of life' and 'frames of reference' and 'conceptual schemes.' There are no norms of reasoning that transcend what is accepted by a society or an epoch, no objective justifications for belief that everyone must respect on pain of cognitive malfunction. To be valid is to be taken to be valid, and different people can have legitimately different patterns of taking. In the end, the only justifications for belief have the form 'justified for me.' " (Note the narcissism or intense subjectivism.)

McGinn continues: "In such a view, objectivity, if it exists at all, is a function of social relations; a matter of social consensus, not of acknowledging truths and principles that obtain whether or not any society recognizes them. The norms of reasoning are ultimately like the norms of fashion."

Nagel shows, and McGinn agrees, that all of those claims are self-contradictory. This is the path also taken by Habermas, and, indeed, I extensively made the same argument in the Introduction to *The Eye of Spirit* (and earlier in SES, and again in chapter 9 of *Sense and Soul* [see July 9 for a short example of this]). But leave it to Nagel to nail it. McGinn: "The subjectivist holds that reason is nothing other than a manifestation of local and relative contingencies, and that its results have no authority beyond the parochial domain; in trying to go beyond the local, reason overreaches itself and produces empty assertions. This is clearly a theory about the nature of reason: it purports to tell us what

---

32. Colin McGinn, "Reason the Need," *The New Republic*, August 4, 1997.

reason is, what its place in the world amounts to. But the point is that this theory is offered as the *truth* about reason, as something that ought to command the assent of all rational beings. It is not offered as merely true for its propounder or his speech community. No, it is meant as a non-relatively true account of the very nature of reason. In propounding it, therefore, the subjectivist himself employs principles of reasoning and commitments to truth which are taken to have more than relative validity."

McGinn then drives to Nagel's inescapable conclusion: "But this is to presuppose the very thing that the subjectivist is claiming to call into question. There is a dilemma here: either announce the debunking account of reason as the objective truth, or put it forward as merely an instance of its own official conception of truth. In the former case, the subjectivist contradicts himself, claiming a status for his utterance that according to him no utterance can have; but in the latter case, the claim is merely true for him and has no authority over anyone else's beliefs. If the subjectivist's statement is true, then we can ignore it; if it is not, then it is false. In either case it is not a claim we can take seriously. And so subjectivism is refuted."

McGinn states that Nagel's argument "is absolutely decisive. Nagel applies his general anti-subjectivist argument in a number of areas, including language, logic, arithmetic and ethics. In each of these areas he argues convincingly that the content of the judgments involved cannot be construed in subjectivist fashion, but must be taken as affording objective reasons with universal prescriptive force."

My own view, of course, is that there are *universal* deep features with *relative* surface features—unitas multiplex, universal pluralism. The deep features are generally similar wherever we find them, while the surface features are local, culturally constructed, and relative, usually differing from culture to culture. But in making the culturally relative surface features the *entire* story, the extreme postmodernists have devastated human and spiritual understanding, which always includes a universal/transcendental component. "The case that Nagel presents should disturb all those who have been lulled, or bludgeoned, into the flabby relativism that is so rampant in contemporary intellectual culture. Richard Rorty comes in for some stern critical words from Nagel, and they are richly deserved."

McGinn says that "Nagel's argument is not only correct, it is also urgent." Why urgent? Because it is required to combat the rampant narcissism that is at the heart of the relativist/constructivist game, which claims for itself a truth that it denies to all others, or, at the very least, anchors all truth in subjectivist, egocentric preferences. "First-person avowals" are the only "truth" acknowledged. In this insane view, says Nagel, "Nothing is right, and instead we are all expressing our personal or cultural points of view. The actual result has been a growth in the already extreme intellectual laziness of contemporary culture and the collapse of serious argument throughout the lower reaches of the humanities and social sciences, together with a refusal to take seriously, as anything other than first-person avowals, the objective arguments of others." Narcissism and fragmentation have replaced truth and communication, and this is called cultural studies.

McGinn gets very close to the heart of the matter. "*The Last Word* is a book that should be read and pondered in this golden age of subjectivism [egocentrism, narcissism]. As to why such leanings exist and are so prevalent today . . . I have a notion." And his notion is that universal truths, as opposed to subjectivist views, "clash with a popular and misguided ideal of freedom." Universal truth "constrains our thinking. We must obey its mandates. Yet people don't want to be constrained; they want to feel they can choose their beliefs, like beans in a supermarket. They want to be able to follow their impulses and not be reined in by impersonal [let alone transpersonal] demands. [This] feels like a violation of the inalienable right to do whatever one wants to do."

In plain language, universal truths curb narcissism; they constrain the ego; they force us outside of our subjectivist wishes, there to confront a reality not merely of our own making. It has become increasingly obvious that extreme social constructivism is the grand refuge of subjectivism/narcissism (which is precisely why it is so popular with my generation; if boomers have one reputation, it is for self-absorption). Wanting nothing to violate one's egocentric priorities—the "misguided ideal of freedom"—it is necessary to make facts plastic. Feminists don't like the relative advantage that males have in physical strength and mobility, so simply claim all biology is socially constructed. New-agers don't like conventional restraints, so claim they are socially constructed. Deep ecologists, ecofeminists, retro-Romantics, new-paradigmers, all would have recourse to social constructivism as a prelude to denying any realities they didn't happen to like and replacing them with ones of their own subjective choosing.

Many critics have harshly noted, therefore, that a boomer-driven, narcissistically based cultural studies would have these features: *social constructivism* (so I can deconstruct whatever I want), *relativism* (no universal truths to constrain me), *equation of science and poetry* (no objective facts to get in my way), *extreme contextualism* (no universal truths except my own), *all interpretation is reader-response* (I create all meaning), *no meta-narratives or big pictures* (except my own big picture about why all other big pictures are invalid), *antirationalism* (there is no objective truth except my own), *antihierarchy* (because there is nothing higher than me). Unfortunately those are the exact characteristics of most academic cultural studies in America—*and* some of the central features of the Person-Centered Civil Religion (another reason the PCCR is so rarely transformative; it rests, in part, on a series of unfortunate self-contradictions, embedded in antihierarchism, relativism, and subjectivism, and thus it can't get any traction for transformation [see September 23]).

Just as SUNY Press is the purveyor of much of extreme postmodernism in this country, Blackwell is in Britain. So I was fascinated to see that its most recent *A Dictionary of Cultural and Critical Theory*, which one would expect to be chock full of postmodern post-structuralist tenets, in fact contains a Nagel-like attack on most postmodern theories of constructivism and relativism. "Therefore it follows, supposedly, that all truth talk, whether in the natural or more theory-prone human sciences, comes down to a choice of the right sort of metaphor (or the optimum rhetorical strategy) for conjuring assent from others engaged in the same communal enterprise. Scientists have understandably considered this an implausible account of how advances come about through the joint application of theory and empirical research. Hence the recent emergence of causal-realist or anti-conventionalist [universal and anti-subjectivist] approaches which offer a far better understanding of our knowledge of the growth of knowledge. After all, there seems rather little to be said for a philosophy of science that effectively leaves itself nothing to explain by reducing 'science' to just another species of preferential language game, rhetoric, discourse, conceptual scheme, or whatever. The current revival of realist ontologies betokens a break with this whole misdirected—as it now appears—line of thought."

While I am obviously in major agreement with these decisive attacks on extreme postmodernism (by Habermas, Otto-Apel, Ernst Gellner, Charles Taylor, Nagel, McGinn, among others), I have always taken a slightly different approach. These critics tend to simply demolish the extreme postmodernists altogether, and give them not an inch of ground on which to stand. My approach has been that there are *some important but partial truths in postmodernism*, and that what needs to be attacked

are the extremist versions that take relativism, constructivism, and contextualism to be the only truths in existence—at which point they all
become self-contradictory and unworthy of respect. But buried in the
postmodern agenda are several noble impulses, I believe, yet in order to
salvage them, they must themselves be placed in a larger context, which
both limits their claims and completes their aims.

The noble impulses are those of freedom, tolerance, aperspectival embrace, and liberation from unnecessary or unfair conventions. The lib-
eral/postmodern agenda has been to cherish cultural differences and
multiple perspectives, including previously marginalized cultures and
groups (women, minorities, gays, etc.). That stance—namely, *universal
pluralism*—is a very high developmental achievement, coming into existence *only* at the worldcentric, postconventional level of growth. The
liberal/postmodern stance, *at its best*, is generated at and from that high
level of consciousness evolution.

But in their zeal to "transgress" and "subvert" conventional levels in
favor of postconventional freedom, the extreme liberal/postmodernists
ended up championing any and all stances (extreme diversity and multiculturalism), including many stances that are frankly ethnocentric and
egocentric (since all stances are to be equally valued). This allowed, and
often encouraged, regressive trends, a devolution from worldcentric to
ethnocentric to egocentric—to a rampant subjectivism and narcissism,
in fact, which then anchored the entire (and at this point completely
misguided) agenda. Noble impulses horribly skewed—there is the best
that can be said for liberal/postmodernism. The noble vision of universal
pluralism was devastated, the *universal* part was completely ditched or
denied, and rampant *pluralism*, driven by rampant narcissism, came to
carry the day.

It is against this vulgar pluralism—which actually dissolves and destroys the liberal stance itself, destroys the demand for evolution to the
worldcentric, postconventional levels which alone can support and protect the pluralistic vision—that the recent attacks have been directed.
Habermas, Nagel, and crew are simply pointing out that the very claim
of pluralism has, in fact, a universal component, and unless this universal component is acknowledged and included, the entire liberal/post-
modern agenda self-destructs. I totally agree. But let us not forget the
noble impulses hidden in that agenda, and let us not forget that those
impulses can be *redeemed*, and the original liberal/postmodern vision
can be fulfilled, if we retire pluralism and return to universal pluralism
and unitas multiplex: universal deep features, local surface features.

These universal features are accessed by empathy and compassion. And the liberal/postmodern vision itself can be protected *only* if it includes, in its own agenda, a cultural encouragement that individuals do their best to grow and evolve from egocentric to sociocentric to worldcentric, there to stand open to universal spiritual glories.

Freedom—the core of the liberal values—does not lie in egocentric or ethnocentric realms. Real freedom, true freedom, lies in the vast expanse of worldcentric awareness, which itself opens onto the infinite expanse of pure Spirit and primordial Self, a Self common in and to all sentient beings as such, and therefore a domain in which Freedom radiates in all directions. That is why we must move in a postliberal, not preliberal, fashion. So it is the irony of ironies that liberal/postmodernism, in searching for freedom for all, has championed modes of intense unfreedom: the egocentric is not free, for he is a slave to his impulses; the ethnocentric is not free, for he is a slave to his skin color; only in worldcentric awareness, which sets a mature individuality in the context of all individuals and moves easily in that vastly expanded space, does a real freedom begin to dawn, a freedom that opens onto pure Spirit in a timeless embrace of the All. Let liberalism continue to move in that original direction, of progressive growth and evolution, and cease the self-contradictory and mindless championing of any subjectivist impulse that comes down the pike.

It is the narrow, misguided, narcissistic, relativistic sludge that is being so effectively demolished by these critics, and rightly so. *Make no mistake*: if postmodernism is right, there is and can be no Spirit whatsoever. If Spirit is anything, it is universal. If Spirit is anything, it is all-encompassing. If Spirit is anything, it is the Ground of manifestation everywhere, equally, radiantly. But if there is nothing universal—and that is the claim of the extreme postmodernists—then there is nothing genuinely spiritual anywhere in the universe, nor can there ever be. So while I hold open the noble impulses in the original vision—that of universal pluralism and unitas multiplex—I join in the attack on those who have forgotten the unitas and offer only the multiplex.

Monday, November 24

Roger, Frances, Kate, and T George have all convened in San Francisco for the annual conference of the American Academy of Religion, running the 22nd through the 25th. Roger, in particular, has attended these regularly in the past, mostly out of professional responsibility, but he always reports the same thing: these scholars are involved in almost nothing but translative spirituality, and then not even in an engaged fashion, but merely as an object of dreary, detached, desiccated study. Roger says to attend most of these talks is to take boredom into uncharted waters.

When I was a youngster, and being the mad scientist type, I used to collect insects. Central to this endeavor was the killing jar. You take an empty mayonnaise jar, put lethal carbon tetrachloride on cotton balls, and place them in the bottom of the jar. You then drop the insect—moth, butterfly, whatnot—into the jar, and it quickly dies, but without being outwardly disfigured. You then mount it, study it, display it.

Academic religion is the killing jar of Spirit.

Thursday, November 27

Marci cooked a huge Thanksgiving dinner, to which we invited Kate. The dinner was fabulous, though at first I thought the turkey was going to burn, it was so large and had to cook so long. Which reminded me of Gracie Allen's instructions on how to cook a chicken. "I always burn everything I cook. But I finally figured out how to cook a chicken correctly. You put a large chicken and a small chicken in a hot oven. When the small chicken burns, the large one is done."

Saturday, November 29

Marci took me to *The Nutcracker*, which was sweet. I feel truly fortunate to have her in my life. With love, the frontal gets an intense glow, the deeper psychic resonates with virtue, the Witness embraces all. But it's like the old Yiddish saying: "I've been rich and I've been poor; rich is better." Same with being in love.

Sunday, November 30

There are four major stages or phases of spiritual unfolding: belief, faith, direct experience, and permanent adaptation: you can believe in Spirit, you can have faith in Spirit, you can directly experience Spirit, you can become Spirit.

1. *Belief* is the earliest (and therefore, the most common) stage of spiritual orientation. Belief originates at the *mental level*, generally, since it requires images, symbols, and concepts. But the mind itself goes

through several transitional phases in its own development—magic, mythic, rational, and vision-logic—and *each of those is the basis of a type (and stage) of spiritual or religious belief.*

Magic belief is egocentric, with subject and object often fused, thus marked by the notion that the individual self can dramatically affect the physical world and other people through mental wishes—voodoo and word magic being the most well-known examples. *Mythic belief* (which is usually sociocentric/ethnocentric, since different people have different myths that are mutually exclusive: if Jesus is the one and only savior of humankind, Krishna is kaput) invests its spiritual intuitions in one or more physically disembodied gods or goddesses, who have ultimate power over human actions. *Rational belief*—to the extent that reason chooses to believe at all—attempts to *demythologize* religion and portray God or the Goddess, not as an anthropomorphic deity, but as an ultimate Ground of Being. This rationalization reaches its zenith with *vision-logic belief*, where sciences such as systems theory are often used to explain this Ground of Being as a Great Holistic System, Gaia, Goddess, Eco-Spirit, the Web of Life, and so forth.

All of those are mental *beliefs*, usually accompanied by strong emotional sentiments or feelings; but they are not necessarily direct experiences of *supramental* spiritual realities. As such, they are merely forms of translation: they can be embraced without changing one's present level of consciousness in the least. But as those merely translative gestures begin to mature, and as direct emergence of the higher domains increasingly presses against the self, mere belief gives way to faith.

2. *Faith* begins, if at all, when belief loses its power to compel. Sooner or later, *any* mental belief—precisely because it is mental and not supramental or spiritual—will begin to lose its forcefulness. For example, the mental belief in spirit as the Web of Life will begin to pale in its power to persuade: no matter how much you keep believing in the Web of Life, you still feel like a separate, isolated ego, beset with hope and fear. You try to believe harder; it still doesn't work. Mere belief might have provided you with a type of translative meaning, but not with an actual *transformation*, and this slowly, painfully, becomes obvious. (It might even be worse if you are involved in magic or mythic beliefs, because not only do these not usually transform you, they often act as a regressive force in your awareness, moving you not toward, but away from, the transrational.)

Still, there is often a genuine, spiritual, transmental intuition behind the mental belief in Gaia or the Web of Life, namely, an intuition of the

Oneness of Life. But this intuition cannot be fully realized as long as belief grips consciousness. For all *beliefs* are ultimately divisive and dualistic—holistic beliefs are ultimately just as dualistic as analytic beliefs, because both make sense only in terms of their opposites. You are not supposed to *think* the All, you are supposed to *be* the All, and as long as you are clinging to beliefs *about* the All, it will never happen. Mere beliefs are cardboard nutrition for the soul, spiritually empty calories, and sooner or later they cease to fascinate and console.

But usually between letting go of belief, on the one hand, and finding direct experience, on the other, the person is carried only by faith. If the *belief* in Oneness can no longer offer much consolation, still the person has *faith* that Oneness is there, somehow, calling out to him or her. And they are right. Faith soldiers on when belief becomes unbelievable, for faith hears the faint but direct call of a higher reality—of Spirit, of God, of Goddess, of Oneness—a higher reality that, being beyond the mind, is *beyond belief*. Faith stands on the threshold of direct supramental, transrational experience. Lacking dogmatic beliefs, it has no sense of security; not yet having direct experience, it has no sense of certainty. Faith is thus a no-man's-land—a thousand questions, no answers—it possesses only a dogged determination to find its spiritual abode, and, pulled on by its own hidden intuition, it might eventually find direct experience.

3. *Direct experience* decisively answers the nagging questions inherent in faith. There are usually two phases of direct experience: peak experiences and plateau experiences.

Peak experiences are relatively brief, usually intense, often unbidden, and frequently life-changing. They are actually "peek experiences" into the transpersonal, supramental levels of one's own higher potentials. *Psychic* peak experiences are a glimpse into nature mysticism (gross-level oneness); *subtle* peak experiences are a glimpse into deity mysticism (subtle-level oneness); *causal* peak experiences are a glimpse into emptiness (causal-level oneness); and *nondual* peak experiences are a glimpse into One Taste. As Roger Walsh has pointed out, the higher the level of the peak experience, the rarer it is. (This is why most experiences of "cosmic consciousness" are actually just a glimpse of nature mysticism or gross-level oneness, the shallowest of the mystical realms. Many people mistake this for One Taste, unfortunately. This confusion, in my opinion, is epidemic among eco-theorists.)

Most people remain, understandably, at the stage of belief or faith (and usually magical or mythical at that). Occasionally, however, individuals will have a strong peak experience of a genuinely transpersonal realm, and it completely shatters them, often for the better, sometimes for the worse. But you can tell they aren't merely repeating a belief they read in a book, or giving merely translative chitchat: they have truly seen a higher realm, and they are never quite the same.

(This is not always a good thing. Someone at the concrete-literal mythic level, for example, can have a peak experience of, say, the subtle level, whereupon the authority of the subtle is injected into their concrete myths, and the result is a reborn fundamentalist: their particular mythic god-figure is the *only* figure that can save the entire world, and they will burn your body to save your soul. Someone at the vision-logic level can have a psychic-level peak experience, and then their "new eco-paradigm" is the *only* thing that can save the planet, and they will gladly march lock-step in eco-fascism to save you from yourself. Religious fanaticism of such ilk is almost impossible to dismantle, because it is an intense mixture of higher truth with lower structure. The higher truth is often a very genuine spiritual experience, a true "peek" experience of a higher domain; but precisely because it is a brief, temporary experience—and not an enduring, steady, clear awareness—it gets immediately snapped up and translated downward into the lower level, where it confers an almost unshakable legitimacy on even the ugliest of beliefs.)

Whereas peak experiences are usually of brief duration—a few minutes to a few hours—*plateau experiences* are more constant and enduring, verging on becoming a permanent adaptation. Whereas peak experiences can, and usually do, come spontaneously, in order to sustain them and turn them from a peak into a plateau—from a brief *altered state* into a more *enduring trait*—prolonged practice is required. Whereas almost anybody, at any time, at any age, can have a brief peak experience, I know of few bona fide cases of plateau experiences that did not involve years of sustained spiritual practice. Thus, whereas belief and faith are by far the most common types of spiritual orientation, and while peak experiences are rare but authentic spiritual experiences, from this point on in spiritual unfolding, we usually find only those who are involved in sustained, intense, prolonged, profound spiritual practice.

Plateau experiences, like peak experiences, can be of the psychic, subtle, causal, or nondual domains. I will give one example, taken from Zen, that covers all four. Typically, individuals practicing Zen meditation will start by counting the breaths, one to ten, repeatedly. When they can do that for half an hour without losing count, they might be assigned a koan (such as the syllable *mu*, which was my first koan). For the next three or four years, they will practice several hours each day, concentrating on the sound *mu* and attempting not to drop it (there is, simultaneously, an intense inquiry into "What is the meaning of *mu*?" or "Who is it that is concentrating on *mu*?"). Several times each year, they will attend seven-day sesshins or intense practice sessions, where they will be encouraged to practice throughout the day and into the night.

The first important plateau experience occurs when students can uninterruptedly hold on to *mu* for most of their waking hours. *Mu* has become such a part of consciousness, such a part of you—in fact, you become *mu*—that you can hold it in awareness, in an unbroken fashion, all day, literally. In other words, a type of witnessing awareness is now a *constant* capacity throughout the gross-waking state. Students are then told that if they truly want to penetrate *mu*, they must continue working on it even during their sleep. (When I first heard this, I thought it was a joke, a type of macho initiation humor, of the sort, "If you want to be part of the fighting First Infantry, mister, you have to eat three live snakes." I thought they were just trying to scare me; they were actually trying to help.) Another one or two years, and dedicated students do indeed continue a subtle concentration on *mu* right into the dream state. There is now a *constant* witnessing awareness even in the subtle-dream realm.[33] At this point, as students approach the causal unmanifest (or pure absorption), they are on the verge of

---

33. Of course, the dream state is only one of the many types of subtle-realm phenomena; the classic subtle state is *savikalpa samadhi*, "nondual absorption with form," which introduces one to the subtle realm while awake. The dream state is said to be a subclass of the subtle, in that there are no gross material phenomena in the dream state (only images and forms). Thus, to enter the dream state *consciously* has always been seen as an analog of *savikalpa samadhi*. (As we might put it: in both there is alpha-waking and theta-dreaming present simultaneously). The effect on the evolution of consciousness is quite similar in both cases: you have to some degree objectified the subtle—consciously seen it as an object, while awake—and thus it has lost its power over you: you have transcended it, and thus can begin to move into causal development.

Nirvikalpa samadhi is the classic state of causal consciousness: formless, unmanifest, pure cessation (one type of emptiness), which introduces you to the causal domain while awake (*nirvikalpa* matures into *jnana samadhi*, or radically pure formlessness, and in some traditions, into *nirodh*, or the complete extinction of objects altogether). Just as *savikalpa* and pellucid dreaming are analogs, so maintaining awareness during deep dreamless sleep and *nirvikalpa* are analogs. In both *nirvikalpa* and pellucid deep sleep, alpha-waking and delta-formlessness are present simultaneously: you have brought consciousness even into the formless realm, thus freeing consciousness from that realm, and open-the explosion known as satori, which is a breakthrough from the "frozen ice" of pure causal absorption to the Great Liberation of One Taste. At first, this One Taste is itself a peak experience, but it, too, will become, with further practice, a plateau experience, then a permanent adaptation.[34]

---

ing it to the nondual. The causal has been transcended, and *nirvikalpa/jnana* (gnosis) gives way to *sahaja*, or effortless, spontaneous, ever-present One Taste.

In order to make a good deal of progress, one does not necessarily have to be able to pellucid dream or pellucid deep sleep. *Savikalpa samadhi* and *nirvikalpa samadhi* can be adequately attained during the waking state. It is just that, when practitioners gain competency of *savikalpa*, they often begin to pellucid dream—precisely because those are analogs. Likewise, a mastery of *nirvikalpa* is often accompanied by pellucid deep sleep. And conversely, pursuing one's meditation into the dream and deep sleep state is a dramatic and extremely effective way to enter *savikalpa* and *nirvikalpa*, and thus more easily stand open to *sahaja*. The Yoga of the Dream State has always been held to be one of the fastest, most efficient ways of reaching a plateau experience of subtle and causal realms, thus quickly opening the door to stable adaptation at—and transcendence of—those realms.

34. The stages of adaptation leading from causal/nirvikalpa/nirvana to nondual One Taste (or sahaja) are known as *post-nirvanic* stages, of which three or four are usually given. There are several variations on these stages, but they all center around constant consciousness, or the unbroken access to witnessing awareness through all three states—first as a plateau, then an adaptation—and then the disappearance of witnessing into nondual One Taste—first as a peak, then as a plateau, then an adaptation.

Once One Taste has been stabilized as an *adaptation*, the *post-enlightenment* stages unfold. These are said to result in *bhava samadhi*, or the complete bodily translation of the human into the Divine; or, alternatively, "the complete extinction of all things into the *dharmata*"; or, another alternative, the achievement of a permanent light body. (See *The Eye of Spirit* for a discussion of post-nirvanic and post-enlightenment stages of development.)

The *post-nirvanic* stages (the essence of Mahayana and Vajrayana, which do not merely embrace Formlessness—nirvana—but integrate that with the entire world of Form—samsara—to result in pure nondual One Taste) have always made sense to me; and, based on my own experience, I can testify to the existence of constant consciousness and One Taste, both of them as prolonged and recurrent plateau experiences, sometimes lasting uninterruptedly 24–36 hours (although, in one case, constant consciousness persisted day and night for eleven days). Neither is a permanent adaptation in my case, but there are several teachers I have met who, I believe, are in such, and the literature is replete with them. All of these post-nirvanic stages inherently make sense because they are, after all, simply the stages of adapting to nonduality (the stages of integrating nirvana and samsara, Spirit and manifestation, Emptiness and Form). More-

4. *Adaptation* simply means *a constant, permanent access to a given level of consciousness*. Most of us have already adapted (or evolved) to matter, body, and mind (which is why you have access to all three of them virtually any time you want). And some of us have had peak experiences into the transpersonal levels (psychic, subtle, causal, or nondual). But with actual practice, we can evolve into plateau experiences of these higher realms, and these plateau experiences, with further practice, can become permanent adaptations: *constant access* to psychic, subtle, causal, and nondual occasions—constant access to nature mysticism, deity mysticism, formless mysticism, and integral mysticism—all as easily available to consciousness as matter, body, and mind now are. And this is likewise evidenced in a constant consciousness (sahaja) through all three states—waking, dreaming (or savikalpa samadhi), and sleeping (or nirvikalpa samadhi). It then becomes obvious why "That which is not present in deep dreamless sleep is not real." The Real must be *present in all three states*, including deep dreamless sleep, and pure Consciousness is the only thing that is present in all three. This Fact becomes perfectly obvious when you rest as pure, empty, formless Consciousness and "watch" all three states arise, abide, and pass, while you remain Unmoved, Unchanged, Unborn, released into the pure Emptiness that is all Form, the One Taste that is the radiant All.

. . .

Those are some of the major phases we tend to go through as we adapt to the higher levels of our own spiritual nature: *belief* (magic, mythic, rational, holistic); *faith* (which is an intuition, but not yet a direct experience, of the higher realms); *peak experience* (of the psychic, subtle,

---

over, with the EEG data now being gathered by Alexander and others, we seem to have hard corroborating evidence that such stages do in fact exist.

But the *post-enlightenment* stages have never made much sense to me, nor have I ever met anybody who was believably at those stages. Those stages, as they are described, have always struck me as a holdover from magic—they always include items such as one's body going up in light, being able to perform extraordinary miracles of transformation, etc.—none of which has any credible, reproducible evidence. As for the notion of "the extinction of all things into the *dharmata*," this sounds indistinguishable from *jnana* or *nirodh*—a regression from One Taste, not a development beyond it. I am not saying these stages do not exist; I am saying that, compared with all the other stages that the traditions offer (and that I briefly outlined above, including the post-nirvanic stages), the post-enlightenment stages have the least amount of evidence—possibly because they are so rare, possibly because they are not there.

causal, or nondual—in no particular order, because peak experiences are usually one-time hits); *plateau experience* (of the psychic, subtle, causal, and nondual—almost always in that order, because competence at one stage is generally required for the next); and *permanent adaptation* (to the psychic, subtle, causal, and nondual, also in that order, for the same reason).

Several important points:

· You can be at a relatively high level of spiritual development and still be at a relatively low level in other lines (e.g., the deeper psychic can be progressing while the frontal is quite retarded). We all know people who are spiritually developed but still rather immature in sexual relations, emotional intimacy, physical health, and so on. Even if you have constant access to One Taste, that will not make your muscles grow stronger, will not necessarily get you that new job, won't get you the girl, and won't cure all your neuroses. You can still have deep pockets of shadow material that are not necessarily dug up as you advance into higher stages of spiritual practice or meditation (precisely because meditation is *not*, contra the popular view, primarily an uncovering technique; if it were, most of our meditation teachers wouldn't need psychotherapy, whereas most of them do, like everybody else. Meditation is not primarily *uncovering* the repressed unconscious, but allowing the *emergence* of higher domains—which usually leaves the lower, repressed domains still lower, and still repressed.)

So even as you advance in your own spiritual unfolding, consider combining it with a good psychotherapeutic practice, because spiritual practice, as a rule, will not adequately expose the psychodynamic unconscious. Nor will it appropriately exercise the physical body—so try weightlifting. Nor will it exercise the pranic body—trying adding t'ai chi ch'uan. Nor will it work with group or community dynamic, so add . . . Well, the point, of course, is to take up *integral practice* as the only sound and balanced way to proceed with one's own higher development.

· This is especially important because the Person-Centered Civil Religion (and the 415 Paradigm) is anchored predominantly in the stage of *holistic belief*. In order for most people to move beyond those mental translations, a genuine transformative practice is required. *Integral practice* is very likely the most effective. It emphasizes transformation not just in the I, but in all four quadrants—or the Big Three of I, we, and it—transformative practices in the self, with relationships and community, and with nature [see June 18], not merely as a change in type of belief but in level of consciousness. In short: exercise body, mind, soul, and spirit in self, culture, and nature.

• Even though I have described higher stages whose access usually takes at least five or six years of arduous practice (and whose highest stages often take thirty years or more), don't let that put you off if you are a beginner. *Simply begin practice*—five or six years will go by in a blink, but you will be reaping the abundant rewards. On the other hand, if you listen to those teachers who are selling nothing but beliefs (magic, mythic, rational, or holistic), you will be nothing but five or six years older. (Holistic beliefs are fine—and quite accurate—*for the mental realm*. But spirituality is about the *transmental* realm, the supramental realm, the superconscious realm, and no amount of mind translations will help you transcend the mind. And no amount of Person-Centered Civil Religion will deliver you from yourself.) Rather, you must take up a contemplative, transpersonal, supramental practice. So no matter how daunting practice seems, simply begin. As the old joke has it: How do you eat an elephant? One bite at a time.

• The fact is, a few bites into the elephant and you will already start gaining considerable benefits. You might begin, say, twenty minutes a day of centering prayer as taught by Father Thomas Keating. Many people report almost immediate effects—calming, opening, caring, listening: the heart melts a little bit, and so do you. Zikr for a half hour; vipassana for 40 minutes; yoga exercises twice a day, worked into your schedule; Tantric visualization; prayer of the heart; counting your breaths for 15 minutes each morning before you get out of bed. Any of those are fine; whatever works for you, just take the first few bites. . . .

• We need to be gentle with ourselves, it is true; but we also need to be firm. Treat yourself with real compassion, not idiot compassion, and therefore begin to challenge yourself, engage yourself, push yourself: begin to practice.

• As any of these practices start to take hold, you might find it appropriate to attend an intensive retreat for a few days each year. This will give you a chance to extend the little "peeks" of practice into the beginning plateaus of practice. The years will go by, yes, but you will be ripening along with them, slowly but surely transcending the lesser aspects of yourself and opening to the greater. There will come a day when you will look back on all that time as if it were just dream, because in fact it is a dream, from which you will soon awaken.

• The point is simple: If you are interested in genuine transformative spirituality, find an authentic spiritual teacher and *begin practice*. Without practice, you will never move beyond the phases of belief, faith, and random peak experiences. You will never evolve into plateau experiences, nor from there into permanent realization. You will remain, at best, a brief visitor in the territory of your own higher estate, a tourist in your own true Self.

December

This self-luminous, vividly clear, present wakefulness and
    awareness,
In which Form and Emptiness are nondual,
Is the consciousness in which the three states *[waking,
    dream, sleep]* are spontaneously present.
Maintain it day and night in a continuous practice, my
    heart children.
This is how nonduality is the natural freedom.
                    —TSOGDRUK RANGDROL

Tuesday, December 2

Marci has finished her thesis, so we celebrate for the day. Rented *Lonesome Dove* ("The only education you're gonna get is listening to me talk"), drank wine, floated downstream.

Wednesday, December 3

Spirit is not an altered state of consciousness (ASC) or a nonordinary state (NOSC). There is no alternative to it. There is only Spirit, within which the world rolls out. There is only One State, within which different states arise. There is only One Taste, through which different tastes flow. But One Taste itself neither comes nor goes; it is beyond motion and stillness, commotion and quiet, movement or rest. Look to the ends of the world, you will only find One Taste. Let your mind wander to the edge of the universe, you will only find One Taste. Let your awareness expand to infinity, you will still only find One Taste.

So where is this amazing One Taste? Well, who is reading this page? Who is looking out from those eyes? Who is hearing with those ears? Who is seeing this world right now? That Seer, that ever-present Witness, which is your own immediate Self, stands on the edge of the nondual revelation in this and every moment. Rest as your very own Self; rest as the clear seeing of this page, this room, this world; rest as the vast pure Emptiness in which the entire world is arising . . . and then see if that world isn't one with that Self. For in this moment of simple resting as the Witness, notice that the *feeling* of the Witness and the *feeling* of the world are one and the same feeling ("When I heard the bell ring, there was no I and no bell, just the ringing"). In the simple Feeling of Being, you are the World.

Look! It's *just this*.

And once you taste One Taste, no matter how fleetingly at first, an entirely new motivation will arise from the depths of your very own being and become a constant atmosphere which your every impulse breathes, and that atmosphere is compassion. Once you taste One Taste, and see the fundamental problems of existence evaporate in the blazing sun of obviousness, you will never again be the same person, deep within your heart. And you will want—finally, profoundly, and most of all—that others, too, may be relieved of the burden of their sleep-walking dreams, relieved of the agony of the separate self, relieved of the inherent torture called time and the gruesome tragedy called space.

No matter that lesser motivations will dog your path, no matter that anger and envy, shame and pity, pride and prejudice will remind you daily how much more you can always grow: still, and still, under it all, around it all, above it all, the heartbeat of compassion will resound. A constant cloud of caring will rain on your every parade. And you will be driven, in the best sense of the word, by this ruthless taskmaster, but only because you, eons ago, made a secret promise to let this motivation rule you until all souls are set free in the ocean of infinity.

Because of compassion, you will strive harder. Because of compassion, you will get straight. Because of compassion, you will work your fingers to the bone, push at the world until you literally bleed, toil till the tears stain your vision, struggle until life itself runs dry. And in the deepest, deepest center of your Heart, the World is already thanking you.

Friday, December 5

I was sorry to see that Leon Forrest died (cancer, age sixty). Forrest used a type of stream-of-consciousness writing to delve into the African-

American experience. *Divine Days* left a deep and unsettling impression on me—seven or eight days in southside Chicago.

The slavery issue in this country is tragic. Of the dozens—more like hundreds—of different ethnic cultures that came to this country, only one was brought against its will. Only one was boiled and fried in the melting pot. Bereft of background culture and supporting social contexts, African-Americans have had to fight a brutal uphill battle to gain meaning, roots, self-determination, and economic power. The wonder is that African-Americans have accomplished the extraordinary amount that they have. It is often said that there are only two original American art forms: jazz and tap dance. Both, we note, are black inventions. In the arts, in sports, in politics, in academia, African-Americans have made profound contributions.

The issue of blame, however, is a dead-end. Historically, slavery was often practiced by Africans on Africans, and Africans sold Africans to white slave traders. Nobody has anything to be proud of in this particular regard. Moreover, the real issue of culpability lies elsewhere, for the most part. *All* types of pre-industrial societies had slavery, with no exceptions—foraging (hunting and gathering), herding, horticultural, maritime, and agrarian. Up to 90% of some societal types—herding and horticultural, for example—had slavery. Only with industrialization does the rate of slavery drop to 0%. In fact, in a one-hundred-year period, roughly 1770–1870, sanctioned slavery was eradicated from every industrialized nation on the face of the planet. It was America's ill fortune to have come of age when that transition was being made—the transition from a mythic-agrarian structure (which happily sanctions slavery) to a rational-industrial structure (which is abhorred by it).

What I find so unfortunate in the "race debate" is how cheaply each side tries to make points, without a certain sensitivity to the historical growth of consciousness itself. The values that liberal Westerners tend to share, the values of the Enlightenment (the values of rational-industrialism)—namely, liberty, equality, and freedom—were simply *not* the values of *any* other societal type, *ever*. Foragers occasionally had a type of diffuse egalitarianism, but physical strength in fact determined a covert male dominance. Horticultural societies—about a third of which were matrifocal, with Great Mother mythologies—had an 84% rate of slavery, one of the very worst in all of history. With the agrarian structure—which was almost entirely patriarchal—the percentage of societies engaged in slavery drops to around 54%. And with patriarchal industrialization, the rate drops to 0%—with the *concomitant* values of equality, liberty, and freedom—the first time, anywhere in history, where these values were implemented on a large scale, as part of the organizing principles of society.

Although whites engaged in slavery—as every pre-industrial race and societal type did—nonetheless, whites set in motion those ideas (the Enlightenment) and those structures (industrialism) that would, within one century, eradicate slavery for the first time in the history of the human race.

The difficulty is that both sides of the debate (by which I mean, roughly, liberal and conservative) get caught up with the wrong sides of the equation. Liberals tend to think that slavery is simply something that mean white people did to nice black people, failing to see that in pre-industrial societies, pretty much everybody did it to pretty much everybody else. The structures of pre-industrial societies simply were not strong enough to dispense with forced human labor. We are shocked that Thomas Jefferson—a deeply agrarian mind—could condone slavery, but this is, in fact, no surprise whatsoever. What is lamentable is how pompously liberals can climb on their high-horses and apply *today's* rational-industrial values to yesterday's agrarian ruminations. (This is also what is so profoundly confused and misleading about Spielberg's *Amistad*—a deeply liberal look at a deeply agrarian time, brutally misinterpreting the context.)

Conservatives fare no better. Modern liberalism came into existence with the rational Enlightenment, and shares its rational-industrial values: liberty, equality, freedom. But conservatism reaches back much further, with its roots thoroughly sunk in the soil of mythic-agrarian values: civic, hierarchical, aristocratic, ethnocentric, with a mythic-fundamentalist belief in a patriarchal God—and a belief in the rightness of slavery. And so even with today's typical conservative, you often get the sense that they think blacks simply deserved it: they were weaker, we were stronger, that's the way it goes. And indeed, that is the way it goes to the mythic-agrarian mind.

Well, a pox on both the liberals and conservatives in this particular regard. Whites are not to blame for slavery; pre-industrial conditions are to blame for slavery. And African-Americans certainly did not "deserve" any such treatment (nor did any other race on the face of the planet, including whites, that was enslaved by others). But it is only with rational-industrialism that machines could do the labor that men otherwise would force other men to do.

What I find so deeply sad about the African-American experience is not just the slavery, but the diaspora. After all, in many cases of slavery, you moved next door; horrible as it was, you were still in your own culture. But to be dispossessed of freedom and culture simultaneously is as brutal an insult as any can endure. But there, I think, is also the beginning of the extraordinary strength of the African-American soul. Starting in the death ships, Africans—they were not yet African-Americans—reached deep into their collective soul and brought forth a thing of brilliance and beauty, sharing and caring, strength and courage, the likes of which history has rarely seen.

What an extraordinarily rich addition to American culture. Muhammed Ali famously said, "I'm glad my great-great-granddaddy caught that ship." It will be a happy day when, on the other side of the color divide, more white Americans share that sentiment.

Sunday, December 7

Transcendence restores humor. Spirit brings smiling. Suddenly, laughter returns. Too many representatives of too many movements—even very good movements, such as feminism, ecology, and spiritual studies—seem to lack humor altogether. In other words, they lack lightness, they lack a distance from themselves, a distance from the ego and its grim game of forcing others to conform to its contours. There is self-transcending humor, or there is the game of egoic power. But we have chosen egoic power and politically correct thought police; grim Victorian reformers pretending to be defending civil rights; messianic new-paradigm thinkers who are going to save the planet and heal the world. No wonder Mencken wrote that "Every third American devotes himself to improving and lifting up his fellow citizens, usually by force; this messianic delusion is our national disease." Perhaps we should all trade two pounds of ego for one ounce of laughter.

Monday, December 8

Speaking of humor, Marci and I want to go see Bobbie Louise Hawkins, who writes brilliantly funny essays, stories, and poetry. She often teaches and performs at Naropa. She is not, alas, taken as seriously as is her due, precisely because she can be so funny. The ego wears grimness around its neck like a garland of garlic to ward off the evils of transcendence and humorous release. Bobbie wrote a very funny piece about funny pieces not being taken seriously, but it wasn't taken seriously.

Tuesday, December 9

Marci has her thesis presentation and defense this Saturday, and she is very nervous and apprehensive, in an endearing sort of way. She can't sleep, so she watches me meditate during the night, and I am aware of her doing so. It's very sweet.

Midnight in the Garden of Good and Evil, the film. Well, I liked it. "This place is like *Gone with the Wind* on mescaline. Everybody is heavily armed and drunk. New York is boring. I'm staying."

Rented *Coldblooded,* a very dark comedy, about a young hit man apprentice. "You've never had a girlfriend?" "No, never. I have been seeing the same hooker for a while." "Doesn't really count." But, of all things, he is saved by a good woman and . . . yoga.

Wednesday, December 10

THE STORY OF THE LOST AND FOUND GOD
A Theoretical Play of Political Redemption and Release,
in Three Acts with an Important Postscript

ACT I

Scene 1

In 1712, in Geneva, Jean-Jacques Rousseau's mother died giving him birth. He was abused and beaten by his father, then abandoned at age ten. By age sixteen he had made it to Savoy, where he was tutored in the ways of the mind, and the body, by Madame de Warens; by age thirty, Rousseau was in Paris, a minor figure in the philosophical circle of Diderot and d'Alembert, editors of the *Encyclopédie,* bastion of Enlightenment thought. Within a decade he had so alienated his former friends—including David Hume and Voltaire—that he fled city life for the countryside, where, for much of the next twenty years, until his death, he lived with Thérèse Levasseur, an unschooled laundry maid. They had five children, each of whom they abandoned to orphanages. Isaac Kramnick tells us that Rousseau "wore shabby, thread-bare and often bizarre clothing; he was tactless and direct, oafish and vulgar." Hume called him "absolutely lunatic." Diderot said, "That man is insane." Sir Isaiah Berlin labeled him "the most sinister and most formidable enemy of liberty in the whole history of modern thought."

Scene 2

Rousseau's legacy is profound, paradoxical, and often contradictory. In modern times, he was the first great retro-Romantic; the first influential deep ecologist; the first major totalitarian; and the first great glorifier of narcissistic self-absorption. He was also the first great advocate of a more democratic society, geared to the many rather than the few; a compelling arguer for justice, but also for greatness; he condemned the inequalities of culture, even though he championed those of nature.

Perhaps the most commonly remembered—and influential—proclamation of Rousseau is the opening line of chapter 1 of *The Social Contract*: "Man is born free, and is everywhere in chains." Rousseau's thought on this matter was actually quite complex, but the general idea—at least as it entered popular imagination—is simply this: people are born good, but that natural goodness is slowly suffocated and buried by the forces of society. Nature is good, culture is suffocating; nature is authentic, society is artificial. The notion—which is the central tenet of Romanticism—is that we start out in a type of natural unity and wholeness, but that wholeness is fractured, broken, and repressed by the world of culture, speech, and reason. Thus our task is to *recapture* the prior wholeness and goodness, perhaps in a "more mature" form, or "on a higher level," but recaptured nonetheless.

Scene 3

"They're going to hunt you tomorrow," said the twins. So begins the last chilling incident in William Golding's classic novel, *Lord of the Flies*. A group of young boys, aged six to twelve, have been stranded on an uninhabited island. Left to their own devices, their true natures begin to emerge, and it is a progressive descent into savagery. By the end of the novel, the boys are naked, filthy, painted with crude designs . . . and hunting, in order to kill and roast, the only two remaining boys who will not join their "natural" displays.

Scene 4

The life of men and women in the state of nature is "solitary, poor, nasty, brutish, and short." With those five famous words, three of which most people remember, Thomas Hobbes staked out, more or less exactly, the opposite of the Romantic view. Hobbes believed that children are born concerned only with themselves. It is the job of education and training to widen their interests to include a concern for others, and perhaps, eventually, for all of humankind. But most people, he believed, only manage to extend the circle of care from themselves to their families.

Such is exactly the importance of civil society, according to Hobbes. It is only by subsuming the state of nature—where self-survival rules—that men and women can join together, beyond mere self-survival, and create a greater good, marked by moral virtues that lead to a peaceful and stable coexistence. We start out wretched, but we can join together and grow into goodness. Otherwise, "They're going to hunt you tomorrow," said the twins.

ACT 2

Scene 1

These two points of view—let us call them "recaptured goodness" and "growth to goodness"—have proven to be two of the most durable, and apparently incompatible, notions of the direction of human growth: devolution, or a downhill slide from a paradisiacal state, a slide that must be reversed in some sense; and evolution, or growth and unfolding from a lesser to a greater good.

The first view almost always uses the metaphor of *healing*; the second, that of *growth*. Healing, because the recaptured-goodness school believes that we were once whole—in childhood, in the noble savage, in Eden—but this wholeness was fractured, broken, buried, or torn, and thus we are in need of healing. *Healing implies that health was once present, but then was lost*, and it needs to be recaptured or restored. The metaphor of healing almost always signals a hidden, or not so hidden, retro-Romantic viewpoint.

Growth, on the other hand, implies not that we are attempting to recapture anything we had yesterday, but that we are *evolving to our own higher possibilities*. The acorn becomes an oak, not by recapturing something it had yesterday, but by growing. The metaphor of growth almost always signals a developmental or evolutionary view.

The first school often uses the metaphor of *uncovering*; the second, that of *emergence*. Uncovering, because the goodness that we need was once present but was buried, and thus all that is required is to scrape off the layers of civilization to retrieve it. Emergence, because the goodness that we need was never present, but will emerge only if higher growth and development occurs.

In short, for the first school, we start out good, become bad, and must recapture that goodness in order to heal ourselves and heal the world.

For the second, we start out, if not bad, then lacking good, a goodness that can only emerge if we grow and develop our fullest potential.

Scene 2

The first school, or natural goodness, is one of the prime ingredients in political *liberalism*; the second, or natural nastiness, of political *conservatism*. The liberal notion is that children start out good, and the job of social institutions is to not disturb that natural goodness. Institutions are usually repressive, oppressive, or stifling of the natural goodness present in children, and these artificial conventions should not be allowed to get in the way of innate goodness. If they do—if social institutions interfere with the natural goodness of people—then a revolutionary liberation is required—a subverting, a transgression, a freeing from the stifling limitations that society has placed on nature and natural goodness.

The conservative notion is that children start out selfcentric, and the job of institutions is to curb their primitive ways, or, we might say, expand their narrow views. When institutions break down, the savage breaks out. "Conservative" usually means the opposite of "progressive"; but in this case, the conservative view is progressive from childhood to adulthood (i.e., children must develop into moral goodness, because it is not given by nature or at birth), whereupon the conservative view indeed becomes *very* conservative: once this fragile growth to adult moral goodness has occurred, don't meddle with the social institutions that precariously hold it in place.

For the first school, social institutions often repress or oppress natural goodness, and they should be quickly abandoned if they become burdensome. Abandoning social institutions is not inherently problematic, according to this view, because under these artificial institutions there is only natural goodness awaiting us. For the second school, social institutions are not "artificial"; they are the means whereby we rise above the nasty, brutish, and short state of nature, and tampering lightly with these institutions is more likely to unleash the beast than the best.

Scene 3

Each school has its representative extremes. Rousseau, at least to many, has stood as the figure sanctioning reckless subversion and rebellion, always in the name of a natural goodness and recaptured innocence. The classic example, of course, is the French Revolution itself, where, as Simon Schama reports, "Their faith was the possibility of a collective moral and political revolution in which the innocence of childhood might be preserved into adulthood." Not figuratively, literally. The result, equally as certain, was the Reign of Terror, where those not innocent enough were simply beheaded by the newly invented guillotine, and the world watched in horror as natural goodness and noble savages ran riot through the streets of Paris. "They're going to hunt you tomorrow," said the twins.

And today as well. Most Marxists—radical liberals—believe in a primitive communism that would be recaptured in the post-proletariat world. More than one scholar (e.g., Cranston) has seen Rousseau as the father of the student rebellions of the sixties, indiscriminately tearing down institutions because institutions per se "restricted" their "natural freedom"—failing, as Romantics often do, to see that there is a massive difference between preconventional license (where you are a slave to your impulses) and postconventional freedom (where you are liberated into moral depth); the former belongs to nature, the latter, to culture.

Most recently, Ted Kaczynski, the Unabomber, lived the life of Rousseau—in a shack, alone, communing with nature, fighting "restrictive" institutions, and—as his manifesto made clear—"The positive ideal we propose is Nature." Kirkpatrick Sale, the little Robespierre to the Unabomber's Rousseau, wrote that "Unless [the Unabomber's] message is somehow heeded . . . we are truly a doomed society hurtling toward a catastrophic breakdown." Joe Klein, in an essay called "The Unabomber and the Left," correctly points out how much this message is essentially that of liberalism—namely, culture represses our natural goodness, so we must throw culture overboard and embrace nature, or else. . . . Eco-terrorism is just one of a dozen variations on the Reign of Terror that is inherently let loose when humans head in the preconventional direction in search of their "natural goodness."

If Rousseau is the extreme figure of natural goodness, back to nature, the noble savage, and the overthrow of restrictive culture, so Nietzsche is the extreme figure of growth and evolution, leading to the superman. Nietzsche railed against the notion that if you scrape off a social institution, all you will find is natural goodness underneath; he tore into those "political and social visionaries who with fiery eloquence demand a revolutionary overthrow of all social orders in the belief that the proudest temple of fair humanity will then at once rise up as though of its own accord. In these perilous dreams there is still an echo of Rousseau's superstition, which believes in a miraculous primeval but as it were *buried* goodness of human nature and ascribes all the blame for this burying to the institutions of culture in the form of society, state and education. The experiences of history have taught us, unfortunately, that every such revolution brings about with it the resurrection of the most savage energies in the shape of a long-buried dreadfulness." Rather, Nietzsche believed, we have to grow, evolve, into our own highest estate, not go treasure hunting in the regressive past.

Just as Rousseau, rightly or wrongly, was causally implicated in the Reign of Terror, so Nietzsche, rightly or wrongly, was appropriated by the Nazis. It turns out, historians agree, quite wrongly, but you can see how inviting it was for National Socialism to embrace evolution to the superman as one of their reigning ideals. Wherever there is a growth model, as opposed to a recapture or regressive model, then you must work hard for a future that is not yet, and not simply slide back into (or regain) a past that once was. Work, not permissiveness, pervades the growth agenda. The fascists, everybody agreed, got the trains to run on time.

Extreme liberalism, ending in *communism* enforced with terror, on the one hand; and extreme conservatism, ending in *fascism*, also enforced with terror, on the other. These two extremes exist precisely because both of these views—recaptured goodness, growth to goodness—are half right, half wrong, and if the half wrong aspect of either view is pressed into widespread action, hellish nightmares await. Communism, or extreme liberalism, sacrifices excellence for the lowest common denominator; it scrapes off the top of the pyramid of growth in order to feed the bottom, with the ultimate permissive society demanding no individual growth whatsoever, for all are to be equally and fully cherished, which in effect lets all equally rot. Fascism does precisely the reverse—it kills the bottom to feed the top—and as it works hard for a growth toward the superman, the gas chambers await those who are, rightly or wrongly (always wrongly), perceived to be subhuman.

ACT 3

Scene 1

Aside from the extremes, there clearly are merits to both schools—the extremes showing starkly what happens if the two approaches are not integrated and balanced. There is much truth to the growth-to-goodness notion, for not all goods are given at birth. And there is much truth to the idea of a recaptured goodness, because during growth itself, many potentials are lost that need to be regained. This translates as well quite directly to liberalism and conservatism, both of which have strengths to embrace, weaknesses to reject.

If we are only dealing with the arc of human evolution—both phylo-genetically and ontogenetically—then the issues, if not the solutions, are fairly clear. But in the area of *spiritual* studies, we are also dealing, in some sense, with the arc of *involution*, whereupon things become much more complicated.

To start with evolution (and let us focus on ontogeny, or the growth of the individual). As it turns out, this issue has already been generally decided. As leading researcher Larry Nucci puts it, "Developmental psychologists have, since the 1960s, reached a measure of agreement on the process by which children acquire moral and social values."[35] And that agreement is: *growth to goodness.*

On the one hand, it is true that children come biologically prepared to make moral distinctions as they socially interact. Children as young as age two have a conception of right and wrong, based largely on emotional responses, and even young children show a capacity for a certain type of emotional empathy and remorse. Nonetheless, all of those will be enriched and expanded dramatically as cognitive, social, and moral growth proceed through their various stages. The child's major capacities, barring pathology, *become more and more encompassing, not less and less.* Summary: children are what Nucci calls *emerging moral agents*, and the growth-to-goodness, not recaptured-goodness, rather decisively takes the debate.

The sequence egocentric to sociocentric to worldcentric is still a good, simple summary of this growth to goodness, not as rigid stages, but as unfolding waves and capacities. Research has continued to confirm that boys and girls both develop through that same general hierarchy, but boys do so with an emphasis on justice, girls on care. Reasons for this, however, are hotly debated, some feeling it is due to biological factors, others cultural conditioning. (My sense is that it has a strong biological grounding, molded by culture.)

Just as pioneers Piaget and Kohlberg thought that the deep features of moral growth-to-goodness are universal, not relative, so leading contemporary researchers, such as Nucci and Turiel, agree. "Turiel has found that, unlike standards regarding dress, etiquette, and the like,

---

35. This is from an essay in *The Sciences*. Nucci also uses the example of Rousseau versus *Lord of the Flies*. I had long been using these as prime examples of the two opposing views, and Nucci does so wonderfully.

standards regarding harm and justice are shared by children from a wide range of cultural backgrounds, suggesting that the development of these moral principles, including their differentiation from social conventions, is universal." There are, of course, enormous local variations in content, so that, once again, "unitas multiplex" is still the best motto: universal deep features, but culturally relative surface features, are what we find in the growth to goodness.

It's the narrowness of the child's cognitive and interpersonal world that makes the child, if not quite the savage some imagine, nonetheless lacking a depth of goodness. As only one example, research has demonstrated that, as David Berreby summarizes it, "Direct learning has less to do with the way racial thinking develops than is often imagined. Substantial aspects of children's racial cognitions do not appear to be derived from adult culture." Put bluntly, it appears children are born racists.

And born narcissists. And born lacking a capacity to take global concerns into account: born lacking a love of Gaia, lacking a global depth, lacking a capacity to take the role of other, lacking a true compassion and love—and locked instead into the narrow, tight, suffocating world of their own sensations. Dear Rousseau, in this regard, got it exactly backwards: You are not born free and everywhere end up in chains; you are born in chains and everywhere can evolve into freedom.

Scene 2

Nonetheless, the Romantic view is very true in this regard: at each stage of growth and development to goodness, something can go wrong. Whatever goodness *emerges* at any stage, just that can indeed be repressed, and *that* repressed good needs to be *uncovered* and reintegrated. (This, incidentally, is why Freud has been classified as both a Rationalist and a Romantic, which has confused many people because it seems so contradictory, but really isn't: he was a Rationalist in that he believed fundamentally in a growth to goodness out of the primitive, natural id; but if, in this growth, we too harshly deny the id, repress it and distort it—if we become our own little fascists—then we must relax the repression barrier, undergo Romantic regression in service of the ego, recapture these lost or repressed aspects of ourselves, and reintegrate them with the ego, thus facilitating our continued growth to goodness).

So, even in the evolutionary arc itself, we want to balance the growth-to-goodness model and the recaptured-goodness model, both of which have much to offer. In practical terms, with the child's development, we do not want to be excessively permissive (liberal), because little Johnny isn't the saint, full of natural goodness, that many parents (and Rousseau) like to imagine. Mere permissiveness—no demands, no constraints, so Johnny can stay close to his natural goodness—actually lets little Johnny rot, and he will eventually unleash an interior Reign of Terror as he wallows in his natural self. He will fail altogether to engage the demanding growth toward goodness; he will behead his own greater future; he will unleash the Unabomber on his own being.

At the same time, we do not want to be excessively authoritarian (conservative), and try to pipe in "family values" and "build character" for little Johnny, because character building is largely a developmental process that occurs as much on the inside as the outside, of its own unfolding accord, and trying to force this is like trying to make a plant grow by yelling at it. The result of excessive authoritarianism is that Johnny will become his own little interior fascist, repressing those aspects of himself that don't live up to the excessively high ideals and standards of the little Hitlers called his parents. And with this internal repression, little Johnny will send to the gas chambers aspects of his own self, lost and repressed potentials that will actually cripple his own growth to goodness.

Scene 3

But what of involution? And the Romantic intuition, not that we have lost some lower potential, but that we have lost, quite literally, our awareness of union with Spirit?

Well, indeed we have incurred such loss, according to the perennial philosophy. But this loss occurred, not at the beginning of evolution—or during the early years of life—but at the beginning of *involution*—or what happens to us prior to our birth in time. Those Romantic souls who intuit this horrible loss of Spirit are quite right; they have simply confused the date of its occurrence. And if we must think of this loss in historical or temporal terms, then the perennial philosophy gives three related definitions of when it occurred, which are simultaneously three related definitions of involution: the loss occurred prior to the Big Bang; prior to your individual conception; prior to your next breath.

Involution means, roughly, the movement from a higher to a lower—in this case, the movement from spirit to soul to mind to body to matter. Each step down renders the senior level "unconscious" (or involved and absorbed in the lower), so that the final result is a Big Bang that blows the material world into existence, a material world out of which evolution will then proceed in the reverse or recapitulating order, matter to body to mind to soul to spirit, with each step unfolding (evolving) that which was previously enfolded (involved), not in any rigidly set pattern or clunk-clunking of stages, but as unfolding atmospheres of subtler possibilities, unfolding waves of being in the Kosmos.

The perennial philosophy, particularly its Eastern and early Western form, maintains that this basic cycle of involution/evolution also occurs with individual souls as they transmigrate. Upon death, one evolves, if one has not already, into the higher levels of soul and spirit; if these are consciously recognized, then the forced cycle of rebirth is ended. If not, then involution occurs, from spirit to soul to mind to body, whereupon one is conceived, as a material body, in a womb, from there to commence one's own personal evolution and development, body to mind to soul to spirit.

Finally, this general involution/evolution sequence is also said to be the very structure of *this moment's experience* (this is the most important meaning of all, and the only one that is required to penetrate the sequence). In each moment, we start out nakedly exposed to One Taste in all its purity, but in each moment most of us fail to recognize it. We contract in the face of infinity and embrace our separate selves, whereupon we become involved with the stream of time, destiny, suffering, and death. But in each moment, we can recognize One Taste and bring the entire cycle to rest. We then cease the torment of life and death, being and nonbeing, existing and perishing, simply because we rest in the timeless, birthless, deathless moment, prior to time and cycles altogether.

In each of those three definitions of the "loss" of the awareness of Spirit, the loss occurs *in early involution*—it occurs as soon as Spirit "steps down" into souls and minds and bodies. It does *not* occur in early evolution, where bodies are starting to climb back or evolve to Spirit. By the time bodies show up on the scene, the *entire* loss has *already* occurred. In fact, according to the perennial philosophy, the early stages of evolution are *the most alienated*, because they are farthest from a conscious recognition of Spirit.

Yet the Romantics imagine that *the early stages of evolution* (both phylogenetic and ontogenetic) are a great paradisiacal state, the state of "natural goodness" that will be subsequently, horribly lost, and thus must be recaptured. But all that is actually lost is an unconscious wholeness (or fusion) with the material world and bodily domains, the lowest dimensions in the Great Nest of Being. Those lowest stages of evolution are a type of "unity" or "fusion," but a fusion with the basement—precisely the shallowest identity that *must* be differentiated and transcended if growth to goodness is to occur.

But once again, let us appreciate the importance of both the Romantic (recaptured goodness) and the evolutionary (growth to goodness) models. The Romantics are absolutely right: we did once walk with God and the Goddess, and bathe in the garden of eternal delights. But that garden didn't actually or historically exist *yesterday*. We did not lose Spirit when we went from foraging to horticulture, or from horticulture to agrarian—we did not lose Spirit at *any* point in evolution, time, or history. We "lost" Spirit in involution, which is what happens when Spirit steps down into time in the first place. And when did that occur? Prior to the Big Bang; prior to your own birth; but most important, prior to the point right now where you recoil from infinity. Growth to goodness is indeed a *recaptured* goodness, but a goodness lost in involution, not evolution. With that simple understanding, both views can be honored.

AN IMPORTANT POSTSCRIPT

Here follows a set of ironies.

I described today's typical conservative as subscribing to a growth-to-goodness view, and that is generally true; but equally typically, that growth only extends from preconventional nature to conventional society, and does not easily continue into postconventional, worldcentric domains. Much of typical conservatism has its roots in the mythic-agrarian age, whose values were civic, aristocratic, hierarchical, militaristic, ethnocentric, patriarchal, and usually sunk in a context of a mythic-concrete God(s). As dismal as we moderns might find that type of society, nonetheless it arose around the globe, ubiquitously, for a five-thousand-year period, where it served its purposes, and served them quite well.

When the Rational-Industrial Age dawned, with its postconventional, worldcentric moral atmosphere, a new political vision became available to men and women: that of the liberal Enlightenment. In many ways this was a decisive break with the mythic and monarchical past: rationality would fight mythology, democracy would fight aristocracy, equality would fight hierarchy, and freedom would fight slavery. That, at its best, was the vision of modernity, and liberalism was the political agenda that captured those lofty ideals.

But modernity, critics have noted, was not always, and certainly not only, lofty. There was a downside to modernity—many downsides, perhaps, but all summarized in the notion of "flatland." Due largely to a rampant scientific materialism, coupled with material industrialism, all forms of holarchy—even the good, beneficial, and spiritual forms, such as the Great Nest of Being—were collapsed into a flat and faded view of the world, composed of nothing but systems of interwoven objects, interwoven its, with no I's and no We's to speak of. Gone was soul and gone was mind and gone was spirit, and in their place an unending flatland of material bodies, which alone were thought to be real (body-ism). The disenchantment of the world, one-dimensional man, the dis-qualified universe, the desacrilization of the world . . . were a few of the famous phrases critics used to summarize this dreary state of affairs.

Liberalism, too, as a child of modernity, was thoroughly caught in this collapse, and therefore instead of coming to an accurate self-under-standing of its own interior foundations (namely, in the growth from egocentric to ethnocentric to worldcentric, liberalism represents world-centric awareness), liberalism instead became *the political champion of flatland*. Instead of interior growth and development (Left Hand), liber-alism came to advocate almost solely exterior, Right Hand, economic development as a means of freedom. Since, according to flatland, there are no interiors—and since morals are interior realities—then in suc-cumbing to the modern flatland, liberalism abdicated its basic moral intuition (that of worldcentric freedom, a stance *from which* all are treated fairly, but a stance *to which* all should be encouraged to grow).

Sadly, inevitably perhaps, liberalism abdicated its moral voice and settled for demanding exterior, material, economic freedom alone, fail-ing to realize that without *interior* freedom (found, as Kant knew, only in postconventional awareness), exterior freedom is largely meaningless. Left-Hand development was abandoned, Right-Hand development alone remained. And as for the interiors: since there are none, none can be better than others, and so permissiveness is fine, extreme diversity is fine, extreme multiculturalism is fine—all bask in the same natural good-ness that a demand for growth only corrupts.

And so it came about that liberalism, representing a higher level of collective growth, was caught in the first great modern pathology: flat-land. Flatland liberalism was thus a sick version of a higher level of collective evolution.

This left the *conservatives*—whose values, embracing the mythic-agrarian age, did not easily submit to the modern collapse—*holding the interior domains*: of religion, of values, of meaning, of a demand for interior growth-to-goodness. The only problem was, these were, for the most part, mythic-agrarian values: the religion was (and is) mythological, the growth-to-goodness reaches only to the conventional/sociocentric stages (and actively fights worldcentric, postconventional modes), the values are agrarian through and through (aristocratic, patriarchal, militaristic, often ethnocentric, often biblical-fundamentalist). These values were quite healthy, for the most part, during the mythic-agrarian era: they were the best to which one could aspire under the conditions of those times.

So there are our political choices in today's world: a healthy lower level (conservative) versus a sick higher level (liberal).

A refurbished, postliberal awareness is therefore, I believe, the only sane course to pursue. This would combine the very best of the conservative vision—including the need for growth to goodness, the importance of holarchical relationships and therefore *meaning* (self, family, community, nation, world, Spirit), the stress on equal opportunity instead of mindless equality. But all of those conservative values need to be raised up into a modern, postconventional, worldcentric awareness.

This means, likewise, that liberalism itself must abandon any remnant of a return to "natural goodness," and again become *progressive*, evolutionary. The irony here is that permissive liberalism (and extreme postmodernism) is actually and deeply *reactionary*, because it fails to engage the difficult demand for growth to postconventional goodness. The only place we can *protect* true diversity and multiculturalism is *from* the postconventional, worldcentric stance, and unless liberalism can encourage growth to that stance, it sabotages its own agenda. Idiot compassion, advocated by liberalism, is killing liberalism.

In short, liberalism must become truly progressive, not just in exterior, flatland, economic terms, but in the interior growth of consciousness, from egocentric to sociocentric to worldcentric, preconventional to conventional to postconventional (there to stand open to post-postconventional). *Not* as a state-sponsored agenda (the state shall neither favor nor sponsor a particular version of the good life), but as an atmosphere of encouragement—in its theoretical writings, in the example of its leaders, in the vision to which it calls us all, in its heart and mind and soul.

As it is now, liberalism, with its background belief in natural goodness and its foreground belief in extreme diversity, is simply fostering an atmosphere of regression—in everything from identity politics to ethnocentric revivals to egocentric license. I am not suggesting that liberals legislate against that (people are free to do whatever they want, bar harming others); I am simply suggesting that they stop encouraging it under the demonstrably false notion of natural goodness and the utterly self-contradictory theory of egalitarianism (which maintains that egalitarianism itself is *better* than the alternatives, when *all* are supposed to be equal). Those two pillars of liberalism are unquestionably false, and certainly indefensible, and at the very least, ought to be quietly dropped, while liberalism goes on about the postliberal task of finding ways to foster an atmosphere of growth to goodness.

And, of course, it is my own belief that this postconservative, postliberal vision would open us to post-postconventional awareness, by any other name, Spirit. The debate, truly, has been decided: You are born in chains, and can everywhere grow into freedom, finding, finally, your own Original Face.

Thursday, December 11

The sleep cycle is fascinating. The *body* goes to sleep, and that leaves the *subtle* (mind and soul) and the *causal* (formless Witness). So as the body goes to sleep, the subtle mind and soul appear vividly in dreams, visions, images, and occasionally archetypal illuminations—the typical dreaming state. At some point the subtle then also goes to sleep—the mind goes to sleep, the soul goes to sleep—and that leaves only formlessness, or deep dreamless sleep, which is actually the Witness or primordial Self in its own naked nature, with no objects of any sort. (This procession from gross to subtle to causal is one version of the evolutionary or ascending arc, although there are many variations on that theme—e.g., many people start the cycle by plunging into dreamless sleep.)

At some point during the deep dreamless state, the soul stirs, awakens, and emerges from its sleep in formlessness, and dreaming begins. Since the limitations and restrictions of the gross body are not present in the dream state, the subtle mind and soul (the deeper psychic) can express their deepest wishes (to merely think or wish a thing is to see it materialize instantly in the dream)—which is why prophets, saints, sages, and depth psychologists have always given so much attention to dreams: a deeper self is speaking here, so for goodness' sake pay attention. Shankara, Freud, and Jimminy Cricket all agree: "A dream is a wish your heart makes, when you're fast asleep."

As the dream state comes to a close (there are often several cycles between subtle-dreaming and causal-dreamless), then the gross body begins to stir, and the subtle mind is slowly submerged as the gross egoic orientation and the gross body awaken from their slumber. The body wakes up, the ego wakes up (the gross ego and gross body are interlinked)—in short, the frontal personality wakes up—and the person remembers very little, if anything, of the extraordinary tour that just occurred. (That movement from causal to subtle to gross—from Unborn to deeper psychic to frontal, from Self to soul to ego—is one version of the involutionary or descending arc.)

Each "step down" in that descending arc is accompanied, in the usual individual, with a forgetting, an anamnesis. In the deep dreamless state, individuals revert to their pure formless Self, but when the subtle arises, they forget the Self and identify with the soul, with luminosities and images and ecstatic visions—they are lost in the dream state, already mistaking it for reality. Then, as the gross ego-body awakens from its slumber in the dream, it generally forgets most of that subtle state itself, unless it struggles to remember a particular dream, which is only a fragment of the wonders of the subtle. Instead, the gross ego-body looks out upon the sensorimotor world—the smallest world of all—and takes that for ultimate reality. It has forgotten both its causal Self and its subtle soul, and it sees merely the gross and the sensorimotor. It has lost its Spirit and lost its soul and damn near lost its mind, and what is left it proudly calls reality.

(Incidentally, that sequence—gross dissolving into subtle dissolving into causal, upon which, if there are karmas present, causal giving rise to subtle giving rise to gross, whereupon one "awakens" to find oneself trapped in a gross body in a gross world—is the same sequence described in the *Tibetan Book of the Dead*, for that sequence is said to be *identical* in the process of death [gross dissolves into subtle dissolves into causal] and rebirth [causal gives rise to subtle gives rise to gross, with a "forgetting" at each step]. To *consciously* master the waking-dreaming-sleeping cycle is therefore said to be the same as being able to *consciously* choose one's rebirth: to master one is to master the other, for they are identical cycles through the Great Nest of Being, gross to subtle to causal and back again. Even so, that cycle, however exalted, is nothing but the cycle of samsara, of the endless rounds of torturous birth and death. Mastering that cycle is, at best, an aid to the ultimate goal: the recognition of One Taste. For only in One Taste does one step off that brutal cycle altogether, there to rest as the All. Neither gross nor subtle nor causal are the ultimate estate, which is the simple Feeling of Being, the simple Feeling of One Taste.)

Most individuals, then, have forgotten their own higher states—forgotten their soul, forgotten their Self, forgotten the One and Only Taste. But as consciousness becomes a little stronger—through growth, through meditation, through evolution—then the transitions between the three great states are not met with blacking out or forgetting or anamnesis. With constant Witnessing, you gain your first real Release from the world, because you are no longer its victim but its Witness. With One Taste you recognize a deeper Release, which is that you are free of the entire world because you *are* the entire world. Even the smallest glimmer of One Taste and you will never be the same. You will inhale galaxies with every breath and sleep as the stars all night. Suns and moons and glorious novas will rush and rumble through your veins, your heart will pulse and beat in time with the entire loving universe. And you will never move at all in this radiant display of your very own Self, for you will long ago have disappeared into the fullness of the night.

Friday, December 12

Tomorrow Marci gives her thesis presentation and defense. Then there is a big celebration for the graduates. This is the start of the party season. Goodbye Witness, hello cruel world.

Saturday, December 13

Marci passed her defense with flying colors. She used a developmental hierarchy (including Maslow's) and applied it to "internal management" in business, or how a company can "sell itself" to its employees by offering services that allow and encourage their own growth in the workplace—thus making employees happier and more productive in their jobs and the company more attractive to new employees—a superb win-win situation. As an unbiased and objective onlooker, I found it brilliant, provocative, novel, compelling, and utterly absorbing.

Then out for a big celebration.

Monday, December 15

BELL HOOKS: "I'm so disturbed when my women students behave as though they can only read women, or black students behave as though they can only read blacks, or white students behave as though they can only identify with a white writer. I think the worst thing that can happen to us is to lose sight of the power of empathy and compassion."

MAYA ANGELOU: "Absolutely. Then we become brutes. Then we risk being consumed by brutism. There's a statement which I use in all my classes, no matter what I'm teaching. I put on the board the statement, "I am a human being. Nothing human can be alien to me." Then I put it down in Latin, "Homo cum humani nil a me alienum puto." And then I show them its origin. The statement was made by Publius Terentius Afer, known as Terence. He was an African and a slave to a Roman senator. Freed by that senator, he became the most popular playwright in Rome. Six of his plays and that statement have come down to us from 154 BCE. This man, not born white, not born free, said *I am a human being.*"

— Discussion in the *Shambhala Sun*, January 1998

Neither hooks nor Angelou (nor Sara Bates) is denying differences or downplaying them, but simply setting our rich cultural differences in a universal context of a common humanity, accessed, as bell beautifully says, by empathy and compassion: postconventional worldcentric awareness, universal pluralism, unitas multiplex.

"Unitas multiplex" is actually a good motto for my work, and there are signs that it is itself an idea whose time has truly come. After modernity went through a period of rigid universalism or uniformitarianism (which denied any significant cultural differences by seeing the world only through the lens of the propertied white male), and after postmodernity went through a period of chaotic diversity amounting to glorified fragmentation (which denied any universal truths at all, except its own), we are in a position to take the best of both worlds: *universal pluralism,* unitas multiplex. And we are seeing signs of this new, integral understanding across the board—in psychology, philosophy, business, economics. . . .

The July issue of *Wired,* for example, has a superb interview with Larry Summers, Clinton's chief advisor on international trade, called "The Integrationists vs. the Separatists," which spells out the disasters of protectionism and separatism in world trade. The title pretty much says it all, but if it needs any explanation, the same issue contains a positively brilliant article, "The Long Boom," by my old acquaintance Peter Schwartz and Peter Leyden. They point out that five waves of technology, now already in motion (personal computers, telecommunications, biotechnology, nanotechnology, and alternative energy), will have several almost inevitable consequences, among which may be a fully integrated world by roughly the year 2020. This interconnected, networked, integral world, they point out, will not, contrary to critics, deny local cultural differences but embrace and cherish them. It will be a truly multicultural, inclusive world—a unitas multiplex. "We're entering an age where diversity is truly valued—the more options the better. Our ecosystem works best that way. Our market economy works best that way. Our civilization, the realm of our ideas, works best that way, too." But *only* if all of them are firmly set in a truly integrated world, not a world where diversity, by itself, is championed—that is the way of the "separatist," clearly the bad guy in their scenario.

They also point out that this growth toward an integral world, although driven in part by technology, depends equally on several *interior* values, particularly those of *openness* and *tolerance*, without which technology can (and will) be put to the most heinous uses. In other words, Right-Hand factors alone will *not* carry the day; certain Left-Hand values and awareness are mandatory if technology is not to be used to increase alienation and separation. Openness and tolerance— universal pluralism—are values of the postconventional, worldcentric level of development. *The conclusion is obvious*: if we are indeed to reach an integrated world—the long boom of prosperity, ecological sustainability, and cultural tolerance—then in addition to the *exterior* waves of technology that the authors outline, humanity will have to commit itself to the *interior* waves of development from egocentric to sociocentric to worldcentric awareness, there to find the openness and tolerance that can cherish individual differences and prevent technology from spelling doom instead of boom.

There are massive, irreversible forces now developing the exterior waves; who will speak for the interior development that alone will divert catastrophe?

Tuesday, December 16

Another Christmas party, this time for the staff and residents of the Developmental Disabilities Center. Marci and I were some of the main dance partners for the residents, and we spent about three hours dancing, if that's the right word. Allen stood in the middle of the floor and didn't move a muscle; but he was smiling. Tavio spun his wheelchair in circles. Sandy bobbed back and forth at a terrifying rate; I tried to keep up with her, but she was too fast for me. Tom jumped up and down, swirling his arms like helicopter blades, also too fast for me. There were perhaps one hundred residents present, about half of whom danced, often simultaneously. Holding hands in a circle and kicking up our feet seemed to be the group dance of choice, when we could get everybody facing the same direction.

I have often written about what I think are the three main types of value in the world: intrinsic value, extrinsic value, and Ground value. Intrinsic value is the value a thing has in itself. Extrinsic value is the value a thing has for others. And Ground value is the value that all things have by virtue of being manifestations of Spirit.

Intrinsic value is ranked according to its degree of inclusiveness and wholeness. A molecule, for example, has more intrinsic value than an atom, because molecules contain atoms. Molecules, being more inclusive, contain more being in their own makeup, and thus their intrinsic value is greater. Cells have more intrinsic value than molecules; organisms, more than cells; and so on. Likewise, worldcentric has more intrinsic value than sociocentric, which has more than egocentric, because the former, in each case, has more depth and more wholeness.

But to say a cell has more intrinsic value than a molecule is *not* to say the molecule has no value at all. It's a sliding scale, depending upon how much of the universe is *embraced* in a holon. The more being that is internal to a holon, the more intrinsic value it has. The greater the depth, the greater the wholeness, the greater the intrinsic value.

Extrinsic value is pretty much the opposite of intrinsic. An atom has more extrinsic value than a molecule, because more holons depend for their existence on atoms than on molecules. Molecules themselves depend for their existence on atoms—but not vice versa—so atoms have more extrinsic value, or value for others.

It's pretty easy to see: the higher a holon is on the Great Holarchy, the more intrinsic value it has. The lower a holon is on the Chain, the more extrinsic value it has. Both are absolutely mandatory, because they can't exist without each other. Without the higher, the lower would have no meaning; without the lower, the higher would have no manifest existence.

Intrinsic value is the value a thing has by virtue of being a *whole* with *agency* (and the greater the depth of the whole—or the more levels it contains—then the greater its intrinsic value, or the more of the universe it embraces and enfolds in its own being). Extrinsic value, on the other hand, is the value a thing has by virtue of being a *part* in *communion* (and the more things it is a part of, the greater its extrinsic value). Agency concerns *rights* (we are individual wholes with individual rights, grounded in justice); communion concerns *responsibilities* (we are also parts or members of many relationships, grounded in care). All things are wholes that are also parts (all holons, without exception, are agency-in-communion), and thus all holons have *both* intrinsic and extrinsic value, both rights and responsibilities.

Intrinsic and extrinsic are relative values; Ground value is absolute. Ground value is the value that each and every holon has by virtue of being a radiant manifestation of Spirit, of Godhead, of Emptiness. All holons, high or low, have the *same* Ground value—namely, One Taste. Holons can have greater or lesser intrinsic value (the greater the depth, the greater the value), but all holons have absolutely equal Ground value: they all share equal Suchness, Thusness, Isness, which is the face of Spirit as it shines in manifestation, One Taste in all its wonder.[36]

Whenever I am with dear people who have been disadvantaged in their own growth and development—crippled in their own depth—I am so much more easily reminded of their Ground value, green emeralds each and all, perfect in their glory. I am reminded that intrinsic and extrinsic fall away in One Taste, where all Spirit's children equally shine in the infinity that they are. I know this for a fact, because last night I spent three hours dancing with buddhas, and who would dare deny that?

Thursday, December 18

Twenty years ago, when Buddhism was first making headway in this country, you couldn't even broach the topic of combining meditation with psychotherapy, because Buddhism was maintained to be a "complete system," so therapy wasn't needed if you were doing Buddhism correctly. *A similar reluctance* has beset virtually every religion in the modern world: only believe in Christ, and all will be well; pray, and your psyche will heal; zikr will cure all; davening will suffice; yoga says it all. The clear implication is that if you have enough faith or spiritual practice, you would *never* need psychotherapy of any sort; and conversely, if you need therapy, something is seriously wrong with your faith. The relation of spirituality to science in general, and psychother-

---

36. See *A Brief History of Everything* for a further discussion of this topic.

apy in particular, is *the* pressing issue for spirituality in the modern world, and most religions are not, it seems, handling this very well.

Even though my actual practice has mostly been Buddhist (and Vedantic), nonetheless my works have usually been looked upon with suspicion in Buddhist circles: that Wilber fellow is implying that Buddhism alone isn't enough. Many Buddhists refused to read anything I had written, and several told me so in quite un-Buddhist terms.

Twenty years later, it's a different story. By now almost every well-known American Buddhist teacher has, in fact, undergone considerable psychotherapy (although many of them still lamentably hide this fact from their students). But most of them realize, at least privately, that there are issues that meditation simply does not (and cannot) address. The same might be said for centering prayer, satsang, zikr, yoga, and so on. The fact is, spiritual practice and psychological practice are, in part, different streams in the great waves of consciousness, and if you are having trouble in one it does not necessarily mean you are a wretch in the other. Neurosis is not a sin.

So, a year ago, when the *Shambhala Sun* (a major Buddhist magazine) approached me with an interview offer, I was reluctant. Nonetheless, one wants to support contemplative magazines of integrity, so I consented. The interview began with the standard "How can you say Buddhism isn't a complete path?," but it quickly moved in a more fruitful direction. And even though this discussion is specifically about Buddhist practice, I would emphasize exactly the same points with any other spiritual practice, Christian to Jewish to Islamic to Taoist. Followers of other faiths can translate the following sentiments directly into their own practice, for the issues here are absolutely crucial, I believe, in getting religion and therapy to talk to each other.[37]

SUN: I read your ideas about the evolution of consciousness in a pair of your most recent books that seem to go together: *Sex, Ecology, Spirituality* is the big one, 800 pages. *A Brief History of Everything* seems to be a summary written for the common man and woman. Who did you write that book for?

KW: Yes, *Brief History* is much shorter and more accessible. At least I hope it is. The common man and woman? Well, anybody reading this

---

37. The following is a slightly condensed version of the original, for which see "Big Map: The Kosmos According to Ken Wilber," *Shambhala Sun*, September 1996.

magazine is already very uncommon, wouldn't you say? I wrote the book for the same not so common people, I guess, nut cases like you and me who are interesting in waking up and other silly notions like that. This book is not going to knock Deepak off the charts. I suppose it's more for anybody who is looking for something like an overall world philosophy, an approach to consciousness and history that takes the best of the East and the West into account, and attempts to honor them both.

SUN: And what effect do you hope to have? What can knowing your philosophy do for the advancement of consciousness?

KW: Not very much, frankly. Each of us still has to find a genuine contemplative practice—maybe yoga, maybe Zen, maybe Shambhala Training, maybe contemplative prayer, or any number of authentic transformative practices. That is what advances consciousness, not my linguistic chitchat and book junk.

But if you want to know how your particular practices fit with the other approaches to truth that are out there, then these books will help you get started. They offer one map of how things fit together, that's all. But none of this will substitute for practice.

SUN: But what if I am, say, a hardcore, born-again Buddhist, who doesn't use other systems of self-development or self-transformation. I get the idea from *Brief History* that I must be leaving something out of my self-culture. You have Buddhism listed in only one of four quadrants, so I must be leaving something out. When I gain enlightenment, won't it be incomplete according to you?

KW: If by "enlightenment" you mean the direct and radical recognition of Emptiness, no, that won't leave anything out at all. Emptiness doesn't have any parts, so you can't leave some of it behind. But there is absolute bodhichitta and there is relative bodhichitta [roughly, absolute and relative truth], and although you might have direct recognition of the absolute, that does not mean you have mastered all the details of the relative. You can be fairly enlightened and still not be able to explain, say, the mathematics of the Schroedinger wave equation. My books deal more with all these relative details, some of which are not covered by Buddhism, or any of the world's wisdom traditions, for that matter. But for the direct recognition of radical Emptiness and spontaneous luminosity, Buddhism is right on the money, yes?

SUN: Then why do I need your history of consciousness when I've got all the Buddhist teachings to play with?

KW: You don't. Unless you happen to find it interesting, or fun, or engaging. Then you'll do it just to do it. The Buddhist teachings don't specifically cover Mexican cooking, either, but you still might like to take that up.

SUN: We could also put it this way: What do you know that the Buddha doesn't?

KW: How to drive a Jeep.

SUN: As you note in *Brief History*, there are already plenty of progressive theories of history and theories of spiritual evolution. Sometimes your theory sounds like Hegel's dialectic, sometimes like Darwin, sometimes like various Asian views of world mind theory. What makes it different from these other systems?

KW: Well, that's sort of the point. It sounds like all of those theories because it takes all of them into account and attempts to synthesize the best of each of them. That's also what makes it different, in that none of those other theories take the others into account. I'm trying to pull these approaches together, which is something they are not interested in.

SUN: You don't divide up your world into atoms, or elements, or psychological states, but rather into units you call *holons*. These sound a lot like the *dharmas* of Buddhist Abhidharma. How influential was Buddhist Abhidharma in your theory?

KW: Well, I'm a long-time practicing Buddhist, and many of the key ideas in my approach are Buddhist or Buddhist-inspired. First and foremost, Nagarjuna and Madhyamika; pure Emptiness and primordial Purity is the "central philosophy" of my approach as well. Also Yogachara, Hua Yen, a great deal of Dzogchen and Mahamudra, and yes, the fundamentals of Abhidharma. The analysis of experience into *dharmas* is also quite similar to Whitehead's actual occasions. My presentation of holons was influenced by all of those. Again, I'm trying to take the best from each of these traditions and bring them together in what I hope is a fruitful fashion.

SUN: Your own worldview is complicated enough. Meditators might just say, "Why do I need to have a global-historical view at all? Leave me alone to just meditate." What would you say to them?

KW: Just meditate.

SUN: You have some interesting criticisms of conventional modernism and postmodernism. You seem to accept their positions and yet at the same time to transcend them, to put them in their place. Can you explain that?

KW: Yes, the idea is that all of the various approaches and theories and practices have something important to tell us, but none of them probably has the whole truth in all its details. So each approach is true but partial, and the trick is then to figure out how all of these true but partial truths fit together. Not, who's right and who's wrong, but how can they all be right? How can they all fit together into one rainbow coalition? So that's why I both accept these positions, but also attempt to transcend them, or "put them in their place," as you say. Whether or not I have succeeded remains to be seen.

SUN: You use the word "Kosmos" instead of "cosmos." Why?

KW: *Kosmos* is an old Pythagorean term, which means the entire universe in all its many dimensions—physical, emotional, mental, and spiritual. *Cosmos* today usually means just the physical universe or physical dimension. So we might say the Kosmos includes the physiosphere or cosmos, the biosphere or life, the noosphere or mind, all of which are radiant manifestations of pure Emptiness, and are not other to that Emptiness.

One of the catastrophes of modernity is that the Kosmos is no longer a fundamental reality to us; only the cosmos is. In other words, what is "real" is just the world of scientific materialism, the world of "flatland," the flat and faded view of the modern and postmodern world, where the cosmos alone is real. And one of the things these two books try to do is rehabilitate the Kosmos as a believable concept.

SUN: You write of the Kosmos as "the pattern that connects" all domains of existence. This reminds me of Gregory Bateson's *Mind and Nature: A Necessary Unity*. How did these modern, sort of New Age movements in the social sciences influence your thought?

KW: Not very much, I must say. I don't find Bateson a very useful theorist, although I know many bright people who do. But the book you mention is what I would call a very "flatland" book, monological, it-language, one-dimensional—not very good, frankly. But that's just my opinion.

SUN: Do you think Foucault, Derrida, and company were getting at points that Asian absolutists had already articulated in some way? Or have their post-structuralist approaches been completely fresh?

KW: The post-structuralist approaches are both more novel or fresh, and much less profound. The great Eastern traditions are, in essence, profound techniques of transformation, of liberation, of release in radical Emptiness. The post-structuralists have none of that; they simply offer new ways of *translation*, not *transformation*. They are interesting twists on relative truth, not a yoga of absolute truth. But within the relative truth, the post-structuralists have a few similarities with the relative aspects of some of the Eastern traditions, such as nonfoundationalism, the contextuality of truth, the sliding nature of signification, the relativity of meaning, and so on.

These are interesting and important similarities, and I try to take them into account, but they are all quite secondary to the real issue, which is *moksha, kensho, satori, rigpa, yeshe, shikan-taza*: none of that will you find in Foucault, Derrida, Lyotard, and company.

SUN: Does the Tibetan Buddhist cosmological thought play any special role in the development of your philosophy? Sometimes it reminds me of the apocalyptic approaches of the Kalachakra school.

KW: Vajrayana in almost all of its forms has been very important to me personally, and yes, to the overall view I have outlined. Kalachakra, as anuttaratantra, is very profound; also the Ati teachings, semde, longde, and upadesa. But really, I feel a great sympathy with all of the schools.

SUN: You want to integrate Freud with the Buddha, or, as you call them, "depth psychology" with "height psychology." Why is this necessary? Do you think that without this integration both systems are incomplete?

KW: Well, I think everything is incomplete, because the Kosmos keeps moving on. New truths emerge, new revelations unfold, new Buddhas keep popping up, it is endless, no? Freud and Buddha are just two examples of some very important truths that can benefit from a mutual dialogue. Emptiness does not depend on either of them; but the manifest world is a big place, plenty of room for both of these pioneers. And yes, I think they can each help the other's path proceed more rapidly.

SUN: Do you think, indeed, that the ancient systems of spiritual transformation are inadequate in modern times, since they leave out so much of the material you include in your synthesis?

KW: Inadequate? Not in absolute truth, no; in relative manifestation, sure, simply because Emptiness keeps manifesting in different forms, doesn't it? You can't find instructions for operating a computer in any of the Sutras or Tantras. You can't find out about DNA or medical anesthesia or kidney transplants in those texts, either. Likewise, the West has contributed a thing or two to psychological and psychotherapeutic understanding, and these contributions are altogether beneficial and helpful, and they don't have many parallels in any of the ancient teachings.

But it's not really a matter of inadequacy; it's a matter of making use of whatever is available. If your practice is working for you, excellent. If it seems to be stuck, maybe a little therapy might help. I myself don't think either side has to be threatened by this. It's a really big universe, very spacious, plenty of room for Freud and Buddha.

SUN: While we're on this topic, what do you think of the inner tantras, such as kundalini yoga and what we Buddhists do with *prana, nadi,* and *bindu* [certain interior spiritual visions]? The reality upon which they rely is not admitted by science and yet it occupies two higher levels in your system, the subtle and the causal. This is confusing, because a lot of spiritual practitioners never admit the existence of those levels and never do those practices. Yet you make them seem to be a necessity of higher development. Or am I misunderstanding you?

KW: I don't think they are a necessity. It's rather that, at those two higher stages that you mentioned (the subtle and causal), these types of processes may occur. Or they may not. It depends on the type of practice, among other things. It's just that, at a certain point in your own meditative practice, various gross processes tend to be replaced by subtle and then very subtle phenomena, and these sometimes include energy currents, *prana, bindu,* and so on. But in other cases it might simply be an increase in clarity and panoramic awareness. I was simply cataloging all the different types of meditative phenomena that can occur as meditation itself unfolds from gross to subtle to very subtle consciousness. Much of what I include here is pretty standard stuff in the traditions.

SUN: Why do some spiritual practitioners seem to make advances in some ways and still be primitive assholes in other ways?

KW: [*laughing*] Well, one of the things I try to do with the developmental model of consciousness is outline two different things, which we can call streams and waves. The streams are the different developmental lines, such as cognitive development, emotional development, interpersonal development, spiritual development, and so on. Each of these streams goes through various stages or waves of its own development. What research indicates is that, one, these different streams can develop fairly independently of each other: you can be advanced in one stream, such as the spiritual, and "retarded" in others, such as emotional or interpersonal. And two, even though these streams develop independently, they all share the same basic stages or waves of development. For example, they all go from preconventional to conventional to postconventional forms.

So we have numerous different streams of development, yet each traverses the same general waves or stages of consciousness unfolding. And people can definitely be advanced in one stream and a "primitive asshole" in others. (I summarize this research in *The Eye of Spirit: An Integral Vision for a World Gone Slightly Mad.*)

But about your point, yes, development can be rather uneven. Most of the great wisdom traditions train people for higher or postconventional awareness and cognition, and for higher or postconventional affect, such as love and compassion. But they tend to neglect interpersonal and emotional development, especially in the conventional domains. We all know advanced meditators who are, well, unpleasant people. This, of course, is where Western psychotherapy excels—although it goes to the other extreme and almost completely neglects and leaves out the higher or transpersonal waves, another reason we need to get Freud and Buddha together.

SUN: Every old-timer in the contemplative game knows this is true—that growth is usually uneven. But some say the neurotic bits are actual regressions: a person made a real advance in meditation but then, seduced by samsara, abandoned it and thus got caught up in samsaric neurosis. Others say that meditation actually scoops up hidden, compacted neuroses in the advanced practitioner, making him or her suddenly and mysteriously become a jerk. Do you think there is any truth in such views, or is your view altogether different?

KW: No, I think each of those points you mentioned is sometimes true. People often do make real progress in meditation, only to abandon it because the demands are too great, and when they return to their "old" ways, their neurosis is even worse, because they have the same ole problem but now their sensitivity is increased, so it simply hurts even more.

And your second scenario is also common. Particularly at advanced stages of meditation, the really deeply buried complexes start to become exposed to awareness. Advanced practitioners can become very exaggerated people, because they have already worked through all the smooth and easy problems, and all that is left are the karmas from when you murdered twenty nuns in your last lifetime. I'm sort of kidding, but you get the idea: some really deep-seated problems can rush to the surface in advanced practice, and this can confuse people, because this does not look like "progress." But it's sort of like frostbite: at first you don't feel anything, because you're frozen. You don't even think you have a problem. But then you start to warm up the frozen part, and it hurts like hell. The cure, the warming up, is horrible. Advanced meditation is especially a fast warming up, a waking up, and it usually hurts like hell.

SUN: But you have some other scenarios as to why things can "go bad" in meditation.

KW: Yes, the idea is that, as we were saying, development consists of several different streams that develop through the basic stages or waves of consciousness unfolding. The great wisdom traditions tend to emphasize two or three of these streams, such as the cognitive (awareness), the spiritual (and moral), the higher affect (love and compassion). But they tend to neglect other streams, such as emotional, interpersonal, relationships, and conventional interactions.

Thus, as you tend to make progress in some of these streams—perhaps the meditative/cognitive—you can become a little "unbalanced" in your overall development. Other developmental lines become neglected, withered, atrophied. Your psyche is saddled with one giant and a dozen pygmies. And the *more* your meditation practice advances, the *worse* the imbalance becomes. You start to get very weird, and you are told to *increase* your meditative effort, and pretty soon you come apart at the seams like a cheap suit. Yes?

So one of the things that we might want to look at are ways to bring a more integral practice to bear on our lives, an integral practice that includes the best of ancient wisdom and modern knowledge, and blends the contemplative with the conventional. I don't have the answers here, but these books are, I hope, a way to begin this dialogue in good faith and good will.

SUN: When you earlier said that meditators could "just meditate," was that perhaps being just a little glib? Because it doesn't seem that you really think that meditation alone is enough.

KW: Well, you didn't ask if I thought meditation alone was enough. You asked what I would tell somebody who said "Leave me alone to just meditate." I'd say, Just meditate. I have no desire to interfere with anybody's practice. But if you asked instead, "What other practices do you think meditators could use to facilitate their growth?," then I would answer more or less as I just did. In other words, a judicious blend of Eastern contemplative approaches with Western psychodynamic approaches is an interesting and I think healthy way to proceed. And if you want a more comprehensive worldview in general, including both absolute and relative truths, then certainly there are numerous items that the West will bring to the feast. Any of those approaches taken in and by themselves are demonstrably partial by comparison.

Incidentally, if you're put off by all this, you don't have to come. But everybody has an invitation to this dance, I think. It's a real Shambhala

Ball. Seriously. Chögyam Trungpa's Shambhala vision, as I understand it, was a secular and integral weaving of the Dharma into the vast cultural currents in which it finds itself. *A Brief History of Everything* outlines many of those currents, and suggests one way that the Dharma can enrich—and be enriched by—those currents. This is very simple, I think.

SUN: Fair enough. What I would like to do now is to ask a few very technical questions. Okay?

KW: Okay.

SUN: One of the most confusing things about being a practitioner of Asian mystical traditions is the fact that before the Enlightenment the West had a thousand-year tradition of a civilization based on a highly mystical religion: Christianity. And yet in *Sex, Ecology, Spirituality* you characterize this thousand-year period as one that promised but did not deliver genuine transcendence. Why do you say that? How could a whole civilization miss the point for so long when it had expressions of the idea in Plato, the Corpus Hermeticum, Neoplatonism, mystical Christianity, and so on?

KW: Imagine if, the very day Buddha attained his enlightenment, he was taken out and hanged precisely because of that realization. And if any of his followers claimed to have the same realization, they were also hanged. Speaking for myself, I would find this something of a disincentive.

But that's exactly what happened with Jesus of Nazareth. "Why do you stone me?" he asks at one point. "Is it for good deeds?" And the crowd responds, "No, it is because you, being a man, make yourself out to be God." The individual Atman is not allowed to realize that it is one with Brahman. "I and my Father are One"—among other complicated factors, that realization got this gentleman crucified.

The reasons for this are involved, but the fact remains: as soon as any spiritual practitioner began to get too close to the realization that Atman and Brahman are one—that one's own mind is intrinsically one with primordial Spirit—then frighteningly severe repercussions usually followed. Of course there were wonderful currents of Neoplatonic and other very high teachings operating in the background (and underground) in the West, but wherever the Church had political influence—and it dominated the Western scene for a thousand years—if you stepped over that line between Atman and Brahman, you were in very dangerous waters. Saint John of the Cross and his friend Saint Teresa of Ávila stepped over the line, but couched their journeys in such careful and pious language they pulled it off, barely. Meister Eckhart stepped over the line, a little too boldly, and had his teachings officially condemned, which meant he wouldn't fry in hell but his words apparently would. Giordano Bruno stepped way over the line, and was burned at the stake. This is a typical pattern.

SUN: You say the reasons are complicated, and I'm sure they are, but could you briefly mention a few?

KW: Well, I'll give you one, which is perhaps the most interesting. The early history of the Church was dominated by traveling "pneumatics," those in whom "spirit was alive." Their spirituality was based largely on direct experience, a type of Christ consciousness, we might suppose ("Let this consciousness be in you which was in Christ Jesus"). We might charitably say that the Nirmanakaya of each pneumatic realized the Dharmakaya of Christ via the Sambhogakaya of the transformative fire of the Holy Ghost—not to put too fine a point on it. But they were clearly alive to some very real, very direct spiritual experiences.

But over a several-hundred-year span, with the codification of the Canon and the Apostle's Creed, a series of necessary *beliefs* replaced actual *experience*. The Church slowly switched from the pneumatics to the *ekklesia*, the ecclesiastic assembly of Christ, and the governor of the *ekklesia* was the local bishop, who possessed "right dogma," and not the pneumatic or prophet, who might possess spirit but couldn't be "controlled." The Church was no longer defined as the assembly of realizers but as the assembly of bishops.

With Tertullian the relationship becomes almost legal, and with Cyprian spirituality actually is bound to the *legal office* of the Church. You could become a priest merely by ordination, not by awakening. A priest was no longer holy (*sanctus*) if he was personally awakened or enlightened or sanctified, but if he held the office. Likewise, you could become "saved" not by waking up yourself, but merely by taking the legal sacraments. As Cyprian put it, "He who does not have the Church as Mother cannot have God as Father."

Well, that puts a damper on it, what? Salvation now belonged to the lawyers. And the lawyers said, basically, we will allow that one megadude became fully one with God, but that's it! No more of that pure Oneness crap.

SUN: But why?

KW: This part of it was simple, raw, political power. Because, you know, the unsettling thing about direct mystical experience is that it has a nasty habit of going straight from Spirit to you, thus bypassing the middleman, namely, the bishop, not to mention the middleman's collection plate. This is the same reason the oil companies do not like solar power.

And so, anybody who had a direct pipeline to God was thus pronounced guilty not only of *religious heresy*, or the violation of the legal codes of the Church, for which you could have your heavenly soul eternally damned; but also of *political treason*, for which you could have your earthly body separated into several sections.

For all these reasons, the summum bonum of spiritual awareness—the supreme identity of Atman and Brahman, or ordinary mind and intrinsic spirit—was officially taboo in the West for a thousand years, more or less. All the wonderful currents that you mention, from Neoplatonism to Hermeticism, were definitely present but severely marginalized, to put it mildly. And thus the West produced an extraordinary number of subtle-level (or Sambhogakaya) mystics, who only claimed that the soul and God can share a *union*; but very few causal (Dharmakaya) and very few nondual (Svabhavikakaya) mystics, who went further and claimed not just a union but a supreme *identity* of soul and God in pure Godhead: just that claim got you toasted.

SUN: As for some of these more profound currents that became marginalized. What is the relationship between Plato's concept of "remembering" and enlightenment? Ever since I read the *Meno* I've thought there was one. But I couldn't quite figure out what it was.

KW: Yes, I think there is a very direct relationship. If we make the assumption, pretty safe with this crowd, that every sentient being has Buddha-mind, and if we agree that with enlightenment we are not attaining this mind but simply acknowledging or recognizing it, then it amounts to the same thing if we say that enlightenment is the remembering of Buddha-mind, or the direct recognition or re-cognition of pure Emptiness.

In other words, we can't attain Buddha-nature any more than we can attain our feet. We can simply look down and notice that we have feet, we can remember that we have them. It sometimes helps, if we think that we do not have feet, to have somebody come along and point to them. A Zen Master will be glad to help. When you earnestly say, "I don't have any feet," the Master will stomp on your toes and see who yells out loud. Then he looks at you: "No feet, eh?"

These "pointing-out instructions" do not point to something that we do not have and need to acquire; they point to something that is fully, totally, completely present right now, but we have perhaps forgotten. Enlightenment in the most basic sense is this simple remembering, recognizing, or simply noticing our feet—that is, noticing that this simple, clear, ever-present awareness is primordial Purity just as it is. In that sense, it is definitely a simple remembering.

SUN: And you think Plato was actually involved in that type of recognition?

KW: Oh, I think so. It becomes extremely obvious in the succeeding Neoplatonic teachers, and in these areas, the apples rarely fall far from the tree. Plato himself says that we were once whole, but a "failure to remember"—*amnesis*—allows us to fall from that wholeness. And we will "recover" from our fragmentation when we *remember* who and what we really are. Plato is very specific. I'll read this: "It is not something that can be put into words like other branches of learning; only after long partnership in a [contemplative community] devoted to this very thing does truth flash upon the soul, like a flame kindled by a leaping spark." Sudden illumination. He then adds, and this is very important: "No treatise by me concerning it exists or ever will exist."

SUN: Purely wordless.

KW: Yes, I think so. Very like, "A special transmission outside the scriptures; Not dependent upon words or letters; Direct pointing to the mind; Seeing into one's Nature and recognizing Buddhahood." We have to be a little careful with quick and easy comparisons, but again, if all sentient beings possess Buddha-mind, and if you are not yet going to be crucified for remembering it, then it is likely enough that souls of such caliber as Parmenides and Plato and Plotinus would remember who and what they are in suchness. And yes, it very much is a simple remembering, like looking in the mirror and going "Oh!" As Philosophia said to Boethius in his distress, "You have forgotten who you are."

SUN: I'd like to ask you a specific question about the connection between ultimate and relative truth. You said that the Buddha's teachings are completely adequate for the realization of Ultimate Truth, but that relative manifestation keeps on changing because "Emptiness takes on different forms." But really in Buddhist teachings there is just one intelligence. The Ati tantras call it *rigpa*. It's basically supposed to be the same as *vipashyana* or *prajna*. I'm wondering if you agree about this one intelligence? Is this the same intelligence that understands calculus? Is it the same intelligence that discovers quantum physics? Is it the same intelligence that microbiologists use to map the human genome?

KW: And you ask because . . . ?

SUN: They are supposed to be the same "one intelligence" but they don't look the same. These scientific and philosophical teachings of the

West seem to be examples of relative truth that were not discovered in Asia. You obviously believe that the Asians were the world's experts on finding or identifying the mind that cognizes Emptiness. But how can we reconcile this if there is only one intelligence? Put succinctly, why didn't *rigpa* discover calculus or quantum physics or human DNA?

KW: Because there is not simply one intelligence, not the way you mean it. Remember, even in the Madhyamaka, where we have the Two Truths doctrine, there is a corresponding Two Modes of Knowing— *samvritti*, which is responsible for the relative truths of science and philosophy, and *paramartha*, or the recognition of pure Emptiness. Whatever relative manifestation there is, it is illumined or lit by *rigpa*, as the one intelligence in the entire universe, which is true enough. But within that absolute space of Emptiness/*rigpa*, there arise all sorts of relative truths and relative objects and relative knowledge, and Emptiness/*rigpa* lights them all equally. It does not choose sides, it doesn't "push" anything. It doesn't push against anything because nothing is outside it.

SUN: Could this be summarized by saying whether there is one intelligence or not?

KW: One intelligence that flashes in many different forms. As the Christian mystics put it, we have the eye of flesh, the eye of mind, and the eye of contemplation—all of which are ultimately lit by *rigpa*, or one intelligence, or Big Mind, but each of which nonetheless has its own domain, its own truths, its own knowing. And, most important, mastering one eye does not necessarily mean you master the others. As we were saying, these are relatively independent streams.

SUN: So the eye of contemplation is capable of disclosing absolute truth or Emptiness, whereas the eye of mind and the eye of flesh can disclose only relative truth and conventional realities.

KW: Yes, I think that is a fair summary of what are after all some very complex issues.

The traditional analogy is the ocean and its waves, which is a really boring analogy, but bear with me. The wetness of the water is Suchness (or Spirit). All waves are equally wet. One wave isn't wetter than another. And thus, if I discover the wetness of any wave, I have discovered the wetness of all. When I directly recognize Suchness or Emptiness, or the wetness of my own being, right here, right now, then I have discovered the ultimate truth of all other waves as well. Emptiness is not a Really Big Wave set apart from little waves, but is the wetness equally present in all waves, high or low, big or small, sacred or profane—which is why Emptiness cannot be used to prefer one wave over another.

Enlightenment is thus not catching a really big wave, but noticing the already present wetness of whatever wave I'm on. Moreover, I am then radically liberated from the narrow identification with this little wave called me, because I am fundamentally one with all other waves—no wetness is outside of me. I am *literally* One Taste with the entire ocean and all its waves. And that taste is wetness, suchness, Emptiness, the utter transparency of the Great Perfection.

At the same time, I do not know all the details of all the other waves: their height, their weight, the number of them, and so on. These relative truths I will have to discover wave by wave, endlessly. No *Sutra of Wetness* will tell about that, nor could it. And no *Tantra of the Soggy* will clue me in on this.

That's why I earlier said that contemplation is sufficient for ultimate truth: it will directly show you the wetness of all waves, the radical suchness of all phenomena, the Emptiness in the Heart of the Kosmos itself, the primordial purity that is your own intrinsic awareness in this moment, and this moment, and this. But meditation will not, and really cannot, tell you about all the details of all the various waves that nevertheless arise as the ceaseless play of Emptiness and spontaneous luminosity. As you say, it will not automatically give you calculus, or the human genome, or quantum physics. And historically, it definitely did not, which should tell us something right there.

SUN: I have a question about the Great Chain of Being, and it dawned on me that the Great Chain might be related to what you are saying about manifestation and relative truth.

KW: Yes, they are very similar notions. In other words, the Great Chain theorists—from Yogachara and Vedanta in the East to Neoplatonism and Kabbalah in the West—maintain that Emptiness (or the "One," meaning the Nondual) manifests as a series of dimensions, or levels, or *koshas*, or *vijnanas*—or "waves"—a spectrum of being and consciousness. The spectrum of levels is the relative or manifest truth, and the vast expanse in which the spectrum appears is Emptiness or absolute truth. Ultimately the absolute and the relative are "not two" or nondual, because Emptiness is not a thing apart from other things but the suchness of all things, the wetness of all waves. And *rigpa* is the flash, the recognition, of that nondual isness, the simplicity of your present, clear, ordinary awareness—the opening or clearing in which the entire universe arises, just so.

But, of course, that is not merely an abstract concept. One Taste is a simple, direct, clear recognition, in which it becomes perfectly obvious that you do not see the sky, you are the sky. You do not touch the earth, you are the earth. The wind does not blow on you, it blows within you. In this simple One Taste, you can drink the Pacific Ocean in a single gulp, and swallow the universe whole. Supernovas are born and die all within your heart, and galaxies swirl endlessly where you thought your head was, and it is all as simple as the sound of a robin singing on a crystal clear dawn.

SUN: The different forms of Emptiness, the different waves of the Great Perfection.

KW: Yes, in the relative world, new truths are constantly emerging; they emerge within Emptiness, within this brilliantly clear opening that is your own awareness in this moment. And whether what arises in the vast expanse of your own primordial awareness is calculus, physics, pottery, or how to make yak butter, will depend on a thousand relative truths and relative forces, none of which individually can be equated with Emptiness, and yet all of which arise as gestures of the Great Perfection or Emptiness itself—that is, all of which arise in this simple, clear, ever-present awareness, the wetness or the transparency of your very own being.

So within "one intelligence" or "Big Mind," all sorts of small minds and stepped-down intelligences arise—that's the Great Chain—and those relative truths, like the clouds in the sky and the waves in the ocean, have an appointment with their own relative karmas and a date with their own destinies.

The West has its relative truths, the East has its relative truths. And mostly in the East we further get a clear understanding of absolute truth, because the toaster was not your fate for dabbling therein. And definitely, my theme is that a judicious blend of relative truths, East and West, set in the primordial context of radical Emptiness, is a very sane approach to the human situation.

Sunday, December 21

Several late-breaking news items on the national astrology debate.

Ivan Kelly sent me a copy of his paper "Modern Astrology: A Critique," and I must say, it is fairly devastating. We last left the debate with astrology hanging, definitely but weakly, by nothing but the Gauquelin thread. Will Keepin tried to also point to the anecdotal evidence collected by Tarnas and Grof, but Roger pointed out that those studies are "uncontrolled (that is, employ no control subjects), not blind (that is, the experimenters usually know the identity of the subjects), retrospective (assessed after the fact), and without reliability tests of the measurement procedures." The Grof/Tarnas studies, in other words, are lacking proof or even corroboration, and will remain biased and anecdotal until the controls Roger outlines are diligently applied.

The Gauquelin studies, on the other hand, were compelling to believers and nonbelievers alike, and were the only studies to be so. On the basis of that *evidence*—and since we must always follow the evidence—I suggested a theory to account for the Gauquelin effects. Contrary to Will's suggestion—that the astral effects were emanating from the World Soul (the psychic level) and, via downward causation, effecting individual minds (or character traits)—I suggested that they were emanating from a merely physical level (geomagnetic, gravitational) and, via upward causation, having a small but discernible effect (via hormonal or neuronal interactions) on individual minds (or character traits). I still maintain that hypothesis, but if and only if the Gauquelin data base is sound. If it is not, then astrology in all forms is simply kaput, as far as the evidence is concerned, and we need no explanatory hypothesis at all.

From Kelly's paper I learn that P. Seymour recently "attempted to strengthen the case for the Gauquelin planetary-occupation findings by proposing a mechanism based on . . . the response of our neural networks to fluctuations in the earth's geomagnetic field which, in turn, interacts with the gravitational fields of the planets." Similar to my suggestion.

But, Kelly points out, although those are plausible hypotheses, the data has not supported them, and worse, they all rest on the reliability of the original Gauquelin data base, which, far from being an invincible edifice, is under sharp attack. Among others, the Dutch mathematician Nienhuys has apparently delivered an effective challenge to the very foundation of the Gauquelin effects.

I am still willing to follow the evidence, but I must say, the total web of evidence at this point is crushingly against astrology in any form. If the Gauquelin data base holds up, I will revert to my original geomagnetic hypothesis; but at this point, it appears astrology is a belief without corroborating evidence.

What I see people yearning for, when they turn to astrology, is a sense of connection to the cosmos. But they would do better to turn to the Kosmos. That is, instead of plugging into the gross dimension of physical planets connected to their personal egos, let their awareness rise gently into the transpersonal realms. Not merely a horizontal connection to physical planets, but a vertical connection to soul and spirit, subtle and causal, ultimate and nondual. The spiritual impulse hidden in astrology and diverted into the cosmos needs to be released into the Kosmos, released into that ultimate Embrace which holds the planets in the palm of its hand, and spins galaxies in its stride. Not psyche and cosmos, but psyche and Kosmos, holds the secret to the connection long sought.

Thursday, December 25

Marci and I spent the day alone, wonderfully.

Monday, December 29

The year is coming to a close—is dying, as tradition has it. Death: the mystics are unanimous that death contains the secret to life—to eternal life, in fact. As Eckhart put it, echoing the mystics everywhere: "No one gets as much of God as those who are thoroughly dead." Or Ramana Maharshi: "You will know in due course that your glory lies where you cease to exist." Or the *Zenrin*: "While alive, live as a dead person, thoroughly dead."

They don't mean physically dead; they mean dead to the separate-self sense. And you can "test" your own spiritual awareness in relation to death by trying to imagine the following items:

1. A famous Zen koan says, "Show me your Original Face, the Face you had before your parents were born." This is not a trick question or a symbolic question; it is very straightforward, with a clear and simple answer. Your Original Face is simply the pure formless Witness, prior to the manifest world. The pure Witness, itself being timeless or prior to time, is equally present at all points of time. So of course this is the Self you had before your parents were born; it is the Self you had before the Big Bang, too. And it is the Self you will have after your body—and the entire universe—dissolves.

This Self existed prior to your parents, and prior to the Big Bang, because it exists prior to time, period. And you can *directly* contact the Self you had before your parents were born by simply resting in the pure Witness *right now*. They are one and the same formless Self, right now, and right now, and right now.

By "imagining" what you were like before your parents were born, you are forced to drop all identity with your present body and ego. You are forced to find that in you which actually goes beyond you—namely, the pure, empty, formless, timeless Witness or primordial Self. To the extent you can actually rest as the timeless Witness ("I am not this, not that"), then you have died to the separate self—and discovered your Original Face, the face you had before your parents were born, before the Big Bang was born, before time was born. You have found, in fact, the great Unborn, which is *just this*.

2. Similarly, imagine what the world will be like a hundred years after you die. You don't have to imagine specific details, just realize that the world will be going on a century after you are gone. Imagine that world without you. So many things will have changed—different people, different technologies, different cars and planes. . . . *But one thing will not have changed*; one thing will be the same: Emptiness, One Taste, Spirit. Well, you can taste that *right now*. One and the same formless Witness will look out from all eyes, hear with all ears, touch with all hands . . . the same formless Witness that is your own primordial Self right now, the same One Taste that is yours, right now, the same radiant Spirit that is yours, right now.

Were you somebody different a thousand years ago? Will you be somebody different a thousand years from now? What is this One Self that is forever your own deepest being? Must you believe the lies of time? Must you swallow the insanity that One Spirit does not exist? Can you right now show me your Original Face, of which there is One and Only One in all the entire World?

Listen to Erwin Schroedinger, the Nobel Prize–winning cofounder of quantum mechanics, and how can I convince you that he means this *literally*?

> Consciousness is a singular of which the plural is unknown.

> It is not possible that this unity of knowledge, feeling, and choice which you call *your own* should have sprung into being from nothingness at a given moment not so long ago; rather, this knowledge, feeling, and choice are essentially eternal and unchangeable and numerically *one* in all people, nay in all sensitive beings.

> The conditions for your existence are almost as old as the rocks. For thousands of years men have striven and suffered and begot-

ten and women have brought forth in pain. A hundred years ago [there's the test], another man sat on this spot; like you he gazed with awe and yearning in his heart at the dying light on the glaciers. Like you he was begotten of man and born of woman. He felt pain and brief joy as you do. *Was* he someone else? Was it not you yourself?

WAS IT NOT YOU, YOUR PRIMORDIAL SELF? Are you not humanity itself? Do you not touch all things human, because you are its only Witness? Do you not therefore love the world, and love all people, and love the Kosmos, because you are its only Self? Do you not weep when one person is hurt, do you not cry when one child goes hungry, do you not scream when one soul is tortured? You *know* you suffer when others suffer. You already know this! "*Was* it someone else? Was it not you yourself?"

3. By thinking of what you were like a thousand years ago or a thousand years hence, you drop your identity with the present body and ego, and find that in you which goes beyond you—namely, the pure, formless, timeless Self or Witness of the entire World. And once every twenty-four hours you completely drop your egoic identity, not as a mere imaginative exercise but as a fact. Every night, in deep dreamless sleep, you are plunged back into the formless realm, into the realm of pure consciousness without an object, into the realm of the formless, timeless Self.

This is why Ramana Maharshi said, "That which is not present in deep dreamless sleep is not real." The Real must be present in all three states, including deep dreamless sleep, and the *only* thing that is present in all three states is the formless Self or pure Consciousness. And each night you die to the separate-self sense, die to the ego, and are plunged back into the ocean of infinity that is your Original Face.

All three of those cases—the Self you had before your parents were born, the Self you will have a hundred years from now, and the Self you have in deep dreamless sleep—point to one and the same thing: the timeless Witness in you which goes beyond you, the pure Emptiness that is one with all Form, the primordial Self that embraces the All in radical One Taste. And *That*, which is *just this*, has not changed, will not change, will never change, because it never enters the corrupting stream of time with all its tears and terror.

The ultimate "spiritual test," then, is simply your relation to death (for all three of those cases are examples of death). If you want to know the "ultimate truth" of what you are doing right now, simply submit it to any of those tests. Practicing astrology? If it is not present in deep dreamless sleep, it is not real. Running with wolves? If it is not present a hundred years from now, it is not real. Care of the Soul? If it is not present in deep dreamless sleep, it is not real. Healing your inner child? If it was not present prior to your parents' birth, it is not real. You remember your reincarnated past lives? If it is not present in deep dreamless sleep, it is not real. Using diet for spiritual cleansing? If it is not present a hundred years from now, it is not real. Worshipping Gaia? If it is not present in deep dreamless sleep, it is not real.

All of those relative practices and translative beliefs are fine, and can be very useful—I truly don't wish to belittle any of them—but never forget they are secondary to the great Unborn, your Original Face, the Face of Spirit in all its radiant forms, the forms of your very own being and becoming, now and again, now and forever, always and already.

"*Was* it someone else? Was it not you yourself?"

Wednesday, December 31—Denver

Marci and I spent New Year's Eve at our favorite local hideaway, the Oxford Hotel in the LoDo district, Denver. Dinner at Jax's, drinks at the Cruise Bar, a midnight embrace, kiss the year goodbye.

Thursday, January 1, 1998—Boulder

A year ago today I was wondering what to do with *Sense and Soul*. It's been a wild ride, this year. In two weeks I go to Manhattan to meet with major book reviewers, all arranged by Ann. Then in March I'll do a six-city book tour, small but unprecedented for me. I will still, I trust, be in love with Marci, one of the most beautiful women and dearest souls I have ever known. I will be editing the *Collected Works*, and will be plowing through the reading for volume 2. I will be nine months away from my fiftieth birthday.

And none of that, of course, is present in deep dreamless sleep, or present a thousand years from now, or prior to my parents' birth, or in the formless realm itself, where I-I alone shine, where IAMness fills the timeless world to all infinity and back. None of it, in other words, touches the purest Emptiness that alone is Real, that bathes my being in delight and sends my mind to heaven. Yet all of that is a compassionate gesture of my very Self, the Self of each and every being without lack or limitation, the Self of all that truly is and truly ever shall be.

It is always already undone, you see, and always already over. In the simple feeling of Being, worlds are born and die—they live and dance and sing a while and melt back into oblivion, and nothing ever really happens here, in the simple world of One Taste. A thousand forms will come and go, a million worlds will rise and fall, a billion souls will love and laugh and languish fast and die, and One Taste alone will embrace them all. And I-I will be there, as I-I always have been, to Witness the rise and miraculous fall of my infinite easy Worlds, happening now and forever, now and forever, now and always forever it seems.

And then again, I might just stay here, and watch the sunset one more time, through the misty rain that is now falling, quietly all around.

BOOKS BY KEN WILBER

The Spectrum of Consciousness (1977)

No Boundary: Eastern and Western Approaches to Personal Growth (1979)

The Atman Project: A Transpersonal View of Human Development (1980)

Up from Eden: A Transpersonal View of Human Evolution (1981)

The Holographic Paradigm and Other Paradoxes: Exploring the Leading Edge of Science (1982)

A Sociable God: Toward a New Understanding of Religion (1983)

Eye to Eye: The Quest for the New Paradigm (1983)

Quantum Questions: Mystical Writings of the World's Great Physicists (1984)

Transformations of Consciousness: Conventional and Contemplative Perspectives on Development, by Ken Wilber, Jack Engler, and Daniel P. Brown (1986)

Spiritual Choices: The Problems of Recognizing Authentic Paths to Inner Transformation, edited by Dick Anthony, Bruce Ecker, and Ken Wilber (1987)

Grace and Grit: Spirituality and Healing in the Life and Death of Treya Killam Wilber (1991)

Sex, Ecology, Spirituality: The Spirit of Evolution (1995)

A Brief History of Everything (1996)

The Eye of Spirit: An Integral Vision for a World Gone Slightly Mad (1997)

The Marriage of Sense and Soul: Integrating Science and Religion (1998)

One Taste: The Journals of Ken Wilber (1999)

Integral Psychology (2000)

INDEX